SQL Server 2008 Query Performance Tuning Distilled

Grant Fritchey and Sajal Dam

Apress®

SQL Server 2008 Query Performance Tuning Distilled

ISBN-13 (pbk): 978-1-4302-1902-6

ISBN-13 (electronic): 978-1-4302-1903-3

Printed and bound in the United States of America 9 8 7 6 5 4 3 2 1

Lead Editor: Jonathan Gennick
Development Editor: Douglas Pundick
Technical Reviewer: Joseph Sack

Project Manager: Richard Dal Porto
Copy Editor: Kim Wimpsett
Associate Production Director: Kari Brooks-Copony
Production Editor: Kelly Winquist
Compositor: Patrick Cunningham
Proofreader: April Eddy
Indexer: John Collin
Artist: April Milne
Cover Designer: Kurt Krames
Manufacturing Director: Tom Debolski

Distributed to the book trade worldwide by Springer-Verlag New York, Inc., 233 Spring Street, 6th Floor, New York, NY 10013. Phone 1-800-SPRINGER, fax 201-348-4505, e-mail orders-ny@springer-sbm.com, or visit http://www.springeronline.com.

For information on translations, please contact Apress directly at 2855 Telegraph Avenue, Suite 600, Berkeley, CA 94705. Phone 510-549-5930, fax 510-549-5939, e-mail info@apress.com, or visit http://www.apress.com.

Apress and friends of ED books may be purchased in bulk for academic, corporate, or promotional use. eBook versions and licenses are also available for most titles. For more information, reference our Special Bulk Sales–eBook Licensing web page at http://www.apress.com/info/bulksales.

The source code for this book is available to readers at http://www.apress.com.

Contents at a Glance

Contents

CHAPTER 2 System Performance Analysis

About the Author

GRANT FRITCHEY works for FM Global, an industry-leading engineering and insurance company, as a principal DBA. He's done development of large-scale applications in languages such as VB, C#, and Java and has worked in SQL Server since version 6.0. In addition, he has worked in finance and consulting and for three failed dot coms. He is the author of *Dissecting SQL Server Execution Plans* (Simple Talk Publishing, 2008).

SAJAL DAM has a master's of technology degree in computer science from the Indian Institute of Science, Bangalore, and has been working with Microsoft technologies for more than 16 years. He has developed an extensive background in designing database applications and managing software development. Sajal also possesses significant experience in troubleshooting and optimizing the performance of Microsoft-based applications, from front-end web pages to back-end databases. He has extensive experience in working with large, Fortune 500 customers to design scalable database solutions and maximize the performance of their database environments.

About the Technical Reviewer

JOSEPH SACK works for Microsoft as a dedicated support engineer on the Premier Field Engineering team. Since 1997, he has been developing and supporting SQL Server environments for clients in the financial services, IT consulting, manufacturing, retail, and real estate industries. He is the author of *SQL Server 2008 Transact-SQL Recipes* (Apress, 2008), *SQL Server 2005 T-SQL Recipes* (Apress, 2005), and *SQL Server 2000 Fast Answers for DBAs and Developers* (Glasshaus, 2003).

Acknowledgments

Holy cats! Writing a book is really hard. Fortunately, there's this incredible support team that gathers around as you write these things. From Apress: Jonathan Gennick, thank you for the opportunity and support; Richard Dal Porto, thanks for keeping everything organized; Douglas Pundick, nice work on the edits, and I'm sorry there was so much for you to do; Kim Wimpsett and Kelly Winquist, same thing. My technical editor, well, "I'm not worthy" is the best that can be said, but my sincere appreciation goes to Joseph Sack for the absolutely outstanding work he did on this book. You've all done amazing work. Anything that's wrong with the book now is my responsibility, not yours.

I have to also show appreciation to all the folks over at the SQL Server Central forums. Steve Jones and Andy Warren created quite a community over there. Steve, Gail, Jeff, Jack, Barry, Lynn, and all the rest I haven't mention specifically, thank you for all the help over the years.

I work for a fantastic company with great people where I've had opportunities to learn and grow. Thanks to Jack Dewar, my manager, and Bill Hawkins, his boss. My thanks to the DBA team who have taught me so much: Peter, Ted, Basem, AJ, Dave M., Dave H., Chris K., Chris P., Yuting, Ray, Raj, and Det.

I want to thank the folks at Red Gate for making terrific tools including SQL Prompt, which I used to write and format all the T-SQL code in the book.

Finally, before someone starts playing music and pushing me off the stage, I want to show appreciation to the family—my wife and kids. This is the second book you've allowed me to write. Thank you for putting up with me so well.

Grant Fritchey

Introduction

Performance is frequently one of the last things on anyone's minds when they're developing a system. Unfortunately, that means it usually becomes the biggest problem after that system goes to production. You can't simply rely on getting a phone call that tells you that procedure X on database Y that runs on server Z is running slow. You have to have a mechanism in place to find this information for yourself. You also can't work off the general word *slow*. Slow compared to what? Last week? Last month? The way it ran in development? And once you've identified something as running slow, you need to identify why. Does it need an index? Does it have an index that it isn't using? Is it the CPU, the disk, the memory, the number of users, the amount of data? Now you've identified what and why, but you have to do something about it. How? Rewrite the query? Change the `WHERE` clause? The questions that will come your way when you start performance tuning are endless.

This book provides you with the tools you need to answer those questions. I'll show you how to set up mechanisms for collecting performance data on your server for the SQL Server instances and databases living there. I'll go over the more tactical methods of collecting data on individual T-SQL calls. Along the way, I'll be discussing index structure, choice, and maintenance; how best to write your T-SQL code; and a whole slew of other topics. One of my goals when writing this book was to deliver all these things using examples that resemble the types of queries you'll see in the real world, at your desk. The tools and methods presented are mostly available with SQL Server Standard Edition, although some are available only with SQL Server Enterprise Edition. These are called out whenever you might encounter them.

The main point is to learn how to answer all those questions that are going to be presented to you. This book gives you the tools to do that and to answer those questions in a methodical manner that eliminates much of the guesswork that is so common in performance optimization today. Performance problems aren't something to be feared. With the right tools, you can tackle performance problems with a calmness and reliability that will earn the respect of your peers and your clients and that will contribute directly to their success.

Who This Book Is For

This book is for just about anyone responsible for the performance of the system. Database administrators, certainly, are targeted because they're responsible for setting up the systems, creating the infrastructure, and monitoring it over time. Developers are too, because who else is going to generate all the well-formed and highly performant T-SQL code? Database developers, more than anyone, are the target audience, if only because that's what I do for work. Anyone who has the capability to write T-SQL, design tables, implement indexes, or manipulate server settings on the SQL Server system is going to need this information to one degree or another.

How This Book Is Structured

The purpose of this was to use as many "real-looking" queries as possible. To do this, I needed a "real" database. I could have created one and forced everyone to track down the download. Instead, I chose to use the sample database created by Microsoft, called `AdventureWorks2008`. This is available through CodePlex (`http://www.codeplex.com/MSFTDBProdSamples`). I suggest keeping a copy of the restore handy and resetting your sample database after you have read a couple of topics from the book. Microsoft updates these databases over time, so you might see different sets of data or different behavior of some of the queries than that listed in the book. To a degree, the book builds on the knowledge presented from previous chapters. However, most of the chapters present information unique within that topic, so it is possible for you to jump in and out of particular chapters. You will still receive the most benefit by a sequential read of Chapter 1 through Chapter 16.

- Chapter 1, "SQL Query Performance Tuning," introduces the iterative process of performance tuning. You'll get a first glimpse at establishing a performance baseline, identifying bottlenecks, resolving the problems, and quantifying the improvements.
- Chapter 2, "System Performance Analysis," starts you off with monitoring the Windows system on which SQL Server runs. Performance Monitor and user-defined functions are shown as a mechanism for collecting data.
- Chapter 3, "SQL Query Performance Analysis," defines the best ways to look "under the hood" and see what kind of queries are being run on your system. It provides a detailed look at the Profiler and trace tools. Several of the most useful dynamic management views and functions used to monitor queries are first identified in this chapter.
- Chapter 4, "Index Analysis," explains indexes and index architecture. It defines the differences between clustered and nonclustered indexes. It shows which types of indexes work best with different types of querying. Basic index maintenance is also introduced.
- Chapter 5, "Database Engine Tuning Advisor," covers the Microsoft tool Database Engine Tuning Advisor. The chapter goes over in detail how to use the Database Engine Tuning Advisor; you're introduced to the various mechanisms for calling the tool and shown how it works under real loads.
- Chapter 6, "Bookmark Lookup Analysis," takes on the classic performance problem, the key lookup, which is also known as the *bookmark lookup*. This chapter explores various solutions to the bookmark lookup operation.
- Chapter 7, "Statistics Analysis," introduces the concept of statistics. The optimizer uses statistics to make decisions regarding the execution of the query. Maintaining statistics, understanding how they're stored, learning how they work, and learning how they affect your queries are all topics within this chapter.
- Chapter 8, "Fragmentation Analysis," shows how indexes fragment over time. You'll learn how to identify when an index is fragmented. You'll see what happens to your queries as indexes fragment. You'll learn mechanisms to eliminate index fragmentation.

- Chapter 9, "Execution Plan Cache Analysis," presents the mechanisms that SQL Server uses to store execution plans. Plan reuse is an important concept within SQL Server. You'll learn how to identify whether plans are being reused. You'll get various mechanisms for looking at the cache. This chapter also introduces new dynamic management views that allow more access to the cache than ever before.
- Chapter 10, "Stored Procedure Recompilation," displays how and when SQL Server will recompile plans that were stored in cache. You'll learn how plan recompiles can hurt or help the performance of your system. You'll pick up mechanisms for forcing a recompile and for preventing one.
- Chapter 11, "Query Design Analysis," reveals how to write queries that perform well within your system. Common mistakes are explored, and solutions are provided. You'll learn several best practices to avoid common bottlenecks.
- Chapter 12, "Blocking Analysis," teaches the best ways to recognize when various sessions on your server are in contention for resources. You'll learn how to monitor for blocking along with methods and techniques to avoid blocked sessions.
- Chapter 13, "Deadlock Analysis," shows how deadlocks occur on your system. You'll get methods for identifying sessions involved with deadlocks. The chapter also presents best practices for avoiding deadlocks or fixing your code if deadlocks are already occurring.
- Chapter 14, "Cursor Cost Analysis," diagrams the inherent costs that cursors present to set-oriented T-SQL code. However, when cursors are unavoidable, you need to understand how they work, what they do, and how best to tune them within your environment if eliminating them outright is not an option.
- Chapter 15, "Database Workload Optimization," demonstrates how to take the information presented in all the previous chapters and put it to work on a real database workload. You'll identify the worst-performing procedures and put them through various tuning methods to arrive at better performance.
- Chapter 16, "SQL Server Optimization Checklist," summarizes all the preceding chapters into a set of checklists and best practices. The goal of the chapter is to enable you to have a place for quickly reviewing all you have learned from the rest of the book.

Downloading the Code

You can download the code examples used in this book from the Source Code section of the Apress website (`http://www.apress.com`). Most of the code is straight T-SQL stored in `.sql` files, which can be opened and used in any SQL Server T-SQL editing tool. There is one PowerShell script that will have to be run through a PowerShell command line.

Contacting the Author

You can contact the author, Grant Fritchey, at `grantedd@google.com`. You can visit his blog at `http://scarydba.wordpress.com`.

CHAPTER 1

SQL Query Performance Tuning

Query performance tuning is an important part of today's database applications. Often you can achieve large savings in both time and money with proper query performance tuning. Hardware performance is constantly improving, which can lead to an attitude suggesting that other methods of performance tuning are no longer important. Upgrades to SQL Server—especially to the optimizer, which helps determine how a query is executed, and the query engine, which executes the query—lead to better performance all on their own. The beauty of query performance tuning is that, in many cases, a small change to an index or a SQL query can result in a far more efficient application at a very low cost.

There are, however, many pitfalls for the unwary. As a result, a proven process is required to ensure that you correctly identify and resolve performance bottlenecks. To whet your appetite for the types of topics essential to honing your query optimization skills, here is a quick list of the query optimization aspects I cover in this book:

- Identifying problematic SQL queries
- Analyzing a query execution plan
- Evaluating the effectiveness of the current indexes
- Avoiding bookmark lookups
- Evaluating the effectiveness of the current statistics
- Analyzing and resolving fragmentation
- Optimizing execution plan caching
- Analyzing and avoiding stored procedure recompilation
- Minimizing blocking and deadlocks
- Analyzing the effectiveness of cursor use
- Applying performance-tuning processes, tools, and optimization techniques to optimize SQL workload

Before jumping straight in to these topics, let's first examine why we go about performance tuning the way we do. In this chapter, I discuss the basic concepts of performance tuning for a SQL Server database system. I detail the main performance bottlenecks and show just how important it is to design a database-friendly application, which is the consumer of the data, as well as how to optimize the database. Specifically, I cover the following topics:

- The performance-tuning process
- Performance vs. price
- The performance baseline
- Where to focus efforts in tuning
- The top 11 SQL Server performance killers

The Performance-Tuning Process

The performance-tuning process consists of identifying performance bottlenecks, troubleshooting their causes, applying different resolutions, and then quantifying performance improvements. It is necessary to be a little creative, since most of the time there is no one silver bullet to improve performance. The challenge is to narrow down the list of possible causes and evaluate the effects of different resolutions. You can even undo modifications as you iterate through the tuning process.

The Core Process

During the tuning process, you must examine various hardware and software factors that can affect the performance of a SQL Server–based application. You should be asking yourself the following general questions during the performance analysis:

- Is any other resource-intensive application running on the same server?
- Is the hardware subsystem capable of withstanding the maximum workload?
- Is SQL Server configured properly?
- Is the database connection between SQL Server and the database application efficient?
- Does the database design support the fastest data retrieval (and modification for an updatable database)?
- Is the user workload, consisting of SQL queries, optimized to reduce the load on SQL Server?
- What processes are causing the system to slow down as reflected in the measurement of various wait states?
- Does the workload support the maximum concurrency?

If any of these factors is not configured properly, then the overall system performance may suffer. Let's briefly examine these factors.

Having another resource-intensive application on the same server can limit the resources available to SQL Server. Even an application running as a service can consume a good part of the system resources and limit the resources available to SQL Server. For example, running Windows Task Manager continuously on the server is not recommended. Windows Task

Manager is also an application, `taskmgr.exe`, which runs at a higher priority than the SQL Server process. *Priority* is the weight given to a resource that pushes the processor to give it greater preference when executing. To determine the priority of a process, follow these steps:

1. Launch Windows Task Manager.
2. Select View ➤ Select Columns.
3. Select the Base Priority check box.
4. Click the OK button.

These steps will add the `Base Priority` column to the list of processes. Subsequently, you will be able to determine that the SQL Server process (`sqlservr.exe`) by default runs at Normal priority, whereas the Windows Task Manager process (`taskmgr.exe`) runs at High priority. Therefore, to allow SQL Server to maximize the use of available resources, you should look for all the nonessential applications/services running on the SQL Server machine and ensure that they are not acting as resource hogs.

Improperly configuring the hardware can prevent SQL Server from gaining the maximum benefit from the available resources. The main hardware resources to be considered are processor, memory, disk, and network. For example, in a server with more than 4GB of memory, an improper memory configuration will prevent SQL Server from using the memory beyond 4GB. Furthermore, if the capacity of a particular resource is small, then it can soon become a performance bottleneck for SQL Server. Chapter 2 covers these hardware bottlenecks in detail.

You should also look at the configuration of SQL Server, since proper configuration is essential for an optimized application. There is a long list of SQL Server configurations that define the generic behavior of a SQL Server installation. These configurations can be viewed and modified using a system stored procedure, `sp_configure`. Many of these configurations can be managed interactively through SQL Server Enterprise Manager.

Since the SQL Server configurations are applicable for the complete SQL Server installation, a standard configuration is usually preferred. The good news is that, generally, you need not modify these configurations; the default settings work best for most situations. In fact, the general recommendation is to keep the SQL Server configurations at the default values. I discuss the configuration parameters in detail throughout the book.

Poor connectivity between SQL Server and the database application can hurt application performance. One of the questions you should ask yourself is, How good is the database connection? For example, the query executed by the application may be highly optimized, but the database connection used to submit this query may add considerable overhead to the query performance. Based on the distribution of the application and the database, different network protocols should be used to reduce the network overhead. Additionally, the data access layer used to manage the database connectivity above the network connection may not be efficient. The data access layer technology or the way the data access layer is used by the application may not be optimal.

The design of the database should also be analyzed while troubleshooting performance. This helps you understand not only the entity-relationship model of the database but also why a query may be written in a certain way. Although it may not always be possible to modify a database design because of wider implications on the database application, a good understanding of the database design helps you focus in the right direction and understand the impact of a resolution. This is especially true of the primary and foreign keys and the clustered indexes used in the tables.

The application may be slow because of poorly built queries, the queries might not be able to use the indexes, or perhaps even the indexes themselves are incorrect or missing. If any of the queries are not optimized sufficiently, they can seriously impact other queries' performance. I cover index optimization in depth in Chapters 3, 4, 5, and 6. The next question at this stage should be, Is a query slow because of its resource intensiveness or because of concurrency issues with other queries? You can find in-depth information on blocking analysis in Chapter 12.

When processes run on a server, even one with multiple processors, at times one process will be waiting on another to complete. You can get a fundamental understanding of the root cause of slowdowns by identifying what is waiting and what is causing it to wait. You can realize this through operating system counters that you access through dynamic management views within SQL Server. I cover this information in Chapter 2 and in Chapter 12.

The challenge is to find out which factor is causing the performance bottleneck. For example, with slow-running SQL queries and high pressure on the hardware resources, you may find that both poor database design and a nonoptimized workload are to blame. In such a case, you must diagnose the symptoms further and correlate the findings with possible causes. Because performance tuning can be time consuming and tiresome, you should ideally take a preventive approach by designing the system for optimum performance from the outset.

To strengthen the preventive approach, every lesson that you learn during the optimization of poor performance should be considered an optimization guideline when implementing new database applications. There are also proven best practices that you should consider while implementing database applications. I present these best practices in detail throughout the book, and Chapter 18 is dedicated to outlining many of the optimization best practices.

Please ensure that you take the performance optimization techniques into consideration at the early stages of your database application development. Doing so will help you roll out your database projects without big surprises later.

Unfortunately, we rarely live up to this ideal and often find database applications needing performance tuning. Therefore, it is important to understand not only how to improve the performance of a SQL Server–based application but also how to diagnose the causes of poor performance.

Iterating the Process

Performance tuning is an iterative process, where you identify major bottlenecks, attempt to resolve them, measure the impact of your changes, and return to the first step until performance is acceptable. While applying your solutions, you should follow the golden rule of making only one change at a time. Any change usually affects other parts of the system, so you must reevaluate the effect of each change on the performance of the overall system.

As an example, adding an index may fix the performance of a specific query, but it could cause other queries to run more slowly, as explained in Chapter 4. Consequently, it is preferable to conduct a performance analysis in a test environment to shield users from your diagnosis attempts and intermediate optimization steps. In such a case, evaluating one change at a time also helps in prioritizing the implementation order of the changes on the production server, based on their relative contributions.

You can keep on chipping away at performance bottlenecks and improving the system performance gradually. Initially, you will be able to resolve big performance bottlenecks and achieve significant performance improvements, but as you proceed through the iterations, your returns will gradually diminish. Therefore, to use your time efficiently, it is worthwhile to quantify the performance objectives first (for example, an 80 percent reduction in the time taken for a certain query, with no adverse effect anywhere else on the server) and then work toward them.

The performance of a SQL Server application is highly dependent on the amount and distribution of user activity (or workload) and data. Both the amount and distribution of workload and data change over time, and differing data can cause SQL Server to execute SQL queries differently. The performance resolution applicable for a certain workload and data may lose its effect over a period of time. Therefore, to ensure an optimum system performance on a continuing basis, you will need to analyze performance at regular intervals. Performance tuning is a never-ending process, as shown in Figure 1-1.

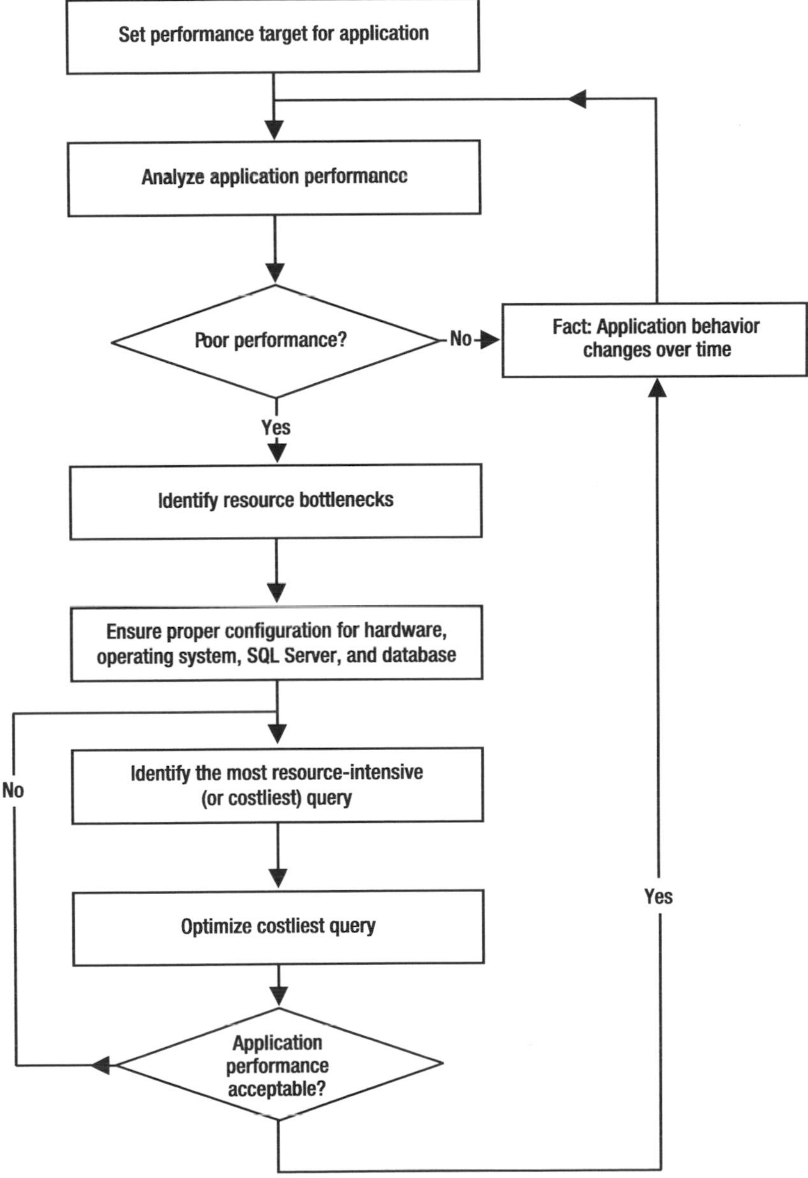

Figure 1-1. *Performance-tuning process*

You can see that the steps to optimize the costliest query make for a complex process, which also requires multiple iterations to troubleshoot the performance issues within the query and apply one change at a time. Figure 1-2 shows the steps involved in the optimization of the costliest query.

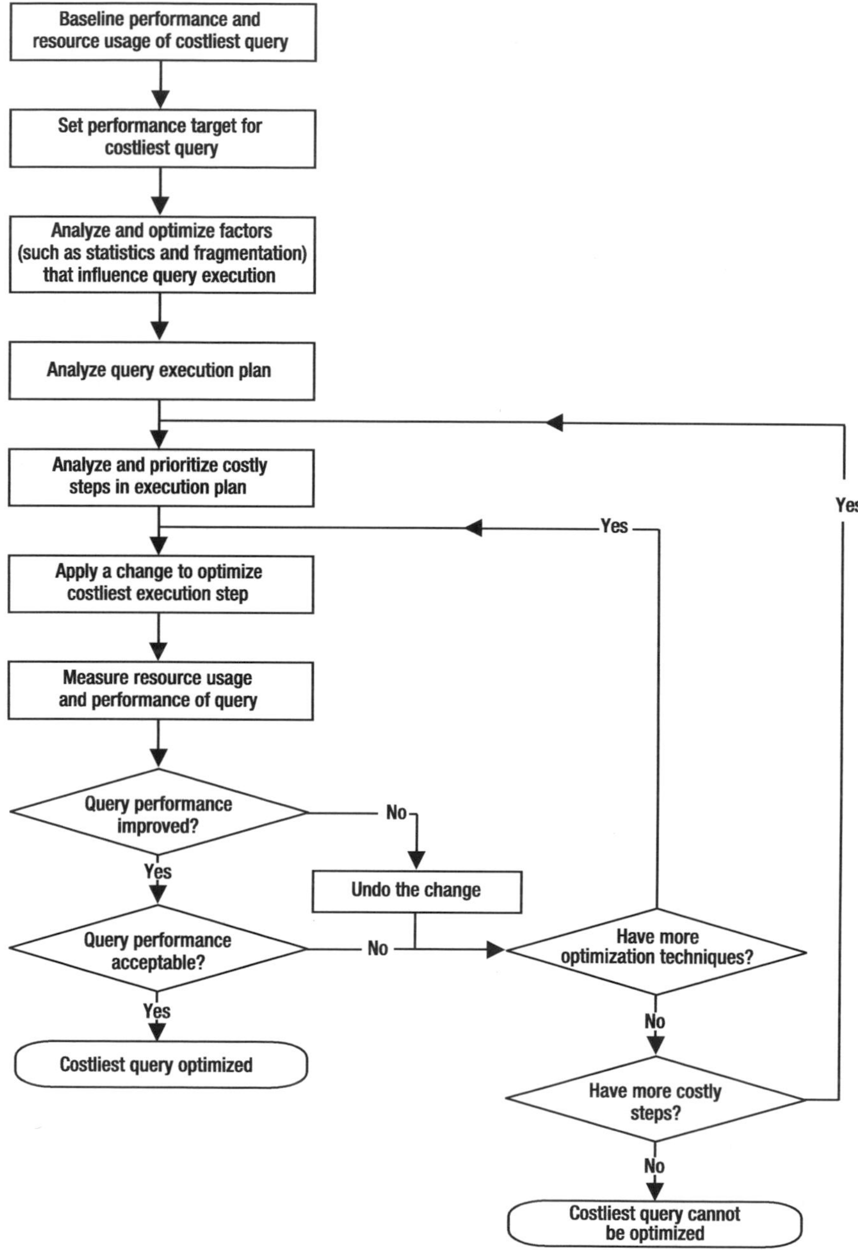

Figure 1-2. *Optimization of the costliest query*

As you can see from this process, there is quite a lot to do to ensure that you correctly tune the performance of a given query. It is important to use a solid process like this in performance tuning to focus on the main identified issues.

Having said this, it also helps to keep a broader perspective about the problem as a whole, since sometimes you may believe that you are trying to solve the correct performance bottleneck when in reality something else is causing the problem.

Performance vs. Price

One of the points I touched on earlier is that to gain increasingly small performance increments, you need to spend increasingly large amounts of time and money. Therefore, to ensure the best return on your investment, you should be very objective while optimizing performance. Always consider the following two aspects:

- What is the acceptable performance for your application?
- Is the investment worth the performance gain?

Performance Targets

To derive maximum efficiency, you must realistically estimate your performance requirements. You can follow many best practices to improve performance—for example, you can have your database files on the most efficient disk subsystem. However, before applying a best practice, you should consider how much you may gain from it and whether the gain will be worth the investment.

Sometimes it is really difficult to estimate the performance gain without actually making the enhancement. That makes properly identifying the source of your performance bottlenecks even more important. Are you CPU, memory, or disk bound? Is the cause code, data structure, or indexing, or are you simply at the limit of your hardware? Be sure you can make these possibly costly decisions from a known point rather than guessing. A practical approach can be to increase a resource in increments and analyze the application's scalability with the added resource. A scalable application will proportionately benefit from an incremental increase of the resource, if the resource was truly causing the scalability bottleneck. If the results appear to be satisfactory, then you can commit to the full enhancement. Experience also plays a very important role here.

"Good Enough" Tuning

Instead of tuning a system to the theoretical maximum performance, the goal should be to tune until the system performance is "good enough." This is a commonly adopted performance-tuning approach. The cost investment after such a point usually increases exponentially in comparison to the performance gain. The 80:20 rule works very well: by investing 20 percent of your resources, you may get 80 percent of the possible performance enhancement, but for the remaining 20 percent possible performance gain, you may have to invest an additional 80 percent of resources. It is therefore important to be realistic when setting your performance objectives.

A business benefits not by considering pure performance but by considering price performance. However, if the target is to find the scalability limit of your application (for various reasons, including marketing the product against its competitors), then it may be worthwhile investing as much as you can. Even in such cases, using a third-party stress test lab may be a better investment decision.

Performance Baseline

One of the main objectives of performance analysis is to understand the underlying level of system use or pressure on different hardware and software subsystems. This knowledge helps you in the following ways:

- Allows you to analyze resource bottlenecks.
- Enables you to troubleshoot by comparing system utilization patterns with a preestablished baseline.
- Assists you in making accurate estimates in capacity planning and scheduling hardware upgrades.
- Aids you in identifying low-utilization periods when the database administrative activities can be executed.
- Helps you estimate the nature of possible hardware downsizing or server consolidation. Why would a company downsize? Well, in the past, some companies leased very high-end systems expecting strong growth, but because of poor growth, they are now forced to downsize their system setups. And consolidation? Companies may sometimes buy too many servers or realize that the maintenance and licensing costs are too high. This would make using fewer servers very attractive.

Therefore, to better understand your application's resource requirements, you should create a *baseline* for your application's hardware and software usage. A baseline serves as a statistic of your system's current usage pattern and as a reference with which to compare future statistics. Baseline analysis helps you understand your application's behavior during a stable period, how hardware resources are used during such periods, and what the software characteristics are. With a baseline in place, you can do the following:

- Measure current performance and express your application's performance goals.
- Compare other hardware or software combinations against the baseline.
- Measure how the workload and/or data changes over time.
- Evaluate the peak and nonpeak usage pattern of the application. This information can be used to effectively distribute database administration activities, such as full database backup and database defragmentation during nonpeak hours.

You can use the System Monitor tool (also referred to as Performance Monitor) to create a baseline for SQL Server's hardware and software resource utilization. Similarly, you may baseline the SQL Server workload using the SQL Profiler tool, which can help you understand the average resource utilization and execution time of SQL queries when conditions are stable. You can also get snapshots of this information by using dynamic management views and dynamic management functions. You will learn in detail how to use these tools and queries in Chapters 2 and 3.

One other option is to take advantage of one of the many tools that can generate an artificial load on a given server or database. Numerous third-party tools are available. Microsoft offers SQLIO (available at `http://www.microsoft.com/downloads/details.aspx?familyid=9a8b005b-84e4-4f24-8d65-cb53442d9e19&displaylang=en`), which measures the I/O capacity of your system. Microsoft also has SQLIOSim, a tool for generating SQL Server–specific calls and simulated loads (available at `http://download.microsoft.com/download/3/8/0/3804cb1c-a911-4d12-8525-e5780197e0b5/SQLIOSimX86.exe`). Many third-party tools are available that can also help with this. If your system is not yet in production, using one of these tools to simulate a load to test the system is a very good idea.

Where to Focus Efforts

When you tune a particular system, pay special attention to the application layer (the database queries and stored procedures executed by Visual Basic/ADO or otherwise that are used to access the database). You will usually find that you can positively affect performance in the application layer far more than if you spend an equal amount of time figuring out how to tune the hardware, operating system, or SQL Server configuration. Although a proper configuration of hardware, operating system, and SQL Server is essential for the best performance of a database application, these fields have standardized so much that you usually need to spend only a limited amount of time configuring them properly for performance. Application design issues such as query design and indexing strategies, on the other hand, are application dependent. Consequently, there is usually more to optimize in the application layer than in the hardware, operating system, or SQL Server configuration. Thus, for a unit of time spent in each area, work in the application layer usually yields the maximum performance benefit, as illustrated in Figure 1-3.

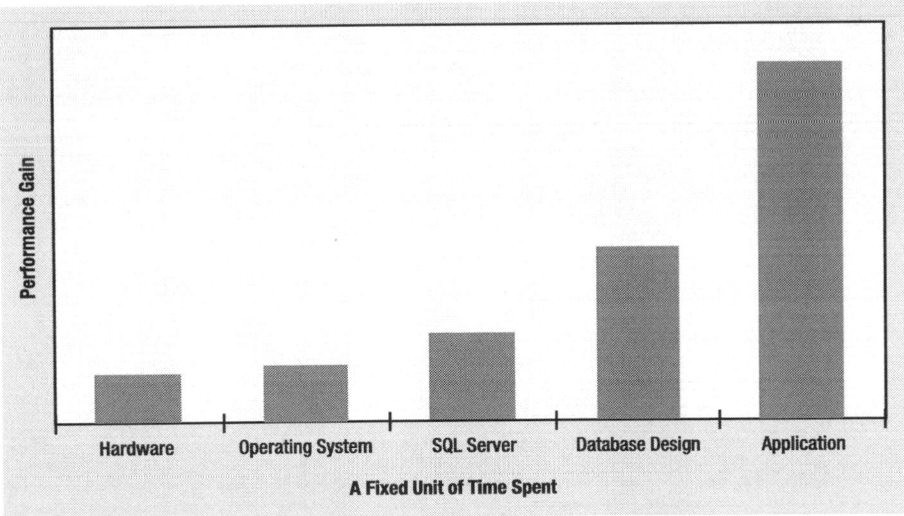

Figure 1-3. *Time spent vs. performance gain*

In my experience, you can obtain the greatest improvement in database application performance by looking first at the area of application design, including logical/physical database design, query design, and index design.

Sure, if you concentrate on hardware configuration and upgrades, you may obtain a satisfactory performance gain. However, a bad SQL query sent by the application can consume all the hardware resources available, no matter how much you have. Therefore, a poor application design can make the hardware upgrade requirements very high, even beyond your limits. In the presence of a heavy SQL workload, concentrating on hardware configurations and upgrades usually produces a poor return on investment.

You should analyze the stress created by an application on a SQL Server database at two levels:

- *High level*: Analyze how much stress the database application is creating on individual hardware resources and what the overall behavior of the SQL Server installation is. The best measures for this are the various wait states. This information can help you in two ways. First, it helps you identify the area to concentrate on within a SQL Server application where there is poor performance. Second, it helps you identify any lack of proper configuration at the higher levels. You can then decide which hardware resource may be upgraded if you are not able to tune the application using the Performance Monitor tool, as explained in Chapter 2.
- *Low level*: Identify the exact culprits within the application—in other words, the SQL queries that are creating most of the pressure visible at the overall higher level. This can be done using the SQL Profiler tool and various dynamic management views, as explained in Chapter 3.

SQL Server Performance Killers

Let's now consider the major problem areas that can degrade SQL Server performance. By being aware of the main performance killers in SQL Server in advance, you will be able to focus your tuning efforts on the likely causes.

Once you have optimized the hardware, operating system, and SQL Server settings, the main performance killers in SQL Server are as follows, in a rough order (with the worst appearing first):

- Poor indexing
- Inaccurate statistics
- Excessive blocking and deadlocks
- Non-set-based operations, usually T-SQL cursors
- Poor query design
- Poor database design
- Excessive fragmentation
- Nonreusable execution plans
- Poor execution plans, usually caused by parameter sniffing

- Frequent recompilation of execution plans
- Improper use of cursors
- Improper configuration of the database log
- Excessive use or improper configuration of `tempdb`

Let's take a quick look at each of these, before considering them in more depth in later chapters.

Poor Indexing

Poor indexing is usually one of the biggest performance killers in SQL Server. In the absence of proper indexing for a query, SQL Server has to retrieve and process much more data while executing the query. This causes high amounts of stress on the disk, memory, and CPU, increasing the query execution time significantly. Increased query execution time then leads to excessive blocking and deadlocks in SQL Server. You will learn how to determine the indexing strategies and resolve indexing problems in Chapters 4, 5, and 6.

Generally, indexes are considered to be the responsibility of the database administrator (DBA). However, the DBA cannot define how to use the indexes, since the use of indexes is determined by the database queries and stored procedures written by the developers. Therefore, defining the indexes must be a shared responsibility since the developers usually have more knowledge of the data to be retrieved and the DBAs have a better understanding of how indexes work. Indexes created without the knowledge of the queries serve little purpose.

■ **Note** Because indexes created without the knowledge of the queries serve little purpose, database developers need to understand indexes at least as well as they know T-SQL.

Inaccurate Statistics

SQL Server relies heavily on cost-based optimization, so accurate data-distribution statistics are extremely important for the effective use of indexes. Without accurate statistics, SQL Server's built-in query optimizer cannot accurately estimate the number of rows affected by a query. Because the amount of data to be retrieved from a table is highly important in deciding how to optimize the query execution, the query optimizer is much less effective if the data distribution statistics are not maintained accurately. You will look at how to analyze statistics in Chapter 7.

Excessive Blocking and Deadlocks

Because SQL Server is fully atomicity, consistency, isolation, and durability (ACID) compliant, the database engine ensures that modifications made by concurrent transactions are properly isolated from one another. By default, a transaction sees the data either in the state before another concurrent transaction modified the data or after the other transaction completed—it does not see an intermediate state.

Because of this isolation, when multiple transactions try to access a common resource concurrently in a noncompatible way, *blocking* occurs in the database. A *deadlock* occurs when two resources attempt to escalate or expand locked resources and conflict with one another. The query engine determines which process is the least costly to roll back and chooses it as the *deadlock victim*. This requires that the database request be resubmitted for successful execution. The execution time of a query is adversely affected by the amount of blocking and deadlock it faces.

For scalable performance of a multiuser database application, properly controlling the isolation levels and transaction scopes of the queries to minimize blocking and deadlock is critical; otherwise, the execution time of the queries will increase significantly, even though the hardware resources may be highly underutilized. I cover this problem in depth in Chapters 12 and 13.

Non-Set-Based Operations

Transact-SQL is a set-based scripting language, which means it operates on sets of data. This forces you to think in terms of columns rather than in terms of rows. Non-set-based thinking leads to excessive use of cursors and loops rather than exploring more efficient joins and subqueries. The T-SQL language offers rich mechanisms for manipulating sets of data. For performance to shine, you need to take advantage of these mechanisms rather than trying to force a row-by-row approach to your code, which will kill performance. Examples of how to do this are available throughout the book; also, I address T-SQL best practices in Chapter 11 and cursors in Chapter 14.

Poor Query Design

The effectiveness of indexes depends entirely on the way you write SQL queries. Retrieving excessively large numbers of rows from a table, or specifying a filter criterion that returns a larger result set from a table than is required, renders the indexes ineffective. To improve performance, you must ensure that the SQL queries are written to make the best use of new or existing indexes. Failing to write cost-effective SQL queries may prevent SQL Server from choosing proper indexes, which increases query execution time and database blocking. Chapter 11 covers how to write effective queries.

Query design covers not only single queries but also sets of queries often used to implement database functionalities such as a queue management among queue readers and writers. Even when the performance of individual queries used in the design is fine, the overall performance of the database can be very poor. Resolving this kind of bottleneck requires a broad understanding of different characteristics of SQL Server, which can affect the performance of database functionalities. You will see how to design effective database functionality using SQL queries throughout the book.

Poor Database Design

A database should be adequately normalized to increase the performance of data retrieval and reduce blocking. For example, if you have an undernormalized database with customer and order information in the same table, then the customer information will be repeated in all the order rows of the customer. This repetition of information in every row will increase the I/Os required to fetch all the orders placed by a customer. At the same time, a data writer working on a customer's order will reserve all the rows that include the customer information and thus block all other data writers/data readers trying to access the customer profile.

Overnormalization of a database is as bad as undernormalization. Overnormalization increases the number and complexity of joins required to retrieve data. An overnormalized database contains a large number of tables with a very small number of columns.

Having too many joins in a query may also be because database entities have not been partitioned very distinctly or the query is serving a very complex set of requirements that could perhaps be better served by creating a new view or stored procedure.

Database design is a large subject. I will provide a few pointers in Chapter 18 and throughout the rest of the book. Because of the size of the topic, I won't be able to treat it in the complete manner it requires. However, if you want to read a book on database design, with an emphasis on introducing the subject, I recommend reading *Data Modeling for Everyone* by Sharon Allen (Apress, 2003).

Excessive Fragmentation

While analyzing data retrieval operations, you can usually assume that the data is organized in an orderly way, as indicated by the index used by the data retrieval operation. However, if the pages containing the data are fragmented in a nonorderly fashion or if they contain a small amount of data because of frequent page splits, then the number of read operations required by the data retrieval operation will be much higher than might otherwise be required. The increase in the number of read operations caused by fragmentation hurts query performance. In Chapter 8, you will learn how to analyze and remove fragmentation.

Nonreusable Execution Plans

To execute a query in an efficient way, SQL Server's query optimizer spends a fair amount of CPU cycles creating a cost-effective execution plan. The good news is that the plan is cached in memory, so you can reuse it once created. However, if the plan is designed so that you cannot plug variable values into it, SQL Server creates a new execution plan every time the same query is resubmitted with different variable values. So, for better performance, it is extremely important to submit SQL queries in forms that help SQL Server cache and reuse the execution plans. I will also address topics such as plan freezing, forcing query plans, and the problems associated with parameter sniffing. You will see in detail how to improve the reusability of execution plans in Chapter 9.

Poor Execution Plans

The same mechanisms that allow SQL Server to establish an efficient stored procedure and reuse that procedure again and again instead of recompiling can, in some cases, work against you. A bad execution plan can be a real performance killer. Bad plans are frequently caused by a process called *parameter sniffing*, which comes from the mechanisms that the query optimizer uses to determine the best plan based on statistics. It's important to understand how statistics and parameters combine to create execution plans and what you can do to control them. I cover statistics in depth in Chapter 7 and execution plan analysis in Chapter 9.

Frequent Recompilation of Execution Plans

One of the standard ways of ensuring a reusable execution plan, independent of variable values used in a query, is to use a stored procedure. Using a stored procedure to execute a set of SQL queries allows SQL Server to create a *parameterized execution plan.*

A parameterized execution plan is independent of the parameter values supplied during the execution of the stored procedure, and it is consequently highly reusable. However, the execution plan of the stored procedure can be reused only if SQL Server does not have to recompile the execution plan every time the stored procedure is run. Frequent recompilation of a stored procedure increases pressure on the CPU and the query execution time. SQL Server has partially addressed this problem with the addition of statement-level recompilation, but it's not a complete fix to the issue. I will discuss in detail the various causes and resolutions of stored procedure, and statement, recompilation in Chapter 10.

Improper Use of Cursors

By preferring a cursor-based (row-at-a-time) result set—or as Jeff Moden has so aptly termed it, Row By Agonizing Row (RBAR; pronounced "ree-bar")—instead of a regular set-based SQL query, you add a large amount of overhead on SQL Server. Use set-based queries whenever possible, but if you are forced to deal with cursors, be sure to use efficient cursor types such as fast-forward only. Excessive use of inefficient cursors increases stress on SQL Server resources, slowing down system performance. I discuss how to work with cursors, if you must, properly in Chapter 14.

Improper Configuration of the Database Log

By failing to follow the general recommendations in configuring a database log, you can adversely affect the performance of an Online Transaction Processing (OLTP)–based SQL Server database. For optimal performance, SQL Server heavily relies on accessing the database logs effectively.

Chapter 2 covers how to configure the database log properly.

Excessive Use or Improper Configuration of tempdb

There is only one `tempdb` for any SQL Server instance. Since temporary storage such as operations involving user objects such as temporary tables and table variables, system objects such as cursors or hash tables for joins, and operations such as sorts and row versioning all use the `tempdb` database, `tempdb` can become quite a bottleneck. All these options and others that you can use lead to space, I/O, and contention issues within `tempdb`. I cover some configuration options to help with this in Chapter 2 and other options in other chapters appropriate to the issues addressed by that chapter.

Summary

In this introductory chapter, you have seen that SQL Server performance tuning is an iterative process, consisting of identifying performance bottlenecks, troubleshooting their cause, applying different resolutions, quantifying performance improvements, and then going back to the start until your required performance level is reached.

To assist in this process, you should create a system baseline to compare with your modifications. Throughout the performance-tuning process, you need to be very objective about the amount of tuning you want to perform—you can always make a query run a little bit faster, but is the effort worth the cost? Finally, since performance depends on the pattern of user activity and data, you must reevaluate the database server performance on a regular basis.

To derive the optimal performance from a SQL Server database system, it is extremely important that you understand the stresses on the server created by the database application. In the next two chapters, I discuss how to analyze these stresses, both at a higher system level and at a lower SQL Server activities level. Then I show how to combine the two.

In the rest of the book, you will examine in depth the biggest SQL Server performance killers, as mentioned earlier in the chapter. You will learn how these individual factors can affect performance if used incorrectly and how to resolve or avoid these traps.

CHAPTER 2

System Performance Analysis

In the first chapter, I stressed the importance of having a performance baseline that you can use to measure performance changes. In fact, this is one of the first things you should do when starting the performance-tuning process, since without a baseline you will not be able to quantify improvements. In this chapter, you will learn how to use the Performance Monitor tool to accomplish this and how to use the different performance counters that are required to create a baseline.

Specifically, I cover the following topics:

- The basics of the Performance Monitor tool
- How to analyze hardware resource bottlenecks using Performance Monitor
- How to retrieve Performance Monitor data within SQL Server using dynamic management views
- How to resolve hardware resource bottlenecks
- How to analyze the overall performance of SQL Server
- How to create a baseline for the system

Performance Monitor Tool

Windows Server 2008 provides a tool called *Performance Monitor*, although all the documentation for it refers to *System Monitor*. This tool is part of a larger suite of data collection tools called the Reliability and Performance Monitor. Performance Monitor collects detailed information about the utilization of operating system resources. It allows you to track nearly every aspect of system performance, including memory, disk, processor, and the network. In addition, SQL Server 2008 provides extensions to the Performance Monitor tool to track a variety of functional areas within SQL Server.

Performance Monitor tracks resource behavior by capturing performance data generated by hardware and software components of the system such as a processor, a process, a thread, and so on. The performance data generated by a system component is represented by a *performance object*. A performance object provides *counters* that represent specific aspects of a component, such as `% Processor Time` for a `Processor` object.

There can be multiple instances of a system component. For instance, the `Processor` object in a computer with two processors will have two instances represented as instances 0 and 1. Performance objects with multiple instances may also have an instance called `_Total` to represent the total value for all the instances. For example, the processor usage of a computer with four processors can be determined using the following performance object, counter, and instance (as shown in Figure 2-1):

- *Performance object*: `Processor`
- *Counter*: `% Processor Time`
- *Instance*: `_Total`

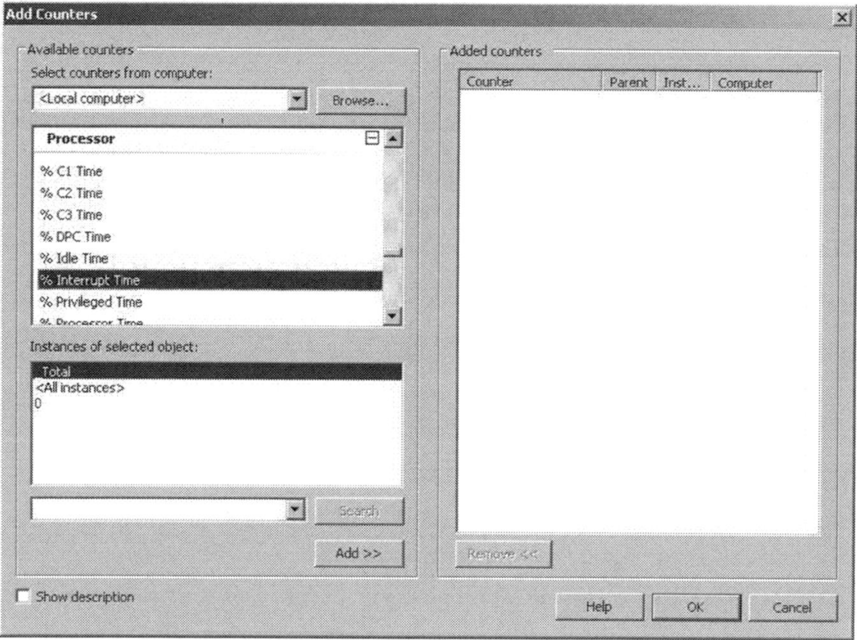

Figure 2-1. *Adding a Performance Monitor counter*

System behavior can be either tracked in real time in the form of graphs or captured as a log (called a *counter log*) for offline analysis.

To run the Performance Monitor tool, execute `perfmon` from a command prompt, which will open the Reliability and Performance Monitor suite. You can also right-click the Computer icon on the desktop or Start menu, expand Diagnostics, and then expand the Reliability and Performance Monitor. Both will allow you to open the Performance Monitor utility.

You will learn how to set up the individual counters in the "Creating a Baseline" section later in this chapter. First you will examine which counters you should choose in order to identify system bottlenecks and also how you can resolve some of these bottlenecks.

Dynamic Management Views

To get an immediate snapshot of a large amount of data that was formerly available only in Performance Monitor, SQL Server now offers the same data internally through a set of dynamic management views (DMVs) and dynamic management functions (DMFs). These are extremely useful mechanisms for capturing a snapshot of the current performance of your system. I'll introduce several of these throughout the book, but I'll focus on a few that are the most important for monitoring performance and for establishing a baseline.

The `sys.dm_os_performance_counters` view displays the SQL Server counters within a query, allowing you to apply the full strength of T-SQL to the data immediately. For example, this simple query will return the current value for `Logins/sec`:

```
SELECT  cntr_value
FROM    sys.dm_os_performance_counters
WHERE   OBJECT_NAME = 'MSSQL$GF2008:General Statistics'
        AND counter_name = 'Logins/sec'
```

This returns the value of 15 for my server. For your server, you'll need to substitute the appropriate server name in the `OBJECT_NAME` comparison.

There are a large number of DMVs and DMFs that can be used to gather information about the server. Rather than cover them all, I'll introduce one more that you will find yourself accessing on a regular basis, `sys.dm_os_wait_stats`. This DMV shows an aggregated view of the threads within SQL Server that are waiting on various resources, collected since the last time SQL Server was started or the counters were reset. Identifying the types of waits that are occurring within your system is one of the easiest mechanisms to begin identifying the source of your bottlenecks. You can sort the data in various ways, but for the first example, I'll look at the waits that have the longest current count using this simple query:

```
SELECT TOP (10)
        *
FROM    sys.dm_os_wait_stats
ORDER BY wait_time_ms DESC
```

Figure 2-2 displays the output.

	wait_type	waiting_tasks_count	wait_time_ms	max_wait_time_ms	signal_wait_time_ms
1	FT_IFTS_SCHEDULER_IDLE_WAIT	448	35901278	600001	1
2	LAZYWRITER_SLEEP	12280	12258720	1460	607
3	SQLTRACE_BUFFER_FLUSH	3064	12255623	4597	6
4	REQUEST_FOR_DEADLOCK_SEARCH	2452	12255005	5003	12255005
5	XE_TIMER_EVENT	410	12241728	30002	12240002
6	SLEEP_TASK	19995	6228098	2967	333
7	BROKER_TO_FLUSH	5979	6126764	1069	28
8	LOGMGR_QUEUE	64	4888389	3643154	2682
9	CHECKPOINT_QUEUE	4	105705	104426	3
10	BROKER_TASK_STOP	6	38912	10000	0

Figure 2-2. *Output from `sys.dm_os_wait_stats`*

You can see not only the cumulative time that particular waits have occurred but also a count of how often they have occurred and the maximum time that something had to wait. From here, you can identify the wait type and begin troubleshooting. One of the most common types of waits is I/O. If you see `ASYNCH_IO_COMPLETION`, `IO_COMPLETION`, `LOGMGR`, `WRITELOG`, or `PAGEIOLATCH` in your top ten wait types, you may be experiencing I/O contention, and you now know where to start working. For a more detailed analysis of wait types and how to use them as a monitoring tool within SQL Server, read the Microsoft white paper "SQL Server 2005 Waits and Queues" (`http://www.microsoft.com/technet/prodtechnol/sql/bestpractice/performance_tuning_waits_queues.mspx`). Although it was written for SQL Server 2005, it is equally applicable to SQL Server 2008.

Hardware Resource Bottlenecks

Typically, SQL Server database performance is affected by stress on the following hardware resources:

- Memory
- Disk I/O
- Processor
- Network

Stress beyond the capacity of a hardware resource forms a bottleneck. To address the overall performance of a system, you need to identify these bottlenecks, because they form the limit on overall system performance.

Identifying Bottlenecks

There is usually a relationship between resource bottlenecks. For example, a processor bottleneck may be a symptom of excessive paging (memory bottleneck) or a slow disk (disk bottleneck). If a system is low on memory, causing excessive paging, and has a slow disk, then one of the end results will be a processor with high utilization since the processor has to spend a significant number of CPU cycles to swap pages in and out of the memory and to manage the resultant high number of I/O requests. Replacing the processor with a faster one may help a little, but it would not be the best overall solution. In a case like this, increasing memory is a more appropriate solution, because it will decrease pressure on the disk and processor as well. Even upgrading the disk will probably be a better solution than upgrading the processor.

■ **Note** The most common performance problem is usually I/O, either from memory or from the disk.

One of the best ways of locating a bottleneck is to identify resources that are waiting for some other resource to complete its operation. You can use Performance Monitor counters or DMVs such as `sys.dm_os_wait_stats` to gather that information. The response time of a request served by a resource includes the time the request had to wait in the resource queue, as well as the time taken to execute the request, so end user response time is directly proportional to the amount of queuing in a system.

For example, consider that the disk subsystem has a disk queue length of 10. Since the disk subsystem already has pending disk requests on it, a new disk request has to wait until the previous disk requests complete. If the time taken by an average disk transfer is one second, then the new disk request has to wait for about ten seconds before getting the attention of the disk subsystem. Therefore, the total response time of the disk request will be ten seconds wait time, plus one second disk transfer time.

Be aware that the absence of a queue does not mean that there is no bottleneck. When queue lengths start growing, however, it is a sure sign that the system is not able to keep up with the demand.

Not all resources have specific counters that show queuing levels, but most resources have some counters that represent an overcommittal of that resource. For example, memory has no such counter, but a large number of hard page faults represents the overcommittal of physical memory (hard page faults are explained later in the chapter in the section "Pages/sec and Page Faults/sec Counters"). Other resources, such as the processor and disk, have specific counters to indicate the level of queuing. For example, the counter `Page Life Expectancy` indicates how long a page will stay in the buffer pool without being referenced. This is an indicator of how well SQL Server is able to manage its memory, since a longer life means that a piece of data in the buffer will be there, available, waiting for the next reference. However, a shorter life means that SQL Server is moving pages in and out of the buffer quickly, possibly suggesting a memory bottleneck.

You will see which counters to use in analyzing each type of bottleneck shortly.

Bottleneck Resolution

Once you have identified bottlenecks, you can resolve them in two ways:

- You can increase resource throughput.
- You can decrease the arrival rate of requests to the resource.

Increasing the throughput usually requires extra resources such as memory, disks, processors, or network adapters. You can decrease the arrival rate by being more selective about the requests to a resource. For example, when you have a disk subsystem bottleneck, you can either increase the throughput of the disk subsystem or decrease the amount of I/O requests.

Increasing the throughput means adding more disks or upgrading to faster disks. Decreasing the arrival rate means identifying the cause of high I/O requests to the disk subsystem and applying resolutions to decrease their number. You may be able to decrease the I/O requests, for example, by adding appropriate indexes on a table to limit the amount of data accessed or by partitioning a table between multiple disks.

Memory Bottleneck Analysis

Memory can be a problematic bottleneck because a bottleneck in memory will manifest on other resources, too. This is particularly true for a system running SQL Server. When SQL Server runs out of cache (or memory), a process within SQL Server (called *lazy writer*) has to work extensively to maintain enough free internal memory pages within SQL Server. This consumes extra CPU cycles and performs additional physical disk I/O to write memory pages back to disk.

SQL Server Memory Management

SQL Server manages memory for databases, including memory requirements for data and query execution plans, in a large pool of memory called the *memory pool*. The memory pool consists of a collection of 8KB buffers to manage data pages and plan cache pages, free pages, and so forth. The memory pool is usually the largest portion of SQL Server memory. SQL Server manages memory by growing or shrinking its memory pool size dynamically.

You can configure SQL Server for dynamic memory management in SQL Server Management Studio (SSMS). Go to the Memory folder of the Server Properties dialog box, as shown in Figure 2-3.

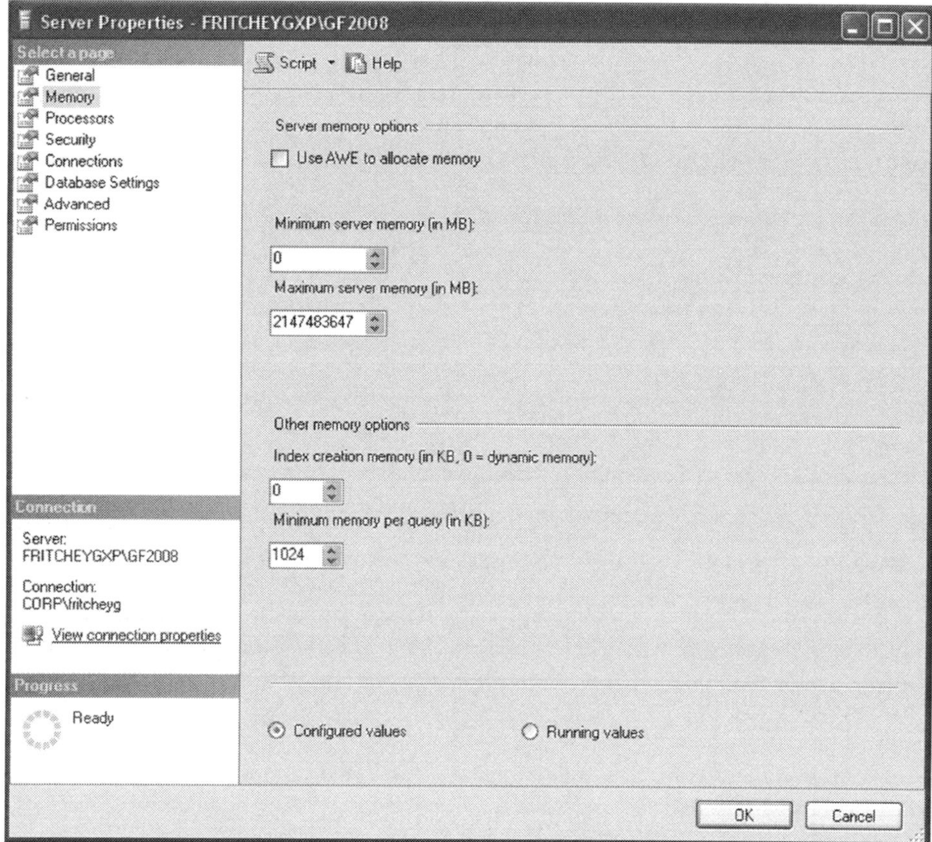

Figure 2-3. *SQL Server memory configuration*

The dynamic memory range is controlled through two configuration properties: `Minimum(MB)` and `Maximum(MB)`.

- `Minimum(MB)`, also known as `min server memory`, works as a floor value for the memory pool. Once the memory pool reaches the same size as the floor value, SQL Server can continue committing pages in the memory pool, but it cannot be shrunk to less than the floor value. Note that SQL Server does not start with the `min server memory` configuration value but commits memory dynamically, as needed.
- `Maximum(MB)`, also known as `max server memory`, serves as a ceiling value to limit the maximum growth of the memory pool. These configuration settings take effect immediately and do not require a restart.

Microsoft recommends that you use dynamic memory configuration for SQL Server, where `min server memory` will be 0 and `max server memory` will be the maximum physical memory of the system, assuming a single instance on the machine. You should not run other memory-intensive applications on the same server as SQL Server, but if you must, I recommend you first get estimates on how much memory is needed by other applications and then configure SQL Server with a `max server memory` value set to prevent the other applications from starving SQL Server of memory. On a system where SQL Server is running on its own, I prefer to set the minimum server memory equal to the max value and simply dispatch with dynamic management. On a server with multiple SQL Server instances, you'll need to adjust these memory settings to ensure each instance has an adequate value. Just make sure you've left enough memory for the operating system and external processes, as well as non-buffer-pool memory (which used to be called `MemToLeave`).

Memory within SQL Server can be roughly divided into buffer pool memory, which represents data pages and free pages, and nonbuffer memory, which consists of threads, DLLs, linked servers, and others. Most of the memory used by SQL Server goes into the buffer pool.

■ **Note** SQL Server does consume more memory than simply that specified by the `max_server_memory` setting.

You can also manage the configuration values for `min server memory` and `max server memory` by using the `sp_configure` system stored procedure. To see the configuration values for these parameters, execute the `sp_configure` stored procedure as follows:

```
exec sp_configure 'min server memory (MB)'
exec sp_configure 'max server memory (MB)'
```

Figure 2-4 shows the result of running these commands.

	name	minimum	maximum	config_value	run_value
1	min server memory (MB)	0	2147483647	0	8

	name	minimum	maximum	config_value	run_value
1	max server memory (MB)	16	2147483647	2147483647	2147483647

Figure 2-4. *SQL Server memory configuration properties*

Note that the default value for the min server memory setting is 0MB, and for the max server memory setting it is 2147483647MB. Also, max server memory cannot be set to less than 4MB.

You can also modify these configuration values using the sp_configure stored procedure. For example, to set max server memory to 200MB and min server memory to 100MB, execute the following set of statements (set_memory.sql in the download):

```
USE master
EXEC sp_configure 'show advanced option', '1'
RECONFIGURE
exec sp_configure 'min server memory (MB)', 100
exec sp_configure 'max server memory (MB)', 200
RECONFIGURE WITH OVERRIDE
```

The min server memory and max server memory configurations are classified as advanced options. By default, the sp_configure stored procedure does not affect/display the advanced options. Setting show advanced option to 1 as shown previously enables the sp_configure stored procedure to affect/display the advanced options.

The RECONFIGURE statement updates the memory configuration values set by sp_configure. Since ad hoc updates to the system catalog containing the memory configuration values are not recommended, the OVERRIDE flag is used with the RECONFIGURE statement to force the memory configuration. If you do the memory configuration through Management Studio, Management Studio automatically executes the RECONFIGURE WITH OVERRIDE statement after the configuration setting.

In some rare circumstances, you may need to allow for SQL Server sharing a system's memory. To elaborate, consider a computer with SQL Server and Exchange Server running on it. Both servers are heavy users of memory and thus keep pushing each other for memory. The dynamic-memory behavior of SQL Server allows it to release memory to Exchange Server at one instance and grab it back as Exchange Server releases it. You can avoid this dynamic-memory management overhead by configuring SQL Server for a fixed memory size. However, please keep in mind that since SQL Server is an extremely resource-intensive process, it is highly recommended that you have a dedicated SQL Server production machine.

Now that you understand SQL Server memory management, let's consider the performance counters you can use to analyze stress on memory, as shown in Table 2-1.

Table 2-1. *Performance Monitor Counters to Analyze Memory Pressure*

Object(Instance[,InstanceN])	Counter	Description	Values
Memory	Available Bytes	Free physical memory	System dependent
	Pages/sec	Rate of hard page faults	Average value < 50
	Page Faults/sec	Rate of total page faults	Compare with its baseline value for trend analysis
	Pages Input/sec	Rate of input page faults	
	Pages Output/sec	Rate of output page faults	

Object(Instance[,InstanceN])	Counter	Description	Values
SQLServer:Buffer Manager	Buffer cache hit ratio	Percentage of requests served out of buffer cache	Average value ≥ 90%
	Page Life Expectancy	Time page spends in buffer	Average value > 300
	Checkpoint Pages/sec	Pages written to disk by checkpoint	Average value < 30
	Lazy writes/sec	Dirty aged pages flushed from buffer	Average value < 20
SQLServer:Memory Manager	Memory Grants Pending	Number of processes waiting for memory grant	Average value = 0
	Target Server Memory (KB)	Maximum physical memory SQL Server can consume on the box	Close to size of physical memory
	Total Server Memory (KB)	Physical memory currently assigned to SQL Server	Close to Target Server Memory (KB)
Process	Private Bytes	Size, in bytes, of memory that this process has allocated that cannot be shared with other processes	

I'll now walk you through these counters to get a better idea of what you can use them for.

Available Bytes

The Available Bytes counter represents free physical memory in the system. For good performance, this counter value should not be too low. If SQL Server is configured for dynamic memory usage, then this value will be controlled by calls to a Windows API that determines when and how much memory to release. Extended periods of time with this value very low and SQL Server memory not changing indicates that the server is under severe memory stress.

Pages/sec and Page Faults/sec Counters

To understand the importance of the Pages/sec and Page Faults/sec counters, you first need to learn about *page faults*. A page fault occurs when a process requires code or data that is not in its *working set* (its space in physical memory). It may lead to a soft page fault or a hard page fault. If the faulted page is found elsewhere in physical memory, then it is called a *soft page fault*. A *hard page fault* occurs when a process requires code or data that is not in its working set or elsewhere in physical memory and must be retrieved from disk.

The speed of a disk access is in the order of milliseconds, whereas a memory access is in the order of nanoseconds. This huge difference in the speed between a disk access and a memory access makes the effect of hard page faults significant compared to that of soft page faults.

The Pages/sec counter represents the number of pages read from or written to disk per second to resolve hard page faults. The Page Faults/sec performance counter indicates the total page faults per second—soft page faults plus hard page faults—handled by the system.

Hard page faults, indicated by Pages/sec, should not be consistently high. If this counter is consistently very high, then SQL Server is probably starving other applications. There are no hard and fast numbers for what indicates a problem, because these numbers will vary widely between systems based on the amount and type of memory as well as the speed of disk access on the system.

If the Pages/sec counter is very high, then you can break it up into Pages Input/sec and Pages Output/sec:

- Pages Input/sec: An application will wait only on an input page, not on an output page.
- Pages Output/sec: Page output will stress the system, but an application usually does not see this stress. Pages output are usually represented by the application's dirty pages that need to be backed out to the disk. Pages Output/sec is an issue only when disk load become an issue.

Also, check Process:Page Faults/sec to find out which process is causing excessive paging in case of high Pages/sec. The Process object is the system component that provides performance data for the processes running on the system, which are individually represented by their corresponding instance name.

For example, the SQL Server process is represented by the sqlservr instance of the Process object. High numbers for this counter usually do not mean much unless Pages/sec is high. Page Faults/sec can range all over the spectrum with normal application behavior, with values from 0 to 1,000 per second being acceptable. This entire data set means a baseline is essential to determine the expected normal behavior.

Buffer Cache Hit Ratio

The *buffer cache* is the pool of buffer pages into which data pages are read, and it is often the biggest part of the SQL Server memory pool. This counter value should be as high as possible, especially for OLTP systems that should have fairly regimented data access, unlike a warehouse or reporting system. It is extremely common to find this counter value as 99 percent or more for most production servers. A low Buffer cache hit ratio value indicates that few requests could be served out of the buffer cache, with the rest of the requests being served from disk.

When this happens, either SQL Server is still warming up or the memory requirement of the buffer cache is more than the maximum memory available for its growth. If this is consistently low, you should consider getting more memory for the system.

Page Life Expectancy

Page Life Expectancy indicates how long a page will stay in the buffer pool without being referenced. Generally, a low number for this counter means that pages are being removed from the buffer, lowering the efficiency of the cache and indicating the possibility of memory pressure. On reporting systems, as opposed to OLTP systems, this number may remain at a lower value since more data is accessed from reporting systems. A reasonable value to expect to see here is 300 seconds or more.

Checkpoint Pages/sec

The `Checkpoint Pages/sec` counter represents the number of pages that are moved to disk by a checkpoint operation. These numbers should be relatively low, for example, less than 30 per second for most systems. A higher number means more pages are being marked as dirty in the cache. A dirty page is one that is modified while in the buffer. When it's modified, it's marked as dirty and will get written back to the disk during the next checkpoint. Higher values on this counter indicate a larger number of writes occurring within the system, possibly indicative of I/O problems.

Lazy writes/sec

The `Lazy writes/sec` counter records the number of buffers written each second by the buffer manager's lazy write process. This process is where the dirty, aged buffers are removed from the buffer by a system process that frees the memory up for other uses. A dirty, aged buffer is one that has changes and needs to be written to the disk. Higher values on this counter possibly indicate I/O issues or even memory problems. The `Lazy writes/sec` values should consistently be less than 20 for the average system.

Memory Grants Pending

The `Memory Grants Pending` counter represents the number of processes pending for a memory grant within SQL Server memory. If this counter value is high, then SQL Server is short of memory. Under normal conditions, this counter value should consistently be 0 for most production servers.

Another way to retrieve this value, on the fly, is to run queries against the DMV `sys.dm_exec_query_memory_grants`. A `null` value in the column `grant_time` indicates that the process is still waiting for a memory grant. This is one method you can use to troubleshoot query timeouts by identifying that a query (or queries) is waiting on memory in order to execute.

Target Server Memory (KB) and Total Server Memory (KB)

`Target Server Memory (KB)` indicates the total amount of dynamic memory SQL Server is willing to consume. `Total Server Memory (KB)` indicates the amount of memory currently assigned to SQL Server. The `Total Server Memory (KB)` counter value can be very high if the system is dedicated to SQL Server. If `Total Server Memory (KB)` is much less than `Target Server Memory (KB)`, then either the SQL Server memory requirement is low, the `max server memory` configuration parameter of SQL Server is set at too low a value, or the system is in *warm-up phase*. The warm-up phase is the period after SQL Server is started when the database server is in the process of expanding its memory allocation dynamically as more data sets are accessed, bringing more data pages into memory.

You can confirm a low memory requirement from SQL Server by the presence of a large number of free pages, usually 5,000 or more.

Memory Bottleneck Resolutions

When there is high stress on memory, indicated by a large number of hard page faults, you can resolve memory bottleneck using the flowchart shown in Figure 2-5.

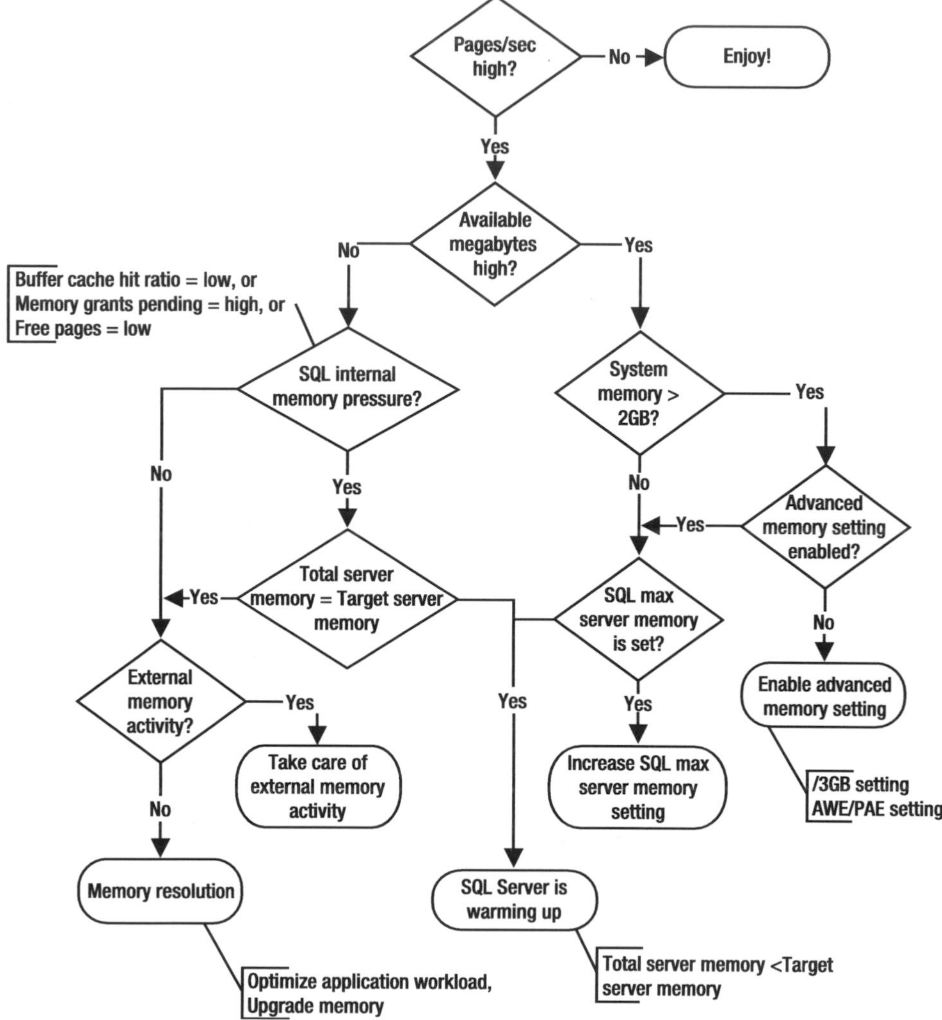

Figure 2-5. *Memory bottleneck resolution chart*

A few of the common resolutions for memory bottlenecks are as follows:

- Optimizing application workload
- Allocating more memory to SQL Server
- Increasing system memory
- Changing from a 32-bit to a 64-bit processor
- Enabling 3GB of process space
- Using memory beyond 4GB within 32-bit SQL Server

Let's take a look at each of these in turn.

Optimizing Application Workload

Optimizing application workload is the most effective resolution most of the time, but because of the complexity and challenges involved in this process, it is usually considered last. To identify the memory-intensive queries, capture all the SQL queries using SQL Profiler (which you will learn how to use in Chapter 3), and then group the trace output on the `Reads` column. The queries with the highest number of logical reads contribute to most of the memory stress. You will see how to optimize those queries in more detail throughout this book.

Allocating More Memory to SQL Server

As you learned in the "SQL Server Memory Management" section, the `max server memory` configuration can limit the maximum size of the SQL Server memory pool. If the memory requirement of SQL Server is more than the `max server memory` value, which you can tell through the number of hard page faults, then increasing the value will allow the memory pool to grow. To benefit from increasing the `max server memory` value, ensure that enough physical memory is available in the system.

Increasing System Memory

The memory requirement of SQL Server depends on the total amount of data processed by SQL activities. It is not directly correlated to the size of the database or the number of incoming SQL queries. For example, if a memory-intensive query performs a cross join between two small tables without any filter criteria to narrow down the result set, it can cause high stress on the system memory.

One of the easiest and cheapest resolutions is to simply increase system memory. However, it is still important to find out what is consuming the physical memory, because if the application workload is extremely memory intensive, you will soon be limited by the maximum amount of memory a system can access. To identify which queries are using more memory, you can query the `sys.dm_exec_query_memory_grants` DMV. Just be careful when running queries against this DMV using a `JOIN` or an `ORDER BY` statement because, if your system is already under memory stress, these actions can lead to your query needing its own memory grant.

Something to keep in mind is the memory needed by SQL Server outside the buffer pool. This is referred to as *nonbuffer memory* and used to be called `MemToLeave`. One of the worst memory problems for queries occurs when the size of the query itself, not the data returned but the T-SQL code, exceeds 8KB in size. This memory is allocated at startup using the `-g` switch. If your queries are large (again, greater than 8KB in size), they will need to take advantage of this memory allocation. You will need to make sure you have enough memory available on your server for this. Using extended stored procedures, distributed queries, and automation objects also places a strain on this memory space.

Changing from a 32-bit to a 64-bit Processor

Switching the physical server from a 32-bit processor to a 64-bit processor (and the attendant Windows Server software upgrade) radically changes the memory management capabilities of SQL Server. The limitations on SQL Server for memory go from 3GB (not counting up to 64GB of additional data cache available through Address Windowing Extensions [AWE]) to a limit of up to 8TB depending on the version of the operating system and the specific processor type.

Limitations experienced with the AWE are removed since the memory used in 64-bit systems can be used for both data and the procedure cache, unlike AWE memory. No other switches or extra mechanisms are needed for SQL Server to take advantage of this memory space.

Enabling 3GB of Process Space

Standard 32-bit addresses can map a maximum of 4GB of memory. The standard address spaces of 32-bit Windows operating systems processes are therefore limited to 4GB. Out of this 4GB process space, by default the upper 2GB is reserved for the operating system, and the lower 2GB is made available to the application. If you specify a `/3GB` switch in the `boot.ini` file of the 32-bit OS, the operating system reserves only 1GB of the address space, and the application can access up to 3GB. This is also called *4-gig tuning* (4GT). No new APIs are required for this purpose.

Therefore, on a machine with 4GB of physical memory and the default Windows configuration, you will find available memory of about 2GB or more. To let SQL Server use up to 3GB of the available memory, you can add the `/3GB` switch in the `boot.ini` file as follows:

```
[boot loader]
timeout=30
default=multi(0)disk(0)rdisk(0)partition(1)\WINNT
[operating systems]
multi(0)disk(0)rdisk(0)partition(1)\WINNT=
"Microsoft Windows Server 2008 Advanced Server"
/fastdetect /3GB
```

The `/3GB` switch should not be used for systems with more than 16GB of physical memory, as explained in the following section, or for systems that require a higher amount of kernel memory.

SQL Server 2008 on 64-bit systems can support up to 8TB on an x64 platform and up to 7TB on the IA64. There is a further limit on Windows 2003 of 1TB. As more memory is available from the OS, the limits imposed by SQL Server are reached. This is without having to use any other switches or extended memory schemes.

Using Memory Beyond 4GB Within SQL Server

All processors based on the IA-32 architecture, beginning with the Intel Pentium Pro, support a new 36-bit physical addressing mode called Physical Address Extension (PAE). PAE allows up to 64GB of physical memory, depending upon the operating system. The PAE mode kernel requires an Intel Architecture processor (Pentium Pro or newer) and more than 4GB of RAM.

Windows Server operating systems that are 32-bit implement Address Windowing Extensions to access up to 64GB of physical memory with the PAE addressing mode. This memory is available for the buffer cache, for data storage only, but cannot be used by operations and tasks to increase the number of, for example, databases available on the system.

Accessing memory beyond 4GB in a 32-bit Windows Server OS requires configuration at two levels: the operating system level and the application level. To enable the operating system to access more than 4GB of physical memory, add a /PAE switch in the boot.ini file as follows:

```
[boot loader]
timeout=30
default=multi(0)disk(0)rdisk(0)partition(1)\WINNT
[operating systems]
multi(0)disk(0)rdisk(0)partition(1)\WINNT=
"Microsoft Windows Server 2008 Advanced Server"
/fastdetect /PAE
```

Once you have modified boot.ini, you can use sp_configure to enable SQL Server 2008 to access more than 4GB of physical memory. The following example (set_5GigMemory.sql in the download) shows how to enable 5GB:

```
sp_configure 'show advanced options', 1
RECONFIGURE
GO
sp_configure 'awe enabled', 1
RECONFIGURE
GO
sp_configure 'max server memory', 5120
RECONFIGURE
GO
```

The operating system must be restarted for the /PAE switch to take effect. The associated restart of SQL Server puts the AWE configuration into effect.

Instances of SQL Server 2008 do not dynamically manage the size of the address space when AWE memory is enabled; therefore, setting the max server memory configuration parameter of SQL Server is mandatory while using AWE memory. On a dedicated SQL Server machine, max server memory may be set to (total physical memory - 200MB) so that enough physical memory is kept aside for the operating system and other essential tools/applications.

While running multiple instances of SQL Server 2008 on the same computer, you must ensure the following with each instance using AWE memory:

- Each instance has a max server memory setting.
- When setting max server memory, you need to take into account the amount of nonbuffer pool memory (formerly called MemToLeave) that you may need for SQL Server to operate.
- The sum of the max server memory values for all the instances should be less than the amount of physical memory in the computer.

Considering the preceding factors, in a SQL Server 2008 cluster environment with two nodes and AWE/PAE enabled, the max server memory value on each node should be less than half the system physical memory.

■ **Note** If you use the /3GB feature along with AWE/PAE, then an instance of SQL Server will be limited to a maximum of 16GB of extended memory.

This limitation is because of the internal design of the Windows Server operating system. Limiting the system space within the process space to 1GB using the /3GB switch allows the Windows Server operating system to manage physical memory up to 16GB. Therefore, to access memory beyond 16GB, you should not use the /3GB switch.

Disk Bottleneck Analysis

SQL Server is a heavy user of the hard disk, and since disk speeds are comparatively much slower than memory and processor speeds, a contention in disk resources can significantly degrade SQL Server performance. Analysis and resolution of any disk resource bottleneck can improve SQL Server performance significantly.

Disk Counters

To analyze disk performance, you can use the counters shown in Table 2-2.

Table 2-2. *Performance Monitor Counters to Analyze I/O Pressure*

Object(Instance[,InstanceN])	Counter	Description	Value
PhysicalDisk(Data-disk, Log-disk)	% Disk Time	Percentage of time disk was busy	Average value < 85%
	Current Disk Queue Length	Number of outstanding disk requests at the time performance data is collected	Average value < 2 per disk
	Avg. Disk Queue Length	Average number of queued disk requests during the sample interval	Average value < 2 per disk
	Disk Transfers/sec	Rate of read/write operations on disk	Maximum value < 100 per disk
	Disk Bytes/sec	Amount of data transfer to/from per disk per second	Maximum value < 10MB per second
	Avg. Disk Sec/Read	Average time in ms to read from disk	Average value < 10 ms
	Avg. Disk Sec/Write	Average time in ms to write to disk	Average value < 10 ms

The PhysicalDisk counters represent the activities on a physical disk. LogicalDisk counters represent logical subunits (or partitions) created on a physical disk. If you create two partitions, say C: and D: on a physical disk, then you can monitor the disk activities of the individual logical disks using logical disk counters. However, because a disk bottleneck ultimately occurs on the physical disk, not on the logical disk, it is usually preferable to use the PhysicalDisk counters.

Note that for a hardware redundant array of independent disks (RAID) subsystem (see the "Using a RAID Array" section for more on RAID), the counters treat the array as a single physical disk. For example, even if you have ten disks in a RAID configuration, they will all be represented as one physical disk to the operating system, and subsequently you will have only one set of PhysicalDisk counters for that RAID subsystem. The same point applies to storage area network (SAN) disks (see the "Using a SAN System" section for specifics).

% Disk Time

The % Disk Time counter monitors the percentage of time the disk is busy with read/write activities. It should not be continuously high. If this counter value is consistently more than 85 percent, then you must take steps to bring it down. You could upgrade the disk subsystem, but a more effective solution is to avoid going to the data disk as much as possible. Even a consistent disk usage of 5 percent may adversely affect performance.

For performance, it is always beneficial to cache the disk contents in memory since disk access is in the order of milliseconds, whereas memory access is in the order of nanoseconds. SQL Server adopts this strategy by caching the data pages in its buffer cache. But if SQL Server has to go to disk often, as indicated by a high % Disk Time value, then the slow access time of the disk compared to that of the memory will hurt the performance of the database.

Current Disk Queue Length

Current Disk Queue Length is the number of requests outstanding on the disk subsystem at the time the performance data is collected. It includes requests in service at the time of the snapshot. A disk subsystem will have only one disk queue. You should use this counter value to support the conclusion made from the % Disk Time counter. A consistent disk queue length of two per disk indicates the possibility of a bottleneck on the disk.

For example, in a RAID configuration with 10 disks, a consistent disk queue length of 2 per disk, or 20 (= 10 disks × 2 per disks), for the complete disk subsystem indicates a disk bottleneck. RAID controllers usually distribute disk I/Os uniformly across all disks in the disk subsystem, but because of the obvious chances of nonuniform disk I/O, consider the following range of values for the Current Disk Queue Length counter:

- Less than (2 + # of spindles) is an *excellent* value to see. In the worst case, the two requests in the queue may be pending on the same disk.
- Less than (2 × # of spindles) is a *fair* value to see. In the best case, the queued requests may be uniformly distributed across all the disks in the disk subsystem with two requests pending per disk.

If you do not suspect dynamic variation in disk loads, then you may use the `Avg. Disk Queue Length` counter since this counter represents the average of the instantaneous values provided by the `Current Disk Queue Length` counter. If you think you may have a disk issue based on the queue length, you should also check the `Average Disk Seconds Per Transfer` value for the same disk. Finally, check the wait states of your processes to see whether you are experiencing I/O waits.

Disk Transfers/sec

`Disk Transfers/sec` monitors the rate of read and write operations on the disk. A typical disk today can do about 180 disk transfers per second for sequential I/O and 100 disk transfers per second for random I/O. In the case of random I/O, `Disk Transfers/sec` is lower because more disk arm and head movements are involved. OLTP workloads, which are workloads for doing mainly singleton operations, small operations, and random access, are typically constrained by disk transfers per second. So, in the case of an OLTP workload, you are more constrained by the fact that a disk can do only 100 disk transfers per second than by its throughput specification of 10MB per second.

Because of the inherent slowness of a disk, it is recommended that you keep disk transfers per second as low as possible. You will see how to do this next.

Disk Bytes/sec

The `Disk Bytes/sec` counter monitors the rate at which bytes are transferred to or from the disk during read or write operations. A typical disk can transfer about 10MB per second. Generally, OLTP applications are not constrained by the disk transfer capacity of the disk subsystem since the OLTP applications access small amounts of data in individual database requests. If the amount of data transfer exceeds the capacity of the disk subsystem, then a backlog starts developing on the disk subsystem, as reflected by the `Disk Queue Length` counters.

Avg. Disk Sec/Read and Avg. Disk Sec/Write

`Avg. Disk Sec/Read` and `Avg. Disk Sec/Write` track the average amount of time it takes in milliseconds to read from or write to a disk. Having an understanding of just how well the disks are handling the writes and reads that they receive can be a very strong indicator of where problems lie. If it's taking more than about 10 ms to move the data from or to your disk, you may need to take a look at the hardware and configuration to be sure everything is working correctly. You'll need to get even better response times for the transaction log to perform well.

Disk Bottleneck Resolutions

A few of the common disk bottleneck resolutions are as follows:

- Optimizing application workload
- Using a faster disk drive
- Using a RAID array
- Using a SAN system
- Aligning disks properly
- Using a battery-backed controller cache
- Adding system memory
- Creating multiple files and filegroups
- Placing the table and the index for that table on different disks
- Saving the log file to a separate physical drive
- Using partitioned tables

I'll now walk you through each of these resolutions in turn.

Optimizing Application Workload

I cannot stress enough how important it is to optimize an application's workload in resolving a performance issue. The queries with the highest number of reads will be the ones that cause a great deal of disk I/O. I'll cover the strategies for optimizing those queries in more detail throughout the rest of this book.

Using a Faster Disk Drive

One of the easiest resolutions, and one that you will adopt most of the time, is to use disk drives with faster disk transfers per second. However, you should not just upgrade disk drives without further investigation; you need to find out what is causing the stress on the disk.

Using a RAID Array

One way of obtaining disk I/O parallelism is to create a single pool of drives to serve all SQL Server database files, excluding transaction log files. The pool can be a single RAID array, which is represented in Windows Server 2008 as a single physical disk drive. The effectiveness of a drive pool depends on the configuration of the RAID disks.

Out of all available RAID configurations, the most commonly used RAID configurations are the following (see Figure 2-6):

- *RAID 0*: Striping with no fault tolerance
- *RAID 1*: Mirroring
- *RAID 5*: Striping with parity
- *RAID 1+0*: Striping with mirroring

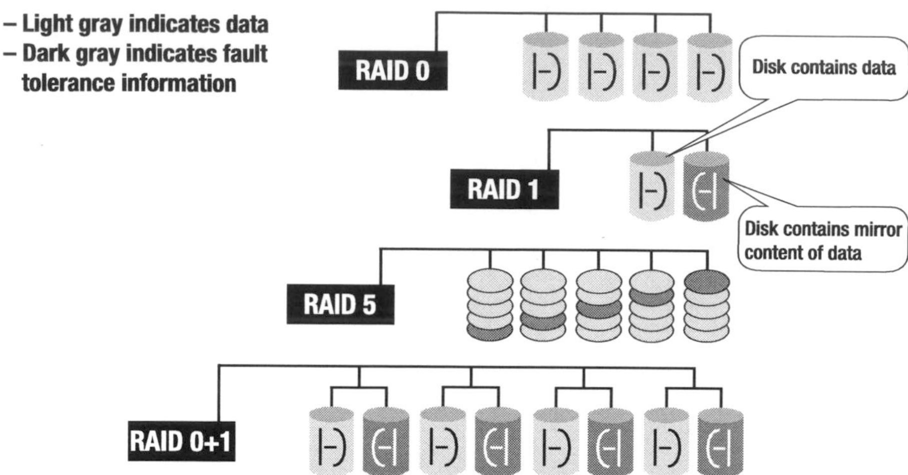

Figure 2-6. *RAID configurations*

RAID 0

Since this RAID configuration has no fault tolerance, you can use it only in situations where the reliability of data is not a concern. The failure of any disk in the array will cause complete data loss in the disk subsystem. Therefore, you cannot use it for any data file or transaction log file that constitutes a database, except for the system temporary database called `tempdb`.

The number of I/Os per disk in RAID 0 is represented by the following equation:

I/Os per disk = (Reads + Writes) / Number of disks in the array

In this equation, `Reads` is the number of read requests to the disk subsystem, and `Writes` is the number of write requests to the disk subsystem.

RAID 1

RAID 1 provides high fault tolerance for critical data by mirroring the data disk onto a separate disk. It can be used where the complete data can be accommodated in one disk only. Database transaction log files for user databases, operating system files, and SQL Server system databases (`master` and `msdb`) are usually small enough to use RAID 1.

The number of I/Os per disk in RAID 1 is represented by the following equation:

I/Os per disk =(Reads + 2 × Writes) / 2

RAID 5

This configuration is a good option in many cases. It provides reasonable fault tolerance by effectively using only one extra disk to save the computed parity of the data in other disks, as shown in Figure 2-6. When there is a disk failure in RAID 5 configuration, I/O performance becomes terrible, although the system does remain usable while operating with the failed drive.

Any data where writes make up more than 10 percent of the total disk requests is not a good candidate for RAID 5. Thus, use RAID 5 on read-only volumes or volumes with a low percentage of disk writes.

The number of I/Os per disk in RAID 5 is represented by the following equation:

I/Os per disk = (Reads + 4 × Writes) / Number of disks in the array

As shown in the preceding equation, the write operations on the RAID 5 disk subsystem are magnified four times. For each incoming write request, the following are the four corresponding I/O requests on the disk subsystem:

- One read I/O to read existing data from the data disk whose content is to be modified
- One read I/O to read existing parity information from the corresponding parity disk
- One write I/O to write the new data to the data disk whose content is to be modified
- One write I/O to write the new parity information to the corresponding parity disk

Therefore, the four I/Os for each write request consist of two read I/Os and two write I/Os.

In an OLTP database, all the data modifications are immediately written to the transaction log file as part of the database transaction, but the data in the data file itself is synchronized with the transaction log file content asynchronously in batch operations. This operation is managed by the internal process of SQL Server called the *checkpoint process*. The frequency of this operation can be controlled by using the `recovery interval (min)` configuration parameter of SQL Server.

Because of the continuous write operation in the transaction log file for a highly transactional OLTP database, placing transaction log files on a RAID 5 array will significantly degrade the array's performance. Although you should not place the transactional log files on a RAID 5 array, the data files may be placed on RAID 5, since the write operations to the data files are intermittent and batched together to improve the efficiency of the write operation.

RAID 1+0 (RAID 10)

RAID 1+0 (also referred to as 0+1 and 10) configuration offers a high degree of fault tolerance by mirroring every data disk in the array. It is a much more expensive solution than RAID 5, since double the number of data disks are required to provide fault tolerance. This RAID configuration should be used where a large volume is required to save data and more than 10 percent of disk requests are writes. Since RAID 1+0 supports *split seeks* (the ability to distribute the read operations onto the data disk and the mirror disk and then converge the two data streams), read performance is also very good. Thus, use RAID 1+0 wherever performance is critical.

The number of I/Os per disk in RAID 1+0 is represented by the following equation:

I/Os per disk = (Reads + 2 × Writes) / Number of disks in the array

Using a SAN System

Storage area networks (SANs) remain largely the domain of large-scale enterprise systems, although the cost is coming down. A SAN can be used to increase performance of a storage subsystem by simply providing more spindles and disk drives to read from and write to.

A "drive" as seen by the operating system is striped across multiple redundant drives in a SAN in a manner similar to that of RAID 5 but without the overhead of RAID 5 or the performance loss caused by disk failures. Because of their size, complexity, and cost, SANs are not necessarily a good solution in all cases. Also, depending on the amount of data, direct attached storage (DAS) can be configured to run faster. The principal strength of SAN systems is not reflected in performance but rather in the areas of scalability, availability, and maintenance.

Aligning Disks Properly

Aligning a disk drive is not a well-known issue, but more and more DBAs are becoming aware of it. The way data is stored on a disk is in a series of sectors (also referred to as *blocks*) that are stored on tracks. A disk is out of alignment when the size of the track, determined by the vendor, consists of a number of sectors different from the default size that you're writing to. This will mean that one sector will be written correctly, but the next one will have to cross two tracks. This can more than double the amount of I/O required to write or read from the disk. The key is to align the partition so that you're storing the correct number of sectors for the track.

Using a Battery-Backed Controller Cache

For best performance, use a caching RAID controller for SQL Server files, because the controller guarantees that data entrusted to it is written to disk eventually, no matter how large the queue is or even if power fails. When using a controller cache, the write requests to the RAID controller are written to the controller cache, and the subsequent disk operations are scheduled asynchronously. This asynchronous technique of doing I/Os for the write requests improves the performance of database queries significantly. The amount of performance improvement depends on the size of the controller cache and number of write requests.

When there is an unreliable battery backup, power disruptions will cause a loss of new/modified data (that is, dirty data) in the controller cache that was not flushed to the disk. If this dirty data belonged to a committed transaction, then the consistency of the data will be compromised.

For example, if a user commits a database transaction, the dirty data for the transaction will be written to the controller cache, and the user will be informed about a successful completion of the transaction. But should the power go down before this committed data is written to the disk, then all the data in the cache will be lost unless the controller has a reliable battery backup.

To avoid data inconsistency, ensure from your disk vendor that the controller cache has a reliable battery backup.

Adding System Memory

When physical memory is scarce, the system starts writing the contents of memory back to disk and reading smaller blocks of data more frequently, causing a lot of paging. The less memory the system has, the more the disk subsystem is used. This can be resolved using the memory bottleneck resolutions enumerated in the previous section.

Creating Multiple Files and Filegroups

In SQL Server, each user database consists of one or more data files and one or more transaction log files. The data files belonging to a database can be grouped together in one or more filegroups for administrative and data allocation/placement purposes. For example, if a data file is placed in a separate filegroup, then write access to all the tables in the filegroup can be controlled collectively by making the filegroup read-only (transaction log files do not belong to any filegroup).

You can create a filegroup for a database from SQL Server Management Studio, as shown in Figure 2-7. The filegroups of a database are presented in the Filegroups pane of the Database Properties dialog box.

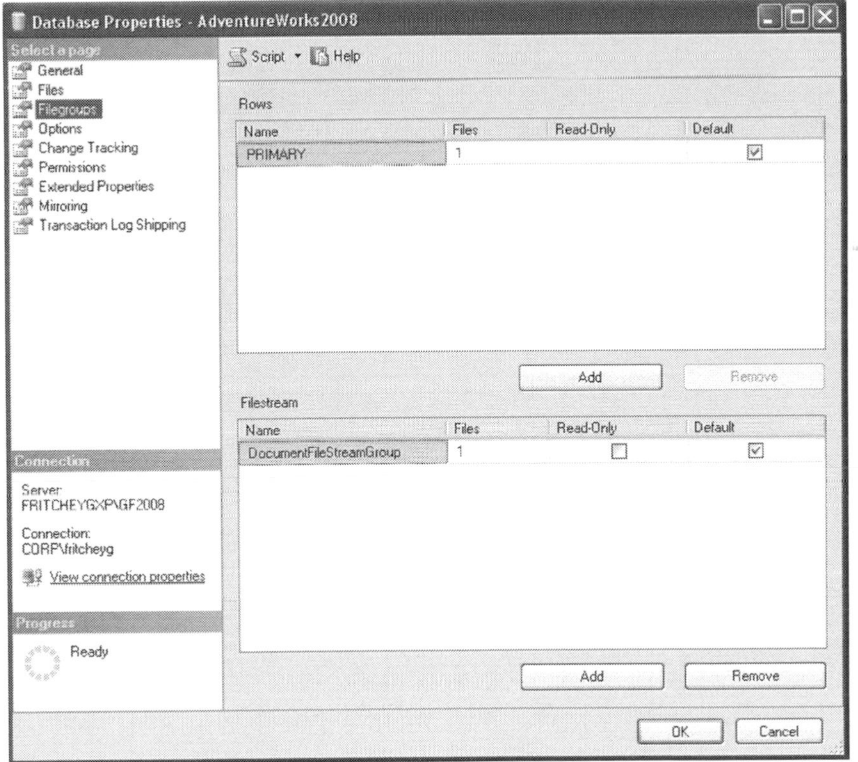

Figure 2-7. *Filegroups configuration*

In Figure 2-7, you can see that there is only a single filegroup created by default with AdventureWorks2008. You can add multiple files to multiple filegroups distributed across drives so that work can be done in parallel across the groups and files.

You can add a data file to a filegroup in the Database Properties dialog box in the Files window by selecting from the drop-down list, as shown in Figure 2-8.

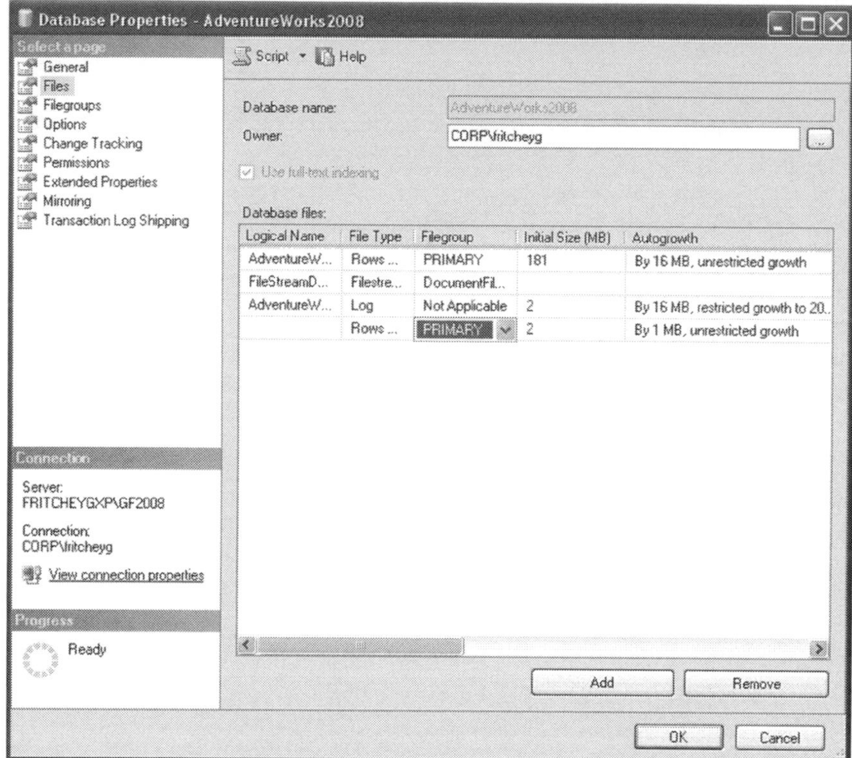

Figure 2-8. *Data files configuration*

You can also do this programmatically, as follows (`filegroup.sql` in the download):

```
ALTER DATABASE AdventureWorks2008 ADD FILEGROUP INDEXES ;

ALTER DATABASE AdventureWorks2008 ADD FILE
(NAME = AdventureWorks2008_Data2,
  FILENAME = 'C:\Program Files\Microsoft SQL ➥
Server\MSSQL10.GF2008\MSSQL\DATA\AdventureWorks2008_2.ndf',
  SIZE = 1MB,
  FILEGROWTH = 10%) TO FILEGROUP Indexes;
```

In a system with multiple processors, SQL Server can take advantage of multiple files and filegroups by performing multiple parallel scans on the data files. As tables in a file are accessed sequentially, a thread is created to read the associated data file. If a filegroup consists of four data files, then four threads will be created to read data in parallel. If the data files are placed on four different physical disks, then all the disk spindles can work simultaneously. Therefore, in a multidisk subsystem, it is usually advantageous to have multiple files in the filegroup.

Using multiple files and filegroups also enables you to improve the performance of join operations. By separating tables that are frequently joined into separate filegroups and then putting files within the filegroups on separate disks or LUNS, the separated I/O paths can result in improved performance. For example, consider the following query:

```
SELECT  *
FROM    t1
        INNER JOIN t2
        ON t1.c1 = t2.c2
```

If the tables t1 and t2 are placed in separate filegroups containing one file each, then on a multiple-processor system a separate thread will be created for each table. With the files of the two filegroups on different physical disks, data from both the tables can be retrieved simultaneously.

It is recommended for performance and recovery purposes that, if multiple filegroups are to be used, the primary filegroup should be used only for system objects and secondary filegroups should be used only for user objects. This approach improves disk I/O and the ability to recover from corruption. The recoverability of a database is higher if the primary data file and the log files are intact. Use the primary filegroup for system objects only, and store all user-related objects on a secondary filegroup.

Spreading a database into multiple files, even onto the same drive, makes it easy to move the database files onto separate drives, making future disk upgrades easier. For example, to move a user database file (AdventureWorks2008_2.ndf) to a new disk subsystem (F:), you can follow these steps:

1. Detach the user database as follows (file_move.sql in the code download):

```
USE master;
GO
sp_detach_db 'AdventureWorks2008';
GO
```

2. Copy the data file AdventureWorks2008_2.ndf to a folder F:\Data\ on the new disk subsystem.

3. Reattach the user database by referring files at appropriate locations, as shown here:

```
USE master;
GO
sp_attach_db 'AdventureWorks2008'
, 'C:\Program Files\Microsoft SQL
Server\MSSQL10.GF2008\MSSQL\DATA\AdventureWorks2008.mdf'
, 'F:\DATA\AdventureWorks2008_2.ndf '
, 'C:\Program Files\Microsoft SQL
Server\MSSQL10.GF2008\MSSQL\DATA\AdventureWorks2008.ldf ';
GO
```

4. To verify the files belonging to a database, execute the following commands:

```
USE Adventureworks2008
GO
SELECT * FROM sys.database_files
GO
```

You may have noticed in Figure 2-8 that one of the files in the AdventureWorks2008 database is of type FileStream. The FileStream data storage was introduced with SQL Server 2008. Its purpose is to separate the work of maintaining unstructured data, large binary files, XML, and so on, from the database, moving that work to the Windows Server file system. So, although the data in a FileStream column can be treated as a column in a table, the processing of the data is not handled by the database engine, thereby decreasing the workload of the SQL Server.

You can insert, update, and delete filestream data through T-SQL commands or by calling directly to streaming interfaces using OpenFile() and WriteFile() from .NET programming languages. For larger sets of unstructured data, when the data stored in the large object column is larger than 1MB, using FileStream provides a serious increase in performance. Smaller data sets are better off being stored within the database using more traditional types such as VARCHAR(MAX) or VARBINARY(MAX).

Placing the Table and Index on Separate Disks

If a system has multiple processors, SQL Server can take advantage of multiple filegroups by accessing tables and corresponding nonclustered indexes using separate I/O paths. A nonclustered index can be created on a specific filegroup as follows:

```
CREATE INDEX i1 ON t1 (c1) ON Indexes
```

■ **Tip** The nonclustered index and other types of indexes are explained in Chapter 4.

Saving Log Files to a Separate Physical Disk

SQL Server log files should always, where possible, be located on a separate hard disk drive from all other SQL Server database files. Transaction log activity primarily consists of sequential write I/O, unlike the nonsequential (or random) I/O required for the data files. Separating transaction log activity from other nonsequential disk I/O activity can result in I/O performance improvements, because it allows the hard disk drives containing log files to concentrate on sequential I/O.

The major portion of time required to access data from a hard disk is spent on the physical movement of the disk spindle head to locate the data. Once the data is located, the data is read electronically, which is much faster than the physical movement of the head. With only sequential I/O operations on the log disk, the spindle head of the log disk can write to the log disk with a minimum of physical movement. If the same disk is used for data files, however, the spindle head has to move to the correct location before writing to the log file. This increases the time required to write to the log file and thereby hurts performance.

Furthermore, for SQL Server with multiple OLTP databases, the transaction log files should be physically separated from each other on different physical drives to improve performance. An exception to this requirement is a read-only database or a database with very few database changes. Since no online changes are made to the read-only database, no write operations are performed on the log file. Therefore, having the log file on a separate disk is not required for the read-only databases.

Partitioning Tables

In addition to simply adding files to filegroups and letting SQL Server distribute the data between them, it's possible to define a horizontal segmentation of data called a *partition* so that data is divided up between multiple files by the partition. A filtered set of data is a *segment*; for example, if the partition is by month, the segment of data is any given month. Creating a partition moves the segment of data to a particular file and only that file. This provides a massive increase in speed because, when querying against well-defined partitions, only the files with the partitions of data you're interested in will be accessed during a given query. If you assume for a moment that data is partitioned by month, then each month's data file can be set to read-only as each month ends. That read-only status means that no locking will occur on a file as read queries are run against it, further increasing the performance of your queries. Partitions can actually be mapped to the same files within a filegroup, which won't offer any performance improvements but can be used for easier maintenance of the data.

Processor Bottleneck Analysis

SQL Server 2008 makes heavy use of any processor resource available. You can use the Performance Monitor counters in Table 2-3 to analyze pressure on the processor resource.

Table 2-3. *Performance Monitor Counters to Analyze CPU Pressure*

Object(Instance[,InstanceN])	Counter	Description	Value
Processor(_Total)	% Processor Time	Percentage of time processor was busy	Average value < 80%
	% Privileged Time	Percentage of processor time spent in privileged mode	Average value < 10%
System	Processor Queue Length	Number of requests outstanding on the processor	Average value < 2
	Context Switches/sec	Rate at which processor is switched per processor from one thread to another	Average value < 1,000
SQL Server:SQL Statistics	Batch Requests/sec	SQL command batches received per second	Based on your standard workload
	SQL Compilations/sec	Number of times SQL is compiled	Average value > 100
	SQL Recompilations/sec	Number of recompiles	

I'll now walk you through these counters in more detail.

% Processor Time

`% Processor Time` should not be consistently high (greater than 75 percent). The effect of any sustained processor time greater than 90 percent is the same as that with 100 percent. If `% Processor Time` is consistently high and disk and network counter values are low, your first priority must be to reduce the stress on the processor.

For example, if `% Processor Time` is 85 percent and `% Disk Time` is 50 percent, then it is quite likely that a major part of the processor time is spent on managing the disk activities. This will be reflected in the `% Privileged Time` counter of the processor, as explained in the next section. In that case, it will be advantageous to optimize the disk bottleneck first. Further, remember that the disk bottleneck in turn can be because of a memory bottleneck, as explained earlier in the chapter.

You can track processor time as an aggregate of all the processors on the machine, or you can track the percentage utilization individually to particular processors. This allows you to segregate the data collection in the event that SQL Server runs on three processors of a four-processor machine.

% Privileged Time

Processing on a Windows server is done in two modes: *user mode* and *privileged* (or *kernel*) mode. All system-level activities, including disk access, are done in privileged mode. If you find that `% Privileged Time` on a dedicated SQL Server system is 20 to 25 percent or more, then the system is probably doing a lot of I/O—likely more than you need. The `% Privileged Time` counter on a dedicated SQL Server system should be at most 5 to 10 percent.

Processor Queue Length

`Processor Queue Length` is the number of threads in the processor queue. (There is a single processor queue, even on computers with multiple processors.) Unlike the disk counters, the `Processor Queue Length` counter does not read threads that are already running. On systems with lower CPU utilization, the `Processor Queue Length` counter is typically 0 or 1.

A sustained `Processor Queue Length` counter of greater than 2 generally indicates processor congestion. Because of multiple processors, you may need to take into account the number of schedulers dealing with the processor queue length. A processor queue length more than two times the number of schedulers (usually 1:1 with processors) can also indicate a processor bottleneck. Although a high `% Processor Time` counter indicates a busy processor, a sustained high `Processor Queue Length` counter is a more certain indicator. If the recommended value is exceeded, this generally indicates that there are more threads ready to run than the current number of processors can service in an optimal way.

Context Switches/sec

The `Context Switches/sec` counter monitors the combined rate at which all processors on the computer are switched from one thread to another. A context switch occurs when a running thread voluntarily relinquishes the processor, is preempted by a higher-priority ready thread, or switches between user mode and privileged mode to use an executive or a subsystem service. It is the sum of `Thread:Context Switches/sec` for all threads running on all processors in the computer, and it is measured in numbers of switches.

A figure of 300 to 1,000 `Context Switches/sec` per processor is excellent to fair. Abnormally high rates, greater than 20,000 per second, can be caused by page faults due to memory starvation.

Batch Requests/sec

`Batch Requests/sec` gives you a good indicator of just how much load is being placed on the system, which has a direct correlation to how much load is being placed on the processor. Since you could see a lot of low-cost queries on your system or a few high-cost queries, you can't look at this number by itself but must reference the other counters defined in this section; 1,000 requests in a second would be considered a busy system. Greater values may be cause for concern. The best way to know which value has meaning within your own systems is to establish a baseline and then monitor from there.

SQL Compilations/sec

The `SQL Compilations/sec` counter shows both batch compiles and statement recompiles as part of its aggregation. This number can be extremely high when a server is first turned on (or after a failover or any other startup type event), but it will stabilize over time. Once stable, 100 or more compilations in one second will certainly manifest as problems in the processor. Chapter 9 covers SQL compilation in detail.

SQL Recompilations/sec

`SQL Recompilations/sec` is a measure of the recompiles of both batches and statements. A high number of recompiles will lead to processor stress. Because statement recompiles are part of this count, it can be much higher than in versions of SQL Server prior to 2005. Chapter 10 covers query recompilation in detail.

Processor Bottleneck Resolutions

A few of the common processor bottleneck resolutions are as follows:

- Optimizing application workload
- Eliminating or reducing excessive compiles/recompiles
- Using more or faster processors
- Using a large L2/L3 cache
- Running with more efficient controllers/drivers
- Not running unnecessary software

Let's consider each of these resolutions in turn.

Optimizing Application Workload

To identify the processor-intensive queries, capture all the SQL queries using SQL Profiler (which I will discuss in the next chapter), and then group the Profiler trace output on the `CPU` column. The queries with the highest amount of CPU time contribute the most to the CPU stress. You should then analyze and optimize those queries to reduce stress on the CPU. You can also query directly against the `sys.dm_exec_query_stats` view to see immediate issues in real time. Finally, using both a query hash and a query plan hash, you can identify and tune common queries or common execution plans (this is discussed in detail in Chapter 9). Most of the rest of the chapters in this book are concerned with optimizing application workload.

Eliminating Excessive Compiles/Recompiles

A certain number of query compiles and recompiles is simply to be expected. It's when there is a large number of these over sustained periods that a problem exists. It's also worth noting the ratio between them. A high number of compiles and a very low number of recompiles means that few queries are being reused within the system (query reuse is covered in detail in Chapter 9). A high number of recompiles will cause high processor use. Methods for addressing recompiles are covered in Chapter 10.

Using More or Faster Processors

One of the easiest resolutions, and one that you will adopt most of the time, is to increase system processing power. However, because of the high cost involved in a processor upgrade, you should first optimize CPU-intensive operations as much as possible.

The system's processing power can be increased by increasing the power of individual processors or by adding more processors. When you have a high `% Processor Time` counter and a low `Processor Queue Length` counter, it makes sense to increase the power of individual processors. In the case of both a high `% Processor Time` counter and a high `Processor Queue Length` counter, you should consider adding more processors. Increasing the number of processors allows the system to execute more requests simultaneously.

Using a Large L2/L3 Cache

Modern processors have become so much faster than memory that they need at least two levels of memory cache to reduce latency. On Pentium-class machines, the fast L1 cache holds 8KB of data and 8KB of instructions, while the slower L2 cache holds up to 6MB of mixed code and data. New processors are shipping with an L3 cache on top of the others varying in size from 6MiB to 256MiB and 2MB (MiB refers to *mebibyte*, a binary representation, 2^{20}, that is very similar in size to but not exactly the same as a megabyte, which is 10^6). References to content found in the L1 cache cost one cycle, references to the L2/L3 cache cost four to seven cycles, and references to the main memory cost dozens of processor cycles. With the increase in processing power, the latter figure will soon exceed 100 cycles. In many ways, the cache is like small, fast, virtual memory inside the processor.

Database engines like L2/L3 caches because they keep processing off the system bus. The processor does not have to go through the system bus to access memory; it can work out of the L2/L3 cache. Not having enough L2/L3 cache can cause the processor to wait a longer period of time for the data/code to move from the main memory to the L2/L3 cache. A processor with a high clock speed but a low L2/L3 cache may waste a large number of CPU cycles waiting on the small L2/L3 cache. A large L2/L3 cache helps maximize the use of CPU cycles for actual processing instead of waiting on the L2/L3 cache.

Today, it is very common to have megabyte caches on four-way systems. With new four- and eight-way systems, you will often get up to a 6MB L2 cache and, as mentioned earlier, 256MiB on L3. For example, sometimes you may get a performance improvement of 20 percent or more simply by using a 512KB L2 cache instead of a 256KB L2 cache.

Running More Efficient Controllers/Drivers

There is a big difference in `% Privileged Time` consumption between different controllers and controller drivers on the market today. The techniques used by controller drivers to do I/O are quite different and consume different amounts of CPU time. If you can change to a controller that frees up 4 to 5 percent of `% Privileged Time`, you can improve performance.

Not Running Unnecessary Software

If you have screen savers running on your system, they may use a large amount of processor time. This is particularly true of screen savers that use OpenGL (a software interface that supports the production of high-quality, three-dimensional color imaging), because they can easily take away 15 percent of processor time on a server that lacks an OpenGL graphics card. Because you can run your servers with the monitor switched off for the majority of the time, simply disable any screen savers on your server or, as a preventive measure, use the blank screen saver. Please do remember to lock your server for security.

When possible, no unnecessary software should be running on the same server as SQL Server. Exterior applications that have nothing to do with maintaining the Windows Server or SQL Server are best placed on a different machine.

Network Bottleneck Analysis

In SQL Server OLTP production environments, you find few performance issues that are because of problems with the network. Most of the network issues you face in the OLTP environment are in fact hardware or driver limitations or issues with switches or routers. Most of these issues can be best diagnosed with the Network Monitor tool. However, Performance Monitor also provides objects that collect data on network activity, as shown in Table 2-4.

Table 2-4. *Performance Monitor Counters to Analyze Network Pressure*

Object(Instance[,InstanceN])	Counter	Description	Value
`Network Interface(Network card)`	`Bytes Total/sec`	Rate at which bytes are transferred on the NIC	Average value < 50% of NIC capacity
`Network Segment`	`% Net Utilization`	Percentage of network bandwidth in use on a network segment	Average value < 80% of network bandwidth

Bytes Total/sec

You can use the `Bytes Total/sec` counter to determine how the network interface card (NIC) or network adapter is performing. The `Bytes Total/sec` counter should report high values to indicate a large number of successful transmissions. Compare this value with that reported by the `Network Interface\Current Bandwidth` performance counter, which reflects each adapter's bandwidth.

To allow headroom for spikes in traffic, you should usually average no more than 50 percent of capacity. If this number is close to the capacity of the connection and if processor and memory use are moderate, then the connection may well be a problem.

% Net Utilization

The `% Net Utilization` counter represents the percentage of network bandwidth in use on a network segment. The threshold for this counter depends on the type of network. For Ethernet networks, for example, 30 percent is the recommended threshold when SQL Server is on a shared network hub. For SQL Server on a dedicated full-duplex network, even though near 100 percent usage of the network is acceptable, it is advantageous to keep the network utilization below an acceptable threshold to keep room for the spikes in the load.

■ **Note** You must install the Network Monitor Driver to collect performance data using the `Network Segment` object counters.

In Windows Server 2008, you can install the Network Monitor Driver from the local area connection properties for the network adapter. The Network Monitor Driver is available in the network protocol list of network components for the network adapter.

Network Bottleneck Resolutions

A few of the common network bottleneck resolutions are as follows:

- Optimizing application workload
- Adding network adapters
- Moderating and avoiding interruptions

Let's consider these resolutions in more detail.

Optimizing Application Workload

To optimize network traffic between a database application and a database server, make the following design changes in the application:

- Instead of sending a long SQL string, create a stored procedure for the SQL query. Then, you just need to send over the network the name of the stored procedure and its parameters.
- Group multiple database requests into one stored procedure. Then, only one database request will be required across the network for the set of SQL queries implemented in the stored procedure.
- Request a small data set. Do not request table columns that are not used in the application logic.
- Move data-intensive business logic into the database as stored procedures or database triggers to reduce network round-trips.

Adding Network Adapters

You can add network adapters so that you have one network adapter per processor. Generally, you should add a network adapter only if you need the increased bandwidth, because each additional network adapter has some intrinsic overhead. However, if one of the processors is nearly always active (that is, `Processor\% Processor Time` consistently equals 100 percent) and more than half of its time is spent servicing deferred procedure calls (that is, `Processor\% DPC Time` exceeds 50 percent), then adding a network card is likely to improve system performance.

If a network adapter does not use Network Driver Interface Specification (NDIS) miniport drivers, you cannot modify the distribution of deferred procedure calls (DPCs) for better performance. An NDIS miniport driver (also called a *miniport driver*) manages a NIC and interfaces with higher-level drivers. It communicates with its NIC and higher-level drivers through the NDIS library.

To be able to modify the distribution of DPCs and because other NDIS optimizations might be unavailable, you may consider upgrading an individual network adapter instead of adding a new adapter.

Moderating and Avoiding Interruptions

When adding or upgrading network adapters, choose adapters with drivers that support *interrupt moderation* and/or *interrupt avoidance*. Interrupt moderation allows a processor to process interrupts more efficiently by grouping several interrupts into a single hardware interrupt. Interrupt avoidance allows a processor to continue processing interrupts without new interrupts queued until all pending interrupts are completed.

SQL Server Overall Performance

To analyze the overall performance of a SQL Server, besides examining hardware resource utilization, you should also examine some general aspects of SQL Server itself. You can use the performance counters presented in Table 2-5.

Table 2-5. *Performance Monitor Counters to Analyze Generic SQL Pressure*

Object(Instance[,InstanceN])	Counter
SQLServer:Access Methods	FreeSpace Scans/sec Full Scans/sec Table Lock Escalations/sec Worktables Created/sec
SQLServer:Latches	Total Latch Wait Time (ms)
SQLServer:Locks(_Total)	Lock Timeouts/sec Lock Wait Time (ms) Number of Deadlocks/sec
SQLServer:SQL Statistics	Batch Requests/sec SQL Re-Compilations/sec
SQLServer:General Statistics	Processes Blocked User Connections

Let's take a look at each of these counters in context.

Missing Indexes

To analyze the possibility of missing indexes causing table scans or large data set retrievals, you can use the counters in Table 2-6.

Table 2-6. *Performance Monitor Counter to Analyze Excessive Data Scans*

Object(Instance[,InstanceN])	Counter
SQLServer:Access Methods	FreeSpace Scans/sec Full Scans/sec

FreeSpace Scans/sec

This counter represents inserts into a table with no physical ordering of its rows—such a table is also called a *heap table.* Extra processing is required to define and store a heap table since SQL Server normally uses the clustered index as a storage mechanism for the table data. A heap table requires an additional, internal column called a *uniquifier* to be generated for each row inserted. Therefore, it is usually recommended that you physically order the table rows by using a clustered index on the table. You will learn about heap tables and clustered indexes in Chapter 5.

Full Scans/sec

This counter monitors the number of unrestricted full scans on base tables or indexes. A few of the main causes of high `Full Scans/sec` are as follows:

- Missing indexes
- Too many rows requested

To further investigate queries producing the preceding problems, use SQL Profiler to identify the queries (I will cover this tool in the next chapter). Queries with missing indexes or too many rows requested will have a large number of logical reads and an increased CPU time.

Be aware of the fact that full scans may be performed for the temporary tables used in a stored procedure, because most of the time you will not have indexes (or you will not need indexes) on temporary tables. Still, adding this counter to the baseline helps identify the possible increase in the use of temporary tables, which are usually not good for performance.

Dynamic Management Views

Another way to check for missing indexes is to the query the dynamic management view `sys.dm_db_missing_index_details`. This management view returns information that can suggest candidates for indexes based on the execution plans of the queries being run against the database. The view `sys.dm_db_missing_index_details` is part of a series of DMVs collectively referred to as the *missing indexes feature*. These DMVs are based on data generated from execution plans stored in the cache. You can query directly against this view to gather data to decide whether you want to build indexes based on the information available from within the view. Missing indexes will also be shown within the XML execution plan for a given query, but I'll cover that more in the next chapter.

The opposite problem to a missing index is one that is never used. The DMV `sys.dm_db_index_usage_stats` shows which indexes have been used, at least since the last reboot of the system. You can also view the indexes in use with a lower-level DMV, `sys.dm_db_index_operational_stats`. It will help to show where indexes are slowing down because of contention or I/O. I'll cover these both in more detail in Chapter 10.

Database Blocking

To analyze the impact of database blocking on the performance of SQL Server, you can use the counters shown in Table 2-7.

Table 2-7. *Performance Monitor Counters to Analyze SQL Server Locking*

Object(Instance[,InstanceN])	Counter
`SQLServer:Latches`	`Total Latch Wait Time (ms)`

`SQLServer:Locks(_Total)`	`Lock Timeouts/sec`
	`Lock Wait Time (ms)`
	`Number of Deadlocks/sec`

Total Latch Wait Time (ms)

Latches are used internally by SQL Server to protect the integrity of internal structures, such as a table row, and are not directly controlled by users. This counter monitors total latch wait time (in milliseconds) for latch requests that had to wait in the last second. A high value for this counter indicates that SQL Server is spending too much time waiting on its internal synchronization mechanism.

Lock Timeouts/sec and Lock Wait Time (ms)

You should expect `Lock Timeouts/sec` to be 0 and `Lock Wait Time (ms)` to be very low. A nonzero value for `Lock Timeouts/sec` and a high value for `Lock Wait Time (ms)` indicate that excessive blocking is occurring in the database.

Two approaches can be adopted in this case:

- You can identify the costly queries using data from SQL Profiler or by querying `sys.dm_exec_query_stats` and then optimize the queries appropriately.
- You can use blocking analysis to diagnose the cause of excessive blocking. It is usually advantageous to concentrate on optimizing the costly queries first, because this, in turn, reduces blocking for others. In Chapter 12, you will learn how to analyze and resolve blocking.

Number of Deadlocks/sec

You should expect to see a 0 value for this counter. If you find a nonzero value, then you should identify the victimized request and either resubmit the database request automatically or suggest that the user do so. More important, an attempt should be made to troubleshoot and resolve the deadlock. Again, Chapter 12 shows how to do this.

Nonreusable Execution Plans

Since generating an execution plan for a stored procedure query requires CPU cycles, you can reduce the stress on the CPU by reusing the execution plan. To analyze the number of stored procedures that are recompiling, you can look at the counter in Table 2-8.

Table 2-8. *Performance Monitor Counter to Analyze Execution Plan Reusability*

Object(Instance[,InstanceN])	Counter
`SQLServer:SQL Statistics`	`SQL Re-Compilations/sec`

Recompilations of stored procedures add overhead on the processor. You should see a value close to zero for the `SQL Re-Compilations/sec` counter. If you consistently see nonzero values, then you should use SQL Profiler to further investigate the stored procedures undergoing recompilations. Once you identify the relevant stored procedures, you should attempt to analyze and resolve the cause of recompilations. In Chapter 10, you will learn how to analyze and resolve various causes of recompilation.

General Behavior

SQL Server provides additional performance counters to track some general aspects of a SQL Server system. Table 2-9 lists a few of the most commonly used counters.

Table 2-9. *Performance Monitor Counters to Analyze Volume of Incoming Requests*

Object(Instance[,InstanceN])	Counter
`SQLServer:General Statistics`	`User Connections`
`SQLServer:SQL Statistics`	`Batch Requests/sec`

User Connections

Multiple read-only SQL Servers can work together in a load-balancing environment (where SQL Server is spread over several machines) to support a large number of database requests. In such cases, it is better to monitor the `User Connections` counter to evaluate the distribution of user connections across multiple SQL Server instances. `User Connections` can range all over the spectrum with normal application behavior. This is where a normal baseline is essential to determine the expected behavior. You will see how you can establish this baseline shortly.

Batch Requests/sec

This counter is a good indicator of the load on SQL Server. Based on the level of system resource utilization and `Batch Requests/sec`, you can estimate the number of users SQL Server may be able to take without developing resource bottlenecks. This counter value, at different load cycles, also helps you understand its relationship with the number of database connections. This also helps you understand SQL Server's relationship with `Web Request/sec`, that is, `Active Server Pages.Requests/sec` for web applications using Microsoft Internet Information Services (IIS) and Active Server Pages (ASP). All this analysis helps you better understand and predict system behavior as the user load changes.

The value of this counter can range over a wide spectrum with normal application behavior. A normal baseline is essential to determine the expected behavior. Let's move on to look at creating one now.

Creating a Baseline

Now that you have looked at a few of the main performance counters, let's see how to bring these counters together to create a system baseline. These are the steps you need to follow:

1. Create a reusable list of performance counters.
2. Create a counter log using your list of performance counters.
3. Minimize Performance Monitor overhead.

Creating a Reusable List of Performance Counters

Run the Performance Monitor tool on a Windows Server 2008 machine connected to the same network as that of the SQL Server system. Add performance counters to the View Chart display of the Performance Monitor through the Properties ➤ Data ➤ Add Counters dialog box, as shown in Figure 2-9.

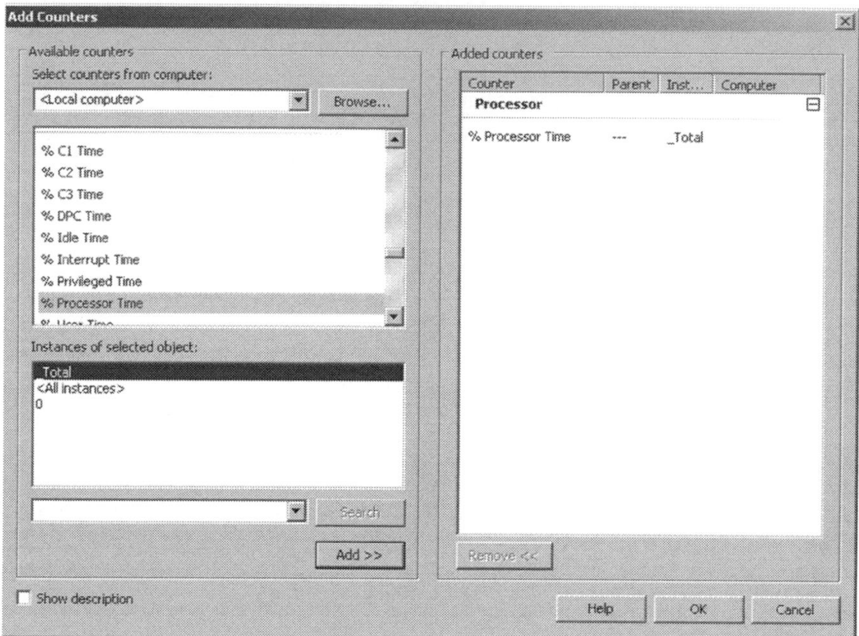

Figure 2-9. *Adding Performance Monitor counters*

For example, to add the performance counter `Processor(_Total)\% Processor Time`, follow these steps:

1. Select the option Select Counters from Computer, and specify the computer name running SQL Server in the corresponding entry field.
2. Click the box next to the performance object `Processor`.
3. Choose the `% Processor Time` counter from the list of performance counters.
4. Choose `instance _Total` from the instances in the Instances of Selected Object list.
5. Click the Add button to add this performance counter to the list of counters to be added.
6. Continue as needed with other counters. When finished, click the OK button.

When creating a reusable list for your baseline, you can repeat the preceding steps to add all the performance counters listed in Table 2-10.

Table 2-10. *Performance Monitor Counters to Analyze SQL Server Performance*

Object(Instance[,InstanceN])	Counter
Memory	Available MBytes Pages/sec
PhysicalDisk(Data-disk, Log-disk)	% Disk Time Current Disk Queue Length Disk Transfers/sec Disk Bytes/sec
Processor(_Total)	% Processor Time % Privileged Time
System	Processor Queue Length Context Switches/sec
Network Interface(Network card)	Bytes Total/sec
Network Segment	% Net Utilization
SQLServer:Access Methods	FreeSpace Scans/sec Full Scans/sec
SQLServer:Buffer Manager	Buffer cache hit ratio Free pages
SQLServer:Latches	Total Latch Wait Time (ms)
SQLServer:Locks(_Total)	Lock Timeouts/sec Lock Wait Time (ms) Number of Deadlocks/sec
SQLServer:Memory Manager	Memory Grants Pending Target Server Memory (KB) Total Server Memory (KB)
SQLServer:SQL Statistics	Batch Requests/sec SQL Re-Compilations/sec
SQLServer:General Statistics	User Connections

Once you have added all the performance counters, close the Add Counters dialog box. To save the list of counters as an `.htm` file, right-click anywhere in the right frame of Performance Monitor, and select the Save As menu item.

The `.htm` file lists all the performance counters that can be used as a base set of counters to create a counter log, or to view Performance Monitor graphs interactively, for the same SQL Server machine. To also use this list of counters for other SQL Server machines, open the `.htm` file in an editor such as Notepad, and replace all instances of `\\SQLServerMachineName` with '' (a blank string), without the quotes.

You can also use this counter list file to view Performance Monitor graphs interactively in an Internet browser, as shown in Figure 2-10.

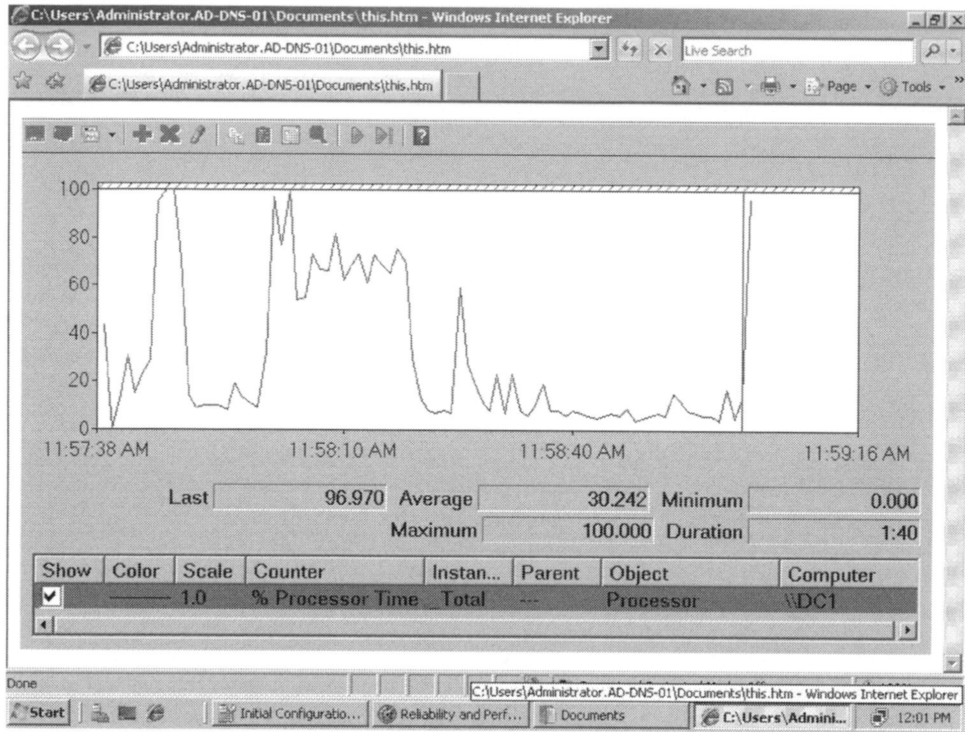

Figure 2-10. *Performance Monitor in Internet browser*

Creating a Counter Log Using the List of Performance Counters

Performance Monitor provides a counter log facility to save the performance data of multiple counters over a period of time. You can view the saved counter log using Performance Monitor to analyze the performance data. It is usually convenient to create a counter log from a defined list of performance counters. Simply collecting the data rather than viewing it through the GUI is the preferred method of automation to prepare for troubleshooting your server's performance or establishing a baseline.

Expand Data Collector Sets ➤ User Defined. Right-click, and select New ➤ Data Collector Set. Define the name of the set, and make this a manual creation by clicking the appropriate radio button; then click Next. You'll have to define what type of data you're collecting. In this case, select the check box Performance Counters under the Create Data Logs radio button, and then click Next. Here you can define the performance objects you want to collect using the same Add Counters dialog box as shown earlier in Figure 2-9. Clicking Next allows you to define the destination folder. Click Next, then select the radio button Open Properties for This Data Collector Set, and click Finish. You can schedule the counter log to automatically start at a specific time and stop after a certain time period or at a specific time. You can configure these settings through the Schedule pane. Figure 2-11 shows the summary of which counters have been selected as well as the frequency with which the counters will be collected.

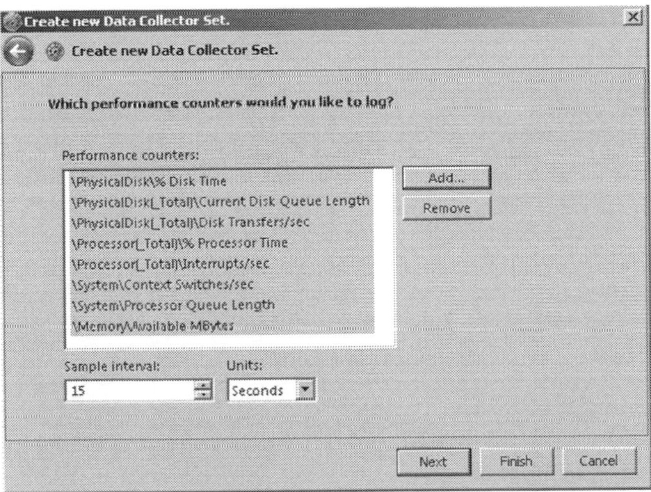

Figure 2-11. *Defining a Performance Monitor counter log*

Tip I'll offer additional suggestions for these settings in the section that follows.

For additional information on how to create counter logs using Performance Monitor, please refer to the Microsoft Knowledge Base article "Performance Tuning Guidelines for Windows Server 2008" at `http://download.microsoft.com/download/9/c/5/9c5b2167-8017-4bae-9fde-d599bac8184a/Perf-tun-srv.docx`.

Minimizing Performance Monitor Overhead

The Performance Monitor tool is designed to add as little overhead as possible, if used correctly. To minimize the impact of using this tool on a system, consider the following suggestions:

- Limit the number of counters, specifically performance objects.
- Use counter logs instead of viewing Performance Monitor graphs interactively.
- Run Performance Monitor remotely while viewing graphs interactively.
- Save the counter log file to a different local disk.
- Increase the sampling interval.

Let's consider each of these points in more detail.

Limit the Number of Counters

Monitoring large numbers of performance counters with small sampling intervals could incur some amount of overhead on the system. The bulk of this overhead comes from the number of performance objects you are monitoring, so selecting them wisely is important. The number of counters for the selected performance objects does not add much overhead, because it gives only an attribute of the object itself. Therefore, it is important to know what objects you want to monitor and why.

Prefer Counter Logs

Use counter logs instead of viewing a Performance Monitor graph interactively, because Performance Monitor graphing is more costly in terms of overhead. Monitoring current activities should be limited to short-term viewing of data, troubleshooting, and diagnosis. Performance data reported via a counter log is *sampled*, meaning that data is collected periodically rather than traced, whereas the Performance Monitor graph is updated in real time as events occur. Using counter logs will reduce that overhead.

View Performance Monitor Graphs Remotely

Since viewing the live performance data using Performance Monitor graphs creates a fair amount of overhead on the system, run the tool remotely on a different machine, and connect to the SQL Server system through the tool. To remotely connect to the SQL Server machine, run the Performance Monitor tool on a machine connected to the network to which the SQL Server machine is connected.

As shown in Figure 2-9, type the computer name (or IP address) of the SQL Server machine in the Select Counters from Computer box. Be aware that if you connect to the production server through a Windows Server 2008 terminal service session, the major part of the tool will still run on the server.

Save Counter Log Locally

Collecting the performance data for the counter log does not incur the overhead of displaying any graph. So, while using counter log mode, it is more efficient to log counter values locally on the SQL Server system instead of transferring the performance data across the network. Put the counter log file on a local disk other than the ones that are monitored.

Increase the Sampling Interval

Because you are mainly interested in the resource utilization pattern during baseline monitoring, you can easily increase the performance data sampling interval to 60 seconds or more to decrease the log file size and reduce demand on disk I/Os. You can use a short sampling interval to detect and diagnose timing issues. Even while viewing Performance Monitor graphs interactively, increase the sampling interval from the default value of one second per sample. Just remember, changing the sampling size, up or down, can affect the granularity of the data as well as the quantity. You have to weigh these choices carefully.

System Behavior Analysis Against Baseline

The default behavior of a database application changes over time because of various factors such as the following:

- Change of data
- Change of user group
- Change in usage pattern of the application
- Addition to or change in application functionalities
- Change in software environment because of the installation of new service packs or software upgrades
- Change in hardware environment

Because of the preceding changes, the baseline created for the database server slowly loses its significance. It may not always be accurate to compare the current behavior of the system with an old baseline. Therefore, it is important to keep the baseline up-to-date by creating a new baseline at regular time intervals. It is also beneficial to archive the previous baseline logs so that they can be referred to later, if required.

The counter log for the baseline or the current behavior of the system can be analyzed using the Performance Monitor tool by following these steps:

1. Open the counter log. Use Performance Monitor's toolbar item View Log File Data, and select the log file name.
2. Add all the performance counters to analyze the performance data. Note that only the performance objects, counters, and instances selected during the counter log creation are shown in the selection lists.
3. Analyze the system behavior at different parts of the day by adjusting the time range accordingly, as shown in Figure 2-12.

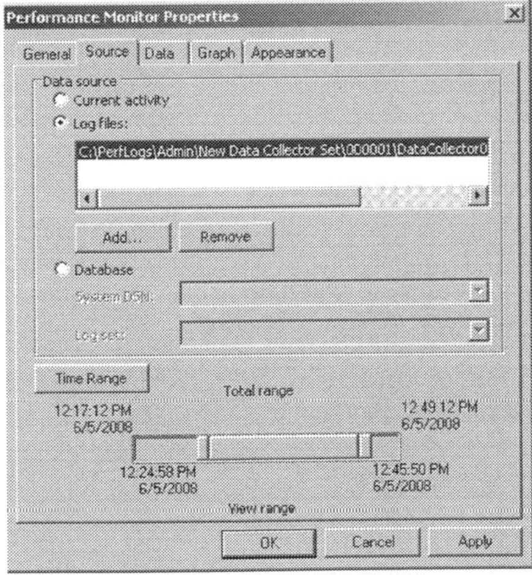

Figure 2-12. *Defining time range for log analysis*

During a performance review, you can analyze the system-level behavior of the database by comparing the current value of performance counters with the latest baseline. Take the following considerations into account while comparing the performance data:

- Use the same set of performance counters in both cases.
- Compare the minimum, maximum, or average value of the counters as applicable for the individual counters. I explained the specific values for the counters earlier.
- Some counters have an absolute good/bad value as mentioned previously. The current value of these counters need not be compared with the baseline values. For example, if the current average value of the `Pages/sec` counter is 100, then it indicates that the system has developed a memory bottleneck. Even though it does not require a comparison with the baseline, it is still advantageous to review the corresponding baseline value, because the memory bottleneck might have existed for a long time. Having the archived baseline logs helps detect the first occurrence of the memory bottleneck.
- Some counters do not have a definitive good/bad value. Because their value depends on the application, a relative comparison with the corresponding baseline counters is a must. For example, the current value of the `User Connections` counter for SQL Server does not signify anything good or bad with the application. But comparing it with the corresponding baseline value may reveal a big increase in the number of user connections, indicating an increase in the workload.
- Compare a range of value for the counters from the current and the baseline counter logs. The fluctuation in the individual values of the counters will be normalized by the range of values.
- Compare logs from the same part of the day. For most applications, the usage pattern varies during different parts of the day. To obtain the minimum, maximum, and average value of the counters for a specific time, adjust the time range of the counter logs as shown previously.

Once the system-level bottleneck is identified, the internal behavior of the application should be analyzed to determine the cause of the bottleneck. Identifying and optimizing the source of the bottleneck will help use the system resources efficiently.

Summary

In this chapter, you learned that you can use the Performance Monitor tool to analyze the effect on system resources of a slow-performing database application, as well as the overall behavior of SQL Server. For every resultant system bottleneck, there are two types of resolutions: hardware resolutions and application optimization. Of course, it is always beneficial to optimize the database application before considering a hardware upgrade.

In the next chapter, you will learn how to analyze the workload of a database application for performance tuning.

CHAPTER 3

SQL Query Performance Analysis

A common cause of slow SQL Server performance is a heavy database application workload—the nature of the queries themselves. Thus, to analyze the cause of a system bottleneck, it is important to examine the database application workload and identify the SQL queries causing the most stress on system resources. To do this, you use the SQL Profiler and Management Studio tools.

In this chapter, I cover the following topics:

- The basics of the SQL Profiler tool
- How to analyze SQL Server workload and identify costly SQL queries using SQL Profiler
- How to combine the baseline measurements with data collected from SQL Profiler
- How to analyze the processing strategy of a costly SQL query using Management Studio
- How to track query performance through dynamic management views
- How to analyze the effectiveness of index and join strategies for a SQL query
- How to measure the cost of a SQL query using SQL utilities

The SQL Profiler Tool

SQL Profiler is a GUI and set of system stored procedures that can be used to do the following:

- Graphically monitor SQL Server queries
- Collect query information in the background
- Analyze performance
- Diagnose problems such as deadlocks
- Debug a Transact-SQL (T-SQL) statement
- Replay SQL Server activity in a simulation

You can also use SQL Profiler to capture activities performed on a SQL Server instance. Such a capture is called a *Profiler trace.* You can use a Profiler trace to capture events generated by various subsystems within SQL Server. You can run traces from the graphical front end or through direct calls to the procedures. The most efficient way to define a trace is through the system procedures, but a good place to start learning about traces is through the GUI.

Profiler Traces

Open the Profiler tool from the Start ➤ Programs ➤ Microsoft SQL Server 2008 ➤ Performance Tools menu, and select File ➤ New ➤ Trace. You can also press Ctrl+N or click the New Trace button. This opens a connection window, so choose the server instance you'll be tracing and then connect. That opens the Trace Properties dialog box shown in Figure 3-1.

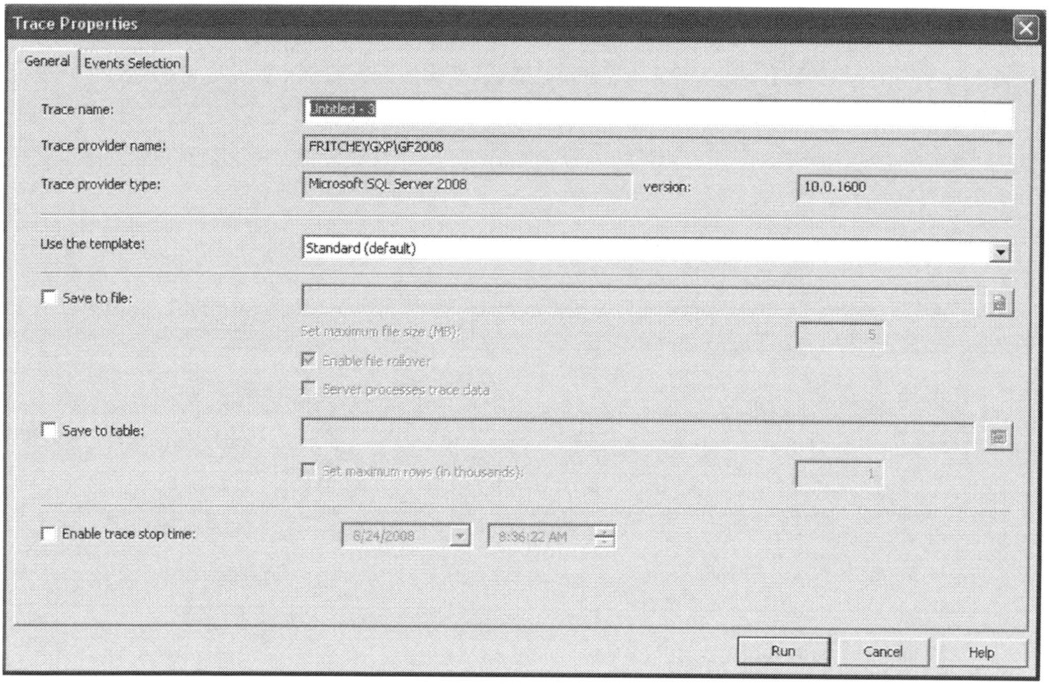

Figure 3-1. *General trace properties*

You can supply a trace name to help categorize your traces later when you have lots of them. Different trace templates are available that quickly help you set up new traces for different purposes. For the moment, I'll stick with the Standard trace. Without additional changes, this trace will run as a graphical trace, but from the Trace Properties dialog box you can define the trace to save its output to a file or to a table. I'll spend more time on these options later in this chapter. Finally, from the General tab, you can define a stop time for the trace. These options combine to give you more control over exactly what you intend to monitor and how you intend to monitor it within SQL Server.

With the initial setup complete, click the Events Selection tab to provide more detailed definition to your trace, as shown in Figure 3-2.

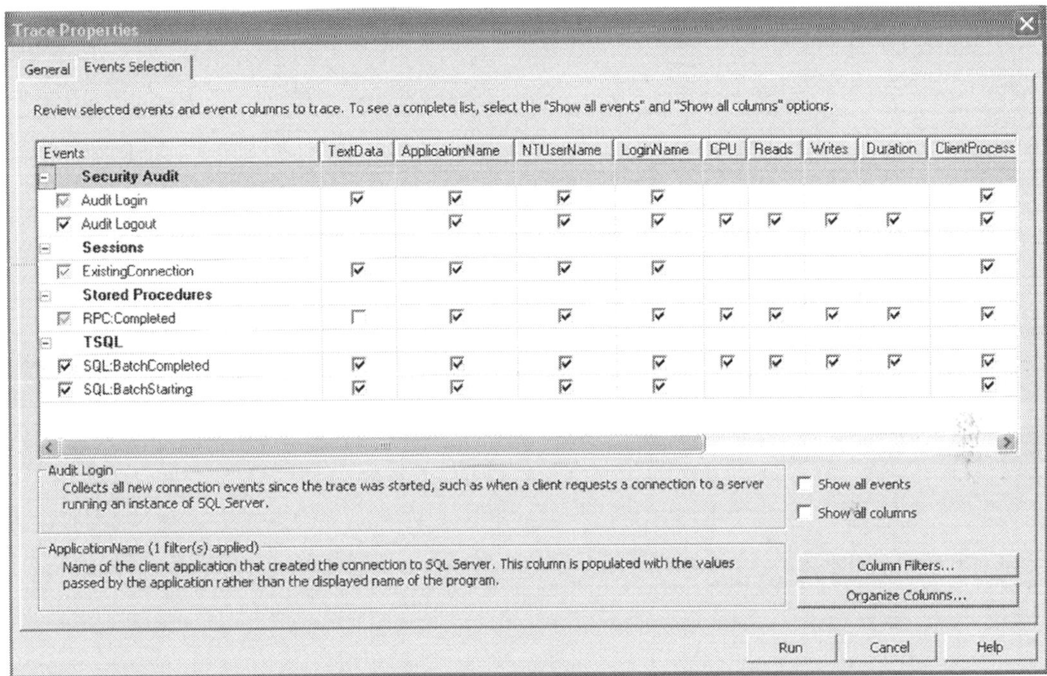

Figure 3-2. *Events Selection tab*

Events

An *event* represents various activities performed in SQL Server. These are categorized for easy classification into *event classes*; cursor events, lock events, stored procedure events, and T-SQL events are a few common event classes.

For performance analysis, you are mainly interested in the events that help you judge levels of resource stress for various activities performed on SQL Server. By *resource stress*, I mean things such as the following:

- What kind of CPU utilization was involved for the SQL activity?
- How much memory was used?
- How much I/O was involved?
- How long did the SQL activity take to execute?
- How frequently was a particular query executed?
- What kind of errors and warnings were faced by the queries?

You can calculate the resource stress of a SQL activity after the completion of an event, so the main events you use for performance analysis are those that represent the completion of a SQL activity. Table 3-1 describes these events.

Table 3-1. *Events to Trace Query Completion*

Event Class	Event	Description
`Stored Procedures`	`RPC:Completed`	An RPC completion event
	`SP:Completed`	A stored procedure completion event
	`SP:StmtCompleted`	A SQL statement completion event within a stored procedure
`TSQL`	`SQL:BatchCompleted`	A T-SQL batch completion event
	`SQL:StmtCompleted`	A T-SQL statement completion event

An RPC event indicates that the stored procedure was executed using the Remote Procedure Call (RPC) mechanism through an OLEDB command. If a database application executes a stored procedure using the T-SQL `EXECUTE` statement, then that stored procedure is resolved as a SQL batch rather than as an RPC. RPC requests are generally faster than `EXECUTE` requests, since they bypass much of the statement parsing and parameter processing in SQL Server.

A *T-SQL batch* is a set of SQL queries that are submitted together to SQL Server. A T-SQL batch is usually terminated by a `GO` command. The `GO` command is not a T-SQL statement. Instead, the `GO` command is recognized by the `sqlcmd` utility, as well as by Management Studio, and it signals the end of a batch. Each SQL query in the batch is considered a T-SQL statement. Thus, a T-SQL batch consists of one or more T-SQL statements. Statements or T-SQL statements are also the individual, discrete commands within a stored procedure. Capturing individual statements with the `SP:StmtCompleted` or `SQL:StmtCompleted` event can be a very expensive operation, depending on the number of individual statements within your queries. Assume for a moment that each stored procedure within your system contains one, and only one, T-SQL statement. In this case, the collection of completed statements is pretty low. Now assume that you have multiple statements within your procedures and that some of those procedures are calls to other procedures with other statements. Collecting all this extra data now becomes a noticeable load on the system. Statement completion events should be collected extremely judiciously, especially on a production system.

After you've selected a trace template, a preselected list of events will already be defined on the Events Selection tab. Only the events you have selected will be displayed. To see the full list of events available, click the Show All Events check box. To add an event to the trace, find the event under an event class in the Event column, and click the check box to the left of it. To remove events not required, deselect the check box next to the event.

Although the events listed in Table 3-1 represent the most common events used for determining performance, you can sometimes use a number of additional events to diagnose the same thing. For example, as mentioned in Chapter 1, repeated recompilation of a stored procedure adds processing overhead, which hurts the performance of the database request. The `Stored Procedures` event class of the Profiler tool includes an event, `SP:Recompile`, to indicate the recompilation of a stored procedure (this event is explained in depth in Chapter 10). Similarly, Profiler includes additional events to indicate other performance-related issues with a database workload. Table 3-2 shows a few of these events.

Table 3-2. *Events to Trace Query Performance*

Event Class	Event	Description
Security Audit	Audit Login Audit Logout	Keeps track of database connections when users connect to and disconnect from SQL Server.
Sessions	ExistingConnection	Represents all the users connected to SQL Server before the trace was started.
Cursors	CursorImplicitConversion	Indicates that the cursor type created is different from the requested type.
Errors and Warnings	Attention	Represents the intermediate termination of a request caused by actions such as query cancellation by a client or a broken database connection.
	Exception	Indicates the occurrence of an exception in SQL Server.
	Execution Warnings	Indicates the occurrence of any warning during the execution of a query or a stored procedure.
	Hash Warning	Indicates the occurrence of an error in a hashing operation.
	Missing Column Statistics	Indicates that the statistics of a column, required by the optimizer to decide a processing strategy, are missing.
	Missing Join Predicate	Indicates that a query is executed with no joining predicate between two tables.
	Sort Warnings	Indicates that a sort operation performed in a query such as SELECT did not fit into memory.
Locks	Lock:Deadlock	Flags the presence of a deadlock.
	Lock:Deadlock Chain	Shows a trace of the chain of queries creating the deadlock.
	Lock:Timeout	Signifies that the lock has exceeded the timeout parameter, which is set by SET LOCK_TIMEOUT timeout_period(ms).
Stored Procedures	SP:Recompile	Indicates that an execution plan for a stored procedure had to be recompiled, because one did not exist, a recompilation was forced, or the existing execution plan could not be reused.
	SP:Starting	Represents the starting of a stored SP:StmtStarting procedure and a SQL statement within a stored procedure, respectively. They are useful to identify queries that started but could not finish because of an operation that caused an Attention event.
Transactions	SQLTransaction	Provides information about a database transaction, including information such as when a transaction started/completed, the duration of the transaction, and so on.

Data Columns

Events are represented by different attributes called *data columns*. The data columns represent different attributes of an event, such as the class of the event, the SQL statement for the event, the resource cost of the event, and the source of the event.

The data columns that represent the resource cost of an event are CPU, Reads, Writes, and Duration. As a result, the data columns you will use most for performance analysis are shown in Table 3-3.

Table 3-3. *Data Columns to Trace Query Completion*

Data Column	Description
EventClass	Type of event, for example, SQL:StatementCompleted.
TextData	SQL statement for an event, such as SELECT * FROM sysobjects.
CPU	CPU cost of an event in milliseconds (ms). For example, CPU = 100 for a SELECT statement indicates that the statement took 100 ms to execute.
Reads	Number of logical reads performed for an event. For example, Reads = 800 for a SELECT statement indicates that the statement required a total of 800 reads.
Writes	Number of logical writes performed for an event.
Duration	Execution time of an event in ms.
SPID	SQL Server process identifier used for the event.
StartTime	Start time of an event.

Each logical read and write consists of an 8KB page activity in memory, which may require zero or more physical I/O operations. To find the number of physical I/O operations on a disk subsystem, use the System Monitor tool; I'll cover more about combining the output of Profiler and System Monitor later in this chapter.

You can add a data column to a Profiler trace by simply clicking the check box for that column. If no check box is available for a given column, then the event in question cannot collect that piece of data. Like the events, initially only the data columns defined by the template are displayed. To see the complete list of data columns, click the Show All Columns check box.

You can use additional data columns from time to time to diagnose the cause of poor performance. For example, in the case of a stored procedure recompilation, the Profiler tool indicates the cause of the recompilation through the EventSubClass data column. (This data column is explained in depth in Chapter 10.) A few of the commonly used additional data columns are as follows:

- BinaryData
- IntegerData
- EventSubClass
- DatabaseID
- ObjectID

- IndexID
- TransactionID
- Error
- EndTime

The BinaryData and IntegerData data columns provide specific information about a given SQL Server activity. For example, in the case of a cursor, they specify the type of cursor requested and the type of cursor created. Although the names of these additional data columns indicate their purpose to a great extent, I will explain the usefulness of these data columns in later chapters as you use them.

Column data can be rearranged to make the screen more pleasing, and they can be grouped to provide aggregates of the data collected. To control the column data placement, click the Organize Columns button. This opens the Organize Columns dialog box shown in Figure 3-3.

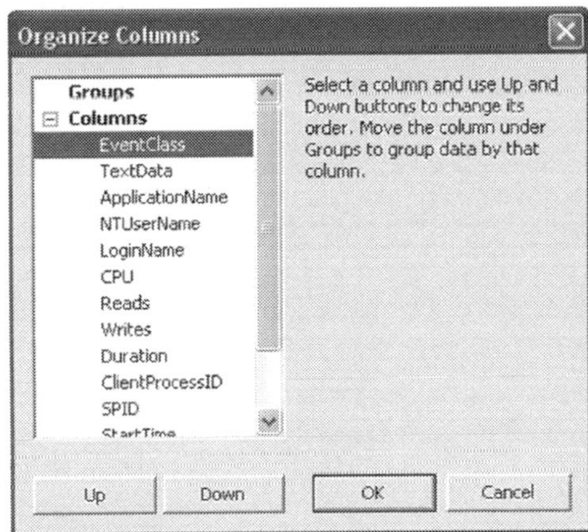

Figure 3-3. *Organize Columns dialog box*

You can change the position of a column by clicking the Up and Down buttons. Moving a column into the Groups category means it will become an aggregation column.

Filters

In addition to defining events and data columns for a Profiler trace, you can also define various filter criteria. These help keep the trace output small, which is usually a good idea. Table 3-4 describes the filter criteria that you will commonly use during performance analysis.

Table 3-4. *SQL Trace Filters*

Events	Filter Criteria Example	Use
ApplicationName	Not like: SQL Profiler	This filters out the events generated by Profiler. This is the default behavior.
DatabaseID	Equals: <ID of the database to monitor>	This filters out events generated by a particular database. You can determine the ID of a database from its name as follows: SELECT DB_ID('Northwind').
Duration	Greater than or equal: 2	For performance analysis, you will often capture a trace for a large workload. In a large trace, there will be many event logs with a Duration that is less than what you're interested in. Filter out these event logs, because there is hardly any scope for optimizing these SQL activities.
Reads	Greater than or equal: 2	This is similar to the criterion on the Duration data column.
SPID	Equals: <Database users to monitor>	This troubleshoots queries sent by a specific database user.

Figure 3-4 shows a snippet of the preceding filter criteria selection in SQL Profiler.

■ **Note** For a complete list of filters available in SQL Profiler, please refer to the MSDN article "Limiting Traces" (http://msdn.microsoft.com/library/default.asp?url=/library/en-us/adminsql/ad_mon_perf_6nxd.asp).

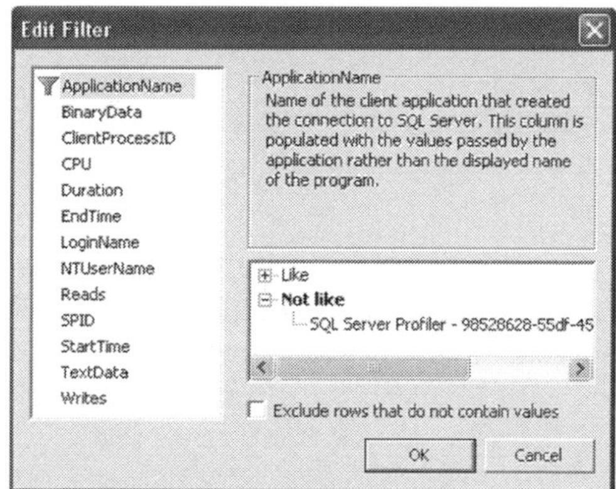

Figure 3-4. *Trace definition with filters*

Trace Templates

In the previous section, you learned how to define a new Profiler trace to monitor activities using SQL Server. However, instead of defining a new trace every time you want to use one, you can create a trace template with your customized events, data columns, and filters and then reuse the trace template to capture a trace. The procedure for defining a new trace template is similar to that of defining a new trace:

1. Create a new trace.
2. Define the events, data columns, and filters the same way as shown earlier.
3. Save the trace definition as a trace template from the File ➤ Save As menu choice. Profiler will automatically populate its Templates list with your new template.

Trace Data

After you've defined a trace, clicking the Run button will begin capturing events and displaying them on your screen, as shown in Figure 3-5. You will see a series of events scrolling by, and you can watch your system perform in what I've always called SQL TV. You have control over the trace more or less like a DVD player, so you can pause, start, and stop the trace (sorry, no fast-forward) using the buttons on the toolbar. You can even pause the trace and make changes to it as you work.

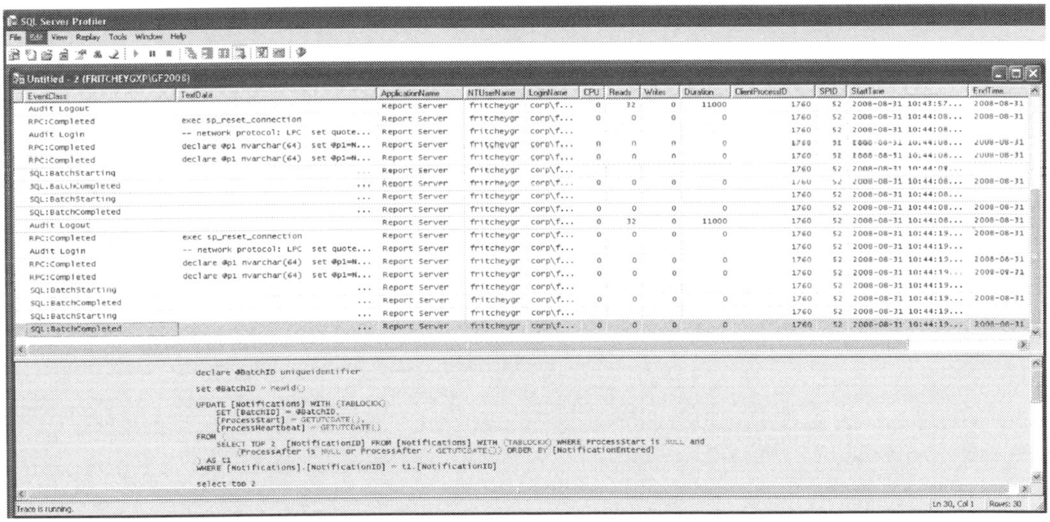

Figure 3-5. *Events and data captured within a trace*

Once you finish capturing your SQL Server activities, you can save the trace output to a *trace file* or a *trace table*. Trace output saved to a trace file is in a native format and can be opened by Profiler to analyze the SQL queries. Saving the trace output to a trace table allows the SQL queries in the trace output to be analyzed by Profiler as well as by SELECT statements on the trace table.

Profiler creates a trace table dynamically as per the definition of the data columns in the trace output. The ability to analyze the trace output using SELECT statements adds great flexibility to the analysis process. For example, if you want to find out the number of query executions with a response time of less than 500 ms, you can execute a SELECT statement on the trace table as follows:

```
SELECT COUNT(*) FROM <Trace Table>
WHERE Duration > 500
```

You will look at some sample queries in the "Identifying Costly Queries" section later in the chapter, but first I'll describe how to automate Profiler and simultaneously reduce the amount of memory and network bandwidth that the Profiler process uses.

Trace Automation

The Profiler GUI makes collecting Profiler trace information easy. Unfortunately, that ease comes at a cost. The events captured by the Profiler tool go into a cache in memory in order to feed across the network to the GUI. Your GUI is dependent on your network. Network traffic can slow things down and cause the cache to fill. This will, to a small degree, impact performance on the server. Further, when the cache fills, the server will begin to drop events in order to avoid seriously impacting server performance. How do you avoid this? Use the system stored procedures to generate a scripted trace that outputs to a file.

Capturing a Trace Using the GUI

You can create a scripted trace in one of two ways, manually or with the GUI. Until you get comfortable with all the requirements of the scripts, the easy way is to use the Profiler tool's GUI. These are the steps you'll need to perform:

1. Define a trace.
2. Click the menu File ➤ Export ➤ Script Trace Definition.
3. You must select the target server type, in this instance, For SQL Server 2005/2008.
4. Give the file a name, and save it.

These steps will generate all the script commands that you need to capture a trace and output it to a file. You can also script trace events that will be used with the new 2008 Data Collector service, but that functionality is beyond the scope of this book.

To manually launch this new trace, use Management Studio as follows:

1. Open the file.
2. Replace where it says `InsertFileNameHere` with the appropriate name and path for your system.
3. Execute the script. It will return a single column result set with the `TraceId`.

You may want to automate the execution of this script through the SQL Agent, or you can even run the script from the command line using the `sqlcmd.exe` utility. Whatever method you use, the script will start the trace. If you have not defined a trace stop time, you will need to stop the trace manually using the `TraceId`. I'll show how to do that in the next section.

Capturing a Trace Using Stored Procedures

If you look at the scripts defined in the previous section, you will see a series of commands, called in a specific order:

- `sp_trace_create`: Create a trace definition.
- `sp_trace_setevent`: Add events and event columns to the trace.
- `sp_trace_setfilter`: Apply filters to the trace.

Once the SQL trace has been defined, you can run the trace using the stored procedure `sp_trace_setstatus`.

The tracing of SQL activities continues until the trace is stopped. Since the SQL tracing continues as a back-end process, the Management Studio session need not be kept open. You can identify the running traces by using the SQL Server built-in function `fn_trace_getinfo`, as shown in the following query:

```
SELECT * FROM ::fn_trace_getinfo(default);
```

Figure 3-6 shows the output of the function.

	traceid	property	value
1	2	1	0
2	2	2	c:\mytrace.trc.trc
3	2	3	5
4	2	4	NULL
5	2	5	1

Figure 3-6. *Output of fn_trace_getinfo*

The number of unique `traceid`s in the output of the function `fn_trace_getinfo` indicates the number of traces active on SQL Server. The data value of the column `value` for the property of 5 indicates whether the trace is running (value = 1) or stopped (value = 0). You can stop a specific trace, say `traceid = 1`, by executing the stored procedure `sp_trace_setstatus`:

```
EXEC sp_trace_setstatus 1, 0;
```

After a trace is stopped, its definition must be closed and deleted from the server by executing `sp_trace_setstatus`:

```
EXEC sp_trace_setstatus 1, 2;
```

To verify that the trace is stopped successfully, reexecute the function `fn_trace_getinfo`, and ensure that the output of the function doesn't contain the `traceid`.

The format of the trace file created by this technique is the same as that of the trace file created by Profiler. Therefore, this trace file can be analyzed in the same way as a trace file created by Profiler.

Capturing a SQL trace using stored procedures as outlined in the previous section avoids the overhead associated with the Profiler GUI. It also provides greater flexibility in managing the tracing schedule of a SQL trace than is provided by the Profiler tool. In Chapter 16, you will learn how to control the schedule of a SQL trace while capturing the activities of a SQL workload over an extended period of time.

■Note The time captured through a trace defined as illustrated in this section is stored in microseceonds, not milliseconds. This difference between units can cause confusion if not taken into account.

Combining Trace and Performance Monitor Output

In Chapter 2, I showed how to capture Performance Monitor data to a file. In the preceding section, I showed how to capture Profiler data to a file as well. If you automate the collection of both of these sets of data so that they cover the same time periods, you can use them together inside the SQL Profiler GUI. Be sure that your trace has both the `StartTime` and `Endtime` data fields. Follow these steps:

1. Open the trace file.
2. Click the File ➤ Import Performance Data.
3. Select the Performance Monitor file to be imported.

Performing these actions will open the dialog box shown in Figure 3-7, which allows you to pick Performance Monitor counters for inclusion.

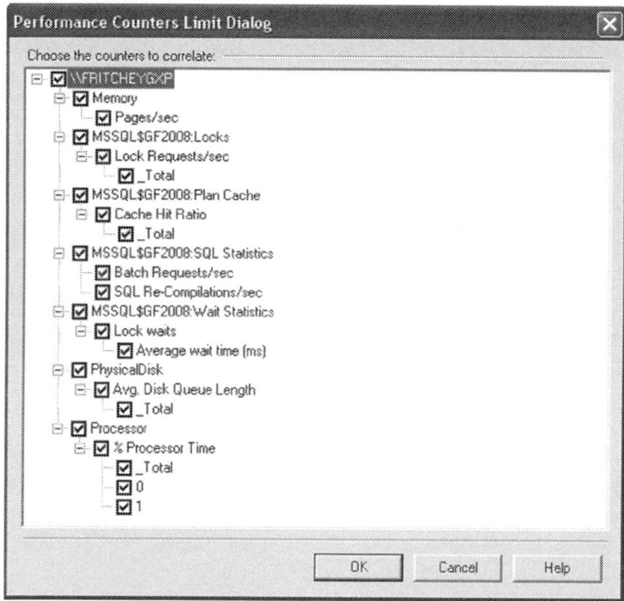

Figure 3-7. *Counters available for display in Profiler*

Once you've selected the counters you want to include, clicking OK will open the Profiler and Performance Monitor data together, as you can see in Figure 3-8. Now you can begin to use the trace data and the Performance Monitor data together. If you select an event in the top window, it will place a red line within the Performance Monitor data, showing where the event occurred within the time frame of that data. Conversely, you can click within the Performance Monitor data, and the event that represents that time frame will be selected. These capabilities work so well together that you'll be using them regularly during tuning sessions to identify the bottlenecks and stress points and to determine which specific queries are causing them.

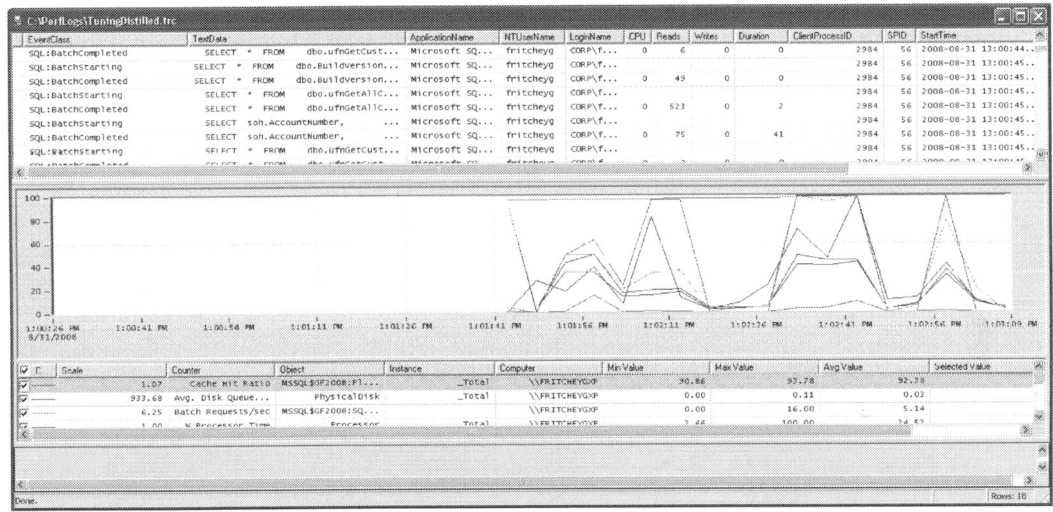

Figure 3-8. *Profiler data next to Performance Monitor data*

SQL Profiler Recommendations

You have already seen how to set some filters on a trace to help minimize the impact of Profiler on system resources. To further minimize the impact, consider the following suggestions:

- Limit the number of events and data columns.
- Discard start events for performance analysis.
- Limit trace output size.
- Avoid online data column sorting.
- Run Profiler remotely.

In the following sections, I cover each of these suggestions in more depth.

Limiting the Number of Events and Data Columns

While tracing SQL queries, you can decide which SQL activities should be captured by filtering events and data columns. Choosing extra events contributes to the bulk of tracing overhead. Data columns do not add much overhead, since they are only attributes of an event class. Therefore, it is extremely important to know why you want to trace each event selected and to select your events based only on necessity.

Minimizing the number of events to be captured prevents SQL Server from wasting the bandwidth of valuable resources generating all those events. Capturing events such as locks and execution plans should be done with caution, because these events make the trace output very large and degrade SQL Server's performance.

It's important to reduce the number of events while analyzing a production server, since you don't want the profiler to add a large amount of load to the production server. On a test server, the amount of load contributed by Profiler is a lesser consideration than the ability to analyze every activity on SQL Server. Therefore, on a test server, you need not compromise so much with the information you might be interested in.

Some events come with added cost. I mentioned earlier in the chapter that the statement completion events can be costly, but other events could negatively impact your system while you're attempting to capture information about that system.

FILTERING STAGES

There are two stages of filtering: prefiltering, which is performed by SQL Server, and postfiltering, which is performed by the user. *Prefiltering* is the online stage of capturing the SQL Server activities. Prefiltering offers several advantages:

- It reduces the impact on the performance of SQL Server, since a limited number of events are generated.
- It reduces trace output size.
- It simplifies postfiltering operations because fewer events are being captured in the first place.

The only disadvantage to prefiltering is that you may miss some vital information that might be required for thorough analysis. As with many things, choosing when and how much to prefilter involves making good judgment calls.

Postfiltering is the stage where you analyze the captured trace file. It is an offline stage, incurring no overhead on SQL Server. Once you filter an existing trace file, you can save the postfiltered information to a new trace file. For example, while identifying the problematic queries, you might be interested in queries with an execution time greater than 500 ms. To identify such queries, you can apply a postfilter on the trace output for a `Duration` greater than or equal to 500 and save this filtered trace output as a separate trace file. This means that the next time you need to look at the same criteria, you do not have to load the original trace file and do filtering again; you can just use the new trace file.

Discarding Start Events for Performance Analysis

The information you want for performance analysis revolves around the resource cost of a query. Start events, such as `SP:StmtStarting`, do not provide this information, because it is only after an event completes that you can compute the amount of I/O, the CPU load, and the duration of the query. Therefore, while tracking slow-running queries for performance analysis, you need not capture the start events. This information is provided by the corresponding completion events.

So, when should you capture start events? Well, you should capture start events when you don't expect some SQL queries to finish execution because of error conditions or when you find frequent Attention events. An Attention event usually indicates that the user cancelled the query midway or the query timeout expired, probably because the query was running for a long time.

Limiting the Trace Output Size

Besides prefiltering events and data columns, other filtering criteria limit the trace output size. Again, limiting size may cause you to miss interesting events if you're looking at overall system behavior. But if you're focusing on costly queries, a filter helps. From the Edit Filter dialog box, accessed by clicking the Column Filters button on the Events Selection tab, consider the following settings:

- *Duration – Greater than or equal: 2*: SQL queries with a Duration equal to 0 or 1 ms cannot be further optimized.
- *Reads – Greater than or equal: 2*: SQL queries with number of logical reads equal to 0 or 1 ms cannot be further optimized.

Avoiding Online Data Column Sorting

During performance analysis, you usually sort a trace output on different data columns (such as Duration, CPU, and Reads) to identify queries with the largest corresponding figures. If you sort offline, you reduce the activities Profiler has to perform while interacting with SQL Server. This is how to sort a captured SQL trace output:

1. Capture the trace without any sorting (or grouping).
2. Save the trace output to a trace file.
3. Open the trace file and sort (or group) the trace file output on specific data columns as required.

Running Profiler Remotely

It is usually not a good practice to run test tools directly on the production server. Profiler has a heavy user interface; therefore, it is better to run it on another machine. Similar to System Monitor, Profiler should not be run through a terminal service session, because a major part of the tool still runs on the server. When collecting a trace output directly to a file, save the file locally where Profiler is being run. This is still a more resource-intensive operation than running Profiler through the system stored procedures as a server-side trace. That remains the best option.

Limiting the Use of Certain Events

Some events are more costly than others. As I mentioned previously, depending on the nature of the queries being generated, the statement completion events can be very costly. Other events to use judiciously, especially on a system that's already experiencing stress, are the Showplan XML events Performance:Showplan XML, Performance:Showplan XML for Query Compile, and Performance:Showplan XML Statistics Profile. Although these events can be useful, keep them off the production machine.

Query Performance Metrics Without Profiler

Setting up a trace allows you to collect a lot of data for later use, but the collection can be somewhat expensive, and you have to wait on the results. If you need to immediately capture performance metrics about your system, especially as they pertain to query performance, then the dynamic management view `sys.dm_exec_query_stats` is what you need. If you still need a historical tracking of when queries were run and their individual costs, a trace is still the better tool. But if you just need to know, at this moment, the longest-running queries or the most physical reads, then you can get that information from `sys.dm_exec_query_stats`.

Since `sys.dm_exec_query_stats` is just a view, you can simply query against it and get information about the statistics of query plans on the server. Table 3-5 shows some of the data returned from the query.

Table 3-5. *`sys.dm_exec_query_stats` Output*

Column	Description
`Plan_handle`	Pointer that refers to the execution plan
`Creation_time`	Time that the plan was created
`Last_execution time`	Last time the plan was used by a query
`Execution_count`	Number of times the plan has been used
`Total_worker_time`	Total CPU time used by the plan since it was created
`Total_logical_reads`	Total number of reads used since the plan was created
`Total_logical_writes`	Total number of writes used since the plan was created
`Query_hash`	A binary hash that can be used to identify queries with similar logic
`Query_plan_hash`	A binary hash that can be used to identify plans with similar logic

Table 3-5 is just a sampling. For complete details, see Books Online.

To filter the information returned from `sys.dm_exec_query_stats`, you'll need to join it with other dynamic management functions such as `sys.dm_exec_sql_text`, which shows the query text associated with the plan, or `sys.dm_query_plan`, which has the execution plan for the query. Once joined to these other DMFs, you can limit the database or procedure that you want to filter. These other DMFs are covered in detail in other chapters of the book.

Costly Queries

Now that you have seen what you need to consider when using the Profiler tool, let's look at what the data represents: the costly queries themselves. When the performance of SQL Server goes bad, two things are most likely happening:

- First, certain queries create high stress on system resources. These queries affect the performance of the overall system, because the server becomes incapable of serving other SQL queries fast enough.
- Additionally, the costly queries block all other queries requesting the same database resources, further degrading the performance of those queries. Optimizing the costly queries improves not only their own performance but also the performance of other queries by reducing database blocking and pressure on SQL Server resources.

You can use Profiler to capture the SQL Server workload, as explained previously in this chapter. Define a trace. Then run the queries in `trace_queries.sql`. Figure 3-9 shows a sample trace output. On a live production server, the trace output may be quite large; the solution is to use filter criteria, as explained in the earlier "Filters" section, to limit the size of the trace output.

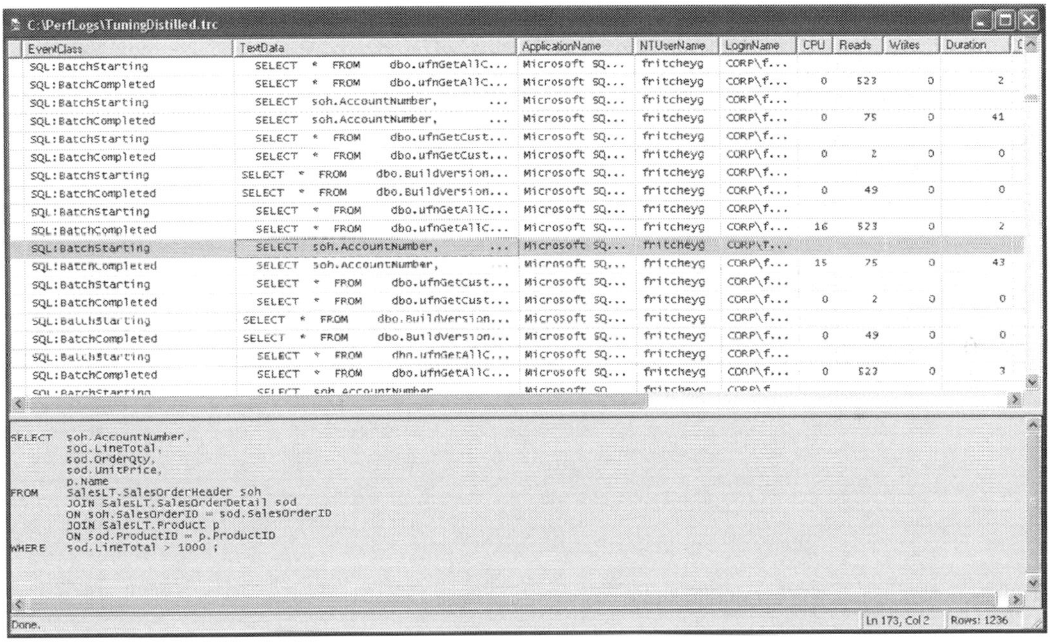

Figure 3-9. *A sample trace output*

Once you have captured the set of SQL queries representing a complete workload, you should analyze the trace to identify two sets of queries:

- Costly queries that are causing a great deal of pressure on the system resources
- Queries that are slowed down the most

Identifying Costly Queries

The goal of SQL Server is to return result sets to the user in the shortest time. To do this, SQL Server has a built-in, cost-based optimizer called the *query optimizer*, which generates a cost-effective strategy called a *query execution plan*. The query optimizer weighs many factors, including (but not limited to) the usage of CPU, memory, and disk I/O required to execute a query, all derived from the statistics maintained by indexes or generated on the fly, and it then creates a cost-effective execution plan. Although minimizing the number of I/Os is not a requirement for a cost-effective plan, you will often find that the least costly plan has the fewest I/Os because I/O operations are expensive.

In the data returned from a trace, the CPU and Reads columns also show where a query costs you. The CPU column represents the CPU time used to execute the query. The Reads column represents the number of logical pages (8KB in size) a query operated on and thereby indicates the amount of memory stress caused by the query. It also provides an indication of disk stress, since memory pages have to be backed up in the case of action queries, populated during first-time data access, and displaced to disk during memory bottlenecks. The higher the number of logical reads for a query, the higher the possible stress on the disk could be. An excessive number of logical pages also increases load on the CPU in managing those pages.

The queries that cause a large number of logical reads usually acquire locks on a correspondingly large set of data. Even reading (as opposed to writing) requires share locks on all the data. These queries block all other queries requesting this data (or a part of the data) for the purposes of modifying it, not for reading it. Since these queries are inherently costly and require a long time to execute, they block other queries for an extended period of time. The blocked queries then cause blocks on further queries, introducing a chain of blocking in the database. (Chapter 12 covers lock modes.)

As a result, it makes sense to identify the costly queries and optimize them first, thereby doing the following:

- Improving the performance of the costly queries themselves
- Reducing the overall stress on system resources
- Reducing database blocking

The costly queries can be categorized into the following two types:

- *Single execution*: An individual execution of the query is costly.
- *Multiple executions*: A query itself may not be costly, but the repeated execution of the query causes pressure on the system resources.

You can identify these two types of costly queries using different approaches, as explained in the following sections.

Costly Queries with a Single Execution

You can identify the costly queries by analyzing a SQL Profiler trace output file or by querying sys.dm_exec_query_stats. Since you are interested in identifying queries that perform a large number of logical reads, you should sort the trace output on the Reads data column. You can access the trace information by following these steps:

1. Capture a Profiler trace that represents a typical workload.
2. Save the trace output to a trace file.
3. Open the trace file for analysis.
4. Open the Properties window for the trace, and click the Events Selection tab.
5. Open the Organize Columns window by clicking that button.
6. Group the trace output on the Reads column. To do this, move the Reads column under the Groups section, described earlier in this chapter, as shown in Figure 3-10.
7. You can work with the trace grouped, or you can look at it sorted by changing the display using Ctrl+E.

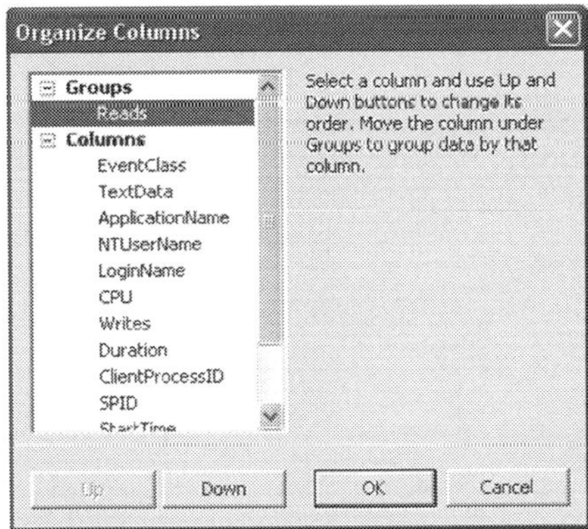

Figure 3-10. *Trace definition sorted on the* `Reads` *column*

This process will group the trace output on the `Reads` column, as shown in Figure 3-11. The trace output is sorted on `Reads` in ascending order. From there, you can select a few of the costliest queries and analyze and optimize them appropriately.

In some cases, you may have identified a large stress on the CPU from the System Monitor output. The pressure on the CPU may be because of a large number of CPU-intensive operations, such as stored procedure recompilations, aggregate functions, data sorting, hash joins, and so on. In such cases, you should sort the Profiler trace output on the `CPU` column to identify the queries taking up a large number of processor cycles.

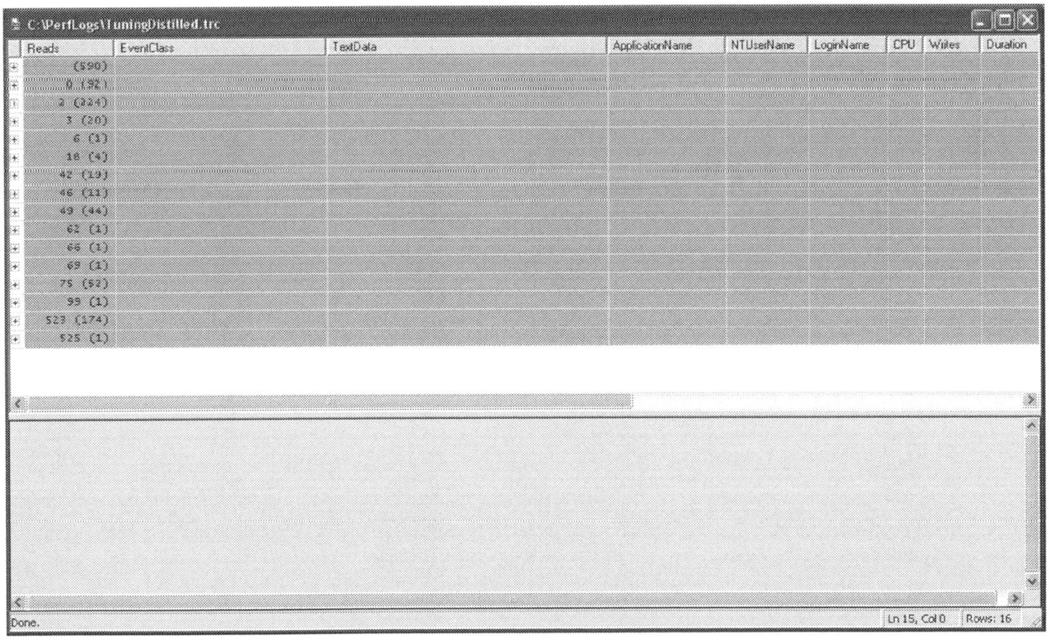

Figure 3-11. *Trace output sorted on the* `Reads` *column*

Costly Queries with Multiple Executions

As I mentioned earlier, sometimes a query may not be costly by itself, but the cumulative effect of multiple executions of the same query might put pressure on the system resources. Sorting on the Reads column won't help you identify this type of costly query. You instead want to know the total number of reads performed by multiple executions of the query. Unfortunately, Profiler doesn't help here directly, but you can still get this information in the following ways:

- Group the trace output in Profiler on the following columns: EventClass, TextData, and Reads. For the group of rows with the same EventClass and TextData, manually calculate the total of all the corresponding Reads. This approach doesn't sound very user friendly!
- Save the trace output to a trace table by selecting File ➤ Save As ➤ Trace Table in Profiler. Also, you can import the trace file output of Profiler to a trace table by using the built-in function fn_trace_gettable.
- Access the sys.dm_exec_query_stats DMV to retrieve the information from the production server. This assumes that you're dealing with an immediate issue and not looking at a historical problem.

In this case, I'll load the data into a table on the database so that I can run queries against it using the following script:

```
SELECT * INTO Trace_Table
FROM ::fn_trace_gettable('C:\PerformanceTrace.trc', default)
```

Once the SQL trace is imported into a database table, execute a SELECT statement to find the total number of reads performed by the multiple executions of the same query as follows (reads.sql in the download):

```
SELECT COUNT(*) AS TotalExecutions, EventClass, TextData
  , SUM(Duration) AS Duration_Total
  , SUM(CPU) AS CPU_Total
  , SUM(Reads) AS Reads_Total
  , SUM(Writes) AS Writes_Total
FROM Trace_Table
GROUP BY EventClass, TextData
ORDER BY Reads_Total DESC
```

The TotalExecutions column in the preceding script indicates the number of times a query was executed. The Reads_Total column indicates the total number of reads performed by the multiple executions of the query.

However, there is a little problem. The data type of the TextData column for the trace table created by Profiler is NTEXT, which can't be specified in the GROUP BY clause—SQL Server 2008 doesn't support grouping on a column with the NTEXT data type. Therefore, you may create a table similar to the trace table, with the only exception being that the data type of the TextData column should be NVARCHAR(MAX) instead of NTEXT. Using the MAX length for the NVARCHAR data type allows you not to worry about how long the NTEXT data is.

Another approach is to use the CAST function as follows:

```
SELECT COUNT(*) AS TotalExecutions, EventClass
  , CAST(TextData AS NVARCHAR(MAX)) TextData
  , SUM(Duration) AS Duration_Total
  , SUM(CPU) AS CPU_Total
  , SUM(Reads) AS Reads_Total
  , SUM(Writes) AS Writes_Total
FROM Trace_Table
GROUP BY EventClass, CAST(TextData AS NVARCHAR(MAX))
ORDER BY Reads_Total DESC
```

The costly queries identified by this approach are a better indication of load than the costly queries with single execution identified by Profiler. For example, a query that requires 50 reads might be executed 1,000 times. The query itself may be considered cheap enough, but the total number of reads performed by the query turns out to be 50,000 (= 50 × 1,000), which cannot be considered cheap. Optimizing this query to reduce the reads by even 10 for individual execution reduces the total number of reads by 10,000 (= 10 × 1,000), which can be more beneficial than optimizing a single query with 5,000 reads.

The problem with this approach is that most queries will have a varying set of criteria in the WHERE clause or that procedure calls will have different values and numbers of parameters passed in. That makes the simple grouping by TextData impossible. You can take care of this problem with a number of approaches. One of the better ones is outlined on the Microsoft Developers Network at http://msdn.microsoft.com/en-us/library/aa175800(SQL.80).aspx. Although it was written originally for SQL Server 2000, it will work fine with SQL Server 2008.

Getting the same information out of the sys.dm_exec_query_stats view simply requires a query against the DMV:

```
SELECT  ss.sum_execution_count
       ,t.TEXT
       ,ss.sum_total_elapsed_time
       ,ss.sum_total_worker_time
       ,ss.sum_total_logical_reads
       ,ss.sum_total_logical_writes
FROM    (SELECT s.plan_handle
               ,SUM(s.execution_count) sum_execution_count
               ,SUM(s.total_elapsed_time) sum_total_elapsed_time
               ,SUM(s.total_worker_time) sum_total_worker_time
               ,SUM(s.total_logical_reads) sum_total_logical_reads
               ,SUM(s.total_logical_writes) sum_total_logical_writes
         FROM   sys.dm_exec_query_stats s
         GROUP BY s.plan_handle
        ) AS ss
        CROSS APPLY sys.dm_exec_sql_text(ss.plan_handle) t
ORDER BY sum_total_logical_reads DESC
```

This is so much easier than all the work required to gather trace data that it makes you wonder why you would ever use trace data. The main reason is precision. The sys.dm_exec_query_stats view is a running aggregate for the time that a given plan has been in memory.

A trace, on the other hand, is a historical track for whatever time frame you ran it in. You can even add traces together within a database and have a list of data that you can generate totals in a more precise manner rather than simply relying on a given moment in time. But understand that a lot of troubleshooting of performance problems is focused on that moment in time when the query is running slowly. That's when `sys.dm_exec_query_stats` becomes irreplaceably useful.

Identifying Slow-Running Queries

Because a user's experience is highly influenced by the response time of their requests, you should regularly monitor the execution time of incoming SQL queries and find out the response time of slow-running queries. If the response time (or duration) of slow-running queries becomes unacceptable, then you should analyze the cause of performance degradation. Not every slow-performing query is caused by resource issues, though. Other concerns such as blocking can also lead to slow query performance. Blocking is covered in detail in Chapter 12.

To discover the slow-running SQL queries, group a trace output on the `Duration` column. This will sort the trace output, as shown in Figure 3-12.

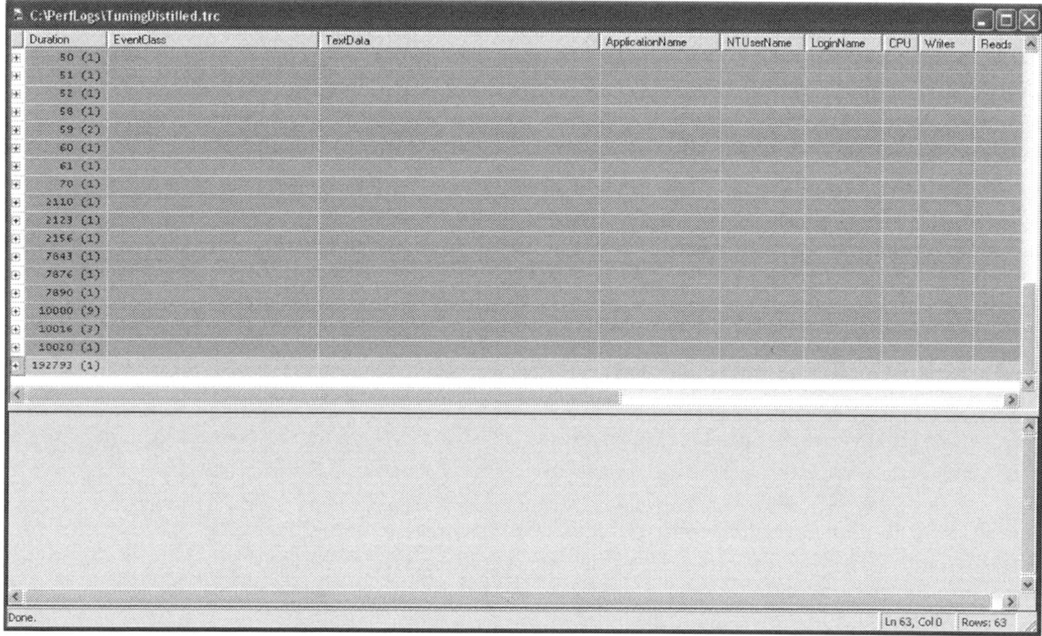

Figure 3-12. *Trace output sorted on the* `Duration` *column*

For a slow-running system, you should note the duration of slow-running queries before and after the optimization process. After you apply optimization techniques, you should then work out the overall effect on the system. It is possible that your optimization steps may have adversely affected other queries, making them slower.

Execution Plans

Once you have identified a costly query, you need to find out *why* it is so costly. You can identify the costly query from SQL Profiler or sys.dm_exec_query_stats, rerun it in Management Studio, and look at the execution plan used by the query optimizer. An execution plan shows the processing strategy (including multiple intermediate steps) used by the query optimizer to execute a query.

To create an execution plan, the query optimizer evaluates various permutations of indexes and join strategies. Because of the possibility of a large number of potential plans, this optimization process may take a long time to generate the most cost-effective execution plan. To prevent the overoptimization of an execution plan, the optimization process is broken into multiple phases. Each phase is a set of transformation rules that evaluate various permutations of indexes and join strategies.

After going through a phase, the query optimizer examines the estimated cost of the resulting plan. If the query optimizer determines that the plan is cheap enough, it will use the plan without going through the remaining optimization phases. However, if the plan is not cheap enough, the optimizer will go through the next optimization phase. I will cover execution plan generation in more depth in Chapter 9.

SQL Server displays a query execution plan in various forms and from two different types. The most commonly used forms in SQL Server 2008 are the graphical execution plan and the XML execution plan. Actually, the graphical execution plan is simply an XML execution plan parsed for the screen. The two types of execution plan are the estimated plan and the actual plan. The *estimated* plan includes the results coming from the query optimizer, and the *actual* plan is the plan used by the query engine. The beauty of the estimated plan is that it doesn't require the query to be executed. These plan types can differ, but most of the time they will be the same. The graphical execution plan uses icons to represent the processing strategy of a query. To obtain a graphical estimated execution plan, select Query ➤ Display Estimated Execution Plan. An XML execution plan contains the same data available through the graphical plan but in a more immediately accessible format. Further, with the XQuery capabilities of SQL Server 2008, XML execution plans can be queried as if they were tables. An XML execution plan is produced by the SET SHOWPLAN_XML and SET STATISTICS XML statements. You can also right-click a graphical execution plan and select Showplan XML.

You can obtain the estimated XML execution plan for the costliest query identified previously using the SET SHOWPLAN_XML command as follows (set_showplan.sql in the download):

```
SET SHOWPLAN_XML ON
GO
SELECT  soh.AccountNumber,
        sod.LineTotal,
        sod.OrderQty,
        sod.UnitPrice,
        p.Name
FROM    Sales.SalesOrderHeader soh
        JOIN Sales.SalesOrderDetail sod
        ON soh.SalesOrderID = sod.SalesOrderID
        JOIN Production.Product p
        ON sod.ProductID = p.ProductID
```

```
WHERE   sod.LineTotal > 1000 ;
GO
SET SHOWPLAN_XML OFF
GO
```

Running this query results in a link to an execution plan, not an execution plan or any data. Clicking the link will open an execution plan. Although the plan will be displayed as a graphical plan, right-clicking the plan and selecting Show Execution Plan XML will display the XML data. Figure 3-13 shows a portion of the XML execution plan output.


```xml
<ShowPlanXML xmlns="http://schemas.microsoft.com/sqlserver/2004/07/showplan" Version="1.1" Build="10.0.1600.22">
  <BatchSequence>
    <Batch>
      <Statements>
        <StmtSimple StatementText="SELECT  soh.AccountNumber,&#xD;&#xA;        sod.LineTotal,&#xD;&#xA;        sod.OrderQty,&#xD;&#xA;
          <StatementSetOptions QUOTED_IDENTIFIER="true" ARITHABORT="true" CONCAT_NULL_YIELDS_NULL="true" ANSI_NULLS="true" ANSI_PADDIN
          <QueryPlan CachedPlanSize="40" CompileTime="2058" CompileCPU="1752" CompileMemory="904">
            <MissingIndexes>
              <MissingIndexGroup Impact="46.345">
                <MissingIndex Database="[AdventureWorks2008]" Schema="[Sales]" Table="[SalesOrderDetail]">
                  <ColumnGroup Usage="INEQUALITY">
                    <Column Name="[LineTotal]" ColumnId="9" />
                  </ColumnGroup>
                  <ColumnGroup Usage="INCLUDE">
                    <Column Name="[SalesOrderID]" ColumnId="1" />
                    <Column Name="[OrderQty]" ColumnId="4" />
                    <Column Name="[ProductID]" ColumnId="5" />
                    <Column Name="[UnitPrice]" ColumnId="7" />
                  </ColumnGroup>
                </MissingIndex>
              </MissingIndexGroup>
            </MissingIndexes>
            <RelOp NodeId="0" PhysicalOp="Hash Match" LogicalOp="Inner Join" EstimateRows="26293.6" EstimateIO="0" EstimateCPU="0.2048
              <OutputList>
                <ColumnReference Database="[AdventureWorks2008]" Schema="[Sales]" Table="[SalesOrderHeader]" Alias="[soh]" Column="Acc
                <ColumnReference Database="[AdventureWorks2008]" Schema="[Sales]" Table="[SalesOrderDetail]" Alias="[sod]" Column="Ord
                <ColumnReference Database="[AdventureWorks2008]" Schema="[Sales]" Table="[SalesOrderDetail]" Alias="[sod]" Column="Uni
                <ColumnReference Table="[sod]" Column="LineTotal" ComputedColumn="1" />
                <ColumnReference Database="[AdventureWorks2008]" Schema="[Production]" Table="[Product]" Alias="[p]" Column="Name" />
              </OutputList>
```


Figure 3-13. *XML execution plan output*

Analyzing a Query Execution Plan

Let's start with the costly query identified in `set_showplan.sql`. Copy it (minus the `SET SHOWPLAN_XML` statements) into Management Studio, and turn on Include Actual Execution Plan. Now, on executing this query, you'll see the execution plan in Figure 3-14.

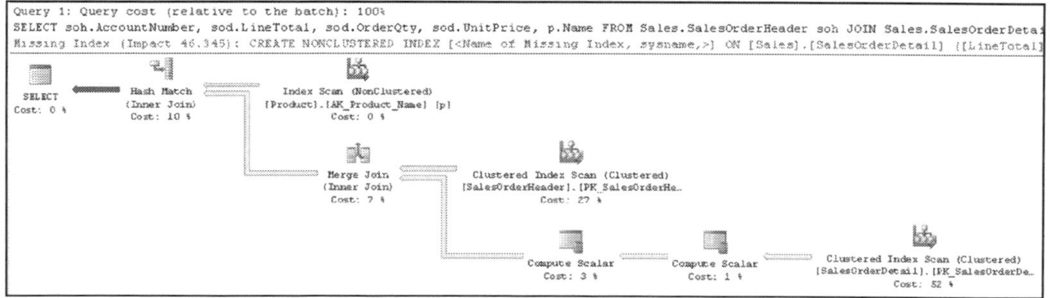

Figure 3-14. *Query execution plan*

Read the execution plan from right to left and from top to bottom. Each step represents an operation performed to get the final output of the query. Some of the aspects of a query execution represented by an execution plan are as follows:

- If a query consists of a batch of multiple queries, the execution plan for each query will be displayed in the order of execution. Each execution plan in the batch will have a relative estimated cost, with the total cost of the whole batch being 100 percent.
- Every icon in an execution plan represents an operator. They will each have a relative estimated cost, with the total cost of all the nodes in an execution plan being 100 percent.
- Usually a starting operator in an execution represents a data-retrieval mechanism from a database object (a table or an index). For example, in the execution plan in Figure 3-14, the three starting points represent retrievals from the `SalesOrderHeader`, `SalesOrderDetail`, and `Product` tables.
- Data retrieval will usually be either a table operation or an index operation. For example, in the execution plan in Figure 3-11, all three data retrieval steps are index operations.
- Data retrieval on an index will be either an index scan or an index seek. For example, the first and third index operations in Figure 3-14 are index scans, and the second one is an index seek.
- The naming convention for a data-retrieval operation on an index is `[Table Name].[Index Name]`.
- Data flows from right to left between two operators and is indicated by a connecting arrow between the two operators.
- The thickness of a connecting arrow between operators represents a graphical representation of the number of rows transferred.
- The joining mechanism between two operators in the same column will be either a nested loop join, a hash match join, or a merge join. For example, in the execution plan shown in Figure 3-14, there is one nested loop join and one hash match.
- Running the mouse over a node in an execution plan shows a pop-up window with some details, as you can see in Figure 3-15.
  - A complete set of details about an operator is available in the Properties window, which you can open by right-clicking the operator and selecting Properties. This is visible in Figure 3-16.
  - An operator detail shows both physical and logical operation types at the top. Physical operations represent those actually used by the storage engine, while the logical operations are the constructs used by the optimizer to build the estimated execution plan. If logical and physical operations are the same, then only the physical operation is shown. It also displays other useful information, such as row count, I/O cost, CPU cost, and so on.
  - The Argument section in an operator detail pop-up window is especially useful in analysis, because it shows the filter or join criterion used by the optimizer.

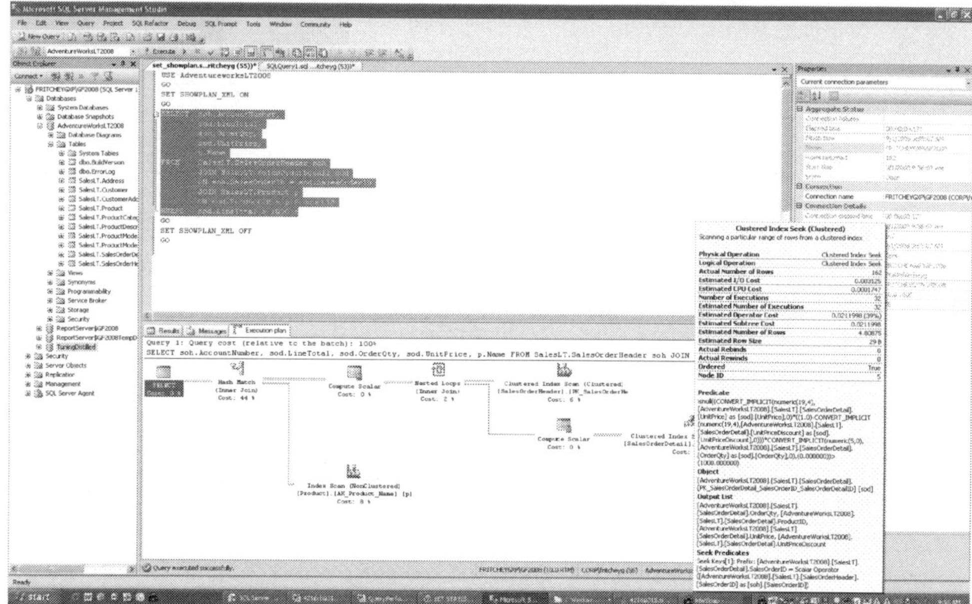

Figure 3-15. *Execution plan node detail*

Figure 3-16. *Clustered index scan properties*

Identifying the Costly Steps in an Execution Plan

Your main interest in the execution plan is to find out which steps are relatively costly. These steps are the starting point for your query optimization. You can choose the starting steps by adopting the following techniques:

- Each node in an execution plan shows its relative cost in the complete execution plan, with the total cost of the whole plan being 100 percent. Therefore, focus attention on the node(s) with the highest relative cost. For example, the execution plan in Figure 3-14 has two steps with 34 percent cost each.
- An execution plan may be from a batch of statements, so you may also need to find the most costly statement. In Figure 3-15 and Figure 3-14, you can see at the top of the plan the text "Query 1." In a batch situation, there will be multiple plans, and they will be numbered in the order they occurred within the batch.
- Observe the thickness of the connecting arrows between nodes. A very thick connecting arrow indicates a large number of rows being transferred between the corresponding nodes. Analyze the node to the left of the arrow to understand why it requires so many rows. Check the properties of the arrows too. You may see that the estimated rows and the actual rows are different. This can be caused by out-of-date statistics, among other things.
- Look for hash join operations. For small result sets, a nested loop join is usually the preferred join technique. You will learn more about hash joins compared to nested loop joins later in this chapter.
- Look for bookmark lookup operations. A bookmark operation for a large result set can cause a large number of logical reads. I will cover bookmark lookups in more detail in Chapter 6.
- There may be warnings, indicated by an exclamation point on one of the operators, which are areas of immediate concern. These can be caused by a variety of issues, including a join without join criteria or an index or a table with missing statistics. Usually resolving the warning situation will help performance.
- Look for steps performing a sort operation. This indicates that the data was not retrieved in the correct sort order.

Analyzing Index Effectiveness

To examine a costly step in an execution plan further, you should analyze the data-retrieval mechanism for the relevant table or index. First, you should check whether an index operation is a seek or a scan. Usually, for best performance, you should retrieve as few rows as possible from a table, and an index *seek* is usually the most efficient way of accessing a small number of rows. A *scan* operation usually indicates that a larger number of rows have been accessed. Therefore, it is generally preferable to seek rather than scan.

Next, you want to ensure that the indexing mechanism is properly set up. The query optimizer evaluates the available indexes to discover which index will retrieve data from the table in the most efficient way. If a desired index is not available, the optimizer uses the next best index. For best performance, you should always ensure that the best index is used in a data-retrieval operation. You can judge the index effectiveness (whether the best index is used or not) by analyzing the Argument section of a node detail for the following:

- A data-retrieval operation
- A join operation

Let's look at the data-retrieval mechanism for the `Product` table in the previous execution plan (Figure 3-14). Figure 3-17 shows the operator properties.

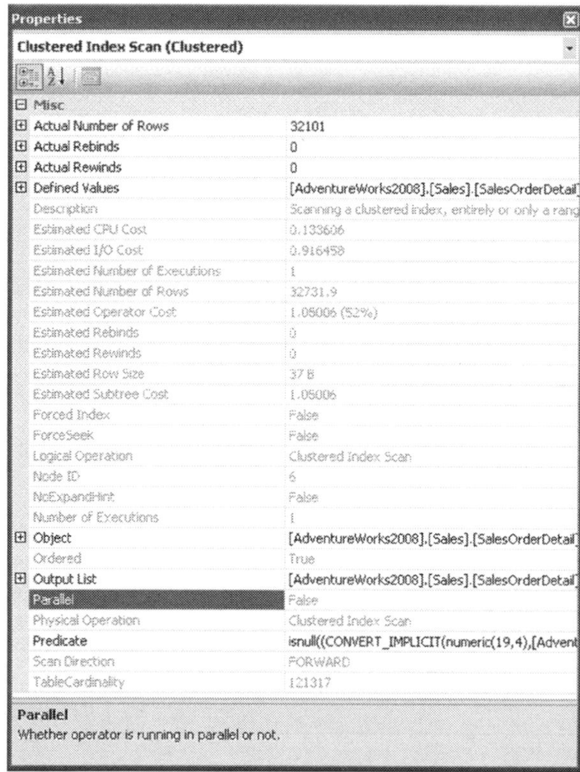

Figure 3-17. *Data-retrieval mechanism for the `SalesOrderDetail` table*

In the operator properties for the `SalesOrderDetail` table, the `Object` property specifies the index used, `PK_SalesOrderDetail`. It uses the following naming convention: `[Database].[Owner].[Table Name].[Index Name]`. The `Seek Predicates` property specifies the column, or columns, used to seek into the index. The `SalesOrderDetail` table is joined with the `SalesOrderHeader` table on the `SalesOrderId` column. The `SEEK` works on the fact that the join criteria, `SalesOrderId`, is the leading edge of the clustered index and primary key, `PK_SalesOrderDetail`.

Sometimes you may have a different data-retrieval mechanism, as shown in Figure 3-18.

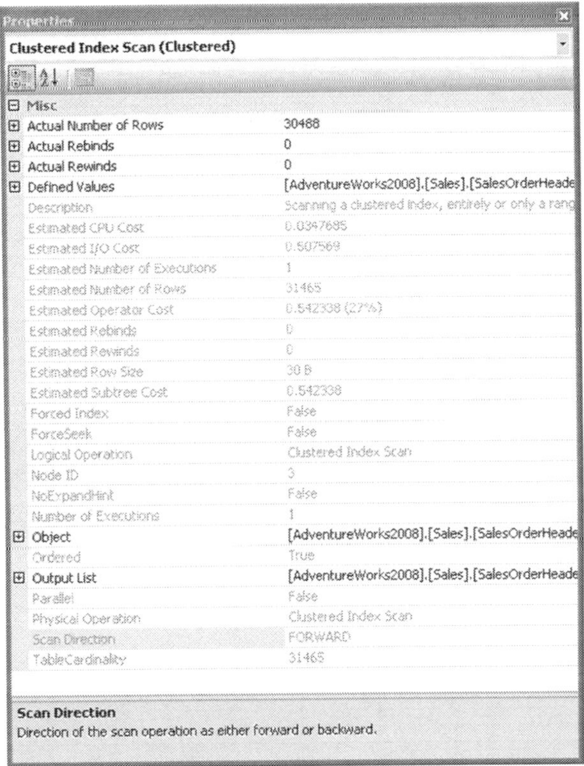

Figure 3-18. *A variation of the data-retrieval mechanism*

In the properties in Figure 3-18, there is no predicate. The lack of predicate means that the entire table, remembering that a clustered index is the table, is being scanned as input to the merge join operator (refer to the earlier Figure 3-14).

Analyzing Join Effectiveness

In addition to analyzing the indexes used, you should examine the effectiveness of join strategies decided by the optimizer. SQL Server uses three types of joins:

- Hash joins
- Merge joins
- Nested loop joins

In many simple queries affecting a small set of rows, nested loop joins are far superior to both hash and merge joins. The join types to be used in a query are decided dynamically by the optimizer.

Hash Join

To understand SQL Server's hash join strategy, consider the following simple query (`hash.sql` in the download):

```
SELECT  p.*
FROM    Production.Product p
        JOIN Production.ProductSubCategory spc
        ON p.ProductSubCategoryID = spc.ProductSubCategoryID
```

Table 3-6 shows the two tables' indexes and number of rows.

Table 3-6. *Indexes and Number of Rows of the* `Products` *and* `ProductCategory` *Tables*

Table	Indexes	Number of Rows
`Product`	Clustered index on `ProductID`	295
`ProductCategory`	Clustered index on `ProductCategoryId`	41

Figure 3-19 shows the execution plan for the preceding query.

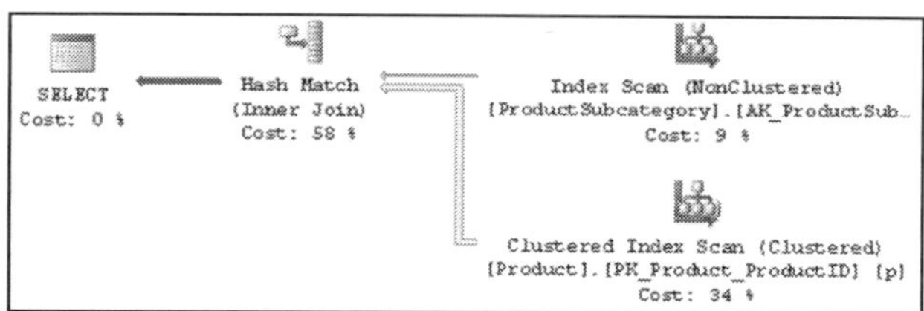

Figure 3-19. *Execution plan with a hash join*

You can see that the optimizer used a hash join between the two tables.

A hash join uses the two join inputs as a *build input* and a *probe input*. The build input is shown as the top input in the execution plan, and the probe input is shown as the bottom input. The smaller of the two inputs serves as the build input.

The hash join performs its operation in two phases: the *build phase* and the *probe phase*. In the most commonly used form of hash join, the *in-memory hash join*, the entire build input is scanned or computed, and then a hash table is built in memory. Each row is inserted into a hash bucket depending on the hash value computed for the *hash key* (the set of columns in the equality predicate).

This build phase is followed by the probe phase. The entire probe input is scanned or computed one row at a time, and for each probe row, a hash key value is computed. The corresponding hash bucket is scanned for the hash key value from the probe input, and the matches are produced. Figure 3-20 illustrates the process of an in-memory hash join.

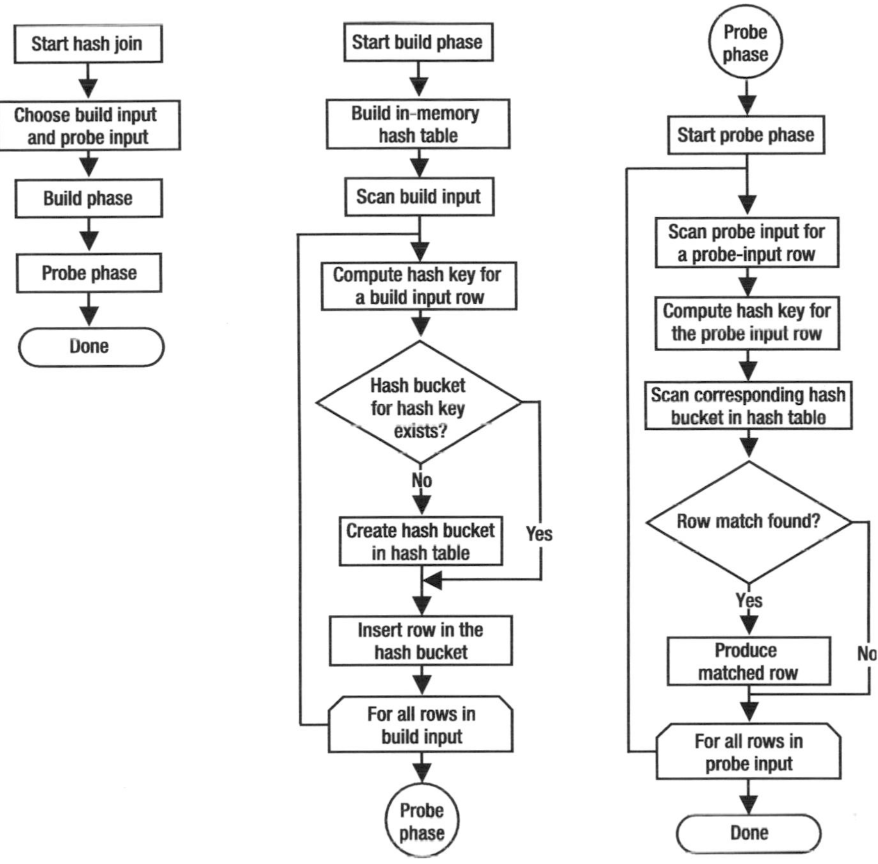

Figure 3-20. *Workflow for an in-memory hash join*

The query optimizer uses hash joins to process large, unsorted, nonindexed inputs efficiently. Let's now look at the next type of join: the merge join.

Merge Join

In the previous case, input from the `Product` table is larger, and the table is not indexed on the joining column (`ProductCategoryID`). Using the following simple query (`merge.sql` in the download), you can see different behavior:

```
SELECT  pm.*
FROM    Production.ProductModel pm
        JOIN Production.ProductModelProductDescriptionCulture pmpd
        ON pm.ProductModelID = pmpd.ProductModelID
```

Figure 3-21 shows the resultant execution plan for this query.

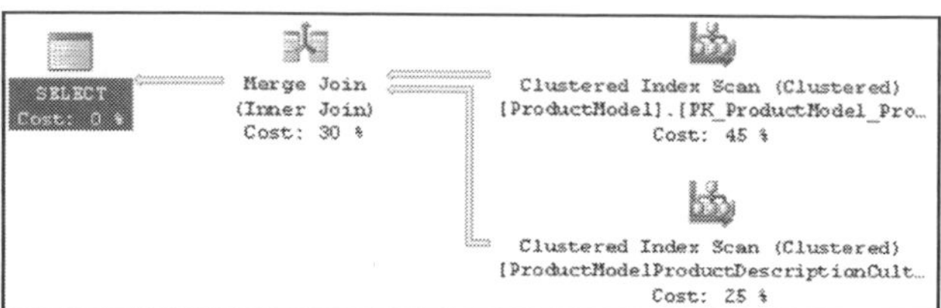

Figure 3-21. *Execution plan with a merge join*

For this query, the optimizer used a merge join between the two tables. A merge join requires both join inputs to be sorted on the merge columns, as defined by the join criterion. If indexes are available on both joining columns, then the join inputs are sorted by the index. Since each join input is sorted, the merge join gets a row from each input and compares them for equality. A matching row is produced if they are equal. This process is repeated until all rows are processed.

In this case, the query optimizer found that the join inputs were both sorted (or indexed) on their joining columns. As a result, the merge join was chosen as a faster join strategy than the hash join.

Nested Loop Join

The final type of join I'll cover here is the nested loop join. For better performance, you should always access a limited number of rows from individual tables. To understand the effect of using a smaller result set, decrease the join inputs in your query as follows (`loop.sql` in the download):

```
SELECT  soh.*
FROM    Sales.SalesOrderHeader soh
        JOIN Sales.SalesOrderDetail sod
        ON soh.SalesOrderID = sod.SalesOrderID
WHERE   soh.SalesOrderID = 71832
```

Figure 3-22 shows the resultant execution plan of the new query.

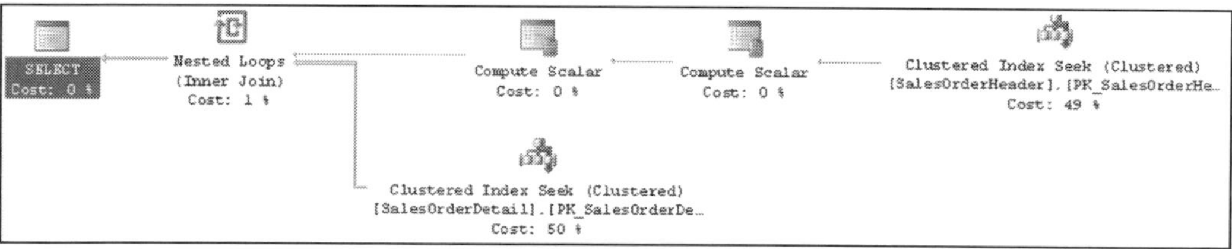

Figure 3-22. *Execution plan with a nested loop join*

As you can see, the optimizer used a nested loop join between the two tables.

A nested loop join uses one join input as the outer input table and the other as the inner input table. The outer input table is shown as the top input in the execution plan, and the inner input table is shown as the bottom input table. The outer loop consumes the outer input table row by row. The inner loop, executed for each outer row, searches for matching rows in the inner input table.

Nested loop joins are highly effective if the outer input is quite small and the inner input is large but indexed. In many simple queries affecting a small set of rows, nested loop joins are far superior to both hash and merge joins. Joins operate by gaining speed through other sacrifices. A loop join is fast because it uses memory to take a small set of data and compare it quickly to a second set of data. A merge join similarly uses memory and a bit of `tempdb` to do its ordered comparisons. A hash join uses memory and `tempdb` to build out the hash tables for the join. Although a loop join is faster, it will consume more memory than a hash or merge as the data sets get larger, which is why SQL Server will use different plans in different situations for different sets of data.

Even for small join inputs, such as in the previous query, it's important to have an index on the joining columns. As you saw in the preceding execution plan, for a small set of rows, indexes on joining columns allow the query optimizer to consider a nested loop join strategy. A missing index on the joining column of an input will force the query optimizer to use a hash join instead.

Table 3-7 summarizes the use of the three join types.

Table 3-7. *Characteristics of the Three Join Types*

Join Type	Index on Joining Columns	Usual Size of Joining Tables	Presorted	Join Clause
Hash	Inner table: Not indexed Outer table: Optional Optimal condition: Small outer table, large inner table	Any	No	Equi-join
Merge	Both tables: Must Optimal condition: Clustered or covering index on both	Large	Yes	Equi-join
Nested loop	Inner table: Must Outer table: Preferable	Small	Optional	All

■ Note The outer table is usually the smaller of the two joining tables in the hash and loop joins.

I will cover index types, including clustered and covering indexes, in Chapter 4.

Actual vs. Estimated Execution Plans

There are estimated and actual execution plans. Although these two types of plans are generally, to a degree, interchangeable, sometimes one is clearly preferred over the other. There are even situations where the estimated plans will not work at all. Consider the following stored procedure (`create_p1.sql` in the download):

```
IF (SELECT  OBJECT_ID('p1')
   ) IS NOT NULL
    DROP PROC p1
GO
CREATE PROC p1
AS
    CREATE TABLE t1 (c1 INT);

    INSERT  INTO t1
            SELECT  productid
            FROM    Production.Product
    SELECT  *
    FROM    t1;

    DROP TABLE t1;
GO
```

You may try to use SHOWPLAN_XML to obtain the estimated XML execution plan for the query as follows (showplan.sql in the download):

```
SET SHOWPLAN_XML ON
GO
EXEC p1;
GO
SET SHOWPLAN_XML OFF
GO
```

But this fails with the following error:

```
Server: Msg 208, Level 16, State 1, Procedure p1, Line 4
Invalid object name 't1'.
```

Since SHOWPLAN_XML doesn't actually execute the query, the query optimizer can't generate an execution plan for INSERT and SELECT statements on the table (t1).

Instead, you can use STATISTICS XML as follows:

```
SET STATISTICS XML ON
GO
EXEC p1;
GO
SET STATISTICS XML OFF
GO
```

Since STATISTICS XML executes the query, a different process is used that allows the table to be created and accessed within the query. Figure 3-23 shows part of the textual execution plan provided by STATISTICS XML.

```
<ShowPlanXML xmlns="http://schemas.microsoft.com/sqlserver/2004/07/showplan" Version="1.1" Build="10.0.1600.22">
  <BatchSequence>
    <Batch>
      <Statements>
        <StmtSimple StatementText="INSERT  INTO t1&#xD;&#xA;              SELECT  ProductID&#xD;&#xA;              FROM
          <StatementSetOptions QUOTED_IDENTIFIER="true" ARITHABORT="true" CONCAT_NULL_YIELDS_NULL="true" ANSI_NULLS
          <QueryPlan DegreeOfParallelism="1" CachedPlanSize="8" CompileTime="0" CompileCPU="0" CompileMemory="72">
            <RelOp NodeId="0" PhysicalOp="Table Insert" LogicalOp="Insert" EstimateRows="295" EstimateIO="0.01" Est
              <OutputList />
              <RunTimeInformation>
                <RunTimeCountersPerThread Thread="0" ActualRows="295" ActualEndOfScans="1" ActualExecutions="1" />
```


Figure 3-23. *STATISTICS PROFILE output*

■ **Tip** Remember to switch Query ➤ Show Execution Plan off in Management Studio, or you will see the graphical, rather than textual, execution plan.

Plan Cache

One final place to access execution plans is to read them directly from the memory space where they are stored, the plan cache. Dynamic management views and functions are provided from SQL Server to access this data. To see a listing of execution plans in cache, run the following query:

```
SELECT p.query_plan,
    t.text
FROM sys.dm_exec_cached_plans r
CROSS APPLY sys.dm_exec_query_plan(r.plan_handle) p
CROSS APPLY sys.dm_exec_sql_text(r.plan_handle) t
```

The query returns a list of XML execution plan links. Opening any of them will show the execution plan. Working further with columns available through the dynamic management views will allow you to search for specific procedures or execution plans.

Query Cost

Even though the execution plan for a query provides a detailed processing strategy and the estimated relative costs of the individual steps involved, it doesn't provide the actual cost of the query in terms of CPU usage, reads/writes to disk, or query duration. While optimizing a query, you may add an index to reduce the relative cost of a step. This may adversely affect a dependent step in the execution plan, or sometimes it may even modify the execution plan itself. Thus, if you look only at the execution plan, you can't be sure that your query optimization benefits the query as a whole, as opposed to that one step in the execution plan. You can analyze the overall cost of a query in different ways.

You should monitor the overall cost of a query while optimizing it. As explained previously, you can use SQL Profiler to monitor the `Duration`, `CPU`, `Reads`, and `Writes` information for the query. To reduce the overhead of Profiler on SQL Server, you should set a filter criterion on

SPID (for example, an identifier inside SQL Server to identify a database user) equal to the SPID of your Management Studio window. However, using Profiler still adds a consistent overhead on SQL Server in filtering out the events for other database users or SPIDs. I will explain SPID in more depth in Chapter 12.

There are other ways to collect performance data that are more immediate than running Profiler.

Client Statistics

Client statistics capture execution information from the perspective of your machine as a client of the server. This means that any times recorded include the time it takes to transfer data across the network, not merely the time involved on the SQL Server machine itself. To use them, simply click Query ➤ Include Client Statistics. Now, each time you run a query, a limited set of data is collected including execution time, the number of rows affected, roundtrips to the server, and more. Further, each execution of the query is displayed separately on the Client Statistics tab, and a column aggregating the multiple executions shows the averages for the data collected. The statistics will also show whether a time or count has changed from one run to the next, showing up as arrows, as shown in Figure 3-24.

For example, consider this query:

```
SELECT TOP 100 p.*
FROM Production.Product p
```

The client statistics information for the query should look something like that shown in Figure 3-24.

	Trial 2		Trial 1		Average
Client Execution Time	13:59:00		12:04:03		
Query Profile Statistics					
Number of INSERT, DELETE and UPDATE statements	0	→	0	→	0.0000
Rows affected by INSERT, DELETE, or UPDATE statem...	0	→	0	→	0.0000
Number of SELECT statements	1	→	1	→	1.0000
Rows returned by SELECT statements	100	→	100	→	100.0000
Number of transactions	0	→	0	→	0.0000
Network Statistics					
Number of server roundtrips	1	→	1	→	1.0000
TDS packets sent from client	1	→	1	→	1.0000
TDS packets received from server	70	→	70	→	70.0000
Bytes sent from client	118	→	118	→	118.0000
Bytes received from server	284748	→	284748	→	284748.0000
Time Statistics					
Client processing time	15	↑	0	→	7.5000
Total execution time	15	↑	0	→	7.5000
Wait time on server replies	0	→	0	→	0.0000

Figure 3-24. *Client statistics*

Although capturing client statistics can be a useful way to gather data, it's a limited set of data, and there is no way to show how one execution is different from another. You could even run a completely different query, and its data would be mixed in with the others, making the averages useless. If you need to, you can reset the client statistics. Select the Query menu and then the Reset Client Statistics menu item.

Execution Time

Both Duration and CPU represent the time factor of a query. To obtain detailed information on the amount of time (in milliseconds) required to parse, compile, and execute a query, use SET STATISTICS TIME as follows (timestats.sql in the download):

```
SET STATISTICS TIME ON
GO
SELECT  soh.AccountNumber,
        sod.LineTotal,
        sod.OrderQty,
        sod.UnitPrice,
        p.Name
FROM    Sales.SalesOrderHeader soh
        JOIN Sales.SalesOrderDetail sod
        ON soh.SalesOrderID = sod.SalesOrderID
        JOIN Production.Product p
        ON sod.ProductID = p.ProductID
WHERE   sod.LineTotal > 1000 ;
GO
SET STATISTICS TIME OFF
GO
```

The output of STATISTICS TIME for the preceding SELECT statement is as follows:

```
SQL Server parse and compile time:
   CPU time = 0 ms, elapsed time = 0 ms.

(32101 row(s) affected)

 SQL Server Execution Times:
   CPU time = 140 ms,  elapsed time = 763 ms.
SQL Server parse and compile time:
   CPU time = 0 ms, elapsed time = 0 ms.
```

The CPU time = 140 ms part of the execution times represents the CPU value provided by the Profiler tool and the Server Trace option. Similarly, the corresponding Elapsed time = 763 ms represents the Duration value provided by the other mechanisms.

A 0 ms parse and compile time signifies that the optimizer reused the existing execution plan for this query and therefore didn't have to spend any time parsing and compiling the query again. If the query is executed for the first time, then the optimizer has to parse the query first for syntax and then compile it to produce the execution plan. This can be easily verified by clearing out the cache using the system call DBCC FREEPROCCACHE and then rerunning the query:

```
SQL Server parse and compile time:
   CPU time = 32 ms, elapsed time = 39 ms.

(162 row(s) affected)

 SQL Server Execution Times:
   CPU time = 187 ms,  elapsed time = 699 ms.
SQL Server parse and compile time:
   CPU time = 0 ms, elapsed time = 0 ms.
```

This time, SQL Server spent 32 ms of CPU time and a total of 39 ms parsing and compiling the query.

Note You should not run DBCC FREEPROCCACHE on your production systems unless you are prepared to incur the not insignificant cost of recompiling every query on the system. In some ways, this will be as costly to your system as a reboot.

STATISTICS IO

As discussed in the "Identifying Costly Queries" section earlier in the chapter, the number of reads in the Reads column is frequently the most significant cost factor among Duration, CPU, Reads, and Writes. The total number of reads performed by a query consists of the sum of the number of reads performed on all tables involved in the query. The reads performed on the individual tables may vary significantly, depending on the size of the result set requested from the individual table and the indexes available.

To reduce the total number of reads, it will be useful to find all the tables accessed in the query and their corresponding number of reads. This detailed information helps you concentrate on optimizing data access on the tables with a large number of reads. The number of reads per table also helps you evaluate the impact of the optimization step (implemented for one table) on the other tables referred to in the query.

In a simple query, you determine the individual tables accessed by taking a close look at the query. This becomes increasingly difficult the more complex the query becomes. In the case of a stored procedure, database views, or functions, it becomes more difficult to identify all the tables actually accessed by the optimizer. You can use STATISTICS IO to get this information, irrespective of query complexity.

To turn STATISTICS IO on, navigate to Query ➤ Query Options ➤ Advanced ➤ Set Statistics IO in Management Studio. You may also get this information programmatically as follows (iostats.sql in the download):

```
SET STATISTICS IO ON
GO
SELECT  soh.AccountNumber,
        sod.LineTotal,
        sod.OrderQty,
        sod.UnitPrice,
        p.Name
FROM    Sales.SalesOrderHeader soh
        JOIN Sales.SalesOrderDetail sod
        ON soh.SalesOrderID = sod.SalesOrderID
        JOIN Production.Product p
        ON sod.ProductID = p.ProductID
WHERE   sod.SalesOrderId = 71856;
GO
SET STATISTICS IO OFF
GO
```

If you run this query and look at the execution plan, it consists of three clustered index seeks with two loop joins. If you remove the WHERE clause and run the query again, you get a set of scans and some hash joins. That's an interesting fact—but you don't know how it affects the query cost! You can use SET STATISTICS IO as shown previously to compare the cost of the query (in terms of logical reads) between the two processing strategies used by the optimizer.

You get following STATISTICS IO output when the query uses the hash join:

```
Table 'Worktable'. Scan count 0, logical reads 0, physical reads 0…
Table 'SalesOrderDetail'. Scan count 1, logical reads 1240, physical reads 0…
Table 'SalesOrderHeader'. Scan count 1, logical reads 686, physical reads 0…
Table 'Product'. Scan count 1, logical reads 5, physical reads 0…
```

Now when you add the WHERE clause to appropriately filter the data, the resultant STATISTICS IO output turns out to be this:

```
Table 'Product'. Scan count 0, logical reads 4, physical reads 0…
Table 'SalesOrderDetail'. Scan count 1, logical reads 3, physical reads 0…
Table 'SalesOrderHeader'. Scan count 0, logical reads 3, physical reads 0…
```

Logical reads for the SalesOrderDetail table have been cut from 1,240 to 3 because of the index seek and the loop join. It also hasn't significantly affected the data retrieval cost of the Product table.

While interpreting the output of STATISTICS IO, you mostly refer to the number of logical reads. Sometimes you also refer to the scan count, but even if you perform few logical reads per scan, the total number of logical reads provided by STATISTICS IO can still be high. If the number of logical reads per scan is small for a specific table, then you may not be able to improve the indexing mechanism of the table any further. The number of physical reads and read-ahead reads will be nonzero when the data is not found in the memory, but once the data is populated in memory, the physical reads and read-ahead reads will tend to be zero.

There is another advantage to knowing all the tables used and their corresponding reads for a query. Both the `Duration` and `CPU` values may fluctuate significantly when reexecuting the same query with no change in table schema (including indexes) or data because the essential services and background applications running on the SQL Server machine usually affect the processing time of the query under observation.

During optimization steps, you need a nonfluctuating cost figure as a reference. The reads (or logical reads) don't vary between multiple executions of a query with a fixed table schema and data. For example, if you execute the previous `SELECT` statement ten times, you will probably get ten different figures for `Duration` and `CPU`, but `Reads` will remain the same each time. Therefore, during optimization, you can refer to the number of reads for an individual table to ensure that you really have reduced the data access cost of the table.

Even though the number of logical reads can also be obtained from Profiler or the Server Trace option, you get another benefit when using `STATISTICS IO`. The number of logical reads for a query shown by Profiler or the Server Trace option increases as you use different `SET` statements (mentioned previously) along with the query. But the number of logical reads shown by `STATISTICS IO` doesn't include the additional pages that are accessed as `SET` statements are used with a query. Thus, `STATISTICS IO` provides a consistent figure for the number of logical reads.

Summary

In this chapter, you saw that you can use the Profiler tool or SQL tracing to identify the queries causing a high amount of stress on the system resources in a SQL workload. Collecting the trace data can, and should be, automated using system stored procedures. For immediate access to statistics about running queries, use the DMV `sys.dm_exec_query_stats`. You can further analyze these queries with Management Studio to find the costly steps in the processing strategy of the query. For better performance, it is important to consider both the index and join mechanisms used in an execution plan while analyzing a query. The number of data retrievals (or reads) for the individual tables provided by `SET STATISTICS IO` helps concentrate on the data access mechanism of the tables with most number of reads. You also should focus on the CPU cost and overall time of the most costly queries.

Once you identify a costly query and finish the initial analysis, the next step should be to optimize the query for performance. Because indexing is one of the most commonly used performance-tuning techniques, in the next chapter I will discuss in depth the various indexing mechanisms available in SQL Server.

CHAPTER 4

Index Analysis

The right index on the right column, or columns, is the basis on which query tuning begins. On the other hand, a missing index or an index placed on the wrong column, or columns, can be the basis for all performance problems starting with basic data access, continuing through joins, and ending in filtering clauses. For these reasons, it is extremely important for everyone—not just the DBA—to understand the different indexing techniques that can be used to optimize the database design.

In this chapter, I cover the following topics:

- What an index is
- The benefits and overhead of an index
- General recommendations for index design
- Clustered and nonclustered index behavior and comparisons
- Recommendations for clustered and nonclustered indexes
- Advanced indexing techniques: covering indexes, index intersections, index joins, filtered indexes, distributed indexes, indexed views, and index compression
- Special index types
- Additional characteristics of indexes

What Is an Index?

One of the best ways to reduce disk I/O and logical reads is to use an index. An index allows SQL Server to find data in a table without scanning the entire table. An index in a database is analogous to an index in a book. Say, for example, that you wanted to look up the phrase *table scan* in this book. Without the index at the back of the book, you would have to peruse the entire book to find the text you needed. With the index, you know exactly where the information you want is stored.

While tuning a database for performance, you create indexes on the different columns used in a query to help SQL Server find data quickly. For example, the following query against the `Production.Product` table results in the data shown in Figure 4-1 (the first six of 500+ rows):

```
SELECT  p.ProductID,
        p.[Name],
        p.StandardCost,
        p.[Weight],
        ROW_NUMBER() OVER (ORDER BY p.Name DESC) AS RowNumber
FROM    Production.Product p;
```

	ProductID	Name	StandardCost	Weight	RowNumber
1	1	Adjustable Race	0.00	NULL	1
2	879	All-Purpose Bike Stand	59.466	NULL	2
3	712	AWC Logo Cap	6.9223	NULL	3
4	3	BB Ball Bearing	0.00	NULL	4
5	2	Bearing Ball	0.00	NULL	5
6	877	Bike Wash - Dissolver	2.9733	NULL	6

Figure 4-1. *Sample `Production.Product` table*

If you need to retrieve all the products where `StandardCost` is greater than 150, without an index the table will have to be scanned, checking the value of `StandardCost` at each row to determine which rows contain a value greater than 150. An index on the `StandardCost` column could speed up this process by providing a mechanism that allows a structured search against the data rather than a row-by-row check. You can take two different, and fundamental, approaches for creating this index:

- *Like a dictionary*: A dictionary is a distinct listing of words in alphabetical order. An index can be stored in a similar fashion. The data is ordered, although it will still have duplicates. The first six rows, ordered by `StandardCost` instead of by `Name`, would look like the data shown in Figure 4-2. Notice the `RowNumber` column shows the original placement of the row when ordering by `Name`.

	ProductID	Name	StandardCost	Weight	RowNumber
200	513	Touring Rim	0.00	460....	472
201	873	Patch Kit/8 Patches	0.8565	NULL	365
202	922	Road Tire Tube	1.4923	NULL	375
203	921	Mountain Tire Tube	1.8663	NULL	327
204	870	Water Bottle - 30 oz.	1.8663	NULL	498
205	923	Touring Tire Tube	1.8663	NULL	474

Figure 4-2. *Product table sorted on `StandardCost`*

So now if you wanted to find all the rows where `StandardCost` is greater than 150, the index would allow you to find them immediately by moving down to the first value greater than 150. An index that orders the data stored based on the index order is known as a *clustered index*. Because of how SQL Server stores data, this is one of the most important indexes in your database design. I explain this in detail later in the chapter.

- *Like a book's index*: An ordered list can be created without altering the layout of the table, similar to the way the index of a book is created. Just like the keyword index of a book lists the keywords in a separate section with a page number to refer to the main content of the book, the list of `StandardCost` values is created as a separate structure and refers to the corresponding row in the `Product` table through a pointer. For the example, I'll use `RowNumber` as the pointer. Table 4-1 shows the structure of the manufacturer index.

Table 4-1. *Structure of the Manufacturer Index*

StandardCost	RowNumber
0.8565	365
1.4923	375
1.8663	327
1.8663	498
1.8663	474

SQL Server can scan the manufacturer index to find rows where `StandardCost` is greater than 150. Since the `StandardCost` values are arranged in a sorted order, SQL Server can stop scanning as soon as it encounters the row with a value of 150. This type of index is called a *nonclustered index*, and I explain it in detail later in the chapter.

In either case, SQL Server will be able to find all the products where `StandardCost` is greater than 150 more quickly than without an index under most circumstances.

You can create indexes on either a single column (as described previously) or a combination of columns in a table. SQL Server automatically creates indexes for certain types of constraints (for example, `PRIMARY KEY` and `UNIQUE` constraints).

The Benefit of Indexes

SQL Server has to be able to find data, even when no index is present on a table. When no clustered index is present to establish a storage order for the data, the storage engine will simply read through the entire table to find what it needs. A table without a clustered index is called a *heap table*. A heap is just a crude stack of data with a row identifier as a pointer to the storage location. This data is not ordered or searchable except by walking through the data, row-by-row, in a process called a *scan*. When a clustered index is placed on a table, the key values of the index establish an order for the data. Further, with a clustered index, the data is stored with the index so that the data itself is now ordered. When a clustered index is present, the pointer on the nonclustered index consists of the values that define the clustered index. This is a big part of what makes clustered indexes so important.

Since a page has a limited amount of space, it can store a larger number of rows if the rows contain a fewer number of columns. The nonclustered index usually doesn't contain all the columns of the table; it usually contains only a limited number of the columns. Therefore, a page will be able to store more rows of a nonclustered index than rows of the table itself, which contains all the columns. Consequently, SQL Server will be able to read more values for a column from a page representing a nonclustered index on the column than from a page representing the table that contains the column.

Another benefit of the nonclustered index is that, because it is in a separate structure from the data table, it can be put in a different filegroup, with a different I/O path, as explained in Chapter 2. This means that SQL Server can access the index and table concurrently, making searches even faster.

Indexes store their information in a B-tree structure, so the number of reads required to find a particular row is minimized. The following example shows the benefit of a B-tree structure.

Consider a single-column table with 27 rows in a random order and only 3 rows per leaf page. Suppose the layout of the rows in the pages is as shown in Figure 4-3.

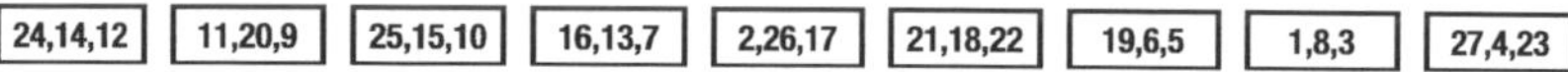

Figure 4-3. *Initial layout of 27 rows*

To search the row (or rows) for the column value of 5, SQL Server has to scan all the rows and the pages, since even the last row in the last page may have the value 5. Because the number of reads depends on the number of pages accessed, nine read operations have to be performed without an index on the column. This content can be ordered by creating an index on the column, with the resultant layout of the rows and pages shown in Figure 4-4.

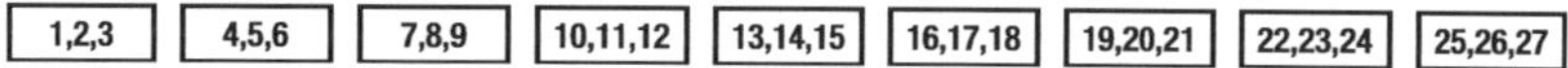

Figure 4-4. *Ordered layout of 27 rows*

Indexing the column arranges the content in a sorted fashion. This allows SQL Server to determine the possible value for a row position in the column with respect to the value of another row position in the column. For example, in Figure 4-4, when SQL Server finds the first row with the column value 6, it can be sure that there are no more rows with the column value 5. Thus, only two read operations are required to fetch the rows with the value 5 when the content is indexed. However, what happens if you want to search for the column value 25? This will require nine read operations! This problem is solved by implementing indexes using the B-tree structure.

A B-tree consists of a starting node (or page) called a *root node* with *branch nodes* (or pages) growing out of it (or linked to it). All keys are stored in the leaves. Contained in each interior node (above the leaf nodes) are pointers to its branch nodes and values representing the smallest value found in the branch node. Keys are kept in sorted order within each node. B-trees use a balanced tree structure for efficient record retrieval—a B-tree is balanced when the leaf nodes are all at the same level from the root node. For example, creating an index on the preceding content will generate the balanced B-tree structure shown in Figure 4-5.

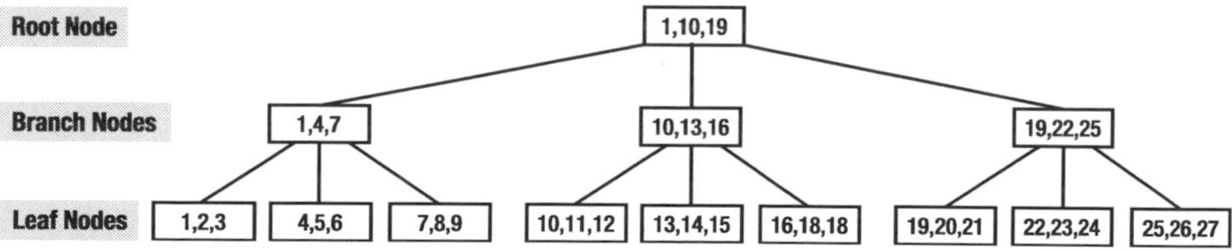

Figure 4-5. *B-tree layout of 27 rows*

The B-tree algorithm minimizes the number of pages to be accessed to locate a desired key, thereby speeding up the data access process. For example, in Figure 4-5, the search for the key value 5 starts at the top root node. Since the key value is between 1 and 10, the search process follows the left branch to the next node. As the key value 5 falls between the values 4 and 7, the search process follows the middle branch to the next node with the starting key value of 4. The search process retrieves the key value 5 from this leaf page. If the key value 5 doesn't exist in this page, the search process will stop since it's the leaf page. Similarly, the key value 25 can also be searched using the same number of reads.

Index Overhead

The performance benefit of indexes does come at a cost. Tables with indexes require more storage and memory space for the index pages in addition to the data pages of the table. Data manipulation queries (`INSERT`, `UPDATE`, and `DELETE` statements, or the CUD part of create, read, update, delete [CRUD]) can take longer, and more processing time is required to maintain the indexes of constantly changing tables. This is because, unlike a `SELECT` statement, data manipulation queries modify the data content of a table. If an `INSERT` statement adds a row to the table, then it also has to add a row in the index structure. If the index is a clustered index, the overhead is greater still, because the row has to be added to the data pages themselves in the right order, which may require other data rows to be repositioned below the entry position of the new row. The `UPDATE` and `DELETE` data manipulation queries change the index pages in a similar manner.

When designing indexes, you'll be operating from two different points of view: the existing system, already in production, where you need to measure the overall impact of an index, and the tactical approach where all you worry about is the immediate benefits of an index, usually when initially designing a system. When you have to deal with the existing system, you should ensure that the performance benefits of an index outweigh the extra cost in processing resources. You can do this by using the Profiler tool (explained in Chapter 3) to do an overall workload optimization (explained in Chapter 16). When you're focused exclusively on the immediate benefits of an index, SQL Server supplies a series of dynamic management views that provide detailed information about the performance of indexes, `sys.dm_db_index_operational_stats` or `sys.dm_db_index_usage_stats`. The view `sys.dm_db_index_operational stats` shows the low-level activity, such as locks and I/O, on an index that is in use. The view `sys.dm_db_index_usage_stats` returns statistical counts of the various index operations that have occurred to an index over time. Both of these will be used more extensively in Chapter 12 when I discuss blocking.

To understand the overhead cost of an index on data manipulation queries, consider the following example. First, create a test table with 10,000 rows (`create_test.sql` in the download):

```
IF (SELECT  OBJECT_ID('t1')
   ) IS NOT NULL
    DROP TABLE dbo.t1 ;
GO
CREATE TABLE dbo.t1 (c1 INT, c2 INT, c3 CHAR(50)) ;
SELECT TOP 10000
        IDENTITY( INT,1,1 ) AS n
INTO    #Nums
```

```
FROM    Master.dbo.SysColumns sc1
       ,Master.dbo.SysColumns sc2 ;

INSERT  INTO dbo.t1 (c1, c2, c3)
        SELECT  n
               ,n
               ,'C3'
        FROM    #Nums ;

DROP TABLE #Nums ;
```

If you then run an UPDATE statement, like so:

```
UPDATE dbo.t1
SET     c1 = 1, c2 = 1
WHERE   c2 = 1 ;
```

the number of logical reads reported by SET STATISTICS IO is as follows:

```
Table 't1'. Scan count 1, logical reads 87
```

After adding an index on column c1, like so:

```
CREATE CLUSTERED INDEX i1 ON t1(c1)
```

the resultant number of logical reads for the same UPDATE statement increases from 87 to 95:

```
Table 't1'. Scan count 1, logical reads 95
```

Even though it is true that the amount of overhead required to maintain indexes increases for data manipulation queries, be aware that SQL Server must first find a row before it can update or delete it; therefore, indexes can be helpful for UPDATE and DELETE statements with complex WHERE clauses as well. The increased efficiency in using the index to locate a row usually offsets the extra overhead needed to update the indexes, unless the table has a lot of indexes.

To understand how an index can benefit even data modification queries, let's build on the example. Create another index on table t1. This time, create the index on column c2 referred to in the WHERE clause of the UPDATE statement:

```
CREATE INDEX i2 ON t1(c2);
```

After adding this new index, run the UPDATE command again:

```
UPDATE t1 SET c1 = 1, c2 = 1 WHERE c2 = 1;
```

the total number of logical reads for this UPDATE statement decreases from 95 to 20 (= 15 + 5):

```
Table 't1'. Scan count 1, logical reads 15
Table 'Worktable'. Scan count 1, logical reads 5
```

■ **Note** A *worktable* is a temporary table used internally by SQL Server to process the intermediate results of a query. Worktables are created in the `tempdb` database and are dropped automatically after query execution.

The examples in this section have demonstrated that although having an index adds some overhead cost to action queries, the overall result is a decrease in cost because of the beneficial effect of indexes on searching.

Index Design Recommendations

The main recommendations for index design are as follows:

- Examine the `WHERE` clause and join criteria columns.
- Use narrow indexes.
- Examine column uniqueness.
- Examine the column data type.
- Consider column order.
- Consider the type of index (clustered vs. nonclustered).

Let's consider each of these recommendations in turn.

Examine the WHERE Clause and Join Criteria Columns

When a query is submitted to SQL Server, the query optimizer tries to find the best data access mechanism for every table referred to in the query. Here is how it does this:

1. The optimizer identifies the columns included in the `WHERE` clause and the join criteria.
2. The optimizer then examines indexes on those columns.
3. The optimizer assesses the usefulness of each index by determining the selectivity of the clause (that is, how many rows will be returned) from statistics maintained on the index.
4. Finally, the optimizer estimates the least costly method of retrieving the qualifying rows, based on the information gathered in the previous steps.

■ **Note** Chapter 7 covers statistics in more depth.

To understand the significance of a `WHERE` clause column in a query, let's consider an example. Let's return to the original code listing that helped you understand what an index is; the query consisted of a `SELECT` statement without any `WHERE` clause, as follows:

```
SELECT  p.ProductID,
        p.[Name],
        p.StandardCost,
        p.[Weight]
FROM    Production.Product p;
```

The query optimizer performs a clustered index scan, the equivalent of a table scan against a heap on a table that has a clustered index, to read the rows as shown in Figure 4-6 (switch on the Show Execution Plan option by using Query Analyzer's Query menu, as well as the Set Statistics IO option by using Query Analyzer's Tools ➤ Options menu).

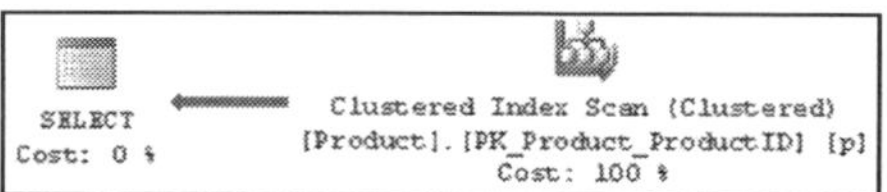

Figure 4-6. *Execution plan with no* `WHERE` *clause*

The number of logical reads reported by `SET STATISTICS IO` for the `SELECT` statement is as follows:

```
Table 'Product'. Scan count 1, logical reads 15
```

To understand the effect of a `WHERE` clause column on the query optimizer's decision, let's add a `WHERE` clause to retrieve a single row:

```
SELECT  p.ProductID,
        p.[Name],
        p.StandardCost,
        p.[Weight]
FROM    Production.Product p
WHERE p.ProductID = 738;
```

With the `WHERE` clause in place, the query optimizer examines the `WHERE` clause column `ProductID`, identifies the availability of index `PK_Product_ProductId` on column `ProductId`, assesses a high selectivity (that is, only one row will be returned) for the `WHERE` clause from the statistics on index `PK_Product_ProductId`, and decides to use that index on column `ProductId`, as shown in Figure 4-7.

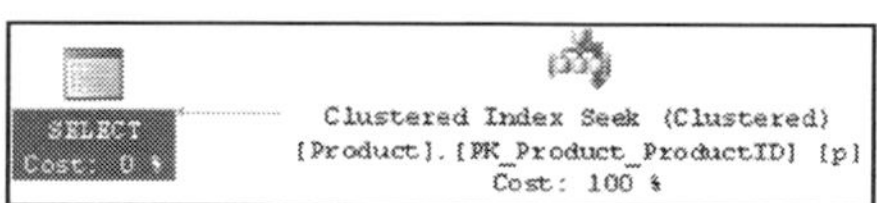

Figure 4-7. *Execution plan with a* `WHERE` *clause*

The resultant number of logical reads is as follows:

```
Table 'Product'. Scan count 0, logical reads 2
```

The behavior of the query optimizer shows that the WHERE clause column helps the optimizer choose an optimal indexing operation for a query. This is also applicable for a column used in the join criteria between two tables. The optimizer looks for the indexes on the WHERE clause column or the join criterion column and, if available, considers using the index to retrieve the rows from the table. The query optimizer considers index(es) on the WHERE clause column(s) and the join criteria column(s) while executing a query. Therefore, having indexes on the frequently used columns in the WHERE clause and the join criteria of a SQL query helps the optimizer avoid scanning a base table.

When the amount of data inside a table is so small that it fits onto a single page (8KB), a table scan may work better than an index seek. If you have a good index in place but you're still getting a scan, consider this issue.

Use Narrow Indexes

You can create indexes on a combination of columns in a table. For the best performance, use as few columns in an index as you can. You should also avoid very wide data type columns in an index. Columns with string data types (CHAR, VARCHAR, NCHAR, and NVARCHAR) sometimes can be quite wide as can binary; unless they are absolutely necessary, minimize the use of wide data type columns with large sizes in an index.

A narrow index can accommodate more rows in an 8KB index page than a wide index. This has the following effects:

- Reduces I/O (by having to read fewer 8KB pages)
- Makes database caching more effective, because SQL Server can cache fewer index pages, consequently reducing the logical reads required for the index pages in the memory
- Reduces the storage space for the database

To understand how a narrow index can reduce the number of logical reads, create a test table with 20 rows and an index (narrowIDX_t1.sql in the download):

```
IF(SELECT OBJECT_ID('t1')) IS NOT NULL
  DROP TABLE dbo.t1
GO
CREATE TABLE dbo.t1(c1 INT, c2 INT);
WITH    Nums
          AS (SELECT    1 AS n
              UNION ALL
              SELECT    n + 1
              FROM      Nums
              WHERE     n < 20
             )
  INSERT INTO t1
  (c1,c2)
  SELECT n,2
  FROM Nums
CREATE INDEX i1 ON t1(c1)
```

Since the indexed column is narrow (the INT data type is 4 bytes), all the index rows can be accommodated in one 8KB index page. As shown in Figure 4-8, you can confirm this in the dynamic management views associated with indexes (base_indx.sql in the download):

```
SELECT  i.Name
       ,i.type_desc
       ,s.page_count
       ,s.record_count
,       s.index_level
FROM    sys.indexes i
        JOIN sys.dm_db_index_physical_stats(DB_ID(N'AdventureWorks2008'),
                                            OBJECT_ID(N'dbo.T1'),
                                            NULL, NULL, 'DETAILED') AS s
        ON i.index_id = s.index_id
WHERE i.OBJECT_ID = OBJECT_ID(N'dbo.T1')
```

	Name	type_desc	page_count	record_count	index_level
1	NULL	HEAP	1	20	0
2	i1	NONCLUSTERED	1	20	0

Figure 4-8. *Number of pages for a narrow, nonclustered index*

The sys.indexes system table is stored in each database and contains the basic information on every index in the database. The dynamic management function, sys.dm_db_index_physical_stats, contains the more detailed information about the statistics on the index (you'll learn more about this DMF in Chapter 7). To understand the disadvantage of a wide index key, modify the data type of the indexed column c1 from INT to CHAR(500) (narrow_alter.sql in the download):

```
DROP INDEX t1.i1
ALTER TABLE t1 ALTER COLUMN c1 CHAR(500)
CREATE INDEX i1 ON t1(c1)
```

The width of a column with the INT data type is 4 bytes, and the width of a column with the CHAR(500) data type is 500 bytes. Because of the large width of the indexed column, two index pages are required to contain all 20 index rows. You can confirm this in the sys.indexes system table by running sysindex_select.sql again (see Figure 4-9).

	Name	type_desc	page_count	record_count	index_level
1	NULL	HEAP	2	25	0
2	i1	NONCLUSTERED	2	20	0
3	i1	NONCLUSTERED	1	2	1

Figure 4-9. *Number of pages for a wide, nonclustered index*

A large index key size increases the number of index pages, thereby increasing the amount of memory and disk activities required for the index. It is always recommended that the index key size is as narrow as possible.

Drop the test table before continuing:

```
DROP TABLE dbo.t1
```

Examine Column Uniqueness

Creating an index on columns with a very low range of possible values (such as gender) will not benefit performance, because the query optimizer will not be able to use the index to effectively narrow down the rows to be returned. Consider a Gender column with only two unique values: M and F. When you execute a query with the Gender column in the WHERE clause, you end up with a large number of rows from the table (assuming the distribution of M and F is even), resulting in a costly table or clustered index scan. It is always preferable to have columns in the WHERE clause with lots of unique rows (or *high selectivity*) to limit the number of rows accessed. You should create an index on those column(s) to help the optimizer access a small result set.

Furthermore, while creating an index on multiple columns, which is also referred to as a *composite index*, column order matters. In some cases, using the most selective column first will help filter the index rows more efficiently.

■ **Note** The importance of column order in a composite index is explained later in the chapter in the "Consider Column Order" section.

From this, you can see that it is important to know the selectivity of a column before creating an index on it. You can find this by executing a query like this one; just substitute the table and column name:

```
SELECT  COUNT(DISTINCT Gender) AS DistinctColValues
        ,COUNT(Gender) AS NumberOfRows
        ,(CAST(COUNT(DISTINCT Gender) AS DECIMAL)
          / CAST(COUNT(Gender) AS DECIMAL)) AS Selectivity
FROM    HumanResources.Employee
```

The column with the highest number of unique values (or selectivity) can be the best candidate for indexing when referred to in a WHERE clause or a join criterion.

To understand how the selectivity of an index key column affects the use of the index, take a look at the Gender column in the HumanResources.Employee table. If you run the previous query, you'll see that it contains only 2 distinct values in more than 290 rows, which is a selectivity of .006. A query to look only for a Gender of F would look like this:

```
SELECT  *
FROM    HumanResources.Employee
WHERE   Gender = 'F'
AND SickLeaveHours = 59
AND MaritalStatus = 'M'
```

This results in the execution plan in Figure 4-10 and the following I/O and elapsed time:

```
Table 'Employee'. Scan count 1, logical reads 9
CPU time = 16 ms,  elapsed time = 103 ms.
```

Figure 4-10. *Execution plan with no index*

The data is returned by scanning the clustered index (where the data is stored) to find the appropriate values where `Gender = 'F'`. (The other operators will be covered in Chapter 9.) If you were to place an index on the column, like so:

```
CREATE INDEX IX_Employee_Test ON HumanResources.Employee (Gender)
```

and run the query again, the execution plan remains the same. The data is just not selective enough for the index to be used, let alone be useful. If instead you use a composite index that looks like this:

```
CREATE INDEX IX_Employee_Test ON
HumanResources.Employee (SickLeaveHours, Gender, MaritalStatus)
WITH (DROP_EXISTING = ON)
```

and then rerun the query to see the execution plan in Figure 4-11 and the performance results, you get this:

```
Table 'Employee'. Scan count 1, logical reads 6
CPU time = 0 ms,  elapsed time = 32 ms.
```

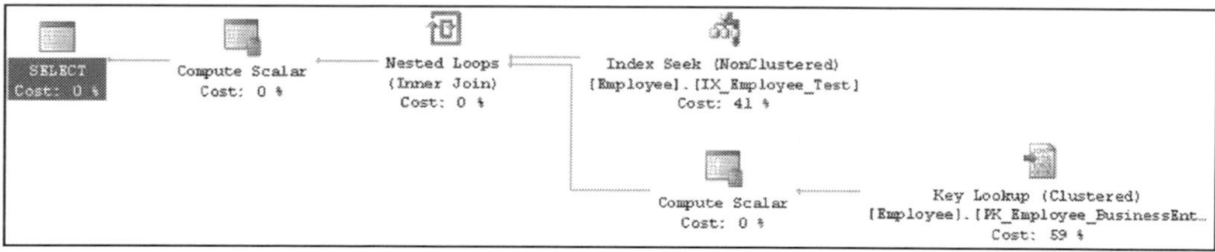

Figure 4-11. *Execution plan with a composite index*

Now you're doing better than you were with the clustered index scan. A nice clean `Index Seek` operation takes about half the time to gather the data. The rest is spent in the `Key Lookup` operation. A `Key Lookup` operation is commonly referred to as a *bookmark lookup.*

■ **Note** You will learn more about bookmark lookups in Chapter 6.

Although none of the columns in question would probably be selective enough on their own to make a decent index, together they provide enough selectivity for the optimizer to take advantage of the index offered.

It is possible to attempt to force the query to use the first test index you created. If you drop the compound index, create the original again, and then modify the query as follows by using a query hint to force the use of the original index:

```
SELECT  *
FROM    HumanResources.Employee WITH (INDEX (IX_Employee_Test))
WHERE   SickLeaveHours = 59
        AND Gender = 'F'
        AND MaritalStatus = 'M'
```

then the results and execution plan shown in Figure 4-12, while similar, are not the same:

```
Table 'Employee'. Scan count 1, logical reads 14
CPU time = 0 ms,  elapsed time = 29 ms.
```

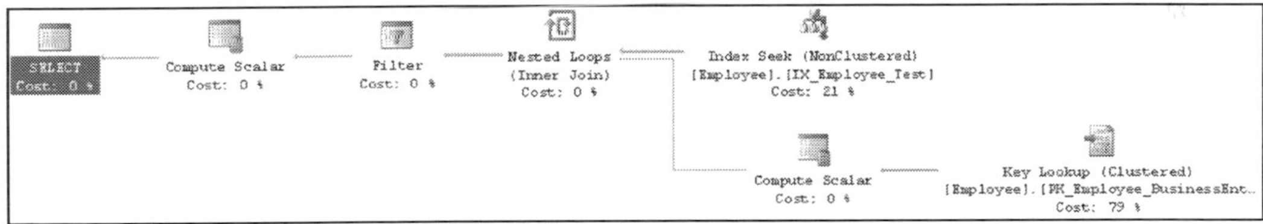

Figure 4-12. *Execution plan when the index is chosen with a query hint*

You see the same index seek, but the number of reads has more than doubled, and the estimated costs within the execution plan have changed. Although forcing the optimizer to choose an index is possible, it clearly isn't always an optimal approach.

Another way to force a different behavior on SQL Server 2008 is the FORCESEEK query hint. FORCESEEK makes it so the optimizer will choose only Index Seek operations. If the query were rewritten like this:

```
SELECT  *
FROM    HumanResources.Employee WITH (FORCESEEK)
WHERE   SickLeaveHours = 59
        AND Gender = 'F'
        AND MaritalStatus = 'M'
```

which changes the I/O, execution time, and execution plan results yet again (Figure 4-13), you end up with these results:

```
Table 'Employee'. Scan count 1, logical reads 170
CPU time = 0 ms,  elapsed time = 39 ms.
```

Limiting the options of the optimizer and forcing behaviors can in some situations help, but frequently, as shown with the results here, an increase in execution time and the number of reads is not helpful.

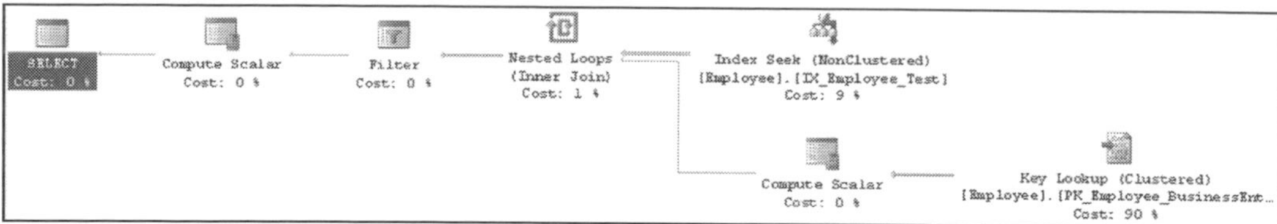

Figure 4-13. *Forcing a Seek operation using FORCESEEK query hint*

■ **Note** To make the best use of your indexes, it is highly recommended that you create the index on a column (or set of columns) with very high selectivity.

Examine the Column Data Type

The data type of an index matters. For example, an index search on integer keys is very fast because of the small size and easy arithmetic manipulation of the INTEGER (or INT) data type. You can also use other variations of integer data types (BIGINT, SMALLINT, and TINYINT) for index columns, whereas string data types (CHAR, VARCHAR, NCHAR, and NVARCHAR) require a string match operation, which is usually costlier than an integer match operation.

Suppose you want to create an index on one column and you have two candidate columns—one with an INTEGER data type and the other with a CHAR(4) data type. Even though the size of both data types is 4 bytes in SQL Server 2008, you will still prefer the INTEGER data type index. Look at arithmetic operations as an example. The value 1 in the CHAR(4) data type is actually stored as 1 followed by three spaces, a combination of the following four bytes: 0x35, 0x20, 0x20, and 0x20. The CPU doesn't understand how to perform arithmetic operations on this data, and therefore it converts to an integer data type before the arithmetic operations, whereas the value 1 in an INTEGER data type is saved as 0x00000001. The CPU can easily perform arithmetic operations on this data.

Of course, most of the time, you won't have the simple choice between identically sized data types, allowing you to choose the more optimal type. Keep this information in mind when designing and building your indexes.

Consider Column Order

An index key is sorted on the first column of the index and then subsorted on the next column within each value of the previous column. The first column in a compound index is frequently referred to as the *leading edge* of the index. For example, consider Table 4-2.

Table 4-2. *Sample Table*

c1	c2
1	1
2	1
3	1
1	2
2	2
3	2

If a composite index is created on the columns (c1, c2), then the index will be ordered as shown in Table 4-3.

Table 4-3. *Composite Index on Columns (c1, c2)*

c1	c2
1	1
1	2
2	1
2	2
3	1
3	2

As shown in Table 4-3, the data is sorted on the first column (c1) in the composite index. Within each value of the first column, the data is further sorted on the second column (c2).

Therefore, the column order in a composite index is an important factor in the effectiveness of the index. You can see this by considering the following:

- Column uniqueness
- Column width
- Column data type

For example, suppose most of your queries on table t1 are similar to the following:

```
SELECT * FROM t1 WHERE c2=12
SELECT * FROM t1 WHERE c2=12 AND c1=11
```

An index on (c2, c1) will benefit both the queries. But an index on (c1, c2) will not be appropriate, because it will sort the data initially on column c1, whereas the first SELECT statement needs the data to be sorted on column c2.

To understand the importance of column ordering in an index, consider the following example. In the Production.Product table, there is a column for StandardCost and another for ListPrice. Create a temporary index on the table like this:

```
CREATE INDEX IX_Test ON Person.Address (City, PostalCode)
```

A simple SELECT statement run against the table that will use this new index will look something like this:

```
SELECT  *
FROM    Person.Address AS a
WHERE   City = 'Warrington'
```

The I/O and execution time for the query is as follows:

```
Table 'Address'. Scan count 1, logical reads 188
CPU time = 0 ms,  elapsed time = 167 ms.
```

And the execution plan in Figure 4-14 shows the use of the index.

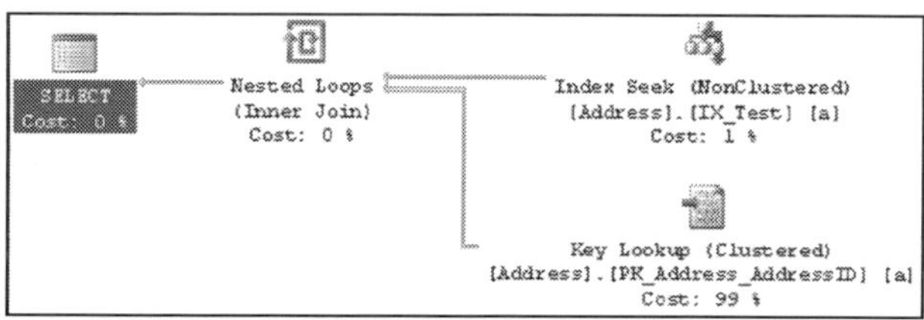

Figure 4-14. *Execution plan for query against leading edge of index*

So, this query is taking advantage of the leading edge of the index to perform a Seek operation to retrieve the data. If, instead of querying using the leading edge, you use another column in the index like the following query:

```
SELECT  *
FROM    Person.Address AS a
WHERE   a.PostalCode = 'WA3 7BH'
```

then the results are as follows:

```
Table 'Address'. Scan count 1, logical reads 173
```

And the execution plan is clearly different, as you can see in Figure 4-15.

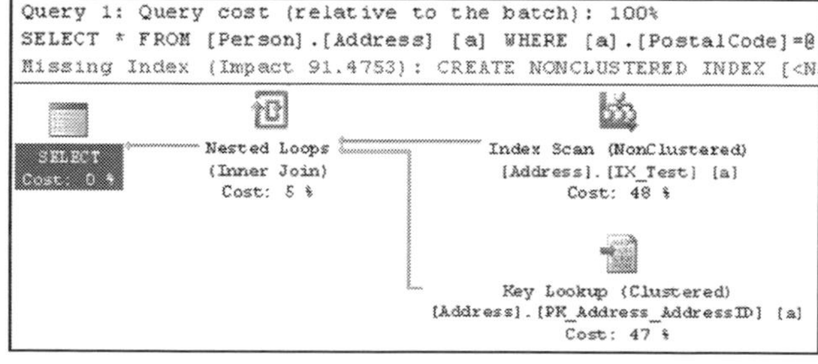

Figure 4-15. *Execution plan for query against inner columns*

The reads for the second query are slightly lower than the first, but when you take into account that the first query returned 86 rows worth of data and the second query returned only 31, you begin to see the difference between the Index Seek operation in Figure 4-14 and the Index Scan operation in Figure 4-15. Also note that because it had to perform a scan, the optimizer marked the column as possibly missing an index.

Finally, to see the order of the index really shine, change the query to this:

```
SELECT  a.AddressID
       ,a.City
       ,a.PostalCode
FROM    Person.Address AS a
WHERE   a.City = 'Warrington'
        AND a.PostalCode = 'WA3 7BH'
```

Executing this query will return the same 31 rows as the previous query, resulting in the following:

```
Table 'Address'. Scan count 1, logical reads 2
```

with the execution plan visible in Figure 4-16.

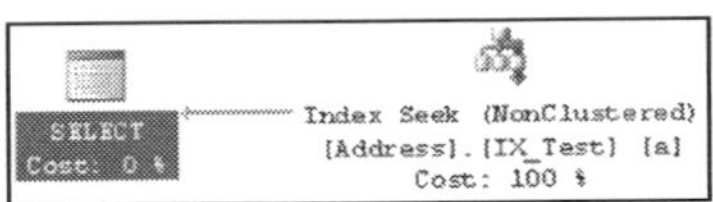

Figure 4-16. *Execution plan using both columns*

The radical changes in I/O and execution plan represent the real use of a compound index, the covering index. This is covered in detail in the section "Covering Indexes" later in the chapter.

When finished, drop the index:

```
DROP INDEX Person.Address.IX_Test
```

Consider the Type of Index

In SQL Server, you have two main index types: *clustered* and *nonclustered*. Both types have a B-tree structure. The main difference between the two types is that the leaf pages in a clustered index are the data pages of the table and are therefore in the same order as the data to which they point. This means that the clustered index is the table. As you proceed, you will see that the difference at the leaf level between the two index types becomes very important when determining the type of index to use.

Clustered Indexes

The leaf pages of a clustered index and the data pages of the table the index is on are one and the same. Because of this, table rows are physically sorted on the clustered index column, and since there can be only one physical order of the table data, a table can have only one clustered index.

■ **Tip** When you create a primary key constraint, SQL Server automatically creates it as a unique clustered index on the primary key if one does not already exist and if it is not explicitly specified that the index should be a unique nonclustered index. This is not a requirement; it's just default behavior. You can change it prior to creating the table.

Heap Tables

As mentioned earlier in the chapter, a table with no clustered index is called a *heap table*. The data rows of a heap table are not stored in any particular order or linked to the adjacent pages in the table. This unorganized structure of the heap table usually increases the overhead of accessing a large heap table when compared to accessing a large nonheap table (a table with a clustered index).

Relationship with Nonclustered Indexes

There is an interesting relationship between a clustered index and the nonclustered indexes in SQL Server. An index row of a nonclustered index contains a pointer to the corresponding data row of the table. This pointer is called a *row locator*. The value of the row locator depends on whether the data pages are stored in a heap or are clustered. For a nonclustered index, the row locator is a pointer to the `RID` for the data row in a heap. For a table with a clustered index, the row locator is the clustered index key value.

For example, say you have a heap table with no clustered index, as shown in Table 4-4.

Table 4-4. *Data Page for a Sample Table*

RowID (Not a Real Column)	c1	c2	c3
1	A1	A2	A3
2	B1	B2	B3

A nonclustered index on column `c1` in a heap will cause the row locator for the index rows to contain a pointer to the corresponding data row in the database table, as shown in Table 4-5.

Table 4-5. *Nonclustered Index Page with No Clustered Index*

c1	Row Locator
A1	Pointer to `RID` = 1
B1	Pointer to `RID` = 2

On creating a clustered index on column `c2`, the row locator values of the nonclustered index rows are changed. The new value of the row locator will contain the clustered index key value, as shown in Table 4-6.

Table 4-6. *Nonclustered Index Page with a Clustered Index on c2*

c1	Row Locator
A1	A2
B1	B2

To verify this dependency between a clustered and a nonclustered index, let's consider an example. In the AdventureWorks2008 database, the table `dbo.DatabaseLog` contains no clustered index, just a nonclustered primary key. If a query is run against it like the following:

```
SELECT  dl.DatabaseLogId
       ,dl.PostTime
FROM    dbo.DatabaseLog AS dl
WHERE   DatabaseLogId = 115
```

then the execution will look like Figure 4-17.

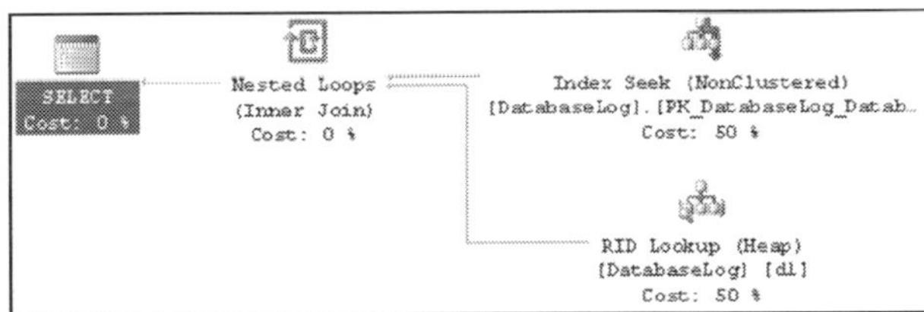

Figure 4-17. *Execution plan against a heap*

As you can see, the index was used in a `Seek` operation. But because the data is stored separately from the nonclustered index, an additional operation, the `RID Lookup` operation, is required in order to retrieve the data, which is then joined back to the information from the `Index Seek` operation through a `Nested Loop` operation. This is a classic example of what is known as a *bookmark lookup*, which is explained in more detail in the "Defining the Bookmark Lookup" section. A similar query run against a table with a clustered index in place will look like this:

```
SELECT  d.DepartmentID
       ,d.ModifiedDate
FROM    HumanResources.Department AS d
WHERE   d.DepartmentID = 10
```

Figure 4-18 shows this execution plan returned.

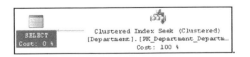

Figure 4-18. *Execution plan with a clustered index*

Although the primary key is used in the same way as the previous query, this time it's against a clustered index. As you now know, this means the data is stored with the index, so the additional column doesn't require a lookup operation to get the data. Everything is returned by the simple clustered `Index Seek` operation.

To navigate from a nonclustered index row to a data row, this relationship between the two index types requires an additional indirection for navigating the B-tree structure of the clustered index. Without the clustered index, the row locator of the nonclustered index would be able to navigate directly from the nonclustered index row to the data row in the base table. The presence of the clustered index causes the navigation from the nonclustered index row to the data row to go through the B-tree structure of the clustered index, since the new row locator value points to the clustered index key.

On the other hand, consider inserting an intermediate row in the clustered index key order or expanding the content of an intermediate row. For example, imagine a clustered index table containing four rows per page, with clustered index column values of 1, 2, 4, and 5. Adding a new row in the table with the clustered index value 3 will require space in the page between values 2 and 4. If enough space is not available in that position, a page split will occur on the data page (or clustered index leaf page). Even though the data page split will cause relocation of the data rows, the nonclustered index row locator values need not be updated. These row locators continue to point to the same logical key values of the clustered index key, even though the data rows have physically moved to a different location. In the case of a data page split, the row locators of the nonclustered indexes need not be updated. This is an important point, since tables often have a large number of nonclustered indexes.

■ **Note** Page splits and their effect on performance are explained in more detail in Chapter 8.

Clustered Index Recommendations

The relationship between a clustered index and a nonclustered index imposes some considerations on the clustered index, which are explained in the sections that follow.

Create the Clustered Index First

Since all nonclustered indexes hold clustered index keys within their index rows, the order of nonclustered and clustered index creation is very important. For example, if the nonclustered indexes are built before the clustered index is created, then the nonclustered index row locator will contain a pointer to the corresponding `RID` of the table. Creating the clustered index later will modify all the nonclustered indexes to contain clustered index keys as the new row locator value. This effectively rebuilds all the nonclustered indexes.

For the best performance, I recommend that you create the clustered index *before* you create any nonclustered index. This allows the nonclustered indexes to have their row locator set to the clustered index keys at the time of creation. This does not have any effect on the final performance, but rebuilding the indexes may be quite a large job.

Keep Indexes Narrow

Since all nonclustered indexes hold the clustered keys as their row locator, for the best performance keep the overall byte size of the clustered index as small as possible. If you create a wide clustered index, say CHAR(500), this will add 500 bytes to every nonclustered index. Thus, keep the number of columns in the clustered index to a minimum, and carefully consider the byte size of each column to be included in the clustered index. A column of the INTEGER data type usually makes a good candidate for a clustered index, whereas a string data type column will be a less-than-optimal choice.

To understand the effect of a wide clustered index on a nonclustered index, consider this example. Create a small test table with a clustered index and a nonclustered index (clust_nonclust.sql in the download):

```
IF (SELECT  OBJECT_ID('t1')) IS NOT NULL
    DROP TABLE t1 ;
GO
CREATE TABLE t1 (c1 INT, c2 INT) ;

WITH    Nums
          AS (SELECT    1 AS n
              UNION ALL
              SELECT    n + 1
              FROM      Nums
              WHERE     n < 20
             )
    INSERT  INTO t1 (c1, c2)
            SELECT  n
                   ,n + 1
            FROM    Nums

CREATE CLUSTERED INDEX icl ON t1 (c2) ;
CREATE NONCLUSTERED INDEX incl ON t1 (c1) ;
```

Since the table has a clustered index, the row locator of the nonclustered index contains the clustered index key value. Therefore:

Width of the nonclustered index row = Width of the nonclustered index column + Width of the clustered index column = size of INT data type + Size of INT data type

= 4 bytes + 4 bytes = 8 bytes

With this small size of a nonclustered index row, all the rows can be stored in one index page. You can confirm this by querying against the index statistics (base_index.sql), as shown in Figure 4-19:

```
SELECT  i.Name
       ,i.type_desc
       ,s.page_count
       ,s.record_count
       ,s.index_level
```

```
FROM    sys.indexes i
        JOIN sys.dm_db_index_physical_stats(DB_ID(N'AdventureWorks2008'),
                                            OBJECT_ID(N'dbo.t1'),
                                            NULL, NULL, 'DETAILED') AS s
        ON i.index_id = s.index_id
WHERE i.OBJECT_ID = OBJECT_ID(N'dbo.t1')
```

	Name	type_desc	page_count	record_count	index_level
1	icl	CLUSTERED	2	20	0
2	icl	CLUSTERED	1	2	1
3	incl	NONCLUSTERED	2	20	0
4	incl	NONCLUSTERED	1	2	1

Figure 4-19. *Number of index pages for a narrow index*

To understand the effect of a wide clustered index on a nonclustered index, modify the data type of the clustered indexed column c2 from INT to CHAR(500):

```
DROP INDEX t1.icl
ALTER TABLE t1 ALTER COLUMN c2 CHAR(500)
CREATE CLUSTERED INDEX icl ON t1(c2)
```

Running sysindex_select2.sql again returns the result in Figure 4-20.

	Name	type_desc	page_count	record_count
1	icl	CLUSTERED	2	20
2	incl	NONCLUSTERED	2	20

Figure 4-20. *Number of index pages for a wide index*

You can see that a wide clustered index increases the width of the nonclustered index row size. Because of the large width of the nonclustered index row, one 8KB index page can't accommodate all the index rows. Instead, two index pages will be required to store all 20 index rows. In the case of a large table, an unreasonable expansion in the size of the nonclustered indexes because of a large clustered index key size can significantly increase the number of pages of the nonclustered indexes.

Therefore, a large clustered index key size not only affects its own width but also widens all nonclustered indexes on the table. This increases the number of index pages for all the indexes on the table, increasing the logical reads and disk I/Os required for the indexes.

Rebuild the Clustered Index in a Single Step

Because of the dependency of nonclustered indexes on the clustered index, rebuilding the clustered index as separate DROP INDEX and CREATE INDEX statements causes all the nonclustered indexes to be rebuilt twice. To avoid this, use the DROP_EXISTING clause of the CREATE INDEX statement to rebuild the clustered index in a single atomic step. Similarly, you can also use the DROP_EXISTING clause with a nonclustered index.

When to Use a Clustered Index

In certain situations, using a clustered index is very helpful. I discuss these in the sections that follow.

Retrieving a Range of Data

Since the leaf pages of a clustered index and the data pages of the table are the same, the order of the clustered index column not only orders the rows of the clustered index but also physically orders the data rows. If the physical order of the data rows matches the order of data requested by a query, then the disk head can read all the rows sequentially, without much disk head movement. For example, if a query requests all the employee records belonging to the database group and the corresponding `Employees` table has a clustered index on the `Group` column, then all the relevant `Employee` rows will be physically arranged together on the disk. This allows the disk head to move to the position of the first row on the disk and then electronically read all the data sequentially with minimal physical movement of the disk head. On the other hand, if the rows are not sorted on the disk in the correct physical order, the disk head has to move randomly from one location to another to fetch all the relevant rows. Since physical movement of the disk head constitutes a major portion of the cost of a disk operation, sorting the rows in the proper physical order on the disk (using a clustered index) optimizes the I/O cost.

One "range" of data that is accessed frequently in relational systems is the foreign key from another table. This data, depending on the access mechanisms of the application, is a great candidate for inclusion in the clustered index.

Retrieving Presorted Data

Clustered indexes are particularly efficient when the data retrieval needs to be sorted. If you create a clustered index on the column or columns that you may need to sort by, then the rows will be physically stored in that order, eliminating the overhead of sorting the data after it is retrieved.

Let's see this in action. Create a test table as follows (`create_sort.sql` in the download):

```
IF (SELECT  OBJECT_ID('od')
   ) IS NOT NULL
    DROP TABLE dbo.od ;
GO
SELECT  *
INTO    dbo.od
FROM    Purchasing.PurchaseOrderDetail AS pod
```

The new table `od` is created with data only. It doesn't have any indexes. You can verify the indexes on the table by executing the following, which returns nothing:

```
sp_helpindex dbo.od
```

To understand the use of a clustered index, fetch a large range of rows ordered on a certain column:

```
SELECT  *
FROM    dbo.od
WHERE   od.ProductID BETWEEN 500 AND 510
ORDER BY od.ProductID
```

You can obtain the cost of executing this query (without any indexes) from the STATISTICS IO output:

```
Table 'od'. Scan count 1, logical reads 79
```

To improve the performance of this query, you should create an index on the WHERE clause column. This query requires both a range of rows and a sorted output. The result set requirement of this query meets the recommendations for a clustered index. Therefore, create a clustered index as follows, and reexamine the cost of the query:

```
CREATE CLUSTERED INDEX i1 ON od(ProductID)
```

When you run the query again, the resultant cost of the query (with a clustered index) is as follows:

```
Table 'od'. Scan count 1, logical reads 8
```

Creating the clustered index reduced the number of logical reads and therefore should contribute to the query performance improvement.

On the other hand, if you create a nonclustered index (instead of a clustered index) on the candidate column, then the query performance may be affected adversely. Let's verify the effect of a nonclustered index in this case:

```
DROP INDEX od.i1
CREATE NONCLUSTERED INDEX i1 on dbo.od(ProductID)
```

The resultant cost of the query (with a nonclustered index) is as follows:

```
Table 'od'. Scan count 1, logical reads 87
```

The nonclustered index significantly increases the number of logical reads, affecting the query performance accordingly. Drop the test table when you're done:

```
DROP TABLE dbo.od
```

■ **Note** For a query that retrieves a large range of rows and/or an ordered output, a clustered index is usually a better choice than a nonclustered index.

When Not to Use a Clustered Index

In certain situations, you are better off not using a clustered index. I discuss these in the sections that follow.

Frequently Updatable Columns

If the clustered index columns are frequently updated, this will cause the row locator of all the nonclustered indexes to be updated accordingly, significantly increasing the cost of the relevant action queries. This also affects database concurrency by blocking all other queries referring to the same part of the table and the nonclustered indexes during that period. Therefore, avoid creating a clustered index on columns that are highly updatable.

Note Chapter 12 covers blocking in more depth.

To understand how the cost of an UPDATE statement that modifies only a clustered key column is increased by the presence of nonclustered indexes on the table, consider the following example. The Sales.SpecialOfferProduct table has a composite clustered index on the primary key, which is also the foreign key from two different tables; this is a classic many-to-many join. In this example, I update one of the two columns using the following statement (note the use of the transaction to keep the test data intact):

```
BEGIN TRAN
SET STATISTICS IO ON;
UPDATE sales.SpecialOfferProduct
SET ProductID = 345
WHERE SpecialOfferID = 1
AND productid = 720;
SET STATISTICS IO OFF;
ROLLBACK TRAN
```

The STATISTICS IO output shows the reads necessary:

```
Table 'Product'. Scan count 0, logical reads 2
Table 'SalesOrderDetail'. Scan count 1, logical reads 1240
Table 'SpecialOfferProduct'. Scan count 0, logical reads 10
```

If you added a nonclustered index to the table, you would see the reads increase:

```
CREATE NONCLUSTERED INDEX ixTest ON  sales.SpecialOfferProduct (ModifiedDate)
```

When you run the same query again, the output of STATISTICS IO changes for the SpecialOfferProduct table:

```
Table 'Product'. Scan count 0, logical reads 2
Table 'SalesOrderDetail'. Scan count 1, logical reads 1240
Table 'SpecialOfferProduct'. Scan count 0, logical reads 19
```

As you can see, the number of reads caused by the update of the clustered index is increased with the addition of the nonclustered index. Be sure to drop the index:

```
DROP INDEX Sales.SpecialOfferProduct.ixTest
```

Wide Keys

Since all nonclustered indexes hold the clustered keys as their row locator, for performance reasons you should avoid creating a clustered index on a very wide column (or columns) or on too many columns. As explained in the preceding section, a clustered index must be as narrow as possible.

Too Many Concurrent Inserts in Sequential Order

If you want to add many new rows concurrently, then it may be better for performance to distribute them across the data pages of the table. However, if you add all the rows in the same order as that imposed by the clustered index, then all the inserts will be attempted on the last page of the table. This may cause a huge "hot spot" on the corresponding sector of the disk. To avoid this disk hot spot, you should not arrange the data rows in the same order as their physical locations. The inserts can be randomized throughout the table by creating a clustered index on another column that doesn't arrange the rows in the same order as that of the new rows. This is an issue only with a large number of simultaneous inserts.

There is a caveat to this recommendation. Allowing inserts on the bottom of the table prevents page splits on the intermediate pages that are required to accommodate the new rows in those pages. If the number of concurrent inserts is low, then ordering the data rows (using a clustered index) in the order of the new rows will prevent intermediate page splits. However, if the disk hot spot becomes a performance bottleneck, then new rows can be accommodated in intermediate pages without causing page splits by reducing the *fill factor* of the table. In addition, the "hot" pages will be in memory, which also benefits performance.

■ **Note** Chapter 8 covers the fill factor in depth.

Nonclustered Indexes

A nonclustered index does not affect the order of the data in the table pages, because the leaf pages of a nonclustered index and the data pages of the table are separate. A pointer (the row locator) is required to navigate from an index row to the data row. As you learned in the earlier "Clustered Indexes" section, the structure of the row locator depends on whether the data pages are stored in a heap or a clustered index. For a heap, the row locator is a pointer to the RID for the data row; for a table with a clustered index, the row locator is the clustered index key.

Nonclustered Index Maintenance

The row locator value of the nonclustered indexes continues to have the same clustered index value, even when the clustered index rows are physically relocated.

To optimize this maintenance cost, SQL Server adds a pointer to the old data page to point to the new data page after a page split, instead of updating the row locator of all the relevant nonclustered indexes. Although this reduces the maintenance cost of the nonclustered indexes, it increases the navigation cost from the nonclustered index row to the data row, since an extra link is added between the old data page and the new data page. Therefore, having a clustered index as the row locator decreases this overhead associated with the nonclustered index.

Defining the Bookmark Lookup

When a query requests columns that are not part of the nonclustered index chosen by the optimizer, a lookup is required. This may be a key lookup when going against a clustered index or an `RID` lookup when performed against a heap. The common term for these lookups comes from the old definition name, *bookmark lookup*. The lookup fetches the corresponding data row from the table by following the row locator value from the index row, requiring a logical read on the data page besides the logical read on the index page. However, if all the columns required by the query are available in the index itself, then access to the data page is not required. This is known as a *covering index*.

These bookmark lookups are the reason that large result sets are better served with a clustered index. A clustered index doesn't require a bookmark lookup, since the leaf pages and data pages for a clustered index are the same.

■ **Note** Chapter 6 covers bookmark lookups in more detail.

Nonclustered Index Recommendations

Since a table can have only one clustered index, you can use the flexibility of multiple nonclustered indexes to help improve performance. I explain the factors that decide the use of a nonclustered index in the following sections.

When to Use a Nonclustered Index

A nonclustered index is most useful when all you want to do is retrieve a small number of rows from a large table. As the number of rows to be retrieved increases, the overhead cost of the bookmark lookup rises proportionately. To retrieve a small number of rows from a table, the indexed column should have a very high selectivity.

Furthermore, there will be indexing requirements that won't be suitable for a clustered index, as explained in the "Clustered Indexes" section:

- Frequently updatable columns
- Wide keys

In these cases, you can use a nonclustered index, since, unlike a clustered index, it doesn't affect other indexes in the table. A nonclustered index on a frequently updatable column isn't as costly as having a clustered index on that column. The `UPDATE` operation on a nonclustered index is limited to the base table and the nonclustered index. It doesn't affect any other nonclustered indexes on the table. Similarly, a nonclustered index on a wide column (or set of columns) doesn't increase the size of any other index, unlike that with a clustered index. However, remain cautious, even while creating a nonclustered index on a highly updatable column or a wide column (or set of columns), since this can increase the cost of action queries, as explained earlier in the chapter.

■ **Tip** A nonclustered index can also help resolve blocking and deadlock issues. I cover this in more depth in Chapters 12 and 13.

When Not to Use a Nonclustered Index

Nonclustered indexes are not suitable for queries that retrieve a large number of rows. Such queries are better served with a clustered index, which doesn't require a separate bookmark lookup to retrieve a data row. Since a bookmark lookup requires an additional logical read on the data page besides the logical read on the nonclustered index page, the cost of a query using a nonclustered index increases significantly for a large number of rows. The SQL Server query optimizer takes this cost into effect and accordingly discards the nonclustered index when retrieving a large result set.

If your requirement is to retrieve a large result set from a table, then having a nonclustered index on the filter criterion (or the join criterion) column will not be useful unless you use a special type of nonclustered index called a *covering index*. I describe this index type in detail later in the chapter.

Clustered vs. Nonclustered Indexes

The main considerations in choosing between a clustered and a nonclustered index are as follows:

- Number of rows to be retrieved
- Data-ordering requirement
- Index key width

- Column update frequency
- Bookmark cost
- Any disk hot spots

Benefits of a Clustered Index over a Nonclustered Index

When deciding upon a type of index on a table with no indexes, the clustered index is usually the preferred choice. Because the index page and the data pages are the same, the clustered index doesn't have to jump from the index row to the base row as required in the case of a nonclustered index.

To understand how a clustered index can outperform a nonclustered index in most circumstances, even in retrieving small number of rows, create a test table with a high selectivity for one column (`cluster_bene.sql` in the download):

```
IF(SELECT OBJECT_ID('t1')) IS NOT NULL
  DROP TABLE t1
GO
CREATE TABLE t1(c1 INT, c2 INT);
SELECT TOP 10000
        IDENTITY( INT,1,1 ) AS n
INTO    #Nums
FROM    Master.dbo.SysColumns sc1
       ,Master.dbo.SysColumns sc2 ;
  INSERT INTO t1
  (c1,c2)
  SELECT n,2
  FROM #Nums
DROP TABLE #Nums ;
```

The following `SELECT` statement fetches only 1 out of 10,000 rows from the table:

```
SELECT  c1
       ,c2
FROM    t1
WHERE   c1 = 1
```

with the graphical execution plan shown in Figure 4-21 and the output of `SET STATISTICS IO` as follows:

```
Table 't1'. Scan count 1, logical reads 22
```

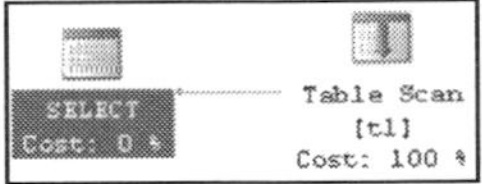

Figure 4-21. *Execution plan with no index*

Considering the small size of the result set retrieved by the preceding SELECT statement, a nonclustered column on c1 can be a good choice:

```
CREATE NONCLUSTERED INDEX incl ON t1(c1)
```

You can run the same SELECT command again. Since retrieving a small number of rows through a nonclustered index is more economical than a table scan, the optimizer used the nonclustered index on column c1, as shown in Figure 4-22. The number of logical reads reported by STATISTICS IO is as follows:

```
Table 't1'. Scan count 1, logical reads 3
```

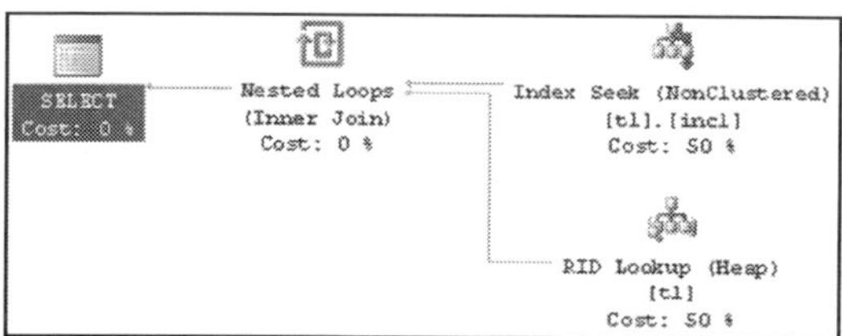

Figure 4-22. *Execution plan with a nonclustered index*

Even though retrieving a small result set using a column with high selectivity is a good pointer toward creating a nonclustered index on the column, a clustered index on the same column can be equally beneficial or even better. To evaluate how the clustered index can be more beneficial than the nonclustered index, create a clustered index on the same column:

```
CREATE CLUSTERED INDEX icl ON t1(c1)
```

Run the same SELECT command again. From the resultant execution plan (see Figure 4-22) of the preceding SELECT statement, you can see that the optimizer used the clustered index (instead of the nonclustered index) even for a small result set. The number of logical reads for the SELECT statement decreased from three to two (Figure 4-23):

```
Table 't1'. Scan count 1, logical reads 2
```

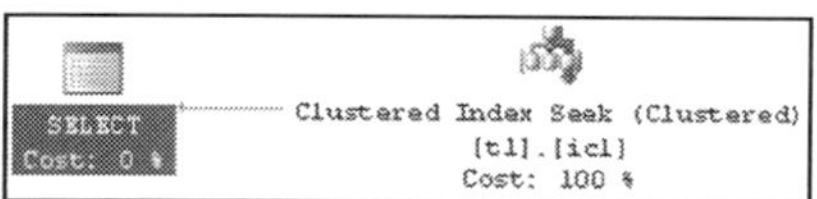

Figure 4-23. *Execution plan with a clustered index*

■ **Note** Even though a clustered index can outperform a nonclustered index in many instances of data retrieval, a table can have only one clustered index. Therefore, reserve the clustered index for a situation in which it can be of the greatest benefit.

Benefits of a Nonclustered Index over a Clustered Index

As you learned in the previous section, a nonclustered index is preferred over a clustered index in the following situations:

- When the index key size is large.
- To avoid the overhead cost associated with a clustered index since rebuilding the clustered index rebuilds all the nonclustered indexes of the table.
- To resolve blocking by having a database reader work on the pages of a nonclustered index, while a database writer modifies other columns (not included in the nonclustered index) in the data page. In this case, the writer working on the data page won't block a reader that can get all the required column values from the nonclustered index without hitting the base table. I'll explain this in detail in Chapter 12.
- When all the columns (from a table) referred to by a query can be safely accommodated in the nonclustered index itself, as explained in this section.

As already established, the data-retrieval performance when using a nonclustered index is generally poorer than that when using a clustered index, because of the cost associated in jumping from the nonclustered index rows to the data rows in the base table. In cases where the jump to the data rows is not required, the performance of a nonclustered index should be just as good as—or even better than—a clustered index. This is possible if the nonclustered index key includes all the columns required from the table.

To understand the situation where a nonclustered index can outperform a clustered index, consider the following example. Assume for our purposes that you need to examine the credit cards that are expiring between the months of June and September of 2008. You may have a query that returns a large number of rows and looks like this:

```
SELECT  cc.CreditCardID
        ,cc.CardNumber
        ,cc.ExpMonth
        ,cc.ExpYear
FROM    Sales.CreditCard cc
WHERE   cc.ExpMonth BETWEEN 6 AND 9
        AND cc.ExpYear = 2008
ORDER BY cc.ExpMonth
```

The following are the I/O results, and Figure 4-24 shows the execution plan:

```
Table 'CreditCard'. Scan count 1, logical reads 189
```

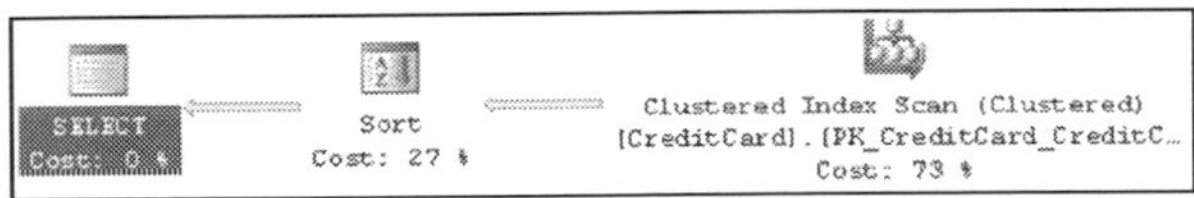

Figure 4-24. *Execution plan scanning the clustered index*

The clustered index is on the primary key, and although most access against the table may be through that key, making the index useful, the cluster in this instance is just not performing in the way you need. Although you could expand the definition of the index to include all the other columns in the query, they're not really needed to make the cluster function, and they would interfere with the operation of the primary key. In this instance, creating a different index is in order:

```
CREATE NONCLUSTERED INDEX ixTest ON Sales.CreditCard (ExpMonth, ExpYear, CardNumber)
```

Now when the query is run again, this is the result:

```
Table 'CreditCard'. Scan count 1, logical reads 30
```

Figure 4-25 shows the corresponding execution plan.

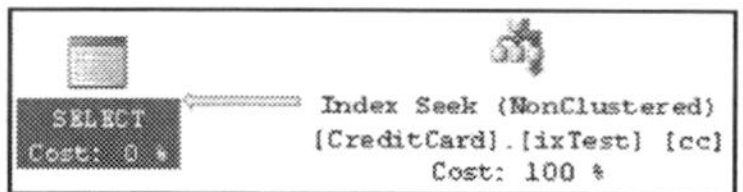

Figure 4-25. *Execution plan with a nonclustered index*

In this case, the SELECT statement doesn't include any column that requires a jump from the nonclustered index page to the data page of the table, which is what usually makes a nonclustered index costlier than a clustered index for a large result set and/or sorted output. This kind of nonclustered index is called a *covering index*.

Clean up the index after the testing is done:

```
DROP INDEX Sales.CreditCard.ixTest
```

Advanced Indexing Techniques

A few of the more advanced indexing techniques that you can also consider are as follows:

- *Covering indexes*: These were introduced in the preceding section.
- *Index intersections*: Use multiple nonclustered indexes to satisfy all the column requirements (from a table) for a query.
- *Index joins*: Use the index intersection and covering index techniques to avoid hitting the base table.
- *Filtered indexes*: To be able to index fields with odd data distributions or sparse columns, a filter can be applied to an index so that it indexes only some data.
- *Indexed views*: This materializes the output of a view on disk.

I cover these topics in more detail in the following sections.

Covering Indexes

A *covering index* is a nonclustered index built upon all the columns required to satisfy a SQL query without going to the base table. If a query encounters an index and does not need to refer to the underlying data table at all, then the index can be considered a covering index.

For example, in the following SELECT statement, irrespective of where the columns are referred, all the columns (StateProvinceId and PostalCode) should be included in the nonclustered index to cover the query fully:

```
SELECT  a.PostalCode
FROM    Person.Address AS a
WHERE   a.StateProvinceID = 42
```

Then all the required data for the query can be obtained from the nonclustered index page, without accessing the data page. This helps SQL Server save logical and physical reads. If you run the query, you'll get the following I/O and execution time as well as the execution plan in Figure 4-26:

```
Table 'Address'. Scan count 1, logical reads 18
CPU time = 15 ms,  elapsed time = 32 ms.
```

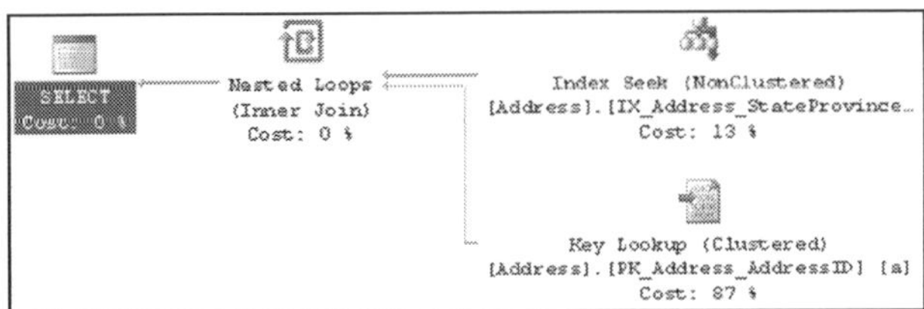

Figure 4-26. *Query without a covering index*

Here you have a classic bookmark lookup with the Key Lookup operator pulling the PostalCode data from the clustered index and joining it with the Index Seek operator against the IX_Address_StateProvinceId index.

Although you can re-create the index with both key columns, another way to make an index a covering index is to use the new INCLUDE operator. This stores data with the index without changing the structure of the index itself. Use the following to re-create the index:

```
CREATE NONCLUSTERED INDEX [IX_Address_StateProvinceID] ON
[Person].[Address] ([StateProvinceID] ASC)
    INCLUDE (PostalCode)
    WITH (
         DROP_EXISTING = ON)
```

If you rerun the query, the execution plan (Figure 4-27), I/O, and execution time change:

```
Table 'Address'. Scan count 1, logical reads 2
CPU time = 0 ms,  elapsed time = 0 ms.
```

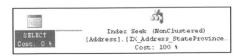

Figure 4-27. *Query with a covering index*

The reads have dropped from 18 to 2, and the execution plan is just about as simple as it's possible to be; it's a single `Index Seek` operation against the new and improved index, which is now covering. A covering index is a useful technique for reducing the number of logical reads of a query. Adding columns using the `INCLUDE` statement makes this functionality easier to achieve without adding to the number of columns in an index or the size of the index key since the included columns are stored only at the leaf level of the index.

The `INCLUDE` is best used in the following cases:

- You don't want to increase the size of the index keys, but you still want to make the index a covering index.
- You're indexing a data type that can't be indexed (except text, ntext, and images).
- You've already exceeded the maximum number of key columns for an index (although this is a problem best avoided).

A Pseudoclustered Index

The covering index physically organizes the data of all the indexed columns in a sequential order. Thus, from a disk I/O perspective, a covering index that doesn't use included columns becomes a clustered index for all queries satisfied completely by the columns in the covering index. If the result set of a query requires a sorted output, then the covering index can be used to physically maintain the column data in the same order as required by the result set—it can then be used in the same way as a clustered index for sorted output. As shown in the previous example, covering indexes can give better performance than clustered indexes for queries requesting a range of rows and/or sorted output. The included columns are not part of the key and therefore wouldn't offer the same benefits for ordering as the key columns of the index.

Recommendations

To take advantage of covering indexes, be careful with the column list in `SELECT` statements. Use as few columns as possible to keep the index key size small for the covering indexes. Add columns using the `INCLUDE` statement in places where it makes sense. Since a covering index includes all columns used in a query, it has a tendency to be very wide, increasing the maintenance cost of the covering indexes. You must balance the maintenance cost with the performance gain that the covering index brings. If the number of bytes from all the columns in the index is small compared to the number of bytes in a single data row of that table and you are certain the query taking advantage of the covered index will be executed frequently, then it may be beneficial to use a covering index.

■ **Tip** Covering indexes can also help resolve blocking and deadlocks, as you will see in Chapters 12 and 13.

Before building a lot of covering indexes, consider how SQL Server can effectively and automatically create covering indexes for queries on the fly using index intersection.

Index Intersections

If a table has multiple indexes, then SQL Server can use multiple indexes to execute a query. SQL Server can take advantage of multiple indexes, selecting small subsets of data based on each index and then performing an intersection of the two subsets (that is, returning only those rows that meet all the criteria). SQL Server can exploit multiple indexes on a table and then employ a join algorithm to obtain the *index intersection* between the two subsets.

In the following SELECT statement, for the WHERE clause columns the table has a nonclustered index on the SalesPersonID column, but it has no index on the OrderDate column:

```
SELECT soh.*
FROM Sales.SalesOrderHeader AS soh
WHERE soh.SalesPersonID = 276
AND soh.OrderDate BETWEEN '4/1/2002' and '7/1/2002'
```

Figure 4-28 shows the execution plan for this query.

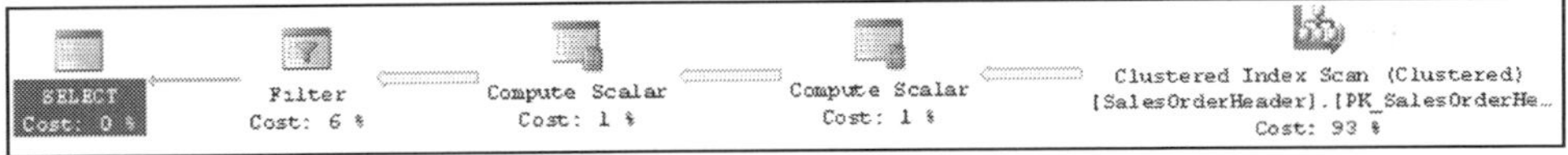

Figure 4-28. *Execution plan with no index on the OrderDate column*

As you can see, the optimizer didn't use the nonclustered index on the SalesPersonID column. Since the value of the OrderDate column is also required, the optimizer chose the clustered index to fetch the value of all the referred columns.

To improve the performance of the query, the OrderDate column can be added to the nonclustered index on the SalesPersonId column or defined as an include column on the same index. But in this real-world scenario, you may have to consider the following while modifying an existing index:

- It may not be permissible to modify an existing index for various reasons.
- The existing nonclustered index key may be already quite wide.
- The cost of the queries using the existing index will be affected by the modification.

In such cases, you can create a new nonclustered index on the OrderDate column:

```
CREATE NONCLUSTERED INDEX IX_Test ON Sales.SalesOrderHeader (OrderDate)
```

Run your SELECT command again.

Figure 4-29 shows the resultant execution plan of the SELECT statement.

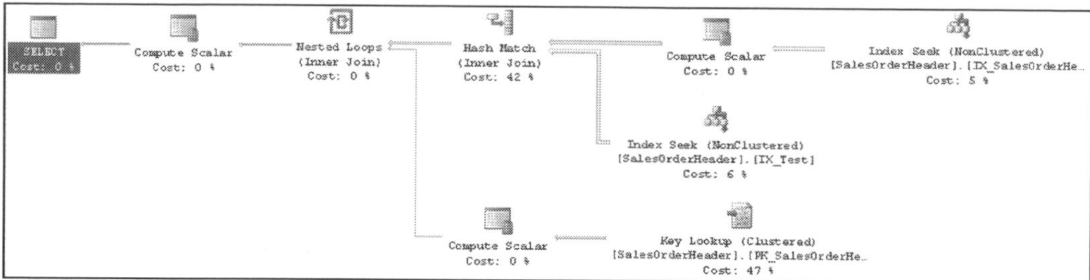

Figure 4-29. *Execution plan with an index on the* `OrderDate` *column*

As you can see, SQL Server exploited both the nonclustered indexes as index seeks (rather than scans) and then employed an intersection algorithm to obtain the index intersection of the two subsets. It then did a `Key Lookup` from the resulting data to retrieve the rest of the data not included in the indexes.

To improve the performance of a query, SQL Server can use multiple indexes on a table. Therefore, instead of creating wide index keys, consider creating multiple narrow indexes. SQL Server will be able to use them together where required, and when not required, queries benefit from narrow indexes. While creating a covering index, determine whether the width of the index will be acceptable and whether using include columns will get the job done. If not, then identify the existing nonclustered indexes that include most of the columns required by the covering index. You may already have two existing nonclustered indexes that jointly serve all the columns required by the covering index. If it is possible, rearrange the column order of the existing nonclustered indexes appropriately, allowing the optimizer to consider an index intersection between the two nonclustered indexes.

At times, it is possible that you may have to create a separate nonclustered index for the following reasons:

- Reordering the columns in one of the existing indexes is not allowed.
- Some of the columns required by the covering index may not be included in the existing nonclustered indexes.
- The total number of columns in the two existing nonclustered indexes may be more than the number of columns required by the covering index.

In such cases, you can create a nonclustered index on the remaining columns. If the combined column order of the new index and an existing nonclustered index meets the requirement of the covering index, the optimizer will be able to use index intersection. While identifying the columns and their order for the new index, try to maximize their benefit by keeping an eye on other queries, too.

Drop the index that was created for the tests:

```
DROP INDEX Sales.SalesOrderHeader.IX_Test
```

Index Joins

The *index join* is a variation of index intersection, where the covering index technique is applied to the index intersection. If no single index covers a query but multiple indexes together can cover the query, SQL Server can use an index join to satisfy the query fully without going to the base table.

Let's look at this indexing technique at work. Make a slight modification to the query from the "Index Intersections" section like this:

```
SELECT soh.SalesPersonID,soh.OrderDate
FROM Sales.SalesOrderHeader AS soh
WHERE soh.SalesPersonID = 276
AND soh.OrderDate BETWEEN '4/1/2002' and '7/1/2002'
```

The execution plan for this query is shown in Figure 4-30, and the reads are as follows:

```
Table 'SalesOrderHeader'. Scan count 1, logical reads 686
```

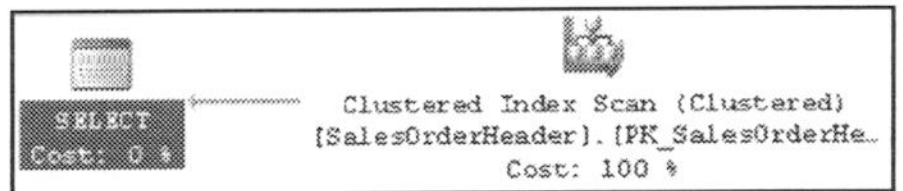

Figure 4-30. *Execution plan with no index join*

As shown in Figure 4-30, the optimizer didn't use the existing nonclustered index on the SalesPersonID column. Since the query requires the value of the OrderDate column also, the optimizer selected the clustered index to retrieve values for all the columns referred to in the query. If an index is created on the OrderDate column like this:

```
CREATE NONCLUSTERED INDEX [IX_Test] ON [Sales].[SalesOrderHeader] ([OrderDate] ASC);
```

and the query is rerun, then Figure 4-31 shows the result, and you can see the reads here:

```
Table 'Worktable'. Scan count 0, logical reads 0
Table 'SalesOrderHeader'. Scan count 2, logical reads 8
```

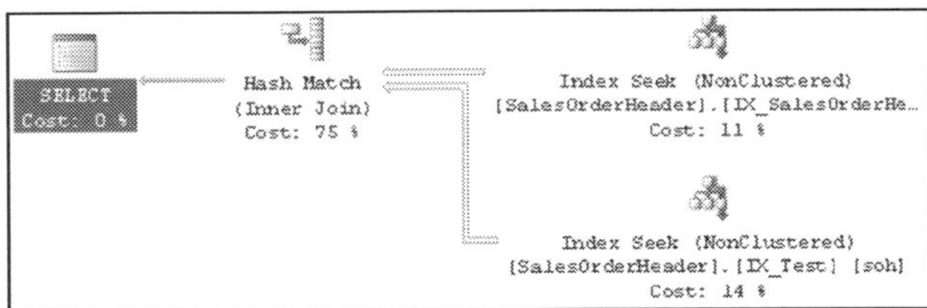

Figure 4-31. *Execution plan with an index join*

The combination of the two indexes acts like a covering index reducing the reads against the table from 686 to 8 because it's using two Index Seek operations joined together instead of a clustered index scan.

But what if the WHERE clause didn't result in both indexes being used? Instead, you know that both indexes exist and that a seek against each would work like the previous query, so you choose to use an index hint:

```
SELECT   soh.SalesPersonID
        ,soh.OrderDate
FROM     Sales.SalesOrderHeader AS soh WITH (INDEX (IX_Test,
                                           IX_SalesOrderHeader_SalesPersonId))
WHERE    soh.OrderDate BETWEEN '4/1/2002' AND '7/1/2002';
```

The results of this new query are shown in Figure 4-32, and the I/O is as follows:

```
Table 'Worktable'. Scan count 0, logical reads 0
Table 'SalesOrderHeader'. Scan count 2, logical reads 62
```

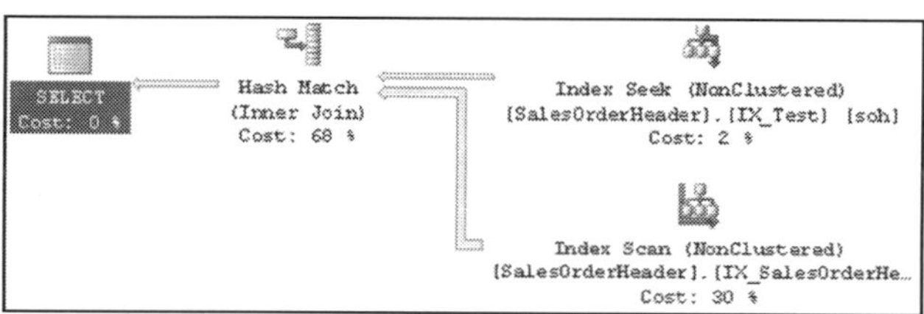

Figure 4-32. *Execution plan with index join through a hint*

The reads have clearly increased, and the estimated costs against the very same indexes that had been picked by the query optimizer are now much higher. Most of the time, the optimizer makes very good choices when it comes to indexes and execution plans. Although query hints are available to allow you to take control from the optimizer, this control can cause as many problems as it solves. In attempting to force an index join as a performance benefit, instead the forced selection of indexes slowed down the execution of the query.

■ **Note** While generating a query execution plan, the SQL Server optimizer goes through the optimization phases not only to determine the type of index and join strategy to be used but also to evaluate the advanced indexing techniques such as index intersection and index join. Therefore, instead of creating wide covering indexes, consider creating multiple narrow indexes. SQL Server can use them together to serve as a covering index yet use them separately where required.

Filtered Indexes

A filtered index is a nonclustered index that uses a filter, basically a WHERE clause, to create a highly selective set of keys against a column or columns that may not have good selectivity otherwise. For example, a column with a large number of null values may be stored as a sparse column to reduce the overhead of those null values. Adding a filtered index to the column will allow you to have an index available on the data that is not `null`. The best way to understand this is to see it in action.

The `Sales.SalesOrderHeader` table has more than 30,000 rows. Of those rows, 27,000 have a `null` value in the `PurchaseOrderNumber` column and the `SalesPersonId` column. If you wanted to get a simple list of purchase order numbers, the query might look like this:

```
SELECT  soh.PurchaseOrderNumber
       ,soh.OrderDate
       ,soh.ShipDate
       ,soh.SalesPersonID
FROM    Sales.SalesOrderHeader AS soh
WHERE   PurchaseOrderNumber LIKE 'PO5%'
        AND soh.SalesPersonID IS NOT NULL;
```

Running the query results in, as you might expect, a clustered index scan, and the following I/O and execution time, as shown in Figure 4-33:

```
Table 'SalesOrderHeader'. Scan count 1, logical reads 686
CPU time = 0 ms,  elapsed time = 619 ms.
```

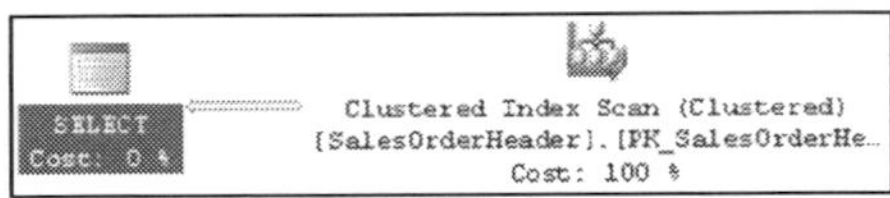

Figure 4-33. *Execution plan without an index*

To fix this, it is possible to create an index and include some of the columns from the query to make this a covering index:

```
CREATE NONCLUSTERED INDEX IX_Test ON Sales.SalesOrderHeader(PurchaseOrderNumber
    ,SalesPersonId)
INCLUDE (OrderDate,ShipDate);
```

When you rerun the query, the performance improvement is fairly radical (see Figure 4-33 and the I/O and time in the following result):

```
Table 'SalesOrderHeader'. Scan count 1, logical reads 5
CPU time = 0 ms,  elapsed time = 139 ms.
```

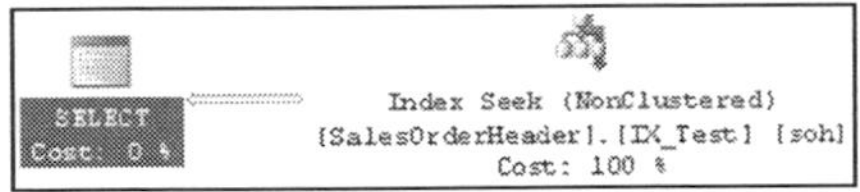

Figure 4-34. *Execution plan with a covering index*

As you can see, the covering index dropped the reads from 686 down to 5 and the time from 619 ms to 139 ms. Normally, this would be enough. Assume for a moment that this query has to be called frequently. Very frequently. Now, every bit of speed you can wring from it will pay dividends. Knowing that so much of the data in the indexed columns is `null`, you can adjust the index so that it filters out the null values, which aren't used by the index anyway, reducing the size of the tree and therefore the amount of searching required:

```
CREATE NONCLUSTERED INDEX IX_Test ON
Sales.SalesOrderHeader(PurchaseOrderNumber
    ,SalesPersonId)
INCLUDE (OrderDate,ShipDate)
WHERE PurchaseOrderNumber IS NOT NULL
AND SalesPersonId IS NOT NULL
WITH (DROP_EXISTING = ON);
```

The final run of the query is visible in the following result and in Figure 4-35:

```
Table 'SalesOrderHeader'. Scan count 1, logical reads 4
CPU time = 0 ms,  elapsed time = 36 ms.
```

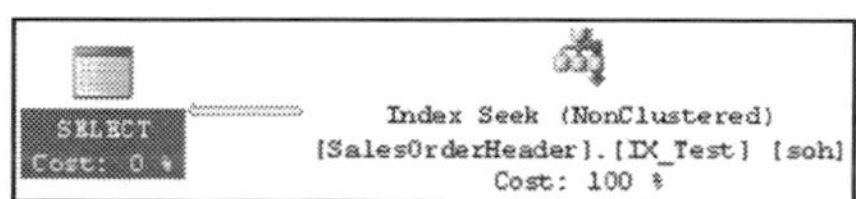

Figure 4-35. *Execution plan with a filtered index*

Although in terms of sheer numbers reducing the reads from 5 to 4 isn't much, it is a 20 percent reduction in the I/O cost of the query, and if this query were running hundreds or even thousands of times in a minute, as some queries do, that 20 percent reduction would be a great payoff indeed. The real payoff is visible in the execution time, which dropped again from 139 ms to 36 ms.

Filtered indexes pay off in many ways:

- Improving the efficiency of queries by reducing the size of the index
- Reducing storage costs by making smaller indexes
- Cutting down on the costs of index maintenance because of the reduced size

One of the first places suggested for their use is just like the previous example, eliminating null values from the index. You can also isolate frequently accessed sets of data with a special index so that the queries against that data perform much faster. You can use the WHERE clause to filter data in a fashion similar to creating an indexed view (covered in more detail in the "Indexed Views" section) without the data maintenance headaches associated with indexed views by creating a filtered index that is a covering index, just like the earlier example.

Filtered indexes require a specific set of ANSI settings when they are accessed or created:

- ON: ANSI_NULLS, ANSI_PADDING, ANSI_WARNINGS, ARITHABORT, CONCAT_NULL_YIELDS_NULL, QUOTED_IDENTIFIER
- OFF: NUMERIC_ROUNDABORT

When completed, drop the testing index:

```
DROP INDEX Sales.SalesOrderHeader.IX_Test;
```

Indexed Views

A database view in SQL Server is like a virtual table that represents the output of a SELECT statement. You create a view using the CREATE VIEW statement, and you can query it exactly like a table. In general, a view doesn't store any data—only the SELECT statement associated with it. Every time a view is queried, it further queries the underlying tables by executing its associated SELECT statement.

A database view can be materialized on the disk by creating a unique clustered index on the view. Such a view is referred to as an *indexed view* or a *materialized view*. After a unique clustered index is created on the view, the view's result set is materialized immediately and persisted in physical storage in the database, saving the overhead of performing costly operations during query execution. After the view is materialized, multiple nonclustered indexes can be created on the indexed view.

Benefit

You can use an indexed view to increase the performance of a query in the following ways:

- Aggregations can be precomputed and stored in the indexed view to minimize expensive computations during query execution.
- Tables can be prejoined, and the resulting data set can be materialized.
- Combinations of joins or aggregations can be materialized.

Overhead

Indexed views can produce major overhead on an OLTP database. Some of the overheads of indexed views are as follows:

- Any change in the base table(s) has to be reflected in the indexed view by executing the view's SELECT statement.
- Any changes to a base table on which an indexed view is defined may initiate one or more changes in the nonclustered indexes of the indexed view. The clustered index will also have to be changed if the clustering key is updated.
- The indexed view adds to the ongoing maintenance overhead of the database.
- Additional storage is required in the database.

The restrictions on creating an indexed view include the following:

- The first index on the view must be a unique clustered index.
- Nonclustered indexes on an indexed view can be created only after the unique clustered index is created.
- The view definition must be *deterministic*—that is, it is able to return only one possible result for a given query. (A list of deterministic and nondeterministic functions is provided in SQL Server Books Online.)
- The indexed view must reference only base tables in the same database, not other views.
- The indexed view may contain float columns. However, such columns cannot be included in the clustered index key.

- The indexed view must be a schema bound to the tables referred to in the view to prevent modifications of the table schema.
- There are several restrictions on the syntax of the view definition. (A list of the syntax limitations on the view definition is provided in SQL Server Books Online.)
- The list of SET options that must be fixed are as follows:
    - ON: ARITHABORT, CONCAT_NULL_YIELDS_NULL, QUOTED_IDENTIFIER, ANSI_NULLS, ANSI_PADDING, and ANSI_WARNING
    - OFF: NUMERIC_ROUNDABORT

Usage Scenarios

Reporting systems benefit the most from indexed views. OLTP systems with frequent writes may not be able to take advantage of the indexed views because of the increased maintenance cost associated with updating both the view and the underlying base tables. The net performance improvement provided by an indexed view is the difference between the total query execution savings offered by the view and the cost of storing and maintaining the view.

An indexed view need not be referenced in the query for the query optimizer to use it during query execution. This allows existing applications to benefit from the newly created indexed views without changing those applications. The query optimizer considers indexed views only for queries with nontrivial cost.

Let's see how indexed views work with the following example. Consider the three queries in Listings 4-1 through 4-3.

Listing 4-1. *Query1.sql*

```
SELECT  p.[Name] AS ProductName
       ,SUM(pod.OrderQty) AS OrderQty
       ,SUM(pod.ReceivedQty) AS ReceivedQty
       ,SUM(pod.RejectedQty) AS RejectedQty
FROM    Purchasing.PurchaseOrderDetail AS pod
        JOIN Production.Product AS p
        ON p.ProductID = pod.ProductID
GROUP BY p.[Name]
```

Listing 4-2. *Query2.sql*

```
SELECT  p.[Name] AS ProductName
       ,SUM(pod.OrderQty) AS OrderQty
       ,SUM(pod.ReceivedQty) AS ReceivedQty
       ,SUM(pod.RejectedQty) AS RejectedQty
FROM    Purchasing.PurchaseOrderDetail AS pod
        JOIN Production.Product AS p
        ON p.ProductID = pod.ProductID
GROUP BY p.[Name]
HAVING (SUM(pod.RejectedQty)/SUM(pod.ReceivedQty)) > .08
```

Listing 4-3. *Query3.sql*

```
SELECT  p.[Name] AS ProductName
       ,SUM(pod.OrderQty) AS OrderQty
       ,SUM(pod.ReceivedQty) AS ReceivedQty
       ,SUM(pod.RejectedQty) AS RejectedQty
FROM    Purchasing.PurchaseOrderDetail AS pod
        JOIN Production.Product AS p
        ON p.ProductID = pod.ProductID
WHERE p.[Name] LIKE 'Chain%'
GROUP BY p.[Name]
```

All the three queries use the aggregation function SUM on columns of the PurchaseOrderDetail table. Therefore, you can create an indexed view to precompute these aggregations and minimize the cost of these complex computations during query execution.

Listings 4-4 through 4-6 show the number of logical reads performed by these queries to access the appropriate tables.

Listing 4-4. *Logical Reads by Query1*

```
Table 'Worktable'. Scan count 0, logical reads 0
Table 'Product'. Scan count 1, logical reads 5
Table 'PurchaseOrderDetail'. Scan count 1, logical reads 66
CPU time = 15 ms,  elapsed time = 100 ms.
```

Listing 4-5. *Logical Reads by Query2*

```
Table 'Worktable'. Scan count 0, logical reads 0
Table 'Product'. Scan count 1, logical reads 5
Table 'PurchaseOrderDetail'. Scan count 1, logical reads 66
CPU time = 16 ms,  elapsed time = 10 ms.
```

Listing 4-6. *Logical Reads by Query3*

```
Table 'PurchaseOrderDetail'. Scan count 5, logical reads 894
Table 'Product'. Scan count 1, logical reads 2
CPU time = 0 ms,  elapsed time = 46 ms.
```

Create an indexed view to precompute the costly computations and join the tables (odView.sql in the download):

```
IF EXISTS ( SELECT  *
            FROM    sys.views
            WHERE   object_id = OBJECT_ID(N'[Purchasing].[IndexedView]') )
    DROP VIEW [Purchasing].[IndexedView]
GO
CREATE VIEW Purchasing.IndexedView
WITH SCHEMABINDING
```

```
AS  SELECT  pod.ProductID
            ,SUM(pod.OrderQty) AS OrderQty
            ,SUM(pod.ReceivedQty) AS ReceivedQty
            ,SUM(pod.RejectedQty) AS RejectedQty
            ,COUNT_BIG(*) AS [Count]
    FROM    Purchasing.PurchaseOrderDetail AS pod
    GROUP BY pod.ProductID
GO
CREATE UNIQUE CLUSTERED INDEX iv ON Purchasing.IndexedView (ProductId) ;
GO
```

Certain constructs such as AVG are disallowed. (For the complete list of disallowed constructs, refer to SQL Server Books Online.) If aggregates are included in the view, as in this one, you must include COUNT_BIG by default.

The indexed view materializes the output of the aggregate functions on the disk. This eliminates the need for computing the aggregate functions during the execution of a query interested in the aggregate outputs. For example, Query3.sql requests the sum of ReceivedQty and RejectedQty for certain products from the PurchaseOrderDetail table. Because these values are materialized in the indexed view for every product in the PurchaseOrderDetail table, you can fetch these preaggregated values using the following SELECT statement on the indexed view:

```
SELECT ProductID,
       ReceivedQty,
       RejectedQty
  FROM Purchasing.IndexedView
```

As shown in the execution plan in Figure 4-36, the SELECT statement retrieves the values directly from the indexed view without accessing the base table (PurchaseOrderDetail).

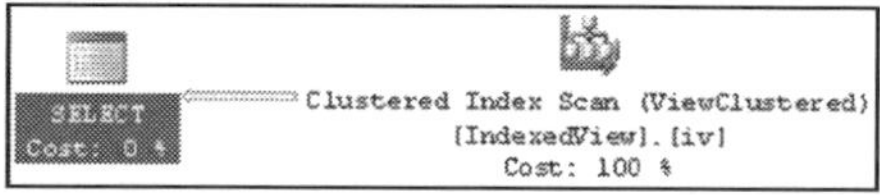

Figure 4-36. *Execution plan with an indexed view*

The indexed view benefits not only the queries based on the view directly but also other queries that may be interested in the materialized data. For example, with the indexed view in place, the three queries on PurchaseOrderDetail benefit without being rewritten (see the execution plan in Figure 4-37 for the execution plan from the first query), and the number of logical reads decreases, as shown in Listings 4-7 through 4-9.

Listing 4-7. *Logical Reads by Query1 with an Indexed View*

```
Table 'Product'. Scan count 1, logical reads 13
Table 'IndexedView'. Scan count 1, logical reads 4
CPU time = 0 ms,  elapsed time = 48 ms.
```

Listing 4-8. *Logical Reads by Query2 with an Indexed View*

```
Table 'Product'. Scan count 1, logical reads 13
Table 'IndexedView'. Scan count 1, logical reads 4
CPU time = 0 ms,  elapsed time = 0 ms.
```

Listing 4-9. *Logical Reads by Query3 with an Indexed View*

```
Table 'IndexedView'. Scan count 0, logical reads 10
Table 'Product'. Scan count 1, logical reads 2
CPU time = 0 ms,  elapsed time = 16 ms.
```

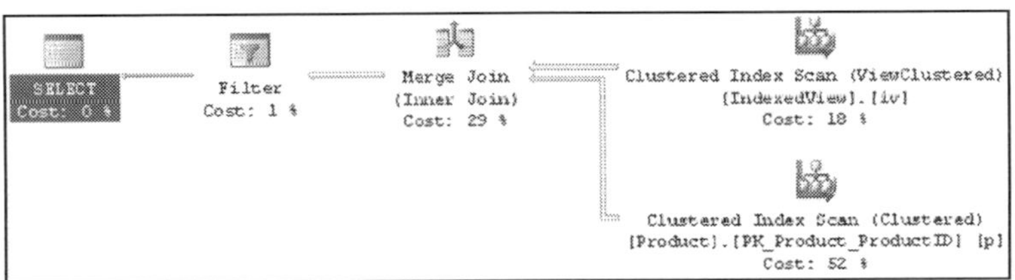

Figure 4-37. *Execution plan with the indexed view automatically used*

Even though the queries are not modified to refer to the new indexed view, the optimizer still uses the indexed view to improve performance. Thus, even existing queries in the database application can benefit from new indexed views without any modifications to the queries.

Index Compression

Data and index compression was introduced in SQL Server 2008 (available in the Enterprise and Developer Editions). *Compressing* an index means getting more key information onto a single page. This can lead to serious performance improvements because fewer pages and fewer index levels are needed to store the index. There will be overhead in the CPU and memory as the key values in the index are compressed and decompressed, so this may not be a solution for all indexes.

By default, an index will be not be compressed. You have to explicitly call for the index to be compressed when you create the index. There are two types of compression: row- and page-level compression. Nonleaf pages in an index receive no compression under the page type. To see it in action, consider the following index (don't run this code since the index already exists):

```
CREATE NONCLUSTERED INDEX [IX_Test] ON
 [Person].[Address] ([City] ASC, [PostalCode] ASC)
```

This index was created earlier in the chapter. If you were to re-create it as defined here

```
CREATE NONCLUSTERED INDEX IX_Comp_Test
ON Person.Address ([City],[PostalCode])
WITH ( DATA_COMPRESSION = ROW ) ;
```

this creates a row type of compression on an index with the same two columns as the first test index IX_Test.

Create one more index:

```
CREATE NONCLUSTERED INDEX IX_Comp_Page_Test
ON Person.Address ([City],[PostalCode])
WITH ( DATA_COMPRESSION = PAGE ) ;
```

To examine the indexes being stored, modify the original query against sys.dm_db_index_physical_stats to add another column, compressed_page_count:

```
SELECT  i.Name
       ,i.type_desc
       ,s.page_count
       ,s.record_count
       ,s.index_level
       ,compressed_page_count
FROM    sys.indexes i
        JOIN sys.dm_db_index_physical_stats(DB_ID(N'AdventureWorks2008'),
                                            OBJECT_ID(N'Person.Address'), NULL,
                                            NULL, 'DETAILED') AS s
        ON i.index_id = s.index_id
WHERE   i.OBJECT_ID = OBJECT_ID(N'Person.Address')
```

Running the query, you get the results in Figure 4-38.

	Name	type_desc	page_count	record_count	index_level	compressed_page_count
1	PK_Address_AddressID	CLUSTERED	340	19614	0	0
2	PK_Address_AddressID	CLUSTERED	1	340	1	0
3	PK_Address_AddressID	CLUSTERED	1	0	0	NULL
4	PK_Address_AddressID	CLUSTERED	1	0	0	NULL
5	AK_Address_rowguid	NONCLUSTERED	56	19614	0	0
6	AK_Address_rowguid	NONCLUSTERED	1	56	1	0
7	IX_Address_AddressLine1_AddressLine2_City_StateP...	NONCLUSTERED	211	19614	0	0
8	IX_Address_AddressLine1_AddressLine2_City_StateP...	NONCLUSTERED	3	211	1	0
9	IX_Address_AddressLine1_AddressLine2_City_StateP...	NONCLUSTERED	1	3	2	0
10	IX_Address_StateProvinceID	NONCLUSTERED	27	19614	0	0
11	IX_Address_StateProvinceID	NONCLUSTERED	1	27	1	0
12	IX_Test	NONCLUSTERED	99	19614	0	0
13	IX_Test	NONCLUSTERED	1	99	1	0
14	IX_Comp_Test	NONCLUSTERED	102	19614	0	0
15	IX_Comp_Test	NONCLUSTERED	1	102	1	0
16	IX_Comp_Page_Test	NONCLUSTERED	27	19614	0	26
17	IX_Comp_Page_Test	NONCLUSTERED	1	27	1	0

Figure 4-38. *sys.dm_db_index_physical_stats output about compressed indexes*

For this index, you can see that the page compression was able move the index from 99 pages down to 27, of which 26 were compressed. The row type compression in this instance didn't make much of a difference; in fact, the overhead associated with compression increased the number of pages it took to define the index.

To see the compression in action, run the following query:

```
SELECT a.City,a.PostalCode
FROM Person.Address AS a
WHERE a.City = 'Newton'
AND a.PostalCode = 'V2M1N7'
```

The optimizer chose, on my system, to use the IX_Comp_Page_Test index. Even if I forced it to use the IX_Test index, thusly,

```
SELECT a.City,a.PostalCode
FROM Person.Address AS a WITH(INDEX = IX_Test)
WHERE a.City = 'Newton'
AND a.PostalCode = 'V2M1N7'
```

the performance was identical. So although one index is taking up radically less room on approximately one quarter as many pages, it's done at no cost in performance.

Compression has a series of impacts on other processes within SQL Server, so further understanding of the possible impacts as well as the possible benefits should be explored thoroughly prior to implementation.

Clean up the indexes after you finish testing:

```
DROP INDEX Person.Address.IX_Test;
DROP INDEX Person.Address.IX_Comp_Test;
DROP INDEX Person.Address IX_Comp_Page_Test;
```

Special Index Types

As special data types and storage mechanisms are introduced to SQL Server by Microsoft, methods for indexing these special storage types are also developed. Explaining all the details possible for each of these special index types is outside the scope of the book. In the following sections, I introduce the basic concepts of each index type in order to facilitate the possibility of their use in tuning your queries.

Full-Text

You can store large amounts of text in SQL Server by using the MAX value in the VARCHAR, NVARCHAR, CHAR, and NCHAR fields. A normal clustered or nonclustered index against these large fields would be unsupportable because a single value can far exceed the page size within an index. So, a different mechanism of indexing text is to use the Full-Text Engine, which must be running to work with full-text indexes. You can also build a full-text index on VARBINARY data.

You need to have one column on the table that is unique. The best candidates for performance are integers: INT or BIGINT. This column is then used along with the word to identify which row within the table it belongs to, as well as its location within the field. SQL Server allows for incremental changes, either change tracking or time based, to the full-text indexes as well as complete rebuilds.

For more details, check out *Pro Full-Text Search in SQL Server 2008* by Hilary Cotter and Michael Coles (Apress, 2008).

Spatial

Introduced in SQL Server 2008 is the ability to store spatial data. This data can be either a geometry type or the very complex geographical type, literally identifying a point on the earth. To say the least, indexing this type of data is complicated. SQL Server stores these indexes in a flat B-tree, similar to regular indexes, except that it is also a hierarchy of four grids linked together. Each of the grids can be given a density of low, medium, or high, outlining how big each grid is. From there it begins to get truly complicated. Suffice to say, there are mechanisms to support indexing of the spatial data types so that different types of queries, such as finding when one object is within the boundaries or near another object, can benefit from performance increases inherent in indexing.

A spatial index can be created only against a column of type geometry or geography. It has to be on a base table, it must have no indexed views, and the table must have a primary key. You can create up to 249 spatial indexes on any given column on a table. Different indexes are used to define different types of index behavior. More information is available in the book *Beginning Spatial with SQL Server 2008* by Alastair Aitchison (Apress, 2009).

XML

Introduced as a data type in SQL Server 2005, XML can be stored not as text but as well-formed XML data within SQL Server. This data can be queries using the XQuery language as supported by SQL Server. To enhance the performance capabilities, a special set of indexes has been defined. An XML column can have one primary and several secondary indexes. The primary XML shreds the properties, attributes, and elements of the XML data and stores it as an internal table. There must be a primary key on the table, and that primary key must be clustered in order to create an XML index. After the XML index is created, the secondary indexes can be created. These indexes have types `Path`, `Value`, and `Property`, depending on how you query the XML. For more details, check out *Pro SQL Server 2008 XML* by Michael Coles (Apress, 2008).

Additional Characteristics of Indexes

Other index properties can affect performance, positively and negatively. A few of these behaviors are explored here.

Different Column Sort Order

SQL Server supports creating a composite index with a different sort order for the different columns of the index. Suppose you want an index with the first column sorted in ascending order and the second column sorted in descending order. You could achieve this as follows:

```
CREATE NONCLUSTERED INDEX i1 ON t1(c1 ASC, c2 DESC)
```

Index on Computed Columns

You can create an index on a computed column, as long as the expression defined for the computed column meets certain restrictions, such as that it references columns only from the table containing the computed column and it is deterministic.

Index on BIT Data Type Columns

SQL Server allows you to create an index on columns with the `BIT` data type. The ability to create an index on a `BIT` data type column by itself is not a big advantage since such a column can have only two unique values. As mentioned previously, columns with such low selectivity (number of unique values) are not usually good candidates for indexing. However, this feature comes into its own when you consider covering indexes. Because covering indexes require including all the columns in the index, the ability to add the `BIT` data type column to an index allows covering indexes to include such a column, if required.

CREATE INDEX Statement Processed As a Query

The `CREATE INDEX` operation is integrated into the query processor. The optimizer can use existing index(es) to reduce scan cost and sort while creating an index.

Take, for example, the `Person.Address` table. A nonclustered index exists on a number of columns: `AddressLine1`, `AddressLine2`, `City`, `StateProvinceId`, and `PostalCode`. If you needed to run queries against the `City` column with the existing index, you'll get a scan of that index. Now create a new index like this:

```
CREATE INDEX IX_Test ON Person.Address(City)
```

You can see in Figure 4-39 that, instead of scanning the table, the optimizer chose to scan the index in order to create the new index because the column needed for the new index was contained within the other nonclustered index.

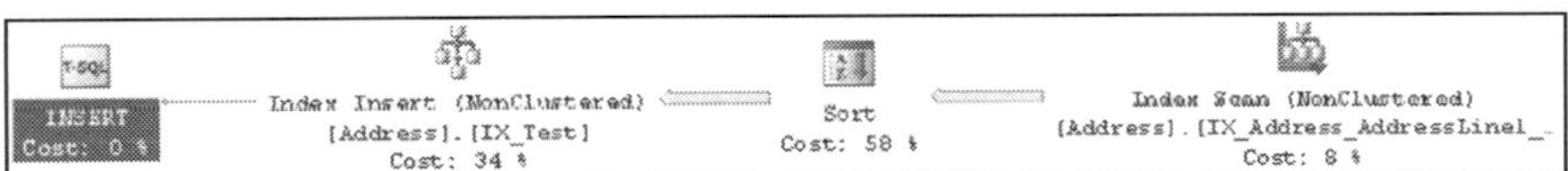

Figure 4-39. *Execution plan for* `CREATE INDEX`

Parallel Index Creation

SQL Server supports parallel plans for a `CREATE INDEX` statement, as supported in other SQL queries. On a multiprocessor machine, index creation won't be restricted to a single processor but will benefit from the multiple processors. You can control the number of processors to be used in a `CREATE INDEX` statement with the `max degree of parallelism` configuration parameter of SQL Server. The default value for this parameter is 0, as you can see by executing the `sp_configure` stored procedure:

```
EXEC sp_configure 'max degree of parallelism'
```

The default value of 0 means that SQL Server can use all the available CPUs in the system for the parallel execution of a T-SQL statement. On a system with four processors, the maximum degree of parallelism can be set to 2 by executing `sp_configure`:

```
EXEC sp_configure 'max degree of parallelism', 2
RECONFIGURE WITH OVERRIDE
```

This allows SQL Server to use up to two CPUs for the parallel execution of a T-SQL statement. This configuration setting takes effect immediately, without a server restart.

The query hint `MAXDOP` can be used for the `CREATE INDEX` statement. Also, be aware that the parallel `CREATE INDEX` feature is available only in SQL Server 2005 and 2008 Enterprise Editions.

Online Index Creation

The default creation of an index is done as an offline operation. This means that exclusive locks are placed on the table, restricting user access while the index is created. It is possible to create the indexes as an online operation. This allows users to continue to access the data while the index is being created. This comes at the cost of increasing the amount of time and resources it takes to create the index. Online index operations are available only in SQL Server 2005 and 2008 Enterprise Editions.

Considering the Database Engine Tuning Advisor

A simple approach to indexing is to use the Database Engine Tuning Advisor tool provided by SQL Server. This tool is a usage-based tool that looks at a particular workload and works with the query optimizer to determine the costs associated with various index combinations. Based on the tool's analysis, you can add or drop indexes as appropriate.

■ **Note** I will cover the Database Engine Tuning Advisor tool in more depth in Chapter 5.

Summary

In this chapter, you learned that indexing is an effective method for reducing the number of logical reads and disk I/O for a query. Although an index may add overhead to action queries, even action queries such as `UPDATE` and `DELETE` can benefit from an index.

To decide the index key columns for a particular query, evaluate the `WHERE` clause and the join criteria of the query. Factors such as column selectivity, width, data type, and column order are important in deciding the columns in an index key. Since an index is mainly useful in retrieving a small number of rows, the selectivity of an indexed column should be very high. It is important to note that nonclustered indexes contain the value of a clustered index key as their row locator, because this behavior greatly influences the selection of an index type.

For better performance, try to cover a query fully using a covering index. Since SQL Server can benefit from multiple indexes, use the index intersection and index join techniques, and consider having multiple narrow indexes instead of one very wide index. When working with special data types, apply the indexes that work with those special data types in order to help performance.

In the next chapter, you will learn more about the Database Engine Tuning Advisor, the SQL Server-provided tool that can help you determine the correct indexes in a database for a given SQL workload.

CHAPTER 5

Database Engine Tuning Advisor

SQL Server's performance largely depends upon having proper indexes on the database tables. However, as the workload and data change over time, the existing indexes may not be entirely appropriate, and new indexes may be required. The task of deciding upon the correct indexes is complicated by the fact that an index change that benefits one set of queries may be detrimental to another set of queries.

To help you through this process, SQL Server provides a tool called the Database Engine Tuning Advisor. This tool helps identify an optimal set of indexes and statistics for a given workload without requiring an expert understanding of the database schema, workload, or SQL Server internals. It can also recommend tuning options for a small set of problem queries. In addition to the tool's benefits, I cover its limitations in this chapter, because it is a tool that can cause more harm than good if used incorrectly.

In this chapter, I cover the following topics:

- How the Database Engine Tuning Advisor works
- How to use the Database Engine Tuning Advisor on a set of problematic queries for index recommendations, including how to define traces
- The limitations of the Database Engine Tuning Advisor

Database Engine Tuning Advisor Mechanisms

You can run the Database Engine Tuning Advisor directly by selecting Microsoft SQL Server 2008 ➤ Performance Tools ➤ Database Engine Tuning Advisor. You can also run it from the command prompt (`dta.exe`), from SQL Profiler (Tools ➤ Database Engine Tuning Advisor), from a query in Management Studio (highlight the required query, and select Query ➤ Analyze Query in Database Engine Tuning Advisor), or from Management Studio (select Tools ➤ Database Engine Tuning Advisor). Once the tool is opened and you're connected to a server, you should see a window like the one in Figure 5-1. I'll run through the options to define and run an analysis in this section and then follow up in the next session with some detailed examples.

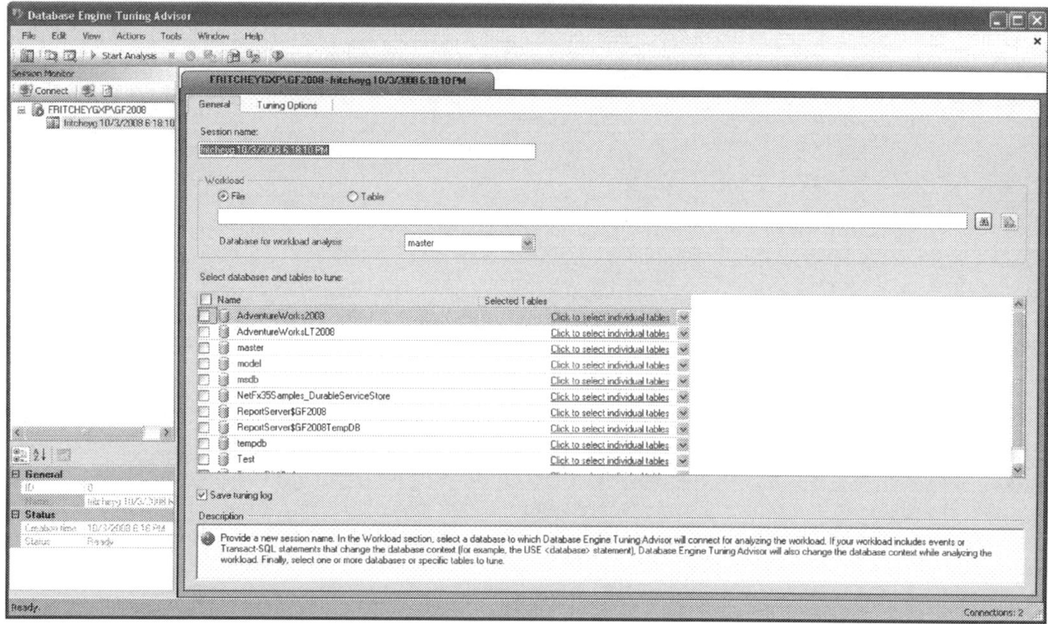

Figure 5-1. *Selecting the server and database in the Database Engine Tuning Advisor*

The Database Engine Tuning Advisor is already connected to a server. From here, you begin to outline the workload and the objects you want to tune. Creating a session name is necessary to label the session for documentation purposes. Then you need to pick a workload, either a file or a table, and browse to the appropriate location. The workload is defined depending on how you launched the Database Engine Tuning Advisor. If you launched it from a query window, you would see a Query radio button, and the File and Table radio buttons would be disabled. You also have to define the Database for Workload Analysis setting and finally select a database to tune.

Tip The Database Engine Tuning Advisor recommends indexed views only for platforms that support them. SQL Server 2008 Enterprise Edition does, but Standard Edition doesn't.

When you select a database, you can also select individual tables to be tuned by clicking the drop-down box on the right side of the screen; you'll see a list of tables like those shown in Figure 5-2.

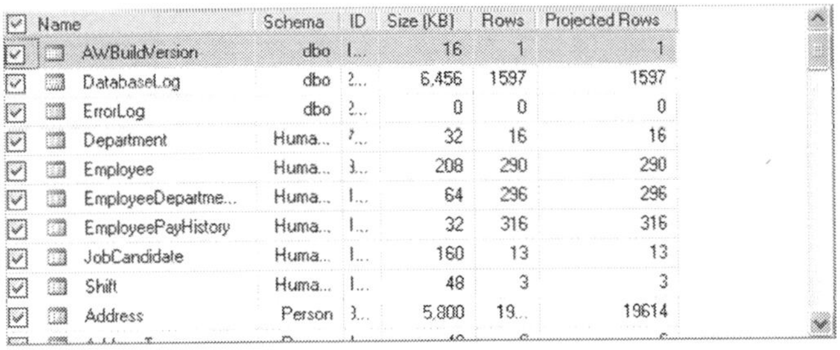

Figure 5-2. *Clicking the boxes defines individual tables for tuning in the Database Engine Tuning Advisor.*

Once you define the workload, you need to select the Tuning Options tab, which is shown in Figure 5-3.

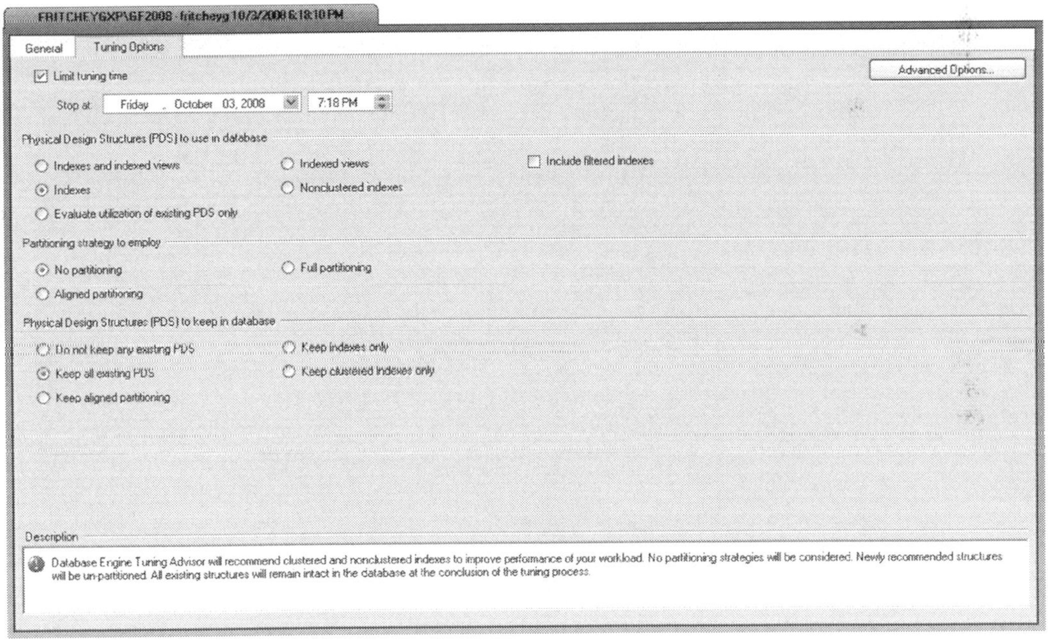

Figure 5-3. *Defining options in the Database Engine Tuning Advisor*

You define the length of time you want the Database Engine Tuning Advisor to run by selecting Limit Tuning Time and then defining a date and time for the tuning to stop. The longer the Database Engine Tuning Advisor runs, the better recommendations it should make. You pick the type of physical design structures to be considered for creation by the Database Engine Tuning Advisor, and you can also set the partitioning strategy so that the tuning advisor knows whether it should consider partitioning the tables and indexes as part of the analysis. Just remember, partitioning isn't necessarily a desirable outcome if your data and structures don't warrant it. Finally, you can define the physical design structures that you want left alone within the database. Changing these options will narrow or widen the choices that the Database Engine Tuning Advisor can make to improve performance.

You can click the Advanced Options button to see even more options, as shown in Figure 5-4.

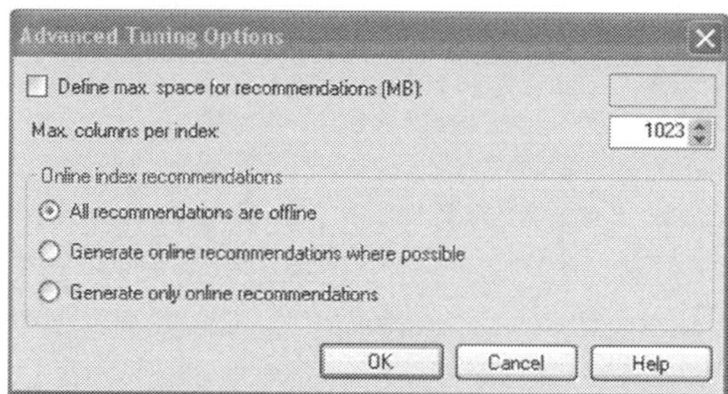

Figure 5-4. *Advanced Tuning Options dialog box*

This dialog box allows you to limit the space of the recommendations and the number of columns that can be included in an index. Finally, you can define whether the new indexes or changes in indexes are done as an online or offline index operation.

Once you've appropriately defined all of these settings, you can start the Database Engine Tuning Advisor by clicking the Start Analysis button. The sessions created are kept in the `msdb` database for any server instance that you run the Database Engine Tuning Advisor against. It displays details about what is being analyzed and the progress made, which you can see in Figure 5-5.

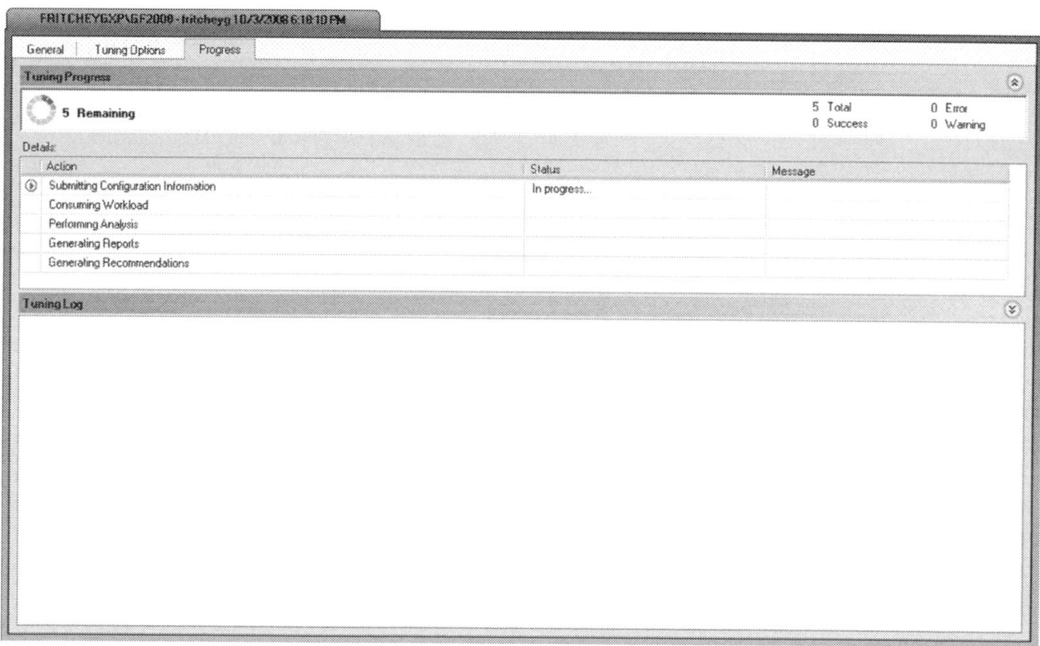

Figure 5-5. *Tuning progress*

You'll see more detailed examples of the progress displayed in the example analysis in the next session.

After the analysis completes, you'll get a list of recommendations (visible in Figure 5-6), and a number of reports become available. Table 5-1 describes the reports.

Table 5-1. *Database Engine Tuning Advisor Reports*

Report Name	Report Description
Column Access	Lists the columns and tables referenced in the workload.
Database Access	Lists each database referenced in the workload and percentage of workload statements for each database.
Event Frequency	Lists all events in the workload ordered by frequency of occurrence.
Index Detail (Current)	Defines indexes and their properties referenced by the workload.
Index Detail (Recommended)	Is the same as the Index Detail (Current) report but shows the information about the indexes recommended by the Database Engine Tuning Advisor.
Index Usage (Current)	Lists the indexes and the percentage of their use referenced by the workload.
Index Usage (Recommended)	Is the same as the Index Usage (Current) report but from the recommended indexes.
Statement Cost	Lists the performance improvements for each statement if the recommendations are implemented.
Statement Cost Range	Breaks down the costs improvements by percentiles to show how much benefit you can achieve for any given set of changes.
Statement Detail	Lists the statements in the workload, their cost, and the reduced cost if the recommendations are implemented.
Statement-to-Index Relationship	Lists the indexes referenced by individual statements. Current and recommended versions of the report are available.
Table Access	Lists the tables referenced by the workload.
View-to-Table Relationship	Lists the tables referenced by materialized views.
Workload Analysis	Gives details about the workload, including the number of statements, the number of statements whose cost is decreased, and the number where the cost remains the same.

Database Engine Tuning Advisor Examples

The best way to learn how to use the Database Engine Tuning Advisor is to use it. It's not a terribly difficult tool to master, so I recommend opening it and getting started.

Tuning a Query

You can use the Database Engine Tuning Advisor to recommend indexes for a complete database by using a workload that fairly represents all SQL activities. You can also use it to recommend indexes for a set of problematic queries.

To learn how you can use the Database Engine Tuning Advisor to get index recommendations on a set of problematic queries, say you have a simple query that is called rather frequently. Because of the frequency, you want a quick turnaround for some tuning. This is the query:

```
SELECT  soh.DueDate
       ,soh.CustomerID
FROM    Sales.SalesOrderHeader AS soh
WHERE   DueDate BETWEEN '1/1/1970' AND '1/1/1971'
        AND Status > 200
```

To analyze the query, right-click it in the query window, and select Analyze Query in the Database Engine Tuning Advisor. The advisor opens with a window where you can change the session name to something meaningful. In this case, I chose Report Query Round 1 – 10/5/2008. The database and tables don't need to be edited. The first tab, General, will look like Figure 5-6 when you're done.

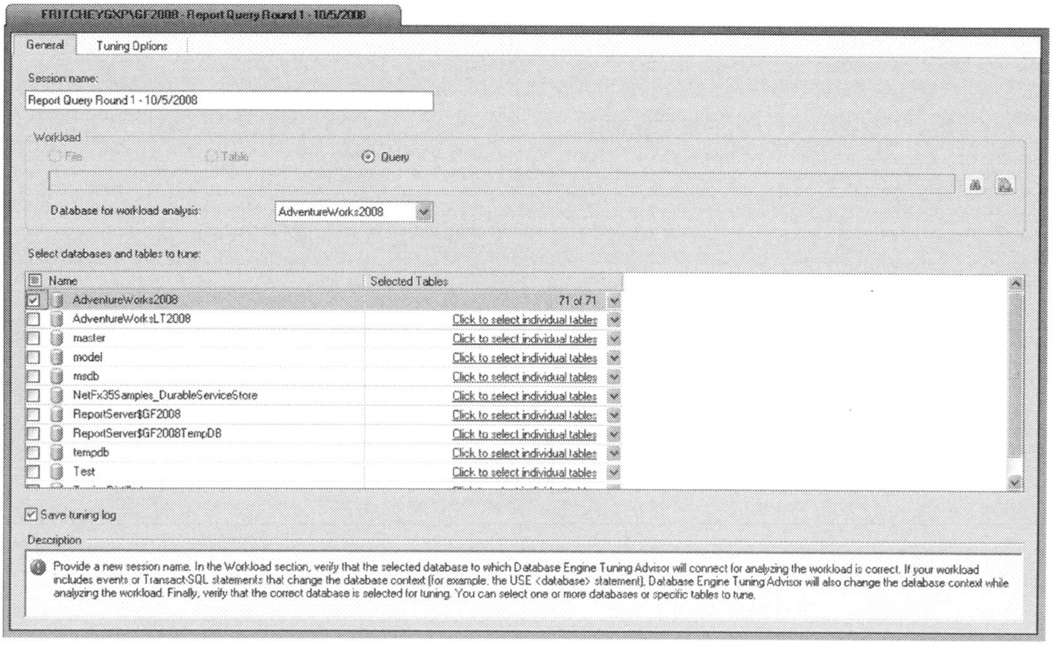

Figure 5-6. *Query tuning general settings*

Because this query is important and tuning it is extremely critical to the business, I'm going to change some settings on the Tuning Options tab. For the purposes of the example, I'm going to let the Database Engine Tuning Advisor run for 15 minutes, but a more realistic approach here would be to let it run for an hour. I'm going to select the Include Filtered Indexes check box so that if a filtered index will help, it can be considered. I'm also going to switch the Partitioning Strategy to Employ setting from No Partitioning to Full Partitioning. Finally, I'm going to allow the Database Engine Tuning Advisor to come up with structural changes if it can find any that will help by switching from Keep All Existing PDS to Do Not Keep Any Existing PDS. Once completed, the Tuning Options tab will look like Figure 5-7.

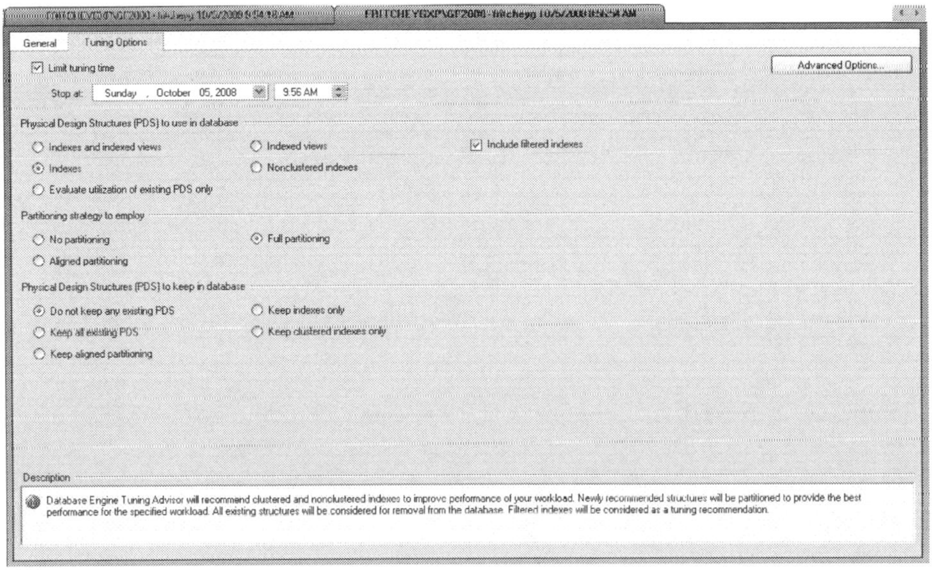

Figure 5-7. *Tuning Options tab adjusted*

After starting the analysis, the progress screen should appear. Although the settings were for 15 minutes of evaluations, it took only about a minute for it to evaluate this query. The initial recommendations were not good. As you can see in Figure 5-8, the Database Engine Tuning Advisor has recommended dropping a huge swath of indexes in the database. This is not the type of recommendation that you want when running the tool.

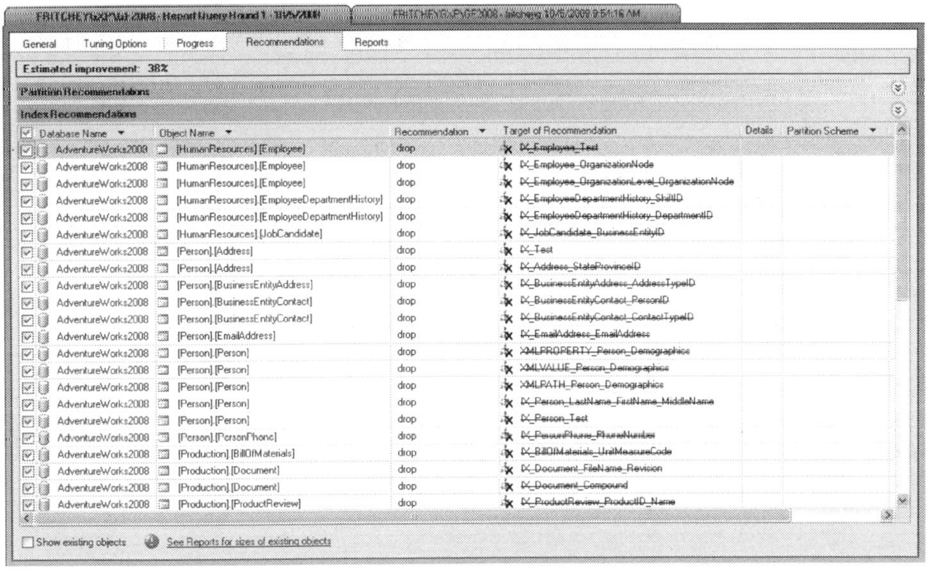

Figure 5-8. *Query tuning initial recommendations*

This is because the Database Engine Tuning Advisor assumes that the load being tested is the full load of the database. If there are indexes not being used, then they should be removed. This is a best practice and one that should be implemented on any database. However, in this case, this is a single query, not a full load of the system. To see whether the advisor can come up with a meaningful recommendation, you must start a new session.

This time, I'll adjust the options so that the Database Engine Tuning Advisor will not be able to drop any of the existing structure. This is set on the Tuning Options tab (shown earlier in Figure 5-7). There I'll change the Physical Design Structure (PDS) to Keep in Database setting from Do Not Keep Any Existing PDS to Keep All Existing PDS. I'll keep the running time the same because the evaluation worked well within the time frame. Running the Database Engine Tuning Advisor again, it finishes in less than a minute and displays the recommendations shown in Figure 5-9.

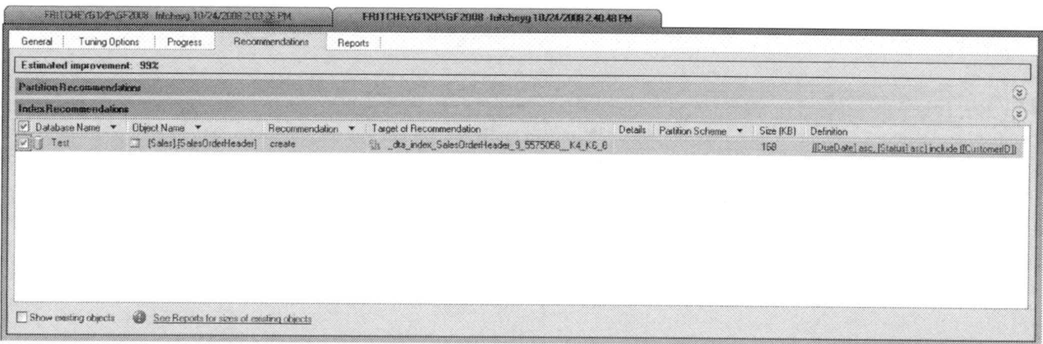

Figure 5-9. *Query tuning recommendations*

The first time through, the Database Engine Tuning Advisor suggested dropping most of the indexes on the tables being tested and a bunch of the related tables. This time it suggests creating a covering index on the two columns referenced in the query. As outlined in Chapter 4, a covering index is one of the most performant methods of indexing. The Database Engine Tuning Advisor was able to recognize that creating an index with all the columns referenced by the query, a covering index, would perform best.

Once you've received a recommendation, you should take a look at the proposed T-SQL command. Finally, you'll want to apply the recommendation. Select Actions ➤ Evaluate Recommendations. This opens a new Database Engine Tuning Advisor session and allows you to evaluate whether the recommendations will work. It looks just like a regular evaluation report. Next select Actions ➤ Apply Recommendation. This opens a dialog box that allows you to apply the recommendation immediately or schedule the application (see Figure 5-10).

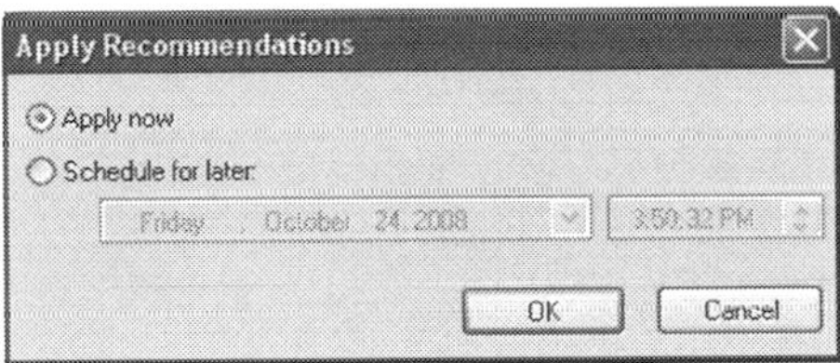

Figure 5-10. *Apply Recommendations dialog box*

If you click the OK button, the Database Engine Tuning Advisor will apply the index to the database where you've been testing queries (see Figure 5-11).

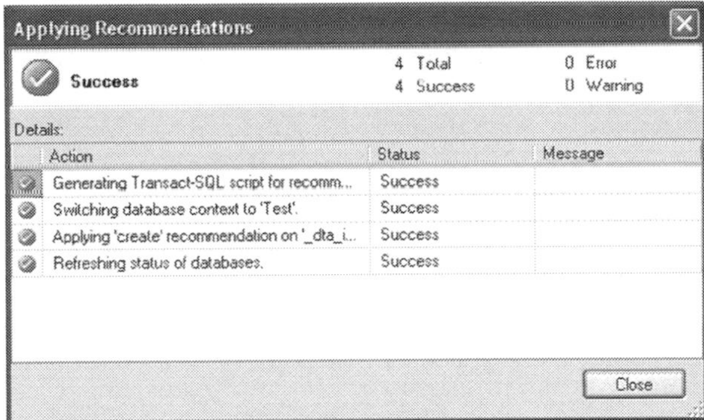

Figure 5-11. *A successful tuning session applied*

After you generate recommendations, you may want to, instead of applying them on the spot, save the T-SQL statements to a file and accumulate a series of changes for release to your production environment during scheduled deployment windows. Remember that applying indexes to tables, especially large tables, can cause a performance impact to processes actively running on the system while the index is being created.

Although getting index suggestions one at a time is nice, it would be better to be able to get large swaths of the database checked all at once. That's where tuning a trace workload comes in.

Tuning a Trace Workload

Capturing a trace from the real-world queries that are running against a production server is a way to feed meaningful data to the Database Engine Tuning Advisor. (Capturing traces was covered in Chapter 3.) The easiest way to define a trace for use in the Database Engine Tuning Advisor is to implement the trace using the Tuning template. Start the trace on the system you need to tune. I generated three different loads by running queries in a loop from the `sqlps.exe` command prompt. This is the PowerShell command prompt with the SQL Server configuration settings. It gets installed with SQL Server.

These are the scripts run (queryload.ps1):

```
$val = 0; while ($val -lt 50) {$val++; Invoke-Sqlcmd
-Server "YourServerName" -Database "AdventureWorks2008"
-InputFile "path\queryload.sql"}
$val = 0; while ($val -lt 20000){$val++; Invoke-sqlcmd
-Server "YourServerName" -Database "AdventureWorks2008"
-Query "EXEC dbo.uspGetEmployeeManagers @BusinessEntityID = $val"}
$val = 0; while ($val -lt 20000){$val++; Invoke-sqlcmd
-Server "YourServerName" -Database "AdventureWorks2008"
-Query "EXEC dbo.uspGetManagerEmployees @BusinessEntityID = $val"}
```

The queryload.sql file is also available in the download file. It's just a collection of queries with various parameters to provide a simulated load.

Note For more information on PowerShell, check out *Pro Windows PowerShell* by Hristo Deshev (Apress, 2008).

Once you've created the trace file, open the Database Engine Tuning Advisor. It defaults to a file type, so you'll only have to browse to the trace file location. Set the appropriate tuning options, and start the analysis. This time, it will take more than a minute to run (see Figure 5-12).

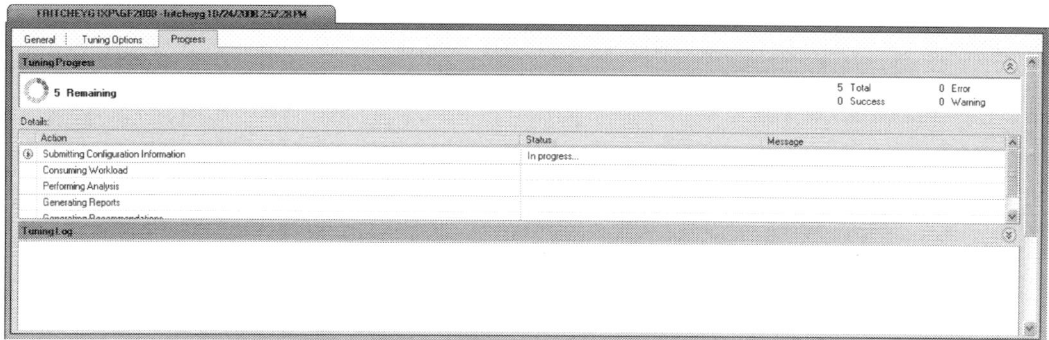

Figure 5-12. *Database tuning engine in progress*

As you can see, simply passing any number to the uspGetEmployeeManagers procedure, and others, can generate instances where no tables were referenced. The processing runs for about 15 minutes on my machine. Then it generates output, shown in Figure 5-13.

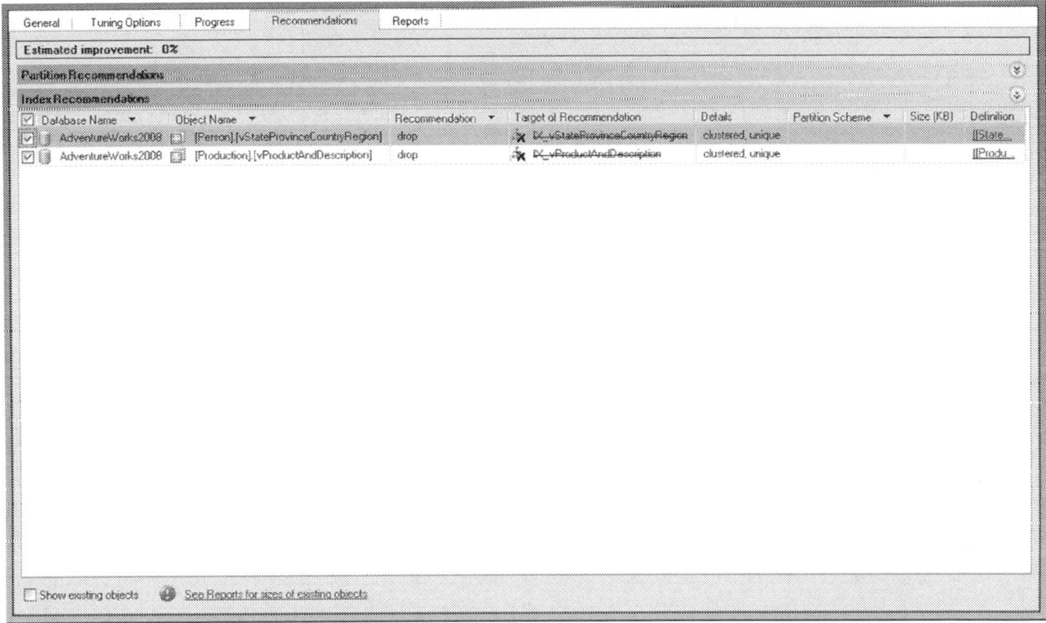

Figure 5-13. *No recommendations*

After running all the queries through the Database Engine Tuning Advisor, the best recommendation it could currently come up with was to drop a couple of indexed views. That doesn't mean there aren't other possible improvements; it just means that the advisor is not always able to recognize all the possible improvements.

Database Engine Tuning Advisor Limitations

The Database Engine Tuning Advisor recommendations are based on the input workload. If the input workload is not a true representation of the actual workload, then the recommended indexes may sometimes have a *negative* effect on some queries that are missing in the workload. But most important, as you saw in the second example of this chapter, the Database Engine Tuning Advisor may not recognize possible tuning opportunities. It has a sophisticated testing engine, but in some scenarios, its capabilities are limited.

For a production server, you should ensure that the SQL trace includes a complete representation of the database workload. For most database applications, capturing a trace for a complete day usually includes most of the queries executed on the database. A few of the other considerations/limitations with the Database Engine Tuning Advisor are as follows:

- *Trace input using the `SQL:BatchCompleted` event*: As mentioned earlier, the SQL trace input to the Database Engine Tuning Advisor must include the `SQL:BatchCompleted` event; otherwise, the wizard won't be able to identify the queries in the workload.
- *Query distribution in the workload*: In a workload, a query may be executed multiple times with the same parameter value. Even a small performance improvement to the most common query can make a bigger contribution to the performance of the overall workload, compared to a large improvement in performance of a query that is executed only once.
- *Index hints*: Index hints in a SQL query can prevent the Database Engine Tuning Advisor from choosing a better execution plan. The wizard includes all index hints used in a SQL query as part of its recommendations. Because these indexes may not be optimal for the table, remove all index hints from queries before submitting the workload to the wizard, bearing in mind that you need to add them back in to see whether they do actually improve performance.

Summary

As you learned in this chapter, the Database Engine Tuning Advisor is a useful tool for analyzing the effectiveness of existing indexes and recommending new indexes for a SQL workload. As the SQL workload changes over time, you can use this tool to determine which existing indexes are no longer in use and which new indexes are required to improve performance. It can be a good idea to run the wizard occasionally just to check that your existing indexes really are the best fit for your current workload. It also provides many useful reports for analyzing the SQL workload and the effectiveness of its own recommendations. Just remember that the limitations of the tool prevent it from spotting all tuning opportunities. If your database is in bad shape, this tool can give you a quick leg up. If you're already monitoring and tuning your queries regularly, you may see no benefit from the recommendations of the Database Engine Tuning Advisor.

Frequently, you will rely on nonclustered indexes to improve the performance of a SQL workload. This assumes that you've already assigned a clustered index to your tables. Because the performance of a nonclustered index is highly dependent on the cost of the bookmark lookup associated with the nonclustered index, you will see in the next chapter how to analyze and resolve a bookmark lookup.

CHAPTER 6

Bookmark Lookup Analysis

To maximize the benefit from nonclustered indexes, you must minimize the cost of the data retrieval as much as possible. A major overhead associated with nonclustered indexes is the cost of excessive key lookups, commonly known as *bookmark lookups*, which are a mechanism to navigate from a nonclustered index row to the corresponding data row in the clustered index or the base table. Therefore, it makes sense to look at the cause of bookmark lookups and to evaluate how to avoid this cost.

In this chapter, I cover the following topics:

- The purpose of bookmark lookups
- Drawbacks of using bookmark lookups
- Analysis of the cause of bookmark lookups
- Techniques to resolve bookmark lookups

Purpose of Bookmark Lookups

When a SQL query requests a small number of rows, the optimizer can use the nonclustered index, if available, on the column(s) in the WHERE or JOIN clause to retrieve the data. If the query refers to columns that are not part of the nonclustered index used to retrieve the data, then navigation is required from the index row to the corresponding data row in the table to access these columns.

For example, in the following SELECT statement, if the nonclustered index used by the optimizer doesn't include all the columns, navigation will be required from a nonclustered index row to the data row in the base table to retrieve the value of those columns:

```
SELECT  p.[Name]
        ,AVG(sod.LineTotal)
FROM    Sales.SalesOrderDetail AS sod
        JOIN Production.Product p
        ON sod.ProductID = p.ProductID
WHERE   sod.ProductID = 776
GROUP BY sod. CarrierTrackingNumber
        ,p.[Name]
HAVING  MAX(OrderQty) > 1
ORDER BY MIN(sod.LineTotal)
```

The `SalesOrderDetail` table has a nonclustered index on the `ProductID` column. The optimizer can use the index to filter the rows from the table. The table has a clustered index on `SalesOrderID` and `SalesOrderDetailID`, so they would be included in the nonclustered index. But since they're not referenced in the query, they won't help the query at all. The other columns (`LineTotal`, `CarrierTrackingNumber`, `OrderQty`, and `LineTotal`) referred to by the query are not available in the nonclustered index. To fetch the values for those columns, navigation from the nonclustered index row to the corresponding data row through the clustered index is required, and this operation is a bookmark lookup. You can see this in action in Figure 6-1.

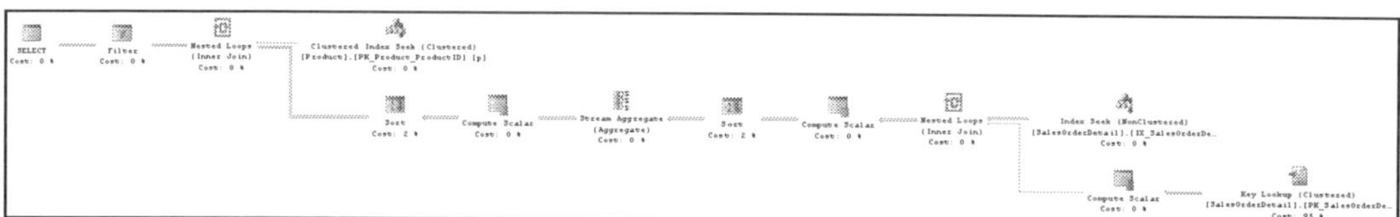

Figure 6-1. *Bookmark lookup in a complicated execution plan*

To better understand how a nonclustered index can cause a bookmark lookup, consider the following `SELECT` statement, which requests only a few rows from the `SalesOrderDetail` table by using a filter criterion on column `ProductID`:

```
SELECT  *
FROM    Sales.SalesOrderDetail AS sod
WHERE   sod.ProductID = 776
```

The optimizer evaluates the `WHERE` clause and finds that the column `ProductID` included in the `WHERE` clause has a nonclustered index on it that filters the number of rows down. Since only a few rows, 223, are requested, retrieving the data through the nonclustered index will be cheaper than scanning the clustered index (containing more than 120,000 rows) to identify the matching rows. The nonclustered index on column `ProductID` will help identify the matching rows quickly. The nonclustered index includes column `ProductID` and the clustered index columns `SalesOrderID` and `SalesOrderDetailID`; all the other columns are not included. Therefore, as you may have guessed, to retrieve the rest of the columns while using the nonclustered index, you require a bookmark lookup.

This is shown in the following metrics and in the execution plan in Figure 6-2 (you can turn on `STATISTICS IO` using the Query ➤ Query Options menu). Look for the `Key Lookup (Clustered)` operator. That is the bookmark lookup in action.

```
Table 'SalesOrderDetail'. Scan count 1, logical reads 709
CPU time = 0 ms,  elapsed time = 323 ms.
```

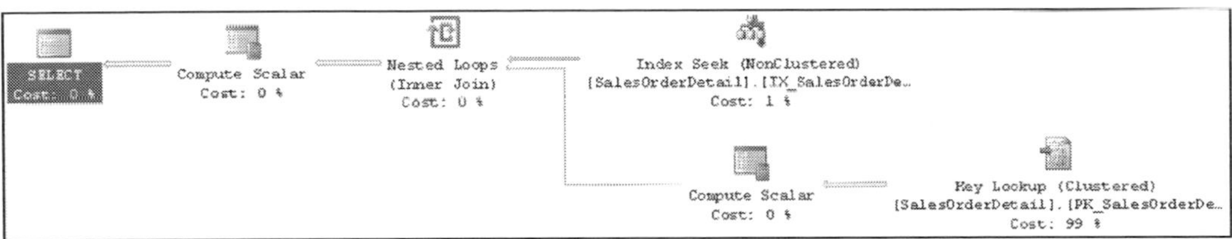

Figure 6-2. *Execution plan with a bookmark lookup*

Drawbacks of Bookmark Lookups

A bookmark lookup requires data page access in addition to index page access. Accessing two sets of pages increases the number of logical reads for the query. Additionally, if the pages are not available in memory, a bookmark lookup will probably require a random (or nonsequential) I/O operation on the disk to jump from the index page to the data page as well as requiring the necessary CPU power to marshal this data and perform the necessary operations. This is because, for a large table, the index page and the corresponding data page usually won't be close to each other on the disk.

The increased logical reads and costly physical reads (if required) make the data-retrieval operation of the bookmark lookup quite costly. This cost factor is the reason that nonclustered indexes are better suited for queries that return a small set of rows from the table. As the number of rows retrieved by a query increases, the overhead cost of a bookmark lookup becomes unacceptable.

To understand how a bookmark lookup makes a nonclustered index ineffective as the number of rows retrieved increases, let's look at a different example. The query that produced the execution plan in Figure 6-2 returned just a few rows from the `SalesOrderDetail` table. Leaving the query the same but changing the parameter to a different value will, of course, change the number of rows returned. If you change the parameter value to look like this:

```
SELECT  *
FROM    Sales.SalesOrderDetail AS sod
WHERE   sod.ProductID = 793
```

then running the query returns more than 700 rows, with different performance metrics and a completely different execution plan (Figure 6-3):

```
Table 'SalesOrderDetail'. Scan count 1, logical reads 1240
CPU time = 15 ms,  elapsed time = 332 ms.
```

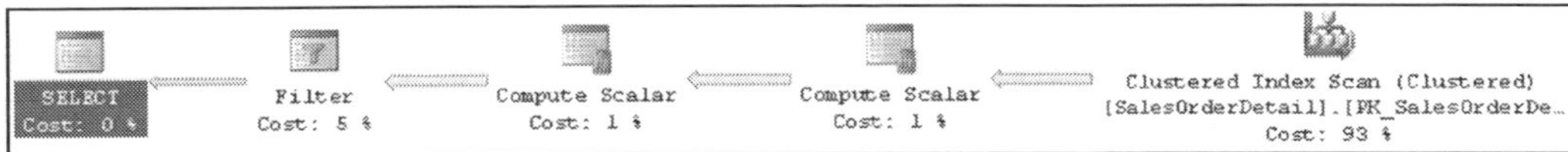

Figure 6-3. *Execution plan with more rows*

To determine how costly it will be to use the nonclustered index, consider the number of logical reads (1,240) performed by the query during the table scan. If you force the optimizer to use the nonclustered index by using an index hint, like this:

```
SELECT  *
FROM    Sales.SalesOrderDetail AS sod WITH (INDEX (IX_SalesOrderDetail_ProductID))
WHERE   sod.ProductID = 793
```

then the number of logical reads increases from 9 to 1,004:

```
Table 'SalesOrderDetail'. Scan count 1, logical reads 2173
CPU time = 0 ms,  elapsed time = 336 ms.
```

Figure 6-4 shows the corresponding execution plan.

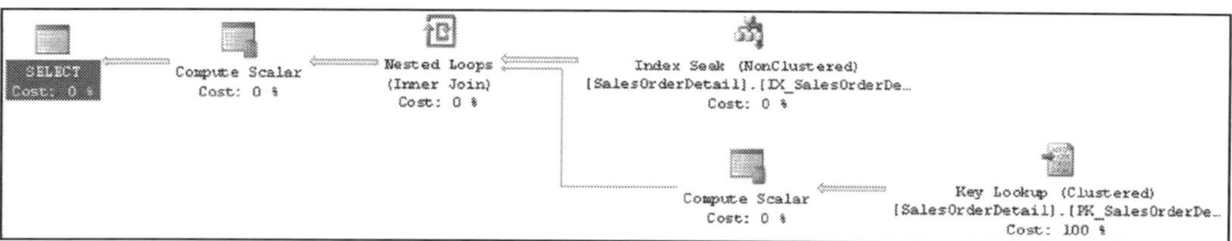

Figure 6-4. *Execution plan for fetching more rows with an index hint*

To benefit from nonclustered indexes, queries should request a relatively small number of rows. Application design plays an important role for the requirements that handle large result sets. For example, search engines on the Web mostly return a limited number of articles at a time, even if the search criterion returns thousands of matching articles. If the queries request a large number of rows, then the increased overhead cost of a bookmark lookup makes the nonclustered index unsuitable; subsequently, you have to consider the possibilities of avoiding the bookmark lookup operation.

Analyzing the Cause of a Bookmark Lookup

Since a bookmark lookup can be a costly operation, you should analyze what causes a query plan to choose a key lookup step in an execution plan. You may find that you are able to avoid the bookmark lookup by including the missing columns in the nonclustered index key or as `INCLUDE` columns at the index page level and thereby avoid the cost overhead associated with the bookmark lookup.

To learn how to identify the columns not included in the nonclustered index, consider the following query, which pulls information from the `HumanResources.Employee` table based on `NationalIDNumber`:

```
SELECT  NationalIDNumber
        ,JobTitle
        ,HireDate
FROM    HumanResources.Employee AS e
WHERE   e.NationalIDNumber = '693168613'
```

This produces the following performance metrics and execution plan (see Figure 6-5):

```
Table 'Employee'. Scan count 0, logical reads 4
CPU time = 0 ms,  elapsed time = 187 ms.
```

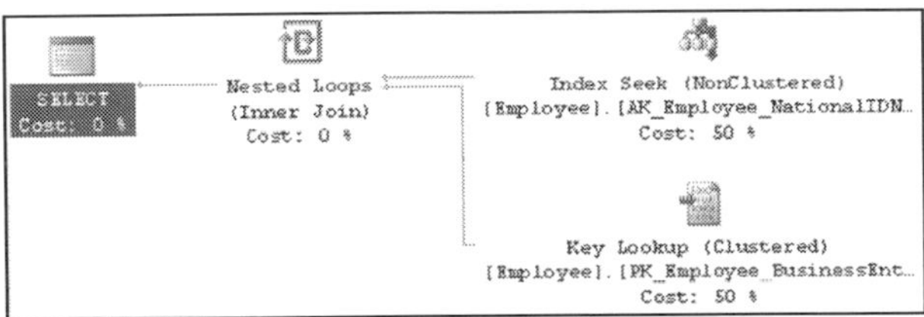

Figure 6-5. *Execution plan with a bookmark lookup*

As shown in the execution plan, you have a key lookup. The `SELECT` statement refers to columns `NationalIDNumber`, `JobTitle`, and `HireDate`. The nonclustered index on column `NationalIDNumber` doesn't provide values for columns `JobTitle` and `HireDate`, so a bookmark lookup operation was required to retrieve those columns from the base table. However, in the real world, it usually won't be this easy to identify all the columns used by a query. Remember that a bookmark lookup operation will be caused if all the columns referred to in any part of the query (not just the selection list) aren't included in the nonclustered index used.

In the case of a complex query based on views and user-defined functions, it may be too difficult to find all the columns referred to by the query. As a result, you need a standard mechanism to find the columns returned by the bookmark lookup that are not included in the nonclustered index.

If you look at the tool tip on the `Key Lookup (Clustered)` operation, you can see the output list for the operation. This shows you the columns being output by the bookmark lookup. However, if the list is very long, it will be quite difficult to read, and you can't copy data from the tool tip. So, to get the list of output columns quickly and easily and be able to copy them, right-click the operator, which in this case is `Key Lookup (Clustered)`. Then select the Properties menu item. Scroll down to the Output List property in the Properties window that opens (Figure 6-6). This property has a plus sign, which allows you to expand the column list, and has plus signs next to each column, which allows you to expand the properties of the column.

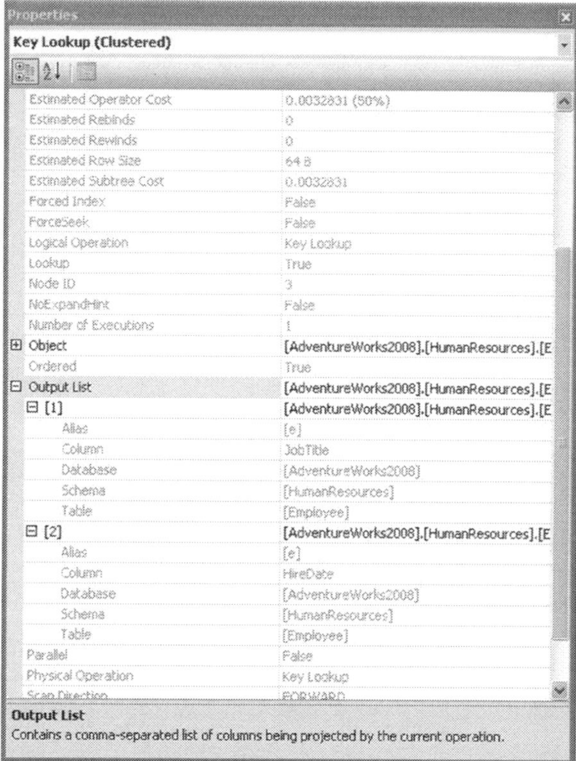

Figure 6-6. *Key lookup Properties window*

To get the list of columns directly from the Properties window, click the ellipsis on the right side of the Output List property. This opens the output list in a text window from which you can copy the data for use when modifying your index (Figure 6-7).

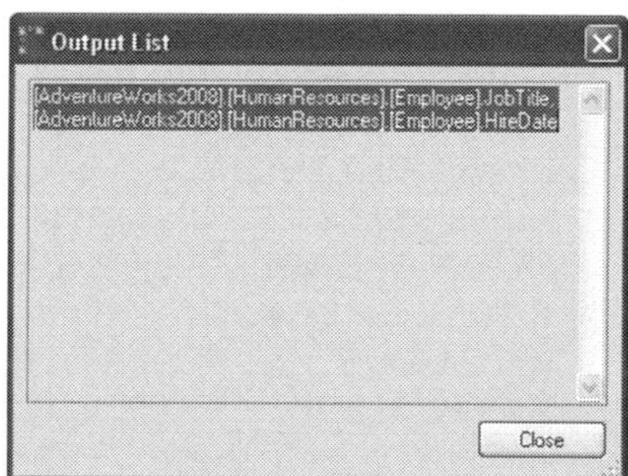

Figure 6-7. *The required columns that were not available in the nonclustered index*

Resolving Bookmark Lookups

Since the relative cost of a bookmark lookup can be very high, you should, wherever possible, try to get rid of bookmark lookup operations. In the preceding section, you needed to obtain the values of columns `JobTitle` and `HireDate` without navigating from the index row to the data row. You can do this in three different ways, as explained in the following sections.

Using a Clustered Index

For a clustered index, the leaf page of the index is the same as the data page of the table. Therefore, when reading the values of the clustered index key columns, the database engine can also read the values of other columns without any navigation from the index row. In the previous example, if you convert the nonclustered index to a clustered index for a particular row, SQL Server can retrieve values of all the columns from the same page.

Simply saying that you want to convert the nonclustered index to a clustered index is easy to do. However, in this case, and in most cases you're likely to encounter, it isn't possible to do so, since the table already has a clustered index in place. The clustered index on this table also happens to be the primary key. You would have to drop all foreign key constraints, drop and re-create the primary key as a nonclustered index, and then re-create the index against `NationalIDNumber`. Not only do you need to take into account the work involved, but you may seriously affect other queries that are dependent on the existing clustered index.

■ **Note** Remember that a table can have only one clustered index.

Using a Covering Index

In Chapter 4, you learned that a covering index is like a pseudoclustered index for the queries, since it can return results without recourse to the table data. So, you can also use a covering index to avoid a bookmark lookup.

To understand how you can use a covering index to avoid a bookmark lookup, examine the query against the `HumanResources.Employee` table again:

```
SELECT  NationalIDNumber
        ,JobTitle
        ,HireDate
FROM    HumanResources.Employee AS e
WHERE   e.NationalIDNumber = '693168613'
```

To avoid this bookmark, you can add the columns referred to in the query, `JobTitle` and `HireDate`, directly to the nonclustered index key. This will make the nonclustered index a covering index for this query because all columns can be retrieved from the index without having to go to the base table or clustered index.

```
CREATE UNIQUE NONCLUSTERED INDEX [AK_Employee_NationalIDNumber] ON
[HumanResources].[Employee]
(
    NationalIDNumber ASC, JobTitle ASC, HireDate ASC
)WITH drop_existing
```

Now when the query gets run, you'll see the following metrics and a different execution plan (Figure 6-8):

```
Table 'Employee'. Scan count 1, logical reads 2
CPU time = 0 ms,  elapsed time = 0 ms.
```

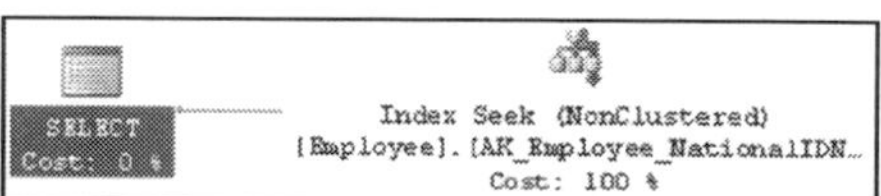

Figure 6-8. *Execution plan with a covering index*

There are a couple of caveats to creating a covering index by changing the key, however. If you add too many columns to a nonclustered index, it becomes too wide, and the index maintenance cost associated with the action queries can increase, as discussed in Chapter 4. Therefore, evaluate closely the number of columns (for size and data type) to be added to the nonclustered index key. If the total width of the additional columns is not too large (best determined through testing and measuring the resultant index size), then those columns can be added in the nonclustered index key to be used as a covering index. Also, if you add columns to the index key, depending on the index, of course, you may be affecting other queries in a negative fashion. They may have expected to see the index key columns in a particular order or may not refer to some of the columns in the key, causing the index to not be used by the optimizer.

Another way to arrive at the covering index, without reshaping the index by adding key columns, is to use the INCLUDE columns. Change the index to look like this:

```
CREATE UNIQUE NONCLUSTERED INDEX [AK_Employee_NationalIDNumber]
ON [HumanResources].[Employee]
(
    NationalIDNumber ASC
) INCLUDE (JobTitle,HireDate)
WITH drop_existing
```

Now when the query is run, you get the following metrics and execution plan (Figure 6-9):

```
Table 'Employee'. Scan count 0, logical reads 2
CPU time = 0 ms,  elapsed time = 0 ms.
```

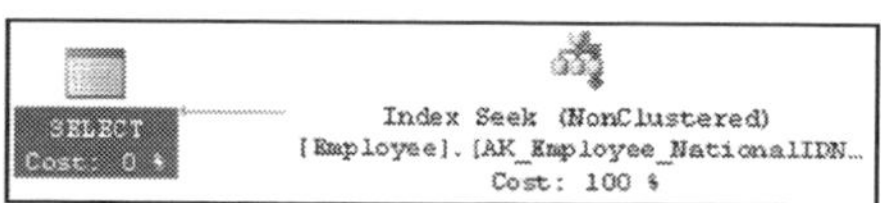

Figure 6-9. *Execution plan with INCLUDE columns*

The index is still covering, exactly as it was in the execution plan displayed in Figure 6-8. Because the data is stored at the leaf level of the index, when the index is used to retrieve the key values, the rest of the columns in the INCLUDE statement are available for use, almost like they were part of the key.

Another way to get a covering index is to take advantage of the structures within SQL Server. If the previous query were modified slightly to retrieve a different set of data instead of a particular NationalIDNumber and its associated JobTitle and HireDate, this time the query would retrieve the NationalIDNumber as an alternate key and the BusinessEntityID, the primary key for the table, over a range of values:

```
SELECT  NationalIDNumber
       ,BusinessEntityID
FROM    HumanResources.Employee AS e
WHERE   e.NationalIDNumber BETWEEN '693168613'
                           AND     '7000000000'
```

The original index on the table doesn't reference the BusinessEntityID column in any way:

```
CREATE UNIQUE NONCLUSTERED INDEX [AK_Employee_NationalIDNumber]
ON [HumanResources].[Employee]
(
    [NationalIDNumber] ASC
)WITH drop_existing
```

When the query is run against the table, you can see the results shown in Figure 6-10.

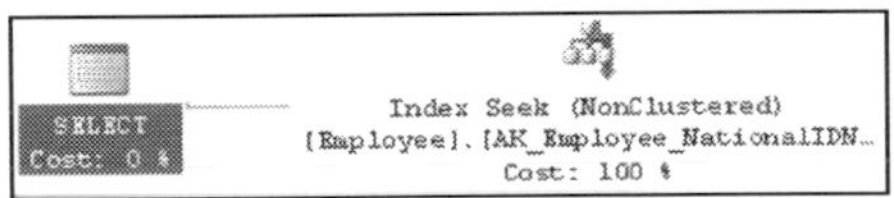

Figure 6-10. *Unexpected covering index*

How did the optimizer arrive at a covering index for this query based on the index provided? It's aware that on a table with a clustered index, the clustered index key, in this case the BusinessEntityID column, is stored as a pointer to the data with the nonclustered index. That means that any query that incorporates a clustered index and a set of columns from a nonclustered index as part of the filtering mechanisms of the query, the WHERE clause, or the join criteria can take advantage of the covering index.

To see how these three different indexes are reflected in storage, you can look at the statistics of the indexes themselves using DBCC SHOW_STATISTICS. When you run the following query against the index, you can see the output in Figure 6-11:

```
DBCC SHOW_STATISTICS('HumanResources.Employee', AK_Employee_NationalIDNumber)
```

	Name	Updated	Rows	Rows Sampled	Steps	Density	Average key length	String Index	Filter Expression	Unfiltered Rows
1	AK_Employee_NationalIDNumber	Oct 9 2008 8:38PM	290	290	177	1	21.66207	YES	NULL	290

	All density	Average Length	Columns
1	0.003448276	17.66207	NationalIDNumber
2	0.003448276	21.66207	NationalIDNumber, BusinessEntityID

Figure 6-11. *DBCC SHOW_STATISTICS output for original index*

As you can see, the `NationalIDNumber` is listed first, but the primary key for the table is included as part of the index, so a second row that includes the `BusinessEntityID` column is there. It makes the average length of the key about 22 bytes. This is how indexes that refer to the primary key values as well as the index key values can function as covering indexes.

If you run the same `DBCC SHOW_STATISTICS` on the first alternate index you tried, with all three columns included in the key, like so:

```
CREATE UNIQUE NONCLUSTERED INDEX [AK_Employee_NationalIDNumber]
ON [HumanResources].[Employee]
(
    NationalIDNumber ASC, JobTitle ASC, HireDate ASC
)WITH drop_existing
```

you will see a different set of statistics (Figure 6-12).

	Name	Updated	Rows	Rows Sampled	Steps	Density	Average key length	String Index	Filter Expression	Unfiltered Rows
1	AK_Employee_NationalIDNumber	Oct 9 2008 8:50PM	290	290	177	1	74.48276	YES	NULL	290

	All density	Average Length	Columns
1	0.003448276	17.66207	NationalIDNumber
2	0.003448276	67.48276	NationalIDNumber, JobTitle
3	0.003448276	70.48276	NationalIDNumber, JobTitle, HireDate
4	0.003448276	74.48276	NationalIDNumber, JobTitle, HireDate, BusinessE...

Figure 6-12. *`DBCC SHOW_STATISTICS` output for a wide key covering index*

You now see the columns added up, all three of the index key columns, and finally the primary key added on. Instead of a width of 22 bytes, it's grown to 74. That reflects the addition of the `JobTitle` column, a `VARCHAR(50)` as well as the 16-byte-wide datetime field.

Finally, looking at the statistics for the second alternate index:

```
CREATE UNIQUE NONCLUSTERED INDEX [AK_Employee_NationalIDNumber]
ON [HumanResources].[Employee]
(
    NationalIDNumber ASC
) INCLUDE (JobTitle,HireDate)
WITH drop_existing
```

With the included columns you'll see the output in Figure 6-13.

	Name	Updated	Rows	Rows Sampled	Steps	Density	Average key length	String Index	Filter Expression	Unfiltered Rows
1	AK_Employee_NationalIDNumber	Oct 9 2008 8:58PM	290	290	177	1	21.66207	YES	NULL	290

	All density	Average Length	Columns
1	0.003448276	17.66207	NationalIDNumber
2	0.003448276	21.66207	NationalIDNumber, BusinessEntityID

Figure 6-13. *`DBCC SHOW_STATISTICS` output for a covering index using `INCLUDE`*

Now the key width is back to the original size because the columns in the `INCLUDE` statement are stored not with the key but at the leaf level of the index.

There is more interesting information to be gleaned from the data stored about statistics, but I'll cover that in Chapter 7.

Using an Index Join

If the covering index becomes very wide, then you might consider an index join technique. As explained in Chapter 4, the index join technique uses an index intersection between two or more indexes to cover a query fully. Since the index join technique requires access to more than one index, it has to perform logical reads on all the indexes used in the index join. Consequently, it requires a higher number of logical reads than the covering index. But since the multiple narrow indexes used for the index join can serve more queries than a wide covering index (as explained in Chapter 4), you can certainly consider the index join as a technique to avoid bookmark lookups.

To better understand how an index join can be used to avoid bookmark lookups, run the following query against the `PurchaseOrderHeader` table in order to retrieve a `PurchaseOrderID` for a particular vendor on a particular date:

```
SELECT  poh.PurchaseOrderID
       ,poh.VendorID
       ,poh.OrderDate
FROM    Purchasing.PurchaseOrderHeader AS poh
WHERE   VendorID = 1636
        AND poh.OrderDate = '12/5/2003'
```

When run, this query results in a `Key Lookup` operation (Figure 6-14) and the following I/O:

```
Table 'PurchaseOrderHeader'. Scan count 1, logical reads 10
CPU time = 0 ms,  elapsed time = 46 ms.
```

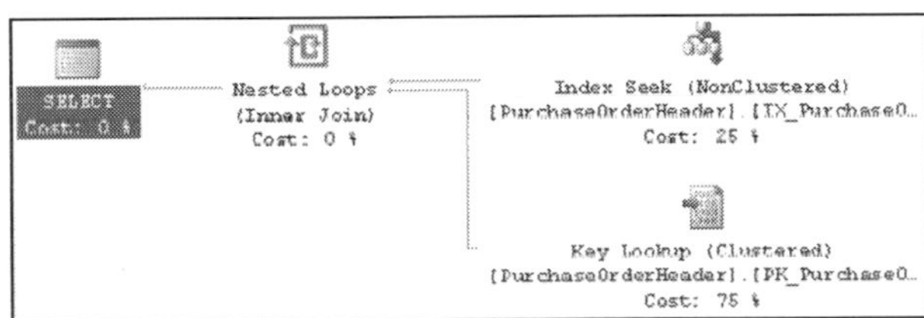

Figure 6-14. *A* `Key Lookup` *operation*

The bookmark lookup is caused since all the columns referred to by the `SELECT` statement and `WHERE` clause are not included in the nonclustered index on column `VendorID`. Using the nonclustered index is still better than not using it, since that would require a scan on the table (in this case, a clustered index scan) with a larger number of logical reads.

To avoid the bookmark lookup, you can consider a covering index on the column `OrderDate` as explained in the previous section. But in addition to the covering index solution, you can consider an index join. As you learned, an index join requires narrower indexes than the covering index and thereby provides the following two benefits:

- Multiple narrow indexes can serve a larger number of queries than the wide covering index.
- Narrow indexes require less maintenance overhead than the wide covering index.

To avoid the bookmark lookup using an index join, create a narrow nonclustered index on column `OrderDate` that is not included in the existing nonclustered index:

```
CREATE NONCLUSTERED INDEX Ix_TEST ON Purchasing.PurchaseOrderHeader(Orderdate)
```

If you run the `SELECT` statement again, the following output and the execution plan shown in Figure 6-15 are returned:

```
Table 'PurchaseOrderHeader'. Scan count 2, logical reads 4
CPU time = 0 ms,  elapsed time = 35 ms.
```

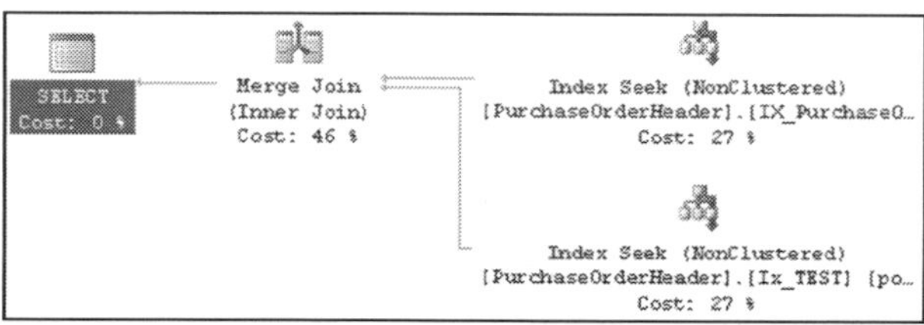

Figure 6-15. *Execution plan without a bookmark lookup*

From the preceding execution plan, you can see that the optimizer used the nonclustered index, `IX_PurchaseOrder_VendorID`, on column `VendorID` and the new nonclustered index, `Ix_TEST`, on column `OrderID` to serve the query fully without hitting the base table. This index join operation avoided the bookmark lookup and consequently decreased the number of logical reads from 10 to 4.

It is true that a covering index on columns `VendorID` and `OrderID` (`c1, c2`) could reduce the number of logical reads further. But it may not always be possible to use covering indexes, since they can be wide and have their associated overhead. In such cases, an index join can be a good alternative.

Summary

As demonstrated in this chapter, the bookmark lookup step associated with a nonclustered index makes data retrieval through a nonclustered index very costly. The SQL Server optimizer takes this into account when generating an execution plan, and if it finds the overhead cost of using a nonclustered index to be very high, it discards the index and performs a table scan (or a clustered index scan if the table contains a clustered index). Therefore, to improve the effectiveness of a nonclustered index, it makes sense to analyze the cause of a bookmark lookup and consider whether you can avoid it completely by adding fields to the index key or to the `INCLUDE` column (or index join) and creating a covering index.

Up to this point, you have concentrated on indexing techniques and presumed that the SQL Server optimizer would be able to determine the effectiveness of an index for a query. In the next chapter, you will see the importance of statistics in helping the optimizer determine the effectiveness of an index.

CHAPTER 7

Statistics Analysis

By now, you should have a good understanding of the importance of indexes. It is equally important for the optimizer to have the necessary statistics on the data distribution so that it can choose indexes effectively. In SQL Server, this information is maintained in the form of *statistics* on the index key.

In this chapter, you'll learn the importance of statistics in query optimization. Specifically, I cover the following topics:

- The role of statistics in query optimization
- The importance of statistics on columns with indexes
- The importance of statistics on nonindexed columns used in join and filter criteria
- Analysis of single-column and multicolumn statistics, including the computation of selectivity of a column for indexing
- Statistics maintenance
- Effective evaluation of statistics used in a query execution

The Role of Statistics in Query Optimization

SQL Server's query optimizer is a cost-based optimizer; it decides on the best data access mechanism and join strategy by identifying the selectivity, how unique the data is, and which columns are used in filtering the data (meaning via the `WHERE` or `JOIN` clause). Statistics exist with an index, but they also exist on columns without an index that are used as part of a predicate. As you learned in Chapter 4, you should use a nonclustered index to retrieve a small result set, whereas for data in related sets, a clustered index works better. With a large result set, going to the clustered index or table directly is usually more beneficial.

Up-to-date information on data distribution in the columns referenced as predicates helps the optimizer determine the query strategy to use. In SQL Server, this information is maintained in the form of statistics, which are essential for the cost-based optimizer to create an effective query execution plan. Through the statistics, the optimizer can make reasonably accurate estimates about how long it will take to return a result set or an intermediate result set and therefore determine the most effective operations to use. As long as you ensure that the default statistical settings for the database are set, the optimizer will be able to do its best to determine effective processing strategies dynamically. Also, as a safety measure while troubleshooting performance, you should ensure that the automatic statistics maintenance routine is doing its job as desired. Where necessary, you may even have to take manual control over the creation and/or maintenance of statistics. (I cover this in the "Manual Maintenance" section, and I cover the precise nature of the functions and shape of statistics in the "Analyzing Statistics" section.) In the following section, I show you why statistics are important to indexed columns and nonindexed columns functioning as predicates.

Statistics on an Indexed Column

The usefulness of an index is fully dependent on the statistics of the indexed columns; without statistics, SQL Server's cost-based query optimizer can't decide upon the most effective way of using an index. To meet this requirement, SQL Server automatically creates the statistics of an index key whenever the index is created. It isn't possible to turn this feature off.

As data changes, the data-retrieval mechanism required to keep the cost of a query low may also change. For example, if a table has only one matching row for a certain column value, then it makes sense to retrieve the matching rows from the table by going through the nonclustered index on the column. But if the data in the table changes so that a large number of rows are added with the same column value, then using the nonclustered index no longer makes sense. To be able to have SQL Server decide this change in processing strategy as the data changes over time, it is vital to have up-to-date statistics.

SQL Server can keep the statistics on an index updated as the contents of the indexed column are modified. By default, this feature is turned on and is configurable through the Properties ➤ Options ➤ Auto Update Statistics setting of a database. Updating statistics consumes extra CPU cycles. To optimize the update process, SQL Server uses an efficient algorithm to decide when to execute the update statistics procedure, based on factors such as the number of modifications and the size of the table:

- When a table with no rows gets a row
- When a table has fewer than 500 rows and is increased by 500 or more rows
- When a table has more than 500 rows and is increased by 500 rows + 20 percent of the number of rows

This built-in intelligence keeps the CPU utilization by each process very low. It's also possible to update the statistics asynchronously. This means when a query would normally cause statistics to be updated, instead that query proceeds with the old statistics, and the statistics are updated offline. This can speed up the response time of some queries, such as when the database is large or when you have a short timeout period.

You can manually disable (or enable) the auto update statistics and the auto update statistics asynchronously features by using the `ALTER DATABASE` command. By default, the auto update statistics feature is enabled, and it is strongly recommended that you keep it enabled. The auto update statistics asynchronously feature is disabled by default. Turn this feature on only if you've determined it will help with timeouts on your database.

■ **Note** I explain ALTER DATABASE later in this chapter in the "Manual Maintenance" section.

Benefits of Updated Statistics

The benefits of performing an auto update usually outweigh its cost on the system resources.

To more directly control the behavior of the data, instead of using the tables in AdventureWorks, for this set of examples you will create one manually. Specifically, create a test table (create_t1.sql in the download) with only three rows and a nonclustered index:

```
IF (SELECT  OBJECT_ID('t1')
   ) IS NOT NULL
    DROP TABLE dbo.t1 ;
GO
CREATE TABLE dbo.t1 (c1 INT, c2 INT IDENTITY) ;
SELECT TOP 1500
        IDENTITY( INT,1,1 ) AS n
INTO    #Nums
FROM    Master.dbo.SysColumns sc1
       ,Master.dbo.SysColumns sc2;

INSERT  INTO dbo.t1 (c1)
        SELECT  n
        FROM    #Nums

DROP TABLE #Nums
CREATE NONCLUSTERED INDEX i1 ON dbo.t1 (c1) ;
```

If you execute a SELECT statement with a very selective filter criterion on the indexed column to retrieve only one row, as shown in the following line of code, then the optimizer uses a nonclustered index seek, as shown in the execution plan in Figure 7-1:

```
SELECT * FROM t1 WHERE c1 = 2 --Retrieve 1 row
```

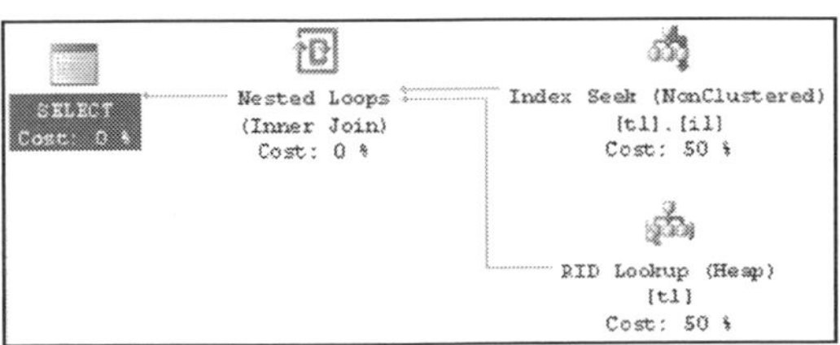

Figure 7-1. *Execution plan for a very small result set*

To understand the effect of small data modifications on a statistics update, create a trace using Profiler. In the trace, add the event `Auto Stats`, which captures statistics update and create events, and add `SQL:BatchCompleted` with a filter on the `TextData` column. The filter should look like `Not Like SET%` when you are done. Add only one row to the table:

```
INSERT INTO t1 (c1) VALUES(2)
```

When you reexecute the preceding `SELECT` statement, you get the same execution plan as shown in Figure 7-1. Figure 7-2 shows the trace events generated by the query.

EventClass	TextData	CPU	Reads	Writes	Duration
SQL:BatchCompleted	SELECT * FROM t1 WHERE c1 = 2 --Ret...	0	4	0	2

Figure 7-2. *Trace output on the addition of a small number of rows*

The trace output doesn't contain any SQL activity representing a statistics update because the number of changes fell below the threshold where any table that has more than 500 rows must have an increase of 500 rows plus 20 percent of the number of rows.

To understand the effect of large data modification on statistics update, add 1,500 rows to the table (`add_rows.sql` in the download):

```
SELECT TOP 1500
        IDENTITY( INT,1,1 ) AS n
INTO    #Nums
FROM    Master.dbo.SysColumns sc1
       ,Master.dbo.SysColumns sc2;
    INSERT INTO dbo.t1 (
        c1
    ) SELECT 2
    FROM #Nums;
DROP TABLE #Nums;
```

Now, if you reexecute the `SELECT` statement, like so:

```
SELECT * FROM dbo.t1 WHERE c1 = 2;
```

a large result set (1,502 rows out of 3,001 rows) will be retrieved. Since a large result set is requested, scanning the base table directly is preferable to going through the nonclustered index to the base table 1,502 times. Accessing the base table directly will prevent the overhead cost of bookmark lookups associated with the nonclustered index. This is represented in the resultant execution plan (see Figure 7-3).

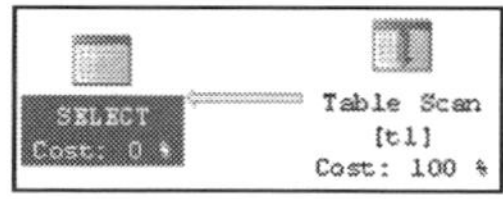

Figure 7-3. *Execution plan for a large result set*

Figure 7-4 shows the resultant Profiler trace output.

EventClass	TextData	CPU	Reads	Writes	Duration
Auto Stats	Updated: t1.i1				7
SQL:BatchCompleted	SELECT * FROM t1 WHERE c1 = 2 --Ret...	0	34	0	101

Figure 7-4. *Trace output on the addition of a large number of rows*

The Profiler trace output includes an `Auto Stats` event since the threshold was exceeded by the large-scale update this time. These SQL activities consume some extra CPU cycles. However, by doing this, the optimizer determines a better data-processing strategy and keeps the overall cost of the query low.

Drawbacks of Outdated Statistics

As explained in the preceding section, the auto update statistics feature allows the optimizer to decide on an efficient processing strategy for a query as the data changes. If the statistics become outdated, however, then the processing strategies decided on by the optimizer may not be applicable for the current data set and thereby will degrade performance.

To understand the detrimental effect of having outdated statistics, follow these steps:

1. Re-create the preceding test table with 1,500 rows only and the corresponding nonclustered index.
2. Prevent SQL Server from updating statistics automatically as the data changes. To do so, disable the auto update statistics feature by executing the following SQL statement:

```
ALTER DATABASE AdventureWorks2008 SET AUTO_UPDATE_STATISTICS OFF
```

3. Add 1,500 rows to the table as before.

Now, reexecute the `SELECT` statement to understand the effect of the outdated statistics on the query optimizer. The query is repeated here for clarity:

```
SELECT * FROM dbo.t1 WHERE c1 = 2
```

Figure 7-5 and Figure 7-6 show the resultant execution plan and the Profiler trace output for this query, respectively.

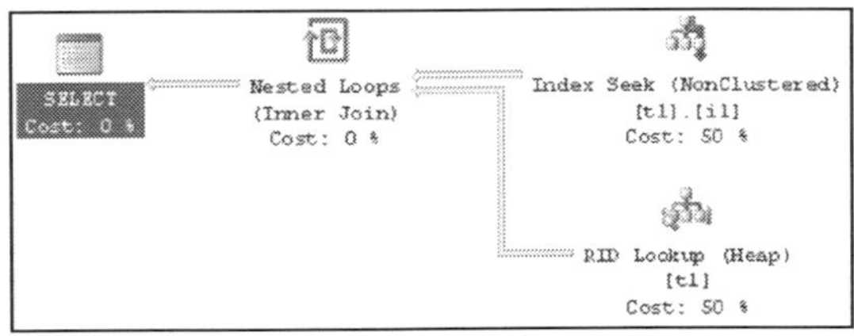

Figure 7-5. *Execution plan with* `AUTO_UPDATE_STATISTICS OFF`

EventClass	TextData	CPU	Reads	Writes	Duration
SQL:BatchCompleted	SELECT * FROM t1 WHERE c1 = 2 --Ret...	15	1509	0	191

Figure 7-6. *Trace output with* `AUTO_UPDATE_STATISTICS OFF`

With the auto update statistics feature switched off, the query optimizer has selected a different execution plan from the one it selected with this feature on. Based on the outdated statistics, which have only one row for the filter criterion (c1 = 2), the optimizer decided to use a nonclustered index seek. The optimizer couldn't make its decision based on the current data distribution in the column. For performance reasons, it would have been better to hit the base table directly instead of going through the nonclustered index, since a large result set (1,501 rows out of 3,000 rows) is requested.

You can see that turning off the auto update statistics feature has a negative effect on performance by comparing the cost of this query with and without updated statistics. Table 7-1 shows the difference in the cost of this query.

Table 7-1. *Cost of the Query with and Without Updated Statistics*

Statistics Update Status	Figure	Cost (SQL:Batch Completed Event)	
		CPU (ms)	**Number of Reads**
Updated	Figure 7-4	0	34
Not updated	Figure 7-6	15	1509

The number of logical reads and the CPU utilization is significantly higher when the statistics are out-of-date even though the data returned is nearly identical and the query was precisely the same. Therefore, it is recommended that you keep the auto update statistics feature on. The benefits of keeping statistics updated outweigh the costs of performing the update. Before you leave this section, turn AUTO_UPDATE_STATISTICS back on (although you can also use sp_autostats):

```
ALTER DATABASE AdventureWorks2008 SET AUTO_UPDATE_STATISTICS ON
```

Statistics on a Nonindexed Column

Sometimes you may have columns in join or filter criteria without any index. Even for such nonindexed columns, the query optimizer is more likely to make the best choice if it knows the data distribution (or statistics) of those columns.

In addition to statistics on indexes, SQL Server can build statistics on columns with no indexes. The information on data distribution, or the likelihood of a particular value occurring in a nonindexed column, can help the query optimizer determine an optimal processing strategy. This benefits the query optimizer even if it can't use an index to actually locate the values. SQL Server automatically builds statistics on nonindexed columns if it deems this information valuable in creating a better plan, usually when the columns are used in a predicate. By default, this feature is turned on, and it's configurable through the Properties ➤ Options ➤ Auto Create Statistics setting of a database. You can override this setting programmatically by using the ALTER DATABASE command. However, for better performance, it is strongly recommended that you keep this feature on.

In general, you should not disable the automatic creation of statistics on nonindexed columns. One of the scenarios in which you may consider disabling this feature is while executing a series of ad hoc SQL activities that you will not execute again. In such a case, you must decide whether you want to pay the cost of automatic statistics creation to get a better plan in this one case and affect the performance of other SQL Server activities. It is worthwhile noting that SQL Server eventually removes statistics when it realizes that they have not been used for a while. So, in general, you should keep this feature on and not be concerned about it.

Benefits of Statistics on a Nonindexed Column

To understand the benefit of having statistics on a column with no index, create two test tables with disproportionate data distributions, as shown in the following code (`create_t1_t2.sql` in the download). Both tables contain 10,001 rows. Table `t1` contains only one row for a value of the second column (`t1_c2`) equal to 1, and the remaining 10,000 rows contain this column value as 2. Table `t2` contains exactly the opposite data distribution.

```
--Create first table with 10001 rows
IF(SELECT OBJECT_ID('dbo.t1')) IS NOT NULL
  DROP TABLE dbo.t1;
GO
CREATE TABLE dbo.t1(t1_c1 INT IDENTITY, t1_c2 INT);
INSERT INTO dbo.t1 (t1_c2) VALUES (1);
SELECT TOP 119026
        IDENTITY( INT,1,1 ) AS n
INTO    #Nums
FROM    Master.dbo.SysColumns sc1
       ,Master.dbo.SysColumns sc2;
    INSERT INTO dbo.t1 (
        t1_c2
    ) SELECT 2
    FROM #Nums
GO
CREATE CLUSTERED INDEX i1 ON dbo.t1(t1_c1)

--Create second table with 10001 rows,
--  but opposite data distribution
IF(SELECT OBJECT_ID('dbo.t2')) IS NOT NULL
  DROP TABLE dbo.t2;
GO
CREATE TABLE dbo.t2(t2_c1 INT IDENTITY, t2_c2 INT);
INSERT INTO dbo.t2(t2_c2) VALUES (2);
    INSERT INTO dbo.t2 (
        t2_c2
    ) SELECT 1
    FROM #Nums;
DROP TABLE #Nums;
GO
CREATE CLUSTERED INDEX i1 ON dbo.t2(t2_c1);
```

Table 7-2 illustrates how the tables will look.

Table 7-2. *Sample Tables*

	Table t1		Table t2	
Column	**t1_c1**	**t1_c2**	**t2_c1**	**t2_c2**
Row1	1	1	1	2
Row2	2	2	2	1
RowN	N	2	N	1
Row10001	10001	2	10001	1

To understand the importance of statistics on a nonindexed column, use the default setting for the auto create statistics feature. By default, this feature is on. You can verify this using the DATABASEPROPERTYEX function (although you can also query the sys.databases view):

```
SELECT DATABASEPROPERTYEX('AdventureWorks2008', 'IsAutoCreateStatistics')
```

■ **Note** You can find a detailed description of configuring the auto create statistics feature later in this chapter.

Use the following SELECT statement (nonindexed_select.sql in the download) to access a large result set from table t1 and a small result set from table t2. Table t1 has 10,000 rows for the column value of t1_c2 = 2, and table t2 has 1 row for t2_c2 = 2. Note that these columns used in the join and filter criteria have no index on either table.

```
SELECT  t1.t1_c2
       ,t2.t2_c2
FROM   dbo. t1
        JOIN dbo.t2
        ON t1.t1_c2 = t2.t2_c2
WHERE   t1.t1_c2 = 2;
```

Figure 7-7 shows the execution plan for this query.

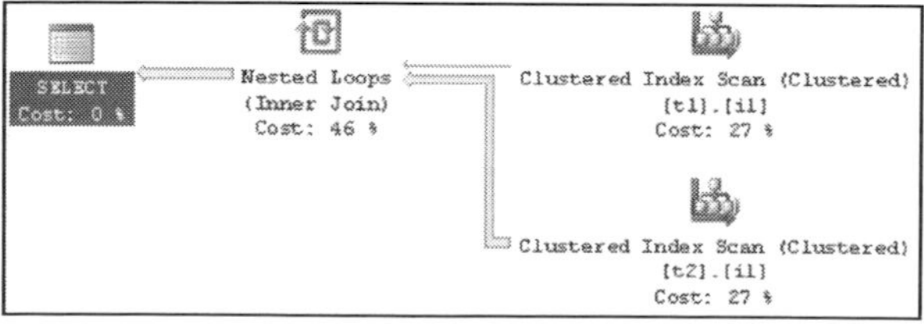

Figure 7-7. *Execution plan with* AUTO_CREATE_STATISTICS ON

Figure 7-8 shows the Profiler trace output with all completed events and the `Auto Stats` event for this query. You can use this to evaluate some of the added costs for a given query.

■ **Tip** To keep the Profiler trace output compact, I used a prefilter on `TextData Not like SET%`. This filters the `SET` statements used to show the graphical execution plan.

The Profiler trace output shown in Figure 7-8 includes two `Auto Stats` events creating statistics on the nonindexed columns referred to in the `JOIN` and `WHERE` clauses, `t2_c2` and `t1_c2`. This activity consumes a few extra CPU cycles (since none could be detected), but by consuming these extra CPU cycles, the optimizer decides upon a better processing strategy for keeping the overall cost of the query low.

EventClass	TextData	CPU	Reads	Writes	Duration
Auto Stats	Created: t2_c2				12
Auto Stats	Created: t1_c2				9
SQL:BatchCompleted	SELECT t1.t1_c2 ,t2.t2_c2 ...	46	143	0	234

Figure 7-8. *Trace output with AUTO_CREATE_STATISTICS ON*

To verify the statistics automatically created by SQL Server on the nonindexed columns of each table, run this `SELECT` statement against the `sys.stats` table:

```
SELECT  *
FROM    sys.stats
WHERE   object_id = OBJECT_ID('t1')
```

Figure 7-9 shows the automatic statistics created for table `t1`.

	object_id	name	stats_id	auto_created	user_created	no_recompute	has_filter	filter_definition
1	1143675122	i1	1	0	0	0	0	NULL
2	1143675122	_WA_Sys_00000002_442B18F2	2	1	0	0	0	NULL

Figure 7-9. *Automatic statistics for table* `t1`

To verify how a different result set size from the two tables influences the decision of the query optimizer, modify the filter criteria of `nonindexed_select.sql` to access an opposite result set size from the two tables (small from `t1` and large from `t2`). Instead of filtering on `t1.t1_c2` = 2, change it to filter on 1:

```
SELECT  t1.t1_c2
       ,t2.t2_c2
FROM  dbo. t1
        JOIN dbo.t2
        ON t1.t1_c2 = t2.t2_c2
WHERE   t1.t1_c2 = 1
```

Figure 7-10 shows the resultant execution plan, and Figure 7-11 shows the Profiler trace output of this query.

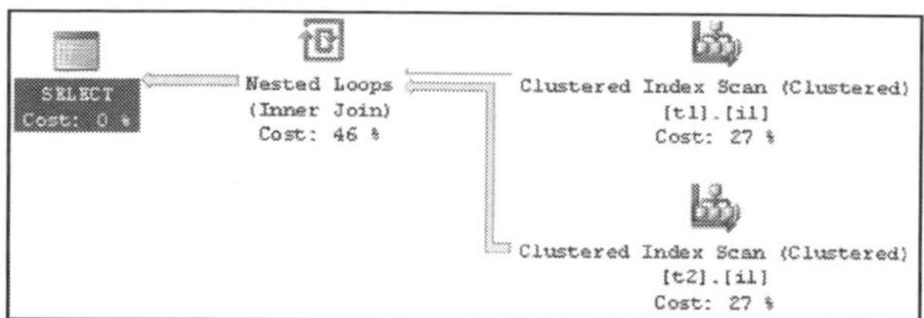

Figure 7-10. *Execution plan for a different result set*

EventClass	TextData	CPU	Reads	Writes	Duration
SQL:BatchCompleted	SELECT t1.t1_c2 ,t2.t2_c2 ...	0	48	0	159

Figure 7-11. *Trace output for a different result set*

The resultant Profiler trace output doesn't perform any additional SQL activities to manage statistics. The statistics on the nonindexed columns (`t1.t1_c2` and `t2.t2_c2`) had already been created during the previous execution of the query.

For effective cost optimization, in each case the query optimizer selected different processing strategies, depending upon the statistics on the nonindexed columns (`t1.t1_c2` and `t2.t2_c2`). You can see this from the last two execution plans. In the first, table `t1` is the outer table for the nested loop join, whereas in the latest one, table `t2` is the outer table. By having statistics on the nonindexed columns (`t1.t1_c2` and `t2.t2_c2`), the query optimizer can create a cost-effective plan suitable for each case.

An even better solution would be to have an index on the column. This would not only create the statistics on the column but also allow fast data retrieval through an `Index Seek` operation, while retrieving a small result set. However, in the case of a database application with queries referring to nonindexed columns in the `WHERE` clause, keeping the auto create statistics feature on still allows the optimizer to determine the best processing strategy for the existing data distribution in the column.

If you need to know which column or columns might be covered by a given statistic, you need to look into the `sys.stats_columns` system table. You can query it in the same way as you did the `sys.stats` table:

```
SELECT  *
FROM    sys.stats_columns
WHERE   object_id = OBJECT_ID('t1')
```

This will show the column or columns being referenced by the automatically created statistics. This will help you if you decide you need to create an index to replace the statistics, because you will need to know which columns to create the statistics on.

Drawback of Missing Statistics on a Nonindexed Column

To understand the detrimental effect of not having statistics on nonindexed columns, drop the statistics automatically created by SQL Server and prevent SQL Server from automatically creating statistics on columns with no index by following these steps:

1. Drop the automatic statistics created on column `t1.t1_c2` through the Manage Statistics dialog box as shown in the section "Benefits of Statistics on a Nonindexed Column," or use the following SQL command:

```
DROP STATISTICS [t1].StatisticsName
```

2. Similarly, drop the corresponding statistics on column `t2.t2_c2`.
3. Disable the auto create statistics feature by deselecting the Auto Create Statistics check box for the corresponding database or by executing the following SQL command:

```
ALTER DATABASE AdventureWorks2008 SET AUTO_CREATE_STATISTICS OFF
```

Now reexecute the `SELECT` statement `nonindexed_select.sql`:

```
SELECT  t1.t1_c2
       ,t2.t2_c2
FROM   dbo. t1
        JOIN dbo.t2
        ON t1.t1_c2 = t2.t2_c2
WHERE   t1.t1_c2 = 2;
```

Figure 7-12 and Figure 7-13 show the resultant execution plan and Profiler trace output, respectively.

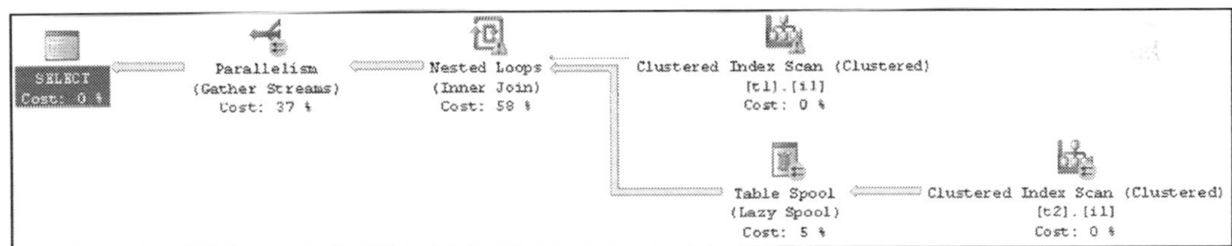

Figure 7-12. *Execution plan with* AUTO_CREATE_STATISTICS OFF

EventClass	TextData	CPU	Reads	Writes	Duration
SQL:BatchCompleted	SELECT t1.t1_c2 ,t2.t2_c2 ...	61	20313	19	303

Figure 7-13. *Trace output with* AUTO_CREATE_STATISTICS OFF

With the auto create statistics feature off, the query optimizer selected a different execution plan compared to the one it selected with the auto create statistics feature on. On not finding statistics on the relevant columns, the optimizer chose the first table (t1) in the FROM clause as the outer table of the nested loop join operation. The optimizer couldn't make its decision based on the actual data distribution in the column. Not only that, but the optimizer and the query engine determined that this query passed the threshold for parallelism, making this a parallel execution (those are the little arrows on the operators, marking them as parallel (more on parallel execution plans in Chapter 9). For example, if you modify the query to reference table t2 as the first table in the FROM clause:

```
SELECT  t1.t1_c2
       ,t2.t2_c2
FROM   dbo. t2
        JOIN dbo.t1
        ON t1.t1_c2 = t2.t2_c2
WHERE   t1.t1_c2 = 2;
```

then the optimizer selects table t2 as the outer table of the nested loop join operation. Figure 7-14 shows the execution plan.

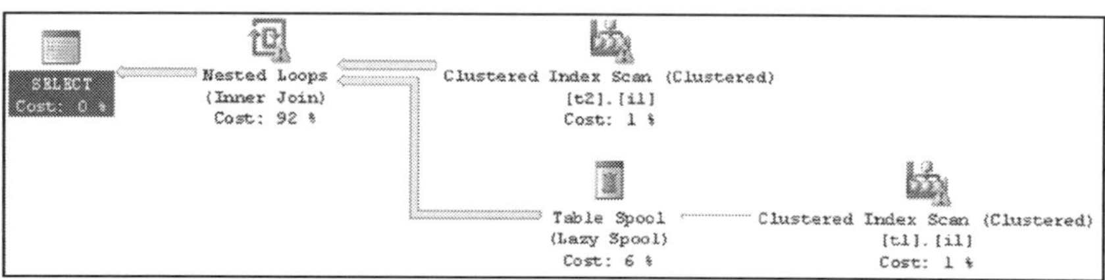

Figure 7-14. *Execution plan with AUTO_CREATE_STATISTICS OFF (a variation)*

You can see that turning off the auto create statistics feature has a negative effect on performance by comparing the cost of this query with and without statistics on a nonindexed column. Table 7-3 shows the difference in the cost of this query.

Table 7-3. *Cost Comparison of a Query with and Without Statistics on a Nonindexed Column*

Statistics on Nonindexed Column	Figure	Cost (SQL:Batch Completed Event)	
		Duration (ms)	**Number of Reads**
With statistics	Figure 7-11	159	48
Without statistics	Figure 7-13	303	20,313

The number of logical reads and the CPU utilization are very high with no statistics on the nonindexed columns. Without these statistics, the optimizer can't create a cost-effective plan.

A query execution plan highlights the missing statistics by placing an exclamation point on the operator that would have used the statistics. You can see this in the clustered index scan operators in the previous execution plan (Figure 7-14), as well as in the detailed description in the Warnings section for a node in a graphical execution plan, as shown in Figure 7-15 for table t2.

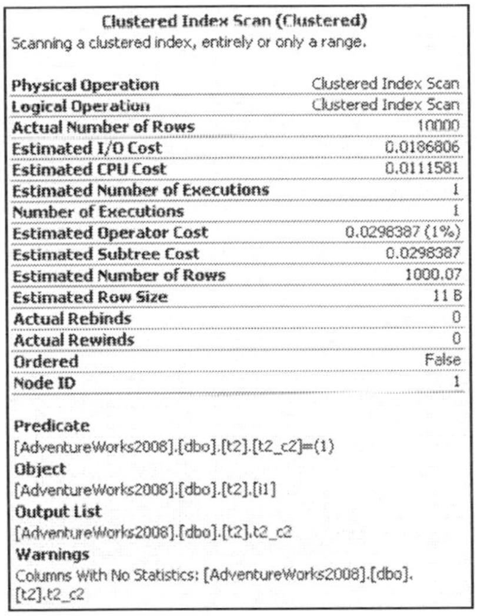

Clustered Index Scan (Clustered)

Scanning a clustered index, entirely or only a range.

Physical Operation	Clustered Index Scan
Logical Operation	Clustered Index Scan
Actual Number of Rows	10000
Estimated I/O Cost	0.0186806
Estimated CPU Cost	0.0111581
Estimated Number of Executions	1
Number of Executions	1
Estimated Operator Cost	0.0298387 (1%)
Estimated Subtree Cost	0.0298387
Estimated Number of Rows	1000.07
Estimated Row Size	11 B
Actual Rebinds	0
Actual Rewinds	0
Ordered	False
Node ID	1

Predicate
[AdventureWorks2008].[dbo].[t2].[t2_c2]=(1)
Object
[AdventureWorks2008].[dbo].[t2].[i1]
Output List
[AdventureWorks2008].[dbo].[t2].t2_c2
Warnings
Columns With No Statistics: [AdventureWorks2008].[dbo].[t2].t2_c2

Figure 7-15. *Missing statistics indication in a graphical plan*

The XML execution plan provides the missing statistics information under the `Warnings` column, as shown in Figure 7-16. Remember that you can obtain the XML execution plan by right-clicking within the graphical execution plan and selecting Show Execution Plan XML or by using `SET STATISTICS XML` in the query window.

```
<Warnings>
  <ColumnsWithNoStatistics>
    <ColumnReference Database="[AdventureWorks2008]" Schema="[dbo]" Table="[t2]" Column="t2_c2" />
  </ColumnsWithNoStatistics>
</Warnings>
```

Figure 7-16. *Missing statistics indication in an XML plan*

■ **Note** In a database application, there is always the possibility of queries using columns with no indexes. Therefore, for performance reasons, leaving the auto create statistics feature of SQL Server databases on is recommended.

Analyzing Statistics

Statistics are collections of information stored as histograms. A *histogram* is a statistical construct that shows how often data falls into varying categories. The histogram stored by SQL Server consists of a sampling of data distribution for a column or an index key (or the first column of a multicolumn index key) of up to 200 rows. The information on the range of index key values between two consecutive samples is called a *step*. These steps consist of varying size intervals between the 200 values stored. A step provides the following information:

- The top value of a given step (RANGE_HI_KEY).
- The number of rows equal to RANGE_HI_KEY (EQ_ROWS).
- The range of rows between the previous top value and the current top value, without counting either of these samples (RANGE_ROWS).
- The number of distinct rows in the range (DISTINCT_RANGE_ROWS). If all values in the range are unique, then RANGE_ROWS equals DISTINCT_RANGE_ROWS.
- The average number of rows equal to a key value within a range (AVG_RANGE_ROWS).

The value of EQ_ROWS for an index key value (RANGE_HI_KEY) helps the optimizer decide how (and whether) to use the index when the indexed column is referred to in a WHERE clause. Because the optimizer can perform a SEEK or SCAN operation to retrieve rows from a table, the optimizer can decide which operation to perform based on the number of matching rows (EQ_ROWS) for the index key value.

To understand how the optimizer's data-retrieval strategy depends on the number of matching rows, create a test table (create_t3.sql in the download) with different data distributions on an indexed column:

```
IF (SELECT  OBJECT_ID('dbo.t1')
   ) IS NOT NULL
    DROP TABLE dbo.t1 ;
GO
CREATE TABLE dbo.t1 (c1 INT, c2 INT IDENTITY) ;
INSERT  INTO dbo.t1 (c1)
VALUES  (1) ;
SELECT TOP 119026
        IDENTITY( INT,1,1 ) AS n
INTO    #Nums ;
INSERT  INTO dbo.t1 (c1)
        SELECT  2
        FROM    #Nums ;
CREATE NONCLUSTERED INDEX i1 ON dbo.t1 (c1) ;
```

When the preceding nonclustered index is created, SQL Server automatically creates statistics on the index key. You can obtain statistics for this nonclustered index key (i1) by executing the DBCC SHOW_STATISTICS command:

```
DBCC SHOW_STATISTICS(t1, i1)
```

Figure 7-17 shows the statistics output.

	Name	Updated	Rows	Rows Sampled	Steps	Density	Average key length	String Index	Filter Expression	Unfiltered Rows
1	i1	Oct 15 2008 8:04PM	10001	10001	2	0	4	NO	NULL	10001

	All density	Average Length	Columns
1	0.5	4	c1

	RANGE_HI_KEY	RANGE_ROWS	EQ_ROWS	DISTINCT_RANGE_ROWS	AVG_RANGE_ROWS
1	1	0	1	0	1
2	2	0	10000	0	1

Figure 7-17. *Statistics on index* i1

Now, to understand how effectively the optimizer decides upon different data-retrieval strategies based on statistics, execute the following two queries requesting different numbers of rows:

```
SELECT * FROM dbo.t1 WHERE c1 = 1 --Retrieve 1 row;
SELECT * FROM dbo.t1 WHERE c1 = 2 --Retrieve 10000 rows;
```

Figure 7-18 shows execution plans of these queries.

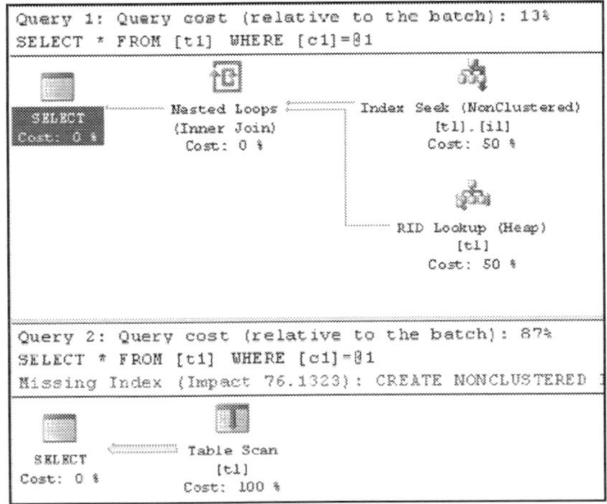

Figure 7-18. *Execution plans of small and large result set queries*

From the statistics, the optimizer can find the number of rows affected by the preceding two queries. Understanding that there is only one row to be retrieved for the first query, the optimizer chose an `Index Seek` operation, followed by the necessary `RID Lookup` to retrieve the data not stored with the clustered index. For the second query, the optimizer knows that a large number of rows (10,000 rows) will be affected and therefore avoided the index to attempt to improve performance. (Chapter 4 explains indexing strategies in detail.)

Besides the information on steps, other useful information in the statistics includes the following:

- The time statistics were last updated
- The number of rows in the table
- The average index key length
- The number of rows sampled for the histogram
- Densities for combinations of columns

Information on the time of the last update can help you decide whether you should manually update the statistics. The average key length represents the average size of the data in the index key column(s). It helps you understand the width of the index key, which is an important measure in determining the effectiveness of the index. As explained in Chapter 4, a wide index is usually costly to maintain and requires more disk space and memory pages.

Density

When creating an execution plan, the query optimizer analyzes the statistics of the columns used in the filter and `JOIN` clauses. A filter criterion with high selectivity limits the number of rows from a table to a small result set and helps the optimizer keep the query cost low. A column with a unique index will have a very high selectivity, since it can limit the number of matching rows to one.

On the other hand, a filter criterion with low selectivity will return a large result set from the table. A filter criterion with very low selectivity makes a nonclustered index on the column ineffective. Navigating through a nonclustered index to the base table for a large result set is usually costlier than scanning the base table (or clustered index) directly because of the cost overhead of bookmark lookups associated with the nonclustered index. You can observe this behavior in the execution plan in Figure 7-18.

Statistics track the selectivity of a column in the form of a density ratio. A column with high selectivity (or uniqueness) will have low density. A column with low density (that is, high selectivity) is suitable for a nonclustered index, because it helps the optimizer retrieve a small number of rows very fast. This is also the principal on which filtered indexes operate since the filter's goal is to increase the selectivity, or density, of the index.

Density can be expressed as follows:

Density = 1 / Number of distinct values for a column

Density will always come out as a number somewhere between 0 and 1. The lower the column density, the more suitable it is for use in a nonclustered index. You can perform your own calculations to determine the density of columns within your own indexes and statistics. For example, to calculate the density of column `c1` from the test table built by `create_t3.sql`, use the following (results in Figure 7-19):

```
SELECT 1.0/COUNT(DISTINCT c1) FROM t1
```

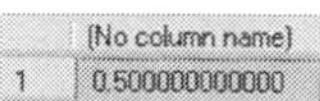

Figure 7-19. *Results of density calculation for column* `c1`

You can see this as actual data in the All density column in the output from DBCC SHOW_STATISTICS. This high-density value for the column makes it a less suitable candidate for an index, even a filtered index. However, the statistics of the index key values maintained in the steps help the query optimizer use the index for the predicate c1 = 1, as shown in the previous execution plan.

Statistics on a Multicolumn Index

In the case of an index with one column, statistics consist of a histogram and a density value for that column. Statistics for a composite index with multiple columns consist of one histogram for the first column only and multiple density values. This is one reason why it's wise to put the more selective column, the one with the lowest density, first when building a compound index or compound statistics. The density values include the density for the first column and for each prefix combination of the index key columns. Multiple density values help the optimizer find the selectivity of the composite index when multiple columns are referred to by predicates in the WHERE and JOIN clauses. Although the first column can help determine the histogram, the final density of the column itself would be the same regardless of column order.

To better understand the density values maintained for a multicolumn index, you can modify the nonclustered index used earlier to include two columns:

```
CREATE NONCLUSTERED INDEX i1 ON dbo.t1(c1,c2) WITH DROP_EXISTING
```

Figure 7-20 shows the resultant statistics provided by DBCC SHOW_STATISTICS.

	Name	Updated	Rows	Rows Sampled	Steps	Density	Average key length	String Index	Filter Expression	Unfiltered Rows
1	i2	Oct 15 2008 8:47PM	10001	10001	2	0	8	NO	NULL	10001

	All density	Average Length	Columns
1	0.5	4	c1
2	9.999E-05	8	c1, c2

	RANGE_HI_KEY	RANGE_ROWS	EQ_ROWS	DISTINCT_RANGE_ROWS	AVG_RANGE_ROWS
1	1	0	1	0	1
2	2	0	10000	0	1

Figure 7-20. *Statistics on the multicolumn index i1*

As you can see, there are two density values under the All density column:

- The density of the first column
- The density of the (first + second) columns

For a multicolumn index with three columns, the statistics for the index would also contain the density value of the (first + second + third) columns. The statistics won't contain a density value for any other combination of columns. Therefore, this index (i1) won't be very useful for filtering rows only on the second column (c2), because the density value of the second column (c2) alone isn't maintained in the statistics.

You can compute the second density value (0.190269999) shown in Figure 7-19 through the following steps. This is the number of distinct values for a column combination of (c1, c2):

```
SELECT 1.0/COUNT(*)
    FROM (SELECT DISTINCT c1, c2 FROM dbo.t1) DistinctRows
```

Statistics on a Filtered Index

The purpose of a filtered index is to change the data that makes up the index and therefore change the density and histogram to make the index more performant. Instead of a test table, this example will use the AdventureWorks2008 database. Create an index on the `Sales.PurchaseOrderHeader` table on the `PurchaseOrderNumber` column:

```
CREATE INDEX IX_Test ON Sales.SalesOrderHeader (PurchaseOrderNumber)
```

Figure 7-21 shows the header and the density of the output from `DBCC SHOW_STATISTICS` run against this new index:

```
DBCC SHOW_STATISTICS('Sales.SalesOrderHeader',IX_Test)
```

	Name	Updated	Rows	Rows Sampled	Steps	Density	Average key length	String Index	Filter Expression	Unfiltered Rows
1	IX_Test	Oct 16 2008 8:22PM	31465	31465	152	1	7.01516	YES	NULL	31465

	All density	Average Length	Columns
1	0.000262674	3.01516	PurchaseOrderNumber
2	3.178134E-05	7.01516	PurchaseOrderNumber, SalesOrderID

Figure 7-21. *Statistics header of an unfiltered index*

If the same index is re-created to deal with values of the column that are not `null`, it would look something like this:

```
CREATE INDEX IX_Test ON Sales.SalesOrderHeader (PurchaseOrderNumber)
WHERE PurchaseOrderNumber IS NOT NULL
WITH DROP_EXISTING
```

And now, in Figure 7-22, take a look at the statistics information.

	Name	Updated	Rows	Rows Sampled	Steps	Density	Average key length	String Index	Filter Expression	Unfiltered Rows
1	IX_Test	Oct 16 2008 8:23PM	3806	3806	151	1	28.92696	YES	([PurchaseOrderNumber] IS NOT NULL)	31465

	All density	Average Length	Columns
1	0.000262743	24.92696	PurchaseOrderNumber
2	0.000262743	28.92696	PurchaseOrderNumber, SalesOrderID

Figure 7-22. *Statistics header for a filtered index*

First you can see that the number of rows that compose the statistics have radically dropped in the filtered index because there is a filter in place. Notice also that the average key length has increased since you're no longer dealing with zero-length strings. A filter expression has been defined rather than the `NULL` value visible in Figure 7-21. But the unfiltered rows of both sets of data are the same.

The density measurements are very interesting. Notice that the density is close to the same for both values, but the filtered density is slightly lower, meaning fewer unique values. This is because the filtered data, while marginally less selective, is actually more accurate, eliminating all the empty values that won't contribute to a search. And the density of the second value, which represents the clustered index pointer, is identical with the value of the density of the `PurchaseOrderNumber` alone because each represents the same amount of unique data. The density of the additional clustered index in the previous column is a much smaller number because of all the unique values of SalesOrderId that are not included in the filtered data because of the elimination of the null values.

One other option open to you is to create filtered statistics. This allows you to create even more fine-tuned histograms on partitioned tables. This is necessary because statistics are not automatically created on partitioned tables and you can't create your own using CREATE STATISTICS. You can create filtered indexes by partition and get statistics or create filtered statistics specifically by partition.

Before going on, clean the indexes created, if any:

```
DROP INDEX Sales.SalesOrderHeader.IX_Test;
```

Statistics Maintenance

SQL Server allows a user to manually override the maintenance of statistics in an individual database. The four main configurations controlling automatic statistics maintenance behavior of SQL Server are as follows:

- New statistics on columns with no index (auto create statistics)
- Updating existing statistics (auto update statistics)
- The degree of sampling used to collect statistics
- Asynchronous updating of existing statistics (auto update statistics async)

You can control the preceding configurations at the levels of a database (all indexes and statistics on all tables) or on a case-by-case basis on individual indexes or statistics. The auto create statistics setting is applicable for nonindexed columns only, because SQL Server always creates statistics for an index key when the index is created. The auto update statistics setting, and the asynchronous version, is applicable for statistics on both indexes and WHERE clause columns with no index.

Automatic Maintenance

By default, SQL Server automatically takes care of statistics. Both the auto create statistics and auto update statistics settings are on by default. These two features together are referred to as *autostats*. As explained previously, it is usually better to keep these settings on. The auto update statistics async setting is off by default.

Auto Create Statistics

The auto create statistics feature automatically creates statistics on nonindexed columns when referred to in the WHERE clause of a query. For example, when this SELECT statement is run against the Sales.SalesOrderHeader table on a column with no index, statistics for the column are created:

```
SELECT  *
FROM    Sales.SalesOrderHeader AS soh
WHERE   ShipToAddressID = 29692
```

Then the auto create statistics feature (make sure it is turned back on if you have turned it off) automatically creates statistics on column `ShipToAddressID`. You can see this in the Profiler trace output in Figure 7-23.

EventClass	TextData	CPU	Reads	Writes	Duration
Auto Stats	Created: ShipToAddressID				41
SQL:BatchCompleted	SELECT * FROM Sales.SalesOrderHead...	63	1407	0	56

Figure 7-23. *Trace output with AUTO_CREATE_STATISTICS ON*

Auto Update Statistics

The auto update statistics feature automatically updates existing statistics on the indexes and columns of a permanent table when the table is referred to in a query, provided the statistics have been marked as out-of-date. The types of changes are action statements, such as `INSERT`, `UPDATE`, and `DELETE`. The threshold for the number of changes depends on the number of rows in the table, as shown in Table 7-4.

Table 7-4. *Update Statistics Threshold for Number of Changes*

Number of Rows	Threshold for Number of Changes
0	> 1 insert
< 500	> 500 changes
> 500	500 + 20% of cardinality changes

In SQL Server, cardinality is counted as the number of rows in the table.

Using an internal threshold reduces the frequency of the automatic update of statistics, and using column changes rather than rows changes further reduces the frequency. For example, consider the following table (`create_t4.sql` in the download):

```
 IF(SELECT OBJECT_ID('dbo.t1')) IS NOT NULL
    DROP TABLE dbo.t1;
CREATE TABLE dbo.t1(c1 INT);
CREATE INDEX ix1 ON dbo.t1(c1);
INSERT INTO dbo.t1 (
    c1
) VALUES ( 0 ) ;
```

After the nonclustered index is created, a single row is added to the table. This outdates the existing statistics on the nonclustered index. If the following `SELECT` statement is executed with a reference to the indexed column in the `WHERE` clause, like so:

```
SELECT * FROM dbo.t1 WHERE c1 = 0
```

then the auto update statistics feature automatically updates statistics on the nonclustered index, as shown in the Profiler trace output in Figure 7-24.

EventClass	TextData	CPU	Reads	Writes	Duration
Auto Stats	Updated: t1.ix1				4
SQL:BatchCompleted	SELECT * FROM t1 WHERE c1 = 0	0	14	0	6

Figure 7-24. *Trace output with* AUTO_UPDATE_STATISTICS ON

Once the statistics are updated, the change-tracking mechanisms for the corresponding tables are set to 0. This way, SQL Server keeps track of the number of changes to the tables and manages the frequency of automatic updates of statistics.

Auto Update Statistics Asynchronously

If auto update statistics asynchronously is set to on, the basic behavior of statistics in SQL Server isn't changed radically. When a set of statistics is marked as out-of-date and a query is then run against those statistics, the statistics update does not interrupt the query, as normally happens. Instead, the query finishes execution using the older set of statistics. Once the query completes, the statistics are updated. The reason this may be attractive is that when statistics are updated, query plans in the procedure cache are removed, and the query being run must be recompiled. So, rather than make a query wait for both the update of the statistics and a recompile of the procedure, the query completes its run. The next time the same query is called, it will have updated statistics waiting for it, and it will have to recompile only.

Although this functionality does make recompiles somewhat faster, it can also cause queries that could benefit from updated statistics and a new execution plan to work with the old execution plan. Careful testing is required before turning this functionality on to ensure it doesn't cause more harm than good.

■ **Note** If you are attempting to update statistics asynchronously, you must also have AUTO_UPDATE_STATISTICS set to ON.

Manual Maintenance

The following are situations in which you need to interfere with the automatic maintenance of statistics:

- *When experimenting with statistics*: Just a friendly suggestion: please spare your production servers from experiments such as the ones you are doing in this book.
- *After upgrading from a previous version to SQL Server 2008*: Since the statistics maintenance of SQL Server 2008 has been upgraded, you should manually update the statistics of the complete database immediately after the upgrade instead of waiting for SQL Server to update it over time with the help of automatic statistics.
- *While executing a series of ad hoc SQL activities that you won't execute again*: In such cases, you must decide whether you want to pay the cost of automatic statistics maintenance to get a better plan in that one case and affect the performance of other SQL Server activities. So, in general, you don't need to be concerned with such one-timers.

- *When you come upon an issue with the automatic statistics maintenance and the only workaround for the time being is to keep the automatic statistics maintenance feature off*: Even in these cases you can turn the feature off for the specific database table that faces the problem instead of disabling it for the complete database.
- *While analyzing the performance of a query, you realize that the statistics are missing for a few of the database objects referred to by the query*: This can be evaluated from the graphical and XML execution plans, as explained earlier in the chapter.
- *While analyzing the effectiveness of statistics, you realize that they are inaccurate*: This can be determined when poor execution plans are being created from what should be good sets of indexes.

SQL Server allows a user to control many of its automatic statistics maintenance features. You can enable (or disable) the automatic statistics creation and update features by using the auto create statistics and auto update statistics settings, respectively, and then you can get your hands dirty.

Manage Statistics Settings

You can control the auto create statistics setting at a database level. To disable this setting, use the `ALTER DATABASE` command:

```
ALTER DATABASE AdventureWorks2008 SET AUTO_CREATE_STATISTICS OFF
```

You can control the auto update statistics setting at different levels of a database, including all indexes and statistics on a table, or at the individual index or statistics level. To disable auto update statistics at the database level, use the `ALTER DATABASE` command:

```
ALTER DATABASE AdventureWorks2008 SET AUTO_UPDATE_STATISTICS OFF
```

Disabling this setting at the database level overrides individual settings at lower levels.

Auto update statistics asynchronously requires that the auto update statistics be on first. Then you can enable the asynchronous update:

```
ALTER DATABASE AdventureWorks2008 SET AUTO_UPDATE_STATISTICS_ASYNC ON
```

To configure auto update statistics for all indexes and statistics on a table in the current database, use the `sp_autostats` system stored procedure:

```
USE AdventureWorks2008
EXEC sp_autostats 'HumanResources.Department', 'OFF'
```

You can also use the same stored procedure to configure this setting for individual indexes or statistics. To disable this setting for the `AK_Department_Name` index on `AdventureWorks2008.HumanResources.Department`, execute the following statements:

```
USE AdventureWorks2008
EXEC sp_autostats ‘HumanResources.Department’, 'OFF', AK_Department_Name
```

You can also use the UPDATE STATISTICS command's WITH NORECOMPUTE option to disable this setting for all or individual indexes and statistics on a table in the current database. The sp_createstats stored procedure also has the NORECOMPUTE option. The NORECOMPUTE option will not disable automatic update of statistics directly, but it will prevent them, which is almost the same.

Avoid disabling the automatic statistics features, unless you have confirmed through testing that this brings a performance benefit. If the automatic statistics features are disabled, then you should manually identify and create missing statistics on the columns that are not indexed and then keep the existing statistics up-to-date.

Reset the automatic maintenance of the index so that it is on where it has been turned off:

```
EXEC sp_autostats 'HumanResources.Department', 'ON'
EXEC sp_autostats 'HumanResources.Department', 'ON', AK_Department_Name
```

Generate Statistics

To create statistics manually, use one of the following options:

- CREATE STATISTICS: You can use this option to create statistics on single or multiple columns of a table or an indexed view. Unlike the CREATE INDEX command, CREATE STATISTICS uses sampling by default.
- sp_createstats: Use this stored procedure to create single-column statistics for all eligible columns for all user tables in the current database. This includes all columns except computed columns; columns with the NTEXT, TEXT, GEOMETRY, GEOGRAPHY, or IMAGE data type; sparse columns; and columns that already have statistics or are the first column of an index.

Similarly, to update statistics manually, use one of the following options:

- UPDATE STATISTICS: You can use this option to update the statistics of individual or all index keys and nonindexed columns of a table or an indexed view.
- sp_updatestats: Use this stored procedure to update statistics of all user tables in the current database.

You may find that allowing the automatic updating of statistics is not quite adequate for your system. Scheduling UPDATE STATISTICS for the database during off-hours is an acceptable way to deal with this issue. UPDATE STATISTICS is the preferred mechanism because it offers a greater degree of flexibility and control. It's possible, because of the types of data inserted, that the sampling method for gathering the statistics, used because it's faster, may not gather the appropriate data. In these cases, you can force a FULLSCAN so that all the data is used to update the statistics just like what happens when the statistics are initially created. This can be a very costly operation, so it's best to be very selective about which indexes receive this treatment and when it is run.

■ **Note** In general, you should always use the default settings for automatic statistics. Consider modifying these settings only after identifying that the default settings appear to detract from performance.

Statistics Maintenance Status

You can verify the current settings for the autostats feature using the following:

- DATABASEPROPERTYEX
- sp_autostats

Status of Auto Create Statistics

You can verify the current setting for auto create statistics by running a query against the sys.databases system table:

```
SELECT is_auto_create_stats_on
FROM sys.databases
WHERE [name] = 'AdventureWorks2008'
```

A return value of 1 means enabled, and a value of 0 means disabled.

You can also verify the status of this feature using the sp_autostats system stored procedure, as shown in the following code. Supplying any table name to the stored procedure will provide the configuration value of auto create statistics for the current database under the Output section of the global statistics settings:

```
USE AdventureWorks2008
EXEC sp_autostats 'HumanResources.Department'
```

Figure 7-25 shows an excerpt of the preceding sp_autostats statement's output.

	Index Name	AUTOSTATS	Last Updated
1	[PK_Department_DepartmentID]	ON	2008-08-06 09:18:18.793
2	[AK_Department_Name]	ON	2008-08-06 09:18:23.237

Figure 7-25. *sp_autostats output*

A return value of ON means enabled, and a value of OFF means disabled.

This stored procedure is more useful when verifying the status of auto update statistics, as explained later in this chapter.

Status of Auto Update Statistics

You can verify the current setting for auto update statistics, and auto update statistics asynchronously, in a similar manner to auto create statistics. Here's how to do it using the function DATABASEPROPERTYEX:

```
SELECT DATABASEPROPERTYEX('AdventureWorks2008', 'IsAutoUpdateStatistics')
```

Here's how to do it using sp_autostats:

```
USE AdventureWorks2008
EXEC sp_autostats 'Sales.SalesOrderDetail'
```

Analyzing the Effectiveness of Statistics for a Query

For performance reasons, it is extremely important to maintain proper statistics on your database objects. Issues with statistics are uncommon. However, you still need to keep your eyes open to the possibility of problems with statistics while analyzing the performance of a query. If an issue with statistics does arise, then it can really take you for a ride. In fact, checking that the statistics are up-to-date at the beginning of a query-tuning session eliminates an easily fixed problem. In this section, you'll see what you can do should you find statistics to be missing or out-of-date.

While analyzing an execution plan for a query, look for the following points to ensure a cost-effective processing strategy:

- Indexes are available on the columns referred to in the filter and join criteria.
- In the case of a missing index, statistics should be available on the columns with no index. It is preferable to have the index itself.
- Since outdated statistics are of no use and can even be misleading, it is important that the estimates used by the optimizer from the statistics are up-to-date.

You analyzed the use of a proper index in Chapter 4. In this section, you will analyze the effectiveness of statistics for a query.

Resolving a Missing Statistics Issue

To see how to identify and resolve a missing statistics issue, consider the following example. To more directly control the data, I'll use a test table instead of one of the AdventureWorks2008 tables. First, disable both auto create statistics and auto update statistics using the `ALTER DATABASE` command:

```
ALTER DATABASE AdventureWorks2008 SET AUTO_CREATE_STATISTICS OFF;
ALTER DATABASE AdventureWorks2008 SET AUTO_UPDATE_STATISTICS OFF;
```

Create a test table with a large number of rows and a nonclustered index (`create_t6.sql` in the download):

```
IF EXISTS ( SELECT  *
            FROM    sys.objects
            WHERE   object_id = OBJECT_ID(N'[dbo].[t1]')
                    AND type IN (N'U') )
    DROP TABLE [dbo].[t1]
GO

CREATE TABLE dbo.t1 (c1 INT, c2 INT, c3 CHAR(50)) ;
INSERT  INTO dbo.t1 (c1, c2, c3)
VALUES  (51, 1, 'c3') ;
INSERT  INTO dbo.t1 (c1, c2, c3)
VALUES  (52, 1, 'c3') ;
CREATE NONCLUSTERED INDEX i1 ON dbo.t1 (c1, c2) ;
```

```
SELECT TOP 10000
        IDENTITY( INT,1,1 ) AS n
INTO    #Nums
FROM    Master.dbo.SysColumns sc1
       ,Master.dbo.SysColumns sc2;

INSERT  INTO dbo.t1 (c1, c2, c3)
        SELECT  n % 50
               ,n
               ,'c3'
        FROM    #Nums;
DROP TABLE #Nums;
```

Since the index is created on (c1, c2), the statistics on the index contain a histogram for the first column, c1, and density values for the prefixed column combinations (c1 and c1 + c2). There are no histograms or density values for column c2.

To understand how to identify missing statistics on a column with no index, execute the following SELECT statement. Since the auto create statistics feature is off, the optimizer won't be able to find the data distribution for the column c2 used in the WHERE clause. You can see this in the execution plan:

```
SELECT * FROM dbo.t1 WHERE t1.c2 = 1;
```

If you right-click the execution plan, you can take a look at the XML data behind it. As shown in Figure 7-26, the XML execution plan indicates missing statistics for a particular execution step under its Warnings element. This shows that the statistics on column t1.c2 are missing.

```
<Warnings>
  <ColumnsWithNoStatistics>
    <ColumnReference Database="[AdventureWorks2008]" Schema="[dbo]" Table="[t1]" Column="c2" />
  </ColumnsWithNoStatistics>
</Warnings>
```

Figure 7-26. *Missing statistics indication in an XML plan*

The information on missing statistics is also provided by the graphical execution plan, as shown in Figure 7-27.

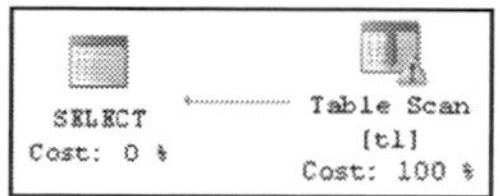

Figure 7-27. *Missing statistics indication in a graphical plan*

The graphical execution plan contains a node with the yellow exclamation point. This indicates some problem with the data-retrieval mechanism (usually missing statistics). You can obtain a detailed description of the error by moving your mouse over the corresponding node of the execution plan to retrieve the tool tip, as shown in Figure 7-28.

Table Scan

Scan rows from a table.

Physical Operation	Table Scan
Logical Operation	Table Scan
Actual Number of Rows	3
Estimated I/O Cost	0.0646065
Estimated CPU Cost	0.0111592
Estimated Number of Executions	1
Number of Executions	1
Estimated Operator Cost	0.0757657 (100%)
Estimated Subtree Cost	0.0757657
Estimated Number of Rows	1000.15
Estimated Row Size	65 B
Actual Rebinds	0
Actual Rewinds	0
Ordered	False
Node ID	0

Predicate
[AdventureWorks2008].[dbo].[t1].[c2]=(1)
Object
[AdventureWorks2008].[dbo].[t1]
Output List
[AdventureWorks2008].[dbo].[t1].c1,
[AdventureWorks2008].[dbo].[t1].c2,
[AdventureWorks2008].[dbo].[t1].c3
Warnings
Columns With No Statistics: [AdventureWorks2008].[dbo].[t1].c2

Figure 7-28. *Tool tip of a graphical plan's node*

Figure 7-28 shows that the statistics for the column are missing. This may prevent the optimizer from selecting the best processing strategy. The current cost of this query as shown by SET STATISTICS IO and SET STATISTICS TIME is as follows:

```
Table 't1'. Scan count 1, logical reads 84
SQL Server Execution Times:
   CPU time = 0 ms,  elapsed time = 44 ms.
```

To resolve this missing statistics issue, you can create the statistics on column t1.c2 by using the CREATE STATISTICS statement:

```
CREATE STATISTICS s1 ON t1(c2);
```

Before rerunning the procedure, be sure to clean out the procedure cache because this query will benefit from simple parameterization:

```
DBCC FREEPROCCACHE();
```

Figure 7-29 shows the resultant execution plan with statistics created on column c2.

```
Table 't1'. Scan count 1, logical reads 43
SQL Server Execution Times:
   CPU time = 0 ms,  elapsed time = 15 ms.
```

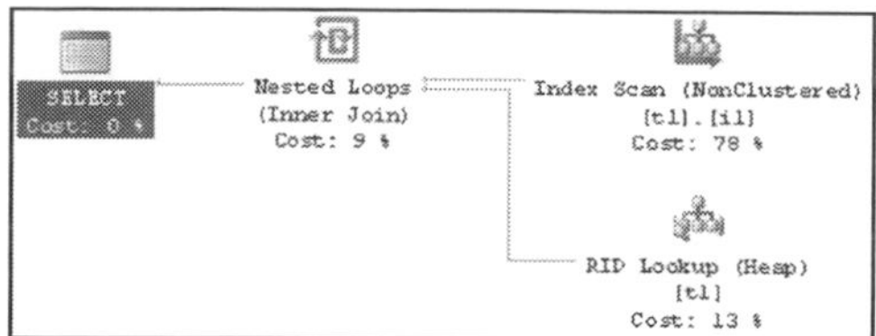

Figure 7-29. *Execution plan with statistics in place*

The query optimizer uses statistics on a noninitial column in a composite index to determine whether scanning the leaf level of the composite index to obtain the bookmarks will be a more efficient processing strategy than scanning the whole table. In this case, creating statistics on column c2 allows the optimizer to determine that instead of scanning the base table, it will be less costly to scan the composite index on (c1, c2) and bookmark lookup to the base table for the few matching rows. Consequently, the number of logical reads has decreased from 87 to 42, but the elapsed time has decreased only slightly.

Resolving an Outdated Statistics Issue

Sometimes outdated or incorrect statistics can be more damaging than missing statistics. Based on old statistics or a partial scan of changed data, the optimizer may decide upon a particular indexing strategy, which may be highly inappropriate for the current data distribution. Unfortunately, the execution plans don't show the same glaring warnings for outdated or incorrect statistics as they do for missing statistics.

To identify outdated statistics, you should examine how close the optimizer's estimation of the number of rows affected is to the actual number of rows affected.

The following example shows you how to identify and resolve an outdated statistics issue. Figure 7-30 shows the statistics on the nonclustered index key on column c1 provided by DBCC SHOW_STATISTICS.

```
DBCC SHOW_STATISTICS(t1, i1);
```

These results say that the density value for column c1 is 0.5. Now consider the following SELECT statement:

```
SELECT * FROM dbo.t1 WHERE c1 = 51;
```

Since the total number of rows in the table is currently 10,002, the number of matching rows for the filter criteria c1 = 51 can be estimated to be 5,001 (= 0.5 × 10,002). This estimated number of rows (5,001) is way off the actual number of matching rows for this column value. The table actually contains only one row for c1 = 51.

	Name	Updated	Rows	Rows Sampled	Steps	Density	Average key length	String Index	Filter Expression	Unfiltered Rows
1	i1	Oct 18 2008 12:40PM	2	2	2	0	8	NO	NULL	2

	All density	Average Length	Columns
1	0.5	4	c1
2	0.5	8	c1, c2

	RANGE_HI_KEY	RANGE_ROWS	EQ_ROWS	DISTINCT_RANGE_ROWS	AVG_RANGE_ROWS
1	51	0	1	0	1
2	52	0	1	0	1

Figure 7-30. *Statistics on index i1*

You can get the information on both the estimated and actual number of rows from the actual execution plan. An estimated plan refers to and uses the statistics only, not the actual data. This means it can be wildly different from the real data, as you're seeing now. The actual execution plan, on the other hand, has both the estimated and actual number of rows available.

Executing the query results in this execution plan (Figure 7-31) and performance:

```
Table 't1'. Scan count 1, logical reads 84
SQL Server Execution Times:
   CPU time = 16 ms,  elapsed time = 2 ms.
```

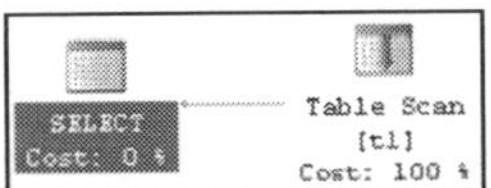

Figure 7-31. *Execution plan with outdated statistics*

To see the estimated and actual rows, you can view the tool tip by hovering over the `Table Scan` operator (Figure 7-32).

Table Scan

Scan rows from a table.

Physical Operation	Table Scan
Logical Operation	Table Scan
Actual Number of Rows	1
Estimated I/O Cost	0.0646065
Estimated CPU Cost	0.0111592
Number of Executions	1
Estimated Number of Executions	1
Estimated Operator Cost	0.0757657 (100%)
Estimated Subtree Cost	0.0757657
Estimated Number of Rows	5001
Estimated Row Size	65 B
Actual Rebinds	0
Actual Rewinds	0
Ordered	False
Node ID	0

Predicate
[AdventureWorks2008].[dbo].[t1].[c1]=(51)
Object
[AdventureWorks2008].[dbo].[t1]
Output List
[AdventureWorks2008].[dbo].[t1].c1,
[AdventureWorks2008].[dbo].[t1].c2,
[AdventureWorks2008].[dbo].[t1].c3

Figure 7-32. *Tool tip showing row count discrepancy*

From the estimated rows value vs. the actual rows value, it's clear that the optimizer made an incorrect estimation based on out-of-date statistics. If the difference between the estimated rows and actual rows is more than a factor of 10, then it's quite possible that the processing strategy chosen may not be very cost effective for the current data distribution. An inaccurate estimation may misguide the optimizer in deciding the processing strategy.

To help the optimizer make an accurate estimation, you should update the statistics on the nonclustered index key on column `c1` (alternatively, of course, you can just leave the auto update statistics feature on):

```
UPDATE STATISTICS t1 i1;
```

If you run the query again, you'll get the following statistics, and the resultant output is as shown in Figure 7-33:

```
Table 't1'. Scan count 1, logical reads 3
SQL Server Execution Times:
   CPU time = 0 ms,  elapsed time = 0 ms.
```

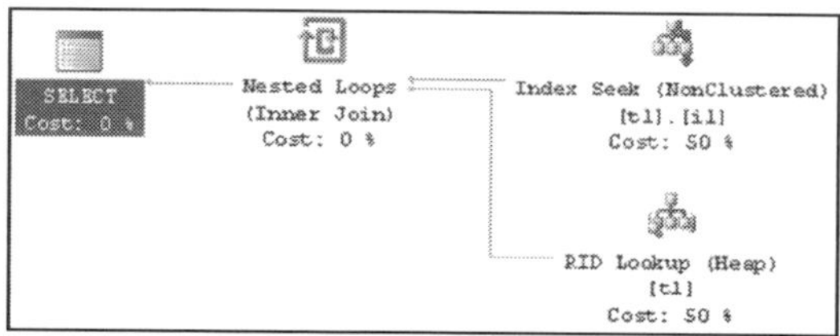

Figure 7-33. *Actual and estimated number of rows with up-to-date statistics*

The optimizer accurately estimated the number of rows using updated statistics and consequently was able to come up with a plan. Since the estimated number of rows is 1, it makes sense to retrieve the row through the nonclustered index on c1 instead of scanning the base table.

Updated, accurate statistics on the index key column help the optimizer come to a better decision on the processing strategy and thereby reduce the number of logical reads from 84 to 3 and reduce the execution time from 16 ms to ~0 ms (there is a ~4 ms lag time).

Before continuing, turn the statistics back on for the database:

```
ALTER DATABASE AdventureWorks2008 SET AUTO_CREATE_STATISTICS ON;
ALTER DATABASE AdventureWorks2008 SET AUTO_UPDATE_STATISTICS ON;
```

Recommendations

Throughout this chapter, I covered various recommendations for statistics. For easy reference, I've consolidated and expanded upon these recommendations in the sections that follow.

Backward Compatibility of Statistics

Statistical information in SQL Server 2008 is different from that in previous versions of SQL Server. However, SQL Server 2008 transfers the statistics during upgrade and, by default, automatically updates these statistics over time. For the best performance, however, manually update the statistics immediately after an upgrade.

Auto Create Statistics

This feature should usually be left on. With the default setting, during the creation of an execution plan, SQL Server determines whether statistics on a nonindexed column will be useful. If this is deemed beneficial, SQL Server creates statistics on the nonindexed column. However, if you plan to create statistics on nonindexed columns manually, then you have to identify exactly for which nonindexed columns statistics will be beneficial.

Auto Update Statistics

This feature should usually be left on, allowing SQL Server to decide on the appropriate execution plan as the data distribution changes over time. Usually the performance benefit provided by this feature outweighs the cost overhead. You will seldom need to interfere with the automatic maintenance of statistics, and such requirements are usually identified while troubleshooting or analyzing performance. To ensure that you aren't facing surprises from the automatic statistics features, it's important to analyze the effectiveness of statistics while diagnosing SQL Server issues.

Unfortunately, if you come across an issue with the auto update statistics feature and have to turn it off, make sure to create a SQL Server job to update the statistics and schedule it to run at regular intervals. For performance reasons, ensure that the SQL job is scheduled to run during off-peak hours.

You can create a SQL Server job to update the statistics from SQL Server Management Studio by following these simple steps:

1. Select ServerName ➤ SQL Server Agent ➤ Jobs, right-click, and select New Job.
2. On the General page of the New Job dialog box, enter the job name and other details, as shown in Figure 7-34.

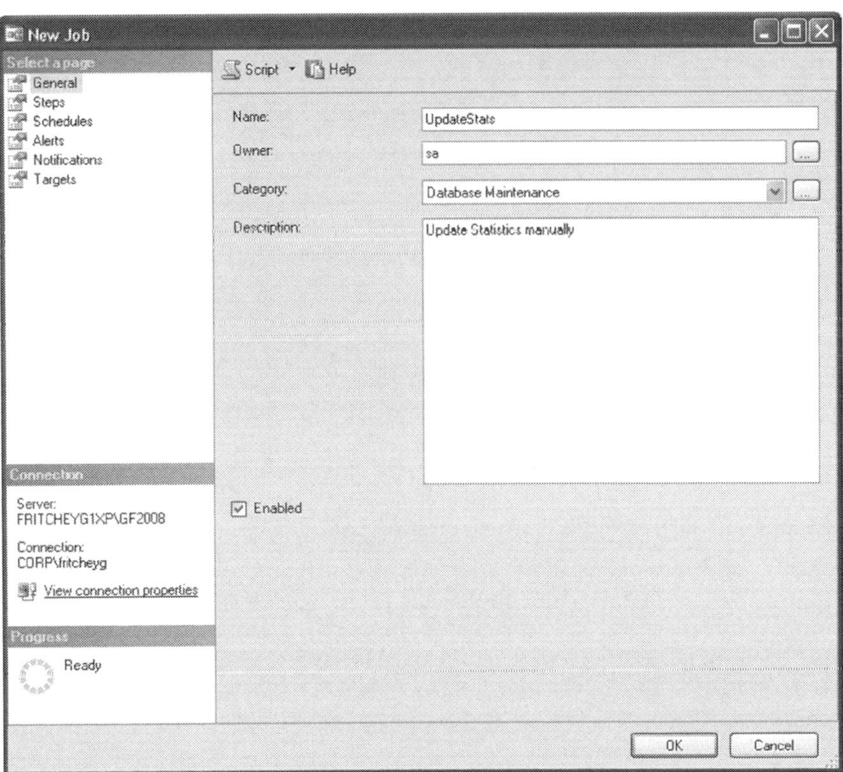

Figure 7-34. *Entering new job information*

3. Choose the Steps page, click New, and enter the SQL command for the user database, as shown in Figure 7-35. I used sp_updatestats here instead of UPDATE STATISTICS because it's a shortcut. I could have run UPDATE STATISTICS against each table in the database a different way, especially if I was interested in taking advantage of all the control offered by UPDATE STATISTICS:

```
EXEC sp_msforeachtable 'UPDATE STATISTICS ? ALL'
```

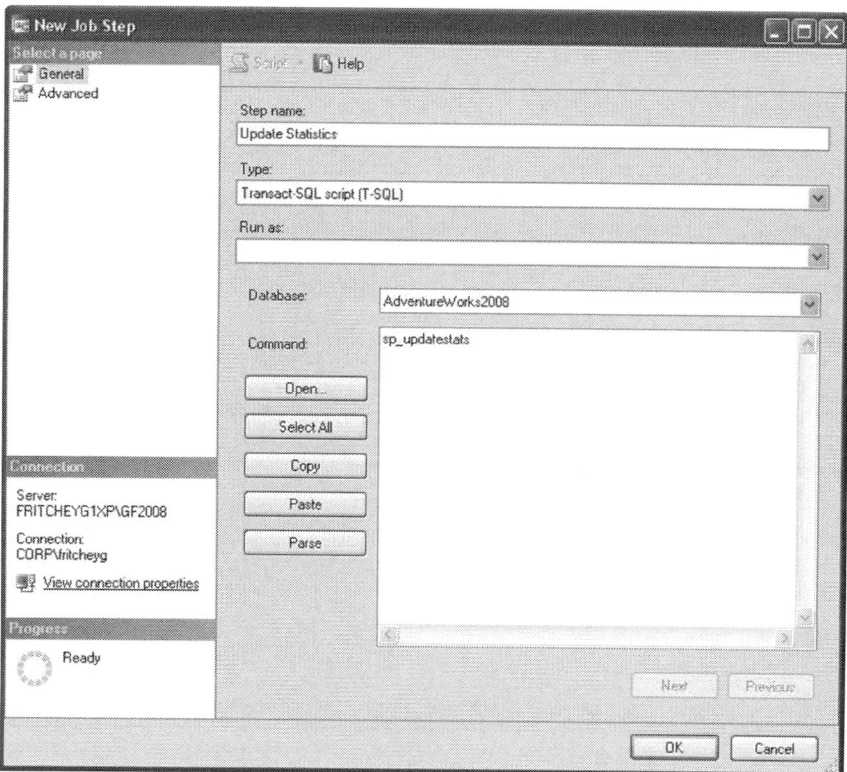

Figure 7-35. *Entering the SQL command for the user database*

4. Return to the New Job dialog box by clicking the OK button.

5. On the Schedules page of the New Job dialog box, click New Schedule, and enter an appropriate schedule to run the SQL Server job, as shown in Figure 7-36.

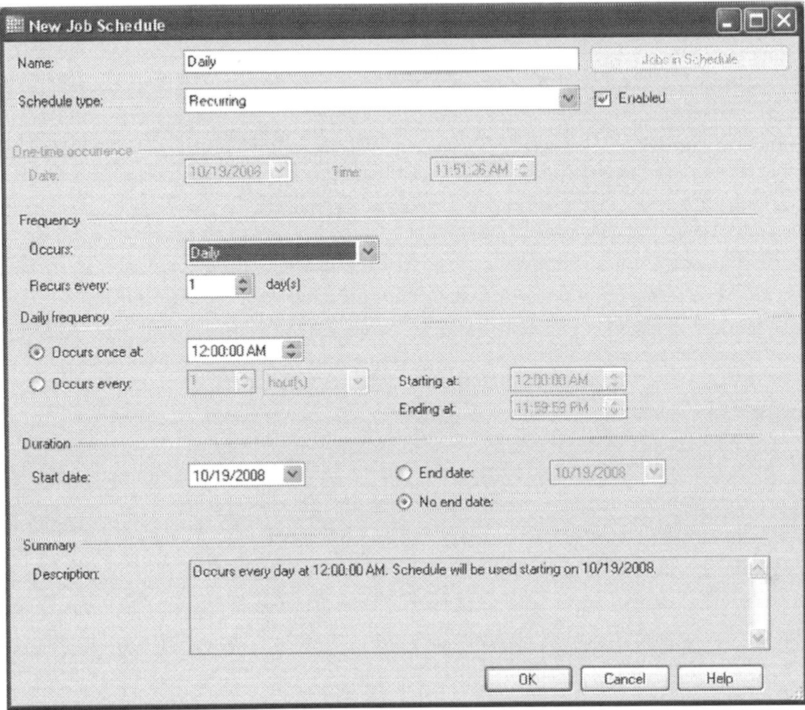

Figure 7-36. *Scheduling the SQL Server job*

6. Return to the New Job dialog box by clicking the OK button.
7. Once you've entered all the information, click OK in the New Job dialog box to create the SQL Server job.
8. Ensure that SQL Server Agent is running so that the SQL Server job is run automatically at the set schedule.

Automatic Update Statistics Asynchronously

Letting statistics update at the beginning of a query, which is the default behavior, will be just fine in most cases. In the very rare circumstances where the statistics update or the execution plan recompiles resulting from that update are very expensive (more expensive than the cost of out-of-date statistics), then you can turn on the asynchronous update of statistics. Just understand that it may mean that procedures that would benefit from more up-to-date statistics will suffer until the next time they are run. Don't forget—you do need automatic update of statistics enabled in order to enable the asynchronous updates.

Amount of Sampling to Collect Statistics

It is generally recommended that you use the default sampling rate. This rate is decided by an efficient algorithm based on the data size and number of modifications. Although the default sampling rate turns out to be best in most cases, if for a particular query you find that the statistics are not very accurate, then you can manually update them with FULLSCAN.

If this is required repeatedly, then you can add a SQL Server job to take care of it. For performance reasons, ensure that the SQL job is scheduled to run during off-peak hours. To identify cases in which the default sampling rate doesn't turn out to be the best, analyze the statistics effectiveness for costly queries while troubleshooting the database performance. Remember that FULLSCAN is expensive, so you should run it only on those tables or indexes that you've determined will really benefit from it.

Summary

As discussed in this chapter, SQL Server's cost-based optimizer requires accurate statistics on columns used in filter and join criteria to determine an efficient processing strategy. Statistics on an index key are always created during the creation of the index, and by default, SQL Server also keeps the statistics on indexed and nonindexed columns updated as the data changes. This enables it to determine the best processing strategies applicable to the current data distribution.

Even though you can disable both the auto create statistics and auto update statistics features, it is recommended that you leave these features *on*, since their benefit to the optimizer is almost always more than their overhead cost. For a costly query, analyze the statistics to ensure that the automatic statistics maintenance lives up to its promise. The best news is that you can rest easy with a little vigilance, since automatic statistics do their job well most of the time. If manual statistics maintenance procedures are used, then you can use SQL Server jobs to automate these procedures.

Even with proper indexes and statistics in place, a heavily fragmented database will incur an increased data-retrieval cost. In the next chapter, you will see how fragmentation in an index can affect query performance, and you'll learn how to analyze and resolve fragmentation.

CHAPTER 8

Fragmentation Analysis

As explained in Chapter 4, index column values are stored in the leaf pages of an index's B-tree structure. When you create an index (clustered or nonclustered) on a table, the cost of data retrieval is reduced by properly ordering the leaf pages of the index and the rows within the leaf pages. In an OLTP database, data changes continually, causing fragmentation of the indexes. As a result, the number of reads required to return the same number of rows increases over time.

In this chapter, I cover the following topics:

- The causes of index fragmentation, including an analysis of page splits caused by `INSERT` and `UPDATE` statements
- The overhead costs associated with fragmentation
- How to analyze the amount of fragmentation
- Techniques used to resolve fragmentation
- The significance of the fill factor in helping to control fragmentation
- How to automate the fragmentation analysis process

Causes of Fragmentation

Fragmentation occurs when data is modified in a table. When you insert or update data in a table (via `INSERT` or `UPDATE`), the table's corresponding clustered indexes and the affected nonclustered indexes are modified. This can cause an index leaf page split if the modification to an index can't be accommodated in the same page. A new leaf page will then be added that contains part of the original page and maintains the logical order of the rows in the index key. Although the new leaf page maintains the *logical* order of the data rows in the original page, this new page usually won't be *physically* adjacent to the original page on the disk. Or, put a slightly different way, the logical key order of the index doesn't match the physical order within the file.

For example, suppose an index has nine key values (or index rows) and the average size of the index rows allows a maximum of four index rows in a leaf page. As explained in Chapter 4, the 8KB leaf pages are connected to the previous and next leaf pages to maintain the logical order of the index. Figure 8-1 illustrates the layout of the leaf pages for the index.

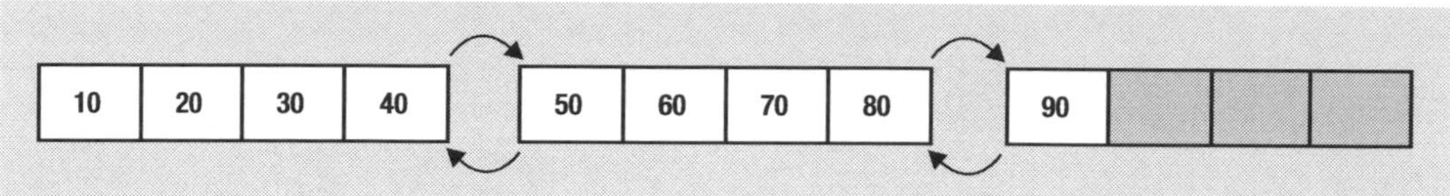

Figure 8-1. *Leaf pages layout*

Since the index key values in the leaf pages are always sorted, a new index row with a key value of 25 has to occupy a place between the existing key values 20 and 30. Because the leaf page containing these existing index key values is full with the four index rows, the new index row will cause the corresponding leaf page to split. A new leaf page will be assigned to the index, and part of the first leaf page will be moved to this new leaf page so that the new index key can be inserted in the correct logical order. The links between the index pages will also be updated so that the pages are logically connected in the order of the index. As shown in Figure 8-2, the new leaf page, even though linked to the other pages in the correct logical order, can be physically out of order.

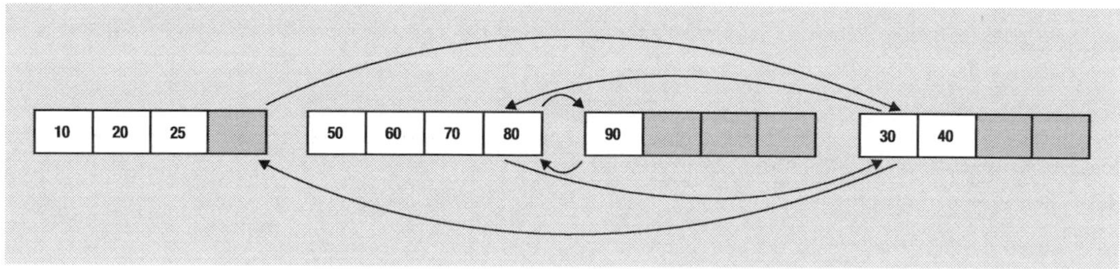

Figure 8-2. *Out-of-order leaf pages*

The pages are grouped together in bigger units called *extents*, which can contain eight pages. SQL Server uses an extent as a physical unit of allocation on the disk. Ideally, the physical order of the extents containing the leaf pages of an index should be the same as the logical order of the index. This reduces the number of switches required between extents when retrieving a range of index rows. However, page splits can physically disorder the pages within the extents, and they can also physically disorder the extents themselves. For example, suppose the first two leaf pages of the index are in extent 1, and say the third leaf page is in extent 2. If extent 2 contains free space, then the new leaf page allocated to the index because of the page split will be in extent 2, as shown in Figure 8-3.

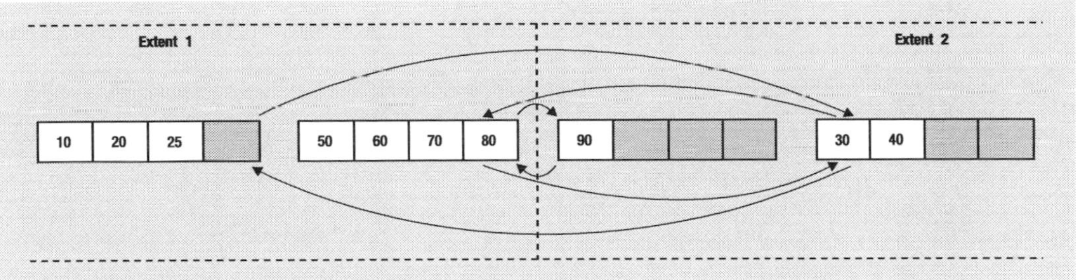

Figure 8-3. *Out-of-order leaf pages distributed across extents*

With the leaf pages distributed between two extents, ideally you expect to read a range of index rows with a maximum of one switch between the two extents. However, the disorganization of pages between the extents can cause more than one extent switch while retrieving a range of index rows. For example, to retrieve a range of index rows between 25 and 90, you will need three extent switches between the two extents, as follows:

- First extent switch to retrieve the key value 30 after the key value 25
- Second extent switch to retrieve the key value 50 after the key value 40
- Third extent switch to retrieve the key value 90 after the key value 80

This type of fragmentation is called *external fragmentation*. External fragmentation is always undesirable.

Fragmentation can also happen within an index page. If an `INSERT` or `UPDATE` operation creates a page split, then free space will be left behind in the original leaf page. Free space can also be caused by a `DELETE` operation. The net effect is to reduce the number of rows included in a leaf page. For example, in Figure 8-3, the page split caused by the `INSERT` operation has created an empty space within the first leaf page. This is known as *internal fragmentation*.

For a highly transactional database, it is desirable to deliberately leave some free space within your leaf pages so that you can add new rows, or change the size of existing rows, without causing a page split. In Figure 8-3, the free space within the first leaf page allows an index key value of 26 to be added to the leaf page without causing a page split.

■ **Note** Note that this index fragmentation is different from disk fragmentation. The index fragmentation cannot be fixed simply by running the disk defragmentation tool, because the order of pages within a SQL Server file is understood only by SQL Server, not by the operating system.

SQL Server 2008 exposes the leaf pages and other data through a dynamic management view called `sys.dm_db_index_physical_stats`. It stores both the index size and the fragmentation. I'll cover it in more detail in the next section. The DMV is much easier to work with than `DBCC SHOWCONTIG`.

Let's now take a look at the mechanics of fragmentation.

Page Split by an UPDATE Statement

To show what happens when a page split is caused by an UPDATE statement, I'll use a constructed table for an example. This small test table will have a clustered index, which orders the rows within one leaf (or data) page as follows (you'll find this code in create_t1.sql in the code download):

```
IF(SELECT OBJECT_ID('t1')) IS NOT NULL
  DROP TABLE t1
GO

CREATE TABLE t1(c1 INT, c2 CHAR(999), c3 VARCHAR(10))
INSERT INTO t1 VALUES(100, 'c2', '')
INSERT INTO t1 VALUES(200, 'c2', '')
INSERT INTO t1 VALUES(300, 'c2', '')
INSERT INTO t1 VALUES(400, 'c2', '')
INSERT INTO t1 VALUES(500, 'c2', '')
INSERT INTO t1 VALUES(600, 'c2', '')
INSERT INTO t1 VALUES(700, 'c2', '')
INSERT INTO t1 VALUES(800, 'c2', '')

CREATE CLUSTERED INDEX i1 ON t1(c1)
```

The average size of a row in the clustered index leaf page (excluding internal overhead) is not just the sum of the average size of the clustered index columns; it's the sum of the average size of all the columns in the table, since the leaf page of the clustered index and the data page of the table are the same. Therefore, the average size of a row in the clustered index is as follows:

= (Average size of [c1]) + (Average size of [c2]) + (Average size of [c3]) bytes

= (Size of INT) + (Size of CHAR(999)) + (Average size of data in [c3]) bytes

= 4 + 999 + 0 = 1,003 bytes

The maximum size of a row in SQL Server is 8,060 bytes. Therefore, if the internal overhead is not very high, all eight rows can be accommodated in a single 8KB page.

To determine the number of leaf pages assigned to the i1 clustered index, execute the SELECT statement against sys.dm_db_index_physical_stats:

```
SELECT  s.avg_fragmentation_in_percent
        ,s.fragment_count
        ,s.page_count
        ,s.avg_page_space_used_in_percent
        ,s.record_count
        ,avg_record_size_in_bytes
FROM    sys.dm_db_index_physical_stats(DB_ID('AdventureWorks2008'),
                                       OBJECT_ID(N'dbo.t1'), NULL, NULL,
                                       'Sampled') AS s
```

You can see the results of this query in Figure 8-4.

	avg_fragmentation_in_percent	fragment_count	page_count	avg_page_space_used_in_percent	record_count	avg_record_size_in_bytes
1	0	1	1	100	8	1010

Figure 8-4. *Physical layout of index* `i1`

From the page_count column in this output, you can see that the number of pages assigned to the clustered index is 1. You can also see the average space used, 100, in the avg_page_space_used_in_percent column. From this you can infer that the page has no free space left to expand the content of c3, which is of type VARCHAR(10) and is currently empty.

Note I'll analyze more of the information provided by sys.dm_db_index_physical_stats in the "Analyzing the Amount of Fragmentation" section later in this chapter.

Therefore, if you attempt to expand the content of column c3 for one of the rows as follows, it should cause a page split:

```
UPDATE  t1
SET     c3 = 'Add data'
WHERE   c1 = 200
```

Selecting the data from sys.dm_db_index_physical_stats results in the information in Figure 8-5.

	avg_fragmentation_in_percent	fragment_count	page_count	avg_page_space_used_in_percent	record_count	avg_record_size_in_bytes
1	50	2	2	50.0741289844329	8	1011.75

Figure 8-5. `i1` *index after a data update*

From the output in Figure 8-5, you can see that SQL Server has added a new page to the index. On a page split, SQL Server generally moves half the total number of rows in the original page to the new page. Therefore, the rows in the two pages are distributed as shown in Figure 8-6.

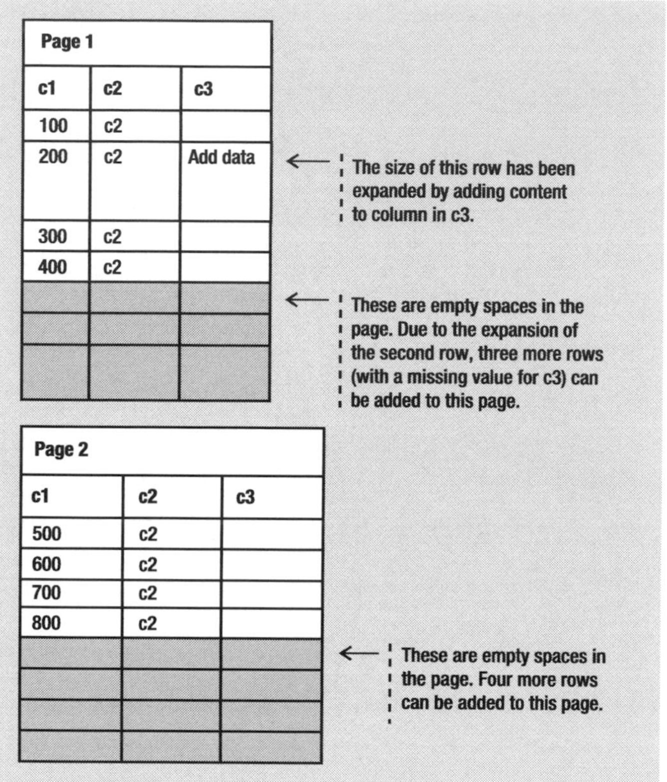

Figure 8-6. *Page split caused by an* UPDATE *statement*

From the preceding tables, you can see that the page split caused by the UPDATE statement results in an internal fragmentation of data in the leaf pages. If the new leaf page can't be written physically next to the original leaf page, there will be external fragmentation as well. For a large table with a high amount of fragmentation, a larger number of leaf pages will be required to hold all the index rows.

To confirm the resultant distribution of rows shown in the previous pages, you can add three trailing rows to the first leaf page and four trailing rows to the second page (`t1_insert.sql` in the download):

```
INSERT INTO t1 VALUES(410, 'c2', '')
INSERT INTO t1 VALUES(420, 'c2', '')
INSERT INTO t1 VALUES(430, 'c2', '')
INSERT INTO t1 VALUES(900, 'c2', '')
INSERT INTO t1 VALUES(1000, 'c2', '')
INSERT INTO t1 VALUES(1100, 'c2', '')
INSERT INTO t1 VALUES(1200, 'c2', '')
```

These seven new rows are accommodated in the existing two leaf pages without causing a page split. You can confirm this by querying `sys.dm_db_index_physical_stats` again (Figure 8-7).

	avg_fragmentation_in_percent	fragment_count	page_count	avg_page_space_used_in_percent	record_count	avg_record_size_in_bytes
1	50	2	2	93.8349394613294	15	1010.933

Figure 8-7. *Pages after the addition of more rows*

Page Split by an INSERT Statement

To understand how a page split can be caused by an `INSERT` statement, create the same test table (`create_t1.sql`) as you did previously, with the eight initial rows and the clustered index. Since the single index leaf page is completely filled, any attempt to add an intermediate row as follows should cause a page split in the leaf page:

```
INSERT INTO t1 VALUES(110, 'c2', '')
```

You can verify this by examining the output of `sys.dm_db_index_physical_stats` (Figure 8-8).

	avg_fragmentation_in_percent	fragment_count	page_count	avg_page_space_used_in_percent	record_count	avg_record_size_in_bytes
1	66.6666666666667	3	3	66.7160859896219	16	1010.875

Figure 8-8. *Pages after insert*

As explained previously, half the rows from the original leaf page are moved to the new page. Once space is cleared in the original leaf page, the new row is added in the appropriate order to the original leaf page. Be aware that a row is associated with only one page; it cannot span multiple pages. Figure 8-9 shows the resultant distribution of rows in the two pages.

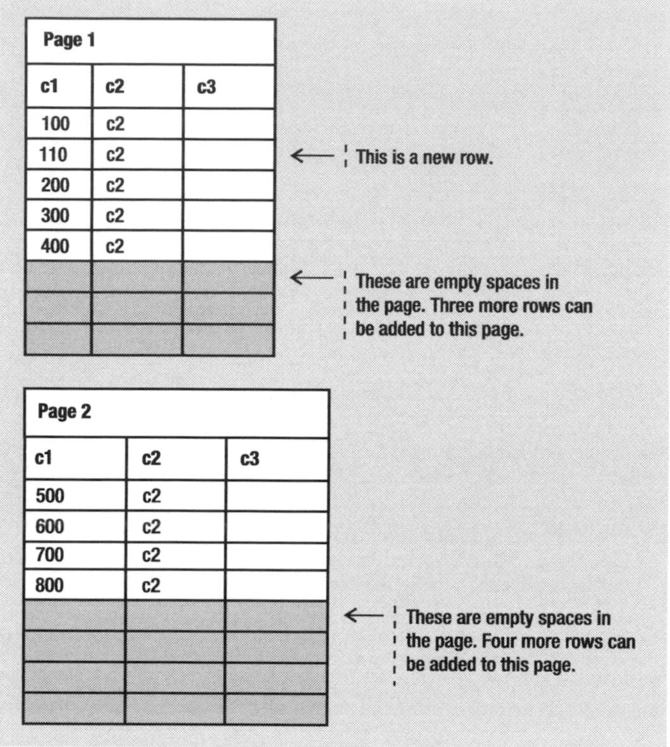

Figure 8-9. *Page split caused by an INSERT statement*

From the previous index pages, you can see that the page split caused by the INSERT statement spreads the rows sparsely across the leaf pages, causing internal fragmentation. It often causes external fragmentation also, since the new leaf page may not be physically adjacent to the original page. For a large table with a high amount of fragmentation, the page splits caused by the INSERT statement will require a larger number of leaf pages to accommodate all the index rows.

To verify the row distribution shown in the index pages, you can run t1_insert.sql again, adding three more rows to the first page and four more rows to the second page:

```
INSERT INTO t1 VALUES(120, 'c2', '')
INSERT INTO t1 VALUES(130, 'c2', '')
INSERT INTO t1 VALUES(140, 'c2', '')
INSERT INTO t1 VALUES(900, 'c2', '')
INSERT INTO t1 VALUES(1000, 'c2', '')
INSERT INTO t1 VALUES(1100, 'c2', '')
INSERT INTO t1 VALUES(1200, 'c2', '')
```

The result is the same as for the previous example: these seven new rows can be accommodated in the two existing leaf pages without causing any page split. Note that in the first page, new rows are added in between the other rows in the page. This won't cause a page split, since free space is available in the page.

What about when you have to add rows to the trailing end of an index? In this case, even if a new page is required, it won't split any existing page. For example, adding a new row with `c1` equal to 1,300 will require a new page, but it won't cause a page split since the row isn't added in an intermediate position. Therefore, if new rows are added in the order of the clustered index, then the index rows will be always added at the trailing end of the index, preventing the page splits otherwise caused by the `INSERT` statements.

Fragmentation caused by page splits hurts data-retrieval performance, as you will see next.

Fragmentation Overhead

Both internal and external fragmentations adversely affect data-retrieval performance. External fragmentation causes a noncontiguous sequence of index pages on the disk, with new leaf pages far from the original leaf pages, and their physical ordering different from their logical ordering. Consequently, a range scan on an index will need more switches between the corresponding extents than ideally required, as explained earlier in the chapter. Also, a range scan on an index will be unable to benefit from read-ahead operations performed on the disk. If the pages are arranged contiguously, then a read-ahead operation can read pages in advance without much head movement.

For better performance, it is preferable to use sequential I/O, since this can read a whole extent (eight 8KB pages together) in a single disk I/O operation. By contrast, a noncontiguous layout of pages requires nonsequential or random I/O operations to retrieve the index pages from the disk, and a random I/O operation can read only 8KB of data in a single disk operation (this may be acceptable, however, if you are retrieving only one row).

In the case of internal fragmentation, rows are distributed sparsely across a large number of pages, increasing the number of disk I/O operations required to read the index pages into memory and increasing the number of logical reads required to retrieve multiple index rows from memory. As mentioned earlier, even though it increases the cost of data retrieval, a little internal fragmentation can be beneficial, because it allows you to perform `INSERT` and `UPDATE` queries without causing page splits. For queries that don't have to traverse a series of pages to retrieve the data, fragmentation can have minimal impact.

To understand how fragmentation affects the cost of a query, create a test table with a clustered index, and insert a highly fragmented data set in the table. Since an `INSERT` operation in between an ordered data set can cause a page split, you can easily create the fragmented data set by adding rows in the following order (`create_t1_fragmented.sql` in the code download):

```
IF (SELECT  OBJECT_ID('t1')
   ) IS NOT NULL
    DROP TABLE t1
GO
CREATE TABLE t1
    (c1 INT
    ,c2 INT
    ,c3 INT
    ,c4 CHAR(2000))
CREATE CLUSTERED INDEX i1 ON t1 (c1) ;
WITH    Nums
          AS (SELECT    1 AS n
              UNION ALL
              SELECT    n + 1
              FROM      Nums
              WHERE     n < 21
             )
    INSERT  INTO t1 (c1, c2, c3, c4)
            SELECT  n
                   ,n
                   ,n
                   ,'a'
            FROM    Nums ;
WITH    Nums
          AS (SELECT    1 AS n
              UNION ALL
              SELECT    n + 1
              FROM      Nums
              WHERE     n < 21
             )
    INSERT  INTO t1 (c1, c2, c3, c4)
            SELECT  41 - n
                   ,n
                   ,n
                   ,'a'
            FROM    Nums
```

To determine the number of logical reads required to retrieve a small result set and a large result set from this fragmented table, execute the two SELECT statements with STATISTICS IO and TIME set to ON (statistics.sql in the download):

```
SELECT * FROM t1 WHERE c1 BETWEEN 21 AND 25 --Reads 6 rows
SELECT * FROM t1 WHERE c1 BETWEEN 1 AND 40  --Reads all rows
```

The number of logical reads performed by the individual queries is, respectively, as follows:

```
Table 't1'. Scan count 1, logical reads 6
CPU time = 0 ms,  elapsed time = 28 ms.
Table 't1'. Scan count 1, logical reads 15
CPU time = 0 ms,  elapsed time = 260 ms.
```

To evaluate how the fragmented data set affects the number of logical reads, rearrange the index leaf pages physically by rebuilding the clustered index:

```
ALTER INDEX i1 ON dbo.t1 REBUILD
```

With the index leaf pages rearranged in the proper order, rerun `statistics.sql`. The number of logical reads required by the preceding two `SELECT` statements reduces to 5 and 13, respectively:

```
Table 't1'. Scan count 1, logical reads 5
CPU time = 0 ms,  elapsed time = 30 ms.
Table 't1'. Scan count 1, logical reads 13
CPU time = 0 ms,  elapsed time = 219 ms.
```

Notice, though, that the execution time wasn't radically reduced, because dropping a single page from the read just isn't likely to increase speed much. The cost overhead because of fragmentation usually increases in line with the number of rows retrieved, because this involves reading a greater number of out-of-order pages. For *point queries* (queries retrieving only one row), fragmentation doesn't usually matter, since the row is retrieved from one leaf page only, but this isn't always the case. Because of the internal structure of the index, fragmentation may increase the cost of even a point query. For instance, the following `SELECT` statement (`singlestat.sql` in the download) performs two logical reads with the leaf pages rearranged properly, but it requires three logical reads on the fragmented data set. To see this in action, run `create_t1_fragmented.sql` again. Now run this query with `STATISTICS IO` and `TIME` enabled:

```
SELECT * FROM t1 WHERE c1 = 10 --Read 1 row
```

The resulting message in the query window for this script is as follows:

```
Table 't1'. Scan count 1, logical reads 3
CPU time = 0 ms,  elapsed time = 0 ms.
```

Once more, rebuild the index using this script:

```
ALTER INDEX i1 ON dbo.t1 REBUILD
```

Running the earlier `SELECT` statement again results in the following output:

```
Table 't1'. Scan count 1, logical reads 2
CPU time = 0 ms,  elapsed time = 0 ms.
```

Remember, this test is on a very small scale, but the number of reads was decreased by a third. Imagine what reducing a third of the number of reads against a table with millions of rows could accomplish.

Note The lesson from this section is that, for better query performance, it is important to analyze the amount of fragmentation in an index and rearrange it if required.

Analyzing the Amount of Fragmentation

You can analyze the fragmentation ratio of an index by using the sys.dm_db_index_physical_stats dynamic management function. For a table with a clustered index, the fragmentation of the clustered index is congruous with the fragmentation of the data pages, since the leaf pages of the clustered index and data pages are the same. sys.dm_db_index_physical_stats also indicates the amount of fragmentation in a heap table (or a table with no clustered index). Since a heap table doesn't require any row ordering, the logical order of the pages isn't relevant for the heap table.

The output of sys.dm_db_index_physical_stats shows information on the pages and extents of an index (or a table). A row is returned for each level of the B-tree in the index. A single row for each allocation unit in a heap is returned. As explained earlier, in SQL Server, eight contiguous 8KB pages are grouped together in an extent that is 64KB in size. For very small tables (much less than 64KB), the pages in an extent can belong to more than one index or table—these are called *mixed extents*. If there are too many small tables in the database, mixed extents help SQL Server conserve disk space.

As a table (or an index) grows and requests more than eight pages, SQL Server creates an extent dedicated to the table (or index) and assigns the pages from this extent. Such an extent is called a *uniform extent*, and it serves up to eight page requests for the same table (or index). Uniform extents help SQL Server lay out the pages of a table (or an index) contiguously. They also reduce the number of page creation requests by an eighth, since a set of eight pages is created in the form of an extent.

To analyze the fragmentation of an index, let's re-create the table with the fragmented data set used in the "Fragmentation Overhead" section (create_t1_fragmented.sql). You can obtain the fragmentation detail of the clustered index (Figure 8-10) by executing the query against the sys.dm_db_index_physical_stats dynamic view used earlier:

```
SELECT  s.avg_fragmentation_in_percent
       ,s.fragment_count
       ,s.page_count
       ,s.avg_page_space_used_in_percent
       ,s.record_count
       ,avg_record_size_in_bytes
FROM    sys.dm_db_index_physical_stats(DB_ID('AdventureWorks2008'),
                                      OBJECT_ID(N'dbo.t1'), NULL, NULL,
                                      'Sampled') AS s
```

	avg_fragmentation_in_percent	fragment_count	page_count	avg_page_space_used_in_percent	record_count	avg_record_size_in_bytes
1	69.2307692307692	10	13	80.6599456387447	42	2019.38

Figure 8-10. *Fragmented statistics*

The dynamic management function sys.dm_db_index_physical_stats scans the pages of an index to return the data. You can control the level of the scan, which affects the speed and the accuracy of the scan. To quickly check the fragmentation of an index, use the Limited option. You can obtain an increased accuracy with only a moderate decrease in speed by using the Sample option, as in the previous example, which scans 1 percent of the pages. For the most accuracy, use the Detailed scan, which hits all the pages in an index. If the index has fewer than 10,000 pages and you select the Sample mode, then the Detailed mode is used instead. This means that despite the choice made in the earlier query, the Detailed scan mode was used.

By defining the different parameters, you can get fragmentation information on different sets of data. By removing the OBJECT_ID function in the earlier query and supplying a NULL value, the query would return information on all indexes within the database. You can also specify the index you want information on or even the partition with a partitioned index.

The output from sys.dm_db_index_physical_stats includes 21 different columns. I selected the basic set of columns used to determine the fragmentation and size of an index. This output represents the following:

- avg_fragmentation_in_percent: This number represents the logical average fragmentation for indexes and heaps as a percentage. If the table is a heap and the mode is Sampled, then this value will be NULL. If average fragmentation is less than 10 to 20 percent, fragmentation is unlikely to be an issue. If the index is between 20 and 40 percent, fragmentation might be an issue, but it can generally be resolved by defragmenting the index through an index reorganization (more information on index reorganization and index rebuild is available in the "Fragmentation Resolutions" section). Large-scale fragmentation, usually greater than 40 percent, may require an index rebuild. Your system may have different requirements than these general numbers

- fragment_count: This number represents the number of fragments, or separated groups of pages, that make up the index. It's a useful number to understand how the index is distributed, especially when compared to the page_count value. fragment_count is NULL when the sampling mode is Sampled.

- page_count: This number is a literal count of the number of index or data pages that make up the statistic. This number is a measure of size but can also help indicate fragmentation. If you know the size of the data or index, you can calculate how many rows can fit on a page. If you then correlate this to the number of rows in the table, you should get a number close to the page_count value. If the page_count value is considerably higher, you may be looking at a fragmentation issue. Refer to the avg_fragmentation_in_percent value for a precise measure.

- avg_page_space_used_in_percent: To get an idea of the amount of space allocated within the pages of the index, use this number. This value is NULL when the sampling mode is Limited.

- record_count: Simply put, this is the number of records represented by the statistics. For indexes, this is the number of records within the current level of the B-tree as represented from the scanning mode. (Detailed scans will show all levels of the B-tree, not simply the leaf level.) For heaps, this number represents the records present, but this number may not correlate precisely to the number of rows in the table since a heap may have two records after an update and a page split.

- avg_record_size_in_bytes: This number simply represents a useful measure for the amount of data stored within the index or heap record.

Running `sys.dm_db_index_physical_stats` with a Detailed scan will return multiple rows for a given index. That is, multiple rows are displayed if that index spans more than one level. Multiple levels exist in an index when that index spans more than a single page. To see what this looks like and to observe some of the other columns of data present in the dynamic management function, run the query this way:

```
SELECT  s.*
FROM    sys.dm_db_index_physical_stats(DB_ID('AdventureWorks2008'),
                                       OBJECT_ID(N'dbo.t1'), NULL, NULL,
                                       'Detailed') AS s
```

To make the data readable, I've broken down the resulting data table into three pieces in a single graphic; see Figure 8-11.

	database_id	object_id	index_id	partition_number	index_type_desc	alloc_unit_type_desc	index_depth	index_level	avg_fragmentation_in_percent
1	7	407672500	1	1	CLUSTERED INDEX	IN_ROW_DATA	2	0	69.2307692307692
2	7	407672500	1	1	CLUSTERED INDEX	IN_ROW_DATA	2	1	0

fragment_count	avg_fragment_size_in_pages	page_count	avg_page_space_used_in_percent	record_count	ghost_record_count
10	1.3	13	80.6599456387447	42	0
1	1	1	2.50803063998023	13	0

version_ghost_record_count	min_record_size_in_bytes	max_record_size_in_bytes	avg_record_size_in_bytes	forwarded_record_count	compressed_page_count
0	2019	2027	2019.38	NULL	0
0	11	14	13.769	NULL	0

Figure 8-11. *Detailed scan of fragmented index*

As you can see, two rows were returned, representing the leaf level of the index (`index_level` = 0) and representing the first level of the B-tree (`index_level` = 1), which is the second row. You can see the additional information offered by `sys.dm_db_index_physical_stats` that can provide more detailed analysis of your indexes. For example, you can see the minimum and maximum record sizes, as well as the index depth (the number of levels in the B-tree) and how many records are on each level. A lot of this information will be less useful for basic fragmentation analysis, which is why I chose to limit the number of columns in the samples as well as use the Sampled scan mode.

Analyzing the Fragmentation of a Small Table

Don't be overly concerned with the output of `sys.dm_db_index_physical_stats` for small tables. For a small table or index with fewer than eight pages, SQL Server uses mixed extents for the pages. For example, if a table (`SmallTable1` or its clustered index) contains only two pages, then SQL Server allocates the two pages from a mixed extent instead of dedicating an extent to the table. The mixed extent may contain pages of other small tables/indexes also, as shown in Figure 8-12.

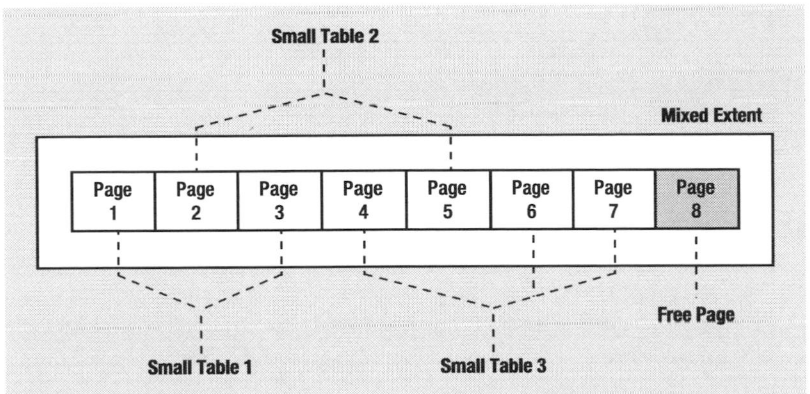

Figure 8-12. *Mixed extent*

The distribution of pages across multiple mixed extents may lead you to believe that there is a high amount of external fragmentation in the table or the index, when in fact this is by design in SQL Server and is therefore perfectly acceptable.

To understand how the fragmentation information of a small table or index may look, create a small table with a clustered index (`create_small_t1_fragmented.sql` in the download):

```
IF(SELECT OBJECT_ID('t1')) IS NOT NULL
  DROP TABLE t1
GO
CREATE TABLE t1(c1 INT, c2 INT, c3 INT, c4 CHAR(2000))
DECLARE @n INT
SET @n = 1
WHILE @n <= 28
BEGIN
  INSERT INTO t1 VALUES(@n, @n, @n, 'a')
  SET @n = @n + 1
END
CREATE CLUSTERED INDEX i1 ON t1(c1)
```

In the preceding table, with each INT taking 4 bytes, the average row size is 2,012 (= 4 + 4 + 4 + 2,000) bytes. Therefore, a default 8KB page can contain up to four rows. After all 28 rows are added to the table, a clustered index is created to physically arrange the rows and reduce fragmentation to a minimum. With the minimum internal fragmentation, seven (= 28 / 4) pages are required for the clustered index (or the base table). Since the number of pages is not more than eight, SQL Server uses pages from mixed extents for the clustered index (or the base table). If the mixed extents used for the clustered index are not side by side, then the output of `sys.dm_db_index_physical_stats` may express a high amount of external fragmentation. But as a SQL user, you can't reduce the resultant external fragmentation. Figure 8-13 shows the output of `sys.dm_db_index_physical_stats`.

	avg_fragmentation_in_percent	fragment_count	page_count	avg_page_space_used_in_percent	record_count	avg_record_size_in_bytes
1	42.8571428571429	4	7	99.8517420311342	28	2019

Figure 8-13. *Fragmentation of a small clustered index*

From the output of `sys.dm_db_index_physical_stats`, you can analyze the fragmentation of the small clustered index (or the table) as follows:

- `avg_fragmentation_in_percent`: Although this index may cross to multiple extents, the fragmentation shown here is not an indication of external fragmentation because this index is being stored on mixed extents.
- `avg_page_space_used_in_percent`: This shows that all or most of the data is stored well within the seven pages displayed in the `page_count` field. This eliminates the possibility of logical fragmentation.
- `fragment_count`: This shows that the data is fragmented and stored on more than one extent, but since it's less than eight pages long, SQL Server doesn't have much choice about where it stores the data.

In spite of the preceding misleading values, a small table (or index) with fewer than eight pages is simply unlikely to benefit from efforts to remove the fragmentation because it will be stored on mixed extents.

Once you determine that fragmentation in an index (or a table) needs to be dealt with, you need to decide which defragmentation technique to use. The factors affecting this decision, and the different techniques, are explained in the following section.

Fragmentation Resolutions

You can resolve fragmentation in an index by rearranging the index rows and pages so that their physical and logical orders match. To reduce external fragmentation, you can physically reorder the leaf pages of the index to follow the logical order of the index. You achieve this through the following techniques:

- Dropping and re-creating the index
- Re-creating the index with the `DROP_EXISTING` clause
- Executing the `ALTER INDEX REBUILD` statement on the index
- Executing the `ALTER INDEX REORGANIZE` statement on the index

Dropping and Re-creating the Index

One of the apparently easiest ways to remove fragmentation in an index is to drop the index and then re-create it. Dropping and re-creating the index reduces fragmentation the most, since it allows SQL Server to use completely new pages for the index and populate them appropriately with the existing data. This avoids both internal and external fragmentation.

Unfortunately, this method has a large number of shortcomings:

- *Blocking*: This technique of defragmentation adds a high amount of overhead on the system, and it causes blocking. Dropping and re-creating the index blocks all other requests on the table (or on any other index on the table). It can also be blocked by other requests against the table.
- *Missing index*: With the index dropped, and possibly being blocked and waiting to be re-created, queries against the table will not have the index available for use. This can lead to the poor performance that the index was intended to remedy.
- *Nonclustered indexes*: If the index being dropped is a clustered index, then all the nonclustered indexes on the table have to be rebuilt after the cluster is dropped. They then have to be rebuilt again after the cluster is re-created. This leads to further blocking and other problems such as stored procedure recompiles (covered in detail in Chapter 10).
- *Unique constraints*: Indexes that are used to define a primary key or a unique constraint cannot be removed using the `DROP INDEX` statement. Also, both unique constraints and primary keys can be referred to by foreign key constraints. Prior to dropping the primary key, all foreign keys that reference the primary key would have to be removed first. Although this is possible, this is a risky and time-consuming method for defragmenting an index.

For all these reasons, dropping and re-creating the index is not a recommended technique for a production database, especially at anything outside off-peak times.

Re-creating the Index with the DROP_EXISTING Clause

To avoid the overhead of rebuilding the nonclustered indexes twice while rebuilding a clustered index, use the `DROP_EXISTING` clause of the `CREATE INDEX` statement. This re-creates the clustered index in one atomic step, avoiding re-creating the nonclustered indexes since the clustered index key values used by the row locators remain the same. To rebuild a clustered key in one atomic step using the `DROP_EXISTING` clause, execute the `CREATE INDEX` statement as follows:

```
CREATE UNIQUE CLUSTERED INDEX pkcl ON t1(c1)
  WITH (DROP_EXISTING = ON)
```

You can use the `DROP_EXISTING` clause for both clustered and nonclustered indexes, and even to convert a nonclustered index to a clustered index. However, you can't use it to convert a clustered index to a nonclustered index.

The drawbacks of this defragmentation technique are as follows:

- *Blocking*: Similar to the DROP and CREATE methods, this technique also causes and faces blocking from other queries accessing the table (or any index on the table).
- *Index with constraints*: Unlike the first method, the CREATE INDEX statement with DROP_EXISTING can be used to re-create indexes with constraints. If the constraint is a primary key or the unique constraint is associated with a foreign key, then failing to include the UNIQUE keyword in the CREATE statement will result in an error like this:

```
Msg 1907, Level 16, State 1, Line 1
Cannot recreate index 'PK_Name'. The new index definition does not match the
constraint being enforced by the existing index.
```

- *Table with multiple fragmented indexes*: As table data fragments, the indexes often become fragmented as well. If this defragmentation technique is used, then all the indexes on the table have to be identified and rebuilt individually.

You can avoid the last two limitations associated with this technique by using ALTER INDEX REBUILD, as explained next.

Executing the ALTER INDEX REBUILD Statement

ALTER INDEX REBUILD rebuilds an index in one atomic step, just like CREATE INDEX with the DROP_EXISTING clause. Since ALTER INDEX REBUILD also rebuilds the index physically, it allows SQL Server to assign fresh pages to reduce both internal and external fragmentation to a minimum. But unlike CREATE INDEX with the DROP_EXISTING clause, it allows an index (supporting either the PRIMARY KEY or UNIQUE constraint) to be rebuilt dynamically without dropping and re-creating the constraints.

To understand the use of ALTER INDEX REBUILD to defragment an index, consider the fragmented table used in the "Fragmentation Overhead" and "Analyzing the Amount of Fragmentation" sections (create_t1_fragmented.sql). This table is repeated here:

```
IF (SELECT  OBJECT_ID('t1')
   ) IS NOT NULL
    DROP TABLE t1
GO
CREATE TABLE t1
    (c1 INT
    ,c2 INT
    ,c3 INT
    ,c4 CHAR(2000))
CREATE CLUSTERED INDEX i1 ON t1 (c1) ;
```

```
WITH    Nums
        AS (SELECT   1 AS n
            UNION ALL
            SELECT   n + 1
            FROM     Nums
            WHERE    n < 21
           )
    INSERT  INTO t1 (c1, c2, c3, c4)
            SELECT  n
                   ,n
                   ,n
                   ,'a'
            FROM    Nums ;
WITH    Nums
        AS (SELECT   1 AS n
            UNION ALL
            SELECT   n + 1
            FROM     Nums
            WHERE    n < 21
           )
    INSERT  INTO t1 (c1, c2, c3, c4)
            SELECT  41 - n
                   ,n
                   ,n
                   ,'a'
            FROM    Nums
```

If you take a look at the current fragmentation, you can see that it is both internally and externally fragmented (Figure 8-14).

	avg_fragmentation_in_percent	fragment_count	page_count	avg_page_space_used_in_percent	record_count	avg_record_size_in_bytes
1	84.6153846153846	12	13	80.6599456387447	42	2019.38

Figure 8-14. *Internal and external fragmentation*

You can defragment the clustered index (or the table) by using the `ALTER INDEX REBUILD` statement:

```
ALTER INDEX i1 ON dbo.t1 REBUILD
```

Figure 8-15 shows the resultant output of the standard `SELECT` statement against `sys.dm_db_index_physical_stats`.

	avg_fragmentation_in_percent	fragment_count	page_count	avg_page_space_used_in_percent	record_count	avg_record_size_in_bytes
1	27.2727272727273	5	11	95.3298739807265	42	2019.38

Figure 8-15. *Fragmentation resolved by* `ALTER INDEX REBUILD`

Compare the preceding results of the query in Figure 8-15 with that from the earlier results in Figure 8-14. You can see that both internal and external fragmentation have been reduced efficiently. Here's an analysis of the output:

- *Internal fragmentation*: The table has 42 rows with an average row size (2,019.38 bytes) that allows a maximum of four rows per page. If the rows are highly defragmented to reduce the internal fragmentation to a minimum, then there should be 11 data pages in the table (or leaf pages in the clustered index). You can observe the following in the preceding output:
  - Number of leaf (or data) pages = `page_count` = 11
  - Amount of defragmentation in a page = `avg_page_space_used_in_percent` = 95.33 percent
- *External fragmentation*: A minimum of two extents is required to hold the 11 pages. For a minimum of external fragmentation, there should not be any gap between the two extents, and all pages should be physically arranged in the logical order of the index. The preceding output illustrates the number of out-of-order pages = `avg_fragmentation_in_percent` = 27.27 percent. Although this may not be a perfect level of fragmentation, being greater than 20 percent, this is adequate considering the size of the index.

As shown previously, the `ALTER INDEX REBUILD` technique effectively reduces fragmentation. You can also use it to rebuild *all* the indexes of a table in one statement:

```
ALTER INDEX ALL ON dbo.t1
```

Although this is the most effective defragmentation technique, it does have some overhead and limitations:

- *Blocking*: Similar to the previous two index-rebuilding techniques, `ALTER INDEX REBUILD` introduces blocking in the system. It blocks all other queries trying to access the table (or any index on the table). It can also be blocked by those queries.
- *Transaction rollback*: Since `ALTER INDEX REBUILD` is fully atomic in action, if it is stopped before completion, then all the defragmentation actions performed up to that time are lost. You can run `ALTER INDEX REBUILD` using the `ONLINE` keyword, which will reduce the locking mechanisms, but it will increase the time involved in rebuilding the index.

Executing the ALTER INDEX REORGANIZE Statement

`ALTER INDEX REORGANIZE` reduces the fragmentation of an index without rebuilding the index. It reduces external fragmentation by rearranging the existing leaf pages of the index in the logical order of the index key. It compacts the rows within the pages, reducing internal fragmentation, and discards the resultant empty pages. This technique doesn't use any new pages for defragmentation.

To avoid the blocking overhead associated with `ALTER INDEX REBUILD`, this technique uses a nonatomic online approach. As it proceeds through its steps, it requests a small number of locks for a short period. Once each step is done, it releases the locks and proceeds to the next step. While trying to access a page, if it finds that the page is being used, it skips that page and never returns to the page again. This allows other queries to run on the table along with the `ALTER INDEX REORGANIZE` operation. Also, if this operation is stopped intermediately, then all the defragmentation steps performed up to then are preserved.

Since `ALTER INDEX REORGANIZE` doesn't use any new pages to reorder the index and it skips the locked pages, the amount of defragmentation provided by this approach is usually less than that of `ALTER INDEX REBUILD`. To observe the relative effectiveness of `ALTER INDEX REORGANIZE` compared to `ALTER INDEX REBUILD`, rebuild the test table (`create_t1_fragmented.sql`) used in the previous section on `ALTER INDEX REBUILD`.

Now, to reduce the fragmentation of the clustered index, use `ALTER INDEX REORGANIZE` as follows:

```
ALTER INDEX i1 ON dbo.t1 REORGANIZE
```

Figure 8-16 shows the resultant output from `sys.dm_db_index_physical_stats`.

	avg_fragmentation_in_percent	fragment_count	page_count	avg_page_space_used_in_percent	record_count	avg_record_size_in_bytes
1	63.6363636363636	8	11	95.3298739807265	42	2019.38

Figure 8-16. *Results of* `ALTER INDEX REORGANIZE`

From the output, you can see that `ALTER INDEX REORGANIZE` doesn't reduce fragmentation as effectively as `ALTER INDEX REBUILD`, as shown in the previous section. For a highly fragmented index, the `ALTER INDEX REORGANIZE` operation can take much longer than rebuilding the index. Also, if an index spans multiple files, `ALTER INDEX REORGANIZE` doesn't migrate pages between the files. However, the main benefit of using `ALTER INDEX REORGANIZE` is that it allows other queries to access the table (or the indexes) simultaneously.

Table 8-1 summarizes the characteristics of these four defragmentation techniques.

Table 8-1. *Characteristics of Four Defragmentation Techniques*

Characteristics/Issues	Drop and Create Index	Create Index with `DROP_EXISTING`	`ALTER INDEX REBUILD`	`ALTER INDEX REORGANIZE`
Rebuild nonclustered indexes on clustered index fragmentation	Twice	No	No	No
Missing indexes	Yes	No	No	No
Defragment index with constraints	Highly complex	Moderately complex	Easy	Easy
Defragment multiple indexes together	No	No	Yes	Yes
Concurrency with others	Low	Low	Medium, depending on concurrent user activity	High
Intermediate cancellation	Dangerous with no transaction	Progress lost	Progress lost	Progress preserved
Degree of defragmentation	High	High	High	Moderate to low
Apply new fill factor	Yes	Yes	Yes	No
Statistics are updated	Yes	Yes	Yes	No

You can also reduce internal fragmentation by compressing more rows within a page, reducing free spaces within the pages. The maximum amount of compression that can be done within the leaf pages of an index is controlled by the fill factor, as you will see next.

When dealing with very large databases and the indexes associated, it may become necessary to split the tables and the indexes up across servers and/or disks using partitioning. Indexes on partitions can also become fragmented as the data within the partition changes. When dealing with a portioned index, you will need to determine whether you want to either `REORGANIZE` or `REBUILD` one, some, or all partitions as part of the `ALTER INDEX` command. Partitioned indexes cannot be rebuilt online. Keep in mind that doing anything that affects all partitions is likely to be a very costly operation.

One of the new features of SQL Server 2008 is data compression. If compression is specified on an index, even on a partitioned index, you must be sure to set the compression while performing the `ALTER INDEX` operation to what it was before; if you don't, it will be lost, and you'll have to rebuild the index again. This is especially important for nonclustered indexes, which will not inherit the compression setting from the table.

Significance of the Fill Factor

The internal fragmentation of an index is reduced by compressing more rows per leaf page in an index. Compressing more rows within a leaf page reduces the total number of pages required for the index and in turn decreases disk I/O and the logical reads required to retrieve a range of index rows. On the other hand, if the index key values are highly transactional, then having fully compressed index pages will cause page splits. Therefore, for a transactional table, a good balance between maximizing the number of rows in a page and avoiding page splits is required.

SQL Server allows you to control the amount of free space within the leaf pages of the index by using the *fill factor*. If you know that there will be enough `INSERT` queries on the table or `UPDATE` queries on the index key columns, then you can pre-add free space to the index leaf page using the fill factor to minimize page splits. If the table is read-only, you can create the index with a high fill factor to reduce the number of index pages.

The default fill factor is 0, which means the leaf pages are packed to 100 percent, although some free space is left in the branch nodes of the B-tree structure. The fill factor for an index is applied only when the index is created. As keys are inserted and updated, the density of rows in the index eventually stabilizes within a narrow range. As you saw in the previous chapter's sections on page splits caused by `UPDATE` and `INSERT`, when a page split occurs, generally half the original page is moved to a new page, which happens irrespective of the fill factor used during the index creation.

To understand the significance of the fill factor, let's use a small test table (`create_t1_fill.sql` in the download) with 24 rows:

```
IF (SELECT  OBJECT_ID('t1')
   ) IS NOT NULL
    DROP TABLE t1
GO
```

```
CREATE TABLE t1 (c1 INT, c2 CHAR(999)) ;
WITH    Nums
          AS (SELECT    1 AS n
              UNION ALL
              SELECT    n + 1
              FROM      Nums
              WHERE     n < 24
             )
     INSERT  INTO t1 (c1, c2)
            SELECT  n * 100
                   ,'a'
            FROM    Nums
```

Compress the maximum number of rows in the leaf (or data) page by creating a clustered index with the default fill factor:

```
CREATE CLUSTERED INDEX i1 ON t1(c1)
```

Since the average row size is 1,010 bytes, a clustered index leaf page (or table data page) can contain a maximum of eight rows. Therefore, at least three leaf pages are required for the 24 rows. You can confirm this in the `sys.dm_db_index_physical_stats` output shown in Figure 8-17.

	avg_fragmentation_in_percent	fragment_count	page_count	avg_page_space_used_in_percent	record_count	avg_record_size_in_bytes
1	66.6666666666667	3	3	100	24	1010

Figure 8-17. *Fill factor set to default value of 0*

Note that avg_page_space_used_in_percent is 100 percent, since the default fill factor allows the maximum number of rows to be compressed in a page. Since a page cannot contain a part row to fill the page fully, avg_page_space_used_in_percent will be often a little less than 100 percent, even with the default fill factor.

To prevent page splits caused by INSERT and UPDATE operations, create some free space within the leaf (or data) pages by re-creating the clustered index with a fill factor as follows:

```
ALTER INDEX i1 ON dbo.t1 REBUILD
    WITH (
         FILLFACTOR=
         75)
```

Because each page has a total space for eight rows, a fill factor of 75 percent will allow six rows per page. Thus, for 24 rows, the number of leaf pages should increase to four, as in the `sys.dm_db_index_physical_stats` output shown in Figure 8-18.

	avg_fragmentation_in_percent	fragment_count	page_count	avg_page_space_used_in_percent	record_count	avg_record_size_in_bytes
1	75	4	4	74.9938225846306	24	1010

Figure 8-18. *Fill factor set to 75*

Note that avg_page_space_used_in_percent is about 75 percent, as set by the fill factor. This allows two more rows to be inserted in each page without causing a page split. You can confirm this by adding two rows to the first set of six rows (c1 = 100 – 600, contained in the first page):

```
INSERT INTO t1 VALUES(110, 'a') --25th row
INSERT INTO t1 VALUES(120, 'a') --26th row
```

Figure 8-19 shows the current fragmentation.

	avg_fragmentation_in_percent	fragment_count	page_count	avg_page_space_used_in_percent	record_count	avg_record_size_in_bytes
1	75	4	4	81.2453669384729	26	1010

Figure 8-19. *Fragmentation after new records*

From the output, you can see that the addition of the two rows has not added any pages to the index. Accordingly, avg_page_space_used_in_percent increased from 74.99 percent to 81.25 percent. With the addition of two rows to the set of the first six rows, the first page should be completely full (eight rows). Any further addition of rows within the range of the first eight rows should cause a page split and thereby increase the number of index pages to five:

```
INSERT INTO t1 VALUES(130, 'a') --27th row
```

Now sys.dm_db_index_physical_stats displays the difference in Figure 8-20.

	avg_fragmentation_in_percent	fragment_count	page_count	avg_page_space_used_in_percent	record_count	avg_record_size_in_bytes
1	80	5	5	67.4919693600198	27	1010

Figure 8-20. *Number of pages goes up*

Note that even though the fill factor for the index is 75 percent, Avg. Page Density (full) has decreased to 67.49 percent, which can be computed as follows:

Avg. Page Density (full)

= Average rows per page / Maximum rows per page

= (27 / 5) / 8

= 67.5%

From the preceding example, you can see that the fill factor is applied when the index is created. But later, as the data is modified, it has no significance. Irrespective of the fill factor, whenever a page splits, the rows of the original page are distributed between two pages, and avg_page_space_used_in_percent settles accordingly. Therefore, if you use a nondefault fill factor, you should ensure that the fill factor is reapplied regularly to maintain its effect.

You can reapply a fill factor by re-creating the index or by using `ALTER INDEX REORGANIZE` or `ALTER INDEX REBUILD`, as was shown. `ALTER INDEX REORGANIZE` takes the fill factor specified during the index creation into account. `ALTER INDEX REBUILD` also takes the original fill factor into account, but it allows a new fill factor to be specified, if required.

Without periodic maintenance of the fill factor, for both default and nondefault fill factor settings, `avg_page_space_used_in_percent` for an index (or a table) eventually settles within a narrow range. Therefore, in most cases, without manual maintenance of the fill factor, the default fill factor is generally good enough.

You should also consider one final aspect when deciding upon the fill factor. Even for a heavy OLTP application, the number of database reads typically outnumbers writes by a factor of 5 to 10. Specifying a fill factor other than the default can degrade read performance by an amount inversely proportional to the fill factor setting, since it spreads keys over a wider area. Before setting the fill factor at a database-wide level, use Performance Monitor to compare the `SQL Server:Buffer Manager\Page reads/sec` counter to the `SQL Server:Buffer Manager\Page writes/sec` counter, and use the fill factor option only if writes are a substantial fraction of reads (greater than 30 percent).

Automatic Maintenance

In a database with a great deal of transactions, tables and indexes become fragmented over time. Thus, to improve performance, you should check the fragmentation of the tables and indexes regularly, and you should defragment the ones with a high amount of fragmentation. You can do this analysis for a database by following these steps:

1. Identify all user tables in the current database to analyze fragmentation.
2. Determine fragmentation of every user table and index.
3. Determine user tables and indexes that require defragmentation by taking into account the following considerations:
    - A high level of fragmentation where `avg_fragmentation_in_percent` is greater than 20 percent
    - Not a very small table/index—that is, `page_count` is greater than 8
4. Defragment tables and indexes with high fragmentation.

A sample SQL stored procedure (`IndexDefrag.sql` in the download) is included here for easy reference. It performs the following actions:

- Walks all databases on the system and identifies indexes on user tables in each database that meets the fragmentation criteria and saves them in a temporary table
- Based on the level of fragmentation, reorganizes lightly fragmented indexes and rebuilds those that are highly fragmented

Here's how to analyze and resolve database fragmentation (store this where appropriate on your system; we have a designated database for enterprise-level scripts):

```
CREATE PROCEDURE IndexDefrag
AS

DECLARE @DBName NVARCHAR(255)
    ,@TableName NVARCHAR(255)
    ,@SchemaName NVARCHAR(255)
    ,@IndexName NVARCHAR(255)
    ,@PctFrag DECIMAL

DECLARE @Defrag NVARCHAR(MAX)

IF EXISTS (SELECT * FROM sys.objects WHERE OBJECT_ID = OBJECT_ID(N'#Frag'))
    DROP TABLE #Frag

CREATE TABLE #Frag
(DBName NVARCHAR(255)
,TableName NVARCHAR(255)
,SchemaName NVARCHAR(255)
,IndexName NVARCHAR(255)
,AvgFragment DECIMAL)

EXEC sp_msforeachdb 'INSERT INTO #Frag (
    DBName,
    TableName,
    SchemaName,
    IndexName,
    AvgFragment
) SELECT  ''?'' AS DBName
       ,t.Name AS TableName
       ,sc.Name AS SchemaName
       ,i.name AS IndexName
       ,s.avg_fragmentation_in_percent
FROM    ?.sys.dm_db_index_physical_stats(DB_ID(''?''), NULL, NULL,
                                NULL, ''Sampled'') AS s
        JOIN ?.sys.indexes i
        ON s.Object_Id = i.Object_id
           AND s.Index_id = i.Index_id
        JOIN ?.sys.tables t
        ON i.Object_id = t.Object_Id
        JOIN ?.sys.schemas sc
        ON t.schema_id = sc.SCHEMA_ID
```

```
WHERE s.avg_fragmentation_in_percent > 20
AND t.TYPE = ''U''
AND s.page_count > 8
ORDER BY TableName,IndexName'

DECLARE cList CURSOR
FOR SELECT * FROM #Frag

OPEN cList
FETCH NEXT FROM cList
INTO @DBName, @TableName,@SchemaName,@IndexName,@PctFrag
WHILE @@FETCH_STATUS = 0
BEGIN
    IF @PctFrag BETWEEN 20.0 AND 40.0
    BEGIN
        SET @Defrag = N'ALTER INDEX ' + @IndexName + ' ON ' + @DBName + '.' +
 @SchemaName + '.' + @TableName + ' REORGANIZE'
        EXEC sp_executesql @Defrag
        PRINT 'Reorganize index: ' + @DBName + '.' + @SchemaName + '.' + @TableName
+'.' + @IndexName
    END
    ELSE IF @PctFrag > 40.0
    BEGIN
        SET @Defrag = N'ALTER INDEX ' + @IndexName + ' ON ' + @DBName + '.' +
@SchemaName + '.' + @TableName + ' REBUILD'
        EXEC sp_executesql @Defrag
        PRINT 'Rebuild index: '+ @DBName + '.' + @SchemaName + '.' + @TableName +'.'
 + @IndexName
    END

    FETCH NEXT FROM cList
    INTO @DBName, @TableName,@SchemaName,@IndexName,@PctFrag

END
CLOSE cList
DEALLOCATE cList

DROP TABLE #Frag
GO
```

To automate the fragmentation analysis process, you can create a SQL Server job from SQL Server Enterprise Manager by following these simple steps:

1. Open Management Studio, right-click the SQL Server Agent icon, and select New ➤ Job.
2. On the General page of the New Job dialog box, enter the job name and other details, as shown in Figure 8-21.

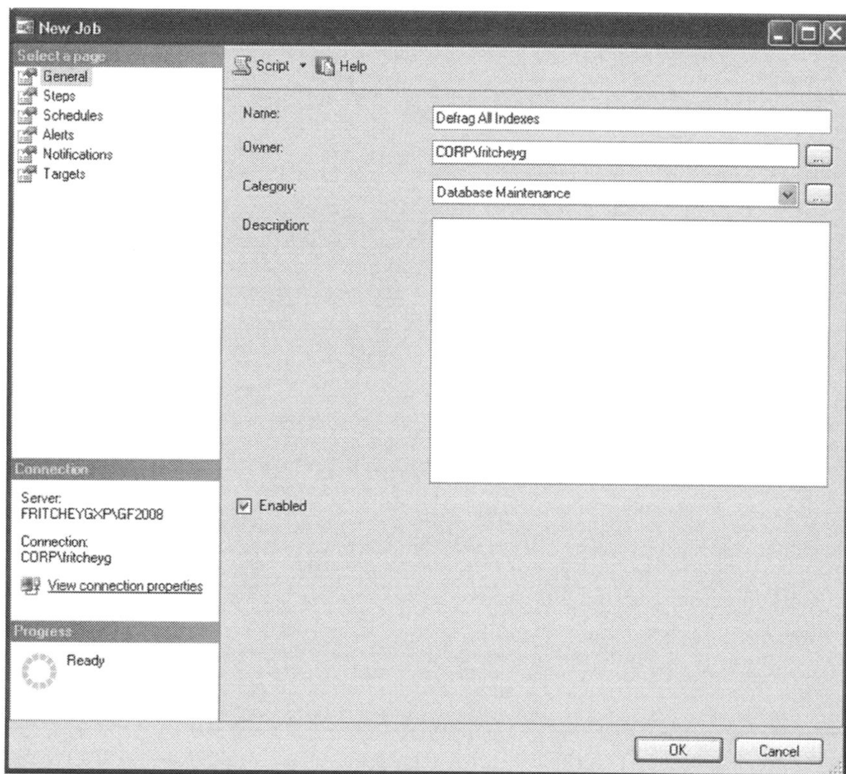

Figure 8-21. *Entering the job name and details*

3. On the Steps page of the New Job dialog box, click New, and enter the SQL command for the user database, as shown in Figure 8-22.
4. On the Advanced page of the New Job Step dialog box, enter an output file name to report the fragmentation analysis outcome, as shown in Figure 8-23.

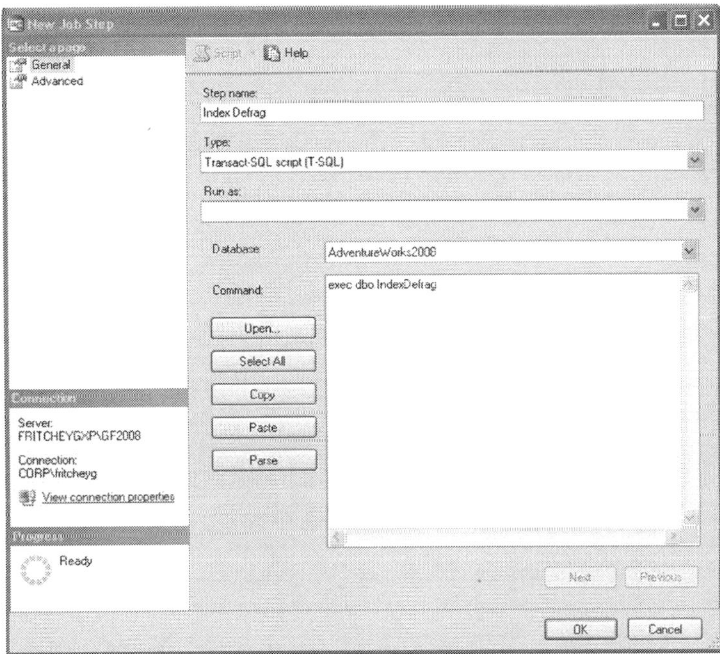

Figure 8-22. *Entering the SQL command for the user database*

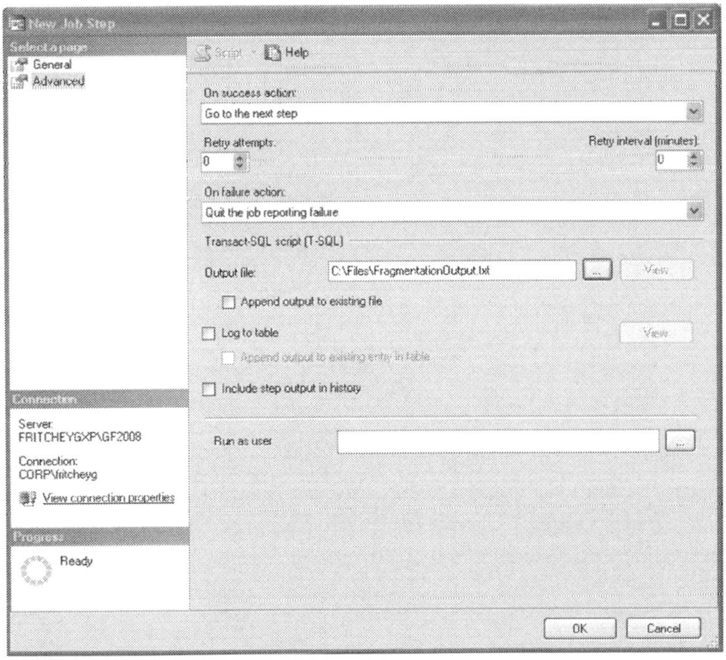

Figure 8-23. *Entering an output file name*

5. Return to the New Job dialog box by clicking OK.
6. On the Schedules page of the New Job dialog box, click New Schedule, and enter an appropriate schedule to run the SQL Server job, as shown in Figure 8-24.

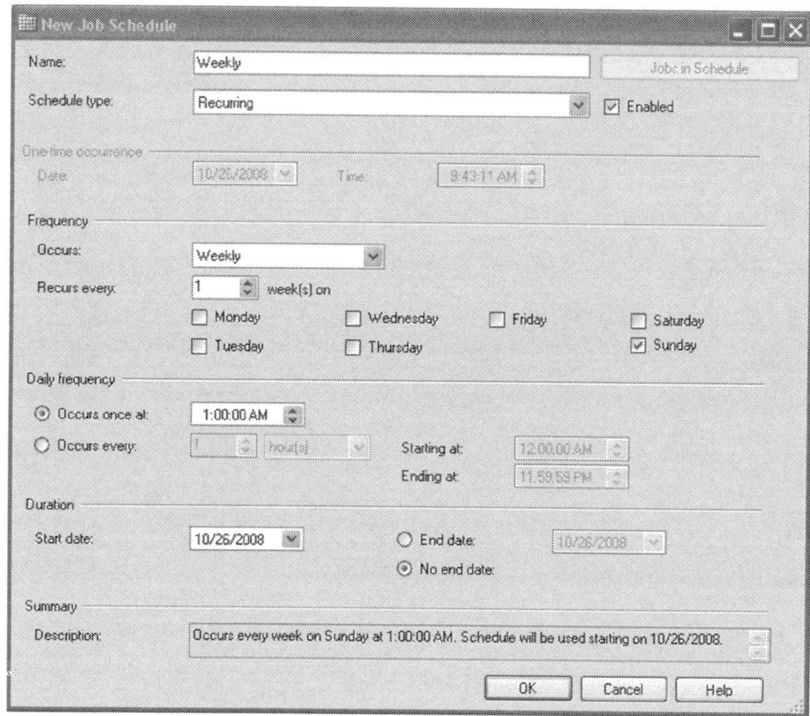

Figure 8-24. *Entering a job schedule*

Schedule this stored procedure to execute during nonpeak hours. To be certain about the usage pattern of your database, log the `SQLServer:SQL Statistics\Batch Requests/sec` performance counter for a complete day. It will show you the fluctuation in load on the database. (I explain this performance counter in detail in Chapter 2.)

7. Return to the New Job dialog box by clicking the OK button.
8. Once you've entered all the information, click OK in the New Job dialog box to create the SQL Server job. A SQL Server job is created that schedules the `sp_IndexDefrag` stored procedure to run at a regular (weekly) time interval.
9. Ensure that SQL Server Agent is running so that the SQL Server job will run automatically according to the set schedule.

The SQL job will automatically analyze and defragment the fragmentation of each database every Sunday at 1 a.m. Figure 8-25 shows the corresponding output of the `FragmentationOutput.txt` file.

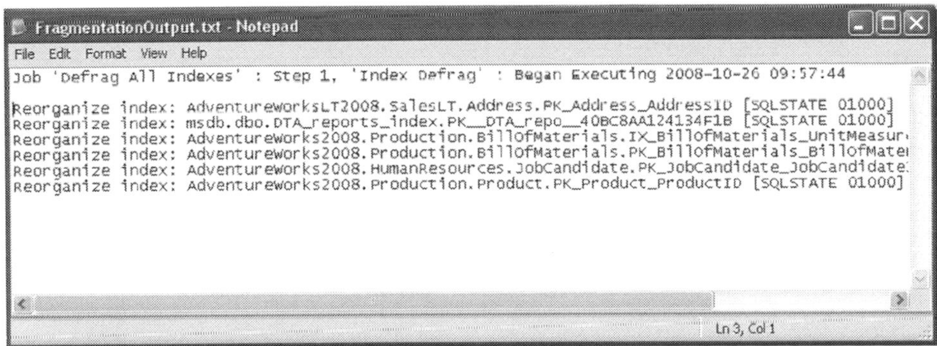

Figure 8-25. `FragmentationOutput.txt` *file output*

The output shows that the job analyzed the fragmentation of the database and identified a series of indexes for defragmentation, specifically for reorganization. Subsequently, it defragments the index. The stored procedure defragmented only the database object that was highly fragmented. Thus, the next run of the SQL job generally won't identify these same indexes for defragmentation.

Summary

As you learned in this chapter, in a highly transactional database page splits caused by `INSERT` and `UPDATE` statements fragment the tables and indexes, increasing the cost of data retrieval. You can avoid these page splits by maintaining free spaces within the pages using the fill factor. Since the fill factor is applied only during index creation, you should reapply it at regular intervals to maintain its effectiveness. You can determine the amount of fragmentation in an index (or a table) using `sys.dm_db_physical_stats`. Upon determining a high amount of fragmentation, you can use either `ALTER INDEX REBUILD` or `ALTER INDEX REORGANIZE`, depending on the required amount of defragmentation and database concurrency.

Defragmentation rearranges the data so that its physical order on the disk matches its logical order in the table/index, thus improving the performance of queries. However, unless the optimizer decides upon an effective execution plan for the query, query performance even after defragmentation can remain poor. Therefore, it is important to have the optimizer use efficient techniques to generate cost-effective execution plans.

In the next chapter, I will delve deeply into execution plan generation and the techniques the optimizer uses to decide upon an effective execution plan.

CHAPTER 9

Execution Plan Cache Analysis

The performance of any query depends on the effectiveness of the execution plan decided upon by the optimizer, as you learned in previous chapters. Because the overall time required to execute a query is the sum of the time required to generate the execution plan plus the time required to execute the query based on this execution plan, it is important that the cost of generating the execution plan itself is low. The cost incurred when generating the execution plan depends on the process of generating the execution plan, the process of caching the plan, and the reusability of the plan from the plan cache. In this chapter, you will learn how an execution plan is generated and how to analyze the execution plan cache for plan reusability.

In this chapter, I cover the following topics:

- Execution plan generation and caching
- The SQL Server components used to generate an execution plan
- Strategies to optimize the cost of execution plan generation
- Factors affecting parallel plan generation
- How to analyze execution plan caching
- Query plan hash and query hash as mechanisms for identifying queries to tune
- Execution plans gone wrong and parameter sniffing
- Ways to improve the reusability of execution plan caching

Execution Plan Generation

As you know by now, SQL Server uses a cost-based optimization technique to determine the processing strategy of a query. The optimizer considers both the metadata of the database objects and the current distribution statistics of the columns referred to in the query when deciding which index and join strategies should be used.

The cost-based optimization allows a database developer to concentrate on implementing a business rule, rather than on the exact syntax of the query. At the same time, the process of determining the query processing strategy remains quite complex and can consume a fair amount of resources. SQL Server uses a number of techniques to optimize resource consumption:

- Syntax-based optimization of the query
- Trivial plan match to avoid in-depth query optimization for simple queries
- Index and join strategies based on current distribution statistics
- Query optimization in multiple phases to control the cost of optimization
- Execution plan caching to avoid the regeneration of query plans

The following techniques are performed in order, as shown in the flowchart in Figure 9-1:

- Parser
- Algebrizer
- Query optimizer
- Execution plan generation, caching, and hash plan generation
- Query execution

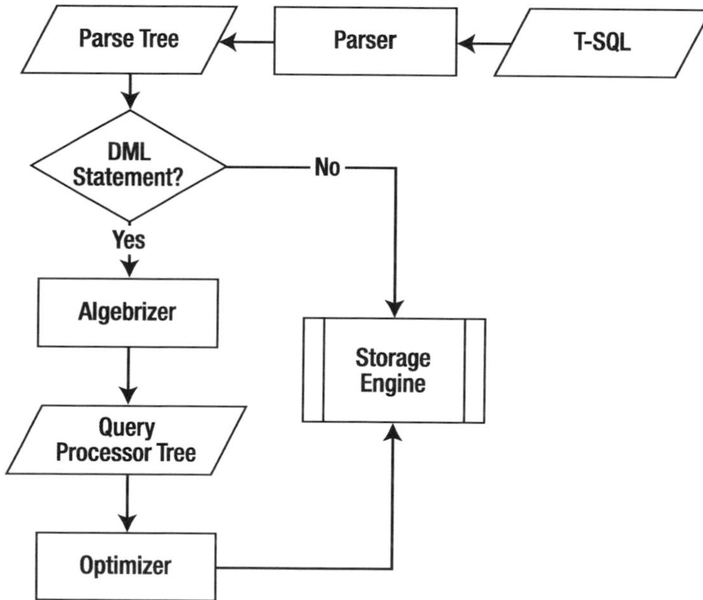

Figure 9-1. *SQL Server techniques to optimize query execution*

Let's take a look at these steps in more detail.

Parser

When a query is submitted, SQL Server passes it to the parser within the *relational engine*. (This relational engine is one of the two main parts of SQL Server, with the other being the *storage engine*, which is responsible for data access, modifications, and caching.) The relational engine takes care of parsing, name and type resolution (the algebrizer), and optimization. It also executes a query as per the query execution plan and requests data from the storage engine.

The parser checks an incoming query, validating it for the correct syntax. The query is terminated if a syntax error is detected. If multiple queries are submitted together as a batch as follows (note the error in syntax):

```
CREATE TABLE t1(c1 INT)
INSERT INTO t1 VALUES(1)
CEILEKT * FROM t1 --Error: I meant, SELECT * FROM t1
GO
```

then the parser checks the complete batch together for syntax and cancels the complete batch when it detects a syntax error. (Note that more than one syntax error may appear in a batch, but the parser goes no further than the first one.) On validating a query for correct syntax, the parser generates an internal data structure called a *parse tree* for the algebrizer. The parser and algebrizer taken together are called *query compilation*.

Algebrizer

The parse tree generated by the parser is passed to the algebrizer for processing. The algebrizer resolves all the names of the different objects, meaning the tables, the columns, and so on, that are being referenced in the T-SQL. It also identifies all the various data types being processed. It even checks for the location of aggregates (such as `GROUP BY` and `MAX`). The output of all these verifications and resolutions is a binary set of data called a *query processor tree*.

To see the algebrizer in action, if the following batch query (`algebrizer_test.sql` in the download) is submitted:

```
CREATE TABLE t1 (c1 INT) ;
INSERT  INTO t1
VALUES  (1) ;
SELECT  'Before Error'
       ,c1
FROM    t1 AS t ;
SELECT  'error'
       ,c1
FROM    no_t1 ; --Error: Table doesn't exist
SELECT  'after error' c1
FROM    t1 AS t ;
```

then the first three statements before the error statement are executed, and the errant statement and the one after it are cancelled.

If a query contains an implicit data conversion, then the normalization process adds an appropriate step to the query tree. The process also performs some syntax-based optimization. For example, if the following query (`syntax_optimize.sql` in the download) is submitted:

```
SELECT  *
FROM    Sales.SalesOrderHeader AS soh
WHERE   soh.SalesOrderID BETWEEN 62500 AND 62550
```

then the syntax-based optimization transforms the syntax of the query, as shown in Figure 9-2, where `BETWEEN` becomes >= and <=.

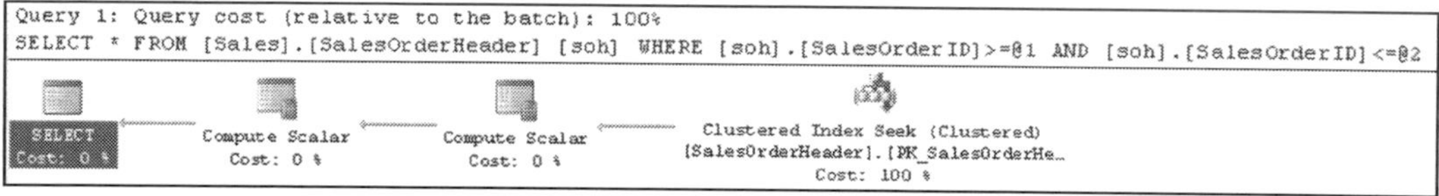

Figure 9-2. *Syntax-based optimization*

For most Data Definition Language (DDL) statements (such as `CREATE TABLE`, `CREATE PROC`, and so on), after passing through the algebrizer, the query is compiled directly for execution, since the optimizer need not choose among multiple processing strategies. For one DDL statement in particular, `CREATE INDEX`, the optimizer can determine an efficient processing strategy based on other existing indexes on the table, as explained in Chapter 4.

For this reason, you will never see any reference to `CREATE TABLE` in an execution plan, although you will see reference to `CREATE INDEX`. If the normalized query is a Data Manipulation Language (DML) statement (such as `SELECT`, `INSERT`, `UPDATE`, or `DELETE`), then the query processor tree is passed to the optimizer to decide the processing strategy for the query.

Optimization

Based on the complexity of a query, including the number of tables referred to and the indexes available, there may be several ways to execute the query contained in the query processor tree. Exhaustively comparing the cost of all the ways of executing a query can take a considerable amount of time, which may sometimes override the benefit of finding the most optimized query. Figure 9-3 shows that, to avoid a high optimization overhead compared to the actual execution cost of the query, the optimizer adopts different techniques, namely:

- Trivial plan match
- Multiple optimization phases
- Parallel plan optimization

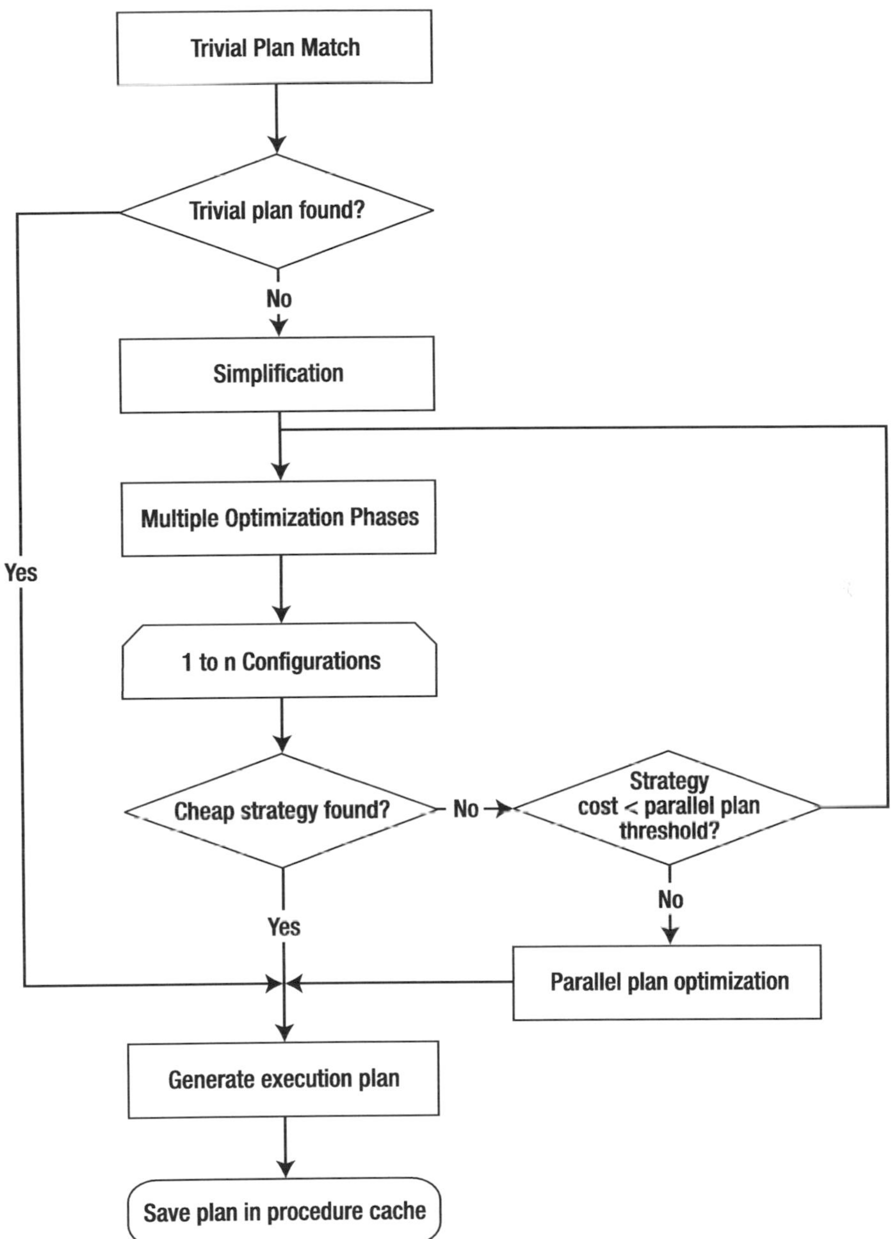

Figure 9-3. *Query optimization steps*

Trivial Plan Match

Sometimes there might be only one way to execute a query. For example, a heap table with no indexes can be accessed in only one way: via a table scan. To avoid the runtime overhead of optimizing such queries, SQL Server maintains a list of trivial plans to choose from. If the optimizer finds a match, then a similar plan is generated for the query without any optimization.

Multiple Optimization Phases

For a complex query, the number of alternative processing strategies to be analyzed can be very high, and it may take a long time to evaluate each option. Therefore, instead of analyzing all the possible processing strategies together, the optimizer breaks them into multiple configurations, each consisting of different index and join techniques.

The index variations consider different indexing aspects, such as single-column index, composite index, index column order, column density, and so forth. Similarly, the join variations consider the different join techniques available in SQL Server: nested loop join, merge join, and hash join. (Chapter 3 covers these join techniques in detail.)

The optimizer considers the statistics of the columns referred to in the `WHERE` clause to evaluate the effectiveness of the index and the join strategies. Based on the current statistics, it evaluates the cost of the configurations in multiple optimization phases. The cost includes many factors, including (but not limited to) usage of CPU, memory, and disk I/O required to execute the query. After each optimization phase, the optimizer evaluates the cost of the processing strategy. If the cost is found to be cheap enough, then the optimizer stops further iteration through the optimization phases and quits the optimization process. Otherwise, it keeps iterating through the optimization phases to determine a cost-effective processing strategy.

Sometimes a query can be so complex that the optimizer needs to extensively iterate through the optimization phases. While optimizing the query, if it finds that the cost of the processing strategy is more than the cost threshold for parallelism, then it evaluates the cost of processing the query using multiple CPUs. Otherwise, the optimizer proceeds with the serial plan.

You can find out some detail of what occurred during the multiple optimization phases via two sources. Take, for example, this query (`non_trivial_query.sql`):

```
SELECT  soh.SalesOrderNumber
       ,sod.OrderQty
       ,sod.LineTotal
       ,sod.UnitPrice
       ,sod.UnitPriceDiscount
       ,p.[Name] AS ProductName
       ,p.ProductNumber
       ,ps.[Name] AS ProductSubCategoryName
       ,pc.[Name] AS ProductCategoryName
FROM    Sales.SalesOrderHeader AS soh
        JOIN Sales.SalesOrderDetail AS sod
        ON soh.SalesOrderID = sod.SalesOrderID
        JOIN Production.Product AS p
        ON sod.ProductID = p.ProductID
        JOIN Production.ProductModel AS pm
        ON p.ProductModelID = pm.ProductModelID
```

```
        JOIN Production.ProductSubcategory AS ps
        ON p.ProductSubcategoryID = ps.ProductSubcategoryID
        JOIN Production.ProductCategory AS pc
        ON ps.ProductCategoryID = pc.ProductCategoryID
WHERE   soh.CustomerID = 29658
```

When this query is run, the execution plan in Figure 9-4, a nontrivial plan for sure, is returned.

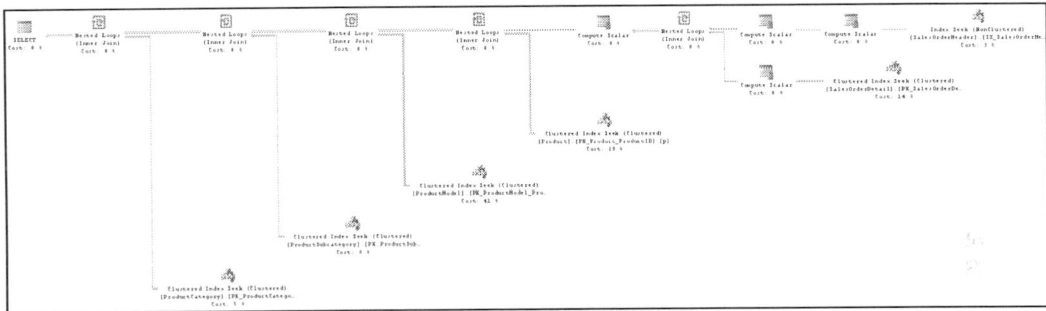

Figure 9-4. *Nontrivial execution plan*

I realize that this execution plan is a little hard to read. The important point to take away is that it involves quite a few tables, each with indexes and statistics that all had to be taken into account to arrive at this execution plan. The first place you can go to look for information about the optimizer's work on this execution plan is the property sheet of the T-SQL SELECT operator at the far left of the execution plan. Figure 9-5 shows the property sheet.

Properties

SELECT

Misc	
Cached plan size	40 B
CompileCPU	21
CompileMemory	744
CompileTime	21
Degree of Parallelism	1
Estimated Number of Rows	13.0278
Estimated Operator Cost	0 (0%)
Estimated Subtree Cost	0.116261
Logical Operation	
Optimization Level	FULL
Physical Operation	
QueryHash	0xE992BC6CFDD9BED9
QueryPlanHash	0x284E4FB1AB059580
Reason For Early Termination Of Statement	Good Enough Plan Found
Set Options	ANSI_NULLS: True, ANSI_PADDING: True, ANSI_
Statement	SELECT soh.SalesOrderNumber ,sod.Ord

Reason For Early Termination Of Statement Optimization
Reason For Early Termination Of Statement Optimization

Figure 9-5. SELECT *operator property sheet*

Starting at the top, you can see information directly related to the creation and optimization of this execution plan:

- The size of the cached plan, which is 40 bytes
- The number of CPU cycles used to compile the plan, which is 21 ms
- The amount of memory used, which is 744KB
- The compile time, which is 21 ms

The Optimization Level property (`StatementOptmLevel` in the XML plan) shows what type of processing occurred within the optimizer. In this case, FULL means that the optimizer did a full optimization. This is further displayed in the property Reason for Early Termination of Statement, which is Good Enough Plan Found. So, the optimizer took 21 ms to track down a plan that it deemed good enough in this situation. You can also see the QueryPlanHash value, also known as the *fingerprint*, for the execution plan (you can find more details on this in the section "Query Plan Hash and Query Hash").

The second source for optimizer information is the dynamic management view `sys.dm_exec_query_optimizer_info`. This DMV is an aggregation of the optimization events over time. It won't show the individual optimizations for a given query, but it will track the optimizations performed. This isn't as immediately handy for tuning an individual query, but if you are working on reducing the costs of a workload over time, being able to track this information can help you determine whether your query tuning is making a positive difference, at least in terms of optimization time. Some of the data returned is for internal SQL Server use only. Figure 9-6 shows a truncated example of the useful data returned in the results from the following query:

```
SELECT  Counter
        ,Occurrence
        ,Value
FROM    sys.dm_exec_query_optimizer_info
```

	counter	occurrence	value
1	optimizations	279	1
2	elapsed time	279	0.0133763440860215
3	final cost	279	0.0363448839674748
4	trivial plan	211	1
5	tasks	68	610.558823529412

Figure 9-6. *Output from* `sys.dm_exec_query_optimizer_info`

Running this query before and after a set of optimizations can show you the changes that have occurred in the number and type of optimizations completed.

Parallel Plan Optimization

The optimizer considers various factors while evaluating the cost of processing a query using a parallel plan. Some of these factors are as follows:

- Number of CPUs available to SQL Server
- SQL Server edition
- Available memory
- Type of query being executed
- Number of rows to be processed in a given stream
- Number of active concurrent connections

If only one CPU is available to SQL Server, then the optimizer won't consider a parallel plan. The number of CPUs available to SQL Server can be restricted using the *affinity mask* setting of the SQL Server configuration. The affinity mask value is a bitmap in that a bit represents a CPU, with the rightmost bit position representing CPU0. For example, to allow SQL Server to use only CPU0 to CPU3 in an eight-way box, execute these statements (`affinity_mask.sql` in the download):

```
USE master
EXEC sp_configure 'show advanced option', '1'
RECONFIGURE
EXEC sp_configure 'affinity mask', 15 --Bit map: 00001111
RECONFIGURE
```

This configuration takes effect immediately. `affinity mask` is a special setting, and I recommend that you use it only in instances where taking control away from SQL Server makes sense, such as when you have multiple instances of SQL Server running on the same machine and you want to isolate them from each other. To set affinity past 32 processors, you have to use the `affinity64 mask` option that is available only in the 64-bit version of SQL Server. You can also bind I/O to a specific set of processors using the affinity mask I/O option in the same way.

Even if multiple CPUs are available to SQL Server, if an individual query is not allowed to use more than one CPU for execution, then the optimizer discards the parallel plan option. The maximum number of CPUs that can be used for a parallel query is governed by the `max degree of parallelism` setting of the SQL Server configuration. The default value is 0, which allows all the CPUs (availed by the `affinity mask` setting) to be used for a parallel query. If you want to allow parallel queries to use no more than two CPUs out of CPU0 to CPU3, limited by the preceding `affinity mask` setting, execute the following statements (`parallelism.sql` in the download):

```
USE master
EXEC sp_configure 'show advanced option', '1'
RECONFIGURE
EXEC sp_configure 'max degree of parallelism', 2
RECONFIGURE
```

This change takes effect immediately, without any restart. The `max degree of parallelism` setting can also be controlled at a query level using the `MAXDOP` query hint:

```
SELECT * FROM t1 WHERE c1 = 1 OPTION(MAXDOP 2)
```

Changing the `max degree of parallelism` setting is best determined by the needs of your system. To limit contention with the operating system, I will usually set the `max degree of parallelism` setting to one less than the number on the server, and I'll set an affinity mask to those CPUs as well.

Since parallel queries require more memory, the optimizer determines the amount of memory available before choosing a parallel plan. The amount of memory required increases with the degree of parallelism. If the memory requirement of the parallel plan for a given degree of parallelism cannot be satisfied, then SQL Server decreases the degree of parallelism automatically or completely abandons the parallel plan for the query in the given workload context.

Queries with a very high CPU overhead are the best candidates for a parallel plan. Examples include joining large tables, performing substantial aggregations, and sorting large result sets, all common operations on reporting systems (less so on OLTP systems). For simple queries usually found in transaction-processing applications, the additional coordination required to initialize, synchronize, and terminate a parallel plan outweighs the potential performance benefit.

Whether or not a query is simple is determined by comparing the estimated execution time of the query with a cost threshold. This cost threshold is controlled by the `cost threshold for parallelism` setting of the SQL Server configuration. By default, this setting's value is 5, which means that if the estimated execution time of the serial plan is more than 5 seconds, then the optimizer considers a parallel plan for the query. For example, to modify the cost threshold to 6 seconds, execute the following statements (`parallelism_threshold.sql` in the download):

```
USE master
EXEC sp_configure 'show advanced option', '1'
RECONFIGURE
EXEC sp_configure 'cost threshold for parallelism', 6
RECONFIGURE
```

This change takes effect immediately, without any restart. If only one CPU is available to SQL Server, then this setting is ignored. I've found that OLTP systems suffer when the cost threshold for parallelism is set this low. Usually increasing the value to somewhere between 15 and 25 will be beneficial.

The DML action queries (`INSERT`, `UPDATE`, and `DELETE`) are executed serially. However, the `SELECT` portion of an `INSERT` statement and the `WHERE` clause of an `UPDATE` or a `DELETE` statement can be executed in parallel. The actual data changes are applied serially to the database. Also, if the optimizer determines that the number of rows affected is too low, it does not introduce parallel operators.

Note that, even at execution time, SQL Server determines whether the current system workload and configuration information allow for parallel query execution. If parallel query execution is allowed, SQL Server determines the optimal number of threads and spreads the execution of the query across those threads. When a query starts a parallel execution, it uses the same number of threads until completion. SQL Server reexamines the optimal number of threads before executing the parallel query the next time.

Once the processing strategy is finalized by using either a serial plan or a parallel plan, the optimizer generates the execution plan for the query. The execution plan contains the detailed processing strategy decided by the optimizer to execute the query. This includes steps such as data retrieval, result set joins, result set ordering, and so on. A detailed explanation of how to analyze the processing steps included in an execution plan is presented in Chapter 3. The execution plan generated for the query is saved in the plan cache for future reuse.

Execution Plan Caching

The execution plan of a query generated by the optimizer is saved in a special part of SQL Server's memory pool called the *plan cache* or *procedure cache*. (The procedure cache is part of the SQL Server buffer cache and is explained in Chapter 2.) Saving the plan in a cache allows SQL Server to avoid running through the whole query optimization process again when the same query is resubmitted. SQL Server supports different techniques such as *plan cache aging* and *plan cache types* to increase the reusability of the cached plans. It also stores two binary values called the *query hash* and the *query plan hash*.

■ **Note** I discuss the techniques supported by SQL Server for improving the effectiveness of execution plan reuse later in this chapter.

Components of the Execution Plan

The execution plan generated by the optimizer contains two components:

- *Query plan*: This represents the commands that specify all the physical operations required to execute a query.
- *Execution context*: This maintains the variable parts of a query within the context of a given user.

I will cover these components in more detail in the next sections.

Query Plan

The query plan is a reentrant, read-only data structure, with commands that specify all the physical operations required to execute the query. The reentrant property allows the query plan to be accessed concurrently by multiple connections. The physical operations include specifications on which tables and indexes to access, how and in what order they should be accessed, the type of join operations to be performed between multiple tables, and so forth. No user context is stored in the query plan. For a single query, there can be two copies of the query plan: the serial plan and the parallel plan (regardless of the degree of parallelism).

Execution Context

The execution context is another data structure that maintains the variable part of the query. Although the server keeps track of the execution plans in the procedure cache, these plans are context neutral. Therefore, each user executing the query will have a separate execution context that holds data specific to their execution, such as parameter values and connection details.

Aging of the Execution Plan

The procedure cache is part of SQL Server's buffer cache, which also holds data pages. As new execution plans are added to the procedure cache, the size of the procedure cache keeps growing, affecting the retention of useful data pages in memory. To avoid this, SQL Server dynamically controls the retention of the execution plans in the procedure cache, retaining the frequently used execution plans and discarding plans that are not used for a certain period of time.

SQL Server keeps track of the frequency of an execution plan's reuse by associating an age field to it. When an execution plan is generated, the age field is populated with the cost of generating the plan. A complex query requiring extensive optimization will have an age field value higher than that for a simpler query.

At regular intervals, the age fields of all the execution plans in the procedure cache are decremented by SQL Server's lazy writer process (which manages most of the background processes in SQL Server). If an execution plan is not reused for a long time, then the age field will eventually be reduced to 0. The cheaper the execution plan was to generate, the sooner its age field will be reduced to 0. Once an execution plan's age field reaches 0, the plan becomes a candidate for removal from memory. SQL Server removes all plans with an age field of 0 from the procedure cache when memory pressure increases to such an extent that there is no longer enough free memory to serve new requests. However, if a system has enough memory and free memory pages are available to serve new requests, execution plans with an age field of 0 can remain in the procedure cache for a long time so that they can be reused later, if required.

As well as aging, execution plans can also find their age field incremented by the cost of generating the plan every time the plan is reused. For example, suppose you have two execution plans with generation costs equal to 100 and 10. Their starting age field values will therefore be 100 and 10, respectively. If both execution plans are reused immediately, their age fields will be incremented to 200 and 20, respectively. With these age field values, the lazy writer will bring down the cost of the second plan to 0 much earlier than that of the first one, unless the second plan is reused more often. Therefore, even if a costly plan is reused less frequently than a cheaper plan, because of the effect of the cost on the age field, the costly plan can remain at a nonzero age value for a longer period of time.

Analyzing the Execution Plan Cache

You can obtain a lot of information about the execution plans in the procedure cache by accessing the dynamic management view `sys.dm_exec_cached_plans`:

```
SELECT * FROM sys.dm_exec_cached_plans
```

Table 9-1 shows some of the useful information provided by `sys.dm_exec_cached_plans` (this is easier to read in Grid view).

Table 9-1. *sys.dm_exec_cached_plans*

Column Name	Description
`refcounts`	Represents the number of other objects in the cache referencing this plan.
`usecounts`	The number of times this object has been used since it was added to the cache.
`size_in_bytes`	The size of the plan stored in the cache.
`cacheobjtype`	What type of plan this is. There are several, but of particular interest are these: Compiled plan: A completed execution plan Compiled plan stub: A marker used for ad hoc queries (you can find more details in the "Ad Hoc Workload" section of this chapter) Parse tree: A plan stored for accessing a view
`Objtype`	The type of object that generated the plan. Again, there are several but these are of particular interest: Proc Prepared Ad hoc View
`Plan_handle`	The identifier for this plan in memory. It is used to retrieve query text and execution plans.

Using the DMV `sys.dm_exec_cached_plans` all by itself gets you only part of the information. The next two parts can be just as important. Using the dynamic management function `sys.dm_exec_query_plan(`*`plan_handle`*`)` in combination with `sys.dm_exec_cached_plans` will also bring back the XML execution plan itself so that you can display it and work with it. If you then bring in `sys.dm_exec_sql_text(`*`plan_handle`*`)`, you can also retrieve the original query text. This may not seem useful while you're running known queries for the examples here, but when you go to your production system and begin to pull in execution plans from the cache, it might be handy to have the original query. To get detailed performance metrics about the cached plan, you can use `sys.dm_exec_query_stats` to return that data. Among other pieces of data, the query hash and query plan hash are stored in this DMF.

In the following sections, I'll explore how the plan cache works with actual queries using `sys.dm_exec_cached_plans` and the other DMVs and DMFs.

Execution Plan Reuse

When a query is submitted, SQL Server checks the procedure cache for a matching execution plan. If one is not found, then SQL Server performs the query compilation and optimization to generate a new execution plan. However, if the plan exists in the procedure cache, it is reused with the private execution context. This saves the CPU cycles that otherwise would have been spent on the plan generation.

Queries are submitted to SQL Server with filter criteria to limit the size of the result set. The same queries are often resubmitted with different values for the filter criteria. For example, consider the following query:

```
SELECT  soh.SalesOrderNumber
       ,soh.OrderDate
       ,sod.OrderQty
       ,sod.LineTotal
FROM    Sales.SalesOrderHeader AS soh
        JOIN Sales.SalesOrderDetail AS sod
        ON soh.SalesOrderID = sod.SalesOrderID
WHERE   soh.CustomerID = 29690
        AND sod.productid = 711
```

When this query is submitted, the optimizer creates an execution plan and saves it in the procedure cache to reuse in the future. If this query is resubmitted with a different filter criterion value—for example, `soh.CustomerID = 29500`—it will be beneficial to reuse the existing execution plan for the previously supplied filter criterion value. But whether the execution plan created for one filter criterion value can be reused for another filter criterion value depends on how the query is submitted to SQL Server.

The queries (or workload) submitted to SQL Server can be broadly classified under two categories that determine whether the execution plan will be reusable as the value of the variable parts of the query changes:

- Ad hoc
- Prepared

■ Tip To test the output of `sys.dm_exec_cached_plans` for this chapter, it will be necessary to remove the plans from cache on occasion by executing `DBCC FREEPROCCACHE`. Do not run this on your production server since flushing the cache will require all execution plans to be rebuilt as they are executed, placing a serious strain on your production system for no good reason.

Ad Hoc Workload

Queries can be submitted to SQL Server without explicitly isolating the variables from the query. These types of queries executed without explicitly converting the variable parts of the query into parameters are referred to as *ad hoc workloads* (or queries). For example, consider this query (`adhoc.sql` in the download):

```
SELECT  soh.SalesOrderNumber
       ,soh.OrderDate
       ,sod.OrderQty
       ,sod.LineTotal
FROM    Sales.SalesOrderHeader AS soh
        JOIN Sales.SalesOrderDetail AS sod
        ON soh.SalesOrderID = sod.SalesOrderID
WHERE   soh.CustomerID = 29690
        AND sod.productid = 711
```

If the query is submitted as is, without explicitly converting either of the variable values to a parameter (that can be supplied to the query when executed), then the query is an ad hoc query.

In this query, the filter criterion value is embedded in the query itself and is not explicitly parameterized to isolate it from the query. This means that you cannot reuse the execution plan for this query unless you use the same variable. However, the variable parts of the queries can be explicitly parameterized in three different ways that are jointly categorized as a prepared workload.

Prepared Workload

Prepared workloads (or queries) explicitly parameterize the variable parts of the query so that the query plan isn't tied to the value of the variable parts. In SQL Server, queries can be submitted as prepared workloads using the following three methods:

- *Stored procedures*: Allows saving a collection of SQL statements that can accept and return user-supplied parameters
- `sp_executesql`: Allows executing a SQL statement or a SQL batch that may contain user-supplied parameters, without saving the SQL statement or batch
- *Prepare/execute model*: Allows a SQL client to request the generation of a query plan that can be reused during subsequent executions of the query with different parameter values, without saving the SQL statement(s) in SQL Server

For example, the `SELECT` statement shown previously can be explicitly parameterized using a stored procedure as follows (`spBasicSalesInfo.sql` in the download):

```
IF(SELECT OBJECT_ID('spBasicSalesInfo')) IS NOT NULL
  DROP PROC dbo.spBasicSalesInfo
GO
CREATE PROC dbo.spBasicSalesInfo
@ProductID INT
,@CustomerId INT
AS
SELECT   soh.SalesOrderNumber
        ,soh.OrderDate
        ,sod.OrderQty
        ,sod.LineTotal
FROM     Sales.SalesOrderHeader AS soh
         JOIN Sales.SalesOrderDetail AS sod
         ON soh.SalesOrderID = sod.SalesOrderID
WHERE    soh.CustomerID = @CustomerId
         AND sod.Productid = @ProductId
```

The plan of the `SELECT` statement included within the stored procedure will embed the parameters `@ProductID` and `@CustomerId`, not variable values. I will cover these methods in more detail shortly.

Plan Reusability of an Ad Hoc Workload

When a query is submitted as an ad hoc workload, SQL Server generates the execution plan and decides whether to cache the plan based upon the cost of generating the execution plan. If the cost of generating the execution plan is very cheap, then SQL Server may not cache the plan to conserve the size of the procedure cache based on the resources available. Instead of flooding the procedure cache with cheap ad hoc queries, SQL Server regenerates the execution plan when the query is resubmitted.

For ad hoc queries with higher execution plan generation costs, SQL Server saves the execution plan in the procedure cache. The values of the variable parts of an ad hoc query are included in the query plan and are not saved separately in the execution context, meaning that you cannot reuse the execution plan for this query unless you use exactly the same variable as you have seen.

To understand this, consider the following ad hoc query (`adhoc.sql` in the download):

```
SELECT  soh.SalesOrderNumber
       ,soh.OrderDate
       ,sod.OrderQty
       ,sod.LineTotal
FROM    Sales.SalesOrderHeader AS soh
        JOIN Sales.SalesOrderDetail AS sod
        ON soh.SalesOrderID = sod.SalesOrderID
WHERE   soh.CustomerID = 29690
        AND sod.productid = 711
```

The execution plan generated for this ad hoc query is based on the exact text of the query, which includes comments, case, trailing spaces, and hard returns. You'll have to use it to pull the information out of `sys.dm_exec_cached_plans`:

```
SELECT  c.usecounts
       ,c.cacheobjtype
       ,c.objtype
FROM    sys.dm_exec_cached_plans c
        CROSS APPLY sys.dm_exec_sql_text(c.plan_handle) t
WHERE   t.TEXT = 'SELECT  soh.SalesOrderNumber
       ,soh.OrderDate
       ,sod.OrderQty
       ,sod.LineTotal
FROM    Sales.SalesOrderHeader AS soh
        JOIN Sales.SalesOrderDetail AS sod
        ON soh.SalesOrderID = sod.SalesOrderID
WHERE   soh.CustomerID = 29690
        AND sod.productid = 711'
```

Figure 9-7 shows the output of `sys.dm_exec_cached_plans`.

	usecounts	cacheobjtype	objtype
1	1	Compiled Plan	Adhoc

Figure 9-7. *sys.dm_exec_cached_plans output*

You can see from Figure 9-7 that a compiled plan is generated and saved in the procedure cache for the preceding ad hoc query. To find the specific query, I used the query itself in the WHERE clause. You can see that this plan has been used once up until now (usecounts = 1). If this ad hoc query is reexecuted, SQL Server reuses the existing executable plan from the procedure cache, as shown in Figure 9-8.

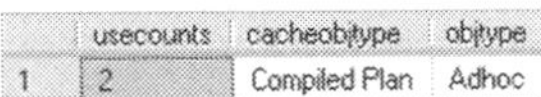

	usecounts	cacheobjtype	objtype
1	2	Compiled Plan	Adhoc

Figure 9-8. *Reusing the executable plan from the procedure cache*

In Figure 9-8, you can see that the usecounts for the preceding query's executable plan has increased to 2, confirming that the existing plan for this query has been reused. If this query is executed repeatedly, the existing plan will be reused every time.

Since the plan generated for the preceding query includes the filter criterion value, the reusability of the plan is limited to the use of the same filter criterion value. Reexecute adhoc1.sql, but change soh.CustomerID to 29500:

```
SELECT  c.usecounts
        ,c.cacheobjtype
        ,c.objtype
FROM    sys.dm_exec_cached_plans c
        CROSS APPLY sys.dm_exec_sql_text(c.plan_handle) t
WHERE   t.TEXT = 'SELECT  soh.SalesOrderNumber
        ,soh.OrderDate
        ,sod.OrderQty
        ,sod.LineTotal
FROM    Sales.SalesOrderHeader AS soh
        JOIN Sales.SalesOrderDetail AS sod
        ON soh.SalesOrderID = sod.SalesOrderID
WHERE   soh.CustomerID = 29500
        AND sod.productid = 711'
```

The existing plan can't be reused, and if the sys.dm_exec_cached_plans is rerun as is, you'll see that the execution count hasn't increased (Figure 9-9).

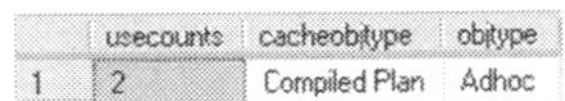

	usecounts	cacheobjtype	objtype
1	2	Compiled Plan	Adhoc

Figure 9-9. *sys.dm_exec_cached_plans shows that the existing plan is not reused.*

Instead, I'll adjust the query against sys.dm_exec_cached_plans:

```
SELECT  c.usecounts
        ,c.cacheobjtype
        ,c.objtype
        ,t.text
FROM    sys.dm_exec_cached_plans c
        CROSS APPLY sys.dm_exec_sql_text(c.plan_handle) t
```

```
WHERE   t.TEXT LIKE 'SELECT  soh.SalesOrderNumber
       ,soh.OrderDate
       ,sod.OrderQty
       ,sod.LineTotal
FROM    Sales.SalesOrderHeader AS soh
        JOIN Sales.SalesOrderDetail AS sod
        ON soh.SalesOrderID = sod.SalesOrderID%'
```

You can see the output from this query in Figure 9-10.

	usecounts	cacheobjtype	objtype	text	plan_handle
1	2	Compiled Plan	Adhoc	SELECT soh.SalesOrderNumber ,soh.OrderD...	0x06000900FB139B22B880490600000000000000000000000
2	1	Compiled Plan	Adhoc	SELECT soh.SalesOrderNumber ,soh.OrderD...	0x060009004D005D22B8A0200600000000000000000000000

Figure 9-10. *`sys.dm_exec_cached_plans` showing that the existing plan can't be reused*

From the `sys.dm_exec_cached_plans` output in Figure 9-8, you can see that the previous plan for the query hasn't been reused; the corresponding `usecounts` value remained at the old value of 2. Instead of reusing the existing plan, a new plan is generated for the query and is saved in the procedure cache with a new `plan_handle`. If this ad hoc query is reexecuted repeatedly with different filter criterion values, a new execution plan will be generated every time. The inefficient reuse of the execution plan for this ad hoc query increases the load on the CPU by consuming additional CPU cycles to regenerate the plan.

To summarize, ad hoc plan caching uses statement-level caching and is limited to an exact textual match. If an ad hoc query is not complex, SQL Server can implicitly parameterize the query to increase plan reusability by using a feature called *simple parameterization*. The definition of a simple query for simple parameterization is limited to fairly simple cases such as ad hoc queries with only one table. As shown in the previous example, a query requiring a join operation cannot be autoparameterized.

Optimize for an Ad Hoc Workload

If your server is going to primarily support ad hoc queries, it is possible to achieve a small degree of performance improvement. One server option is called `optimize for ad hoc workloads`. Enabling this for the server changes the way the engine deals with ad hoc queries. Instead of generating a full compiled plan for the query the first time it's called, a compiled plan stub is created. The stub does not have a full execution plan associated, saving the time of generating that execution plan and the storage space required for it. This option can be enabled without rebooting the server:

```
sp_configure 'optimize for ad hoc workloads', 1;
GO
RECONFIGURE;
```

After changing the option, flush the cache, and then rerun the query `adhoc.sql`. Modify the query against `sys.dm_exec_cached_plans` so that you include the `size_in_bytes` column, and then run it to see the results in Figure 9-11.

	usecounts	cacheobjtype	objtype	TEXT	plan_handle	size_in_bytes
1	1	Compiled Plan Stub	Adhoc	SELECT soh.SalesOrderNumber ,soh.OrderD...	0x06000E00FB139B22C065EF070000000000000000000000000	320

Figure 9-11. *`sys.dm_exec_cached_plans` showing a compiled plan stub*

Figure 9-11 shows in the `cacheobjtype` column that the new object in the cache is a compiled plan stub. Stubs can be created for lots more queries with less impact on the server than full compiled plans. But the next time an ad hoc query is executed, a fully compiled plan is created. To see this in action, run the query `adhoc.sql`, and check the results in `sys.dm_exec_cached_plans`, as shown in Figure 9-12.

	usecounts	cacheobjtype	objtype	TEXT	plan_handle	size_in_bytes
1	1	Compiled Plan	Adhoc	SELECT soh.SalesOrderNumber ,soh.OrderD...	0x06000E00FB139B22B880090800000000000000000000000000	65536

Figure 9-12. *The compiled plan stub has become a compiled plan.*

Not only did the `cacheobjtype` change, but now that a full compiled plan was created, including an execution plan, a new `plan_handle` was created as well. Finally, to see the real difference between a stub and a full plan, check the `size_in_bytes` column in Figure 9-11 and Figure 9-12. The size changed from 320 in the stub to 65,536 in the full plan. This shows precisely the savings available when working with lots of ad hoc queries. Before proceeding, be sure to disable `optimize for ad hoc workloads`:

```
sp_configure 'optimize for ad hoc workloads', 0;
GO
RECONFIGURE;
```

Simple Parameterization

When an ad hoc query is submitted, SQL Server analyzes the query to determine which parts of the incoming text might be parameters. It looks at the variable parts of the ad hoc query to determine whether it will be safe to parameterize them automatically and use the parameters (instead of the variable parts) in the query so that the query plan can be independent of the variable values. This feature of automatically converting the variable part of a query into a parameter, even though not parameterized explicitly (using a prepared workload technique), is called *simple parameterization.*

During simple parameterization, SQL Server ensures that if the ad hoc query is converted to a parameterized template, the changes in the parameter values won't widely change the plan requirement. On determining the simple parameterization to be safe, SQL Server creates a parameterized template for the ad hoc query and saves the parameterized plan in the procedure cache.

The parameterized plan is not based on the dynamic values used in the query. Since the plan is generated for a parameterized template, it can be reused when the ad hoc query is reexecuted with different values for the variable parts.

To understand the simple parameterization feature of SQL Server, consider the following query (`simple_parameterization.sql` in the download):

```
SELECT  a.*
FROM    Person.Address AS a
WHERE   a.AddressID = 42
```

When this ad hoc query is submitted, SQL Server can treat this query as it is for plan creation. However, before the query is executed, SQL Server tries to determine whether it can be safely parameterized. On determining that the variable part of the query can be parameterized without affecting the basic structure of the query, SQL Server parameterizes the query and generates a plan for the parameterized query. You can observe this from the `sys.dm_exec_cached_plans` output shown in Figure 9-13.

	usecounts	cacheobjtype	objtype	text
1	1	Compiled Plan	Adhoc	SELECT c.usecounts ,c.cacheobjtype ,c.objtype ,t.text ,plan_handle ...
2	1	Compiled Plan	Adhoc	SELECT a.* FROM Person.Address AS a WHERE a.AddressID = 42
3	1	Compiled Plan	Prepared	(@1 tinyint)SELECT [a].* FROM [Person].[Address] [a] WHERE [a].[AddressID]=@1

Figure 9-13. *sys.dm_exec_cached_plans output showing an autoparameterized plan*

The `usecounts` of the executable plan for the parameterized query appropriately represents the number of reuses as 1. Also, note that the `objtype` for the autoparameterized executable plan is no longer `Adhoc`; it reflects the fact that the plan is for a parameterized query, Prepared.

The original ad hoc query, even though not executed, gets compiled to create the query tree required for the simple parameterization of the query. The compiled plan for the ad hoc query may or may not be saved in the plan cache depending on the resources available. But before creating the executable plan for the ad hoc query, SQL Server figured out that it was safe to autoparameterize and thus autoparameterized the query for further processing. This is visible as the highlighted line in Figure 9-13.

Since this ad hoc query has been autoparameterized, SQL Server will reuse the existing execution plan if you reexecute `simple_parameterization.sql` with a different value for the variable part:

```
SELECT  a.*
from    Person.Address AS a
where   a.[AddressID] = 52 -previous value was 42
```

Figure 9-14 shows the output of `sys.dm_exec_cached_plans`.

	usecounts	cacheobjtype	objtype	text
1	1	Compiled Plan	Adhoc	SELECT c.usecounts ,c.cacheobjtype ,c.objtype ,t.text FROM s...
2	1	Compiled Plan	Adhoc	SELECT a.* from Person.Address AS a where a.[AddressID] = 52
3	1	Compiled Plan	Adhoc	SELECT a.* FROM Person.Address AS a WHERE a.AddressID = 42
4	2	Compiled Plan	Prepared	(@1 tinyint)SELECT [a].* FROM [Person].[Address] [a] WHERE [a].[AddressID]=@1

Figure 9-14. *sys.dm_exec_cached_plans output showing reuse of the autoparameterized plan*

From Figure 9-14, you can see that although a new plan has been generated for this ad hoc query, the ad hoc one using an `AddressId` value of 52, the existing prepared plan is reused as indicated by the increase in the corresponding `usecounts` value to 2. The ad hoc query can be reexecuted repeatedly with different filter criterion values, reusing the existing execution plan.

There is one more aspect to note in the parameterized query for which the execution plan is cached. In Figure 9-10, observe that the body of the parameterized query doesn't exactly match with that of the ad hoc query submitted. For instance, in the ad hoc query, the words `from` and `where` are in lowercase, and the `AddressID` column is enclosed in square brackets.

On realizing that the ad hoc query can be safely autoparameterized, SQL Server picks a template that can be used instead of the exact text of the query.

To understand the significance of this, consider the following query:

```
SELECT  a.*
FROM    Person.Address AS a
WHERE   a.AddressID BETWEEN 40 AND 60
```

Figure 9-15 shows the output of `sys.dm_exec_cached_plans`.

	usecounts	cacheobjtype	objtype	text
6	1	Compiled Plan	Adhoc	SELECT a.* FROM Person.Address AS a WHERE a.AddressID BETWEEN 40 AND 60
7	1	Compiled Plan	Prepared	(@1 tinyint,@2 tinyint)SELECT [a].* FROM [Person].[Address] [a] WHERE [a].[AddressID]>=@1 AND [a].[AddressID]<=@2

Figure 9-15. *`sys.dm_exec_cached_plans` output showing plan simple parameterization using a template*

From Figure 9-15, you can see that SQL Server autoparameterized the ad hoc query by picking up a template with a pair of >= and <= operators, which are equivalent to the `BETWEEN` operator. That means instead of resubmitting the preceding ad hoc query using the `BETWEEN` clause, if a similar query using a pair of >= and <= is submitted, SQL Server will be able to reuse the existing execution plan. To confirm this behavior, let's modify the ad hoc query as follows:

```
SELECT  a.*
FROM    Person.Address AS a
WHERE   a.AddressID >= 40 AND a.AddressID <=60
```

Figure 9-16 shows the output of `sys.dm_exec_cached_plans`.

	usecounts	cacheobjtype	objtype	text
9	2	Compiled Plan	Prepared	(@1 tinyint,@2 tinyint)SELECT [a].* FROM [Person].[Address] [a] WHERE [a].[AddressID]>=@1 AND [a].[AddressID]<=@2

Figure 9-16. *`sys.dm_exec_cached_plans` output showing reuse of the autoparameterized plan*

From Figure 9-16, you can see that the existing plan is reused, even though the query is syntactically different from the query executed earlier. The autoparameterized plan generated by SQL Server allows the existing plan to be reused not only when the query is resubmitted with different variable values but also for queries with the same template form.

Simple Parameterization Limits

SQL Server is highly conservative during simple parameterization, because the cost of a bad plan can far outweigh the cost of generating a new plan. The conservative approach prevents SQL Server from creating an unsafe autoparameterized plan. Thus, simple parameterization is limited to fairly simple cases, such as ad hoc queries with only one table. An ad hoc query with a join operation between two (or more) tables (as shown in the early part of the "Plan Reusability of an Ad Hoc Workload" section) is not considered safe for simple parameterization.

In a scalable system, do not rely on simple parameterization for plan reusability. The simple parameterization feature of SQL Server makes an educated guess as to which variables and constants can be parameterized. Instead of relying on SQL Server for simple parameterization, you should actually specify it programmatically while building your application.

Forced Parameterization

If the system you're working on consists of primarily ad hoc queries, you may want to attempt to increase the number of queries that accept parameterization. You can modify a database to attempt to force, within certain restrictions, all queries to be parameterized just like in simple parameterization.

To do this, you have to change the database option `PARAMETERIZATION` to `FORCED` using `ALTER DATABASE` like this:

```
ALTER DATABASE AdventureWorks2008 SET PARAMETERIZATION FORCED
```

But before you do, try running this query, which takes only two string literals as inputs and so could be a candidate for simple parameterization (`forced_parameterization.sql` in the download):

```
SELECT  ea.EmailAddress
       ,e.BirthDate
       ,a.City
FROM    Person.Person AS p
        JOIN HumanResources.Employee AS e
        ON p.BusinessEntityID = e.BusinessEntityID
        JOIN Person.BusinessEntityAddress AS bea
        ON e.BusinessEntityID = bea.BusinessEntityID
        JOIN Person.Address AS a
        ON bea.AddressID = a.AddressID
        JOIN Person.StateProvince AS sp
        ON a.StateProvinceID = sp.StateProvinceID
        JOIN Person.EmailAddress AS ea
        ON p.BusinessEntityID = ea.BusinessEntityID
WHERE   ea.EmailAddress LIKE 'david%'
        AND sp.StateProvinceCode = 'WA' ;
```

When you run this query, simple parameterization is not applied, as you can see in Figure 9-17.

	usecounts	cacheobjtype	objtype	text
1	1	Compiled Plan	Adhoc	SELECT c.usecounts ,c.cacheobjtype ,c.objty...
2	1	Compiled Plan	Adhoc	SELECT ea.EmailAddress ,e.BirthDate ,a.City ...
3	2	Parse Tree	View	CREATE FUNCTION sys.dm_exec_sql_text(@handle var...
4	2	Parse Tree	View	create view sys.dm_exec_cached_plans as select * fro...

Figure 9-17. *A more complicated query doesn't get parameterized.*

No prepared plans are visible in the output from `sys.dm_exec_cached_plans`. But if you use the previous script to set `PARAMETERIZATION` to `FORCED`, clear the cache, and rerun the query, the output from `sys.dm_exec_cached_plans` changes so that the output looks different, as shown in Figure 9-18.

	usecounts	cacheobjtype	objtype	text
1	1	Compiled Plan	Adhoc	SELECT c.usecounts ,c.cacheobjtype ,c.objty...
2	1	Compiled Plan	Adhoc	SELECT ea.EmailAddress ,e.BirthDate ,a.City ...
3	1	Compiled Plan	Prepared	(@0 varchar(8000))select ea . EmailAddress , e . BirthDat...
4	2	Parse Tree	View	CREATE FUNCTION sys.dm_exec_sql_text(@handle var...
5	2	Parse Tree	View	create view sys.dm_exec_cached_plans as select * fro...

Figure 9-18. *Forced parameterization changes the plan.*

Now a prepared plan is visible in the third row. However, only a single parameter was supplied, `@0 varchar(8000)`. If you get the full text of the prepared plan out of `sys.dm_exec_query_text` and format it, it looks like this:

```
(@0 varchar(8000))
select  ea.EmailAddress
        ,e.BirthDate
        ,a.City
from    Person.Person as p
        join HumanResources.Employee as e
        on p.BusinessEntityID = e.BusinessEntityID
        join Person.BusinessEntityAddress as bea
        on e.BusinessEntityID = bea.BusinessEntityID
        join Person.Address as a
        on bea.AddressID = a.AddressID
        join Person.StateProvince as sp
        on a.StateProvinceID = sp.StateProvinceID
        join Person.EmailAddress as ea
        on p.BusinessEntityID = ea.BusinessEntityID
where   ea.EmailAddress like 'david%'
        and sp.StateProvinceCode = @0
```

Because of its restrictions, forced parameterization was unable to substitute anything for the string `'david%'`, but it was able to for the string `'WA'`. Worth noting is that the variable was declared as a full 8,000-length `VARCHAR` instead of the three-character `NCHAR` like the actual column in the `Person.StateProvince` table. Although you have a parameter, it might lead to implicit data conversions that could prevent the use of an index.

Before you start using forced parameterization, the following list of restrictions may give you information to help you decide whether forced parameterization will work in your database. (This is a partial list; for the complete list, please consult Books Online.)

- `INSERT ... EXECUTE` queries
- Statements inside procedures, triggers, and user-defined functions since they already have execution plans
- Client-side prepared statements (you'll find more detail on these later in this chapter)
- Queries with the query hint `RECOMPILE`
- Pattern and escape clause arguments used in a `LIKE` statement (as shown earlier)

This gives you an idea of the types of restrictions placed on forced parameterization. Forced parameterization is really going to be helpful only if you are suffering from large amounts of compiles and recompiles because of ad hoc queries. Any other load won't benefit from the use of forced parameterization.

Before continuing, change the database back to `SIMPLE PARAMETERIZATION`:

```
ALTER DATABASE AdventureWorks2008 SET PARAMETERIZATION SIMPLE
```

Plan Reusability of a Prepared Workload

Defining queries as a prepared workload allows the variable parts of the queries to be explicitly parameterized. This enables SQL Server to generate a query plan that is not tied to the variable parts of the query, and it keeps the variable parts separate in an execution context. As you saw in the previous section, SQL Server supports three techniques to submit a prepared workload:

- Stored procedures
- `sp_executesql`
- Prepare/execute model

In the sections that follow, I cover each of these techniques in more depth and point out where it's possible for parameterized execution plans to cause problems.

Stored Procedures

Using stored procedures is a standard technique for improving the effectiveness of plan caching. When the stored procedure is compiled, a combined plan is generated for all the SQL statements within the stored procedure. The execution plan generated for the stored procedure can be reused whenever the stored procedure is reexecuted with different parameter values.

In addition to checking `sys.dm_exec_cached_plans`, you can track the execution plan caching for stored procedures using the Profiler tool. Profiler provides the events listed in Table 9-2 to track the plan caching for stored procedures.

Table 9-2. *Events to Analyze Plan Caching for the* `Stored Procedures` *Event Class*

Event	Description
`SP:CacheHit`	Plan is found in the cache
`SP:CacheMiss`	Plan is not found in the cache
`SP:ExecContextHit`	Execution context for the stored procedure is found in the cache

To track the stored procedure plan caching using Profiler, you can use these events along with the other stored procedure events and data columns shown in Table 9-3.

Table 9-3. *Data Columns to Analyze Plan Caching for Stored Procedures Event Class*

Event	Data Column
SP:CacheHit	EventClass
SP:CacheMiss	TextData
SP:Completed	LoginName
SP:ExecContextHit	SPID
SP:Starting	StartTime
SP:StmtCompleted	

To understand how stored procedures can improve plan caching, reexamine the procedure created earlier called spBasicSalesInfo. The procedure (spBasicSalesInfo.sql) is repeated here for clarity:

```
IF(SELECT OBJECT_ID('spBasicSalesInfo')) IS NOT NULL
  DROP PROC dbo.spBasicSalesInfo
GO
CREATE PROC dbo.spBasicSalesInfo
@ProductID INT
,@CustomerId INT
AS
SELECT  soh.SalesOrderNumber
        ,soh.OrderDate
        ,sod.OrderQty
        ,sod.LineTotal
FROM    Sales.SalesOrderHeader AS soh
        JOIN Sales.SalesOrderDetail AS sod
        ON soh.SalesOrderID = sod.SalesOrderID
WHERE   soh.CustomerID = @CustomerId
        AND sod.Productid = @ProductId
```

To retrieve a result set for soh.CustomerId = 29690 and sod.ProductId=711, you can execute the stored procedure like this:

```
EXEC dbo.spBasicSalesInfo @CustomerId =29690, @ProductId =711
```

Figure 9-19 shows the output of sys.dm_exec_cached_plans.

	usecounts	cacheobjtype	objtype	text
1	1	Compiled Plan	Proc	CREATE PROC dbo.spBasicSalesInfo @ProductID INT ,@CustomerId INT AS SELECT soh.SalesOrd...

Figure 9-19. *sys.dm_exec_cached_plans output showing stored procedure plan caching*

From Figure 9-19, you can see that a compiled plan of type Proc is generated and cached for the stored procedure. The usecounts value of the executable plan is 1 since the stored procedure is executed only once.

Figure 9-20 shows the Profiler trace output for this stored procedure execution.

EventClass	TextData	CPU	Reads	Writes	Duration
SP:CacheMiss	EXEC spBasicSalesInfo @CustomerId =...				
SQL:BatchStarting	EXEC spBasicSalesInfo @CustomerId =...				
SP:CacheInsert	spBasicSalesInfo				
SQL:BatchCompleted	EXEC spBasicSalesInfo @CustomerId =...	0	109	0	16

Figure 9-20. *Profiler trace output showing that the stored procedure plan isn't easily found in the cache*

From the Profiler trace output, you can see that the plan for the stored procedure is not found in the cache. When the stored procedure is executed the first time, SQL Server looks in the procedure cache and fails to find any cache entry for the procedure `spBasicSalesInfo`, causing an `SP:CacheMiss` event. On not finding a cached plan, SQL Server makes arrangements to compile the stored procedure. Subsequently, SQL Server generates and saves the plan and proceeds with the execution of the stored procedure.

If this stored procedure is reexecuted to retrieve a result set for `@ProductId = 777`:

```
EXEC spBasicSalesInfo @CustomerId =29690, @ProductId =777
```

then the existing plan is reused, as shown in the `sys.dm_exec_cached_plans` output in Figure 9-21.

	usecounts	cacheobjtype	objtype	text
1	2	Compiled Plan	Proc	CREATE PROC dbo.spBasicSalesInfo @ProductID INT ...

Figure 9-21. *`sys.dm_exec_cached_plans` output showing reuse of the stored procedure plan*

You can also confirm the reuse of the execution plan from the Profiler trace output, as shown in Figure 9-22.

EventClass	TextData	CPU	Reads	Writes	Duration
SP:CacheMiss	EXEC spBasicSalesInfo @CustomerId =29690, @ProductId =777				
SQL:BatchStarting	EXEC spBasicSalesInfo @CustomerId =29690, @ProductId =777				
SP:CacheHit					
SQL:BatchCompleted	EXEC spBasicSalesInfo @CustomerId =29690, @ProductId =777	0	77	0	0

Figure 9-22. *Profiler trace output showing reuse of the stored procedure plan*

From the Profiler trace output, you can see that the existing plan is found in the procedure cache. On searching the cache, SQL Server finds the executable plan for the stored procedure `p1` causing an `SP:CacheHit` event. Once the existing execution plan is found, SQL reuses the plan to execute the stored procedure.

A few other aspects of stored procedures are worth considering:

- Stored procedures are compiled on first execution.
- Stored procedures have other performance benefits, such as reducing network traffic.
- Stored procedures have additional benefits, such as the isolation of the data.

Stored Procedures Are Compiled on First Execution

The execution plan of a stored procedure is generated when it is executed the first time. When the stored procedure is created, it is only parsed and saved in the database. No normalization and optimization processes are performed during the stored procedure creation. This allows a stored procedure to be created before creating all the objects accessed by the stored procedure. For example, you can create the following stored procedure, even when table no_t1 referred to in the stored procedure does not exist:

```
IF(SELECT OBJECT_ID('p1')) IS NOT NULL
  DROP PROC p1
GO
CREATE PROC p1
AS
  SELECT c1 FROM no_t1 --Table no_t1 doesn't exist
GO
```

The stored procedure will be created successfully, since the normalization process to bind the referred object to the query tree (generated by the command parser during the stored procedure execution) is not performed during the stored procedure creation. The stored procedure will report the error when it is first executed (if table no_t1 is not created by then), since the stored procedure is compiled the first time it is executed.

Other Performance Benefits of Stored Procedures

Besides improving the performance through execution plan reusability, stored procedures provide the following performance benefits:

- *Business logic is close to the data*: The parts of the business logic that perform extensive operations on data stored in the database should be put in stored procedures, since SQL Server's engine is extremely powerful for relational and set theory operations.
- *Network traffic is reduced*: The database application, across the network, sends just the name of the stored procedure and the parameter values. Only the processed result set is returned to the application. The intermediate data doesn't need to be passed back and forth between the application and the database.

Additional Benefits of Stored Procedures

Some of the other benefits provided by stored procedures are as follows:

- *The application is isolated from data structure changes.* If all critical data access is made through stored procedures, then when the database schema changes, the stored procedures can be re-created without affecting the application code that accesses the data through the stored procedures. In fact, the application accessing the database need not even be stopped.
- *Security is increased.* User privileges on database tables can be restricted and can be allowed only through the standard business logic implemented in the stored procedure. For example, if you want user u1 to be restricted from physically deleting rows from table t1 and to be allowed to mark only the rows virtually deleted through stored procedure p1 by setting the rows' status as 'Deleted', then you can execute the DENY and GRANT commands as follows:

```
IF(SELECT OBJECT_ID('t1')) IS NOT NULL
  DROP TABLE t1
GO
CREATE TABLE t1(c1 INT, status VARCHAR(7))
INSERT INTO t1 VALUES(1, 'New')
GO
IF(SELECT OBJECT_ID('p1')) IS NOT NULL
  DROP PROC p1
GO
CREATE PROC p1
@c1 INT
AS
  UPDATE t1 SET status = 'Deleted' WHERE c1 = @c1
GO
--Prevent user u1 from deleting rows
DENY DELETE ON t1 TO u1
--Allow user u1 to mark a row as 'deleted'
GRANT EXECUTE ON p1 TO u1
GO
```

This assumes the existence of user u1. Note that if the query within the stored procedure p1 is built dynamically as a string (@sql) as follows, then granting permission to the stored procedure won't grant any permission to the query, since the dynamic query isn't treated as part of the stored procedure:

```
IF(SELECT OBJECT_ID('p1')) IS NOT NULL
  DROP PROC p1
GO
CREATE PROC p1
@c1 INT
AS
  DECLARE @sql VARCHAR(50)
  SET @sql = 'UPDATE t1 SET status = ''Deleted'' WHERE c1 = ' +
             CAST(@c1 AS VARCHAR(10))
  EXECUTE(@sql)
GO
GRANT EXECUTE ON p1 TO u1
GO
```

Consequently, user u1 won't be able to mark the row as 'Deleted' using the stored procedure p1. (I cover the aspects of using a dynamic query in the stored procedure in the next chapter.)

- *There is a single point of administration*: All the business logic implemented in stored procedures is maintained as part of the database and can be managed centrally on the database itself. Of course, this benefit is highly relative, depending on whom you ask. To get a different opinion, ask a non-DBA!

Since stored procedures are saved as database objects, they add maintenance overhead to the database administration. Many times, you may need to execute just one or a few queries from the application. If these singleton queries are executed frequently, you should aim to reuse their execution plans to improve performance. But creating stored procedures for these individual singleton queries adds a large number of stored procedures to the database, increasing the database administrative overhead significantly. To avoid the maintenance overhead of using stored procedures and yet derive the benefit of plan reuse, submit the singleton queries as a prepared workload using the sp_executesql system stored procedure.

sp_executesql

sp_executesql is a system stored procedure that provides a mechanism to submit one or more queries as a prepared workload. It allows the variable parts of the query to be explicitly parameterized, and it can therefore provide execution plan reusability as effective as a stored procedure. The SELECT statement spBasicSalesInfo.sql can be submitted through sp_executesql as follows (executesql.sql in the download):

```
DECLARE @query NVARCHAR(MAX)
DECLARE @param NVARCHAR(MAX)

SET @query = N'SELECT  soh.SalesOrderNumber
       ,soh.OrderDate
       ,sod.OrderQty
       ,sod.LineTotal
FROM    Sales.SalesOrderHeader AS soh
        JOIN Sales.SalesOrderDetail AS sod
        ON soh.SalesOrderID = sod.SalesOrderID
WHERE   soh.CustomerID = @CustomerId
        AND sod.ProductId = @ProductId'

SET @param = N'@CustomerId INT, @ProductId INT'

EXEC sp_executesql @query, @param, @CustomerId = 29690,@ProductId = 711
```

Note that the strings passed to the sp_executesql stored procedure are declared as NVARCHAR and that they are built with a prefix of N. This is required since sp_executesql uses Unicode strings as the input parameters.

The output of sys.dm_exec_cached_plans is shown next (see Figure 9-23):

```
SELECT  c.usecounts
       ,c.cacheobjtype
       ,c.objtype
       ,t.text
FROM    sys.dm_exec_cached_plans c
        CROSS APPLY sys.dm_exec_sql_text(c.plan_handle) t
```

	usecounts	cacheobjtype	objtype	text
1	1	Compiled Plan	Adhoc	SELECT c.usecounts ,c.cacheobjtype ,c.objty...
2	1	Compiled Plan	Prepared	(@CustomerId INT, @ProductId INT)SELECT soh.Sales...
3	2	Parse Tree	View	CREATE FUNCTION sys.dm_exec_sql_text(@handle var...
4	2	Parse Tree	View	create view sys.dm_exec_cached_plans as select * fro...
5	1	Extended Proc	Proc	sp_executesql

Figure 9-23. *sys.dm_exec_cached_plans output showing a parameterized plan generated using sp_executesql*

In Figure 9-23, you can see that the plan is generated for the parameterized part of the query submitted through `sp_executesql`, line 2. Since the plan is not tied to the variable part of the query, the existing execution plan can be reused if this query is resubmitted with a different value for one of the parameters (`d.ProductID=777`) as follows:

```
...
EXEC sp_executesql @query, @param, @CustomerId = 29690, @ProductId = 711
```

Figure 9-24 shows the output of `sys.dm_exec_cached_plans`.

	usecounts	cacheobjtype	objtype	text
1	1	Compiled Plan	Adhoc	SELECT c.usecounts ,c.cacheobjtype ,c.objtype ...
2	2	Compiled Plan	Prepared	(@CustomerId INT, @ProductId INT)SELECT soh.SalesOrder...
3	1	Compiled Plan	Adhoc	SELECT name, cmptlevel, sid, status FROM dbo.sysdatabases ...
4	2	Parse Tree	View	CREATE FUNCTION sys.dm_exec_sql_text(@handle varbinary...
5	2	Parse Tree	View	create view sys.dm_exec_cached_plans as select * from Ope...
6	2	Parse Tree	View	CREATE VIEW sys.sysdatabases AS SELECT d.name, dbid =...
7	2	Parse Tree	View	CREATE VIEW sys.master_files$ AS SELECT database_id...
8	2	Parse Tree	View	CREATE VIEW sys.databases AS SELECT d.name, d.id AS d...
9	2	Extended Proc	Proc	sp_executesql

Figure 9-24. *sys.dm_exec_cached_plans output showing reuse of the parameterized plan generated using sp_executesql*

From Figure 9-24, you can see that the existing plan is reused (`usecounts` is `2` on the plan on line 2) when the query is resubmitted with a different variable value. If this query is resubmitted many times with different values for the variable part, the existing execution plan can be reused without regenerating new execution plans.

The query for which the plan is created (the `text` column) matches the exact textual string of the parameterized query submitted through `sp_executesql`. Therefore, if the same query is submitted from different parts of the application, ensure that the same textual string is used in all places. For example, if the same query is resubmitted with a minor modification in the query string (`where` in lowercase instead of uppercase letters):

```
...
SET @query = N'SELECT  soh.SalesOrderNumber
        ,soh.OrderDate
        ,sod.OrderQty
        ,sod.LineTotal
FROM    Sales.SalesOrderHeader AS soh
        JOIN Sales.SalesOrderDetail AS sod
        ON soh.SalesOrderID = sod.SalesOrderID
```

```
where   soh.CustomerID = @CustomerId
        AND sod.Productid = @ProductId'
...
```

then the existing plan is not reused, and instead a new plan is created, as shown in the sys.dm_exec_cached_plans output in Figure 9-25.

	usecounts	cacheobjtype	objtype	text
1	1	Compiled Plan	Prepared	(@CustomerId INT, @ProductId INT)SELECT soh.Sales...
2	2	Compiled Plan	Adhoc	SELECT c.usecounts ,c.cacheobjtype ,c.objty...
3	2	Compiled Plan	Prepared	(@CustomerId INT, @ProductId INT)SELECT soh.Sales...
4	1	Compiled Plan	Adhoc	SELECT name, cmptlevel, sid, status FROM dbo.sysdata...
5	2	Parse Tree	View	CREATE FUNCTION sys.dm_exec_sql_text(@handle var...
6	2	Parse Tree	View	create view sys.dm_exec_cached_plans as select * fro...
7	2	Parse Tree	View	CREATE VIEW sys.sysdatabases AS SELECT d.name, ...
8	2	Parse Tree	View	CREATE VIEW sys.master_files$ AS SELECT datab...
9	2	Parse Tree	View	CREATE VIEW sys.databases AS SELECT d.name, d.i...
10	3	Extended Proc	Proc	sp_executesql

Figure 9-25. *sys.dm_exec_cached_plans output showing sensitivity of the plan generated using sp_executesql*

In general, use sp_executesql to explicitly parameterize queries to make their execution plans reusable when the queries are resubmitted with different values for the variable parts. This provides the performance benefit of reusable plans without the overhead of managing any persistent object as required for stored procedures. This feature is exposed by both ODBC and OLEDB through SQLExecDirect and ICommandWithParameters, respectively. As .NET developers or users of ADO.NET (ADO 2.7 or higher), you can submit the preceding SELECT statement using ADO Command and Parameters. If you set the ADO Command Prepared property to FALSE and use ADO Command ('SELECT * FROM "Order Details" d, Orders o WHERE d.OrderID=o.OrderID and d.ProductID=?') with ADO Parameters, ADO.NET will send the SELECT statement using sp_executesql.

Along with the parameters, sp_executesql sends the entire query string across the network every time the query is reexecuted. You can avoid this by using the prepare/execute model of ODBC and OLEDB (or OLEDB .NET).

Prepare/Execute Model

ODBC and OLEDB provide a prepare/execute model to submit queries as a prepared workload. Like sp_executesql, this model allows the variable parts of the queries to be parameterized explicitly. The prepare phase allows SQL Server to generate the execution plan for the query and return a handle of the execution plan to the application. This execution plan handle is used by the execute phase to execute the query with different parameter values. This model can be used only to submit queries through ODBC or OLEDB, and it can't be used within SQL Server itself—queries within stored procedures can't be executed using this model.

The SQL Server ODBC driver provides the SQLPrepare and SQLExecute APIs to support the prepare/execute model. The SQL Server OLEDB provider exposes this model through the ICommandPrepare interface. The OLEDB .NET provider of ADO.NET behaves similarly.

■ **Note** For a detailed description of how to use the prepare/execute model in a database application, please refer to the MSDN article "Preparing SQL Statements" (`http://msdn.microsoft.com/en-us/library/ms175528.aspx`).

Parameter Sniffing

Although the goal of a well-defined workload is to get a plan into the cache that will be reused, it is possible to get a plan into the cache that you don't want to reuse. The first time a procedure is called by SQL Server, the values used are included as a part of generating the plan. If these values are representative of the data and statistics, then you'll get a good plan that will be beneficial to most executions of the stored procedure. But if the data is skewed in some fashion, it can seriously impact the performance of the query.

For example, take the following stored procedure (`spAddressByCity.sql` in the download):

```
IF (SELECT  OBJECT_ID('spAddressByCity')
   ) IS NOT NULL
    DROP PROC dbo.spAddressByCity
GO
CREATE PROC dbo.spAddressByCity @City NVARCHAR(30)
AS
    SELECT  a.AddressID
           ,a.AddressLine1
           ,AddressLine2
           ,a.City
           ,sp.[Name] AS StateProvinceName
           ,a.PostalCode
    FROM    Person.Address AS a
            JOIN Person.StateProvince AS sp
            ON a.StateProvinceID = sp.StateProvinceID
    WHERE   a.City = @City
```

After creating the procedure, run it with this parameter:

```
EXEC dbo.spAddressByCity
    @City = N'London'
```

This will result in the following I/O and execution times as well as the query plan in Figure 9-26:

```
Table 'Address'. Scan count 1, logical reads 216
Table 'StateProvince'. Scan count 1, logical reads 3
CPU time = 0 ms,  elapsed time = 167 ms.
```

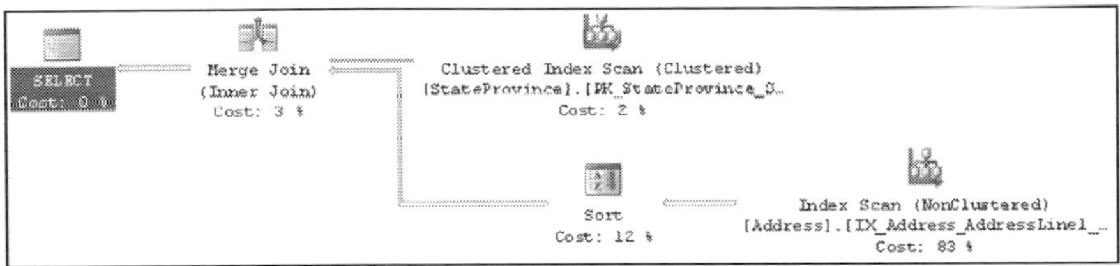

Figure 9-26. *Execution plan of spAddressByCity*

If the stored procedure is run again but this time with a different parameter:

```
EXEC dbo.spAddressByCity
    @City = N'Mentor'
```

then it returns with a different set of I/O and execution times but the same execution plan:

```
Table 'Address'. Scan count 1, logical reads 216
Table 'StateProvince'. Scan count 1, logical reads 3
CPU time = 16 ms,  elapsed time = 75 ms.
```

The I/O looks roughly the same since the same execution plan is reused. You can verify this by taking a look at the output from sys.dm_exec_cached_plans (in Figure 9-27).

	usecounts	cacheobjtype	objtype	text
1	2	Compiled Plan	Proc	CREATE PROC dbo.spAddressByCity @City NVARCHAR(3...

Figure 9-27. *Output from sys.dm_exec_cached_plans verifies procedure reuse*

To show how parameters affect execution plans, you can reverse the order of the execution of the procedures. First flush the buffer cache by running DBCC FREEPROCCACHE. Then rerun the queries in reverse order. The first query, using the parameter Mentor, results in the following I/O and execution plan (Figure 9-28):

```
Table 'StateProvince'. Scan count 0, logical reads 2
Table 'Address'. Scan count 1, logical reads 216
CPU time = 0 ms,  elapsed time = 76 ms
```

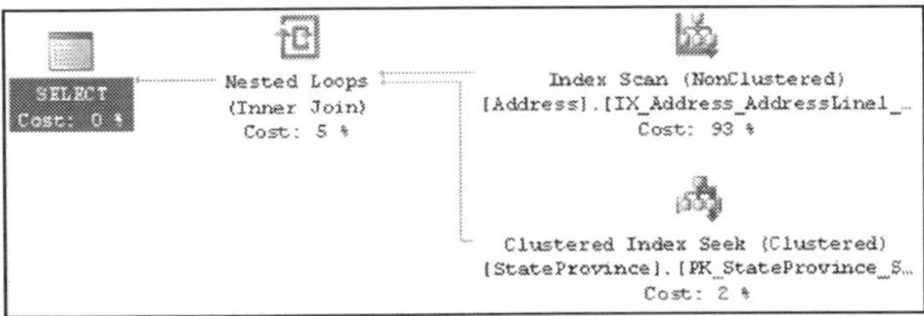

Figure 9-28. *The execution plan changes.*

Figure 9-28 is not the same execution plan as that shown in Figure 9-26. The number of reads drops slightly, but the execution time stays roughly the same. The second execution, using London as the value for the parameter, results in the following I/O and execution times:

```
Table 'StateProvince'. Scan count 0, logical reads 868
Table 'Address'. Scan count 1, logical reads 216
CPU time = 0 ms,  elapsed time = 243 ms.
```

This time the reads are radically higher, and the execution time was increased by more than 100 ms. The plan created in the first execution of the procedure with the parameter London created a plan best suited to retrieve the 1,000+ rows that match that criteria in the database. Then the next execution of the procedure using the parameter value Mentor did well enough using the same plan generated by the first execution. When the order is reversed, a new execution plan was created for the value Mentor that did not work at all well for the value London.

This is a case where having an execution plan in the cache can hurt the performance of your queries. Once you identify the issue for a plan that works well some of the time but doesn't others, you avoid or fix this problem in a number of ways:

- You can force a recompile of the plan either at the time of execution by running sp_recompile against the procedure prior to executing it or by getting it to recompile each time it executes by using the WITH RECOMPILE option.
- Reassign input parameters to local parameters. This popular fix forces the optimizer to make a best guess at the values likely to be used by looking at the statistics of the data being referenced, which can and does eliminate the values being taken into account. The problem with the solution is it eliminates the values being taken into account. You may get worse performing procedures overall.
- You can use a query hint, OPTIMIZE FOR, when you create the procedure and supply it with known good parameters that will generate a plan that works well for most of your queries. However, understand that some percentage of the queries won't work well with the parameter supplied.
- You can use a plan guide, which is a mechanism to get a query to behave a certain way without making modifications to the procedure. This will be covered in detail in Chapter 10.

Just remember that most of the time parameterized queries and plan reuse are not a problem. This type of situation is somewhat rare.

Query Plan Hash and Query Hash

With SQL Server 2008, new functionality around execution plans and the cache was introduced called the *query plan hash* and the *query hash*. These are binary objects using an algorithm against the query or the query plan to generate the binary hash value. These are useful for a very common practice in developing known as *copy and paste*. You will find that very common patterns and practices will be repeated throughout your code. Under the best circumstances, this is a very good thing, because you will see the best types of queries, joins, set-based operations, and so on, copied from one procedure to another as needed. But sometimes, you will see the worst possible practices repeated over and over again in your code. This is where the query hash and the query plan hash come into play.

You can retrieve the query plan hash and the query hash from `sys.dm_exec_query_stats` or `sys.dm_exec_requests`. Although this is a mechanism for identifying queries and their plans, the hash values are not unique. Dissimilar plans can arrive at the same hash, so you can't rely on this as an alternate primary key.

To see the hash values in action, create two queries (`queryhash1.sql` and `queryhash2.sql` in the download):

```
SELECT  *
FROM    Production.Product AS p
        JOIN Production.ProductSubcategory AS ps
        ON p.ProductSubcategoryID = ps.ProductSubcategoryID
        JOIN Production.ProductCategory AS pc
        ON ps.ProductCategoryID = pc.ProductCategoryID
WHERE   pc.[Name] = 'Bikes'
        AND ps.[Name] = 'Touring Bikes'
```

```
SELECT  *
FROM    Production.Product AS p
        JOIN Production.ProductSubcategory AS ps
        ON p.ProductSubcategoryID = ps.ProductSubcategoryID
        JOIN Production.ProductCategory AS pc
        ON ps.ProductCategoryID = pc.ProductCategoryID
where   pc.[Name] = 'Bikes'
        and ps.[Name] = 'Road Bikes'
```

Note that the only substantial difference between the two queries is that `ProductSubCategory.Name` is different, `Touring Bikes` in one and `Road Bikes` in the other. However, also note that the `WHERE` and `AND` keywords in `queryhash2.sql` are lowercase. After you execute each of these queries, you can see the results of these format changes from `sys.dm_exec_query_stats` in Figure 9-29 from the following query:

```
SELECT  s.execution_count
        ,s.query_hash
        ,s.query_plan_hash
        ,t.text
FROM    sys.dm_exec_query_stats s
        CROSS APPLY sys.dm_exec_sql_text(s.plan_handle) t
```

	execution_count	query_hash	query_plan_hash	text
1	1	0x08088CD8B192397F	0x0F296BAA42FA4CDF	SELECT * FROM Production.Product AS...
2	1	0x08088CD8B192397F	0x0F296BAA42FA4CDF	SELECT * FROM Production.Product AS...

Figure 9-29. *sys.dm_exec_query_stats showing the plan hash values*

Two different plans were created because these are not parameterized queries, they are too complex to be considered for simple parameterization, and forced parameterization is off. These two plans have identical hash values because they varied only in terms of the values passed. The differences in case did not matter to the query hash or the query plan hash value. If, however, you changed the SELECT criteria in queryhash2.sql:

```
SELECT  p.ProductID
FROM    Production.Product AS p
        JOIN Production.ProductSubcategory AS ps
        ON p.ProductSubcategoryID = ps.ProductSubcategoryID
        JOIN Production.ProductCategory AS pc
        ON ps.ProductCategoryID = pc.ProductCategoryID
WHERE   pc.[Name] = 'Bikes'
        and ps.[Name] = 'Touring Bikes'
```

then the values would be retrieved from sys.dm_exec_query_stats, as shown in Figure 9-30, and the query would have changes.

	execution_count	query_hash	query_plan_hash	text
1	1	0x08088CD8B192397F	0x0F296BAA42FA4CDF	SELECT * FROM Production.Product AS p J...
2	1	0x08088CD8B192397F	0x0F296BAA42FA4CDF	SELECT * FROM Production.Product AS p J...
3	1	0x15823AE0D4D97753	0x19043ECD2E2ACD44	SELECT p.ProductID FROM Production.Product ...

Figure 9-30. *sys.dm_exec_query_stats showing a different hash*

Although the basic structure of the query is the same, the change in the columns returned was enough to change the query hash value and the query plan hash value.

Because differences in data distribution and indexes can cause the same query to come up with two different plans, the query_hash can be the same, and the query_plan_hash can be different. To illustrate this, create two new queries (queryplanhash1.sql and queryplanhash2.sql in the download):

```
SELECT  p.[Name],
        tha.TransactionDate,
        tha.TransactionType,
        tha.Quantity,
        tha.ActualCost
FROM    Production.TransactionHistoryArchive tha
        JOIN Production.Product p
        ON tha.ProductID = p.ProductID
WHERE   P.ProductID = 461 ;


SELECT  p.[Name],
        tha.TransactionDate,
        tha.TransactionType,
        tha.Quantity,
        tha.ActualCost
FROM    Production.TransactionHistoryArchive tha
        JOIN Production.Product p
        ON tha.ProductID = p.ProductID
WHERE   p.ProductID = 712 ;
```

Like the original queries used earlier, these queries vary only by the values passed to the ProductID column. When both queries are run, you can select data from sys.dm_exec_query_stats to see the hash values (Figure 9-31).

	execution_count	query_hash	query_plan_hash	text
1	1	0xF0CF17CED693193C	0x85EBF074263F0B0A	SELECT p.[Name], tha.TransactionDat...
2	1	0xF0CF17CED693193C	0x7C5E24CA4DE108A6	SELECT p.[Name], tha.TransactionDat...

Figure 9-31. *Differences in the query_plan_hash*

You can see the query_hash values are identical, but the query_plan_hash values are different. This is because the execution plans created, based on the statistics for the values passed in, are radically different, as you can see in Figure 9-32.

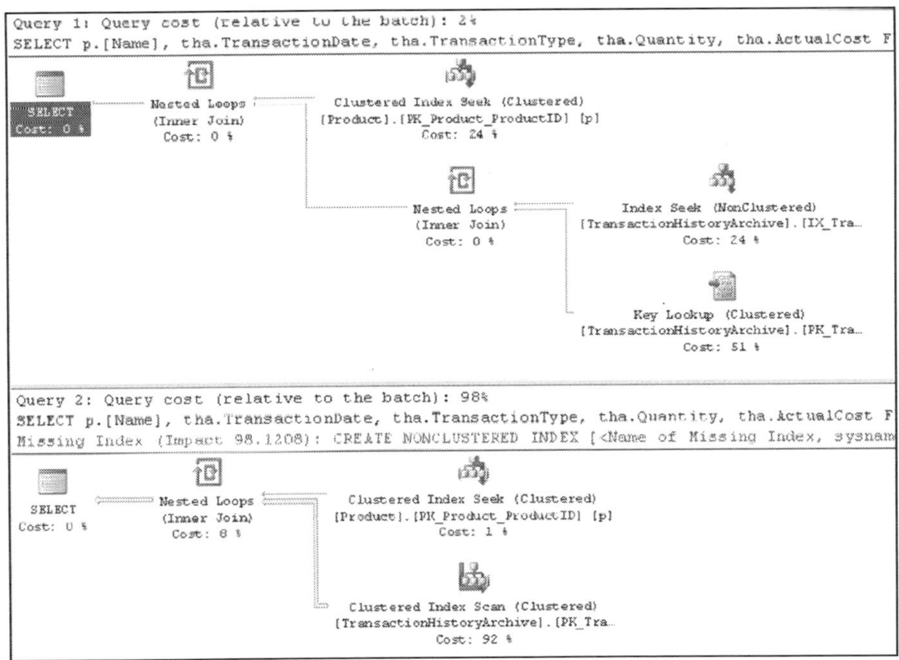

Figure 9-32. *Different parameters result in radically different plans*

The query plan hash and the query hash values can be useful tools for tracking down common issues between disparate queries, but as you've seen, they're not going to retrieve an accurate set of information in every possibility. They do add yet another useful tool in identifying other places where query performance could be poor. They can also be used to track execution plans over time. You can capture the query_plan_hash for a query after deploying it to production and then watch it over time to see whether it changes because of data changes. With this you can also keep track of aggregated query stats by plan, referencing sys.dm_exec_query_stats, although, remember, the aggregated data is reset when the server is restarted. Keep these tools in mind while tuning your queries.

Execution Plan Cache Recommendations

The basic purpose of the plan cache is to improve performance by reusing execution plans. Thus, it is important to ensure that your execution plans actually are reusable. Since the plan reusability of ad hoc queries is inefficient, it is generally recommended that you rely on prepared workload techniques as much as possible. To ensure efficient use of the plan cache, follow these recommendations:

- Explicitly parameterize variable parts of a query.
- Use stored procedures to implement business functionality.
- Use `sp_executesql` to avoid stored procedure maintenance.
- Use the prepare/execute model to avoid resending a query string.
- Avoid ad hoc queries.
- Use `sp_executesql` over `EXECUTE` for dynamic queries.
- Parameterize variable parts of queries with care.
- Avoid modifying environment settings between connections.
- Avoid the implicit resolution of objects in queries.

Let's take a closer look at these points.

Explicitly Parameterize Variable Parts of a Query

A query is often run several times, with the only difference between each run being that there are different values for the variable parts. Their plans can be reused, however, if the static and variable parts of the query can be separated. Although SQL Server has a simple parameterization feature and a forced parameterization feature, they have severe limitations. Always perform parameterization explicitly using the standard prepared workload techniques.

Create Stored Procedures to Implement Business Functionality

If you have explicitly parameterized your query, then placing it in a stored procedure brings the best reusability possible. Since only the parameters need to be sent along with the stored procedure name, network traffic is reduced. Since stored procedures are precompiled, they run faster than ad hoc queries. And stored procedures can also maintain a single parameterized plan for the set of queries included within the stored procedure, instead of maintaining a large number of small plans for the individual queries. This prevents the plan cache from being flooded with separate plans for the individual queries.

Code with sp_executesql to Avoid Stored Procedure Maintenance

If the object maintenance required for the stored procedures becomes a consideration or you are using client-side generated queries, then use `sp_executesql` to submit the queries as prepared workloads. Unlike the stored procedure model, `sp_executesql` doesn't create any persistent objects in the database. `sp_executesql` is suited to execute a singleton query or a small batch query.

The complete business logic implemented in a stored procedure can also be submitted with sp_executesql as a large query string. However, as the complexity of the business logic increases, it becomes difficult to create and maintain a query string for the complete logic.

Implement the Prepare/Execute Model to Avoid Resending a Query String

sp_executesql requires the query string to be sent across the network every time the query is reexecuted. It also requires the cost of a query string match at the server to identify the corresponding execution plan in the procedure cache. In the case of an ODBC or OLEDB (or OLEDB .NET) application, you can use the prepare/execute model to avoid resending the query string during multiple executions, since only the plan handle and parameters need to be submitted.

In the prepare/execute model, since a plan handle is returned to the application, the plan can be reused by other user connections; it is not limited to the user who created the plan.

Avoid Ad Hoc Queries

Do not design new applications using ad hoc queries! The execution plan created for an ad hoc query cannot be reused when the query is resubmitted with a different value for the variable parts. Even though SQL Server has the simple parameterization and forced parameterization features to isolate the variable parts of the query, because of the strict conservativeness of SQL Server in parameterization, the feature is limited to simple queries only. For better plan reusability, submit the queries as prepared workloads.

Prefer sp_executesql over EXECUTE for Dynamic Queries

SQL query strings generated dynamically within stored procedures or a database application should be executed using sp_executesql instead of the EXECUTE command. The EXECUTE command doesn't allow the variable parts of the query to be explicitly parameterized.

To understand the preceding comparison between sp_executesql and EXECUTE, consider the dynamic SQL query string used to execute the SELECT statement in adhoc_sproc.sql:

```
DECLARE @n VARCHAR(3)
SET @n = '776'
DECLARE @sql VARCHAR(MAX)
SET @sql = 'SELECT * FROM Sales.SalesOrderDetail sod '
    + 'JOIN Sales.SalesOrderHeader soh '
    + 'ON sod.SalesOrderID=soh.SalesOrderID '
    + 'WHERE  sod.ProductID=''' + @n
    + ''''
--Execute the dynamic query using EXECUTE statement
EXECUTE (@sql)
```

The EXECUTE statement submits the query along with the value of d.ProductID as an ad hoc query and thereby faces the conservativeness of simple parameterization. For improved plan cache reusability, execute the dynamic SQL string as a parameterized query using sp_executesql:

```
DECLARE @n INT
SET @n = 776
DECLARE @sql NVARCHAR(MAX)
   ,@paramdef NCHAR(6)
SET @sql = 'SELECT * FROM Sales.SalesOrderDetail sod '
    + 'JOIN Sales.SalesOrderHeader soh '
    + 'ON sod.SalesOrderID=soh.SalesOrderID '
    + 'WHERE  sod.ProductID=@1'
SET @paramdef = N'@1 INT'
--Execute the dynamic query using sp_executesql system stored
--procedure
EXECUTE sp_executesql @sql, @paramdef, @1 = @n
```

Executing the query as an explicitly parameterized query using `sp_executesql` generates a parameterized plan for the query and thereby increases the execution plan reusability.

Parameterize Variable Parts of Queries with Care

Be careful while converting variable parts of a query into parameters. The range of values for some variables may vary so drastically that the execution plan for a certain range of values may not be suitable for the other values. This can lead to parameter sniffing. Deal with this as needed within the situation.

Do Not Allow Implicit Resolution of Objects in Queries

SQL Server allows multiple database objects with the same name to be created under different schemas. For example, table `t1` can be created using two different schemas (`u1` and `u2`) under their individual ownership. The default owner in most systems is `dbo` (database owner). If user `u1` executes the following query:

```
SELECT * FROM t1 WHERE c1 = 1
```

then SQL Server first tries to find whether table `t1` exists for user `u1`'s default schema. If not, then it tries to find whether table `t1` exists for the `dbo` user. This implicit resolution allows user `u1` to create another instance of table `t1` under a different schema and access it temporarily (using the same application code) without affecting other users.

On a production database, I recommend using the schema owner and avoiding implicit resolution. If not, using implicit resolution adds the following overhead on a production server:

- It requires more time to identify the objects.
- It decreases the effectiveness of plan cache reusability.

Summary

SQL Server's cost-based query optimizer decides upon an effective execution plan not based on the exact syntax of the query but by evaluating the cost of executing the query using different processing strategies. The cost evaluation of using different processing strategies is done in multiple optimization phases to avoid spending too much time optimizing a query. Then, the execution plans are cached to save the cost of execution plan generation when the same queries are reexecuted. To improve the reusability of cached plans, SQL Server supports different techniques for execution plan reuse when the queries are rerun with different values for the variable parts.

Using stored procedures is usually the best technique to improve execution plan reusability. SQL Server generates a parameterized execution plan for the stored procedures so that the existing plan can be reused when the stored procedure is rerun with the same or different parameter values. However, if the existing execution plan for a stored procedure is invalidated, the plan can't be reused without a recompilation, decreasing the effectiveness of plan cache reusability.

In the next chapter, I will discuss how to troubleshoot and resolve unnecessary stored procedure plan recompilations.

CHAPTER 10

Stored Procedure Recompilation

Stored procedures improve the reusability of an execution plan by explicitly converting the variable parts of the queries into parameters. This allows execution plans to be reused when the queries are resubmitted with the same or different values for the variable parts. Since stored procedures are mostly used to implement complex business rules, a typical stored procedure contains a complex set of SQL statements, making the price of generating the execution plan of a stored procedure a bit costly. Therefore, it is usually beneficial to reuse the existing execution plan of a stored procedure instead of generating a new plan. However, sometimes the existing plan may not be applicable, or it may not provide the best processing strategy during reuse. SQL Server resolves this condition by recompiling statements within stored procedures to generate a new execution plan.

In this chapter, I cover the following topics:

- The benefits and drawbacks of recompilation
- How to identify the statements causing recompilation
- How to analyze the causes of recompilations
- Ways to avoid recompilations

Benefits and Drawbacks of Recompilation

The recompilation of stored procedures can be both beneficial and harmful. Sometimes, it may be beneficial to consider a new processing strategy for a query instead of reusing the existing plan, especially if the data distribution in the table (or the corresponding statistics) has changed or new indexes are added to the table. Recompiles in SQL Server 2008 are at the statement level. This increases the overall number of recompiles that can occur within a procedure, but it reduces the effects and overhead of recompiles in general. Statement-level recompiles reduce overhead because they recompile an individual statement only rather than all the statements within a procedure, whereas the older method of recompiles caused a procedure, in its entirety, to be recompiled over and over. Despite this smaller footprint for recompiles, it's something to be reduced and controlled as much as possible.

To understand how the recompilation of an existing plan can sometimes be beneficial, assume you need to retrieve some information from the Production.WorkOrder table. The stored procedure may look like this (spWorkOrder.sql in the download):

```
IF (SELECT  OBJECT_ID('dbo.spWorkOrder')
   ) IS NOT NULL
    DROP PROCEDURE dbo.spWorkOrder;
GO
CREATE PROCEDURE dbo.spWorkOrder
AS
    SELECT  wo.WorkOrderID
           ,wo.ProductID
           ,wo.StockedQty
    FROM    Production.WorkOrder AS wo
    WHERE   wo.StockedQty BETWEEN 500 AND 700 ;
```

With the current indexes, the execution plan for the SELECT statement, which is part of the stored procedure plan, scans the index PK_WorkOrder_ID, as shown in Figure 10-1.

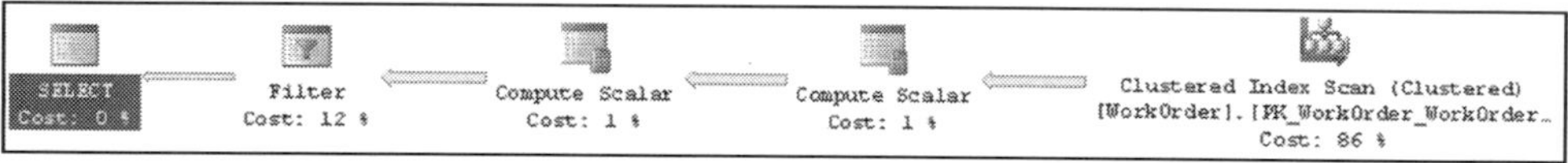

Figure 10-1. *Execution plan for the stored procedure*

This plan is saved in the procedure cache so that it can be reused when the stored procedure is reexecuted. But if a new index is added on the table as follows, then the existing plan won't be the most efficient processing strategy to execute the query:

```
CREATE INDEX IX_Test ON Production.WorkOrder(StockedQty,ProductID)
```

Since index IX_Test can serve as a covering index for the SELECT statement, the cost of a bookmark lookup can be avoided by using index IX_Test instead of scanning PK_WorkOrder_WorkOrderID. SQL Server automatically detects this change and thereby recompiles the existing plan to consider the benefit of using the new index. This results in a new execution plan for the stored procedure (when executed), as shown in Figure 10-2.

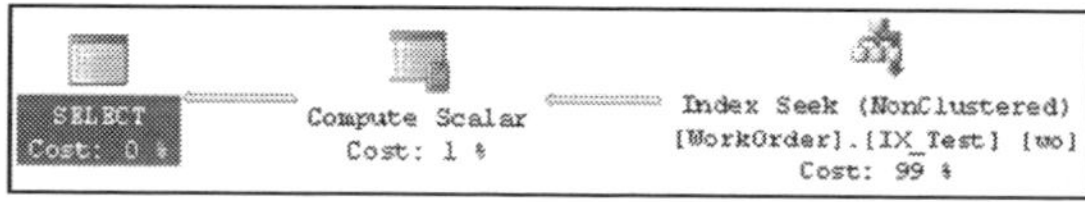

Figure 10-2. *New execution plan for the stored procedure*

In this case, it is beneficial to spend extra CPU cycles to recompile the stored procedure so that you generate a better execution plan.

SQL Server automatically detects the conditions that require a recompilation of the existing plan. SQL Server follows certain rules in determining when the existing plan needs to be recompiled. If a specific implementation of a stored procedure falls within the rules of recompilation (execution plan aged out, SET options changed, and so on), then the stored procedure will be recompiled every time it meets the requirements for a recompile, and SQL Server may not generate a better execution plan. To see this in action, you'll need a different stored procedure. The following procedure returns all the rows from the WorkOrder table (spWorkOrderAll.sql in the download):

```
IF (SELECT  OBJECT_ID('dbo.spWorkOrderAll')
   ) IS NOT NULL
    DROP PROCEDURE dbo.spWorkOrderAll;
GO
CREATE PROCEDURE dbo.spWorkOrderALL
AS
    SELECT  *
    FROM    Production.WorkOrder AS wo
```

Before executing this procedure, drop the index IX_Test:

```
DROP INDEX Production.WorkOrder.IX_Test
```

When you execute this procedure, the SELECT statement returns the complete data set (all rows and columns) from the table and is therefore best served through a table scan on the table WorkOrder. As explained in Chapter 4, the processing of the SELECT statement won't benefit from a nonclustered index on any of the columns. Therefore, ideally, creating the nonclustered index, as follows, before the execution of the stored procedure shouldn't matter:

```
EXEC dbo.spWorkOrderAll
GO
CREATE INDEX IX_Test ON Production.WorkOrder(StockedQty,ProductID)
GO
EXEC dbo.spWorkOrderAll --After creation of index IX_Test
```

But the stored procedure execution after the index creation faces recompilation, as shown in the corresponding Profiler trace output in Figure 10-3.

EventClass	TextData	CPU	Reads	Writes	Duration
Trace Start					
SQL:BatchCompleted	SELECT name, cmptlevel, sid, status...	0	26	0	0
SQL:BatchCompleted	EXEC dbo.spWorkOrderAll;	46	526	0	1489
SQL:BatchCompleted	CREATE INDEX IX_Test ON Production....	172	1488	140	419
SP:Recompile	SELECT * FROM Production.W...				
SQL:BatchCompleted	EXEC dbo.spWorkOrderAll; --After cr...	94	536	0	1458

Figure 10-3. *Nonbeneficial recompilation of the stored procedure*

The SP:Recompile event was used to trace the statement recompiles. You can also use the SQL:StmtRecompile event, even with stored procedures. In this case, the recompilation is of no real benefit to the stored procedure. But unfortunately, it falls within the conditions that cause SQL Server to recompile the stored procedure on every execution. This makes plan caching for the stored procedure ineffective and wastes CPU cycles in regenerating the same plan on this execution. Therefore, it is important to be aware of the conditions that cause the recompilation of stored procedures and to make every effort to avoid those conditions when implementing stored procedures. I will discuss these conditions next, after identifying which statements cause SQL Server to recompile the stored procedure in the respective case.

Identifying the Statement Causing Recompilation

SQL Server can recompile individual statements within a procedure or the entire procedure. Thus, to find the cause of recompilation, it's important to identify the SQL statement that can't reuse the existing plan.

You can use the Profiler tool to track stored procedure recompilation. You can also use Profiler to identify the stored procedure statement that caused the recompilation. Table 10-1 shows the relevant events and data columns you can use (`sprocTrace.tdf` in the download).

Table 10-1. *Events and Data Columns to Analyze Stored Procedure Recompilation for* `Stored Procedures` *Event Class*

Event	Data Column
`SP:Completed`	`EventClass`
`SP:Recompile`	`TextData`
`SP:Starting`	`EventSubClass`
`SP:StmtCompleted` *(Optional)*	`SPID`
`SP:StmtStarting` *(Optional)*	`StartTime`

Consider the following simple stored procedure (`create_p1.sql` in the download):

```
IF(SELECT OBJECT_ID('dbo.p1')) IS NOT NULL
  DROP PROC dbo.p1;
GO
CREATE PROC dbo.p1
AS
CREATE TABLE #t1(c1 INT);
INSERT INTO #t1 (
    c1
) VALUES ( 42 ) ; -- data change causes recompile
GO
```

On executing this stored procedure the first time, you get the Profiler trace output shown in Figure 10-4.

```
EXEC dbo.p1;
```

EventClass	TextData	Duration	EventSubClass
SP:Starting	EXEC dbo.p1		
SP:Recompile	INSERT INTO #t1 (c1) VALUES (...		3 - Deferred compile
SP:Completed	EXEC dbo.p1	1	

Figure 10-4. *Profiler trace output showing an SP:StmtCompleted event causing recompilation*

In Figure 10-4, you can see that you have a recompilation event (SP:Recompile), indicating that the stored procedure went through recompilation. When a stored procedure is executed for the first time, SQL Server compiles the stored procedure and generates an execution plan, as explained in the previous chapter.

Since execution plans are maintained in volatile memory only, they get dropped when SQL Server is restarted. On the next execution of the stored procedure, after the server restart, SQL Server once again compiles the stored procedure and generates the execution plan. These compilations aren't treated as a stored procedure recompilation, since a plan didn't exist in the cache for reuse. An SP:Recompile event indicates that a plan was already there but couldn't be reused.

■ **Note** I discuss the significance of the EventSubClass data column later in the "Analyzing Causes of Recompilation" section.

To see which statement caused the recompile, look at the TextData column within the SP:Recompile event. It shows specifically the statement being recompiled. You can also identify the stored procedure statement causing the recompilation by using the SP:StmtStarting event in combination with a recompile event. The SP:StmtStarting event immediately before the SP:Recompile event indicates the stored procedure statement that caused the recompilation, as shown in Figure 10-5. It's generally easier to use the TextData column, but in very complicated procedures it might make sense to use the SP:StmtStarting event.

EventClass	TextData	Duration	EventSubClass
SP:Starting	EXEC dbo.p1		
SP:StmtStarting	CREATE TABLE #t1(c1 INT);		
SP:StmtCompleted	CREATE TABLE #t1(c1 INT);	0	
SP:StmtStarting	INSERT INTO #t1 (c1) VALUES (...		
SP:Recompile	INSERT INTO #t1 (c1) VALUES (...		3 - Deferred compile
SP:StmtStarting	INSERT INTO #t1 (c1) VALUES (...		
SP:StmtCompleted	INSERT INTO #t1 (c1) VALUES (...	0	
SP:Completed	EXEC dbo.p1	0	

Figure 10-5. *Profiler trace output showing an SP:StmtStarting event causing recompilation*

Note that after the stored procedure recompilation, the stored procedure statement that caused the recompilation is started again to execute with the new plan. You may use either the SP:StmtStarting event or the SP:StmtCompleted event to identify the stored procedure statement causing the recompilation; using both the events will duplicate the information, and the SP:Recompile event will further duplicate the information.

Analyzing Causes of Recompilation

To improve performance, it is important that you analyze the causes of recompilation. Often, recompilation may not be necessary, and you can avoid it to improve performance. Knowing the different conditions that result in recompilation helps you evaluate the cause of a recompilation and determine how to avoid recompiling when it isn't necessary. Stored procedure recompilation occurs for the following reasons:

- The schema of regular tables, temporary tables, or views referred to in the stored procedure statement have changed. Schema changes include changes to the metadata of the table or the indexes on the table.
- Bindings (such as defaults/rules) to the columns of regular or temporary tables have changed.
- Statistics on the table indexes or columns have changed past a certain threshold.
- An object did not exist when the stored procedure was compiled, but it was created during execution. This is called *deferred object resolution*, which is the cause of the preceding recompilation.
- `SET` options have changed.
- The execution plan was aged and deallocated.
- An explicit call was made to the `sp_recompile` system stored procedure.
- There was an explicit use of the `RECOMPILE` clause.

You can see these changes in Profiler. The cause is indicated by the `EventSubClass` data column value for the `SP:Recompile` event, as shown in Table 10-2.

Table 10-2. *`EventSubClass` Data Column Reflecting Causes of Recompilation*

`EventSubClass`	**Description**
1	Schema or bindings to regular table or view changed
2	Statistics changed
3	Object did not exist in the stored procedure plan but was created during execution
4	`SET` options changed
5	Schema or bindings to temporary table changed
6	Schema or bindings of remote rowset changed
7	`FOR BROWSE` permissions changed
8	Query notification environment changed
9	MPI view changed
10	Cursor options changed
11	`WITH RECOMPILE` option invoked

Let's look at some of the reasons listed in Table 10-2 for recompilation in more detail and discuss what you can do to avoid them.

Schema or Bindings Changes

When the schema or bindings to a view, regular table, or temporary table change, the existing stored procedure execution plan becomes invalid. The stored procedure must be recompiled before executing any statement that refers to such an object. SQL Server automatically detects this situation and recompiles the stored procedure.

■ **Note** I talk about recompilation due to schema changes in more detail in the "Benefits and Drawbacks of Recompilation" section.

Statistics Changes

SQL Server keeps track of the number of changes to the table. If the number of changes exceeds the recompilation threshold (RT) value, then SQL Server automatically updates the statistics when the table is referred to in the stored procedure, as you saw in Chapter 7. When the condition for the automatic update of statistics is detected, SQL Server automatically recompiles the stored procedure, along with the statistics update.

The RT is determined by a set of formula that depend on the table being a permanent table or a temporary table (not a table variable) and how many rows are in the table. Table 10-3 shows the basic formula so that you can determine when you can expect to see a statement recompile because of data changes.

Table 10-3. *Formula for Determining Data Changes*

Type of Table	Formula
Permanent table	If number of rows (n) <= 500, RT = 500 IF n > 500, RT = 500 + .2 * n
Temporary table	If n < 6, RT = 6 If 6 <= n <= 500, RT = 500 IF n > 500, RT = 500 + .2 * n

To understand how statistics changes can cause recompilation, consider the following example (`stats_changes.sql` in the download). The stored procedure is executed the first time with only one row in the table. Before the second execution of the stored procedure, a large number of rows are added to the table.

■ **Note** Please ensure that the `AUTO_UPDATE_STATISTICS` setting for the database is `ON`. You can determine the `AUTO_UPDATE_STATISTICS` setting by executing the following query: `SELECT DATABASEPROPERTYEX('AdventureWorks2008', 'IsAutoUpdateStatistics')`.

```
IF EXISTS ( SELECT  *
            FROM    sys.objects
            WHERE   OBJECT_ID = OBJECT_ID(N'[dbo].[NewOrders]')
                    AND TYPE IN (N'U') )
    DROP TABLE [dbo].[NewOrders] ;
GO
SELECT  *
INTO    dbo.NewOrders
FROM    sales.SalesOrderDetail ;
GO
CREATE INDEX IX_NewOrders_ProductID ON dbo.NewOrders (ProductID) ;
GO

IF EXISTS ( SELECT  *
            FROM    sys.objects
            WHERE   object_id = OBJECT_ID(N'[dbo].[spNewOrders]')
                    AND type IN (N'P', N'PC') )
    DROP PROCEDURE [dbo].[spNewOrders] ;
GO
CREATE PROCEDURE dbo.spNewOrders
AS
    SELECT  nwo.OrderQty
           ,nwo.CarrierTrackingNumber
    FROM    dbo.NewOrders nwo
    WHERE   ProductID = 897 ;
GO

SET STATISTICS XML ON ;
EXEC dbo.spNewOrders ;
SET STATISTICS XML OFF ;
GO
```

Next, still in `stats_changes.sql`, you modify a number of rows before reexecuting the stored procedure:

```
UPDATE  dbo.NewOrders
SET     ProductID = 897
WHERE   ProductID BETWEEN 800 AND 900 ;
GO

SET STATISTICS XML ON ;
EXEC dbo.spNewOrders ;
SET STATISTICS XML OFF ;
GO
```

The first time, SQL Server executes the `SELECT` statement of the stored procedure using an `Index Seek` operation, as shown in Figure 10-6.

■ **Note** Please ensure that the setting for the graphical execution plan is `OFF`; otherwise, the output of `STATISTICS XML` won't display.

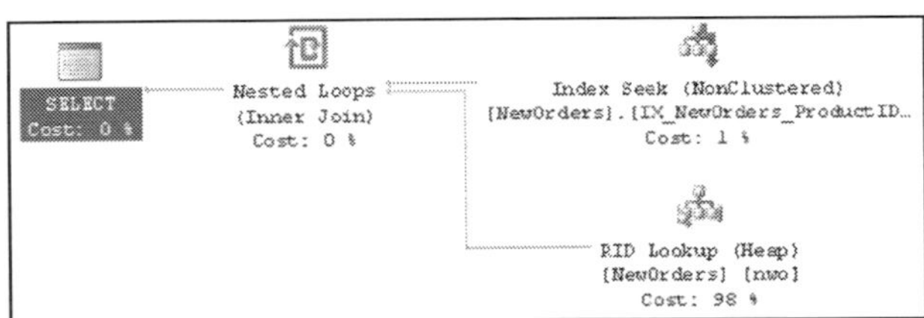

Figure 10-6. *Execution plan prior to data changes*

While reexecuting the stored procedure, SQL Server automatically detects that the statistics on the index have changed. This causes a recompilation of the `SELECT` statement within the procedure, with the optimizer determining a better processing strategy, before executing the `SELECT` statement within the stored procedure, as you can see in Figure 10-7.

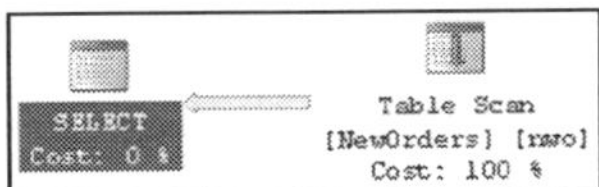

Figure 10-7. *Effect of statistics change on the execution plan*

Figure 10-8 shows the corresponding Profiler trace output (with the `Auto Stats` event added).

EventClass	TextData	Duration	EventSubClass
SP:Starting	EXEC dbo.spNewOrders ;		
SP:Completed	EXEC dbo.spNewOrders ;	0	
SP:Starting	EXEC dbo.spNewOrders ;		
SP:Recompile	SELECT nwo.OrderQty ,n...		2 - Statistics changed
Auto Stats	Updated: dbo.NewOrders.IX_NewOrders...	230	1
SP:Completed	EXEC dbo.spNewOrders ;	839	

Figure 10-8. *Effect of statistics change on the stored procedure recompilation*

In Figure 10-7, you can see that to execute the `SELECT` statement during the second execution of the stored procedure, a recompilation was required. From the value of `EventSubClass` (`2 - Statistics Changed`), you can understand that the recompilation was due to the statistics change. As part of creating the new plan, the statistics are automatically updated, as indicated by the `Auto Stats` event. You can also verify the automatic update of the statistics using the `DBCC SHOW_STATISTICS` statement, as explained in Chapter 7.

Deferred Object Resolution

Stored procedures often dynamically create and subsequently access database objects. When such a stored procedure is executed for the first time, the first execution plan won't contain the information about the objects to be created during runtime. Thus, in the first execution plan, the processing strategy for those objects is deferred until the runtime of the stored procedure. When a DML statement (within the stored procedure) referring to one of those objects is executed, the stored procedure is recompiled to generate a new plan containing the processing strategy for the object.

Both a regular table and a local temporary table can be created within a stored procedure to hold intermediate result sets. The recompilation of the stored procedure due to deferred object resolution behaves differently for a regular table when compared to a local temporary table, as explained in the following section.

Recompilation Due to a Regular Table

To understand the stored procedure recompilation issue by creating a regular table within the stored procedure, consider the following example (`regular.sql` in the download):

```
IF(SELECT OBJECT_ID('dbo.p1')) IS NOT NULL
  DROP PROC dbo.p1;
GO
CREATE PROC dbo.p1
AS
CREATE TABLE dbo.p1_t1(c1 INT); --Ensure table doesn't exist
SELECT * FROM dbo.p1_t1; --Causes recompilation
DROP TABLE dbo.p1_t1;
GO

EXEC dbo.p1; --First execution
EXEC dbo.p1; --Second execution
```

When the stored procedure is executed for the first time, an execution plan is generated before the actual execution of the stored procedure. If the table created within the stored procedure doesn't exist (as expected in the preceding code) before the stored procedure is created, then the plan won't contain the processing strategy for the `SELECT` statement referring to the table. Thus, to execute the `SELECT` statement, the stored procedure needs to be recompiled, as shown in Figure 10-9.

EventClass	TextData	Duration	EventSubClass
SP:Starting	EXEC p1 --First execution		
SP:Recompile	SELECT * FROM p1_t1 --Causes recomp...		3 - Deferred compile
SP:Completed	EXEC p1 --First execution	1	
SP:Starting	EXEC p1 --Second execution		
SP:Recompile	SELECT * FROM p1_t1 --Causes recomp...		1 - Schema changed
SP:Completed	EXEC p1 --Second execution	2	

Figure 10-9. *Profiler trace output showing a stored procedure recompilation because of a regular table*

You can see that the SELECT statement is recompiled when it's executed the second time. Dropping the table within the stored procedure during the first execution doesn't drop the stored procedure plan saved in the procedure cache. During the subsequent execution of the stored procedure, the existing plan includes the processing strategy for the table. However, because of the re-creation of the table within the stored procedure, SQL Server considers it a change to the table schema. Therefore, SQL Server recompiles the stored procedure before executing the SELECT statement during the subsequent execution of the stored procedure. The value of the EventSubClass for the corresponding SP:Recompile event reflects the cause of the recompilation.

Recompilation Due to a Local Temporary Table

Most of the time in the stored procedure you create local temporary tables instead of regular tables. To understand how differently the local temporary tables affect stored procedure recompilation, modify the preceding example by just replacing the regular table with a local temporary table:

```
IF(SELECT OBJECT_ID('dbo.p1')) IS NOT NULL
  DROP PROC dbo.p1;
GO
CREATE PROC dbo.p1
AS
CREATE TABLE #p1_t1(c1 INT); -- # designates local temp table
SELECT * FROM #p1_t1; --Causes recompilation on 1st execution
DROP TABLE #p1_t1; --Optional
GO

EXEC dbo.p1; --First execution
EXEC dbo.p1; --Second execution
```

Since a local temporary table is automatically dropped when the execution of a stored procedure finishes, it's not necessary to drop the temporary table explicitly. But, following good programming practice, you can drop the local temporary table as soon as its work is done.

Figure 10-10 shows the Profiler trace output for the preceding example.

EventClass	TextData	Duration	EventSubClass
Trace Start			
SP:Starting	EXEC dbo.p1; --First execution		
SP:Recompile	SELECT * FROM #p1_t1; --Causes reco...		3 - Deferred compile
SP:Completed	EXEC dbo.p1; --First execution	1	
SP:Starting	EXEC dbo.p1; --Second execution		
SP:Completed	EXEC dbo.p1; --Second execution	0	

Figure 10-10. *Profiler trace output showing a stored procedure recompilation because of a local temporary table*

You can see that the stored procedure is recompiled when executed for the first time. The cause of the recompilation, as indicated by the corresponding EventSubClass value, is the same as the cause of the recompilation on a regular table. However, note that when the stored procedure is reexecuted, it isn't recompiled, unlike the case with a regular table.

The schema of a local temporary table during subsequent execution of the stored procedure remains exactly the same as during the previous execution. A local temporary table isn't available outside the scope of the stored procedure, so its schema can't be altered in any way between multiple executions. Thus, SQL Server safely reuses the existing plan (based on the previous instance of the local temporary table) during the subsequent execution of the stored procedure and thereby avoids the recompilation.

■ **Note** To avoid recompilation, it makes sense to hold the intermediate result sets in the stored procedure using local temporary tables, instead of using temporarily created regular tables as an alternative.

SET Options Changes

The execution plan of a stored procedure is dependent on the environment settings. If the environment settings are changed within a stored procedure, then SQL Server recompiles the stored procedure on every execution. For example, consider the following code (`set.sql` in the download):

```
IF(SELECT OBJECT_ID(' dbo.p1')) IS NOT NULL
  DROP PROC dbo.p1;
GO
CREATE PROC dbo.p1
AS
SELECT 'a' + null + 'b'; --1st
SET CONCAT_NULL_YIELDS_NULL OFF;
SELECT 'a' + null + 'b'; --2nd
SET ANSI_NULLS OFF;
SELECT 'a' + null + 'b'; --3rd
GO

EXEC dbo.p1; --First execution
EXEC dbo.p1; --Second execution
```

Changing the SET options in the stored procedure causes SQL Server to recompile the stored procedure before executing the statement after the SET statement. Thus, this stored procedure is recompiled twice: once before executing the second SELECT statement and once before executing the third SELECT statement. The Profiler trace output in Figure 10-11 shows this.

EventClass	TextData	Duration	EventSubClass
Trace Start			
SP:Starting	EXEC p1 --First execution		
SP:Recompile	SELECT 'a' + null + 'b' --2nd		4 - Set option change
SP:Recompile	SELECT 'a' + null + 'b' --3rd		4 - Set option change
SP:Completed	EXEC p1 --First execution	28	
SP:Starting	EXEC p1 --Second execution		
SP:Completed	EXEC p1 --Second execution	0	

Figure 10-11. *Profiler trace output showing a stored procedure recompilation because of a* SET *option change*

If the procedure were reexecuted, you wouldn't see a recompile since those are now part of the execution plan.

Since SET NOCOUNT does not change the environment settings, unlike the SET statements used to change the ANSI settings as shown previously, SET NOCOUNT does not cause stored procedure recompilation. I explain how to use SET NOCOUNT in detail in Chapter 11.

Execution Plan Aging

SQL Server manages the size of the procedure cache by maintaining the age of the execution plans in the cache, as you saw in Chapter 9. If a stored procedure is not reexecuted for a long time, then the age field of the execution plan can come down to 0, and the plan can be removed from the cache because of memory shortage. When this happens and the stored procedure is reexecuted, a new plan will be generated and cached in the procedure cache. However, if there is enough memory in the system, unused plans are not removed from the cache until memory pressure increases.

Explicit Call to sp_recompile

SQL Server automatically recompiles stored procedures when the schema changes or statistics are altered enough. It also provides the sp_recompile system stored procedure to manually mark stored procedures for recompilation. This stored procedure can be called on a table, view, stored procedure, or trigger. If it is called on a stored procedure or a trigger, then the stored procedure or trigger is recompiled the next time it is executed. Calling sp_recompile on a table or a view marks all the stored procedures and triggers that refer to the table/view for recompilation the next time they are executed.

For example, if sp_recompile is called on table t1, all the stored procedures and triggers that refer to table t1 are marked for recompilation and are recompiled the next time they are executed:

```
sp_recompile 't1'
```

You can use sp_recompile to cancel the reuse of an existing plan when executing dynamic queries with sp_executesql. As demonstrated in the previous chapter, you should not parameterize the variable parts of a query whose range of values may require different processing strategies for the query. For instance, reconsidering the corresponding example, you know that the second execution of the query reuses the plan generated for the first execution. The example is repeated here for easy reference:

```
DBCC FREEPROCCACHE; --Clear the procedure cache
GO
DECLARE @query NVARCHAR(MAX);
DECLARE @param NVARCHAR(MAX);

SET @query = N'SELECT  soh.SalesOrderNumber
       ,soh.OrderDate
       ,sod.OrderQty
       ,sod.LineTotal
FROM    Sales.SalesOrderHeader AS soh
        JOIN Sales.SalesOrderDetail AS sod
        ON soh.SalesOrderID = sod.SalesOrderID
WHERE   soh.CustomerID >= @CustomerId;'

SET @param = N'@CustomerId INT';

EXEC sp_executesql @query, @param, @CustomerId = 1
EXEC sp_executesql @query, @param, @CustomerId = 30118
```

The second execution of the query performs an `Index Scan` operation on the `SalesOrderHeader` table to retrieve the data from the table. As explained in Chapter 4, an `Index Seek` operation may have been preferred on the `SalesOrderHeader` table for the second execution. You can achieve this by executing the `sp_recompile` system stored procedure on the `SalesOrderHeader` table as follows:

```
EXEC sp_recompile 'Sales.SalesOrderHeader'
```

Now, if the query with the second parameter value is reexecuted, the plan for the query will be recompiled as marked by the preceding `sp_recompile` statement. This allows SQL Server to generate an optimal plan for the second execution.

Well, there is a slight problem here: you will likely want to reexecute the first statement again. With the plan existing in the cache, SQL Server will reuse the plan (the `Index Scan` operation on the `SalesOrderHeader` table) for the first statement even though an `Index Seek` operation (using the index on the filter criterion column `soh.CustomerID`) would have been optimal. One way of avoiding this problem can be to create a stored procedure for the query and use a `WITH RECOMPILE` clause, as explained next.

Explicit Use of the RECOMPILE Clause

SQL Server allows a stored procedure to be explicitly recompiled using the `RECOMPILE` clause with the `CREATE PROCEDURE` or `EXECUTE` statement. These methods decrease the effectiveness of plan reusability, so you should consider them only under the specific circumstances explained in the following sections.

RECOMPILE Clause with the CREATE PROCEDURE Statement

Sometimes the plan requirements of a stored procedure may vary as the parameter values to the stored procedure change. In such a case, reusing the plan with different parameter values may degrade the performance of the stored procedure. You can avoid this by using the RECOMPILE clause with the CREATE PROCEDURE statement. For example, for the query in the preceding section, you can create a stored procedure with the RECOMPILE clause:

```
IF(SELECT OBJECT_ID('dbo.spCustomerList')) IS NOT NULL
  DROP PROC dbo.spCustomerList
GO
CREATE PROCEDURE dbo.spCustomerList
@CustomerId INT
WITH RECOMPILE
AS
SELECT   soh.SalesOrderNumber
        ,soh.OrderDate
        ,sod.OrderQty
        ,sod.LineTotal
FROM     Sales.SalesOrderHeader AS soh
         JOIN Sales.SalesOrderDetail AS sod
         ON soh.SalesOrderID = sod.SalesOrderID
WHERE    soh.CustomerID >= @CustomerId;
GO
```

The RECOMPILE clause prevents the caching of the stored procedure plan. Every time the stored procedure is executed, a new plan will be generated. Therefore, if the stored procedure is executed with the soh.CustomerID value as 30118 or 1, like so:

```
EXEC spCustomerList @CustomerId = 1
EXEC spCustomerList @CustomerId = 30118
```

a new plan will be generated during the individual execution, as shown in Figure 10-12.

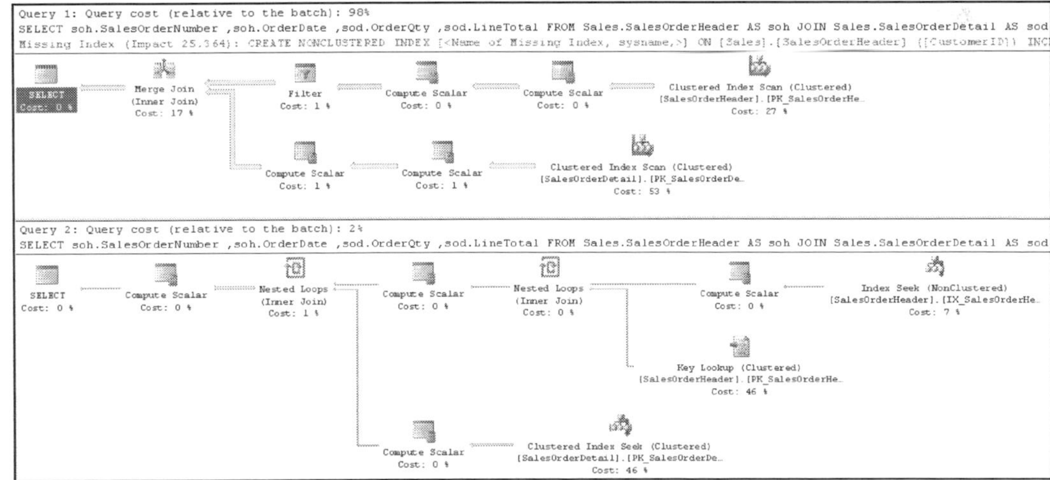

Figure 10-12. *Effect of the* RECOMPILE *clause used in stored procedure creation*

RECOMPILE Clause with the EXECUTE Statement

As shown previously, specific parameter values in a stored procedure may require a different plan, depending upon the nature of the values. You can take the RECOMPILE clause out of the stored procedure and use it on a case-by-case basis when you execute the stored procedure, as follows:

```
EXEC dbo.spCustomerList @CustomerId = 1 WITH RECOMPILE
```

When the stored procedure is executed with the RECOMPILE clause, a new plan is generated temporarily. The new plan isn't cached, and it doesn't affect the existing plan. When the stored procedure is executed without the RECOMPILE clause, the plan is cached as usual. This provides some control over reusability of the existing plan cache rather than using the RECOMPILE clause with the CREATE PROCEDURE statement.

Since the plan for the stored procedure when executed with the RECOMPILE clause is not cached, the plan is regenerated every time the stored procedure is executed with the RECOMPILE clause. However, for better performance, instead of using RECOMPILE, you should consider creating separate stored procedures, one for each set of parameter values that requires a different plan.

Avoiding Recompilations

Sometimes recompilation is beneficial, but at other times it is worth avoiding. If a new index is created on a column referred to in the WHERE or JOIN clause of a query, it makes sense to regenerate the execution plans of stored procedures referring to the table so they can benefit from using the index. However, if recompilation is deemed detrimental to performance, you can avoid it by following these implementation practices:

- Do not interleave DDL and DML statements.
- Avoid recompilation caused by statistics changes:
  - Use the KEEPFIXED PLAN option.
  - Disable the auto update statistics feature on the table.
- Use table variables.
- Avoid changing SET options within the stored procedure.
- Use the OPTIMIZE FOR query hint.
- Use plan guides.

Do Not Interleave DDL and DML Statements

In stored procedures, DDL statements are often used to create local temporary tables and to change their schema (including adding indexes). Doing so can affect the validity of the existing plan and can cause recompilation when the stored procedure statements referring to the tables are executed. To understand how the use of DDL statements for local temporary tables can cause repetitive recompilation of the stored procedure, consider the following example (ddl.sql in the download):

```
IF (SELECT  OBJECT_ID('dbo.spTempTable')
   ) IS NOT NULL
    DROP PROC dbo.spTempTable
GO
CREATE PROC dbo.spTempTable
AS
    CREATE TABLE #MyTempTable (ID INT, Dsc NVARCHAR(50))
    INSERT INTO #MyTempTable (
        ID,
        Dsc
    ) SELECT ProductModelId, [Name]
    FROM Production.ProductModel AS pm;  --Needs 1st recompilation
    SELECT * FROM #MyTempTable AS mtt;
    CREATE CLUSTERED INDEX iTest ON #MyTempTable (ID);
    SELECT  *
    FROM    #MyTempTable AS mtt; --Needs 2nd recompilation
    CREATE TABLE #t2 (c1 INT);
    SELECT  *
    FROM    #t2;
 --Needs 3rd recompilation
GO

EXEC spTempTable --First execution
```

The stored procedure has interleaved DDL and DML statements. Figure 10-13 shows the Profiler trace output of the preceding code.

EventClass	TextData	EventSubClass
SP:Starting	EXEC spTempTable --First execution	
SP:Recompile	INSERT INTO #MyTempTable (ID, ...	3 - Deferred compile
SP:Recompile	SELECT * FROM #MyTempTable AS mtt; ...	3 - Deferred compile
SP:Recompile	SELECT * FROM #MyTempTable...	3 - Deferred compile
SP:Recompile	SELECT * FROM #t2; --Nee...	3 - Deferred compile
SP:Completed	EXEC spTempTable --First execution	

Figure 10-13. *Profiler trace output showing recompilation because of DDL and DML interleaving*

You can see that the stored procedure is recompiled four times:

- The execution plan generated for a stored procedure when it is first executed doesn't contain any information about local temporary tables. Therefore, the first generated plan can never be used to access the temporary table using a DML statement.
- The second recompilation comes from the changes encountered in the data contained within the table as it gets loaded.

- The third recompilation is due to a schema change in the first temporary table (#MyTempTable). The creation of the index on #MyTempTable invalidates the existing plan, causing a recompilation when the table is accessed again. If this index had been created before the first recompilation, then the existing plan would have remained valid for the second SELECT statement too. Therefore, you can avoid this recompilation by putting the CREATE INDEX DDL statement above all DML statements referring to the table.
- The fourth recompilation of the stored procedure generates a plan to include the processing strategy for #t2. The existing plan has no information about #t2 and therefore cannot be used to access #t2 using the third SELECT statement. If the CREATE TABLE DDL statement for #t2 had been placed before all the DML statements that could cause a recompilation, then the first recompilation itself would have included the information on #t2, avoiding the third recompilation.

Avoiding Recompilations Caused by Statistics Change

In the "Analyzing Causes of Recompilation" section, you saw that a change in statistics is one of the causes of recompilation. On a simple table with uniform data distribution, recompilation due to a change of statistics may generate a plan identical to the previous plan. In such situations, recompilation can be unnecessary and should be avoided if it is too costly.

You have two techniques to avoid recompilations caused by statistics change:

- Use the KEEPFIXED PLAN option.
- Disable the auto update statistics feature on the table.

Using the KEEPFIXED PLAN Option

SQL Server provides a KEEPFIXED PLAN option to avoid recompilations due to a statistics change. To understand how you can use KEEPFIXED PLAN, consider stats_changes.sql with an appropriate modification to use the KEEPFIXED PLAN option:

```
--Create a small table with one row and an index
IF (SELECT  OBJECT_ID('dbo.t1')
   ) IS NOT NULL
    DROP TABLE dbo.t1 ;
GO
CREATE TABLE dbo.t1 (c1 INT, c2 CHAR(50)) ;
INSERT  INTO dbo.t1
VALUES  (1, '2') ;
CREATE NONCLUSTERED INDEX i1 ON t1 (c1) ;

--Create a stored procedure referencing the previous table
IF (SELECT  OBJECT_ID('dbo.p1')
   ) IS NOT NULL
    DROP PROC dbo.p1 ;
GO
CREATE PROC dbo.p1
```

```
AS
    SELECT  *
    FROM    t1
    WHERE   c1 = 1
    OPTION  (KEEPFIXED PLAN) ;
GO

--First execution of stored procedure with 1 row in the table
EXEC dbo.p1 ;
 --First execution

--Add many rows to the table to cause statistics change
WITH    Nums
          AS (SELECT    1 AS n
              UNION ALL
              SELECT    n + 1
              FROM      Nums
              WHERE     n < 1000
             )
    INSERT  INTO t1
            SELECT  1
                   ,N
            FROM    Nums
    OPTION  (MAXRECURSION 1000) ;
GO

--Reexecute the stored procedure with a change in statistics
EXEC dbo.p1 --With change in data distribution
```

Figure 10-14 shows the Profiler trace output.

EventClass	TextData	EventSubClass	StartTime
SP:Starting	EXEC dbo.p1; --First execution -...		2008-11-08 07:32:38...
SP:Completed	EXEC dbo.p1; --First execution -...		2008-11-08 07:32:38...
SP:Starting	EXEC dbo.p1 --With change in data d...		2008-11-08 07:32:38...
SP:Completed	EXEC dbo.p1 --With change in data d...		2008-11-08 07:32:38...

Figure 10-14. *Profiler trace output showing the role of the* `KEEPFIXED PLAN` *option in reducing recompilation*

You can see that, unlike in the earlier example with changes in data, there's no `Auto Stats` event (see Figure 10-8). Consequently, there's no recompilation. Therefore, by using the `KEEPFIXED PLAN` option, you can avoid recompilation due to a statistics change.

■ **Note** Before you consider using this option, ensure that any new plans that would have been generated are not superior to the existing plan.

Disable Auto Update Statistics on the Table

You can also avoid recompilation due to a statistics update by disabling the automatic statistics update on the relevant table. For example, you can disable the auto update statistics feature on table t1 as follows:

```
EXEC sp_autostats 't1', 'OFF'
```

If you disable this feature on the table before inserting the large number of rows that causes statistics change, then you can avoid the recompilation due to a statistics change.

However, be very cautious with this technique, since outdated statistics can adversely affect the effectiveness of the cost-based optimizer, as discussed in Chapter 7. Also, as explained in Chapter 7, if you disable the automatic update of statistics, you should have a SQL job to update the statistics regularly.

Using Table Variables

One of the variable types supported by SQL Server 2008 is the table variable. You can create the table variable data type like other data types, using the DECLARE statement. It behaves like a local variable, and you can use it inside a stored procedure to hold intermediate result sets, as you do using a temporary table.

You can avoid the recompilations caused by a temporary table if you use a table variable. Since statistics are not created for table variables, the different recompilation issues associated with temporary tables are not applicable to it. For instance, consider create_p1.sql used in the section "Identifying the Statement Causing Recompilation." It is repeated here for your reference:

```
IF(SELECT OBJECT_ID('dbo.p1')) IS NOT NULL
  DROP PROC dbo.p1;
GO
CREATE PROC dbo.p1
AS
CREATE TABLE #t1(c1 INT);
INSERT INTO #t1 (
    c1
) VALUES ( 42 ) ; -- data change causes recompile
GO

EXEC dbo.p1; --First execution
```

Because of deferred object resolution, the stored procedure is recompiled during the first execution. You can avoid this recompilation caused by the temporary table by using the table variable as follows:

```
IF(SELECT OBJECT_ID('dbo.p1')) IS NOT NULL
  DROP PROC dbo.p1
GO
CREATE PROC dbo.p1
AS
DECLARE @t1 TABLE(c1 INT)
INSERT INTO @t1 (
    C1
) VALUES (42); --Recompilation not needed
GO

EXEC dbo.p1; --First execution
```

Figure 10-15 shows the Profiler trace output for the first execution of the stored procedure. The recompilation caused by the temporary table has been avoided by using the table variable.

EventClass	TextData	EventSubClass	StartTime
SP:Starting	EXEC dbo.p1; --First execution		2008-11-08 15:03:55...
SP:Completed	EXEC dbo.p1; --First execution		2008-11-08 15:03:55...

Figure 10-15. *Profiler trace output showing the role of a table variable in resolving recompilation*

Additional benefits of using the table variables are as follows:

- *No transaction log overhead*: No transaction log activities are performed for table variables, whereas they are for both regular and temporary tables.
- *No lock overhead*: Since table variables are treated like local variables (not database objects), the locking overhead associated with regular tables and temporary tables does not exist.
- *No rollback overhead*: Since no transaction log activities are performed for table variables, no rollback overhead is applicable for table variables. For example, consider the following code (`rollback.sql` in the download):

  ```
  DECLARE @t1 TABLE(c1 INT)
  INSERT INTO @t1 VALUES(1)
  BEGIN TRAN
    INSERT INTO @t1 VALUES(2)
  ROLLBACK
  SELECT * FROM @t1 --Returns 2 rows
  ```

  The ROLLBACK statement won't roll back the second row insertion into the table variable.

However, table variables have their limitations. The main ones are as follows:

- No DDL statement can be executed on the table variable once it is created, which means no indexes or constraints can be added to the table variable later. Constraints can be specified only as part of the table variable's DECLARE statement. Therefore, only one index can be created on a table variable, using the PRIMARY KEY or UNIQUE constraint.
- No statistics are created for table variables, which means they resolve as single-row tables in execution plans. This is not an issue when the table actually contains only a small quantity of data, approximately less than 100 rows. It becomes a major performance problem when the table variable contains more data since appropriate decisions regarding the right sorts of operations within an execution plan are completely dependent on statistics.
- The following statements are not supported on the table variables:
    - INSERT INTO TableVariable EXEC StoredProcedure
    - SELECT SelectList INTO TableVariable FROM Table
    - SET TableVariable = Value

Avoiding Changing SET Options Within a Stored Procedure

It is generally recommended that you not change the environment settings within a stored procedure and thus avoid recompilation because the SET options changed. For ANSI compatibility, it is recommended that you keep the following SET options ON:

- ARITHABORT
- CONCAT_NULL_YIELDS_NULL
- QUOTED_IDENTIFIER
- ANSI_NULLS
- ANSI_PADDING
- ANSI_WARNINGS

NUMERIC_ROUNDABORT should be OFF.

Although the following approach is not recommended, you can avoid the recompilation caused by some of these SET options changes by resetting the options for the connection as shown in the following modifications to set.sql:

```
IF(SELECT OBJECT_ID('p1')) IS NOT NULL
  DROP PROC p1
GO
CREATE PROC p1
AS
SELECT 'a' + null + 'b' --1st
SET CONCAT_NULL_YIELDS_NULL OFF
```

```
SELECT 'a' + null + 'b' --2nd
SET ANSI_NULLS OFF
SELECT 'a' + null + 'b' --3rd
GO

SET CONCAT_NULL_YIELDS_NULL OFF
SET ANSI_NULLS OFF
EXEC p1
SET CONCAT_NULL_YIELDS_NULL ON --Reset to default
SET ANSI_NULLS ON              --Reset to default
```

Figure 10-16 shows the Profiler trace output.

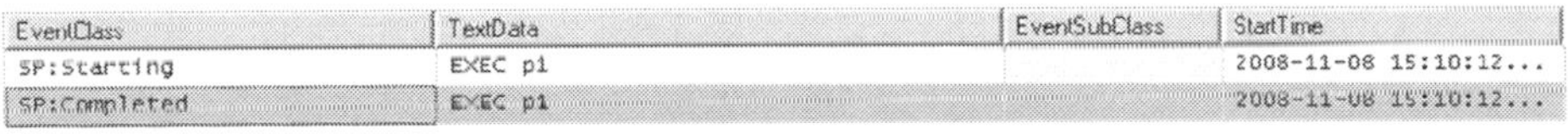

EventClass	TextData	EventSubClass	StartTime
SP:Starting	EXEC p1		2008-11-08 15:10:12...
SP:Completed	EXEC p1		2008-11-08 15:10:12...

Figure 10-16. *Profiler trace output showing effect of the ANSI SET options on stored procedure recompilation*

You can see that there were fewer recompilations when compared to the original `set.sql` code (Figure 10-11). Out of the `SET` options listed previously, the `ANSI_NULLS` and `QUOTED_IDENTIFIER` options are saved as part of the stored procedure when it is created. Therefore, setting these options in the connection outside the stored procedure won't affect any recompilation issues; only re-creating the stored procedure can change these settings.

Using OPTIMIZE FOR Query Hint

Although you may not always be able to reduce or eliminate recompiles, using the `OPTIMIZE FOR` query hint will help ensure you get the plan you want when the recompile does occur. The `OPTIMIZE FOR` query hint uses parameter values supplied by you to compile the plan, regardless of the values of the parameter passed in by the calling application.

For an example, examine `spCustomerList` from earlier in the chapter. You know that if this procedure receives certain values, it will need to create a new plan. Knowing your data, you also know two more important facts: the frequency that this query will return small data sets is exceedingly small, and when this query uses the wrong plan, performance suffers. Rather than recompiling it over and over again, modify it so that it creates the plan that works best most of the time:

```
IF(SELECT OBJECT_ID('dbo.spCustomerList')) IS NOT NULL
  DROP PROC dbo.spCustomerList
GO
CREATE PROCEDURE dbo.spCustomerList
@CustomerId INT
AS
SELECT  soh.SalesOrderNumber
       ,soh.OrderDate
       ,sod.OrderQty
       ,sod.LineTotal
```

```
FROM    Sales.SalesOrderHeader AS soh
        JOIN Sales.SalesOrderDetail AS sod
        ON soh.SalesOrderID = sod.SalesOrderID
WHERE   soh.CustomerID >= @CustomerId
OPTION (OPTIMIZE FOR (@CustomerID = 1));
GO
```

When this query is executed the first time or it's recompiled for any reason, it always gets the same execution plan. To test this, execute the procedure this way:

```
EXEC dbo.spCustomerList @CustomerId = 7920 WITH RECOMPILE;
EXEC dbo.spCustomerList @CustomerId = 30118 WITH RECOMPILE;
```

Just as earlier in the chapter, this will force the procedure to be recompiled each time it is executed. Figure 10-17 shows the resulting execution plans.

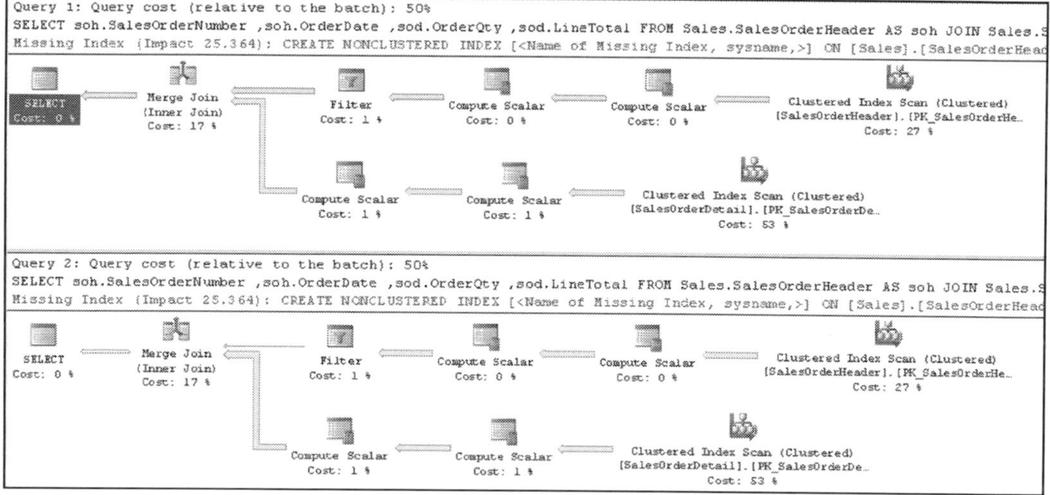

Figure 10-17. `WITH RECOMPILE` *forces identical execution plans.*

Unlike earlier in the chapter, recompiling the procedure now does not result in a new execution plan. Instead, the same plan is generated, regardless of input, because the query optimizer has received instructions to use the value supplied, `@CustomerId = 1`, when optimizing the query.

This can reduce the number of recompiles, and it does help you control the execution plan generated. It requires that you know your data very well. If your data changes over time, you may need to reexamine areas where the `OPTIMIZE FOR` query hint was used.

SQL Server 2008 introduces one more wrinkle on the `OPTIMIZE FOR` query hint. You can specify that the query be optimized using `OPTIMIZE FOR UNKOWN`. This is almost the opposite of the `OPTIMIZE FOR` hint. What you are directing the processor to do is perform the optimization based on statistics, always, and to ignore the actual values passed when the query is optimized. You can use it in combination with `OPTIMIZE FOR <value>`. It will optimize for the value supplied on that parameter but will use statistics on all other parameters.

Using Plan Guides

A plan guide allows you to use query hint or other optimization techniques without having to modify the query or procedure text. This is especially useful when you have a third-party product with poorly performing procedures you need to tune but can't modify. As part of the optimization process, if a plan guide exists when a procedure is compiled or recompiled, it will use that guide to create the execution plan.

In the previous section, I showed you how using `OPTIMIZE FOR` would affect the execution plan created on a procedure. The following is the query from the original procedure, with no hints (`plan_guide.sql` in the download):

```
IF(SELECT OBJECT_ID('dbo.spCustomerList')) IS NOT NULL
  DROP PROC dbo.spCustomerList
GO
IF(SELECT OBJECT_ID('dbo.spCustomerList')) IS NOT NULL
  DROP PROC dbo.spCustomerList
GO
CREATE PROCEDURE dbo.spCustomerList
@CustomerId INT
AS
SELECT  soh.SalesOrderNumber
       ,soh.OrderDate
       ,sod.OrderQty
       ,sod.LineTotal
FROM    Sales.SalesOrderHeader AS soh
        JOIN Sales.SalesOrderDetail AS sod
        ON soh.SalesOrderID = sod.SalesOrderID
WHERE   soh.CustomerID >= @CustomerId
GO
```

Now assume for a moment that this query is part of a third-party application and you are not able to modify it to include `OPTION (OPTIMIZE FOR)`. To provide it with the query hint, `OPTIMIZE FOR`, create a plan guide as follows:

```
sp_create_plan_guide
@name = N'MyGuide',
@stmt = N'SELECT  soh.SalesOrderNumber
       ,soh.OrderDate
       ,sod.OrderQty
       ,sod.LineTotal
FROM    Sales.SalesOrderHeader AS soh
        JOIN Sales.SalesOrderDetail AS sod
        ON soh.SalesOrderID = sod.SalesOrderID
WHERE   soh.CustomerID >= @CustomerId',
@type = N'OBJECT',
@module_or_batch = N'dbo.spCustomerList',
@params = NULL,
@hints = N'OPTION (OPTIMIZE FOR (@CustomerId = 1))'
```

Now, when the procedure is executed with each of the different parameters, even with the `RECOMPILE` being forced, Figure 10-18 shows the results:

```
EXEC dbo.spCustomerList @CustomerId = 7920 WITH RECOMPILE;
EXEC dbo.spCustomerList @CustomerId = 30118 WITH RECOMPILE;
```

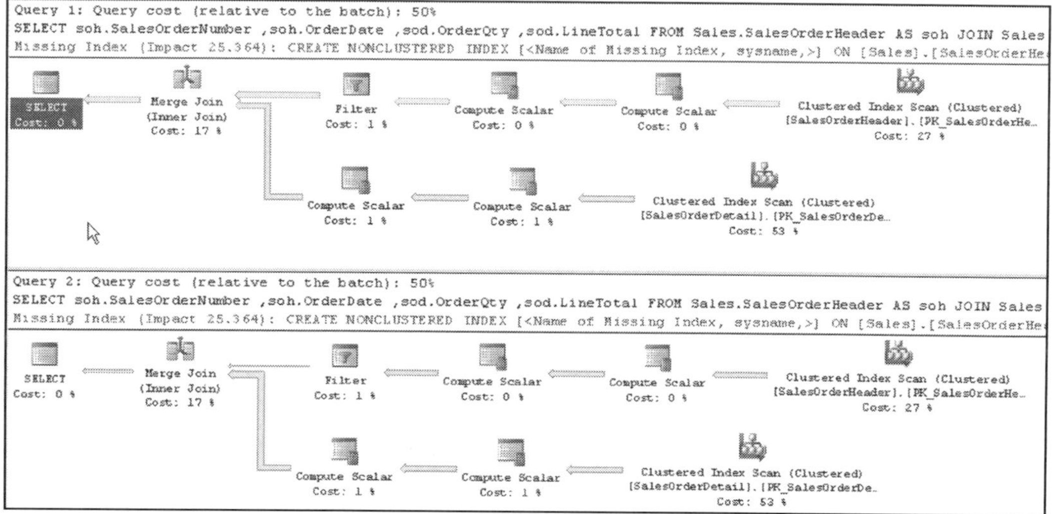

Figure 10-18. *Using a plan guide to apply the `OPTIMIZE FOR` query hint*

The results are the same as when the procedure was modified, but in this case, no modification was necessary.

Various types of plan guides exist. The previous example is an *object* plan guide, which is a guide matched to a particular object in the database, in this case `spCustomerList`. You can also create plan guides for ad hoc queries that come into your system repeatedly by creating a *SQL* plan guide that looks for particular SQL statements. Instead of a procedure, the following query gets passed to your system and needs an `OPTIMIZE FOR` query hint:

```
SELECT  soh.SalesOrderNumber
       ,soh.OrderDate
       ,sod.OrderQty
       ,sod.LineTotal
FROM    Sales.SalesOrderHeader AS soh
        JOIN Sales.SalesOrderDetail AS sod
        ON soh.SalesOrderID = sod.SalesOrderID
WHERE   soh.CustomerID >= 1
```

Running this query results in the execution plan you see in Figure 10-19.

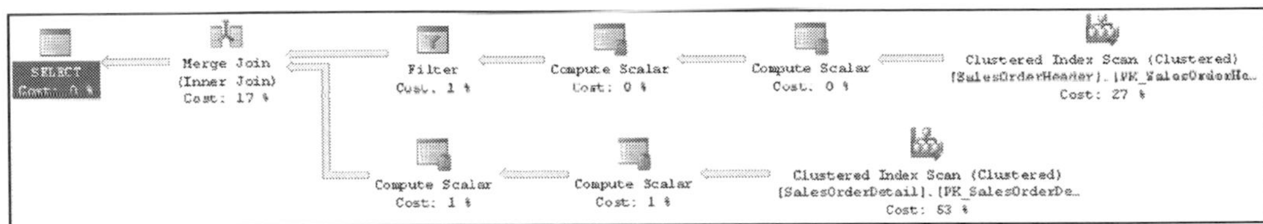

Figure 10-19. *Query uses a different execution plan from the one wanted*

To get a query plan guide, you first need to know the precise format used by the query in case parameterization, forced or simple, changes the text of the query. The text has to be precise. If your first attempt at a query plan guide looked like this (bad_guide.sql in the download):

```
EXECUTE sp_create_plan_guide
@name = N'MyBadSQLGuide',
@stmt = N'SELECT  soh.SalesOrderNumber
,soh.OrderDate
,sod.OrderQty
,sod.LineTotal
from    Sales.SalesOrderHeader AS soh
join Sales.SalesOrderDetail AS sod
on soh.SalesOrderID = sod.SalesOrderID
where   soh.CustomerID >= @CustomerId',
@type = N'SQL',
@module_or_batch = NULL,
@params = N'@CustomerId int',
@hints = N'OPTION (TABLE HINT(soh, FORCESEEK))';
```

then you'll still get the same execution plan when running the select query. This is because the query doesn't look like what was typed in for the bad_guide.sql plan guide. Several things are different such as the spacing and the case on the JOIN statement. You can drop this bad plan guide using the T-SQL statement:

```
EXECUTE sp_control_plan_guide @Operation = 'Drop', @name = N'MyBadSQLGuide'
```

Inputting the correct syntax will create a new plan:

```
EXECUTE sp_create_plan_guide
@name = N'MyGoodSQLGuide',
@stmt = N'SELECT  soh.SalesOrderNumber
       ,soh.OrderDate
       ,sod.OrderQty
       ,sod.LineTotal
FROM    Sales.SalesOrderHeader AS soh
        JOIN Sales.SalesOrderDetail AS sod
        ON soh.SalesOrderID = sod.SalesOrderID
```

```
WHERE    soh.CustomerID >= 1',
@type = N'SQL',
@module_or_batch = NULL,
@params = NULL,
@hints = N'OPTION (TABLE HINT(soh, FORCESEEK))';
```

Now when the query is run, a completely different plan is created, as shown in Figure 10-20.

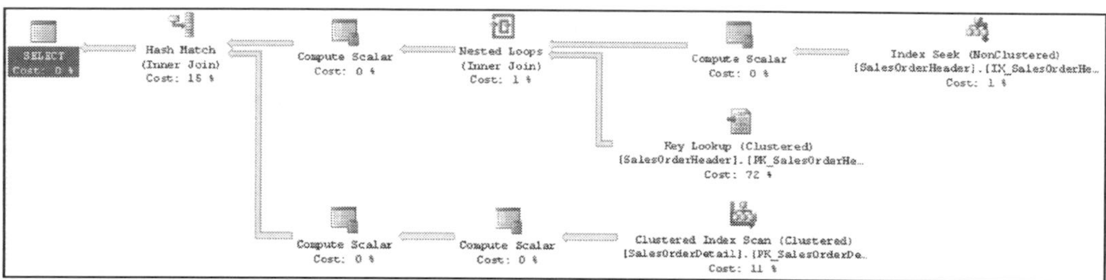

Figure 10-20. *The plan guide forces a new execution plan on the same query.*

One other option exists when you have a plan in the cache that you think performs the way you want. You can capture that plan into a plan guide to ensure that the next time the query is run, the same plan is executed. You accomplish this by running sp_create_plan_guide_from_handle.

To test it, first clear out the procedure cache so you can control exactly which query plan is used:

```
DBCC FREEPROCCACHE
```

With the procedure cache clear and the existing plan guide, MyGoodSQLGuide, in place, rerun the query. It will use the plan guide to arrive at the execution plan displayed in Figure 10-20. To see whether this plan can be kept, first drop the plan guide that is forcing the Index Seek operation:

```
EXECUTE sp_control_plan_guide @Operation = 'Drop', @name = N'MyGoodSQLGuide';
```

If you were to rerun the query now, it would revert to its original plan. However, right now in the plan cache, you have the plan displayed in Figure 10-20. To keep it, run the following script:

```
DECLARE @plan_handle VARBINARY(64)
   ,@start_offset INT
SELECT  @plan_handle = qs.plan_handle
       ,@start_offset = qs.statement_start_offset
FROM    sys.dm_exec_query_stats AS qs
        CROSS APPLY sys.dm_exec_sql_text(sql_handle)
        CROSS APPLY sys.dm_exec_text_query_plan(qs.plan_handle,
                                                qs.statement_start_offset,
                                                qs.statement_end_offset) AS qp
WHERE   text LIKE N'SELECT  soh.SalesOrderNumber%'
```

```
EXECUTE sp_create_plan_guide_from_handle @name = N'ForcedPlanGuide',
    @plan_handle = @plan_handle, @statement_start_offset = @start_offset ;
GO
```

This creates a plan guide based on the execution plan as it currently exists in the cache. To be sure this works, clear the cache again. That way, the query has to generate a new plan. Rerun the query, and observe the execution plan. It will be the same as that displayed in Figure 10-20 because of the plan guide created using sp_create_plan_guide_from_handle.

Plan guides are useful mechanisms for controlling the behavior of SQL queries and stored procedures, but you should use them only when you have a thorough understanding of the execution plan, the data, and the structure of your system.

Summary

As you learned in this chapter, stored procedure recompilation can both benefit and hurt performance. Recompilations that generate better plans improve the performance of the stored procedure. However, recompilations that regenerate the same plan consume extra CPU cycles without any improvement in processing strategy. Therefore, you should look closely at recompilations to determine their usefulness. You can use Profiler to identify which stored procedure statement caused the recompilation, and you can determine the cause from the EventSubClass data column value in Profiler and trace output. Once you determine the cause of the recompilation, you can apply different techniques to avoid the unnecessary recompilations.

Up until now, you have seen how to benefit from proper indexing and plan caching. However, the performance benefit of these techniques depends on the way the queries are designed. The cost-based optimizer of SQL Server takes care of many of the query design issues. However, you should adopt a number of best practices while designing queries. In the next chapter, I will cover some of the common query design issues that affect performance.

CHAPTER 11

Query Design Analysis

A database schema may include a number of performance-enhancement features such as indexes, statistics, and stored procedures. But none of these features guarantees good performance if your queries are written badly in the first place. The SQL queries may not be able to use the available indexes effectively. The structure of the SQL queries may add avoidable overhead to the query cost. Queries may be attempting to deal with data in a row-by-row fashion (or to quote Jeff Moden, Row By Agonizing Row, which is abbreviated to RBAR and pronounced "reebar") instead of in logical sets. To improve the performance of a database application, it is important to understand the cost associated with varying ways of writing a query.

In this chapter, I cover the following topics:

- Aspects of query design that affect performance
- How query designs use indexes effectively
- The role of optimizer hints on query performance
- The role of database constraints on query performance
- Query designs that are less resource intensive
- Query designs that use the procedure cache effectively
- Query designs that reduce network overhead
- Techniques to reduce the transaction cost of a query

Query Design Recommendations

When you need to run a query, you can often use many different approaches to get the same data. In many cases, the optimizer generates the same plan, irrespective of the structure of the query. However, in some situations the query structure won't allow the optimizer to select the best possible processing strategy. It is important that you know when this happens and what you can do to avoid it.

In general, keep the following recommendations in mind to ensure the best performance:

- Operate on small result sets.
- Use indexes effectively.
- Avoid optimizer hints.
- Use domain and referential integrity.
- Avoid resource-intensive queries.
- Reduce the number of network round-trips.
- Reduce the transaction cost.

Careful testing is essential to identify the query form that provides the best performance in a specific database environment. You should be conversant with writing and comparing different SQL query forms so you can evaluate the query form that provides the best performance in a given environment.

Operating on Small Result Sets

To improve the performance of a query, limit the amount of data it operates on, including both columns and rows. Operating on small result sets reduces the amount of resources consumed by a query and increases the effectiveness of indexes. Two of the rules you should follow to limit the data set's size are as follows:

- Limit the number of columns in the select list.
- Use highly selective `WHERE` clauses to limit the rows returned.

It's important to note that you will be asked to return tens of thousands of rows to an OLTP system. Just because someone tells you those are the business requirements doesn't mean they are right. Human beings don't process tens of thousands of rows. Very few human beings are capable of processing thousands of rows. Be prepared to push back on these requests, and be able to justify your reasons.

Limit the Number of Columns in select_list

Use a minimum set of columns in the select list of a `SELECT` statement. Do not use columns that are not required in the output result set. For instance, do not use `SELECT *` to return all columns. `SELECT *` statements render covered indexes ineffective, since it is impractical to include all columns in an index. For example, consider the following query:

```
SELECT  [Name]
       ,TerritoryID
FROM    Sales.SalesTerritory AS st
WHERE   st.[Name] = 'Australia'
```

A covering index on the `Name` column (and through the clustered key, `ProductID`) serves the query quickly through the index itself, without accessing the clustered index. When you have `STATISTICS IO` and `STATISTICS TIME` switched on, you get the following number of logical reads and execution time, as well as the corresponding execution plan (shown in Figure 11-1):

```
Table 'SalesTerritory'. Scan count 0, logical reads 2
CPU time = 0 ms,  elapsed time = 17 ms.
```

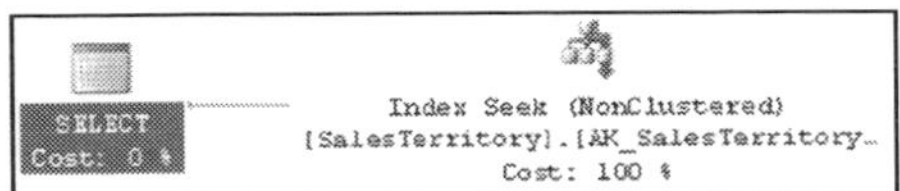

Figure 11-1. *Execution plan showing the benefit of referring to a limited number of columns*

If this query is modified to include all columns in the select list as follows, then the previous covering index becomes ineffective, because all the columns required by this query are not included in that index:

```
SELECT *
FROM Sales.SalesTerritory AS st
WHERE   st.[Name] = 'Australia'
```

Subsequently, the base table (or the clustered index) containing all the columns has to be accessed, as shown next (see Figure 11-2). The number of logical reads and the execution time have both increased:

```
Table 'SalesTerritory'. Scan count 0, logical reads 4
CPU time = 0 ms,  elapsed time = 28 ms
```

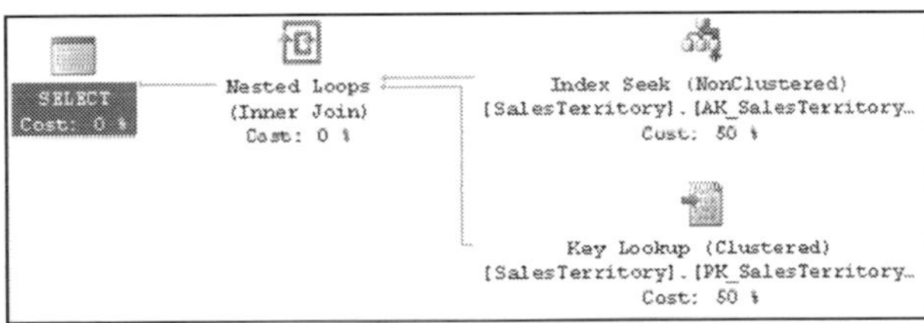

Figure 11-2. *Execution plan showing the added cost of referring to too many columns*

As shown in Figure 11-2, the fewer the columns in the select list, the better the query performance. Selecting too many columns also increases data transfer across the network, further degrading performance.

Use Highly Selective WHERE Clauses

As explained in Chapter 4, the selectivity of a column referred to in the WHERE clause governs the use of an index on the column. A request for a large number of rows from a table may not benefit from using an index, either because it can't use an index at all or, in the case of a nonclustered index, because of the overhead cost of the bookmark lookup. To ensure the use of indexes, the columns referred to in the WHERE clause should be highly selective.

Most of the time, an end user concentrates on a limited number of rows at a time. Therefore, you should design database applications to request data incrementally as the user navigates through the data. For applications that rely on a large amount of data for data analysis or reporting, consider using data analysis solutions such as Analysis Services. Remember, returning huge result sets is costly, and this data is unlikely to be used in its entirety.

Using Indexes Effectively

It is extremely important to have effective indexes on database tables to improve performance. However, it is equally important to ensure that the queries are designed properly to use these indexes effectively. These are some of the query design rules you should follow to improve the use of indexes:

- Avoid nonsargable search conditions.
- Avoid arithmetic operators on the `WHERE` clause column.
- Avoid functions on the `WHERE` clause column.

I cover each of these rules in detail in the following sections.

Avoid Nonsargable Search Conditions

A *sargable* predicate in a query is one in which an index can be used. The word is a contraction of "Search ARGument ABLE." The optimizer's ability to benefit from an index depends on the selectivity of the search condition, which in turn depends on the selectivity of the column(s) referred to in the `WHERE` clause. The search predicate used on the column(s) in the `WHERE` clause determines whether an index operation on the column can be performed.

The sargable search conditions listed in Table 11-1 generally allow the optimizer to use an index on the column(s) referred to in the `WHERE` clause. The sargable search conditions generally allow SQL Server to seek to a row in the index and retrieve the row (or the adjacent range of rows until the search condition remains true).

On the other hand, the *nonsargable* search conditions listed in Table 11-1 generally prevent the optimizer from using an index on the column(s) referred to in the `WHERE` clause. The exclusion search conditions generally don't allow SQL Server to perform `Index Seek` operations as supported by the sargable search conditions. For example, the `!=` condition requires scanning all the rows to identify the matching rows.

Table 11-1. *Common Sargable and Nonsargable Search Conditions*

Type	Search Conditions
Sargable	Inclusion conditions `=`, `>`, `>=`, `<`, `<=`, and `BETWEEN`, and some `LIKE` conditions such as `LIKE '<literal>%'`
Nonsargable	Exclusion conditions `<>`, `!=`, `!>`, `!<`, `NOT EXISTS`, `NOT IN`, and `NOT LIKE IN`, `OR`, and some `LIKE` conditions such as `LIKE '%<literal>'`

Try to implement workarounds for these nonsargable search conditions to improve performance. In some cases, it may be possible to rewrite a query to avoid a nonsargable search condition. For example, consider replacing an `IN`/`OR` search condition with a `BETWEEN` condition, as described in the following section.

BETWEEN vs. IN/OR

Consider the following query, which uses the search condition IN:

```
SELECT  sod.*
FROM    Sales.SalesOrderDetail AS sod
WHERE   sod.SalesOrderID IN (51825, 51826, 51827, 51828)
```

You can replace the nonsargable search condition in this query with a BETWEEN clause as follows:

```
SELECT  sod.*
FROM    Sales.SalesOrderDetail AS sod
WHERE   sod.SalesOrderID BETWEEN 51825 AND 51828
```

On the face of it, the execution plan of both the queries appears to be the same, as shown in the execution plan in Figure 11-3.

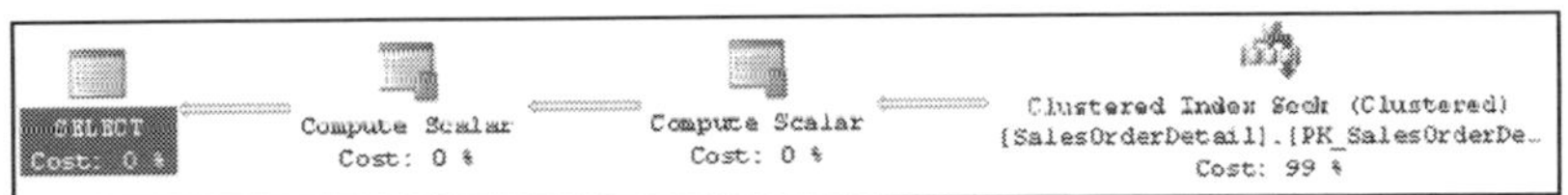

Figure 11-3. *Execution plan for a simple SELECT statement using a BETWEEN clause*

However, taking a closer look at the execution plans reveals the difference in their data-retrieval mechanism, as shown in Figure 11-4. The left box is the IN condition, and the right box is the BETWEEN condition.

Clustered Index Seek (Clustered)
Scanning a particular range of rows from a clustered index.

Physical Operation	Clustered Index Seek
Logical Operation	Clustered Index Seek
Actual Number of Rows	150
Estimated I/O Cost	0.0038657
Estimated CPU Cost	0.0003
Estimated Number of Executions	1
Number of Executions	1
Estimated Operator Cost	0.0041657 (99%)
Estimated Subtree Cost	0.0041657
Estimated Number of Rows	130
Estimated Row Size	95 B
Actual Rebinds	0
Actual Rewinds	0
Ordered	True
Node ID	2

Object
[AdventureWorks2008].[Sales].[SalesOrderDetail].
[PK_SalesOrderDetail_SalesOrderID_SalesOrderDetailID] [sod]
Seek Predicates
[1] Seek Keys[1]: Prefix: [AdventureWorks2008].[Sales].
[SalesOrderDetail].SalesOrderID = Scalar Operator((51825)),
[2] Seek Keys[1]: Prefix: [AdventureWorks2008].[Sales].
[SalesOrderDetail].SalesOrderID = Scalar Operator((51826)),
[3] Seek Keys[1]: Prefix: [AdventureWorks2008].[Sales].
[SalesOrderDetail].SalesOrderID = Scalar Operator((51827)),
[4] Seek Keys[1]: Prefix: [AdventureWorks2008].[Sales].
[SalesOrderDetail].SalesOrderID = Scalar Operator((51828))

Clustered Index Seek (Clustered)
Scanning a particular range of rows from a clustered index.

Physical Operation	Clustered Index Seek
Logical Operation	Clustered Index Seek
Actual Number of Rows	150
Estimated I/O Cost	0.0038657
Estimated CPU Cost	0.0002937
Estimated Number of Executions	1
Number of Executions	1
Estimated Operator Cost	0.0041594 (99%)
Estimated Subtree Cost	0.0041594
Estimated Number of Rows	124.265
Estimated Row Size	95 B
Actual Rebinds	0
Actual Rewinds	0
Ordered	True
Node ID	2

Object
[AdventureWorks2008].[Sales].[SalesOrderDetail].
[PK_SalesOrderDetail_SalesOrderID_SalesOrderDetailID] [sod]
Seek Predicates
Seek Keys[1]: Start: [AdventureWorks2008].[Sales].
[SalesOrderDetail].SalesOrderID >= Scalar Operator([@1]),
End: [AdventureWorks2008].[Sales].
[SalesOrderDetail].SalesOrderID <= Scalar Operator([@2])

Figure 11-4. *Execution plan details for an IN condition (left) and a BETWEEN condition (right)*

As shown in Figure 11-4, SQL Server resolved the IN condition containing four values into four OR conditions. Accordingly, the clustered index (PK_SalesTerritory_TerritoryId) is accessed four times (Scan count 4) to retrieve rows for the four OR conditions, as shown in the following corresponding STATISTICS IO output. On the other hand, the BETWEEN condition is resolved into a pair of >= and <= conditions, as shown in Figure 11-4. SQL Server accesses the clustered index only once (Scan count 1) from the first matching row until the match condition is true, as shown in the following corresponding STATISTICS IO and QUERY TIME output:

- With the IN condition:

```
Table 'SalesOrderDetail'. Scan count 4, logical reads 21
CPU time = 0 ms,  elapsed time = 208 ms.
```

- With the BETWEEN condition:

```
Table 'SalesOrderDetail'. Scan count 1, logical reads 7
CPU time = 0 ms,  elapsed time = 161 ms.
```

Replacing the search condition IN with BETWEEN decreases the number of logical reads for this query from eight to two. As just shown, although both queries use a clustered index seek on OrderID, the optimizer locates the range of rows much faster with the BETWEEN clause than with the IN clause. The same thing happens when you look at the BETWEEN condition and the OR clause. Therefore, if there is a choice between using IN/OR and the BETWEEN search condition, always choose the BETWEEN condition, because it is generally much more efficient than the IN/OR condition. In fact, you should go one step further and use the combination of >= and <= instead of the BETWEEN clause.

Not every WHERE clause that uses exclusion search conditions prevents the optimizer from using the index on the column referred to in the search condition. In many cases, the SQL Server 2008 optimizer does a wonderful job of converting the exclusion search condition to a sargable search condition. To understand this, consider the following two search conditions, which I discuss in the sections that follow:

- The LIKE condition
- The !< condition vs. the >= condition

LIKE Condition

While using the LIKE search condition, try to use one or more leading characters in the WHERE clause if possible. Using leading characters in the LIKE clause allows the optimizer to convert the LIKE condition to an index-friendly search condition. The greater the number of leading characters in the LIKE condition, the better the optimizer is able to determine an effective index. Be aware that using a wildcard character as the leading character in the LIKE condition *prevents* the optimizer from performing a SEEK (or a narrow-range scan) on the index; it relies on scanning the complete table instead.

To understand this ability of the SQL Server 2008 optimizer, consider the following SELECT statement that uses the LIKE condition with a leading character:

```
SELECT  c.CurrencyCode
FROM    Sales.Currency AS c
WHERE   c.[Name] LIKE 'Ice%'
```

The SQL Server 2008 optimizer does this conversion automatically, as shown in Figure 11-5.

Index Seek (NonClustered)
Scan a particular range of rows from a nonclustered index.

Physical Operation	Index Seek
Logical Operation	Index Seek
Actual Number of Rows	1
Estimated I/O Cost	0.003125
Estimated CPU Cost	0.0001581
Number of Executions	1
Estimated Number of Executions	1
Estimated Operator Cost	0.0032831 (100%)
Estimated Subtree Cost	0.0032831
Estimated Number of Rows	1
Estimated Row Size	41 B
Actual Rebinds	0
Actual Rewinds	0
Ordered	True
Node ID	0

Predicate
[AdventureWorks2008].[Sales].[Currency].[Name] as [c].[Name] like N'Ice%'
Object
[AdventureWorks2008].[Sales].[Currency].[AK_Currency_Name] [c]
Output List
[AdventureWorks2008].[Sales].[Currency].CurrencyCode
Seek Predicates
Seek Keys[1]: Start: [AdventureWorks2008].[Sales].[Currency].Name >= Scalar Operator(N'Ice'), End: [AdventureWorks2008].[Sales].[Currency].Name < Scalar Operator(N'IcF')

Figure 11-5. *Execution plan showing automatic conversion of a* `LIKE` *clause with a trailing % sign to an indexable search condition*

As you can see, the optimizer automatically converts the `LIKE` condition to an equivalent pair of >= and < conditions. You can therefore rewrite this `SELECT` statement to replace the `LIKE` condition with an indexable search condition as follows:

```
SELECT  c.CurrencyCode
FROM    Sales.Currency AS c
WHERE   c.[Name] >= 'Ice'
        AND c.[Name] < 'IcF'
```

Note that, in both cases, the number of logical reads, the execution time for the query with the `LIKE` condition, and the manually converted sargable search condition are all the same. Thus, if you include leading characters in the `LIKE` clause, the SQL Server 2008 optimizer optimizes the search condition to allow the use of indexes on the column.

!< Condition vs. >= Condition

Even though both the `!<` and `>=` search conditions retrieve the same result set, they may perform different operations internally. The `>=` comparison operator allows the optimizer to use an index on the column referred to in the search argument, because the `=` part of the operator allows the optimizer to seek to a starting point in the index and access all the index rows from there onward. On the other hand, the `!<` operator doesn't have an `=` element and needs to access the column value for every row.

Or does it? As explained in Chapter 9, the SQL Server optimizer performs syntax-based optimization, before executing a query, to improve performance. This allows SQL Server to take care of the performance concern with the !< operator by converting it to >=, as shown in the execution plan in Figure 11-6 for the two following SELECT statements:

```
SELECT  *
FROM    Purchasing.PurchaseOrderHeader AS poh
WHERE   poh.PurchaseOrderID >= 2975
SELECT  *
FROM    Purchasing.PurchaseOrderHeader AS poh
WHERE   poh.PurchaseOrderID !< 2975
```

As you can see, the optimizer often provides you with the flexibility of writing queries in the preferred T-SQL syntax without sacrificing performance.

Although the SQL Server optimizer can automatically optimize query syntax to improve performance in many cases, you should not rely on it to do so. It is a good practice to write efficient queries in the first place.

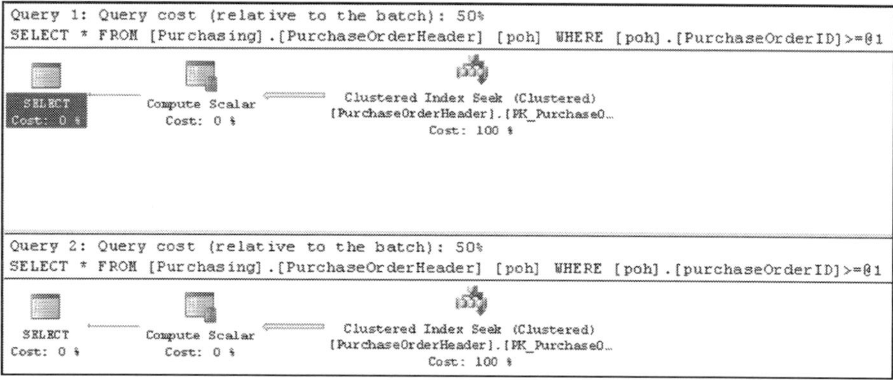

Figure 11-6. *Execution plan showing automatic transformation of a nonindexable !< operator to an indexable >= operator*

Avoid Arithmetic Operators on the WHERE Clause Column

Using an arithmetic operator on a column in the WHERE clause prevents the optimizer from using the index on the column. For example, consider the following SELECT statement:

```
SELECT  *
FROM    Purchasing.PurchaseOrderHeader AS poh
WHERE   poh.PurchaseOrderID * 2 = 3400
```

A multiplication operator, *, has been applied on the column in the WHERE clause. You can avoid this on the column by rewriting the SELECT statement as follows:

```
SELECT  *
FROM    Purchasing.PurchaseOrderHeader AS poh
WHERE   poh.PurchaseOrderID = 3400 / 2
```

The table has a clustered index on the PurchaseOrderID column. As explained in Chapter 4, an Index Seek operation on this index will be suitable for this query since it returns only one row. Even though both queries return the same result set, the use of the multiplication operator on the PurchaseOrderID column in the first query prevents the optimizer from using the index on the column, as you can see in Figure 11-7.

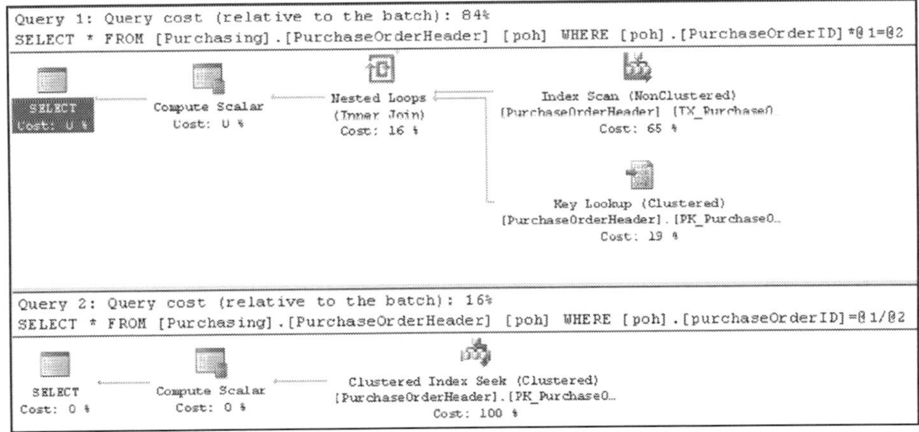

Figure 11-7. *Execution plan showing the detrimental effect of an arithmetic operator on a* WHERE *clause column*

Their corresponding STATISTICS IO and TIME outputs are as follows:

- With the * operator on the PurchaseOrderID column:

```
Table 'PurchaseOrderHeader'. Scan count 1, logical reads 10
CPU time = 0 ms,  elapsed time = 68 ms.
```

- With no operator on the PurchaseOrderID column:

```
Table 'PurchaseOrderHeader'. Scan count 0, logical reads 2
CPU time = 0 ms,  elapsed time = 65 ms.
```

Therefore, to use the indexes effectively and improve query performance, avoid using arithmetic operators on column(s) in the WHERE clause.

■ **Note** For small result sets, even though an index seek is usually a better data-retrieval strategy than a table scan (or a complete clustered index scan), for very small tables (in which all data rows fit on one page) a table scan can be cheaper. I explain this in more detail in Chapter 4.

Avoid Functions on the WHERE Clause Column

In the same way as arithmetic operators, functions on `WHERE` clause columns also hurt query performance—and for the same reasons. Try to avoid using functions on `WHERE` clause columns, as shown in the following two examples:

- `SUBSTRING` vs. `LIKE`
- Date part comparison

SUBSTRING vs. LIKE

In the following `SELECT` statement (`substring.sql` in the download), using the `SUBSTRING` function prevents the use of the index on the `ShipPostalCode` column:

```
SELECT  d.Name
FROM    HumanResources.Department AS d
WHERE   SUBSTRING(d.[Name], 1, 1) = 'F'
```

Figure 11-8 illustrates this.

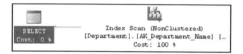

Figure 11-8. *Execution plan showing the detrimental effect of using the `SUBSTRING` function on a `WHERE` clause column*

As you can see, using the `SUBSTRING` function prevented the optimizer from using the index on the `[Name]` column. This function on the column made the optimizer use a clustered index scan. In the absence of the clustered index on the `DepartmentID` column, a table scan would have been performed.

You can redesign this `SELECT` statement to avoid the function on the column as follows:

```
SELECT d.Name
FROM HumanResources.Department AS d
WHERE d.[Name] LIKE 'F%'
```

This query allows the optimizer to choose the index on the `[Name]` column, as shown in Figure 11-9.

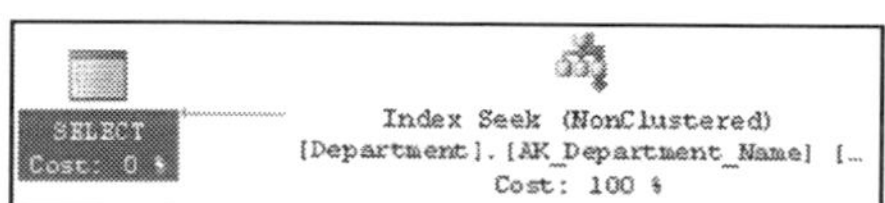

Figure 11-9. *Execution plan showing the benefit of not using the `SUBSTRING` function on a `WHERE` clause column*

Date Part Comparison

SQL Server can store date and time data as separate fields or as a combined DATETIME field that has both. Although you may need to keep date and time data together in one field, sometimes you want only the date, which usually means you have to apply a conversion function to extract the date part from the DATETIME data type. Doing this prevents the optimizer from choosing the index on the column, as shown in the following example.

First, there needs to be a good index on the DATETIME column of one of the tables. Use Sales.SalesOrderHeader, and create the following index:

```
IF EXISTS ( SELECT  *
            FROM    sys.indexes
            WHERE   object_id = OBJECT_ID(N'[Sales].[SalesOrderHeader]')
                    AND name = N'IX_Test' )
    DROP INDEX [AK_SalesOrderHeader_rowguid] ON [Sales].[SalesOrderHeader]
GO
CREATE INDEX IX_Test ON Sales.SalesOrderHeader(OrderDate)
```

To retrieve all rows from Sales.SalesOrderHeader with OrderDate in the month of April in the year 2002, you can execute the following SELECT statement (datetime.sql):

```
SELECT  soh.SalesOrderID
       ,soh.OrderDate
FROM    Sales.SalesOrderHeader AS soh
        JOIN Sales.SalesOrderDetail AS sod
        ON soh.SalesOrderID = sod.SalesOrderID
WHERE   DATEPART(yy, soh.OrderDate) = 2002
        AND DATEPART(mm, soh.OrderDate) = 4
```

Using the DATEPART function on the column OrderDate prevents the optimizer from considering index IX_Test on the column and instead causes a table scan, as shown in Figure 11-10.

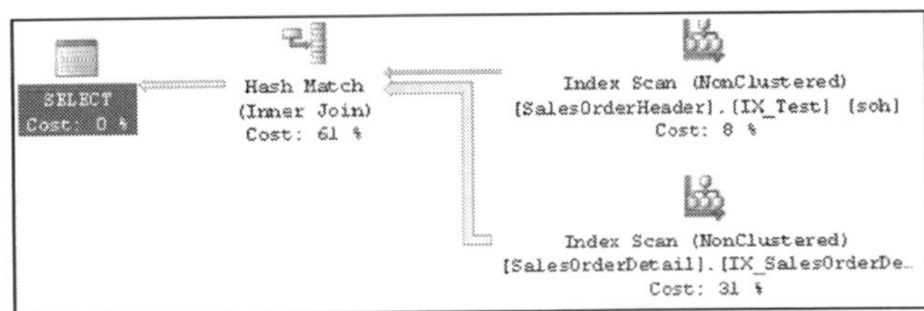

Figure 11-10. *Execution plan showing the detrimental effect of using the DATEPART function on a WHERE clause column*

This is the output of SET STATISTICS IO and TIME:

```
Table 'Worktable'. Scan count 0, logical reads 0
Table 'SalesOrderDetail'. Scan count 1, logical reads 228
Table 'SalesOrderHeader'. Scan count 1, logical reads 61
CPU time = 31 ms,  elapsed time = 67 ms.
```

The date part comparison can be done without applying the function on the DATETIME column:

```
SELECT  soh.SalesOrderID
       ,soh.OrderDate
FROM    Sales.SalesOrderHeader AS soh
        JOIN Sales.SalesOrderDetail AS sod
        ON soh.SalesOrderID = sod.SalesOrderID
WHERE soh.OrderDate >= '2002-04-01'
AND soh.OrderDate < '2002-05-01'
```

This allows the optimizer to consider index IX_Test that was created on the DATETIME column, as shown in Figure 11-11.

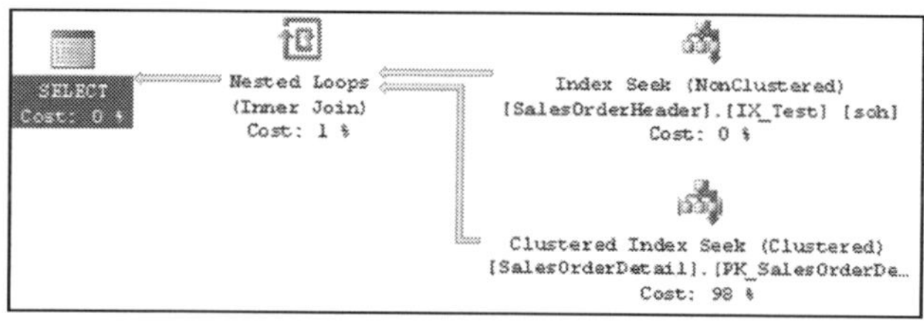

Figure 11-11. *Execution plan showing the benefit of not using the* CONVERT *function on a* WHERE *clause column*

This is the output of SET STATISTICS IO and TIME:

```
Table 'SalesOrderDetail'. Scan count 244, logical reads 814
Table 'SalesOrderHeader'. Scan count 1, logical reads 3
CPU time = 0 ms,  elapsed time = 109 ms
```

Therefore, to allow the optimizer to consider an index on a column referred to in the WHERE clause, always avoid using a function on the indexed column. This increases the effectiveness of indexes, which can improve query performance. In this instance, though, it's worth noting that the performance on the SalesOrderHeader table increased, but the optimizer chose a Nested Loop join rather than the Hash of the plan shown in Figure 11-10. This increased overall performance because of the extra scans against the SalesOrderDetail table.

Be sure to drop the index created earlier:

```
DROP INDEX Sales.SalesOrderHeader.IX_Test;
```

Avoiding Optimizer Hints

SQL Server's cost-based optimizer dynamically determines the processing strategy for a query, based on the current table/index structure and data. This dynamic behavior can be overridden using optimizer hints, taking some of the decisions away from the optimizer by instructing it to use a certain processing strategy. This makes the optimizer behavior static and doesn't allow it to dynamically update the processing strategy as the table/index structure or data changes.

Since it is usually difficult to outsmart the optimizer, the usual recommendation is to avoid optimizer hints. Generally, it is beneficial to let the optimizer determine a cost-effective processing strategy based on the data distribution statistics, indexes, and other factors. Forcing the optimizer (with hints) to use a specific processing strategy hurts performance more often than not, as shown in the following examples for these hints:

- `JOIN` hint
- `INDEX` hint
- `FORCEPLAN` hint

JOIN Hint

As explained in Chapter 3, the optimizer dynamically determines a cost-effective `JOIN` strategy between two data sets, based on the table/index structure and data. Table 11-2 presents a summary of the `JOIN` types supported by SQL Server 2008 for easy reference.

Table 11-2. *`JOIN` Types Supported by SQL Server 2008*

`JOIN` Type	Index on Joining Columns	Usual Size of Joining Tables	Presorted `JOIN` Clause
Nested loop	Inner table must. Outer table preferable.	Small	Optional
Merge	Both tables must. Optimal condition: Clustered or covering index on both.	Large	Yes
Hash	Inner table *not* indexed.	Any Optimal condition: Inner table large. Outer table small.	No

■ **Note** The outer table is usually the smaller of the two joining tables.

You can instruct SQL Server to use a specific `JOIN` type by using the `JOIN` hints in Table 11-3.

Table 11-3. *`JOIN` Hints*

`JOIN` Type	`JOIN` Hint
Nested loop	`LOOP JOIN`
Merge	`MERGE JOIN`
Hash	`HASH JOIN`

To understand how the use of JOIN hints can affect performance, consider the following SELECT statement (join.sql in the download):

```
SELECT  s.[Name] AS StoreName
       ,p.[LastName] + ', ' + p.[FirstName]
FROM    [Sales].[Store] s
        JOIN [Sales].SalesPerson AS sp
        ON s.SalesPersonID = sp.BusinessEntityID
        JOIN HumanResources.Employee AS e
        ON sp.BusinessEntityID = e.BusinessEntityID
        JOIN Person.Person AS p
        ON e.BusinessEntityID = p.BusinessEntityID
```

Figure 11-12 shows the execution plan.

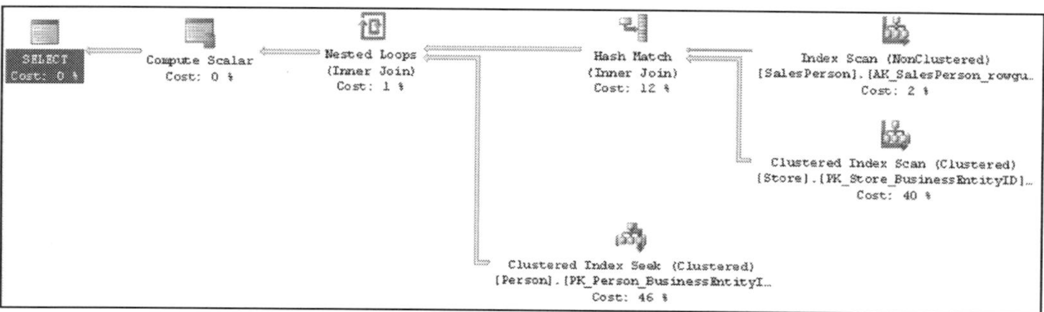

Figure 11-12. *Execution plan showing a simple join between two tables*

As you can see, SQL Server dynamically decided to use a LOOP JOIN to add the data from the Person.Person table and to add a HASH JOIN for the Sales.SalesPerson and Sales.Store tables. As demonstrated in Chapter 3, for simple queries affecting a small result set, the LOOP JOIN generally provides better performance than a HASH JOIN or MERGE JOIN. Since the number of rows coming from the Sales.SalesPerson table is relatively small, it might feel like you could force the JOIN to be a LOOP like this:

```
SELECT  s.[Name] AS StoreName
       ,p.[LastName] + ', ' + p.[FirstName]
FROM    [Sales].[Store] s
        JOIN [Sales].SalesPerson AS sp
        ON s.SalesPersonID = sp.BusinessEntityID
        JOIN HumanResources.Employee AS e
        ON sp.BusinessEntityID = e.BusinessEntityID
        JOIN Person.Person AS p
        ON e.BusinessEntityID = p.BusinessEntityID
OPTION (LOOP JOIN)
```

When this query is run, the execution plan changes, as you can see in Figure 11-13.

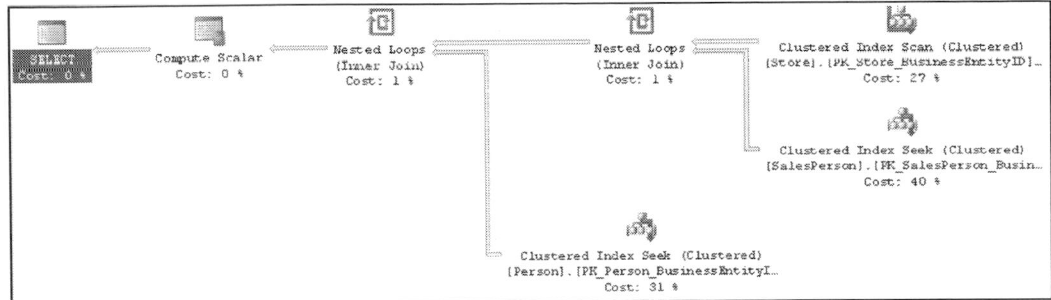

Figure 11-13. *Cost of a query with and without a JOIN hint*

The corresponding STATISTICS IO and TIME outputs for each query are as follows:

- With no JOIN hint:

```
Table 'Person'. Scan count 0, logical reads 2155
Table 'Employee'. Scan count 0, logical reads 1402
Table 'SalesPerson'. Scan count 0, logical reads 1402
Table 'Store'. Scan count 1, logical reads 103
CPU time = 0 ms,  elapsed time = 100 ms.
```

- With a JOIN hint:

```
Table 'Person'. Scan count 0, logical reads 2155
Table 'Employee'. Scan count 0, logical reads 1402
Table 'SalesPerson'. Scan count 0, logical reads 1402
Table 'Store'. Scan count 1, logical reads 103
CPU time = 16 ms,  elapsed time = 139 ms.
```

You can see that the query with the JOIN hint takes longer to run than the query without the hint. It also adds overhead to the CPU.

JOIN hints force the optimizer to ignore its own optimization strategy and use instead the strategy specified by the query. JOIN hints generally hurt query performance because of the following factors:

- Hints prevent autoparameterization.
- The optimizer is prevented from dynamically deciding the joining order of the tables.

Therefore, it makes sense to not use the JOIN hint but to instead let the optimizer dynamically determine a cost-effective processing strategy.

INDEX Hints

As mentioned earlier, using an arithmetic operator on a WHERE clause column prevents the optimizer from choosing the index on the column. To improve performance, you can rewrite the query without using the arithmetic operator on the WHERE clause, as shown in the corresponding example. Alternatively, you may even think of forcing the optimizer to use the index on the column with an INDEX hint (a type of optimizer hint). However, most of the time, it is better to avoid the INDEX hint and let the optimizer behave dynamically.

To understand the effect of an INDEX hint on query performance, consider the example presented in the "Avoid Arithmetic Operators on the WHERE Clause Column" section. The multiplication operator on the PurchaseOrderID column prevented the optimizer from choosing the index on the column. You can use an INDEX hint to force the optimizer to use the index on the OrderID column as follows:

```
SELECT  *
FROM    Purchasing.PurchaseOrderHeader AS poh
WITH (INDEX (PK_PurchaseOrderHeader_PurchaseOrderID))
WHERE   poh.PurchaseOrderID * 2 = 3400
```

Note the relative cost of using the INDEX hint in comparison to not using the INDEX hint, as shown in Figure 11-14.

Also, note the difference in the number of logical reads shown in the following STATISTICS IO outputs:

- No hint (with the arithmetic operator on the WHERE clause column):

```
Table 'PurchaseOrderHeader'. Scan count 1, logical reads 10
CPU time = 0 ms,  elapsed time = 206 ms.
```

- No hint (without the arithmetic operator on the WHERE clause column):

```
Table 'PurchaseOrderHeader'. Scan count 0, logical reads 2
CPU time = 16 ms,  elapsed time = 32 ms.
```

- INDEX hint:

```
Table 'PurchaseOrderHeader'. Scan count 1, logical reads 44
CPU time = 16 ms,  elapsed time = 71 ms.
```

From the relative cost of execution plans and number of logical reads, it is evident that the query with the INDEX hint actually impaired the query performance. Even though it allowed the optimizer to use the index on the PurchaseOrderID column, it did not allow the optimizer to determine the proper index-access mechanism. Consequently, the optimizer used the index scan to access just one row. In comparison, avoiding the arithmetic operator on the WHERE clause column and not using the INDEX hint allowed the optimizer not only to use the index on the PurchaseOrderID column but also to determine the proper index access mechanism: index seek.

Therefore, in general, let the optimizer choose the best indexing strategy for the query, and don't override the optimizer behavior using an INDEX hint. Also, not using INDEX hints allows the optimizer to decide the best indexing strategy dynamically as the data changes over time.

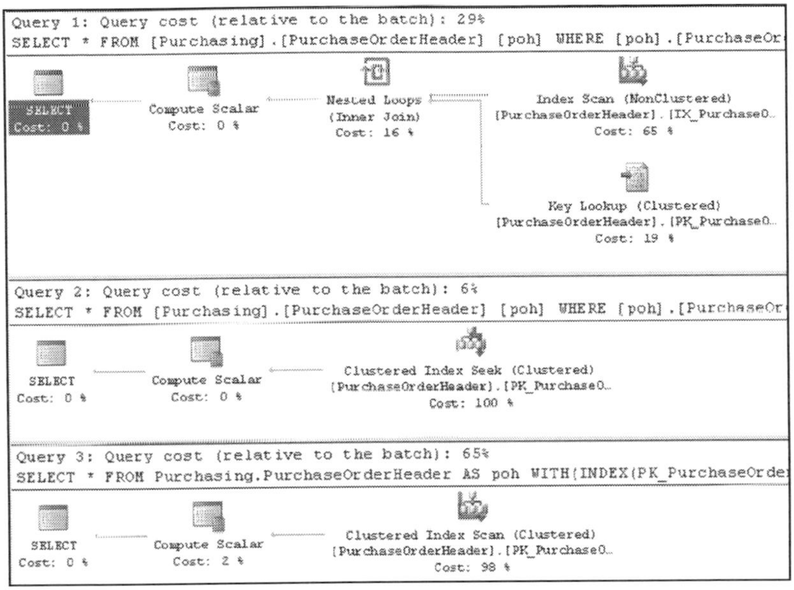

```
Query 1: Query cost (relative to the batch): 29%
SELECT * FROM [Purchasing].[PurchaseOrderHeader] [poh] WHERE [poh].[PurchaseOr

SELECT        Compute Scalar    Nested Loops        Index Scan (NonClustered)
Cost: 0 %     Cost: 0 %         (Inner Join)        [PurchaseOrderHeader].[IX_PurchaseO...
                                Cost: 16 %          Cost: 65 %

                                                    Key Lookup (Clustered)
                                                    [PurchaseOrderHeader].[PK_PurchaseO...
                                                    Cost: 19 %

Query 2: Query cost (relative to the batch): 6%
SELECT * FROM [Purchasing].[PurchaseOrderHeader] [poh] WHERE [poh].[PurchaseOr

SELECT        Compute Scalar    Clustered Index Seek (Clustered)
Cost: 0 %     Cost: 0 %         [PurchaseOrderHeader].[PK_PurchaseO...
                                Cost: 100 %

Query 3: Query cost (relative to the batch): 65%
SELECT * FROM Purchasing.PurchaseOrderHeader AS poh WITH(INDEX(PK_PurchaseOrde

SELECT        Compute Scalar    Clustered Index Scan (Clustered)
Cost: 0 %     Cost: 2 %         [PurchaseOrderHeader].[PK_PurchaseO...
                                Cost: 98 %
```

Figure 11-14. *Cost of a query with and without an INDEX hint*

Using Domain and Referential Integrity

Domain and referential integrity help define and enforce valid values for a column, maintaining the integrity of the database. This is done through column/table constraints.

Since data access is usually one of the most costly operations in a query execution, avoiding redundant data access helps the optimizer reduce the query execution time. Domain and referential integrity help the SQL Server 2008 optimizer analyze valid data values without physically accessing the data, which reduces query time.

To understand how this happens, consider the following examples:

- The `NOT NULL` constraint
- Declarative referential integrity (DRI)

NOT NULL Constraint

The `NOT NULL` column constraint is used to implement domain integrity by defining the fact that a `NULL` value cannot be entered in a particular column. SQL Server automatically enforces this fact at runtime to maintain the domain integrity for that column. Also, defining the `NOT NULL` column constraint helps the optimizer generate an efficient processing strategy when the `ISNULL` function is used on that column in a query.

To understand the performance benefit of the `NOT NULL` column constraint, consider the following example. In the following example, these two queries are intended to return every value that does not equal `'B'`. These two queries are running against similarly sized columns, each of which will require a table scan in order to return the data (`null.sql` in the download):

```
SELECT  p.FirstName
FROM    Person.Person AS p
WHERE   p.FirstName < 'B'
        OR p.Firstname >= 'C';

SELECT  p.MiddleName
FROM    Person.Person AS p
WHERE   p.MiddleName < 'B'
        OR p.MiddleName >= 'C';
```

The two queries use identical execution plans, as you can see in Figure 11-15.

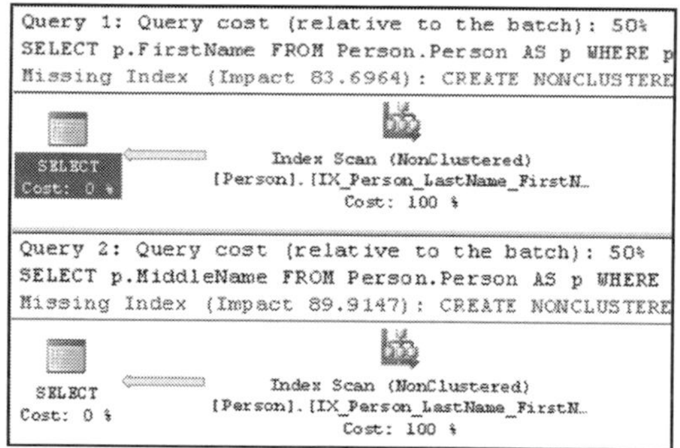

Figure 11-15. *Table scans caused by a lack of indexes*

Since the column `Person.MiddleName` can contain `NULL`, the data returned is incomplete. This is because, by definition, although a `NULL` value meets the necessary criteria of not being in any way equal to "`B`", you can't return `NULL` values in this manner. An added `OR` clause is necessary. That would mean modifying the second query like this:

```
SELECT  p.FirstName
FROM    Person.Person AS p
WHERE   p.FirstName < 'B'
        OR p.Firstname >= 'C';

SELECT  p.MiddleName
FROM    Person.Person AS p
WHERE   p.MiddleName < 'B'
        OR p.MiddleName >= 'C'
OR p.MiddleName IS NULL;
```

Also, as shown in the missing index statements in the execution plan in Figure 11-15, these two queries can benefit from having indexes created on their tables. Creating test indexes like the following should satisfy the requirements:

```
CREATE INDEX IX_Test1 ON Person.Person (MiddleName);
CREATE INDEX IX_test2 ON Person.Person (FirstName);
```

When the queries are reexecuted, Figure 11-16 shows the resultant execution plan for the two SELECT statements.

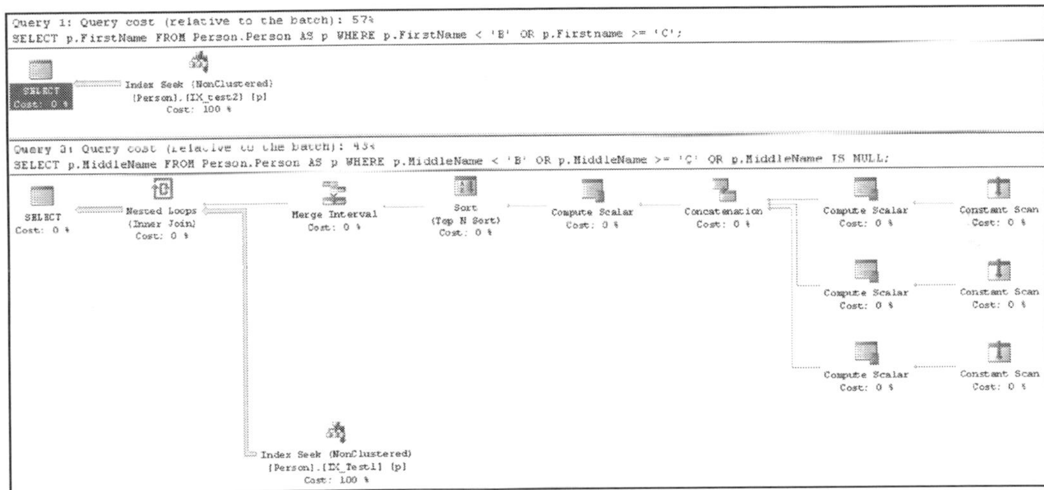

Figure 11-16. *Effect of the* `IS NULL` *option being used*

As shown in Figure 11-16, the optimizer was able to take advantage of the index `IX_Test2` on the `Person.FirstName` column to get a nice clean `Index Seek` operation. Unfortunately, the requirements for processing the `NULL` columns were very different. The index `IX_Test1` was not used in the same way. Instead, three constants were created for each of the three criteria defined within the query. These were then joined together through the `Concatenation` operation, sorted and merged prior to scanning the index three times through the `Nested Loop` operator to arrive at the result set. Although it appears, from the estimated costs in the execution plan, that this was the less costly query (43 percent compared to 57 percent), `STATISTICS IO` and `TIME` tell the more accurate story, which is that the `NULL` queries were more costly:

```
Table 'Person'. Scan count 2, logical reads 59
CPU time = 0 ms,  elapsed time = 336 ms.
```

vs.

```
Table 'Person'. Scan count 3, logical reads 42
CPU time = 0 ms,  elapsed time = 461 ms.
```

Be sure to drop the test indexes that were created:

```
DROP INDEX person.Person.ix_test2
DROP INDEX Person.Person.IX_Test1
```

As much as possible, you should attempt to leave NULL values out of the database. However, when data is unknown, default values may not be possible. That's when NULL will come back into the design. I find it unavoidable, but it's something to minimize as much as you can.

When it is unavoidable and you will be dealing with NULL values, keep in mind that you can use a filtered index that removes NULL values from the index, thereby improving the performance of that index. This was detailed in Chapter 4. Sparse columns, introduced in SQL Server 2008, offer another option to help you deal with NULL values. Sparse columns are primarily aimed at storing NULL values more efficiently and therefore reduce space, at a sacrifice in performance. This option is specifically targeted at business intelligence (BI) databases, not OLTP databases, where large amounts of NULL values in fact tables are a normal part of the design.

Declarative Referential Integrity

Declarative referential integrity is used to define referential integrity between a parent table and a child table. It ensures that a record in the child table exists only if the corresponding record in the parent table exists. The only exception to this rule is that the child table can contain a NULL value for the identifier that links the rows of the child table to the rows of the parent table. For all other values of the identifier in the child, a corresponding value must exist in the parent table. In SQL Server, DRI is implemented using a PRIMARY KEY constraint on the parent table and a FOREIGN KEY constraint on the child table.

With DRI established between two tables and the foreign key columns of the child table set to NOT NULL, the SQL Server 2008 optimizer is assured that for every record in the child table, the parent table has a corresponding record. Sometimes this can help the optimizer improve performance, because accessing the parent table is not necessary to verify the existence of a parent record for a corresponding child record.

To understand the performance benefit of implementing declarative referential integrity, let's consider an example. First eliminate the referential integrity between two tables, Person.Address and Person.StateProvince, using this script:

```
IF EXISTS ( SELECT  *
            FROM    sys.foreign_keys
            WHERE   object_id =
OBJECT_ID(N'[Person].[FK_Address_StateProvince_StateProvinceID]')
                    AND parent_object_id = OBJECT_ID(N'[Person].[Address]') )
    ALTER TABLE [Person].[Address]
DROP CONSTRAINT [FK_Address_StateProvince_StateProvinceID]
```

Consider the following SELECT statement (prod.sql in the download):

```
SELECT  a.AddressID
       ,sp.StateProvinceID
FROM    Person.Address AS a
        JOIN Person.StateProvince AS sp
        ON a.StateProvinceID = sp.StateProvinceID
WHERE   a.AddressID = 27234;
```

Note that the SELECT statement fetches the value of the StateProvinceID column from the parent table (Person.Address). If the nature of the data requires that for every product (identified by StateProvinceId) in the child table (Person.StateProvince) the parent table (Person.Address) contains a corresponding product, then you can rewrite the preceding SELECT statement as follows (prod.sql in the download):

```
SELECT  a.AddressID
       ,a.StateProvinceID
FROM    Person.Address AS a
        JOIN Person.StateProvince AS sp
        ON a.StateProvinceID = sp.StateProvinceID
WHERE   a.AddressID = 27234;
```

Both SELECT statements should return the same result set. Even the optimizer generates the same execution plan for both the SELECT statements, as shown in Figure 11-17.

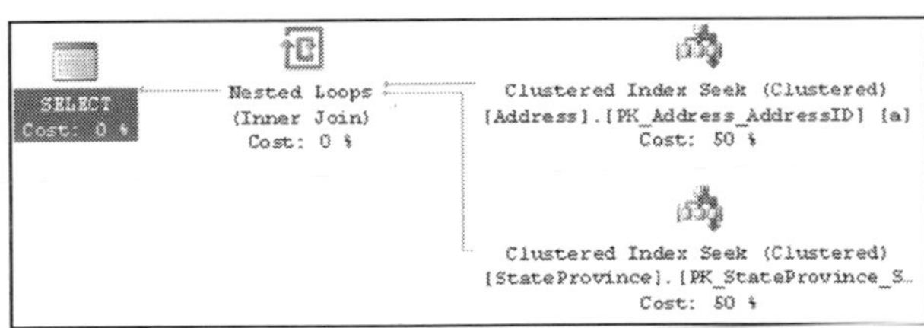

Figure 11-17. *Execution plan when DRI is not defined between the two tables*

To understand how declarative referential integrity can affect query performance, replace the FOREIGN KEY dropped earlier:

```
ALTER TABLE [Person].[Address]
        WITH CHECK
ADD CONSTRAINT [FK_Address_StateProvince_StateProvinceID]
FOREIGN KEY ([StateProvinceID]) REFERENCES [Person].[StateProvince] ([StateProvinceID]);
```

Note There is now referential integrity between the tables.

Figure 11-18 shows the resultant execution plans for the two SELECT statements.

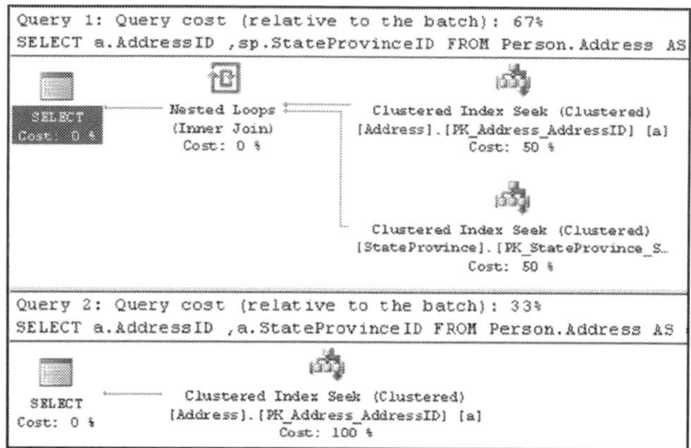

Figure 11-18. *Execution plans showing the benefit of defining DRI between the two tables*

As you can see, the execution plan of the second SELECT statement is highly optimized: the Person.StateProvince table is not accessed. With the declarative referential integrity in place (and Address.StateProvince set to NOT NULL), the optimizer is assured that for every record in the child table, the parent table contains a corresponding record. Therefore, the JOIN clause between the parent and child tables is redundant in the second SELECT statement, with no other data requested from the parent table.

You probably already knew that domain and referential integrity are a Good Thing, but you can see that they not only ensure data integrity but also improve performance. As just illustrated, domain and referential integrity provide more choices to the optimizer to generate cost-effective execution plans and improve performance.

To achieve the performance benefit of DRI, as mentioned previously, the foreign key columns in the child table should be NOT NULL. Otherwise, there can be rows (with foreign key column values as NULL) in the child table with no representation in the parent table. That won't prevent the optimizer from accessing the primary table (Prod) in the previous query. By default—that is, if the NOT NULL attribute isn't mentioned for a column—the column can have NULL values. Considering the benefit of the NOT NULL attribute and the other benefits explained in this section, always mark the attribute of a column as NOT NULL if NULL isn't a valid value for that column.

Avoiding Resource-Intensive Queries

Many database functionalities can be implemented using a variety of query techniques. The approach you should take is to use query techniques that are very resource friendly and set based. A few techniques you can use to reduce the footprint of a query are as follows:

- Avoid data type conversion.
- Use EXISTS over COUNT(*) to verify data existence.
- Use UNION ALL over UNION.

- Use indexes for aggregate and sort operations.
- Avoid local variables in a batch query.
- Be careful naming stored procedures.

I cover these points in more detail in the next sections.

Avoid Data Type Conversion

SQL Server allows, in some instances (defined by the large table of data conversions available in Books Online), a value/constant with different but compatible data types to be compared with a column's data. SQL Server automatically converts the data from one data type to another. This process is called *implicit data type conversion*. Although useful, implicit conversion adds overhead to the query optimizer. To improve performance, use a variable/constant with the same data type as that of the column to which it is compared.

To understand how implicit data type conversion affects performance, consider the following example (`conversion.sql` in the download):

```
IF EXISTS ( SELECT  *
            FROM    sys.objects
            WHERE   object_id = OBJECT_ID(N'[dbo].[t1]')
                    AND type IN (N'U') )
    DROP TABLE [dbo].[t1] ;
CREATE TABLE dbo.t1
    (Id INT IDENTITY(1, 1)
    ,MyKey VARCHAR(50)
    ,MyValue VARCHAR(50)) ;
CREATE UNIQUE CLUSTERED INDEX PK_t1 ON dbo.t1 ([Id] ASC) ;
CREATE UNIQUE NONCLUSTERED INDEX IX_Test ON dbo.t1 (MyKey) ;
GO

SELECT TOP 10000
        IDENTITY( INT,1,1 ) AS n
INTO    #Tally
FROM    Master.dbo.SysColumns sc1
       ,Master.dbo.SysColumns sc2;

INSERT  INTO dbo.t1 (MyKey, MyValue)
        SELECT TOP 10000
                'UniqueKey' + CAST(n AS VARCHAR)
               ,'Description'
        FROM    #Tally ;

DROP TABLE #Tally

SELECT  MyValue
FROM    dbo.t1
WHERE   MyKey = 'UniqueKey333';
```

```
SELECT  MyValue
FROM    dbo.t1
WHERE   MyKey = N'UniqueKey333';
```

After creating the table `t1`, creating a couple of indexes on it, and placing some data, two queries are defined. Both queries return the same result set. As you can see, both queries are identical except for the data type of the variable equated to the `MyKey` column. Since this column is `VARCHAR`, the first query doesn't require an implicit data type conversion. The second query uses a different data type from that of the `MyKey` column, requiring an implicit data type conversion and thereby adding overhead to the query performance. Figure 11-19 shows the execution plans for both queries.

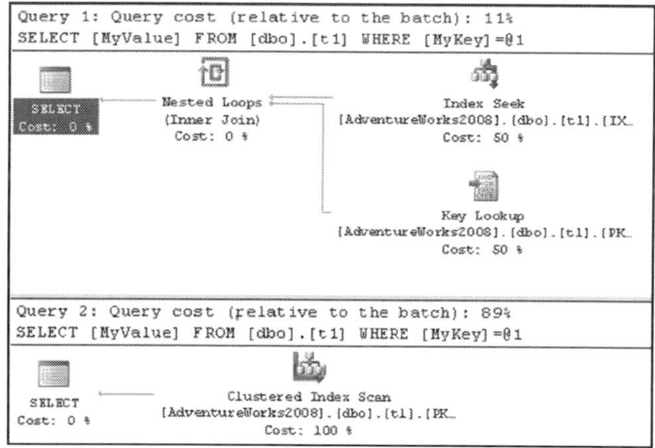

Figure 11-19. *Cost of a query with and without implicit data type conversion*

The complexity of the implicit data type conversion depends on the precedence of the data types involved in the comparison. The data type precedence rules of SQL Server specify which data type is converted to the other. Usually, the data type of lower precedence is converted to the data type of higher precedence. For example, the `TINYINT` data type has a lower precedence than the `INT` data type. For a complete list of data type precedence in SQL Server 2008, please refer to the MSDN article "Data Type Precedence" (`http://msdn.microsoft.com/en-us/library/ms190309.aspx`). For further information about which data type can implicitly convert to which data type, refer to the MSDN article "Data Type Conversion" (`http://msdn.microsoft.com/en-us/library/ms191530.aspx`).

When SQL Server compares a column value with a certain data type and a variable (or constant) with a different data type, the data type of the variable (or constant) is always converted to the data type of the column. This is done because the column value is accessed based on the implicit conversion value of the variable (or constant). Therefore, in such cases, the implicit conversion is always applied on the variable (or constant).

As you can see, implicit data type conversion adds overhead to the query performance both in terms of a poor execution plan and in added CPU cost to make the conversions. Therefore, to improve performance, always use the same data type for both expressions.

Use EXISTS over COUNT(*) to Verify Data Existence

A common database requirement is to verify whether a set of data exists. Usually you'll see this implemented using a batch of SQL queries, as follows (count.sql in the download):

```
DECLARE @n INT
SELECT  @n = COUNT(*)
FROM    Sales.SalesOrderDetail AS sod
WHERE   sod.OrderQty = 1
IF @n > 0
    PRINT 'Record Exists'
```

Using COUNT(*) to verify the existence of data is highly resource intensive, because COUNT(*) has to scan all the rows in a table. EXISTS merely has to scan and stop at the first record that matches the EXISTS criterion. To improve performance, use EXISTS instead of the COUNT(*) approach:

```
IF EXISTS ( SELECT  sod.*
            FROM    Sales.SalesOrderDetail AS sod
            WHERE   sod.OrderQty = 1 )
    PRINT 'Record Exists'
```

The performance benefit of the EXISTS technique over the COUNT(*) technique can be compared using the STATISTICS IO and TIME output, as well as the execution plan in Figure 11-20, as you can see from the output of running these queries:

```
Table 'SalesOrderDetail'. Scan count 1, logical reads 1240
CPU time = 16 ms,  elapsed time = 18 ms.

Table 'SalesOrderDetail'. Scan count 1, logical reads 3
CPU time = 0 ms,  elapsed time = 0 ms.
```

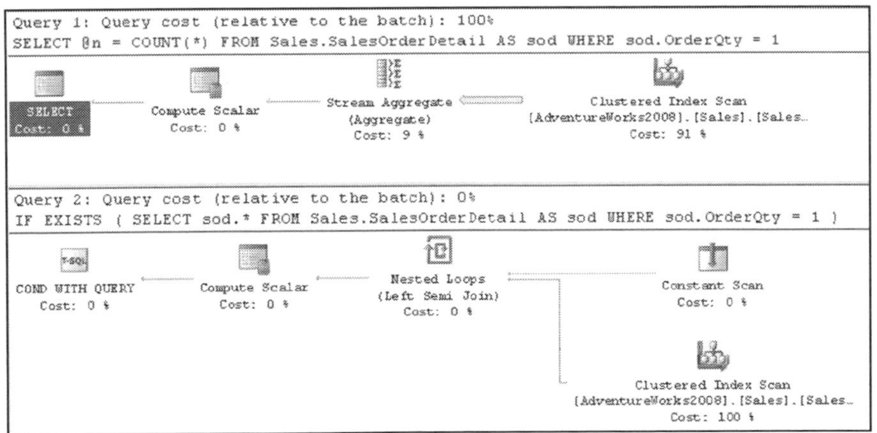

Figure 11-20. *Difference between COUNT and EXISTS*

As you can see, the EXISTS technique used only three logical reads compared to the 1,240 used by the COUNT(*) technique, and the execution time went from 16 ms to effectively 0. Therefore, to determine whether data exists, use the EXISTS technique.

Use UNION ALL Instead of UNION

You can concatenate the result set of multiple SELECT statements using the UNION clause as follows:

```
SELECT  *
FROM    Sales.SalesOrderHeader AS soh
WHERE   soh.SalesOrderNumber LIKE '%47808'
UNION
SELECT  *
FROM    Sales.SalesOrderHeader AS soh
WHERE   soh.SalesOrderNumber LIKE '%65748'
```

The UNION clause processes the result set from the two SELECT statements, removing duplicates from the final result set and effectively running DISTINCT on each query. If the result sets of the SELECT statements participating in the UNION clause are exclusive to each other or you are allowed to have duplicate rows in the final result set, then use UNION ALL instead of UNION. This avoids the overhead of detecting and removing any duplicates, improving performance as shown in Figure 11-21.

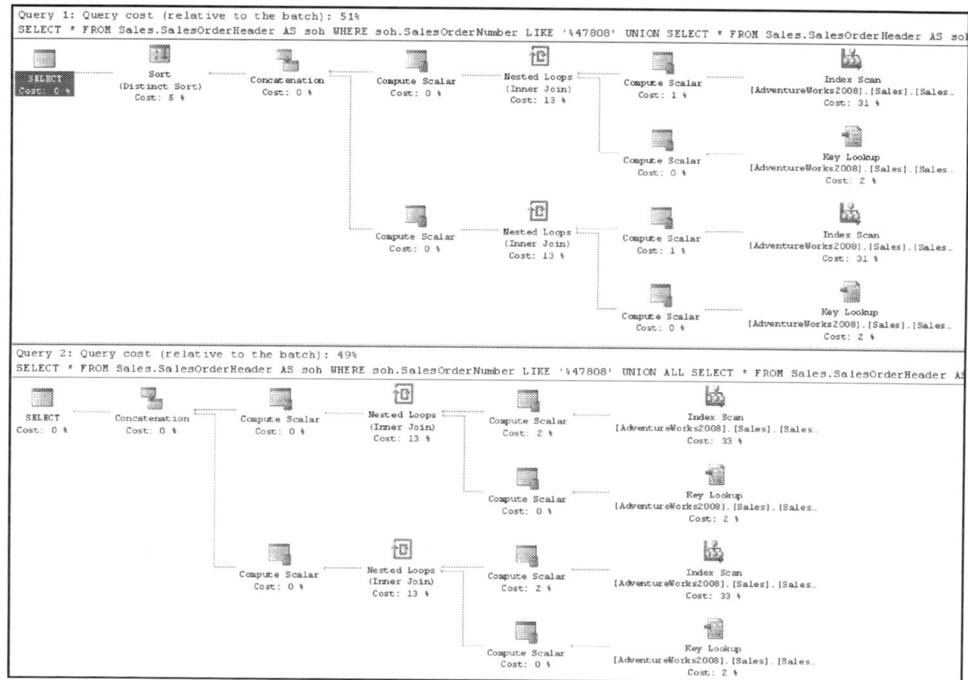

Figure 11-21. *Cost of a query with the UNION clause vs. the UNION ALL clause*

As you can see, in the first case (using UNION), the optimizer used a merge join to process the duplicates while concatenating the result set of the two SELECT statements. Since the result sets are exclusive to each other, you can use UNION ALL instead of the UNION clause. Using the UNION ALL clause avoids the overhead of detecting duplicates and thereby improves performance. The optimizer is smart enough to recognize when two queries will absolutely result in distinct lists and at those times can choose execution plans that are effectively a UNION ALL operation.

Use Indexes for Aggregate and Sort Conditions

Generally, aggregate functions such as MIN and MAX benefit from indexes on the corresponding column. Without any index on the column, the optimizer has to scan the base table (or the clustered index), retrieve all the rows, and perform a stream aggregate on the group (containing all rows) to identify the MIN/MAX value, as shown in the following example:

```
SELECT  MIN(sod.UnitPrice)
FROM    Sales.SalesOrderDetail AS sod
```

The STATISTICS IO and TIME output of the SELECT statement using the MIN aggregate function is as follows:

```
Table 'SalesOrderDetail'. Scan count 1, logical reads 1240
CPU time = 46 ms,  elapsed time = 121 ms.
```

As shown in the STATISTICS output, the query performed more than 1,000 logical reads just to retrieve the row containing the minimum value for the UnitPrice column. If you create an index on the UnitPrice column, then the UnitPrice values will be presorted by the index in the leaf pages:

```
CREATE INDEX IX_Test ON Sales.SalesOrderDetail (UnitPrice ASC)
```

The index on the UnitPrice column improves the performance of the MIN aggregate function significantly. The optimizer can retrieve the minimum UnitPrice value by seeking to the topmost row in the index. This reduces the number of logical reads for the query, as shown in the corresponding STATISTICS output:

```
able 'SalesOrderDetail'. Scan count 1, logical reads 2
CPU time = 0 ms,  elapsed time = 0 ms.
```

Similarly, creating an index on the columns referred to in an ORDER BY clause helps the optimizer organize the result set fast because the column values are prearranged in the index. The internal implementation of the GROUP BY clause also sorts the column values first because sorted column values allow the adjacent matching values to be grouped quickly. Therefore, like the ORDER BY clause, the GROUP BY clause also benefits from having the values of the columns referred to in the GROUP BY clause sorted in advance.

Avoid Local Variables in a Batch Query

Often, multiple queries are submitted together as a batch, avoiding multiple network round-trips. It's common to use local variables in a query batch to pass a value between the individual queries. However, using local variables in the WHERE clause of a query in a batch doesn't allow the optimizer to generate an efficient execution plan.

To understand how the use of a local variable in the WHERE clause of a query in a batch can affect performance, consider the following batch query (batch.sql):

```
DECLARE @id INT = 1;
SELECT  pod.*
FROM    Purchasing.PurchaseOrderDetail AS pod
        JOIN Purchasing.PurchaseOrderHeader AS poh
        ON poh.PurchaseOrderID = pod.PurchaseOrderID
WHERE   poh.PurchaseOrderID >= @id;
```

Figure 11-22 shows the execution plan of this SELECT statement.

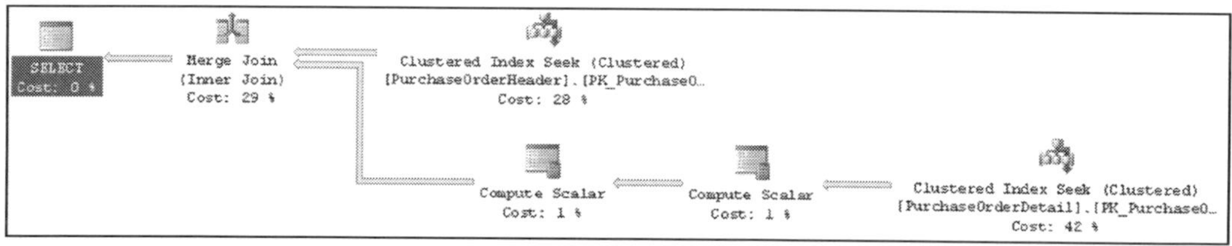

Figure 11-22. *Execution plan showing the effect of a local variable in a batch query*

As you can see, an Index Seek operation is performed to access the rows from the Purchasing.PurchaseOrderDetail table.

If the SELECT statement is executed without using the local variable, by replacing the local variable value with an appropriate constant value as in the following query, then the optimizer makes different choices:

```
SELECT  pod.*
FROM    Purchasing.PurchaseOrderDetail AS pod
        JOIN Purchasing.PurchaseOrderHeader AS poh
        ON poh.PurchaseOrderID = pod.PurchaseOrderID
WHERE   poh.PurchaseOrderID >= 1;
```

Figure 11-23 shows the result.

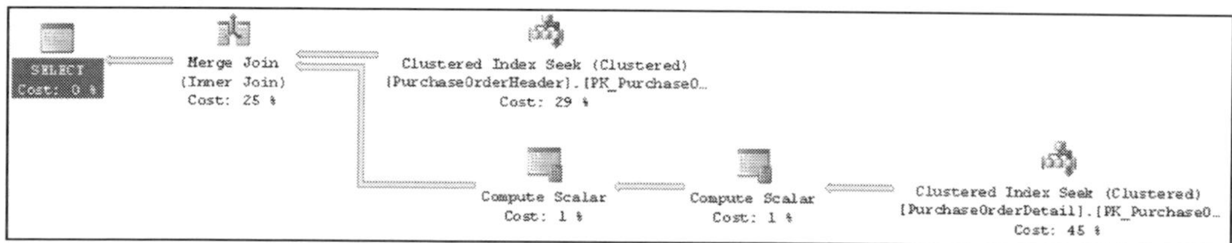

Figure 11-23. *Execution plan for the query when the local variable is not used*

Although these two approaches look identical, on closer examination, interesting differences begin to appear. Notice the estimated cost of some of the operations. For example, the Merge Join is different between Figure 11-22 and Figure 11-23; it's 29 percent in the first and 25 percent in the second. If you look at STATISTICS IO and TIME for each query, other differences appear. First here's the information from the initial query:

```
Table 'PurchaseOrderDetail'. Scan count 1, logical reads 66
Table 'PurchaseOrderHeader'. Scan count 1, logical reads 44
CPU time = 0 ms,  elapsed time = 494 ms.
```

Then here's the second query, without the local variable:

```
Table 'PurchaseOrderDetail'. Scan count 1, logical reads 66
Table 'PurchaseOrderHeader'. Scan count 1, logical reads 44
CPU time = 46 ms,  elapsed time = 360 ms.
```

Notice that the scans and reads are the same, as might be expected of queries with near identical plans. The CPU and elapsed times are different, with the second query (the one without the local variable) consistently being a little less. Based on these facts, you may assume that the execution plan of the first query will be somewhat more costly compared to the second query. But the reality is quite different, as shown in the execution plan cost comparison in Figure 11-24.

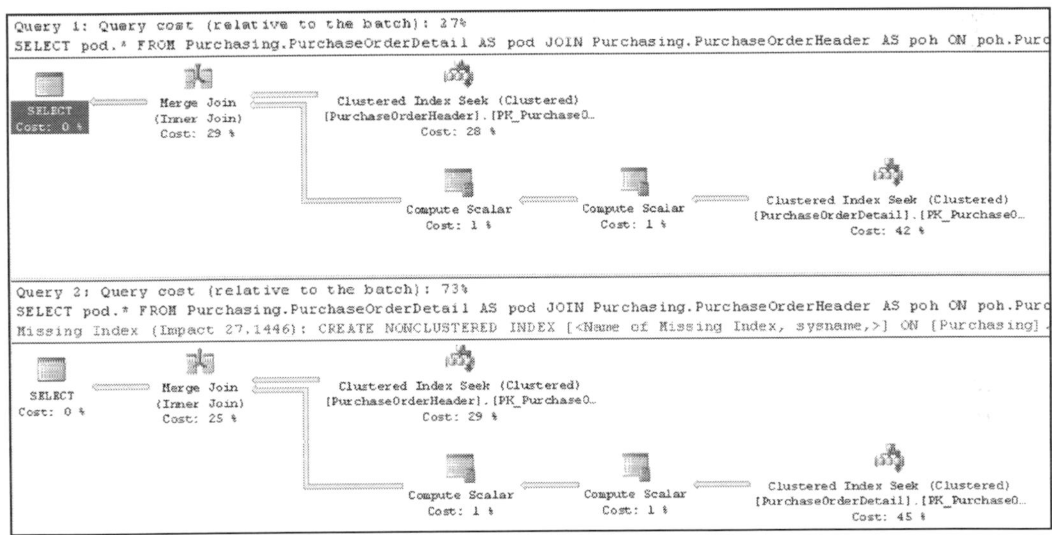

Figure 11-24. *Relative cost of the query with and without the use of a local variable*

From the relative cost of the two execution plans, it appears that the second query isn't cheaper than the first query. However, from the STATISTICS comparison, it appears that the second query should be cheaper than the first query. Which one should you believe: the comparison of STATISTICS or the relative cost of the execution plan? What's the source of this anomaly?

The execution plan is generated based on the optimizer's estimation of the number of rows affected for each execution step. If you take a look at the pop-ups for the various operators in the initial execution plan for the query with the local variable (as shown in Figure 11-22), you may notice a disparity. Take a look at this in Figure 11-25.

Clustered Index Seek (Clustered)
Scanning a particular range of rows from a clustered index.

Physical Operation	Clustered Index Seek
Logical Operation	Clustered Index Seek
Actual Number of Rows	4012
Estimated I/O Cost	0.0120139
Estimated CPU Cost	0.001481
Estimated Number of Executions	1
Number of Executions	1
Estimated Operator Cost	0.0134948 (28%)
Estimated Subtree Cost	0.0134948
Estimated Number of Rows	1203.6
Estimated Row Size	11 B
Actual Rebinds	0
Actual Rewinds	0
Ordered	True
Node ID	1

Object
[AdventureWorks2008].[Purchasing].[PurchaseOrderHeader].
[PK_PurchaseOrderHeader_PurchaseOrderID] [poh]
Output List
[AdventureWorks2008].[Purchasing].
[PurchaseOrderHeader].PurchaseOrderID
Seek Predicates
Seek Keys[1]: Start: [AdventureWorks2008].[Purchasing].
[PurchaseOrderHeader].PurchaseOrderID >= Scalar Operator
([@id])

Figure 11-25. *Clustered index seek details with a local variable*

The disparity you're looking for is the Estimated Number of Rows value compared to the Actual Number of Rows value. In the properties shown in Figure 11-25, there are 1203.6 estimated rows, while the actual number is considerably higher at 4012. If you compare this to the same operator in the second query (the one without the local variable), you may notice something else. Take a look at Figure 11-26.

Clustered Index Seek (Clustered)
Scanning a particular range of rows from a clustered index.

Physical Operation	Clustered Index Seek
Logical Operation	Clustered Index Seek
Actual Number of Rows	4012
Estimated I/O Cost	0.0334954
Estimated CPU Cost	0.0045702
Estimated Number of Executions	1
Number of Executions	1
Estimated Operator Cost	0.0380656 (29%)
Estimated Subtree Cost	0.0380656
Estimated Number of Rows	4012
Estimated Row Size	11 B
Actual Rebinds	0
Actual Rewinds	0
Ordered	True
Node ID	1

Object
[AdventureWorks2008].[Purchasing].[PurchaseOrderHeader].
[PK_PurchaseOrderHeader_PurchaseOrderID] [poh]
Output List
[AdventureWorks2008].[Purchasing].
[PurchaseOrderHeader].PurchaseOrderID
Seek Predicates
Seek Keys[1]: Start: [AdventureWorks2008].[Purchasing].
[PurchaseOrderHeader].PurchaseOrderID >= Scalar Operator
((1))

Figure 11-26. *Clustered index seek details without a local variable*

Here you'll see that the Actual Number of Rows and Estimated Number of Rows values are the same, 4012. From these two measures, you can see that the estimated rows for the execution steps of the first query (using a local variable in the WHERE clause) is way off the actual number of rows returned by the steps. Consequently, the execution plan cost for the first query, which is based on the estimated rows, is somewhat misleading. The incorrect estimation misguides the optimizer and somewhat causes some variations in how the query is executed. You can see this in the return times on the query, even though the number of rows returned is identical.

Any time you find such an anomaly between the relative execution plan cost and the STATISTICS output for the queries under analysis, you should verify the basis of the estimation. If the underlying facts (estimated rows) of the execution plan itself are wrong, then it is quite likely that the cost represented in the execution plan will also be wrong. But since the output of the various STATISTICS measurements shows the actual number of logical reads and the real elapsed time required to perform the query without being affected by the initial estimation, you can rely on the STATISTICS output.

Now let's return to the actual performance issue associated with using local variables in the WHERE clause. As shown in the preceding example, using the local variable as the filter criterion in the WHERE clause of a batch query doesn't allow the optimizer to determine the right indexing strategy. This happens because, during the optimization of the queries in the batch, the optimizer doesn't know the value of the variable used in the WHERE clause and can't determine the right access strategy—it knows the value of the variable only during execution. You can further see this by noting that the second query in Figure 11-24 has a missing index alert, suggesting a possible way to improve the performance of the query, whereas the query with the local variable is unable to make that determination.

To avoid this performance problem, use one of the following approaches:

- Do not use a local variable as a filter criterion in a batch.
- Create a stored procedure for the batch, and execute it as follows (batch_sproc.sql):

```
CREATE PROCEDURE spProductDetails
(
@id INT
)
AS
SELECT  pod.*
FROM    Purchasing.PurchaseOrderDetail AS pod
        JOIN Purchasing.PurchaseOrderHeader AS poh
        ON poh.PurchaseOrderID = pod.PurchaseOrderID
WHERE   poh.PurchaseOrderID >= @id
GO
EXEC spProductDetails @id=1
```

The optimizer generates the same execution plan as the query that does not use a local variable for the ideal case. Correspondingly, the execution time is also reduced. In the case of a stored procedure, the optimizer generates the execution plan during the first execution of the stored procedure and uses the parameter value supplied to determine the right processing strategy.

Be Careful Naming Stored Procedures

The name of a stored procedure does matter. You should not name your procedures with a prefix of sp_. Developers often prefix their stored procedures with sp_ so that they can easily identify the stored procedures. However, SQL Server assumes that any stored procedure with this exact prefix is probably a system stored procedure, whose home is in the master database. When a stored procedure with an sp_ prefix is submitted for execution, SQL Server looks for the stored procedure in the following places in the following order:

- In the master database
- In the current database based on any qualifiers provided (database name or owner)
- In the current database using dbo as the schema, if a schema is not specified

Therefore, although the user-created stored procedure prefixed with sp_ exists in the current database, the master database is checked first. This happens even when the stored procedure is qualified with the database name.

To understand the effect of prefixing sp_ to a stored procedure name, consider the following stored procedure (sp_dont.sql in the download):

```
IF  EXISTS (SELECT * FROM sys.objects WHERE object_id =
OBJECT_ID(N'[dbo].[sp_Dont]') AND type in (N'P', N'PC'))
DROP PROCEDURE [dbo].[sp_Dont]
GO
CREATE PROC [sp_Dont]
AS
  PRINT 'Done!'
GO

EXEC AdventureWorks2008.dbo.[sp_Dont]; --Add plan of sp_p1 to procedure cache
GO
EXEC AdventureWorks2008.dbo.[sp_Dont]; --Use the above cached plan of sp_p1
GO
```

The first execution of the stored procedure adds the execution plan of the stored procedure to the procedure cache. A subsequent execution of the stored procedure reuses the existing plan from the procedure cache unless a recompilation of the plan is required (the causes of stored procedure recompilation are explained in Chapter 10). Therefore, the second execution of the stored procedure sp_Dont shown in Figure 11-27 should find a plan in the procedure cache. This is indicated by an SP:CacheHit event in the corresponding Profiler trace output.

EventClass	TextData	ApplicationName
SP:CacheMiss	EXEC AdventureWorks2008.dbo.[sp_Don...	Microsoft SQ...
SP:CacheMiss		Microsoft SQ...
SP:Completed	EXEC AdventureWorks2008.dbo.[sp_Don...	Microsoft SQ...
SP:CacheMiss	EXEC AdventureWorks2008.dbo.[sp_Don...	Microsoft SQ...
SP:CacheHit		Microsoft SQ...
SP:Completed	EXEC AdventureWorks2008.dbo.[sp_Don...	Microsoft SQ...

Figure 11-27. *Profiler trace output showing the effect of the sp_ prefix on a stored procedure name*

Note that an SP:CacheMiss event is fired before SQL Server tries to locate the plan for the stored procedure in the procedure cache. The SP:CacheMiss event is caused by SQL Server looking in the master database for the stored procedure, even though the execution of the stored procedure is properly qualified with the user database name.

This aspect of the sp_ prefix becomes more interesting when you create a stored procedure with the name of an existing system stored procedure (sp_addmessage.sql in the download):

```
CREATE PROC [sp_addmessage] @param1 NVARCHAR(25)
AS
    PRINT '@param1 = ' + @param1
GO

EXEC AdventureWorks2008.dbo.[sp_addmessage] 'AdventureWorks'
```

The execution of this user-defined stored procedure causes the execution of the system stored procedure sp_addmessage from the master database instead, as you can see in Figure 11-28.

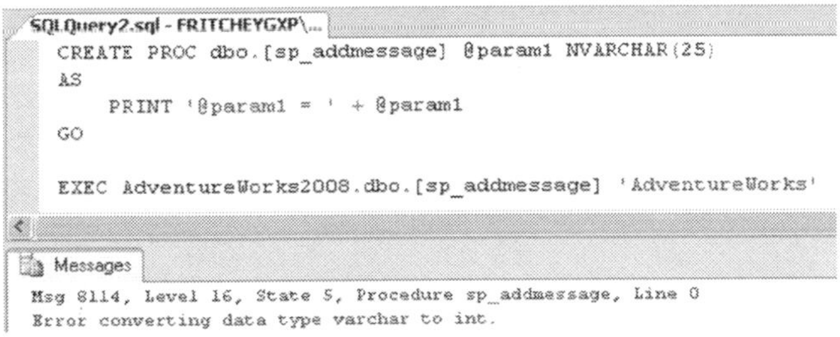

```
SQLQuery2.sql - FRITCHEYGXP\...
CREATE PROC dbo.[sp_addmessage] @param1 NVARCHAR(25)
AS
    PRINT '@param1 = ' + @param1
GO

EXEC AdventureWorks2008.dbo.[sp_addmessage] 'AdventureWorks'

Messages
Msg 8114, Level 16, State 5, Procedure sp_addmessage, Line 0
Error converting data type varchar to int.
```

Figure 11-28. *Execution result for stored procedure showing the effect of the sp_ prefix on a stored procedure name*

Unfortunately, it is not possible to execute this user-defined stored procedure.

Tip As a side note, please don't try to execute the DROP PROCEDURE statement on this stored procedure twice. On the second execution, the system stored procedure will be dropped from the master database.

You can see now why you should not prefix a user-defined stored procedure's name with sp_. Use some other naming convention.

Reducing the Number of Network Round-Trips

Database applications often execute multiple queries to implement a database operation. Besides optimizing the performance of the individual query, it is important that you optimize the performance of the batch. To reduce the overhead of multiple network round-trips, consider the following techniques:

- Execute multiple queries together.
- Use SET NOCOUNT.

Let's look at these techniques in a little more depth.

Execute Multiple Queries Together

It is preferable to submit all the queries of a set together as a batch or a stored procedure. Besides reducing the network round-trips between the database application and the server, stored procedures also provide multiple performance and administrative benefits, as described in Chapter 9. This means that the code in the application will need to be able to deal with multiple result sets. It also means your T-SQL code may need to deal with XML data or other large sets of data, not single-row inserts or updates.

Use SET NOCOUNT

You need to consider one more factor when executing a batch or a stored procedure. After every query in the batch or the stored procedure is executed, the server reports the number of rows affected:

```
(<Number> row(s) affected)
```

This information is returned to the database application and adds to the network overhead. Use the T-SQL statement SET NOCOUNT to avoid this overhead:

```
SET NOCOUNT ON
<SQL queries>
SET NOCOUNT OFF
```

Note that the SET NOCOUNT statement doesn't cause any recompilation issue with stored procedures, unlike some SET statements as explained in Chapter 10.

Reducing the Transaction Cost

Every action query in SQL Server is performed as an *atomic* action so that the state of a database table moves from one *consistent* state to another. SQL Server does this automatically, and it cannot be disabled. If the transition from one consistent state to another requires multiple database queries, then atomicity across the multiple queries should be maintained using explicitly defined database transactions. The old and new state of every atomic action is maintained in the transaction log (on the disk) to ensure *durability*, which guarantees that the outcome of an atomic action won't be lost once it completes successfully. An atomic action during its execution is *isolated* from other database actions using database locks.

Based on the characteristics of a transaction, here are two broad recommendations to reduce the cost of the transaction:

- Reduce logging overhead.
- Reduce lock overhead.

Reduce Logging Overhead

A database query may consist of multiple data manipulation queries. If atomicity is maintained for each query separately, then too many disk writes are performed on the transaction log disk to maintain the durability of each atomic action. Since disk activity is extremely slow compared to memory or CPU activity, the excessive disk activities increase the execution time of the database functionality. For example, consider the following batch query (`logging.sql` in the download):

```
--Create a test table
IF (SELECT  OBJECT_ID('t1')
   ) IS NOT NULL
    DROP TABLE t1;
GO
CREATE TABLE t1 (c1 TINYINT);
GO
--Insert 10000 rows
DECLARE @Count INT = 1;
WHILE @Count <= 10000
    BEGIN
        INSERT  INTO t1
        VALUES  (@Count % 256);
        SET @Count = @Count + 1;
    END
```

Since every execution of the `INSERT` statement is atomic in itself, SQL Server will write to the transaction log for every execution of the `INSERT` statement.

An easy way to reduce the number of log disk writes is to include the action queries within an explicit transaction:

```
--Insert 10000 rows
DECLARE @Count INT = 1;
BEGIN TRANSACTION
WHILE @Count <= 10000
    BEGIN
        INSERT  INTO t1
        VALUES  (@Count % 256);
        SET @Count = @Count + 1;
    END
COMMIT
```

The defined transaction scope (between the `BEGIN TRANSACTION` and `COMMIT` pair of commands) expands the scope of atomicity to the multiple `INSERT` statements included within the transaction. This decreases the number of log disk writes and improves the performance of the database functionality. To test this theory, run the following T-SQL command before and after each of the `WHILE` loops:

```
DBCC SQLPERF(LOGSPACE)
```

This will show you the percentage of log space used. On running the first set of inserts on my database, the log went from 2.6 percent used to 29 percent. When running the second set of inserts, the log grew about 6 percent.

The best way is to work with sets of data rather than individual rows. A WHILE loop can be an inherently costly operation, like a cursor (more details on cursors in Chapter 14). So, running a query that avoids the WHILE loop and instead works from a set-based approach will be even better:

```
SELECT TOP 10000
        IDENTITY( INT,1,1 ) AS n
INTO    #Tally
FROM    Master.dbo.SysColumns sc1
       ,Master.dbo.SysColumns sc2
BEGIN TRANSACTION
INSERT  INTO dbo.t1 (c1)
        SELECT (n % 256)
        FROM    #Tally ;
COMMIT TRANSACTION
DROP TABLE #Tally;
```

Running this query with the DBCC SQLPERF() function before and after showed less than 4 percent growth of the used space within the log, and it ran in 41 ms as compared to more than 2 seconds for the WHILE loop.

One area of caution, however, is that by including too many data manipulation queries within a transaction, the duration of the transaction is increased. During that time, all other queries trying to access the resources referred to in the transaction are blocked.

Reduce Lock Overhead

By default, all four SQL statements (SELECT, INSERT, UPDATE, and DELETE) use database locks to isolate their work from that of other SQL statements. This lock management adds a performance overhead to the query. The performance of a query can be improved by requesting fewer locks. By extension, the performance of other queries are also improved because they have to wait a shorter period of time to obtain their own locks.

By default, SQL Server can provide row-level lock. For a query working on a large number of rows, requesting a row lock on all the individual rows adds a significant overhead to the lock-management process. You can reduce this lock overhead by decreasing the lock granularity, say to the page level or table level. SQL Server performs the lock escalation dynamically by taking into consideration the lock overheads. Therefore, generally, it is not necessary to manually escalate the lock level. But, if required, you can control the concurrency of a query programmatically using lock hints as follows:

```
SELECT * FROM <TableName> WITH(PAGLOCK) --Use page level lock
```

Similarly, by default, SQL Server uses locks for SELECT statements besides those for INSERT, UPDATE, and DELETE statements. This allows the SELECT statements to read data that isn't being modified. In some cases, the data may be quite static, and it doesn't go through much modification. In such cases, you can reduce the lock overhead of the SELECT statements in one of the following ways:

- Mark the database as READ_ONLY:

  ```
  ALTER DATABASE <DatabaseName> SET READ_ONLY
  ```

  This allows users to retrieve data from the database, but it prevents them from modifying the data. The setting takes effect immediately. If occasional modifications to the database are required, then it may be temporarily converted to READ_WRITE mode:

  ```
  ALTER DATABASE <DatabaseName> SET READ_WRITE
  <Database modifications>
  ALTER DATABASE <DatabaseName> SET READ_ONLY
  ```

- Place the specific tables on a filegroup, and mark the filegroup as READONLY:

  ```
  --Add a new filegroup with a file to the database
  ALTER DATABASE AdventureWorks2008
    ADD FILEGROUP ReadOnlyFileGroup
  ALTER DATABASE AdventureWorks2008
    ADD FILE(NAME=ReadOnlyFile, FILENAME='C:\adw_1.ndf')
    TO FILEGROUP ReadOnlyFileGroup

  --Create specific table(s) on the new filegroup
  CREATE TABLE T1(C1 INT, C2 INT) ON ReadOnlyFileGroup
  CREATE CLUSTERED INDEX I1 ON T1(C1)
  INSERT INTO T1 VALUES(1, 1)
  --Or move existing table(s) to the new filegroup
  CREATE CLUSTERED INDEX I1 ON T1(C1)
    WITH DROP_EXISTING ON ReadOnlyFileGroup

  --Set the filegroup property to READONLY
  ALTER DATABASE AdventureWorks2008
    MODIFY FILEGROUP ReadOnlyFileGroup READONLY
  ```

  This allows you to limit the data access to only the tables residing on the specific filegroup to READONLY but keep the data access to tables on other filegroups as READWRITE. This filegroup setting takes effect immediately. If occasional modifications to the specific tables are required, then the property of the corresponding filegroup may be temporarily converted to READWRITE mode:

  ```
  ALTER DATABASE AdventureWorks2008
    MODIFY FILEGROUP ReadOnlyFileGroup READWRITE
  <Database modifications>
  ALTER DATABASE AdventureWorks2008
    MODIFY FILEGROUP ReadOnlyFileGroup READONLY
  ```

- Prevent SELECT statements from requesting any lock:

  ```
  SELECT * FROM <TableName> WITH(NOLOCK)
  ```

  This prevents the SELECT statement from requesting any lock, and it is applicable to SELECT statements only. Although the NOLOCK hint cannot be used directly on the tables referred to in the action queries (INSERT, UPDATE, and DELETE), it may be used on the data-retrieval part of the action queries, as shown here:

  ```
  DELETE Sales.SalesOrderDetail
  FROM Sales.SalesOrderDetail sod WITH(NOLOCK)
  JOIN Production.Product p WITH(NOLOCK)
   ON sod.ProductID = p.ProductID
   AND p.ProductID = 0
  ```

I discuss the different types of lock requests and how to manage lock overhead in the next chapter.

Summary

As discussed in this chapter, to improve the performance of a database application, it is important to ensure that SQL queries are designed properly to benefit from performance-enhancement techniques such as indexes, stored procedures, database constraints, and so on. Ensure that queries are resource friendly, and don't prevent the use of indexes. Even though, in many cases, the optimizer has the ability to generate cost-effective execution plans irrespective of query structure, it is still a good practice to design the queries properly in the first place.

Even after you design individual queries for great performance, the overall performance of a database application may not be satisfactory. It is important not only to improve the performance of individual queries but also to ensure that they work well with other queries without causing serious blocking issues. In the next chapter, you will look into the different blocking aspects of a database application.

CHAPTER 12

Blocking Analysis

You would ideally like your database application to scale linearly with the number of database users and the volume of data. However, it is common to find that performance degrades as the number of users increases and as the volume of data grows. One cause for degradation is blocking. In fact, database blocking is usually the biggest enemy of scalability for database applications.

In this chapter, I cover the following topics:

- The fundamentals of blocking in SQL Server
- The ACID properties of a transactional database
- Database lock granularity, escalation, modes, and compatibility
- ANSI isolation levels
- The effect of indexes on locking
- The information necessary to analyze blocking
- A SQL script to collect blocking information
- Resolutions and recommendations to avoid blocking
- Techniques to automate the blocking detection and information collection processes

Blocking Fundamentals

In an ideal world, every SQL query would be able to execute concurrently, without any blocking by other queries. However, in the real world, queries *do* block each other, similar to the way a car crossing through a green traffic signal at an intersection blocks other cars waiting to cross the intersection. In SQL Server, this traffic management takes the form of the *lock manager*, which controls concurrent access to a database resource to maintain data consistency. The concurrent access to a database resource is controlled across multiple database connections.

I want to make sure things are clear before moving on. Three terms are used within databases that sound the same and are interrelated but have different meanings. These are frequently confused, and people often use the terms incorrectly. These terms are *locking*, *blocking*, and *deadlocking*. Locking is an integral part of the process of SQL Server managing multiple connections. When a connection needs access to a piece of data, a lock of some type is placed on it. This is different from blocking, which is when one connection needs access to a piece of data and has to wait for another connection's lock to clear. Finally, deadlocking is when two connections form what is sometimes referred to as a *deadly embrace*. They are each waiting on the other for a lock to clear. Deadlocking could also be referred to as a permanent blocking situation. Deadlocking will be covered in more detail in Chapter 13. Please understand the differences between these terms and use them correctly. It will help in your understanding of the system, your ability to troubleshoot, and your ability to communicate with other database administrators and developers.

In SQL Server, a database connection is identified by a session ID (SPID). Connections may be from one or many applications and one or many users on those applications; as far as SQL Server is concerned, every connection is treated as a separate session. Blocking between two sessions accessing the same piece of data at the same time is a natural phenomenon in SQL Server. Whenever two sessions try to access a common database resource in conflicting ways, the lock manager ensures that the second session waits until the first session completes its work. For example, a session might be modifying a table record while another session tries to delete the record. Since these two data access requests are incompatible, the second session will be blocked until the first session completes its task.

On the other hand, if the two sessions try to read a table concurrently, both sessions are allowed to execute without blocking, since these data accesses are compatible with each other.

Usually, the effect of blocking on a session is quite small and doesn't affect its performance noticeably. At times, however, because of poor query and/or transaction design (or maybe bad luck), blocking can affect query performance significantly. In a database application, every effort should be made to minimize blocking and thereby increase the number of concurrent users that can use the database.

Understanding Blocking

In SQL Server, a database query can execute as a logical unit of work in itself, or it can participate in a bigger logical unit of work. A bigger logical unit of work can be defined using the `BEGIN TRANSACTION` statement along with `COMMIT` and/or `ROLLBACK` statements. Every logical unit of work must conform to a set of four properties called *ACID* properties:

- Atomicity
- Consistency
- Isolation
- Durability

I cover these properties in the sections that follow, because understanding how transactions work is fundamental to understanding blocking.

Atomicity

A logical unit of work must be *atomic*. That is, either all the actions of the logical unit of work are completed or no effect is retained. To understand the atomicity of a logical unit of work, consider the following example (atomicity.sql in the download):

```
--Create a test table
IF (SELECT  OBJECT_ID('dbo.t1')
   ) IS NOT NULL
    DROP TABLE dbo.t1
GO
CREATE TABLE dbo.t1
    (
     c1 INT CONSTRAINT chk_c1 CHECK (c1 = 1)
    )
GO

--All ProductIDs are added into t1 as a logical unit of work
INSERT  INTO dbo.t1
        SELECT  p.ProductID
        FROM    Production.Product AS p
GO
SELECT  *
FROM    dbo.t1 --Returns 0 rows
```

SQL Server treats the preceding INSERT statement as a logical unit of work. The CHECK constraint on column c1 of table dbo.t1 allows only the value 1. Although the ProductID column in the Production.Product table starts with the value 1, it also contains other values. For this reason, the INSERT statement won't add any records at all to the table dbo.t1, and an error is raised because of the CHECK constraint. This atomicity is automatically ensured by SQL Server.

So far, so good. But in the case of a bigger logical unit of work, you should be aware of an interesting behavior of SQL Server. Imagine that the previous insert task consists of multiple INSERT statements. These can be combined to form a bigger logical unit of work as follows (logical.sql in the download):

```
BEGIN TRAN --Start: Logical unit of work
  --First:
  INSERT INTO dbo.t1
    SELECT p.ProductID FROM Production.Product AS p
  --Second:
  INSERT INTO dbo.t1 VALUES(1)
COMMIT --End: Logical unit of work
GO
```

With table dbo.t1 already created in atomicity.sql, the BEGIN TRAN and COMMIT pair of statements defines a logical unit of work, suggesting that all the statements within the transaction should be atomic in nature. However, the default behavior of SQL Server doesn't ensure that the failure of one of the statements within a user-defined transaction scope will undo the effect of the prior statement(s). In the preceding transaction, the first INSERT statement will fail as explained earlier, whereas the second INSERT is perfectly fine. The default behavior of SQL Server allows the second INSERT statement to execute, even though the first INSERT statement fails. A SELECT statement, as shown in the following code, will return the row inserted by the second INSERT statement:

```
SELECT * FROM dbo.t1 --Returns a row with t1.c1 = 1
```

The atomicity of a user-defined transaction can be ensured in the following two ways:

- SET XACT_ABORT ON
- Explicit rollback

Let's look at these quickly.

SET XACT_ABORT ON

You can modify the atomicity of the INSERT task in the preceding section using the SET XACT_ABORT ON statement:

```
SET XACT_ABORT ON
GO
BEGIN TRAN --Start: Logical unit of work
  --First:
  INSERT INTO dbo.t1 SELECT p.ProductID FROM Production.Product AS p
  --Second:
  INSERT INTO dbo.t1 VALUES(1)
COMMIT --End: Logical unit of work
GO
SET XACT_ABORT OFF
GO
```

The SET XACT_ABORT statement specifies whether SQL Server should automatically roll back and abort an entire transaction when a statement within the transaction fails. The failure of the first INSERT statement will automatically suspend the entire transaction, and thus the second INSERT statement will not be executed. The effect of SET XACT_ABORT is at the connection level, and it remains applicable until it is reconfigured or the connection is closed. By default, SET XACT_ABORT is OFF.

Explicit Rollback

You can also manage the atomicity of a user-defined transaction by using the TRY/CATCH error-trapping mechanism within SQL Server. If a statement within the TRY block of code generates an error, then the CATCH block of code will handle the error. If an error occurs and the CATCH block is activated, then the entire work of a user-defined transaction can be rolled back, and further statements can be prevented from execution, as follows (rollback.sql in the download):

```
BEGIN TRY
    BEGIN TRAN --Start: Logical unit of work
  --First:
    INSERT  INTO dbo.t1
            SELECT  p.ProductID
            FROM    Production.Product AS p
```

```
  --Second:
    INSERT  INTO dbo.t1
    VALUES  (1)
    COMMIT --End: Logical unit of work
END TRY
BEGIN CATCH
    ROLLBACK
    PRINT 'An error occurred'
    RETURN
END CATCH
```

The ROLLBACK statement rolls back all the actions performed in the transaction until that point. For a detailed description of how to implement error handling in SQL Server–based applications, please refer to the MSDN Library article titled "Using TRY...CATCH in Transact SQL" (http://msdn.microsoft.com/en-us/library/ms179296.aspx) or to the introductory article "SQL Server Error Handling Workbench" (http://www.simple-talk.com/sql/t-sql-programming/sql-server-error-handling-workbench/).

Since the atomicity property requires that either all the actions of a logical unit of work are completed or no effects are retained, SQL Server *isolates* the work of a transaction from that of others by granting it exclusive rights on the affected resources so that the transaction can safely roll back the effect of all its actions, if required. The exclusive rights granted to a transaction on the affected resources block all other transactions (or database requests) trying to access those resources during that time period. Therefore, although atomicity is required to maintain the integrity of data, it introduces the undesirable side effect of blocking.

Consistency

A logical unit of work should cause the state of the database to travel from one *consistent* state to another. At the end of a transaction, the state of the database should be fully consistent. SQL Server always ensures that the internal state of the databases is correct and valid by automatically applying all the constraints of the affected database resources as part of the transaction. SQL Server ensures that the state of internal structures, such as data and index layout, are correct after the transaction. For instance, when the data of a table is modified, SQL Server automatically identifies all the indexes, constraints, and other dependent objects on the table and applies the necessary modifications to all the dependent database objects as part of the transaction.

The logical consistency of the data required by the business rules should be ensured by a database developer. A business rule may require changes to be applied on multiple tables. The database developer should accordingly define a logical unit of work to ensure that all the criteria of the business rules are taken care of. SQL Server provides different transaction management features that the database developer can use to ensure the logical consistency of the data.

As just explained, maintaining a consistent logical state requires the use of transactions to define the logical unit of work as per the business rules. Also, to maintain a consistent physical state, SQL Server identifies and works on the dependent database objects as part of the logical unit of work. The atomicity characteristic of the logical unit of work blocks all other transactions (or database requests) trying to access the affected object(s) during that time period. Therefore, even though consistency is required to maintain a valid logical and physical state of the database, it also introduces the undesirable side effect of blocking.

Isolation

In a multiuser environment, more than one transaction can be executed simultaneously. These concurrent transactions should be isolated from one another so that the intermediate changes made by one transaction don't affect the data consistency of other transactions. The degree of *isolation* required by a transaction can vary. SQL Server provides different transaction isolation features to implement the degree of isolation required by a transaction.

Note Transaction isolation levels are explained later in the chapter in the "Isolation Levels" section.

The isolation requirements of a transaction operating on a database resource can block other transactions trying to access the resource. In a multiuser database environment, multiple transactions are usually executed simultaneously. It is imperative that the data modifications made by an ongoing transaction be protected from the modifications made by other transactions. For instance, suppose a transaction is in the middle of modifying a few rows in a table. During that period, to maintain database consistency, you must ensure that other transactions do not modify or delete the same rows. SQL Server logically isolates the activities of a transaction from that of others by blocking them appropriately, which allows multiple transactions to execute simultaneously without corrupting one another's work.

Excessive blocking caused by isolation can adversely affect the scalability of a database application. A transaction may inadvertently block other transactions for a long period of time, thereby hurting database concurrency. Since SQL Server manages isolation using locks, it is important to understand the locking architecture of SQL Server. This helps you analyze a blocking scenario and implement resolutions.

Note The fundamentals of database locks are explained later in the chapter in the "Capturing Blocking Information" section.

Durability

Once a transaction is completed, the changes made by the transaction should be *durable.* Even if the electrical power to the machine is tripped off immediately after the transaction is completed, the effect of all actions within the transaction should be retained. SQL Server ensures durability by keeping track of all pre- and post-images of the data under modification in a transaction log as the changes are made. Immediately after the completion of a transaction, even if SQL Server, the operating system, or the hardware fails (excluding the log disk), SQL Server ensures that all the changes made by the transaction are retained. During restart, SQL Server runs its database recovery feature, which identifies the pending changes from the transaction log for completed transactions and applies them on the database resources. This database feature is called *roll forward.*

The recovery interval period depends on the number of pending changes that need to be applied to the database resources during restart. To reduce the recovery interval period, SQL Server intermittently applies the intermediate changes made by the running transactions as configured by the recovery interval option. The recovery interval option can be configured using the `sp_configure` statement. The process of intermittently applying the intermediate changes is referred to as the *checkpoint* process. During restart, the recovery process identifies all uncommitted changes and removes them from the database resources by using the pre-images of the data from the transaction log.

The durability property isn't a direct cause of blocking since it doesn't require the actions of a transaction to be isolated from those of others. But in an indirect way, it increases the duration of the blocking. Since the durability property requires saving the pre- and post-images of the data under modification to the transaction log on disk, it increases the duration of the transaction and blocking.

■ **Note** Out of the four ACID properties, the isolation property, which is also used to ensure atomicity and consistency, is the main cause of blocking in a SQL Server database. In SQL Server, isolation is implemented using database locks, as explained in the following section.

Database Locks

When a session executes a query, SQL Server determines the database resources that need to be accessed, and if required, the lock manager grants database locks to the session. The query is blocked if another session has already been granted the locks; however, to provide both transaction isolation and concurrency, SQL Server uses different lock granularities and modes, as explained in the sections that follow.

Lock Granularity

SQL Server databases are maintained as files on the physical disk. In the case of a nondatabase file such as an Excel file, the file may be written to by only one user at a time. Any attempt to write to the file by other users fails. However, unlike the limited concurrency on a nondatabase file, SQL Server allows multiple users to modify (or access) contents simultaneously, as long as they don't affect one another's data consistency. This decreases blocking and improves concurrency among the transactions.

To improve concurrency, SQL Server implements lock granularities at the following resource levels:

- Row (`RID`)
- Key (`KEY`)
- Page (`PAG`)
- Extent (`EXT`)

- Heap or B-tree (HoBT)
- Table (TAB)
- Database (DB)

Let's take a look at these lock levels in more detail.

Row-Level Lock

This lock is maintained on a single row within a table and is the lowest level of lock on a database table. When a query modifies a row in a table, an RID lock is granted to the query on the row. For example, consider the transaction on the following test table (rowlock.sql):

```
--Create a test table
IF(SELECT OBJECT_ID('dbo.t1')) IS NOT NULL
  DROP TABLE dbo.t1
GO
CREATE TABLE dbo.t1 (c1 INT)
INSERT INTO dbo.t1 VALUES(1)
GO

BEGIN TRAN
  DELETE dbo.t1 WHERE c1 = 1
  SELECT tl.request_session_id
    ,tl.resource_database_id
    ,tl.resource_associated_entity_id
    ,tl.resource_type
    ,tl.resource_description
    ,tl.request_mode
    ,tl.request_status
  FROM sys.dm_tran_locks tl
ROLLBACK
```

The dynamic management view sys.dm_tran_locks can be used to display the lock status. The query against sys.dm_tran_locks in Figure 12-1 shows that the DELETE statement acquired an RID lock on the row to be deleted.

	request_session_id	resource_database_id	resource_associated_entity_id	resource_type	resource_description	request_mode	request_status
1	52	14	0	DATABASE		S	GRANT
2	52	14	72057594061062144	RID	1:984:0	X	GRANT
3	52	14	72057594061062144	PAGE	1:984	IX	GRANT
4	52	14	823673982	OBJECT		IX	GRANT

Figure 12-1. *sys.dm_tran_locks output showing the row-level lock granted to the DELETE statement*

■ **Note** I explain lock modes later in the chapter in the "Lock Modes" section.

Granting an RID lock to the DELETE statement prevents other transactions from accessing the row.

The resource locked by the RID lock can be represented in the following format from the resource_description column:

```
DatabaseID:FileID:PageID:Slot(row)
```

In the output from the query against sys.dm_tran_locks in Figure 12-1, the DatabaseID is displayed separately under the resource_database_id column. The resource_description column value for the RID type represents the remaining part of the RID resource as 1:984:0. In this case, a FileID of 1 is the primary data file, a PageID of 984 is a page belonging to table dbo.t1 identified by the ObjId column, and a slot (row) of 0 represents the row position within the page. You can obtain the table name and the database name by executing the following SQL statements:

```
SELECT OBJECT_NAME(72057594061127680)
SELECT DB_NAME(14)
```

The row-level lock provides a very high concurrency, since blocking is restricted to the row under effect.

Key-Level Lock

This is a row lock within an index, and it is identified as a KEY lock. As you know, for a table with a clustered index, the data pages of the table and the leaf pages of the clustered index are the same. Since both the rows are the same for a table with a clustered index, only a KEY lock is acquired on the clustered index row, or limited range of rows, while accessing the row(s) from the table (or the clustered index). For example, consider having a clustered index on the table t1 (keylock.sql):

```
CREATE CLUSTERED INDEX i1 ON dbo.t1(c1)
```

If you now rerun the following:

```
BEGIN TRAN
  DELETE dbo.t1 WHERE c1 = 1
  SELECT tl.request_session_id
    ,tl.resource_database_id
    ,tl.resource_associated_entity_id
    ,tl.resource_type
    ,tl.resource_description
    ,tl.request_mode
    ,tl.request_status
  FROM sys.dm_tran_locks tl
ROLLBACK
```

the corresponding output from sys.dm_tran_locks shows a KEY lock instead of the RID lock, as you can see in Figure 12-2.

	request_session_id	resource_database_id	resource_associated_entity_id	resource_type	resource_description	request_mode	request_status
1	52	14	0	DATABASE		S	GRANT
2	55	14	0	DATABASE		S	GRANT
3	55	14	72057594061258752	PAGE	1:986	IX	GRANT
4	55	14	855674096	OBJECT		IX	GRANT
5	55	14	72057594061258752	KEY	(0200c411ba73)	X	GRANT

Figure 12-2. *`sys.dm_tran_locks` output showing the key-level lock granted to the `DELETE` statement*

When you are querying `sys.dm_tran_locks`, you will be able to retrieve the database identifier, `resource_database_id`, and the object, `resource_associated_entity_id`, but to get to the particular resource (in this case, the page on the key), you have to go to the `resource_description` column for the value, which is (0200c411ba73). In this case, the `IndId` of 1 is the clustered index on table `dbo.t1`.

■ **Note** Different values for the `IndId` column and how to determine the corresponding index name are explained later in the "Effect of Indexes on Locking" section.

Like the row-level lock, the key-level lock provides a very high concurrency.

Page-Level Lock

This is maintained on a single page within a table or an index and is identified as a `PAG` lock. When a query requests multiple rows within a page, the consistency of all the requested rows can be maintained by acquiring either `RID`/`KEY` locks on the individual rows or a `PAG` lock on the entire page. From the query plan, the lock manager determines the resource pressure of acquiring multiple `RID`/`KEY` locks, and if the pressure is found to be high, the lock manager requests a `PAG` lock instead.

The resource locked by the `PAG` lock may be represented in the following format in the `resource_description` column of `sys.dm_tran_locks`:

```
DatabaseID:FileID:PageID
```

The page-level lock increases the performance of an individual query by reducing its locking overhead, but it hurts the concurrency of the database by blocking access to all the rows in the page.

Extent-Level Lock

This is maintained on an extent (a group of eight contiguous data or index pages) and is identified as an `EXT` lock. This lock is used, for example, when an `ALTER INDEX REBUILD` command is executed on a table and the pages of the table may be moved from an existing extent to a new extent. During this period, the integrity of the extents is protected using `EXT` locks.

Heap or B-tree Lock

A heap or B-tree lock is used to describe when a lock to either object could be made. This means a lock on an unordered heap table, a table without a clustered index, or a lock on a B-tree object, usually referring to partitions. A setting within the `ALTER TABLE` function, new to SQL Server 2008, allows you to exercise a level of control over how locking escalation (covered in the "Lock Escalation" section) is affected with the partitions. Because partitions are stored across multiple filegroups, each one has to have its own data allocation definition. This is where the HoBT comes into play. It acts like a table-level lock but on a partition instead of on the table itself.

Table-Level Lock

This is the highest level of lock on a table, and it is identified as a `TAB` lock. A table-level lock on a table reserves access to the complete table and all its indexes.

When a query is executed, the lock manager automatically determines the locking overhead of acquiring multiple locks at the lower levels. If the resource pressure of acquiring locks at the row level or the page level is determined to be high, then the lock manager directly acquires a table-level lock for the query.

The resource locked by the `TAB` lock will be represented in `resource_description` in the following format:

```
DatabaseID:ObjectID
```

A table-level lock requires the least overhead compared to the other locks and thus improves the performance of the individual query. On the other hand, since the table-level lock blocks all write requests on the entire table (including indexes), it can significantly hurt database concurrency.

Sometimes an application feature may benefit from using a specific lock level for a table referred to in a query. For instance, if an administrative query is executed during nonpeak hours, then a table-level lock may not affect concurrency much, but it can reduce the locking overhead of the query and thereby improve its performance. In such cases, a query developer may override the lock manager's lock level selection for a table referred to in the query using locking hints:

```
SELECT * FROM <TableName> WITH(TABLOCK)
```

Database-Level Lock

This is maintained on a database and is identified as a `DB` lock. When an application makes a database connection, the lock manager assigns a database-level shared lock to the corresponding SPID. This prevents a user from accidentally dropping or restoring the database while other users are connected to it.

SQL Server ensures that the locks requested at one level respect the locks granted at other levels. For instance, while a user acquires a row-level lock on a table row, another user can't acquire a lock at any other level that may affect the integrity of the row. The second user may acquire a row-level lock on other rows or a page-level lock on other pages, but an incompatible page- or table-level lock containing the row won't be granted to other users.

The level at which locks should be applied need not be specified by a user or database administrator; the lock manager determines that automatically. It generally prefers row-level and key-level locks while accessing a small number of rows to aid concurrency. However, if the locking overhead of multiple low-level locks turns out to be very high, the lock manager automatically selects an appropriate higher-level lock.

Lock Escalation

When a query is executed, SQL Server determines the required lock level for the database objects referred to in the query and starts executing the query after acquiring the required locks. During the query execution, the lock manager keeps track of the number of locks requested by the query to determine the need to escalate the lock level from the current level to a higher level.

The lock escalation threshold is dynamically determined by SQL Server during the course of a transaction. Row locks and page locks are automatically escalated to a table lock when a transaction exceeds its threshold. After the lock level is escalated to a table-level lock, all the lower-level locks on the table are automatically released. This dynamic lock escalation feature of the lock manager optimizes the locking overhead of a query.

It is possible to establish a level of control over the locking mechanisms on a given table. This is the T-SQL syntax to change this:

```
ALTER TABLE schema.table
SET (LOCK_ESCALATION = DISABLE)
```

This syntax will disable lock escalation on the table entirely (except for a few special circumstances). You can also set it to `TABLE`, which will cause the escalation to go to a table lock every single time. You can also set lock escalation on the table to `AUTO`, which will allow SQL Server to make the determination for the locking schema and any escalation necessary.

Lock Modes

The degree of isolation required by different transactions may vary. For instance, consistency of data is not affected if two transactions read the data simultaneously, but the consistency is affected if two transactions are allowed to modify the data simultaneously. Depending on the type of access requested, SQL Server uses different lock modes while locking resources:

- Shared (`S`)
- Update (`U`)
- Exclusive (`X`)
- Intent:
  - Intent Shared (`IS`)
  - Intent Exclusive (`IX`)
  - Shared with Intent Exclusive (`SIX`)

- Schema:
    - Schema Modification (Sch-M)
    - Schema Stability (Sch-S)
- Bulk Update (BU)
- Key-Range

Shared (S) Mode

Shared mode is used for read-only queries, such as a SELECT statement. It doesn't prevent other read-only queries from accessing the data simultaneously, since the integrity of the data isn't compromised by the concurrent reads. But the concurrent data modification queries on the data are prevented to maintain data integrity. The (S) lock is held on the data until the data is read. By default, the (S) lock acquired by a SELECT statement is released immediately after the data is read. For example, consider the following transaction:

```
BEGIN TRAN
SELECT  *
FROM    Production.Product AS p
WHERE   p.ProductID = 1
  --Other queries
COMMIT
```

The (S) lock acquired by the SELECT statement is not held until the end of the transaction. The (S) lock is released immediately after the data is read by the SELECT statement under read_committed, the default isolation level. This behavior of the (S) lock can be altered using a higher isolation level or a lock hint.

Update (U) Mode

Update mode may be considered similar to the (S) lock but with an objective to modify the data as part of the same query. Unlike the (S) lock, the (U) lock indicates that the data is read for modification. Since the data is read with an objective to modify it, more than one (U) lock is not allowed on the data simultaneously in order to maintain data integrity, but concurrent (S) locks on the data are allowed. The (U) lock is associated with an UPDATE statement.

The action of an UPDATE statement actually involves two intermediate steps:

1. Read the data to be modified.
2. Modify the data.

Different lock modes are used in the two intermediate steps to maximize concurrency. Instead of acquiring an exclusive right while reading the data, the first step acquires a (U) lock on the data. In the second step, the (U) lock is converted to an exclusive lock for modification. If no modification is required, then the (U) lock is released; in other words, it's not held until the end of the transaction. Consider the following example, which demonstrates the locking behavior of the UPDATE statement (create_t1.sql in the download):

```
--Create a test table
IF (SELECT  OBJECT_ID('dbo.t1')
   ) IS NOT NULL
    DROP TABLE dbo.t1;
GO
CREATE TABLE dbo.t1 (c1 INT, c2 DATETIME);
INSERT  INTO dbo.t1
VALUES  (1, GETDATE());
GO
```

Consider the following UPDATE statement (update1.sql in the download):

```
BEGIN TRANSACTION Tx1
    UPDATE  dbo.t1
    SET     c2 = GETDATE()
    WHERE   c1 = 1;
COMMIT
```

To understand the locking behavior of the intermediate steps of the UPDATE statement, you need to obtain data from sys.dm_tran_locks at the end of each step. You can obtain the lock status after each step of the UPDATE statement by following the steps outlined next. You're going have three connections open that I'll refer to as Connection 1, Connection 2, and Connection 3. This means three different query windows in Management Studio. You'll run the queries in the connections I list in the order that I specify to arrive at a blocking situation and be able to observe those blocks as they occur. The initial query listed previously is in Connection 1.

1. Block the second step of the UPDATE statement by first executing a transaction from a second connection (update2.sql in the download), Connection 2:

   ```
   --Execute from second connection
   BEGIN TRANSACTION Tx2
     --Retain an (S) lock on the resource
       SELECT  *
       FROM    t1 WITH (REPEATABLEREAD)
       WHERE   c1 = 1;
         --Allow sp_lock to be executed before second step of
         -- UPDATE statement is executed by transaction Tx1
       WAITFOR DELAY '00:00:10';
   COMMIT
   ```

   The REPEATABLEREAD locking hint, running in Connection 2, allows the SELECT statement to retain the (S) lock on the resource.

2. While the transaction Tx2 is executing, execute the UPDATE transaction (update1.sql) from the first connection (repeated here for clarity), Connection 1:

   ```
   BEGIN TRANSACTION Tx1
       UPDATE  dbo.t1
       SET     c2 = GETDATE()
       WHERE   c1 = 1;
   COMMIT
   ```

3. While the UPDATE statement is blocked, query the sys.dm_tran_locks DMV from a third connection, Connection 3, as follows:

```
SELECT tl.request_session_id
  ,tl.resource_database_id
  ,tl.resource_associated_entity_id
  ,tl.resource_type
  ,tl.resource_description
  ,tl.request_mode
  ,tl.request_status
FROM sys.dm_tran_locks tl;
```

The output from sys.dm_tran_locks, in Connection 3, will provide the lock status after the first step of the UPDATE statement since the lock conversion to an exclusive (X) lock by the UPDATE statement is blocked by the SELECT statement.

4. The lock status after the second step of the UPDATE statement will be provided by the query against sys.dm_tran_locks in the UPDATE transaction in Connection 3.

The lock status provided from sys.dm_tran_locks after the individual steps of the UPDATE statement is as follows:

- Figure 12-3 shows the lock status after step 1 of the UPDATE statement (obtained from the output from sys.dm_tran_locks executed on the third connection, Connection 3, as explained previously).

	request_session_id	resource_database_id	resource_associated_entity_id	resource_type	resource_description	request_mode	request_status
1	56	1	72057594041270272	PAGE	1:192	IS	GRANT
2	55	1	72057594041270272	PAGE	1:192	IX	GRANT
3	56	1	72057594041270272	RID	1:192:0	S	GRANT
4	55	1	72057594041270272	RID	1:192:0	U	GRANT
5	55	1	72057594041270272	RID	1:192:0	X	CONVERT
6	56	1	1595152728	OBJECT		IS	GRANT
7	56	1	1611152785	OBJECT		IS	GRANT
8	55	1	1611152785	OBJECT		IX	GRANT

Figure 12-3. *sys.dm_tran_locks output showing the lock conversion state of an UPDATE statement*

■ **Note** The order of these rows is not that important.

- Figure 12-4 shows the lock status after step 2 of the UPDATE statement.

	request_session_id	resource_database_id	resource_associated_entity_id	resource_type	resource_description	request_mode	request_status
1	55	1	72057594041270272	PAGE	1:192	IX	GRANT
2	55	1	72057594041270272	RID	1:192:0	X	GRANT
3	55	1	1611152785	OBJECT		IX	GRANT

Figure 12-4. *sys.dm_tran_locks output showing the final lock status held by the UPDATE statement*

From the sys.dm_tran_locks output after the first step of the UPDATE statement, you can note the following:

- A (U) lock is granted to the SPID on the data row.
- A conversion to an (X) lock on the data row is requested.

From the output of sys.dm_tran_locks after the second step of the UPDATE statement, you can see that the UPDATE statement holds only an (X) lock on the data row. Essentially, the (U) lock on the data row is converted to an (X) lock.

By not acquiring an exclusive lock at the first step, an UPDATE statement allows other transactions to read the data using the SELECT statement during that period, since (U) and (S) locks are compatible with each other. This increases database concurrency.

Note I discuss lock compatibility among different lock modes later in this chapter.

You may be curious to learn why a (U) lock is used instead of an (S) lock in the first step of the UPDATE statement. To understand the drawback of using an (S) lock instead of a (U) lock in the first step of the UPDATE statement, let's break the UPDATE statement into the following two steps:

1. Read the data to be modified using an (S) lock instead of a (U) lock.
2. Modify the data by acquiring an (X) lock.

Consider the following code (split_update.sql in the download):

```
BEGIN TRAN
  --1. Read data to be modified using (S)lock instead of (U)lock.
  --   Retain the (S)lock using REPEATABLEREAD locking hint,
  --   since the original (U)lock is retained until the conversion
  --   to (X)lock.
    SELECT  *
    FROM    t1 WITH (REPEATABLEREAD)
    WHERE   c1 = 1;

  --Allow another equivalent update action to start concurrently
    WAITFOR DELAY '00:00:10';

  --2. Modify the data by acquiring (X)lock
    UPDATE  t1 WITH (XLOCK)
    SET     c2 = GETDATE()
    WHERE   c1 = 1;
COMMIT
```

If this transaction is executed from two connections simultaneously, then it causes a deadlock as follows:

```
Msg 1205, Level 13, State 45, Line 14
Transaction (Process ID 57) was deadlocked on lock resources with another process
and has been chosen as the deadlock victim. Rerun the transaction.
```

Both transactions read the data to be modified using an (S) lock and then request an (X) lock for modification. When the first transaction attempts the conversion to the (X) lock, it is blocked by the (S) lock held by the second transaction. Similarly, when the second transaction attempts the conversion from (S) to (X), lock, it is blocked by the (S) lock held by the first transaction, which in turn is blocked by the second transaction. This causes a circular block and therefore a deadlock.

To avoid this typical deadlock, the UPDATE statement uses a (U) lock instead of an (S) lock at its first intermediate step. Unlike an (S) lock, a (U) lock doesn't allow another (U) lock on the same resource simultaneously. This forces the second concurrent UPDATE statement to wait until the first UPDATE statement completes.

Exclusive (X) Mode

Exclusive lock mode provides an exclusive right on a database resource for modification by data manipulation queries such as INSERT, UPDATE, and DELETE. It prevents other concurrent transactions from accessing the resource under modification. Both the INSERT and DELETE statements acquire (X) locks at the very beginning of their execution. As explained earlier, the UPDATE statement converts to the (X) lock after the data to be modified is read. The (X) locks granted in a transaction are held until the end of the transaction.

The (X) lock serves two purposes:

- It prevents other transactions from accessing the resource under modification so that they see a value either before or after the modification, not a value undergoing modification.
- It allows the transaction modifying the resource to safely roll back to the original value before modification, if needed, since no other transaction is allowed to modify the resource simultaneously.

Intent Shared (IS), Intent Exclusive (IX), and Shared with Intent Exclusive (SIX) Modes

Intent Shared, Intent Exclusive, and Shared with Intent Exclusive intent locks indicate that the query intends to grab a corresponding (S) or (X) lock at a lower lock level. For example, consider the following transaction on the test table (isix.sql in the download):

```
IF (SELECT  OBJECT_ID('t1')
   ) IS NOT NULL
    DROP TABLE t1
GO
CREATE TABLE t1 (c1 INT)
INSERT  INTO t1
VALUES  (1)
GO
```

```
BEGIN TRAN
    DELETE  t1
    WHERE   c1 = 1
     --Delete a row
    SELECT  tl.request_session_id
           ,tl.resource_database_id
           ,tl.resource_associated_entity_id
           ,tl.resource_type
           ,tl.resource_description
           ,tl.request_mode
           ,tl.request_status
    FROM    sys.dm_tran_locks tl ;
ROLLBACK
```

Figure 12-5 shows the output from sys.dm_tran_locks.

	request_session_id	resource_database_id	resource_associated_entity_id	resource_type	resource_description	request_mode	request_status
1	58	1	72057594041335808	PAGE	1:192	IX	GRANT
2	58	1	72057594041335808	RID	1:192:0	X	GRANT
3	58	1	1627152842	OBJECT		IX	GRANT

Figure 12-5. *sys.dm_tran_locks output showing the intent locks granted at higher levels*

The (IX) lock at the table level (TAB) indicates that the DELETE statement intends to acquire an (X) lock at a page level, row level, or key level. Similarly, the (IX) lock at the page level (PAG) indicates that the query intends to acquire an (X) lock on a row in the page. The (IX) locks at the higher levels prevent another transaction from acquiring an incompatible lock on the table or on the page containing the row.

Flagging the intent lock—(IS) or (IX)—at a corresponding higher level by a transaction, while holding the lock at a lower level, prevents other transactions from acquiring an incompatible lock at the higher level. If the intent locks were not used, then a transaction trying to acquire a lock at a higher level would have to scan through the lower levels to detect the presence of lower-level locks. While the intent lock at the higher levels indicates the presence of a lower-level lock, the locking overhead of acquiring a lock at a higher level is optimized. The intent locks granted to a transaction are held until the end of the transaction.

Only a single (SIX) can be placed on a given resource at once. This prevents updates made by other transactions. Other transactions can place (IS) locks on the lower-level resources while the (SIX) lock is in place.

Furthermore, there can be combination of locks requested (or acquired) at a certain level and the intention of having lock(s) at a lower level. There can be (SIU) and (UIX) lock combinations indicating that an (S) or a (U) lock is acquired at the corresponding level and (U) or (X) lock(s) are intended at a lower level.

Schema Modification (Sch-M) and Schema Stability (Sch-S) Modes

Schema Modification and Schema Stability locks are acquired on a table by SQL statements that depend on the schema of the table. A DDL statement, working on the schema of a table, acquires an (Sch-M) lock on the table and prevents other transactions from accessing the table.

An (Sch-S) lock is acquired for database activities that depend on the table schema but do not modify the schema, such as a query compilation. It prevents an (Sch-M) lock on the table, but it allows other locks to be granted on the table.

Since, on a production database, schema modifications are infrequent, (Sch-M) locks don't usually become a blocking issue. And because (Sch-S) locks don't block other locks except (Sch-M) locks, concurrency is generally not affected by (Sch-S) locks either.

Bulk Update (BU) Mode

The Bulk Update lock mode is unique to bulk load operations. These operations are the older-style bcp (bulk copy), the BULK INSERT statement, and inserts from the OPENROWSET using the BULK option. As a mechanism for speeding up these processes, you can provide a TABLOCK hint or set the option on the table for it to lock on bulk load. The key to (BU) locking mode is that it will allow multiple bulk operations against the table being locked but prevent other operations while the bulk process is running.

Key-Range Mode

The Key-Range mode is applicable only while the isolation level is set to Serializable (more on transaction isolation levels in the later "Isolation Levels" section). The Key-Range locks are applied to a series, or range, of key values that will be used repeatedly while the transaction is open. Locking a range during a serializable transaction ensures that other rows are not inserted within the range, possibly changing result sets within the transaction. The range can be locked using the other lock modes, making this more like a combined locking mode rather than a distinctively separate locking mode. For the Key-Range lock mode to work, an index must be used to define the values within the range.

Lock Compatibility

SQL Server provides isolation to a transaction by preventing other transactions from accessing the same resource in an incompatible way. However, if a transaction attempts a compatible task on the same resource, then, to increase concurrency, it won't be blocked by the first transaction. SQL Server ensures this kind of selective blocking by preventing a transaction from acquiring an incompatible lock on a resource held by another transaction. For example, an (S) lock acquired on a resource by a transaction allows other transactions to acquire an (S) lock on the same resource. However, an (Sch-M) lock on a resource by a transaction prevents other transactions from acquiring any lock on that resource.

Isolation Levels

The lock modes explained in the previous section help a transaction protect its data consistency from other concurrent transactions. The degree of data protection or isolation a transaction gets depends not only on the lock modes but also on the isolation level of the transaction. This level influences the behavior of the lock modes. For example, by default, an (S) lock is released immediately after the data is read; it isn't held until the end of the transaction. This behavior may not be suitable for some application functionality. In such cases, you can configure the isolation level of the transaction to achieve the desired degree of isolation.

SQL Server implements six isolation levels, four of them as defined by ISO:

- Read Uncommitted
- Read Committed
- Repeatable Read
- Serializable

Two other isolation levels provide row versioning, which is a mechanism whereby a version of the row is created as part of data manipulation queries. This extra version of the row allows read queries to access the data without acquiring locks against it. The extra two isolation levels are as follows:

- Read Committed Snapshot (actually part of the Read Committed isolation)
- Snapshot

The four ISO isolation levels are listed in increasing order of degree of isolation. You can configure them at either the connection or query level by using the `SET TRANSACTION ISOLATION LEVEL` statement or the locking hints, respectively. The isolation level configuration at the connection level remains effective until the isolation level is reconfigured using the `SET` statement or until the connection is closed. All the isolation levels are explained in the sections that follow.

Read Uncommitted

Read Uncommitted is the lowest of the four isolation levels, and it allows `SELECT` statements to read data without requesting an (S) lock. Since an (S) lock is not requested by a `SELECT` statement, it neither blocks nor is blocked by the (X) lock. It allows a `SELECT` statement to read data while the data is under modification. This kind of data read is called a *dirty read.* For an application in which the amount of data modification is minimal and makes a negligible impact on the accuracy of the data read by the `SELECT` statement, you can use this isolation level to avoid blocking the `SELECT` statement by a data modification activity.

You can use the following `SET` statement to configure the isolation level of a database connection to the Read Uncommitted isolation level:

```
SET TRANSACTION ISOLATION LEVEL READ UNCOMMITTED
```

You can also achieve this degree of isolation on a query basis using the `NOLOCK` locking hint:

```
SELECT * FROM Production.Products WITH(NOLOCK);
```

The effect of the locking hint remains applicable for the query and doesn't change the isolation level of the connection.

The Read Uncommitted isolation level avoids the blocking caused by a `SELECT` statement, but you should not use it if the transaction depends on the accuracy of the data read by the `SELECT` statement or if the transaction cannot withstand a concurrent change of data by another transaction.

It's very important to understand what is meant by a dirty read. Lots of people think this means that while a field is being updated from `Tusa` to `Tulsa` , a query can still read the previous value. Although that is true, much more egregious data problems could occur. Since no locks are placed while reading the data, indexes may be split. This can result in extra or missing rows of data returned to the query. To be very clear, using Read Uncommitted in any environment where data manipulation is occurring as well as data reads can result in unanticipated behaviors. The intention of this isolation level is for systems primarily focused on reporting and business intelligence, not online transaction processing.

Read Committed

The Read Committed isolation level prevents the dirty read caused by the Read Uncommitted isolation level. This means that (S) locks are requested by the SELECT statements at this isolation level. This is the default isolation level of SQL Server. If needed, you can change the isolation level of a connection to Read Committed by using the following SET statement:

```
SET TRANSACTION ISOLATION LEVEL READ COMMITTED
```

The Read Committed isolation level is good for most cases, but since the (S) lock acquired by the SELECT statement isn't held until the end of the transaction, it can cause nonrepeatable read or phantom read issues, as explained in the sections that follow.

The behavior of the Read Committed isolation level can be changed by the database option READ_COMMITTED_SNAPSHOT. When this is set to ON, row versioning is used by data manipulation transactions. This places an extra load on tempdb because previous versions of the rows being changed are stored there while the transaction is uncommitted. This allows other transactions to access data for reads without having to place locks on the data, which can improve the speed and efficiency of all the queries in the system.

To see the row versioning in practice, first you need to create a test database for use with this one sample. Because the AdventureWorks2008 database comes with filestream objects enabled, this prevents row versioning from functioning.

```
CREATE DATABASE VersionTest;
```

Modify the VersionTest database so that READ_COMMITTED_SNAPSHOT is turned on:

```
ALTER DATABASE VersionTest
    SET READ_COMMITTED_SNAPSHOT ON;
```

Load one table into the new VersionTest database for the purposes of testing:

```
USE VersionTest;
GO
SELECT * INTO dbo.Product
FROM AdventureWorks2008.Production.Product;
```

Now imagine a business situation. The first connection and transaction will be pulling data from the Production.Product table, acquiring the color of a particular item (read_commited.sql):

```
BEGIN TRANSACTION;
SELECT  p.Color
FROM    dbo.Product AS p
WHERE   p.ProductID = 711;
```

A second connection is made with a new transaction that will be modifying the color of the same item (change_color.sql).

```
BEGIN TRANSACTION;
UPDATE dbo.Product
SET Color = 'Coyote'
WHERE ProductID = 711;

SELECT p.Color
FROM dbo.Product AS p
WHERE p.ProductID = 711;
```

Running the SELECT statement after updating the color, you can see that the color was updated. But if you switch back to the first connection and rerun the original SELECT statement, you'll still see the color as Blue. Switch back to the second connection, and finish the transaction:

```
COMMIT TRANSACTION
```

Switching again to the first transaction, commit that transaction, and then rerun the original SELECT statement. You'll see the new color updated for the item, Coyote. You can delete the database created before continuing:

```
DROP DATABASE VersionTest;
```

■ **Note** If the tempdb is filled, data modification using row versioning will continue to succeed, but reads may fail since the versioned row will not be available. If you enable any type of row versioning isolation within your database, you must take extra care to maintain free space within tempdb.

Repeatable Read

The Repeatable Read isolation level allows a SELECT statement to retain its (S) lock until the end of the transaction, thereby preventing other transactions from modifying the data during that time. Database functionality may implement a logical decision inside a transaction based on the data read by a SELECT statement within the transaction. If the outcome of the decision is dependent on the data read by the SELECT statement, then you should consider preventing modification of the data by other concurrent transactions. For example, consider the following two transactions:

- Normalize the price for ProductID = 1: For ProductID = 1, if Price > 10, decrease the price by 10.
- Apply a discount: For Products with Price > 10, apply a discount of 40 percent.

Considering the following test table (repeatable.sql in the download):

```
IF (SELECT  OBJECT_ID('dbo.MyProduct')
   ) IS NOT NULL
    DROP TABLE dbo.MyProduct;
GO
CREATE TABLE dbo.MyProduct
    (ProductID INT
    ,Price MONEY);
INSERT  INTO dbo.MyProduct
VALUES  (1, 15.0);
```

you can write the two transactions like this (repeatable_trans.sql):

```
--Transaction 1 from Connection 1
DECLARE @Price INT ;
BEGIN TRAN NormailizePrice
SELECT  @Price = Price
FROM    dbo.MyProduct AS mp
WHERE   mp.ProductID = 1 ;
  /*Allow transaction 2 to execute*/
WAITFOR DELAY '00:00:10'
IF @Price > 10
    UPDATE  dbo.MyProduct
    SET     Price = Price - 10
    WHERE   ProductID = 1 ;
COMMIT
GO

--Transaction 2 from Connection 2
BEGIN TRAN ApplyDiscount
UPDATE  dbo.MyProduct
SET     Price = Price * 0.6 --Discount = 40%
WHERE   Price > 10 ;
COMMIT
```

On the surface, the preceding transactions may look good, and yes, they do work in a single-user environment. But in a multiuser environment where multiple transactions can be executed concurrently, you have a problem here!

To figure out the problem, let's execute the two transactions from different connections in the following order:

- Start transaction 1 first.
- Start transaction 2 within 10 seconds of the start of transaction 1.

As you may have guessed, at the end of the transactions, the new price of the product (with ProductID = 1) will be –1.0. Ouch—it appears that you're ready to go out of business!

The problem occurs because transaction 2 is allowed to modify the data while transaction 1 has finished reading the data and is about to make a decision on it. Transaction 1 requires a higher degree of isolation than that provided by the default isolation level (Read Committed).

As a solution, you want to prevent transaction 2 from modifying the data while transaction 1 is working on it. In other words, provide transaction 1 with the ability to read the data again later in the transaction without being modified by others. This feature is called *repeatable read*. Considering the context, the implementation of the solution is probably obvious. After re-creating the table, you can write this:

```
SET TRANSACTION ISOLATION LEVEL REPEATABLE READ
GO
--Transaction 1 from Connection 1
DECLARE @Price INT ;
BEGIN TRAN NormailizePrice
SELECT  @Price = Price
FROM    dbo.MyProduct AS mp
WHERE   mp.ProductID = 1 ;
  /*Allow transaction 2 to execute*/
WAITFOR DELAY '00:00:10'
IF @Price > 10
    UPDATE  dbo.MyProduct
    SET     Price = Price - 10
    WHERE   ProductID = 1 ;
COMMIT
GO
SET TRANSACTION ISOLATION LEVEL READ COMMITTED --Back to default
GO
```

Increasing the isolation level of transaction 1 to Repeatable Read will prevent transaction 2 from modifying the data during the execution of transaction 1. Consequently, you won't have an inconsistency in the price of the product. Since the intention isn't to release the (S) lock acquired by the `SELECT` statement until the end of the transaction, the effect of setting the isolation level to Repeatable Read can also be implemented at the query level using the lock hint:

```
--Transaction 1 from Connection 1
DECLARE @Price INT ;
BEGIN TRAN NormailizePrice
SELECT  @Price = Price
FROM    dbo.MyProduct AS mp WITH(REPEATABLEREAD)
WHERE   mp.ProductID = 1 ;
  /*Allow transaction 2 to execute*/
WAITFOR DELAY '00:00:10'
IF @Price > 10
    UPDATE  dbo.MyProduct
    SET     Price = Price - 10
    WHERE   ProductID = 1 ;
COMMIT
GO
```

This solution prevents the data inconsistency of `MyProduct.Price`, but it introduces another problem to this scenario. On observing the result of transaction 2, you realize that it could cause a deadlock. Therefore, although the preceding solution prevented the data inconsistency, it is not a complete solution. Looking closely at the effect of the Repeatable Read isolation level on the transactions, you see that it introduced the typical deadlock issue avoided by the internal implementation of an UPDATE statement, as explained previously. The SELECT statement acquired and retained an (S) lock instead of a (U) lock, even though it intended to modify the data later within the transaction. The (S) lock allowed transaction 2 to acquire a (U) lock, but it blocked the (U) lock's conversion to an (X) lock. The attempt of transaction 1 to acquire a (U) lock on the data at a later stage caused a circular blocking, resulting in a deadlock.

To prevent the deadlock and still avoid data corruption, you can use an equivalent strategy as adopted by the internal implementation of the UPDATE statement. Thus, instead of requesting an (S) lock, transaction 1 can request a (U) lock using an UPDLOCK locking hint when executing the SELECT statement:

```
--Transaction 1 from Connection 1
DECLARE @Price INT ;
BEGIN TRAN NormailizePrice
SELECT  @Price = Price
FROM    dbo.MyProduct AS mp WITH(UPDLOCK)
WHERE   mp.ProductID = 1 ;
  /*Allow transaction 2 to execute*/
WAITFOR DELAY '00:00:10'
IF @Price > 10
    UPDATE  dbo.MyProduct
    SET     Price = Price - 10
    WHERE   ProductID = 1 ;
COMMIT
GO
```

This solution prevents both data inconsistency and the possibility of the deadlock. If the increase of the isolation level to Repeatable Read had not introduced the typical deadlock, then it would have done the job. Since there is a chance of a deadlock occurring because of the retention of an (S) lock until the end of a transaction, it is usually preferable to grab a (U) lock instead of holding the (S) lock, as just illustrated.

Serializable

Serializable is the highest of the six isolation levels. Instead of acquiring a lock only on the row to be accessed, the Serializable isolation level acquires a range lock on the row and the next row in the order of the data set requested. For instance, a SELECT statement executed at the Serializable isolation level acquires a (RangeS-S) lock on the row to be accessed and the next row in the order. This prevents the addition of rows by other transactions in the data set operated on by the first transaction, and it protects the first transaction from finding new rows in its data set within its transaction scope. Finding new rows in a data set within a transaction is also called a *phantom read.*

To understand the need for a Serializable isolation level, let's consider an example. Suppose a group (with GroupID = 10) in a company has a fund of $100 to be distributed among the employees in the group as a bonus. The fund balance after the bonus payment should be $0. Consider the following test table (serializable.sql in the download):

```
IF (SELECT  OBJECT_ID('dbo.MyEmployees')
   ) IS NOT NULL
    DROP TABLE dbo.MyEmployees;
GO
CREATE TABLE dbo.MyEmployees
    (EmployeeID INT
    ,GroupID INT
    ,Salary MONEY);
CREATE CLUSTERED INDEX i1 ON dbo.MyEmployees (GroupID);
INSERT  INTO dbo.MyEmployees
VALUES  (1, 10, 1000);
 --Employee 1 in group 10
INSERT  INTO dbo.MyEmployees
VALUES  (2, 10, 1000);
 --Employee 2 in group 10
--Employees 3 & 4 in different groups
INSERT  INTO dbo.MyEmployees
VALUES  (3, 20, 1000);
INSERT  INTO dbo.MyEmployees
VALUES  (4, 9, 1000);
```

The preceding business functionality may be implemented as follows (bonus.sql in the download):

```
DECLARE @Fund MONEY = 100
   ,@Bonus MONEY
   ,@NumberOfEmployees INT
BEGIN TRAN PayBonus
SELECT  @NumberOfEmployees = COUNT(*)
FROM    dbo.MyEmployees
WHERE   GroupID = 10
  /*Allow transaction 2 to execute*/
WAITFOR DELAY '00:00:10'
IF @NumberOfEmployees > 0
    BEGIN
        SET @Bonus = @Fund / @NumberOfEmployees
        UPDATE  dbo.MyEmployees
        SET     Salary = Salary + @Bonus
        WHERE   GroupID = 10
        PRINT 'Fund balance =
          ' + CAST((@Fund - (@@ROWCOUNT * @Bonus)) AS VARCHAR(6)) + ' $'
    END
COMMIT
GO
```

The PayBonus transaction works well in a single-user environment. However, in a multiuser environment, there is a problem.

Consider another transaction that adds a new employee to GroupID = 10 as follows (new_employee.sql in the download) and is executed concurrently (immediately after the start of the PayBonus transaction) from a second connection:

```
--Transaction 2 from Connection 2
BEGIN TRAN NewEmployee
  INSERT INTO MyEmployees VALUES(5, 10, 1000)
COMMIT
```

The fund balance after the PayBonus transaction will be –$50! Although the new employee may like it, the group fund will be in the red. This causes an inconsistency in the logical state of the data.

To prevent this data inconsistency, the addition of the new employee to the group (or data set) under operation should be blocked. Of the five isolation levels discussed, only Snapshot isolation can provide a similar functionality, since the transaction has to be protected not only on the existing data but also from the entry of new data in the data set. The Serializable isolation level can provide this kind of isolation by acquiring a range lock on the affected row and the next row in the order determined by the i1 index on the GroupID column. Thus, the data inconsistency of the PayBonus transaction can be prevented by setting the transaction isolation level to Serializable.

Remember to re-create the table first:

```
SET TRANSACTION ISOLATION LEVEL SERIALIZABLE
GO
DECLARE @Fund MONEY = 100
   ,@Bonus MONEY
   ,@NumberOfEmployees INT
BEGIN TRAN PayBonus
SELECT  @NumberOfEmployees = COUNT(*)
FROM    dbo.MyEmployees
WHERE   GroupID = 10
  /*Allow transaction 2 to execute*/
WAITFOR DELAY '00:00:10'
IF @NumberOfEmployees > 0
    BEGIN
        SET @Bonus = @Fund / @NumberOfEmployees
        UPDATE  dbo.MyEmployees
        SET     Salary = Salary + @Bonus
        WHERE   GroupID = 10
        PRINT 'Fund balance =
          ' + CAST((@Fund - (@@ROWCOUNT * @Bonus)) AS VARCHAR(6)) + ' $'
    END
COMMIT
GO
SET TRANSACTION ISOLATION LEVEL READ COMMITTED --Back to default
GO
```

The effect of the Serializable isolation level can also be achieved at the query level by using the HOLDLOCK locking hint on the SELECT statement, as shown here:

```
DECLARE @Fund MONEY = 100
   ,@Bonus MONEY
   ,@NumberOfEmployees INT
BEGIN TRAN PayBonus
SELECT  @NumberOfEmployees = COUNT(*)
FROM    dbo.MyEmployees WITH(HOLDLOCK)
WHERE   GroupID = 10
  /*Allow transaction 2 to execute*/
WAITFOR DELAY '00:00:10'
IF @NumberOfEmployees > 0
    BEGIN
        SET @Bonus = @Fund / @NumberOfEmployees
        UPDATE  dbo.MyEmployees
        SET     Salary = Salary + @Bonus
        WHERE   GroupID = 10
        PRINT 'Fund balance =
          ' + CAST((@Fund - (@@ROWCOUNT * @Bonus)) AS VARCHAR(6)) + ' $'
    END
COMMIT
GO
```

You can observe the range locks acquired by the PayBonus transaction by querying sys.dm_tran_locks from another connection while the PayBonus transaction is executing, as shown in Figure 12-6.

	request_session_id	resource_database_id	resource_associated_entity_id	resource_type	resource_description	request_mode	request_status
1	54	14	0	DATABASE		S	GRANT
2	53	14	0	DATABASE		S	GRANT
3	55	14	0	DATABASE		S	GRANT
4	52	14	0	DATABASE		S	GRANT
5	54	14	919674324	OBJECT		IX	GRANT
6	53	14	919674324	OBJECT		IS	GRANT
7	53	14	72057594061783040	KEY	(0b00d5206a04)	RangeS-S	GRANT
8	53	14	72057594061783040	KEY	(15003609badb)	RangeS-S	GRANT
9	54	14	72057594061783040	KEY	(15003609badb)	RangeI-N	WAIT
10	54	14	72057594061783040	PAGE	1:984	IX	GRANT
11	53	14	72057594061783040	PAGE	1:984	IS	GRANT
12	54	14	887674210	OBJECT		IX	GRANT
13	53	14	72057594061783040	KEY	(0b003b5ba1b3)	RangeS-S	GRANT

Figure 12-6. *sys.dm_tran_locks output showing range locks granted to the serializable transaction*

The output of sys.dm_tran_locks shows that shared-range (RangeS-S) locks are acquired on three index rows: the first employee in GroupID = 10, the second employee in GroupID = 10, and the third employee in GroupID = 20. These range locks prevent the entry of any new employee in GroupID = 10.

The range locks just shown introduce a few interesting side effects:

- No new employee with a GroupID between 10 and 20 can be added during this period. For instance, an attempt to add a new employee with a GroupID of 15 will be blocked by the PayBonus transaction:

```
--Transaction 2 from Connection 2
BEGIN TRAN NewEmployee
  INSERT INTO dbo.MyEmployees VALUES(6, 15, 1000)
COMMIT
```

- If the data set of the PayBonus transaction turns out to be the last set in the existing data ordered by the index, then the range lock required on the row, after the last one in the data set, is acquired on the last possible data value in the table.

To understand this behavior, let's delete the employees with a GroupID > 10 to make the GroupID = 10 data set the last data set in the clustered index (or table):

```
DELETE dbo.MyEmployees WHERE GroupID > 10
```

Run the updated bonus.sql and new_employee.sql again. Figure 12-7 shows the resultant output of sys.dm_tran_locks for the PayBonus transaction.

	request_session_id	resource_database_id	resource_associated_entity_id	resource_type	resource_description	request_mode	request_status
1	54	14	0	DATABASE		S	GRANT
2	53	14	0	DATABASE		S	GRANT
3	56	14	0	DATABASE		S	GRANT
4	55	14	0	DATABASE		S	GRANT
5	52	14	0	DATABASE		S	GRANT
6	53	14	72057594061783040	KEY	(0c00d5f414a1)	RangeS-S	GRANT
7	53	14	72057594061783040	KEY	(ffffffffffff)	RangeS-S	GRANT
8	54	14	72057594061783040	KEY	(ffffffffffff)	RangeI-N	WAIT
9	54	14	919674324	OBJECT		IX	GRANT
10	53	14	919674324	OBJECT		IS	GRANT
11	53	14	72057594061783040	KEY	(0b00d5206a04)	RangeS-S	GRANT
12	54	14	72057594061783040	PAGE	1:984	IX	GRANT
13	53	14	72057594061783040	PAGE	1:984	IS	GRANT
14	53	14	72057594061783040	KEY	(0b003b5ba1b3)	RangeS-S	GRANT

Figure 12-7. *sys.dm_tran_locks output showing extended range locks granted to the serializable transaction*

The range lock on the last possible row (KEY = ffffffffffff) in the clustered index, as shown in Figure 12-7, will block the addition of employees with all GroupIDs greater than or equal to 10. You know that the lock is on the last row, not because it's displayed in a visible fashion in the output of sys.dm_tran_locks but because you cleaned out everything up to that row previously. For example, an attempt to add a new employee with GroupID = 999 will be blocked by the PayBonus transaction:

```
--Transaction 2 from Connection 2
BEGIN TRAN NewEmployee
  INSERT INTO dbo.MyEmployees VALUES(7, 999, 1000)
COMMIT
```

Guess what will happen if the table doesn't have an index on the `GroupID` column (in other words, the column in the `WHERE` clause)? While you're thinking, I'll re-create the table with the clustered index on a different column:

```
IF (SELECT  OBJECT_ID('dbo.MyEmployees')
   ) IS NOT NULL
    DROP TABLE dbo.MyEmployees
GO
CREATE TABLE dbo.MyEmployees
    (EmployeeID INT
    ,GroupID INT
    ,Salary MONEY)
CREATE CLUSTERED INDEX i1 ON dbo.MyEmployees (EmployeeID)
INSERT  INTO dbo.MyEmployees
VALUES  (1, 10, 1000)
 --Employee 1 in group 10
INSERT  INTO dbo.MyEmployees
VALUES  (2, 10, 1000)
 --Employee 2 in group 10
--Employees 3 & 4 in different groups
INSERT  INTO dbo.MyEmployees
VALUES  (3, 20, 1000)
INSERT  INTO dbo.MyEmployees
VALUES  (4, 9, 1000)
GO
```

Rerun the updated `bonus.sql` and `new_employee.sql`. Figure 12-8 shows the resultant output of `sys.dm_tran_locks` for the `PayBonus` transaction.

	request_session_id	resource_database_id	resource_associated_entity_id	resource_type	resource_description	request_mode	request_status
1	54	14	0	DATABASE		S	GRANT
2	53	14	0	DATABASE		S	GRANT
3	56	14	0	DATABASE		S	GRANT
4	55	14	0	DATABASE		S	GRANT
5	52	14	0	DATABASE		S	GRANT
6	53	14	72057594061914112	KEY	(ffffffffffff)	RangeS-S	GRANT
7	54	14	72057594061914112	KEY	(ffffffffffff)	RangeI-N	WAIT
8	54	14	919674324	OBJECT		IX	GRANT
9	53	14	919674324	OBJECT		IS	GRANT
10	54	14	935674381	OBJECT		IX	GRANT
11	53	14	935674381	OBJECT		IS	GRANT
12	54	14	72057594061914112	PAGE	1:984	IX	GRANT
13	53	14	72057594061914112	PAGE	1:984	IS	GRANT
14	53	14	72057594061914112	KEY	(0500b49e5abb)	RangeS-S	GRANT
15	53	14	72057594061914112	KEY	(0200c411ba73)	RangeS-S	GRANT
16	53	14	72057594061914112	KEY	(0400a4427a09)	RangeS-S	GRANT
17	53	14	72057594061914112	KEY	(0300146b1a34)	RangeS-S	GRANT

Figure 12-8. *`sys.dm_tran_locks` output showing range locks granted to the serializable transaction with no index on the `WHERE` clause column*

Once again, the range lock on the last possible row (KEY = ffffffffffff) in the new clustered index, as shown in Figure 12-8, will block the addition of any new row to the table. I will discuss the reason behind this extensive locking later in the chapter in the "Effect of Indexes on the Serializable Isolation Level" section.

As you've seen, the Serializable isolation level not only holds the share locks until the end of the transaction like the Repeatable Read isolation level but also prevents any new row in the data set (or more) by holding range locks. Because this increased blocking can hurt database concurrency, you should avoid the Serializable isolation level.

Snapshot

Snapshot isolation is the second of the row-versioning isolation levels available in SQL Server 2008. Unlike Read Committed Snapshot isolation, Snapshot isolation requires an explicit call to SET TRANSACTION ISOLATION LEVEL at the start of the transaction in addition to setting the isolation level on the database. Snapshot isolation is meant as a more stringent isolation level than the Read Committed Snapshot isolation. Snapshot isolation will attempt to put an exclusive lock on the data it intends to modify. If that data already has a lock on it, the snapshot transaction will fail. It provides transaction-level read consistency, which makes it more applicable to financial-type systems than Read Committed Snapshot.

Effect of Indexes on Locking

Indexes affect the locking behavior on a table. On a table with no indexes, the lock granularities are RID, PAG (on the page containing the RID), and TAB. Adding indexes to the table affects the resources to be locked. For example, consider the following test table with no indexes (create_t1_2.sql in the download):

```
IF (SELECT  OBJECT_ID('dbo.t1')
   ) IS NOT NULL
    DROP TABLE dbo.t1
GO
CREATE TABLE dbo.t1 (c1 INT, c2 DATETIME)
INSERT  INTO dbo.t1
VALUES  (1, GETDATE())
```

Observe the locking behavior on the table for the transaction (indexlock.sql in the download):

```
BEGIN TRAN LockBehavior
UPDATE  dbo.t1 WITH (REPEATABLEREAD) --Hold all acquired locks
SET     c2 = GETDATE()
WHERE   c1 = 1
  --Observe lock behavior using sp_lock from another connection
WAITFOR DELAY '00:00:10'
COMMIT
```

Figure 12-9 shows the output of sys.dm_tran_locks applicable to the test table.

	request_session_id	resource_database_id	resource_associated_entity_id	resource_type	resource_description	request_mode	request_status
1	53	14	0	DATABASE		S	GRANT
2	52	14	0	DATABASE		S	GRANT
3	53	14	72057594061979648	RID	1:986:0	X	GRANT
4	53	14	72057594061979648	PAGE	1:986	IX	GRANT
5	53	14	951674438	OBJECT		IX	GRANT

Figure 12-9. *`sys.dm_tran_locks` output showing the locks granted on a table with no index*

The following locks are acquired by the transaction:

- An (IX) lock on the table
- An (IX) lock on the page containing the data row
- An (X) lock on the data row within the table

When the `resource_type` is an object, the `resource_associated_entity_id` column value in `sys.dm_tran_locks` indicates the `object_id` of the object on which the lock is placed. You can obtain the specific object name on which the lock is acquired from the `sys.object` system table as follows:

```
SELECT OBJECT_NAME(<object_id>)
```

The effect of the index on the locking behavior of the table varies with the type of index on the `WHERE` clause column. The difference arises from the fact that the leaf pages of the nonclustered and clustered indexes have a different relationship with the data pages of the table. Let's look into the effect of these indexes on the locking behavior of the table.

Effect of a Nonclustered Index

Because the leaf pages of the nonclustered index are separate from the data pages of the table, the resources associated with the nonclustered index are also protected from corruption. SQL Server automatically ensures this. To see this in action, create a nonclustered index on the test table:

```
CREATE NONCLUSTERED INDEX i1 ON dbo.t1(c1)
```

On running the `LockBehavior` transaction (`indexlock.sql`) again, and querying `sys.dm_tran_locks` from a separate connection, you get the result shown in Figure 12-10.

	request_session_id	resource_database_id	resource_associated_entity_id	resource_type	resource_description	request_mode	request_status
1	54	14	0	DATABASE		S	GRANT
2	53	14	0	DATABASE		S	GRANT
3	52	14	0	DATABASE		S	GRANT
4	53	14	72057594061979648	RID	1:986:0	X	GRANT
5	53	14	72057594061979648	PAGE	1:986	IX	GRANT
6	53	14	72057594062045184	KEY	(dc00d3620601)	U	GRANT
7	53	14	951674438	OBJECT		IX	GRANT
8	53	14	0	METADATA	$hash = 0xddde15a2:0xc0f54294:0xba64b4	Sch-S	GRANT
9	53	14	72057594062045184	PAGE	1:23123	IU	GRANT

Figure 12-10. *`sys.dm_tran_locks` output showing the effect of a nonclustered index on locking behavior*

The following locks are acquired by the transaction:

- An (IU) lock on the page containing the nonclustered index row, (IndId = 2)
- A (U) lock on the nonclustered index row within the index page, (IndId = 2)
- An (IX) lock on the table, (IndId = 0)
- An (IX) lock on the page containing the data row, (IndId = 0)
- An (X) lock on the data row within the data page, (IndId = 0)

Note that only the row-level and page-level locks are directly associated with the nonclustered index. The next higher level of lock granularity for the nonclustered index is the table-level lock on the corresponding table.

Thus, nonclustered indexes introduce an additional locking overhead on the table. You can avoid the locking overhead on the index by using the ALLOW_ROW_LOCKS and ALLOW_PAGE_LOCKS options in ALTER INDEX (indexoption.sql in the download):

```
--Avoid KEY lock on the index rows
ALTER INDEX i1 ON dbo.t1
SET (ALLOW_ROW_LOCKS = OFF
    ,ALLOW_PAGE_LOCKS= OFF);
BEGIN TRAN LockBehavior
UPDATE  dbo.t1 WITH (REPEATABLEREAD) --Hold all acquired locks
SET     c2 = GETDATE()
WHERE   c1 = 1;
  --Observe lock behavior using sp_lock from another connection
WAITFOR DELAY '00:00:10';
COMMIT
ALTER INDEX i1 ON dbo.t1
SET (ALLOW_ROW_LOCKS = ON
    ,ALLOW_PAGE_LOCKS= ON);
```

You can use these options when working with an index to enable/disable the KEY locks and PAG locks on the index. Disabling just the KEY lock causes the lowest lock granularity on the index to be the PAG lock. Configuring lock granularity on the index remains effective until it is reconfigured. Modifying locks like this should be a last resort after many other options have been tried. This could cause significant locking overhead that would seriously impact performance of the system.

Figure 12-11 displays the output of sys.dm_tran_locks executed from a separate connection.

	request_session_id	resource_database_id	resource_associated_entity_id	resource_type	resource_description	request_mode	request_status
1	55	14	0	DATABASE		S	GRANT
2	54	14	0	DATABASE		S	GRANT
3	53	14	0	DATABASE		S	GRANT
4	52	14	0	DATABASE		S	GRANT
5	55	14	0	METADATA	$hash = 0xadfe0a4a:0x70a3ea8d:0x21c969	Sch-S	GRANT
6	55	14	951674438	OBJECT		X	GRANT

Figure 12-11. *sys.dm_tran_locks output showing the effect of sp_indexoption on lock granularity*

The only lock acquired by the transaction on the test table is an (X) lock on the table (IndId = 0).

You can see from the new locking behavior that disabling both the KEY lock and the PAG lock on the index using the sp_indexoption procedure escalates lock granularity to the table level. This will block every concurrent access to the table or to the indexes on the table, and consequently it can hurt the database concurrency seriously. However, if a nonclustered index becomes a point of contention in a blocking scenario, then it may be beneficial to disable the PAG locks on the index, thereby allowing only KEY locks on the index.

■ **Note** Using this option can have serious side effects. You should use it only as a last resort.

Effect of a Clustered Index

Since for a clustered index the leaf pages of the index and the data pages of the table are the same, the clustered index can be used to avoid the overhead of locking additional pages (leaf pages) and rows introduced by a nonclustered index. To understand the locking overhead associated with a clustered index, convert the preceding nonclustered index to a clustered index:

```
CREATE CLUSTERED INDEX i1 ON t1(c1) WITH DROP_EXISTING
```

If you run indexlock.sql again and query sys.dm_tran_locks in a different connection, you should see the resultant output for the LockBehavior transaction on t1 in Figure 12-12.

	request_session_id	resource_database_id	resource_associated_entity_id	resource_type	resource_description	request_mode	request_status
1	55	14	0	DATABASE		S	GRANT
2	54	14	0	DATABASE		S	GRANT
3	53	14	0	DATABASE		S	GRANT
4	52	14	0	DATABASE		S	GRANT
5	53	14	951674438	OBJECT		IX	GRANT
6	53	14	72057594062110720	KEY	(0200c411ba73)	X	GRANT
7	53	14	0	METADATA	$hash = 0xddde15a2:0xc0f54294:0xba64b4	Sch-S	GRANT
8	53	14	72057594062110720	PAGE	1:23125	IX	GRANT

Figure 12-12. *sys.dm_tran_locks output showing the effect of a clustered index on locking behavior*

The following locks are acquired by the transaction:

- An (IX) lock on the table, (IndId = 0)
- An (IX) lock on the page containing the clustered index row (IndId = 1)
- An (X) lock on the clustered index row within the table (or clustered index) (IndId = 1)

The locks on the clustered index row and the leaf page are actually the locks on the data row and data page too, since the data pages and the leaf pages are the same. Thus, the clustered index reduced the locking overhead on the table compared to the nonclustered index.

Reduced locking overhead of a clustered index is another benefit of using a clustered index over a nonclustered index.

Effect of Indexes on the Serializable Isolation Level

Indexes play a significant role in determining the amount of blocking caused by the Serializable isolation level. The availability of an index on the WHERE clause column (that causes the data set to be locked) allows SQL Server to determine the order of the rows to be locked. For instance, consider the example used in the section on the Serializable isolation level. The SELECT statement uses a GroupID filter column to form its data set, like so:

```
...
SELECT @NumberOfEmployees = COUNT(*)
  FROM dbo.MyEmployees WITH(HOLDLOCK) WHERE GroupID = 10
...
```

A clustered index is available on the GroupID column, allowing SQL Server to acquire a (RangeS-S) lock on the row to be accessed and the next row in the correct order.

If the index on the GroupID column is removed, then SQL Server cannot determine the rows on which the range locks should be acquired, since the order of the rows is no longer guaranteed. Consequently, the SELECT statement acquires an (IS) lock at the table level instead of acquiring lower-granularity locks at the row level, as shown in Figure 12-13.

	request_session_id	resource_database_id	resource_associated_entity_id	resource_type	resource_description	request_mode	request_status
6	55	14	935674381	OBJECT		IS	GRANT

Figure 12-13. *sys.dm_tran_locks output showing the locks granted to a SELECT statement with no index on the WHERE clause column*

By failing to have an index on the filter column, you significantly increase the degree of blocking caused by the Serializable isolation level. This is another good reason to have an index on the WHERE clause columns.

Capturing Blocking Information

Although blocking is necessary to isolate a transaction from other concurrent transactions, sometimes it may rise to excessive levels, adversely affecting database concurrency. In the simplest blocking scenario, the lock acquired by an SPID on a resource blocks another SPID requesting an incompatible lock on the resource. To improve concurrency, it is important to analyze the cause of blocking and apply the appropriate resolution.

In a blocking scenario, you need the following information to have a clear understanding of the cause of the blocking:

- *The connection information of the blocking and blocked SPIDs*: You can obtain this information from the sys.dm_os_waiting_tasks dynamic management view or the sp_who2 system stored procedure.
- *The lock information of the blocking and blocked SPIDs*: You can obtain this information from the sys.dm_tran_locks DMV.
- *The SQL statements last executed by the blocking and blocked SPIDs*: You can use the sys.dm_exec_requests DMV combined with sys.dm_exec_sql_text and sys.dm_exec_query_plan or SQL Profiler to obtain this information.

You can also obtain the following information from the SQL Server Management Studio by running the Activity Monitor. The Processes page provides connection information of all SPIDs. This shows blocked SPIDS, the process blocking them, and the head of any blocking chain with details on how long the process has been running, its SPID, and other information. It is possible to put Profiler to work using the blocking report to gather a lot of the same information. You can find more on this in the "Profiler Trace and the Blocked Process Report Event" section.

To provide more power and flexibility to the process of collecting blocking information, a SQL Server administrator can use SQL scripts to provide the relevant information listed here.

Capturing Blocking Information with SQL

To arrive at enough information about blocked and blocking processes, you can bring several dynamic management views into play. This query will show information necessary to identify blocked processes based on those that are waiting. You can easily add filtering to only access processes blocked for a certain period of time or only within certain databases, and so on (`blocker.sql`):

```
SELECT  tl.request_session_id AS WaitingSessionID
        ,wt.blocking_session_id AS BlockingSessionID
        ,wt.resource_description
        ,wt.wait_type
        ,wt.wait_duration_ms
        ,DB_NAME(tl.resource_database_id) AS DatabaseName
        ,tl.resource_associated_entity_id AS WaitingAssociatedEntity
        ,tl.resource_type AS WaitingResourceType
        ,tl.request_type AS WaitingRequestType
        ,wrt.[text] AS WaitingTSql
        ,btl.request_type BlockingRequestType
        ,brt.[text] AS BlockingTsql
FROM    sys.dm_tran_locks tl
        JOIN sys.dm_os_waiting_tasks wt
        ON tl.lock_owner_address = wt.resource_address
        JOIN sys.dm_exec_requests wr
        ON wr.session_id = tl.request_session_id
        CROSS APPLY sys.dm_exec_sql_text(wr.sql_handle) AS wrt
        LEFT JOIN sys.dm_exec_requests br
        ON br.session_id = wt.blocking_session_id
        OUTER APPLY sys.dm_exec_sql_text(br.sql_handle) AS brt
        LEFT JOIN sys.dm_tran_locks AS btl
        ON br.session_id = btl.request_session_id;
```

To understand how to analyze a blocking scenario and the relevant information provided by the blocker script, consider the following example (`block_it.sql` in the download). First, create a test table:

```
IF (SELECT  OBJECT_ID('dbo.t1')
   ) IS NOT NULL
    DROP TABLE dbo.t1;
GO
CREATE TABLE dbo.t1
    (c1 INT
    ,c2 INT
    ,c3 DATETIME);
INSERT  INTO dbo.t1
VALUES  (11, 12, GETDATE());
INSERT  INTO dbo.t1
VALUES  (21, 22, GETDATE());
```

Now, open three connections, and run the following two queries concurrently. Once they're run, use the `blocker.sql` script in the third connection. Execute the code in Listing 12-1 first.

Listing 12-1. *Connection 1*

```
BEGIN TRAN User1
UPDATE  dbo.t1
SET     c3 = GETDATE();
```

Execute Listing 12-2 while the `User1` transaction is executing.

Listing 12-2. *Connection 2*

```
BEGIN TRAN User2
  SELECT c2 FROM dbo.t1 WHERE c1 = 11;
COMMIT
```

This creates a simple blocking scenario where the `User1` transaction blocks the `User2` transaction.

The output of the blocker script provides information immediately useful to begin resolving blocking issues. First, you can identify the specific session information including the session ID of both the blocking and waiting sessions. You get an immediate resource description from the waiting resource, the wait type, and the length of time, in milliseconds, that the process has been waiting. It's that value that allows you to provide a filter to eliminate short-term blocks, which are part of normal processing.

The database name is supplied because blocking can occur anywhere in the system, not just in AdventureWorks2008. You'll want to identify it where it occurs. The resources and types from the basic locking information are retrieved for the waiting process.

The blocking request type is displayed, and both the waiting T-SQL and blocking T-SQL, if available, are displayed. Once you have the object where the block is occurring, having the T-SQL so that you can understand exactly where and how the process is either blocking or being blocked is a vital part of the process of eliminating or reducing the amount of blocking. All this information is available from one simple query. Figure 12-14 shows the sample output from the earlier blocked process.

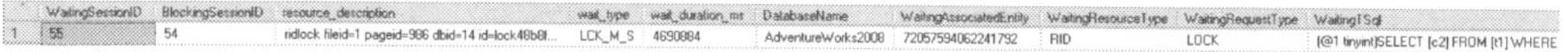

	WaitingSessionID	BlockingSessionID	resource_description	wait_type	wait_duration_ms	DatabaseName	WaitingAssociatedEntity	WaitingResourceType	WaitingRequestType	WaitingTSql
1	55	54	ridlock fileid=1 pageid=986 dbid=14 id=lock48b8...	LCK_M_S	4690884	AdventureWorks2008	72057594062241792	RID	LOCK	(@1 tinyint)SELECT [c2] FROM [t1] WHERE

Figure 12-14. *Output from the blocker script*

Be sure to go back to Connection 1 and commit or roll back the transaction.

Profiler Trace and the Blocked Process Report Event

The Profiler provides an event called "Errors and Warning: Blocked Process Report." This event works off the blocked process threshold that you need to provide to the system configuration. This script sets the threshold to five seconds:

```
EXEC sp_configure 'blocked process threshold', 5 ;
RECONFIGURE;
```

That would normally be a very low value in most systems. A general rule would be to start with a setting at 30 seconds and adjust up or down as seems appropriate for your databases, servers, and their workloads. If you have an established performance service-level agreement (SLA), you could use that as the threshold. Once the value is set, you can configure alerts so that emails or pages are sent if any process is blocked longer than the value you set. It also acts as a trigger for the Profiler event.

To set up a trace that captures the Blocked Process report, first open Profiler. (Although you should use scripts to set up this event and trace in a production environment, I'll show how to use the GUI.) Select a Blank template, navigate to the Events Selection page, and expand Errors and Warnings in order to select Blocked Process Report. You should have something similar to Figure 12-15.

Figure 12-15. *Blocked process report event selected in Trace Properties*

You need to be sure that the TextData column is also selected. If you still have the queries running from the previous section that created the block, all you need to do now is click the Run button to capture the event. Otherwise, go back to Listings 12-1 and 12-2 and run them in two different connections. After the blocked process threshold is passed, you'll see the event fire. And fire. Every five seconds it will fire if that's how you've configured it and you're leaving the connections running from Listings 12-1 and 12-2. What's generated is a rather hard to read XML file:


```
<blocked-process-report>
 <blocked-process>
  <process id="process50801c0" taskpriority="0" logused="0"
waitresource="RID: 14:1:1279:0" waittime="5212" ownerId="9616"
transactionname="User2" lasttranstarted="2008-12-19T10:02:29.617" XDES="0x730bbe0"
lockMode="S" schedulerid="2" kpid="2468" status="suspended" spid="53" sbid="0"
ecid="0" priority="0" trancount="1" lastbatchstarted="2008-12-19T10:02:29.617"
lastbatchcompleted="2008-12-19T10:01:42.990" clientapp="Microsoft SQL Server
Management Studio - Query" hostname="FRITCHEYGXP" hostpid="5748"
loginname="CORP\fritcheyg" isolationlevel="read committed (2)"
xactid="9616" currentdb="14"
lockTimeout="4294967295" clientoption1="671098976" clientoption2="390200">
   <executionStack>
    <frame line="2" stmtstart="24"
sqlhandle="0x020000001be0f42a9b3a6fd8eae5b4ae648e87cc70b1f6ba"/>
    <frame line="2" stmtstart="40" stmtend="114"
sqlhandle="0x020000003c6c8b1b2150baa2bc7c06d7557a87169ea51e5a"/>
   </executionStack>
   <inputbuf>
BEGIN TRAN User2
  SELECT c2 FROM dbo.t1 WHERE c1 = 11;
COMMIT
   </inputbuf>
  </process>
 </blocked-process>
 <blocking-process>
  <process status="sleeping" spid="54" sbid="0" ecid="0" priority="0" trancount="1"
lastbatchstarted="2008-12-19T10:02:27.163"
lastbatchcompleted="2008-12-19T10:02:27.163"
clientapp="Microsoft SQL Server Management Studio - Query"
hostname="FRITCHEYGXP" hostpid="5748" loginname="CORP\fritcheyg"
isolationlevel="read committed (2)" xactid="9615" currentdb="14"
lockTimeout="4294967295" clientoption1="671098976" clientoption2="390200">
   <executionStack/>
   <inputbuf>
BEGIN TRAN User1
UPDATE  dbo.t1
SET     c3 = GETDATE();
--rollback
   </inputbuf>
  </process>
 </blocking-process>
</blocked-process-report>
```

But if you look through it, the elements are clear. <blocked-process> shows information about the process that was blocked including familiar information such as the SPID, the database ID, and so on. It doesn't include some of the other information that you can easily get from T-SQL queries such as the query string of the blocked and waiting process. But with the SPID available, you can get them from the cache, if available, or you can combine the Blocked Process report with other trace events such as `RPC:Starting` to show the query information. However, that will add to the overhead of using this long term within your database. If you know you have a blocking problem, this can be part of a short-term monitoring project to capture the necessary blocking information.

Blocking Resolutions

Once you've analyzed the cause of a block, the next step is to determine any possible resolutions. A few techniques you can use to do this are as follows:

- Optimize the queries executed by blocking and blocked SPIDs.
- Decrease the isolation level.
- Partition the contended data.
- Use a covering index on the contended data.

■ **Note** A detailed list of recommendations to avoid blocking appears later in the chapter in the section "Recommendations to Reduce Blocking."

To understand these resolution techniques, let's apply them in turn to the preceding blocking scenario.

Optimize the Queries

Optimizing the queries executed by the blocking and blocked SPIDs helps reduce the blocking duration. In the blocking scenario, the queries executed by the SPIDs participating in the blocking are as follows:

- Blocking SPID:

```
BEGIN TRAN User1
  UPDATE dbo.t1
SET c3 = GETDATE()
```

- Blocked SPID:

```
BEGIN TRAN User2
  SELECT c2
  FROM dbo.t1
  WHERE c1 = 11
COMMIT
```

Let's analyze the individual SQL statements executed by the blocking and blocked SPIDs to optimize their performance:

- The UPDATE statement of the blocking SPID accesses the data without a WHERE clause. This makes the query inherently costly on a large table. If possible, break the action of the UPDATE statement into multiple batches using appropriate WHERE clauses. If the individual UPDATE statements of the batch are executed in separate transactions, then fewer locks will be held on the resource within one transaction, and for shorter time periods.
- The SELECT statement executed by the blocked SPID has a WHERE clause on column c1. From the index structure on the test table, you can see that there is no index on this column. To optimize the SELECT statement, you should create a clustered index on column c1:

```
CREATE CLUSTERED INDEX i1 ON t1(c1)
```

Note Since the table fits within one page, adding the clustered index won't make much difference to the query performance. However, as the number of rows in the table increases, the beneficial effect of the index will become more pronounced.

Optimizing the queries reduces the duration for which the locks are held by the SPIDs. The query optimization reduces the impact of blocking; it doesn't prevent the blocking completely. However, as long as the optimized queries execute within acceptable performance limits, a small amount of blocking may be neglected.

Decrease the Isolation Level

Another approach to resolve blocking can be to use a lower isolation level, if possible. The SELECT statement of the User2 transaction gets blocked while requesting an (S) lock on the data row. The isolation level of this transaction can be decreased to Read Uncommitted so that the (S) lock is not requested by the SELECT statement. The Read Uncommitted isolation level can be configured for the connection using the SET statement:

```
SET TRANSACTION ISOLATION LEVEL READ UNCOMMITTED
GO
BEGIN TRAN User2
  SELECT c2
  FROM dbo.t1
  WHERE c1 = 11;
COMMIT
GO
SET TRANSACTION ISOLATION LEVEL READ COMMITTED --Back to default
GO
```

The Read Uncommitted isolation level can also be configured for the SELECT statement at a query level by using the NOLOCK locking hint:

```
BEGIN TRAN User2
  SELECT c2
  FROM dbo.t1 WITH(NOLOCK)
  WHERE c1 = 11;
COMMIT
```

The Read Uncommitted isolation level avoids the blocking faced by the User2 transaction.

This example shows the utility of reducing the isolation level. However, as a production solution, this has severe problems. Not only can you get *dirty reads*, which means that the data returned by the select statement is changing or changed, but you can get inconsistent reads. It's possible while reading uncommitted data to get extra rows or fewer rows as pages are split and rearranged by the actions of other queries. Reading uncommitted data is a very popular way to reduce contention and increase performance on the database, but it comes at a very high cost in terms of data accuracy. Be very aware of these costs prior to attempting to use this as an active solution within your database.

Partition the Contended Data

When dealing with very large data sets or data that can be very discretely stored, it is possible to apply table partitioning to the data. Partitioned data is split horizontally, meaning by certain values (for example, splitting sales data up by month). This allows the transactions to execute concurrently on the individual partitions, without blocking each other. These separate partitions are treated as a single unit for querying, updating, and inserting; only the storage and access are separated out by SQL Server. It should be noted that partitioning is available only in the Developer Edition and Enterprise Edition of SQL Server.

In the preceding blocking scenario, the data could be separated by date. This would entail setting up multiple filegroups and splitting the data per a defined rule. Once the UPDATE statement gets a WHERE clause, then it and the original SELECT statement will be able to execute concurrently on two separate partitions.

Partitioning the table does add some overhead to maintain integrity between the parts of the table. However, if done properly, it can improve both performance and concurrency on very large data sets.

Covering Index on Contended Data

In a blocking scenario, you should analyze whether the query of the blocking or the blocked SPID can be fully satisfied using a covering index. If the query of one of the SPIDs can be satisfied using a covering index, then it will prevent the SPID from requesting locks on the contended resource. Also, if the other SPID doesn't need a lock on the covering index (to maintain data integrity), then both SPIDs will be able to execute concurrently without blocking each other.

For instance, in the preceding blocking scenario, the SELECT statement by the blocked SPID can be fully satisfied by a covering index on columns c1 and c2:

```
CREATE NONCLUSTERED INDEX iAvoidBlocking ON dbo.t1(c1, c2)
```

The transaction of the blocking SPID need not acquire a lock on the covering index since it accesses only column c3 of the table. The covering index will allow the SELECT statement to get the values for columns c1 and c2 without accessing the base table. Thus, the SELECT statement of the blocked SPID can acquire an (S) lock on the covering-index row without being blocked by the (X) lock on the data row acquired by the blocking SPID. This allows both transactions to execute concurrently without any blocking.

Consider a covering index as a mechanism to "duplicate" part of the table data whose consistency is automatically maintained by SQL Server. This covering index, if mostly read-only, can allow some transactions to be served from the "duplicate" data while the base table (and other indexes) can continue to serve other transactions.

Recommendations to Reduce Blocking

Single-user performance and the ability to scale with multiple users are both important for a database application. In a multiuser environment, it is important to ensure that the database operations don't hold database resources for a long time. This allows the database to support a large number of operations (or database users) concurrently without serious performance degradation. The following is a list of tips to reduce/avoid database blocking:

- Keep transactions short.
  - Perform the minimum steps/logic within a transaction.
  - Do not perform costly external activity within a transaction, such as sending acknowledgment email or performing activities driven by the end user.
- Optimize queries using indexes.
  - Create indexes as required to ensure optimal performance of the queries within the system.
  - Avoid a clustered index on frequently updated columns. Updates to clustered index key columns require locks on the clustered index and all nonclustered indexes (since their row locator contains the clustered index key).
  - Consider using a covering index to serve the blocked SELECT statements.
- Consider partitioning a contended table.
- Use query timeouts to control runaway queries.
- Avoid losing control over the scope of the transactions because of poor error-handling routines or application logic.
  - Use SET XACT_ABORT ON to avoid a transaction being left open on an error condition within the transaction.
  - Execute the following SQL statement from a client error handler (TRY/CATCH) after executing a SQL batch or stored procedure containing a transaction:

    ```
    IF @@TRANCOUNT > 0 ROLLBACK
    ```
- Use the lowest isolation level required.
  - Use the default isolation level (Read Committed).
  - Consider using row versioning to help reduce contention.

Automation to Detect and Collect Blocking Information

You can automate the process of detecting a blocking condition and collecting the relevant information using SQL Server Agent. SQL Server provides the Performance Monitor counters shown in Table 12-1 to track the amount of wait time.

Table 12-1. *Performance Monitor Counters*

Object	Counter	Instance	Description
SQLServer:Locks (For SQL Server named instance: MSSQL$<InstanceName>:Locks)	Average Wait Time (ms)	_Total	The average amount of wait time for each lock that resulted in a wait
	Lock Wait Time (ms)	_Total	Total wait time for locks in the last second

You can create a combination of the SQL Server alerts and jobs to automate the following process:

1. Determine when the average amount of wait time exceeds an acceptable amount of blocking using the `Average Wait Time (ms)` counter. Based on your preferences, you can use the `Lock Wait Time (ms)` counter instead.
2. Once you've established the minimum wait, set Blocked Process Threshold. When the average wait time exceeds the limit, notify the SQL Server DBA of the blocking situation through email and/or a pager.
3. Automatically collect the blocking information using the blocker script or a trace using the Blocked Process report for a certain period of time.

To set up the Blocked Process report to run automatically, first create the SQL Server job, called Blocking Analysis, so that it can be used by the SQL Server alert created later. You can create this SQL Server job from SQL Server Management Studio to collect blocking information by following these steps:

1. Generate a trace script (as detailed in Chapter 3) using the "`Errors And Warnings: Blocked process report` event. Set a stop time to ten minutes greater than the current time. Using the `sp_trace_create` procedure in the generated script, set the parameter `@stoptime = SELECT DATEADD(mi,10,GETDATE())`.
2. In Management Studio, expand the server by selecting *<ServerName>* ➤ SQL Server Agent ➤ ➤ Jobs; then right-click, and select New Job.

3. On the General page of the New Job dialog box, enter the job name and other details, as shown in Figure 12-16.

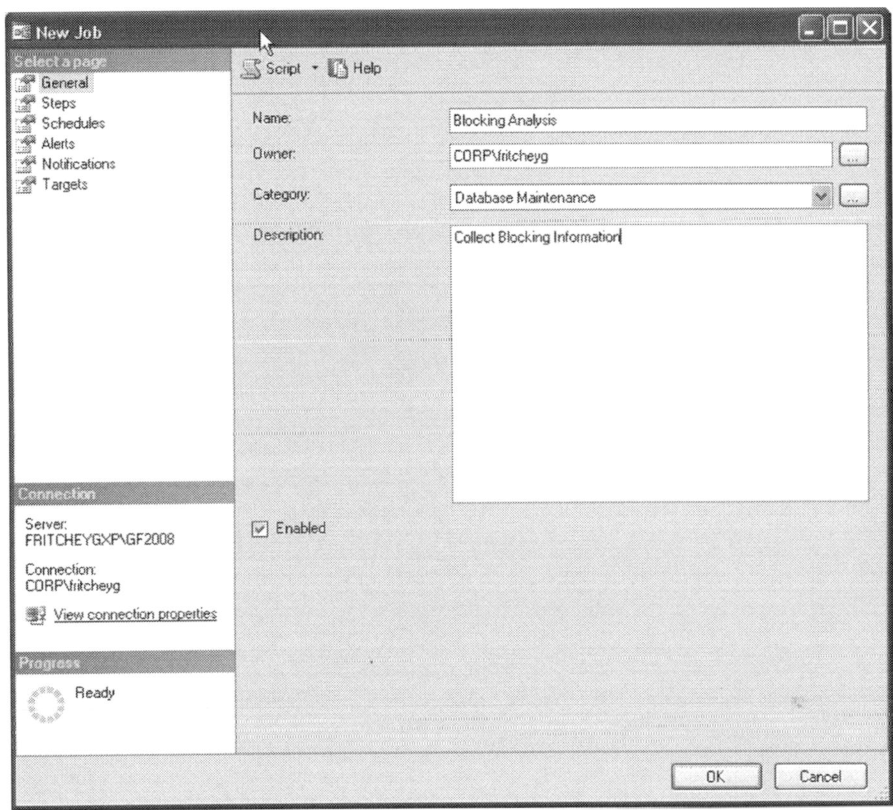

Figure 12-16. *Entering the job name and other details*

4. On the Steps page, click New, and enter the command to run the trace script from a Windows command prompt (or you could run it from PowerShell or create the script as a procedure), as shown in Figure 12-17.

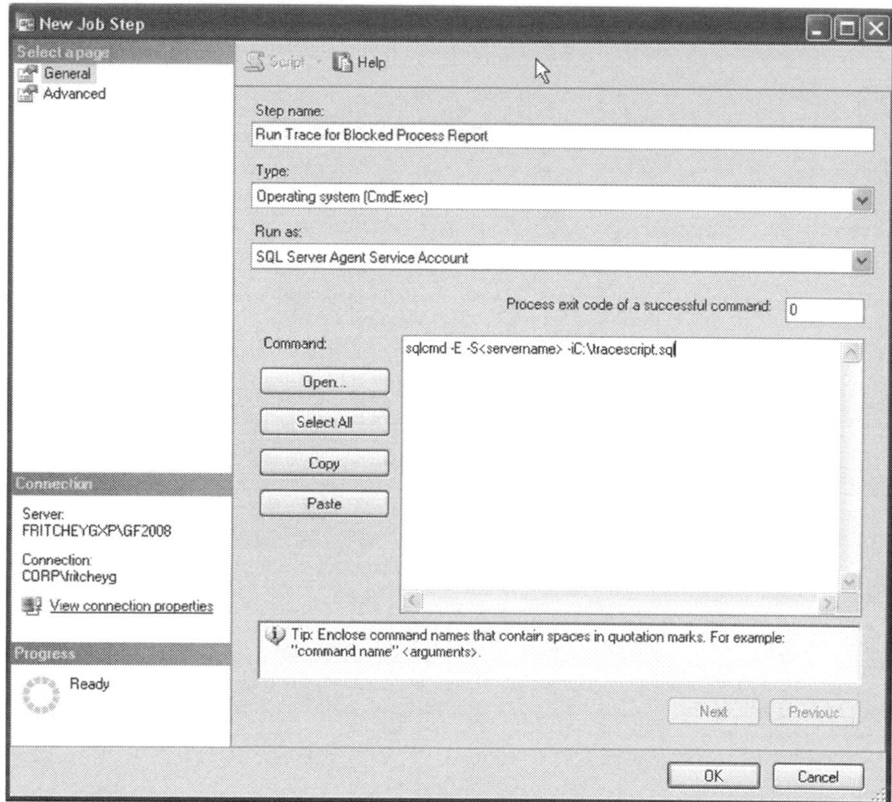

Figure 12-17. *Entering the command to run the blocker script*

You can use the following command:

```
sqlcmd -E -S<servername> -iC:\tracescript.sql
```

The output of the blocker script is determined as part of the trace that you created.

5. Return to the New Job dialog box by clicking OK.
6. Click OK to create the SQL Server job. The SQL Server job will be created with an enabled and runnable state to collect blocking information for ten minutes using the trace script.

You can create a SQL Server alert to automate the following tasks:

- Inform the DBA via email, SMS text, or pager.
- Execute the Blocking Analysis job to collect blocking information for ten minutes.

You can create the SQL Server alert from SQL Server Enterprise Manager by following these steps:

1. In Management Studio, while still in the SQL Agent area of the Object Explorer, right-click Alerts, and select New Alert.
2. On the General page of the new alert's Properties dialog box, enter the alert name and other details, as shown in Figure 12-18. The specific object you need to capture information from for your instance is Locks (MSSQL$GF2008:Locks in Figure 12-18).

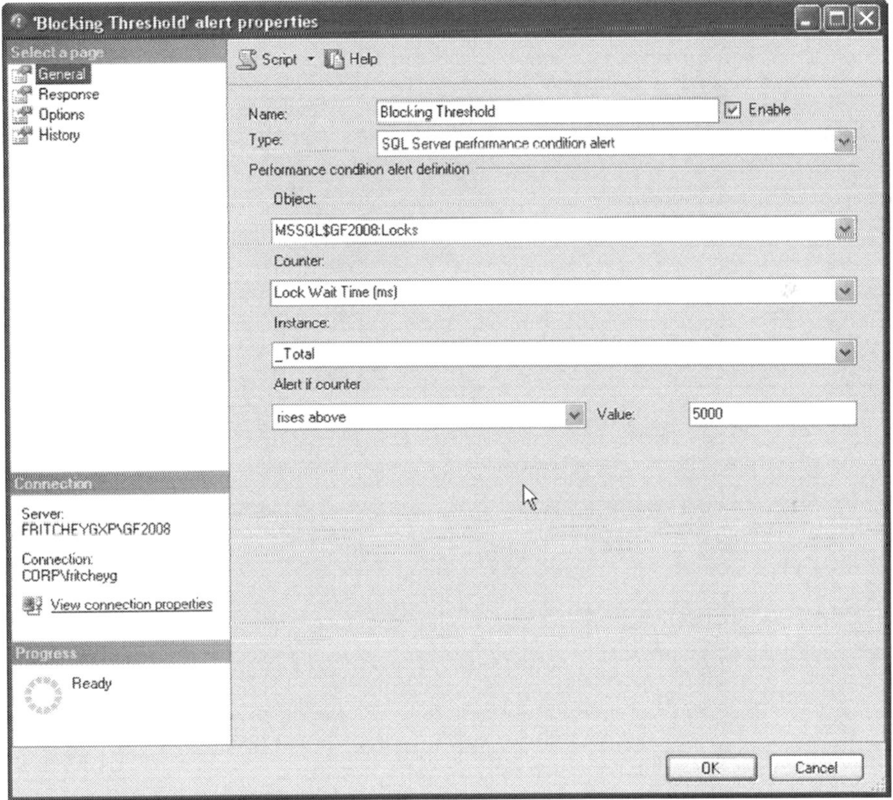

Figure 12-18. *Entering the alert name and other details*

3. On the Response page, click New Operator, and enter the operator details, as shown in Figure 12-19.

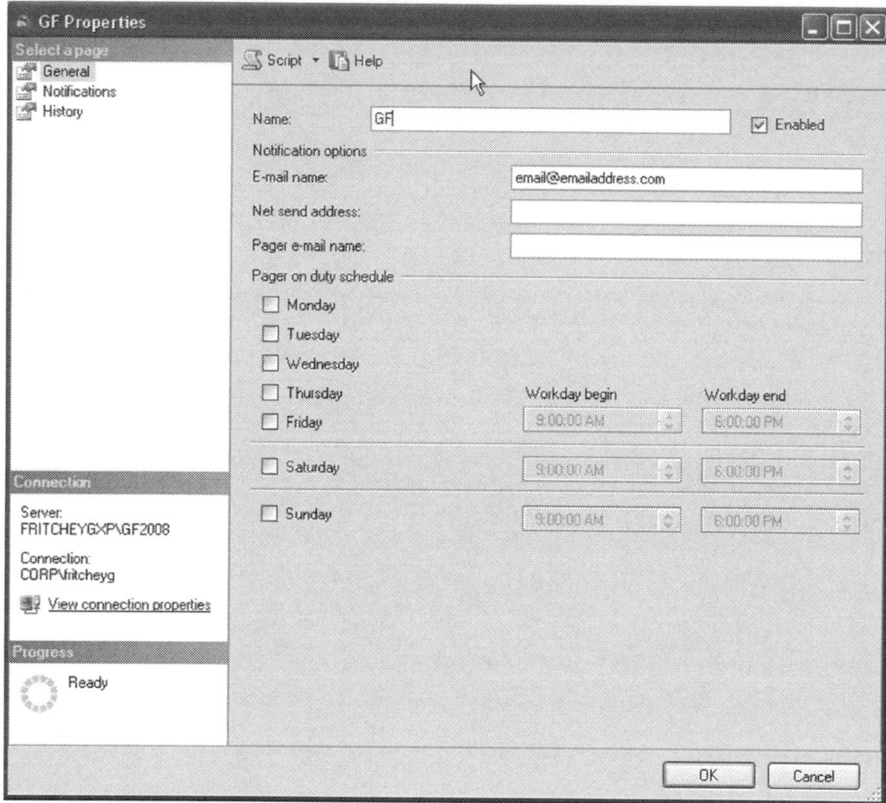

Figure 12-19. *Entering the operator details*

4. Return to the new alert's Properties dialog box by clicking OK.
5. On the Response page, enter the remaining information shown in Figure 12-20.

   The Blocking Analysis job is selected to automatically collect the blocking information.
6. Once you've finished entering all the information, click OK to create the SQL Server alert. The SQL Server alert will be created in the enabled state to perform the intended tasks.
7. Ensure that the SQL Server Agent is running.

The SQL Server alert and the job together will automate the blocking detection and the information collection process. This automatic collection of the blocking information will ensure that a good amount of the blocking information will be available whenever the system gets into a massive blocking state.

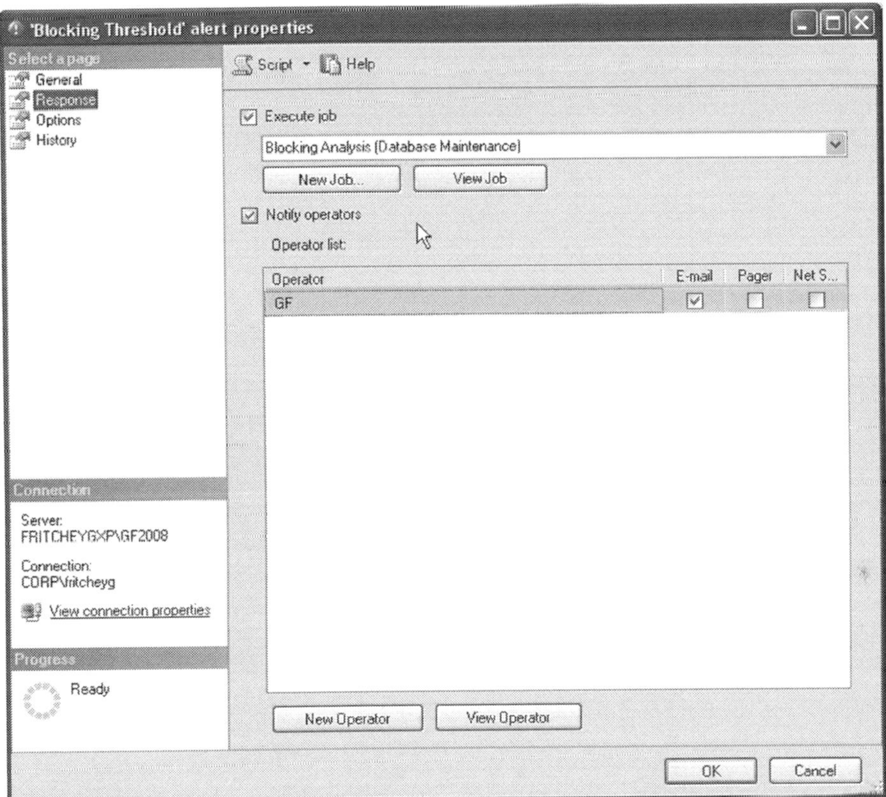

Figure 12-20. *Entering the actions to be performed when the alert is triggered*

Summary

Even though blocking is inevitable and is in fact essential to maintain isolation among transactions, it can sometimes adversely affect database concurrency. In a multiuser database application, you must minimize blocking among concurrent transactions.

SQL Server provides different techniques to avoid/reduce blocking, and a database application should take advantage of these techniques to scale linearly as the number of database users increases. When an application faces a high degree of blocking, you can collect the relevant blocking information using a blocker script to understand the root cause of the blocking and accordingly use an appropriate technique to either avoid or reduce blocking.

Blocking can not only hurt concurrency but can also cause an abrupt termination of a database request in the case of circular blocking. We will cover circular blocking, or deadlocks, in the next chapter.

CHAPTER 13

Deadlock Analysis

When a deadlock occurs between two or more transactions, SQL Server allows one transaction to complete and terminates the other transaction. SQL Server then returns an error to the corresponding application, notifying the user that they have been chosen as a deadlock victim. This leaves the application with only two options: resubmit the transaction or apologize to the end user. To successfully complete a transaction and avoid the apologies, it is important to understand what might cause a deadlock and the ways to handle a deadlock.

In this chapter, I cover the following topics:

- Deadlock fundamentals
- Error handling to catch a deadlock
- Ways to analyze the cause of a deadlock
- Techniques to resolve a deadlock

Deadlock Fundamentals

A *deadlock* is a special blocking scenario in which two sessions get blocked by each other. Each session, while holding its own resources, attempts to access a resource that is locked by the other session. This will lead to a circular blocking scenario, also known as a *deadly embrace*, as illustrated in Figure 13-1.

Deadlocks also frequently occur when two processes attempt to escalate their locking mechanisms on the same resource. In this case, each of the two processes has a shared lock on a resource, such as an `RID`, and they both attempt to promote the lock from shared to exclusive, but neither can do so until the other releases its shared lock. This too leads to one of the processes being chosen as a deadlock victim.

Deadlocks are an especially nasty type of blocking, because a deadlock cannot resolve on its own, even if given an unlimited period of time. A deadlock requires an external process to break the circular blocking.

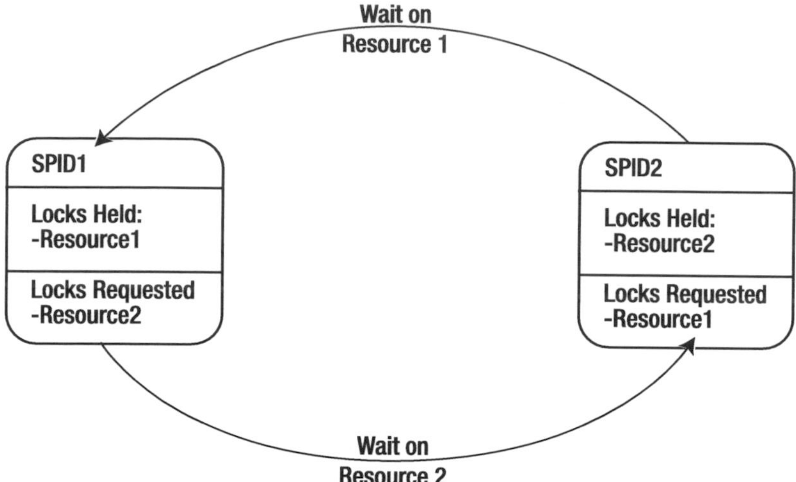

Figure 13-1. *Circular blocking scenario*

SQL Server has a deadlock detection routine, called a *lock monitor,* that regularly checks for the presence of deadlocks in SQL Server. Once a deadlock condition is detected, SQL Server selects one of the sessions participating in the deadlock as a *victim* to break the circular blocking. This process involves withdrawing all the resources held by the victim session. SQL Server does so by rolling back the uncommitted transaction of the session picked as a victim.

Choosing the Deadlock Victim

SQL Server determines the session to be a deadlock victim by evaluating the cost of undoing the transaction of the participating sessions, and it selects the one with the least cost. You can exercise some control over the session to be chosen as a victim by setting the deadlock priority of its connection to `LOW`:

```
SET DEADLOCK_PRIORITY LOW
```

This steers SQL Server toward choosing this particular session as a victim in the event of a deadlock. You can reset the deadlock priority of the connection to its normal value by executing the following `SET` statement:

```
SET DEADLOCK_PRIORITY NORMAL
```

The `SET` statement allows you to mark a session as a `HIGH` deadlock priority too. This won't prevent deadlocks on a given session, but it will reduce the likelihood of a given session being picked as the victim. You can even set the priority level to a number value from –10 for the lowest priority to 10 for the highest.

In the event of a tie, one of the processes is chosen as a victim and rolled back as if it had the least cost. Some processes are invulnerable to being picked as a deadlock victim. These processes are marked as such and will never be chosen as a deadlock victim. The most common example I've seen are processes already involved in a rollback.

Using Error Handling to Catch a Deadlock

When SQL Server chooses a session as a victim, it raises an error with the error number. You can use the TRY/CATCH construct within T-SQL to handle the error. SQL Server ensures the consistency of the database by automatically rolling back the transaction of the victim session. The rollback ensures that the session is back to the same state it was in before the start of its transaction. On determining a deadlock situation in the error handler, it is possible to attempt to restart the transaction within T-SQL a number of times before returning the error to the application.

Take the following T-SQL statement as an example of one method for handling a deadlock error (trap_sample.sql in the download):

```
DECLARE @retry AS TINYINT = 1
   ,@retrymax AS TINYINT = 2
   ,@retrycount AS TINYINT = 0 ;

WHILE @retry = 1
    AND @retrycount <= @retrymax
    BEGIN
        SET @retry = 0 ;
        BEGIN TRY
            UPDATE  HumanResources.Employee
            SET     LoginID = '54321'
            WHERE   BusinessEntityID = 100 ;
        END TRY
        BEGIN CATCH
            IF (ERROR_NUMBER() = 1205)
                BEGIN
                    SET @retrycount = @retrycount + 1 ;
                    SET @retry = 1 ;
                END
        END CATCH
    END
```

The TRY/CATCH methodology allows you to capture errors. You can then check the error number using the ERROR_NUMBER() function to determine whether you have a deadlock. Once a deadlock is established, it's possible to try restarting the transaction a set number of times, in this case, two. Using error trapping will help your application deal with intermittent or occasional deadlocks, but the best approach is to analyze the cause of the deadlock and resolve it, if possible.

Deadlock Analysis

You can sometimes prevent a deadlock from happening by analyzing the causes. You need the following information to do this:

- The sessions participating in the deadlock
- The resources involved in the deadlock
- The queries executed by the sessions

Collecting Deadlock Information

You can collect the deadlock information three ways: using a specific trace event through the Profiler tool, setting trace flag 1222, and setting trace flag 1204. Trace flags are used to customize certain SQL Server behavior such as, in this case, generating the deadlock information.

Profiler provides information on deadlocks through the `Locks:Deadlock` graph event. The deadlock graph generates XML output in the `TextData` field on a trace. After the trace has captured the deadlock events, you can view them within the Profiler tool by bringing up that particular event. You also have the option of exporting an individual event or all deadlock events to a file.

You can open the deadlock graph in Management Studio or Profiler. You can search the XML, but the deadlock graph generated from the XML works almost like an execution plan for deadlocks, as shown in Figure 13-2.

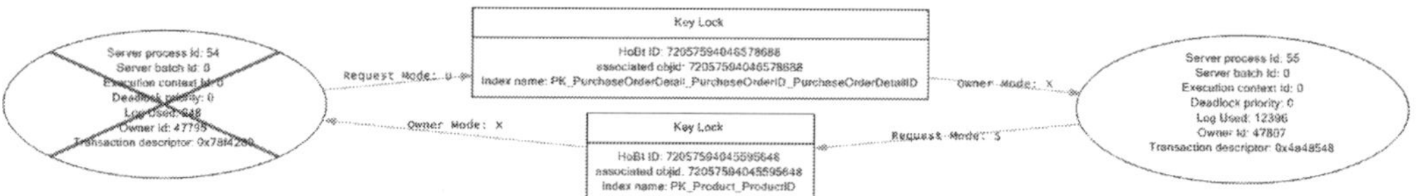

Figure 13-2. *A deadlock graph as displayed in the Profiler*

I'll show you how to use this in the "Analyzing the Deadlock" section.

The two trace flags that generate deadlock information can be used together to generate two sets of information. Usually people will prefer to run one or the other. Trace flag 1222 provides the most detailed information on the deadlock. The trace flags write the information gathered into the log file on the server where the deadlock event occurred.

Trace flag 1204 provides detailed deadlock information that helps you analyze the cause of a deadlock. It sorts the information by each of the nodes involved in the deadlock. Trace flag 1222 also provides detailed deadlock information, but it breaks the information down differently. Trace flag 1222 sorts the information by resource and by processes and provides even more information. Details on both sets of data will be shown in the "Analyzing the Deadlock" section.

The `DBCC TRACEON` statement is used to turn on (or enable) the trace flags. A trace flag remains enabled until it is disabled using the `DBCC TRACEOFF` statement. If the server is restarted, this trace flag will be cleared. You can determine the status of a trace flag using the `DBCC TRACESTATUS` statement. Setting both of the deadlock trace flags looks like this:

```
DBCC TRACEON (1222, -1);
DBCC TRACEON (1204, -1);
```

To ensure that the trace flags are always set, it is possible to make them part of the SQL Server startup in the SQL Server Configuration Manager by following these steps:

1. Open the Properties dialog box of the instance of SQL Server.
2. Switch to the Advanced tab of the Properties dialog box, and find Startup Parameters, as shown in Figure 13-3.

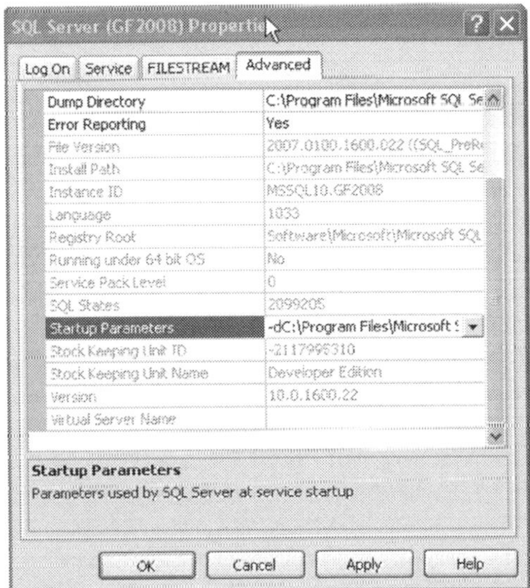

Figure 13-3. *SQL Server instance's Properties dialog box showing the server's advanced properties*

3. Type **;T-1204; T-1222** in the Startup Parameter text box, and click Add to add trace flag 1204, as shown in Figure 13-4. This will set both. I recommend just using trace flag 1222.

```
-dC:\Program Files\Microsoft SQL
Server\MSSQL10.GF2008\MSSQL\DATA\master.mdf;-eC:\Program
Files\Microsoft SQL
Server\MSSQL10.GF2008\MSSQL\Log\ERRORLOG;-lC:\Program
Files\Microsoft SQL Server\MSSQL10.GF2008\MSSQL\DATA\mastlog.ldf;
-t1222;-t1204
```

Figure 13-4. *SQL Server startup parameters settings*

4. Click the OK button to close all the dialog boxes.

These trace flag settings will be in effect after you restart your SQL Server instance.

Analyzing the Deadlock

To analyze the cause of a deadlock, let's consider a straightforward little example. First, make sure you've turned on the deadlock trace flags, 1204 and 1222, and created a trace that uses the deadlock graph event. In one connection, execute this script (`deadlock_1.sql` in the download):

```
BEGIN TRAN
UPDATE  Purchasing.PurchaseOrderHeader
SET     Freight = Freight * 0.9 -- 10% discount on shipping
WHERE   PurchaseOrderID = 1255 ;
```

In a second connection, execute this script (`deadlock_2.sql` in the download):

```
BEGIN TRANSACTION
UPDATE  Purchasing.PurchaseOrderDetail
SET     OrderQty = 2
WHERE   ProductID = 448
        AND PurchaseOrderID = 1255 ;
```

Each of these opens a transaction and manipulates data, but neither one commits or rolls back the transaction. Switch back to the first transaction, and run this query:

```
UPDATE  Purchasing.PurchaseOrderDetail
SET     OrderQty = 4
WHERE   ProductID = 448
        AND PurchaseOrderID = 1255 ;
```

Unfortunately, after possibly a few seconds, the first connection faces a deadlock:

```
Msg 1205, Level 13, State 51, Line 1
Transaction (Process ID 54) was deadlocked on lock resources with another process
and has been chosen as the deadlock victim. Rerun the transaction.
```

Any idea what's wrong here?

Let's analyze the deadlock by first examining the deadlock graph collected through the trace event (see Figure 13-5).

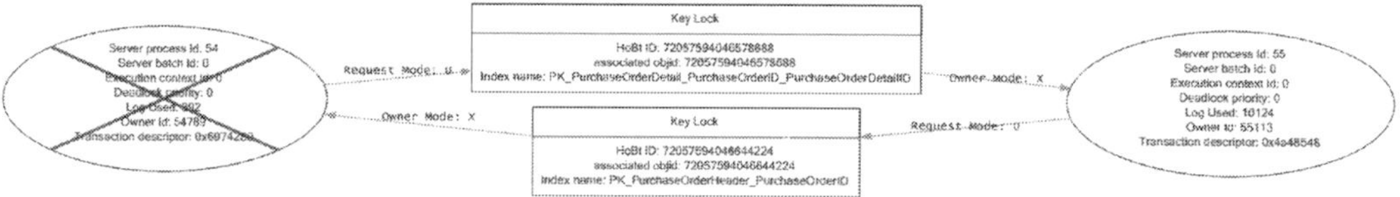

Figure 13-5. *A deadlock graph displayed in the Profiler tool*

From the deadlock graph displayed in Figure 13-5, it's fairly clear that two processes were involved, session 54 and session 55. Session 54, the one with the big blue *X* crossing it out, was chosen as the deadlock victim. Two different keys were in question. The top key was owned by session 55, as demonstrated by the arrow pointing to the session object, named Owner Mode, and marked with an *X* for exclusive. Session 54 was attempting to request the same key for an update. The other key was owned by session 54 with session 55 requesting an update. You can see the exact HoBt ID, object ID, and index name for the objects in question for the deadlock. For a classic, simple deadlock like this, you have most of the information you need. The last piece would be the queries running from each process. These would need to be captured using a different Profiler event.

This visual representation of the deadlock can do the job, but to really understand exactly where deadlocks occurred, what processes caused them, and which objects were involved, the best tool is still the trace flag. As I mentioned earlier, I prefer using trace flag 1222.

Trace flag 1222 also generates deadlock information and stores it in the error log. Table 13-1 shows each statement from trace flag 1222 and the information it represents.

Table 13-1. *Trace Flag 1222 Data*

Entry in Log	Description
`deadlock-list`	The beginning of the deadlock information.
`deadlock victim=process502d720`	Physical memory address of the process picked to be the deadlock victim.
`process-list`	Processes that define the deadlock victim.
`process id=process502d720 taskpriority=0 logused=392 waitresource=KEY: 14:72057594046578688 (f800e6f77703) waittime=4907 ownerId=57602 transactionname=user_transaction lasttranstarted=2008-12-05T23:20:55.960 XDES=0x7eb0c10 lockMode=U schedulerid=2 kpid=3444 status=suspended spid=54 sbid=0 ecid=0 priority=0 trancount=2 lastbatchstarted=2008-12-05T23:21:15.600 lastbatchcompleted=2008-12-05T23:21:15.600 lastattention=2008-12-05T23:07:00.080 clientapp=Microsoft SQL Server Management Studio - Query hostname=FRITCHEYGXP hostpid=2724 loginname=CORP\fritcheyg` **`isolationlevel=read committed`** `(2) xactid=57602 currentdb=14 lockTimeout=4294967295 clientoption1=671098976 clientoption2=390200`	All the information about the session picked as the deadlock victim. Note the highlighted isolation level, which is a key for helping identify the root cause of a deadlock.
`executionStack`	T-SQL that was being executed.
`frame procname=adhoc line=1 stmtstart=64 sqlhandle=0x02000000d0c7f31a30fb1ad425c34357fe8ef6326793e7aa`	The type of query being executed, in this case ad hoc.
`UPDATE [Purchasing].[PurchaseOrderDetail] set [OrderQty] = @1 WHERE [ProductID]=@2 AND [PurchaseOrderID]=@3`	The T-SQL statement generated for the execution plan.
`frame procname=adhoc line=1 sqlhandle=0x020000001472d506ef788e5357d6da47e2652f0e385d481d`	The next statement in the batch.
`UPDATE Purchasing.PurchaseOrderDetail SET OrderQty = 4 WHERE ProductID = 448 AND PurchaseOrderID = 1255 ;`	The query with values.
`Inputbuf`	The statements for the current batch.
`UPDATE Purchasing.PurchaseOrderDetail SET OrderQty = 4 WHERE ProductID = 448 AND PurchaseOrderID = 1255 ;`	The text from the execution plan showing the precise values used by the statement defined earlier.

Continued

Table 13-1. *Continued*

Entry in Log	Description
`process id=processb0fab0 taskpriority=0 logused=10124 waitresource=KEY: 14:72057594046644224 (e700bef11a92) waittime=21088 ownerId=57607 transactionname=user_transaction lasttranstarted=2008-12-05T23:20:59.410 XDES=0x7eb1640 lockMode=U schedulerid=2 kpid=4248 status=suspended spid=53 sbid=0 ecid=0 priority=0 trancount=2 lastbatchstarted=2008-12-05T23:20:59.410 lastbatchcompleted=2008-12-05T23:20:59.410 clientapp=Microsoft SQL Server Management Studio - Query hostname=FRITCHEYGXP hostpid=2724 loginname=CORP\fritcheyg isolationlevel=read committed (2) xactid=57607 currentdb=14 lockTimeout=4294967295 clientoption1=673327200 clientoption2=390200`	The next process in the deadlock. This is the process that succeeded.
`executionStack`	
`frame procname=AdventureWorks2008.Purchasing. uPurchaseOrderDetail line=39 stmtstart=2732 stmtend=3864 sqlhandle=0x03000e00203bb566d83ad7004f9b00000000000000000000`	Note the procname value, `AdventureWorks2008.Purchasing. uPurchaseOrderDetail`. This is a trigger fired by the following code.
`UPDATE [Purchasing].[PurchaseOrderHeader] SET [Purchasing].[PurchaseOrderHeader]. [SubTotal] = (SELECT SUM([Purchasing].[PurchaseOrderDetail]. [LineTotal]) FROM [Purchasing].[PurchaseOrderDetail] WHERE [Purchasing].[PurchaseOrderHeader]. [PurchaseOrderID] = [Purchasing].[PurchaseOrderDetail]. [PurchaseOrderID]) WHERE [Purchasing].[PurchaseOrderHeader]. [PurchaseOrderID] IN (SELECT inserted.[PurchaseOrderID] FROM inserted);`	The T-SQL executed by the trigger.
`frame procname=adhoc line=2 stmtstart=64 sqlhandle=0x02000000d0c7f31a30fb1ad425c34357fe8ef6326793e7aa`	The ad hoc code defined in the listings being run.
`UPDATE [Purchasing].[PurchaseOrderDetail] set [OrderQty] = @1 WHERE [ProductID]=@2 AND [PurchaseOrderID]=@3`	Again, this is the code as presented to the optimizer including parameterization.
`frame procname=adhoc line=2 stmtstart=38 sqlhandle=0x020000008a87202a1b402d77071c771ac5d1b58e896fbf3f`	Definition of the T-SQL.

Entry in Log	Description
UPDATE Purchasing.PurchaseOrderDetail SET OrderQty = 2 WHERE ProductID = 448 AND PurchaseOrderID = 1255 ;	T SQL, including the actual values. This would be the cause of firing of the trigger.
Inputbuf	
BEGIN TRANSACTION UPDATE Purchasing.PurchaseOrderDetail SET OrderQty = 2 WHERE ProductID = 448 AND PurchaseOrderID = 1255 ;	The query with the actual values passed.
resource-list	The objects that caused the conflict.
keylock hobtid=72057594046578688 dbid=14 objectname=AdventureWorks2008.Purchasing. PurchaseOrderDetail indexname=PK_ PurchaseOrderDetail_PurchaseOrderID_ PurchaseOrderDetailID id=lock48b7cc0 mode=X associatedObjectId=72057594046578688	Definition of the primary key from the Purchasing.PurchaseOrderDetail table.
owner-list	The process that owned the object.
owner id=processb0fab0 mode=X	Process definition.
waiter-list	The process that was waiting for access to the object, which is the deadlock victim.
waiter id=process502d720 mode=U requestType=wait	Additional detail about the waiting process.
keylock hobtid=72057594046644224 dbid=14 objectname=AdventureWorks2008. Purchasing.PurchaseOrderHeader indexname=PK_ PurchaseOrderHeader_PurchaseOrderID id=lock48b9100 mode=X associatedObjectId= 72057594046644224	The Purchasing.PurchaseOrderHeader clustered index where the conflict occurred.
owner-list	Owner of the object.
owner id=process502d720 mode=X	Owner definition. Note this was the process waiting for access to the Purchasing.PurchaseOrderDetail table.
waiter-list	Process waiting for access.
waiter id=processb0fab0 mode=U requestType=wait	Process waiting for access. As you can see, this process owned the lock on the Purchasing.PurchaseOrderDetail table.

This information is a bit more difficult to read through than the clean set of data provided by the deadlock graph. However, it is a very similar set of information. You can see, highlighted in bold near the bottom, the definition of one of the keys associated with the deadlock. You can also see, just before it, that the text of the execution plans is available through trace flag 1222, unlike the deadlock graph. In this case, you are much more likely to have everything you need to isolate the cause of the deadlock.

The information collected by trace flag 1204 is completely different from either of the other two sets of data and doesn't provide nearly as much detail as trace flag 1222. Trace flag 1204 is also much more difficult to interpret. For all these reasons, I suggest you stick to using trace flag 1222 to capture deadlock data.

This example demonstrated a classic circular reference. Although not immediately obvious, the deadlock was caused by a trigger on the `Purchasing.PurchaseOrderDetail` table. When `Quantity` is updated on the `Purchasing.PurchaseOrderDetail` table, it attempts to update the `Purchasing.PurchaseOrderHeader` table. When the first two queries are run, each within an open transaction, it's just a blocking situation. The second query is waiting on the first to clear so that it can also update the `Purchasing.PurchaseOrderHeader` table. But when the third query, the second within the first transaction, is introduced, now a circular reference is in place, and the only way to resolve it is to kill one of the processes.

Before proceeding, be sure to roll back the open transaction.

The obvious question at this stage is, can you avoid this deadlock? If the answer is yes, then how?

Avoiding Deadlocks

The methods for avoiding a deadlock scenario depend upon the nature of the deadlock. The following are some of the techniques you can use to avoid a deadlock:

- Accessing resources in the same chronological order
- Decreasing the locking
- Minimizing lock contention

Accessing Resources in the Same Chronological Order

One of the most commonly adopted techniques in avoiding a deadlock is to ensure that every transaction accesses the resources in the same physical order. For instance, suppose that two transactions need to access two resources. If each transaction accesses the resources in the same physical order, then the first transaction will successfully acquire locks on the resources without being blocked by the second transaction. The second transaction will be blocked by the first while trying to acquire a lock on the first resource. This will cause a typical blocking scenario without leading to a circular blocking.

If the resources are not accessed in the same physical order, as follows (and as demonstrated in the earlier deadlock analysis example), this can cause a circular blocking between the two transactions:

- Transaction 1:
  - Access Resource 1
  - Access Resource 2
- Transaction 2:
  - Access Resource 2
  - Access Resource 1

In the current deadlock scenario, the following resources are involved in the deadlock:

- Resource 1, hobtid=72057594046578688: This is the index row within index PK_PurchaseOrderDetail_PurchaseOrderId_PurchaseOrderDetailId on table Purchasing.PurchaseOrderDetail.
- Resource 2, hobtid=72057594046644224: This is the row within clustered index PK_PurchaseOrderHeader_PurchaseOrderId on table Purchasing.PurchaseOrderHeader.

Both sessions attempt to access the resource; unfortunately, the order in which they access the key are different.

Decreasing the Number of Resources Accessed

A deadlock involves at least two resources. A session holds the first resource and then requests the second resource. The other session holds the second resource and requests the first resource. If you can prevent the sessions (or at least one of them) from accessing one of the resources involved in the deadlock, then you can prevent the deadlock. You can achieve this by redesigning the application, which is a solution highly resisted by developers late in the project. However, you can consider using the following features of SQL Server without changing the application design:

- Convert a nonclustered index to a clustered index.
- Use a covering index for a SELECT statement.

Convert a Nonclustered Index to a Clustered Index

As you know, the leaf pages of a nonclustered index are separate from the data pages of the heap or the clustered index. Therefore, a nonclustered index takes two locks: one for the base (either the cluster or the heap) and one for the nonclustered index. However, in the case of a clustered index, the leaf pages of the index and the data pages of the table are the same; it requires one lock, and that one lock protects both the clustered index and the table, since the leaf pages and the data pages are the same. This decreases the number of resources to be accessed by the same query, compared to a nonclustered index.

Use a Covering Index for a SELECT Statement

You can also use a covering index to decrease the number of resources accessed by a SELECT statement. Since a SELECT statement can get everything from the covering index itself, it doesn't need to access the base table. Otherwise, the SELECT statement needs to access both the index and the base table to retrieve all the required column values. Using a covering index stops the SELECT statement from accessing the base table, leaving the base table free to be locked by another session.

Minimizing Lock Contention

You can also resolve a deadlock by avoiding the lock request on one of the contended resources. You can do this when the resource is accessed only for reading data. Modifying a resource will always acquire an (X) lock on the resource to maintain the consistency of the resource; therefore, in a deadlock situation, identify the resource accesses that are read-only, and try to avoid their corresponding lock requests by using the dirty read feature, if possible. You can use the following techniques to avoid the lock request on a contended resource:

- Implement row versioning.
- Decrease the isolation level.
- Use locking hints.

Implement Row Versioning

Instead of attempting to prevent access to resources using a more stringent locking scheme, you could implement row versioning through the READ_COMMITTED_SNAPSHOT isolation level or through the SNAPSHOT isolation level. The row versioning isolation levels are used to reduce blocking as outlined in Chapter 12. Because they reduce blocking, which is the root cause of deadlocks, they can also help with deadlocking. By introducing READ_COMMITTED_SNAPSHOT with the following T-SQL, you can have a version of the rows available in tempdb, thus possibly eliminating the contention caused by the lock escalation in the preceding deadlock scenario:

```
ALTER DATABASE AdventureWorks2008
    SET READ_COMMITTED_SNAPSHOT ON;
```

This will allow any necessary reads without causing lock contention since the reads are on a different version of the data. There is overhead associated with row versioning, especially in tempdb and when marshaling data from multiple resources instead of just the table or indexes used in the query. But that trade-off of increased tempdb overhead vs. the benefit of reduced deadlocking and increased concurrency may be worth the cost.

Decrease the Isolation Level

Sometimes the (S) lock requested by a SELECT statement contributes to the formation of circular blocking. You can avoid this type of circular blocking by reducing the isolation level of the transaction containing the SELECT statement to READ UNCOMMITTED. This will allow the SELECT statement to read the data without requesting an (S) lock and thereby avoid the circular blocking. However, reading uncommitted data carries with it a serious issue by returning bad data to client. You need to be in very dire straights to consider this as a method of eliminating your deadlocks.

Use Locking Hints

You can also resolve the deadlock presented in the preceding technique using the following locking hints:

- NOLOCK
- READUNCOMMITTED

Like the READ UNCOMMITTED isolation level, the NOLOCK or READUNCOMMITTED locking hint will avoid the (S) locks requested by a given session, thereby preventing the formation of circular blocking.

The effect of the locking hint is at a query level and is limited to the table (and its indexes) on which it is applied. The NOLOCK and READUNCOMMITTED locking hints are allowed only in SELECT statements and the data selection part of the INSERT, DELETE, and UPDATE statements.

The resolution techniques of minimizing lock contention introduce the side effect of a dirty read, which may not be acceptable in every transaction. Therefore, use these resolution techniques only in situations in which a dirty read is acceptable.

Summary

As you learned in this chapter, a deadlock is the result of circular blocking and is reported to an application with the error number 1205. You can analyze the cause of a deadlock by collecting the deadlock information using the trace flags 1204 and 1222. You can also capture deadlock graphs using a trace.

You have a number of techniques to avoid a deadlock; which technique is applicable depends upon the type of queries executed by the participating sessions, the locks held and requested on the involved resources, and the business rules governing the degree of isolation required. Generally, you can resolve a deadlock by reconfiguring the indexes and the transaction isolation levels. However, at times you may need to redesign the application or automatically reexecute the transaction on a deadlock.

In the next chapter, I cover the performance aspects of cursors and how to optimize the cost overhead of using cursors.

CHAPTER 14

Cursor Cost Analysis

It is very common to find database applications that use cursors to process one row at a time. Because data manipulation through a cursor in SQL Server incurs significant additional overhead, database applications should avoid using cursors. T-SQL and SQL Server are designed to work best with sets of data, not one row at a time. If a cursor must be used, then use a cursor with the least cost.

In this chapter, I cover the following topics:

- The fundamentals of cursors
- A cost analysis of different characteristics of cursors
- The benefits and drawbacks of a default result set over cursors
- Recommendations to minimize the cost overhead of cursors

Cursor Fundamentals

When a query is executed by an application, SQL Server returns a set of data consisting of rows. Generally, applications can't process multiple rows together, so instead they process one row at a time by walking through the result set returned by SQL Server. This functionality is provided by a *cursor*, which is a mechanism to work with one row at a time out of a multirow result set.

Cursor processing usually involves the following steps:

1. Declare the cursor to associate it with a `SELECT` statement and define the characteristics of the cursor.
2. Open the cursor to access the result set returned by the `SELECT` statement.
3. Retrieve a row from the cursor. Optionally, modify the row through the cursor.
4. Once all the rows in the result set are processed, close the cursor, and release the resources assigned to the cursor.

You can create cursors using T-SQL statements or the data access layers (ADO, OLEDB, and ODBC) used to connect to SQL Server. Cursors created using data access layers are commonly referred to as *client* cursors. Cursors written in T-SQL are referred to as *server* cursors. You can write a T-SQL cursor processing for a table, t1, as follows (cursor.sql in the download):

```
--Associate a SELECT statement to a cursor and define the
--cursor's characteristics
DECLARE MyCursor CURSOR
 /*<cursor characteristics>*/
    FOR SELECT  adt.AddressTypeId
               ,adt.NAME
               ,adt.ModifiedDate
        FROM    Person.AddressType adt
--Open the cursor to access the result set returned by the
--SELECT statement
OPEN MyCursor

--Retrieve one row at a time from the result set returned by
--the SELECT statement
DECLARE @AddressTypeId INT
   ,@Name VARCHAR(50)
   ,@ModifiedDate DATETIME

FETCH NEXT FROM MyCursor INTO @AddressTypeId, @Name, @ModifiedDate
WHILE @@FETCH_STATUS = 0
    BEGIN
        PRINT 'NAME = ' + @Name
  --Optionally, modify the row through the cursor
        UPDATE  Person.AddressType
        SET     Name = Name + 'z'
        WHERE CURRENT OF MyCursor
        FETCH NEXT FROM MyCursor INTO @AddressTypeId, @Name, @ModifiedDate
    END
--Close the cursor and release all resources assigned to the
--cursor
CLOSE MyCursor
DEALLOCATE MyCursor
```

The overhead of the cursor depends on the cursor characteristics. The characteristics of the cursors provided by SQL Server and the data access layers can be broadly classified into three categories:

- *Cursor location*: Defines the location of the cursor creation
- *Cursor concurrency*: Defines the degree of isolation and synchronization of a cursor with the underlying content
- *Cursor type*: Defines the specific characteristics of a cursor

Before looking at the costs of cursors, I'll take a few pages to introduce the various characteristics of cursors. You can undo the changes to the Person.AddressType table with this query:

```
UPDATE Person.AddressType
SET [Name] = LEFT([Name],LEN([Name])-1);
```

Cursor Location

Based on the location of a cursor creation, cursors can be classified into two categories:

- Client-side cursors
- Server-side cursors

The T-SQL cursors are always created on SQL Server. However, the database API cursors can be created on either the client side or the server side.

Client-Side Cursors

As its name signifies, a *client-side cursor* is created on the machine running the application, whether the app is a service, a data access layer, or the front end for the user. It has the following characteristics:

- It is created on the client machine.
- The cursor metadata is maintained on the client machine.
- It is created using the data access layers.
- It works against most of the data access layers (OLEDB providers and ODBC drivers).
- It can be a forward-only or static cursor.

■ **Note** Cursor types, including forward-only and static cursor types, are described later in the chapter in the "Cursor Types" section.

Server-Side Cursors

A *server-side cursor* is created on the SQL Server machine. It has the following characteristics:

- It is created on the server machine.
- The cursor metadata is maintained on the server machine.
- It is created using either data access layers or T-SQL statements.
- A server-side cursor created using T-SQL statements is tightly integrated with SQL Server.
- It can be any type of cursor. (Cursor types are explained later in the chapter.)

Note The cost comparison between client-side and server-side cursors is covered later in the chapter in the "Cost Comparison on Cursor Type" section.

Cursor Concurrency

Depending on the required degree of isolation and synchronization with the underlying content, cursors can be classified into the following concurrency models:

- *Read-only*: A nonupdatable cursor
- *Optimistic*: An updatable cursor that uses the optimistic concurrency model (no locks retained on the underlying data rows)
- *Scroll locks*: An updatable cursor that holds a lock on any data row to be updated

Read-Only

A read-only cursor is nonupdatable; no locks are held on the base table(s). While fetching a cursor row, whether an (S) lock will be acquired on the underlying row or not depends upon the isolation level of the connection and the locking hint used in the SELECT statement for the cursor. However, once the row is fetched, by default the locks are released.

The following T-SQL statement creates a read-only T-SQL cursor:

```
DECLARE MyCursor CURSOR READ_ONLY
    FOR SELECT  adt.Name
        FROM    Person.AddressType AS adt
        WHERE   adt.AddressTypeID = 1
```

The lack of locking makes the read-only type of cursor faster and safer. Just remember that you cannot manipulate data through the read-only cursor, which is the sacrifice you make for performance.

Optimistic

The optimistic with values concurrency model makes a cursor updatable. No locks are held on the underlying data. The factors governing whether an (S) lock will be acquired on the underlying row are the same as for a read-only cursor.

The optimistic concurrency model uses row versioning to determine whether a row has been modified since it was read into the cursor instead of locking the row while it is read into the cursor. Version-based optimistic concurrency requires a TIMESTAMP column in the underlying user table on which the cursor is created. The TIMESTAMP data type is a binary number that indicates the relative sequence of modifications on a row. Each time a row with a TIMESTAMP column is modified, SQL Server stores the current value of the global TIMESTAMP value, @@DBTS, in the TIMESTAMP column and then increments the @@DBTS value.

Before applying a modification through the optimistic cursor, SQL Server determines whether the current TIMESTAMP column value for the row matches the TIMESTAMP column value for the row when it was read into the cursor. The underlying row is modified only if the TIMESTAMP values match, indicating that the row hasn't been modified by another user in the meantime. Otherwise, an error is raised. In case of an error, first refresh the cursor with the updated data.

If the underlying table doesn't contain a TIMESTAMP column, then the cursor defaults to value-based optimistic concurrency, which requires matching the current value of the row with the value when the row was read into the cursor. The version-based concurrency control is more efficient than the value-based concurrency control since it requires less processing to determine the modification of the underlying row. Therefore, for the best performance of a cursor with the optimistic concurrency model, ensure that the underlying table has a TIMESTAMP column.

The following T-SQL statement creates an optimistic T-SQL cursor:

```
DECLARE MyCursor CURSOR OPTIMISTIC
    FOR SELECT  adt.Name
        FROM    Person.AddressType AS adt
        WHERE   adt.AddressTypeID = 1
```

Scroll Locks

A cursor with scroll locks concurrency holds a (U) lock on the underlying row until another cursor row is fetched or the cursor is closed. This prevents other users from modifying the underlying row when the cursor fetches it. The scroll locks concurrency model makes the cursor updatable.

The following T-SQL statement creates a T-SQL cursor with the scroll locks concurrency model:

```
DECLARE MyCursor CURSOR SCROLL_LOCKS
    FOR SELECT  adt.Name
        FROM    Person.AddressType AS adt
        WHERE   adt.AddressTypeID = 1
```

Since locks are held on the underlying rows (until another cursor row is fetched or the cursor is closed), it blocks all the other users trying to modify the row during that period. This hurts database concurrency.

Cursor Types

Cursors can be classified into the following four types:

- Forward-only cursors
- Static cursors
- Keyset-driven cursors
- Dynamic cursors

Let's take a closer look at these four types in the sections that follow.

Forward-Only Cursors

These are the characteristics of forward-only cursors:

- They operate directly on the base table(s).
- Rows from the underlying table(s) are usually not retrieved until the cursor rows are fetched using the cursor `FETCH` operation. However, the database API forward-only cursor type, with the following additional characteristics, retrieves all the rows from the underlying table first:
  - Client-side cursor location
  - Server-side cursor location and read-only cursor concurrency
- They support forward scrolling only (`FETCH NEXT`) through the cursor.
- They allow all changes (`INSERT`, `UPDATE`, and `DELETE`) through the cursor. Also, these cursors reflect all changes made to the underlying table(s).

The forward-only characteristic is implemented differently by the database API cursors and the T-SQL cursor. The data access layers implement the forward-only cursor characteristic as one of the four previously listed cursor types. But the T-SQL cursor doesn't implement the forward-only cursor characteristic as a cursor type; rather, it implements it as a property that defines the scrollable behavior of the cursor. Thus, for a T-SQL cursor, the forward-only characteristic can be used to define the scrollable behavior of one of the remaining three cursor types.

A forward-only cursor with a read-only property can be created using a `fast_forward` statement. The T-SQL syntax provides a specific cursor type option, `FAST_FORWARD`, to create a fast-forward-only cursor. The nickname for the `FAST_FORWARD` cursor is the *fire hose* because it is the fastest way to move data through a cursor and because all the information flows one way. The following T-SQL statement creates a fast-forward-only T-SQL cursor:

```
DECLARE MyCursor CURSOR FAST_FORWARD
    FOR SELECT  adt.Name
        FROM    Person.AddressType AS adt
        WHERE   adt.AddressTypeID = 1
```

The `FAST_FORWARD` property specifies a forward-only, read-only cursor with performance optimizations enabled.

Static Cursors

These are the characteristics of static cursors:

- They create a snapshot of cursor results in the `tempdb` database when the cursor is opened. Thereafter, static cursors operate on the snapshot in the `tempdb` database.
- Data is retrieved from the underlying table(s) when the cursor is opened.

- They support all scrolling options: FETCH FIRST, FETCH NEXT, FETCH PRIOR, FETCH LAST, FETCH ABSOLUTE n, and FETCH RELATIVE n.
- Static cursors are always read-only; data modifications are not allowed through static cursors. Also, changes (INSERT, UPDATE, and DELETE) made to the underlying table(s) are not reflected in the cursor.

The following T-SQL statement creates a static T-SQL cursor:

```
DECLARE MyCursor CURSOR STATIC
    FOR SELECT  adt.Name
        FROM    Person.AddressType AS adt
        WHERE   adt.AddressTypeID = 1
```

Some tests show that a static cursor can perform as well as, and sometimes faster than, a forward-only cursor. Be sure to test this behavior on your own system.

Keyset-Driven Cursors

These are the characteristics of keyset-driven cursors:

- They are controlled by a set of unique identifiers (or keys) known as a *keyset*. The keyset is built from a set of columns that uniquely identify the rows in the result set.
- They create the keyset of rows in the tempdb database when the cursor is opened.
- Membership of rows in the cursor is limited to the keyset of rows created in the tempdb database when the cursor is opened.
- On fetching a cursor row, it first looks at the keyset of rows in tempdb, and then it navigates to the corresponding data row in the underlying table(s) to retrieve the remaining columns.
- They support all scrolling options.
- They allow all changes through the cursor. An INSERT performed outside the cursor is not reflected in the cursor, since the membership of rows in the cursor is limited to the keyset of rows created in the tempdb database on opening the cursor. An INSERT through the cursor appears at the end of the cursor. A DELETE performed on the underlying table(s) raises an error when the cursor navigation reaches the deleted row. An UPDATE on the nonkeyset columns of the underlying table(s) is reflected in the cursor. An UPDATE on the keyset column(s) is treated like a DELETE of an old key value and the INSERT of a new key value. If a change disqualifies a row for membership or affects the order of a row, the row does not disappear or move unless the cursor is closed and reopened.

The following T-SQL statement creates a keyset-driven T-SQL cursor:

```
DECLARE MyCursor CURSOR KEYSET
    FOR SELECT  adt.Name
        FROM    Person.AddressType AS adt
        WHERE   adt.AddressTypeID = 1
```

Dynamic Cursors

These are the characteristics of dynamic cursors:

- They operate directly on the base table(s).
- The membership of rows in the cursor is not fixed, since they operate directly on the base table(s).
- Like forward-only cursors, rows from the underlying table(s) are not retrieved until the cursor rows are fetched using a cursor FETCH operation.
- They support all scrolling options except FETCH ABSOLUTE n, since the membership of rows in the cursor is not fixed.
- They allow all changes through the cursor. Also, all changes made to the underlying table(s) are reflected in the cursor.
- They don't support all properties and methods implemented by the database API cursors. Properties such as AbsolutePosition, Bookmark, and RecordCount, as well as methods such as clone and Resync, are not supported by dynamic cursors but are supported by keyset-driven cursors.

The following T-SQL statement creates a dynamic T-SQL cursor:

```
DECLARE MyCursor CURSOR DYNAMIC
    FOR SELECT  adt.Name
        FROM    Person.AddressType AS adt
        WHERE   adt.AddressTypeID = 1
```

The dynamic cursor is absolutely the slowest possible cursor to use in all situations. Take this into account when designing your system.

Cursor Cost Comparison

Now that you've seen the different cursor flavors, let's look at their costs. If you must use a cursor, you should always use the lightest-weight cursor that meets the requirements of your application. The cost comparisons among the different characteristics of the cursors are detailed next.

Cost Comparison on Cursor Location

The client-side and server-side cursors have their own cost benefits and overhead, as explained in the sections that follow.

Client-Side Cursors

Client-side cursors have the following cost benefits compared to server-side cursors:

- *Higher scalability*: Since the cursor metadata is maintained on the individual client machines connected to the server, the overhead of maintaining the cursor metadata is taken up by the client machines. Consequently, the ability to serve a larger number of users is not limited by the server resources.
- *Fewer network round-trips*: Since the result set returned by the SELECT statement is passed to the client where the cursor is maintained, extra network round-trips to the server are not required while retrieving rows from the cursor.
- *Faster scrolling*: Since the cursor is maintained locally on the client machine, it's faster to walk through the rows of the cursor.
- *Highly portable*: Since the cursor is implemented using data access layers, it works across a large range of databases: SQL Server, Oracle, Sybase, and so forth.

Client-side cursors have the following cost overhead or drawbacks:

- *Higher pressure on client resources*: Since the cursor is managed at the client side, it increases pressure on the client resources. But it may not be all that bad, considering that most of the time the client applications are web applications and scaling out web applications (or web servers) is quite easy using standard load-balancing solutions. On the other hand, scaling out a transactional SQL Server database is still an art!
- *Support for limited cursor types*: Dynamic and keyset-driven cursors are not supported.
- *Only one active cursor-based statement on one connection*: As many rows of the result set as the client network can buffer are arranged in the form of network packets and sent to the client application. Therefore, until all the cursor's rows are fetched by the application, the database connection remains busy, pushing the rows to the client. During this period, other cursor-based statements cannot use the connection.

Server-Side Cursors

Server-side cursors have the following cost benefits:

- *Multiple active cursor-based statements on one connection*: While using server-side cursors, no results are left outstanding on the connection between the cursor operations. This frees the connection, allowing the use of multiple cursor-based statements on one connection at the same time. In the case of client-side cursors, as explained previously, the connection remains busy until all the cursor rows are fetched by the application and therefore cannot be used simultaneously by multiple cursor-based statements.
- *Row processing near the data*: If the row processing involves joining with other tables and a considerable amount of set operations, then it is advantageous to perform the row processing near the data using a server-side cursor.

- *Less pressure on client resources*: It reduces pressure on the client resources. But this may not be that desirable, because if the server resources are maxed out (instead of the client resources), then it will require scaling out the database, which is a difficult proposition.
- *Support for all cursor types*: Client-side cursors have limitations on which types of cursors can be supported. There are no limits on the server-side cursors.

Server-side cursors have the following cost overhead or disadvantages:

- *Lower scalability*: They make the server less scalable since server resources are consumed to manage the cursor.
- *More network round-trips*: They increase network round-trips, if the cursor row processing is done in the client application. The number of network round-trips can be optimized by processing the cursor rows in the stored procedure or by using the cache size feature of the data access layer.
- *Less portable*: Server-side cursors implemented using T-SQL cursors are not readily portable to other databases because the syntax of the database code managing the cursor is different across databases.

Cost Comparison on Cursor Concurrency

As expected, cursors with a higher concurrency model create the least amount of blocking in the database and support higher scalability, as explained in the following sections.

Read-Only

The read-only concurrency model provides the following cost benefits:

- *Lowest locking overhead*: The read-only concurrency model introduces the least locking and synchronization overhead on the database. Since (S) locks are not held on the underlying row after a cursor row is fetched, other users are not blocked from accessing the row. Furthermore, the (S) lock acquired on the underlying row while fetching the cursor row can be avoided by using the `NOLOCK` locking hint in the `SELECT` statement of the cursor.
- *Highest concurrency*: Since locks are not held on the underlying rows, the read-only cursor doesn't block other users from accessing the underlying table(s).

The main drawback of the read-only cursor is as follows:

- *Nonupdatable*: The content of underlying table(s) cannot be modified through the cursor.

Optimistic

The optimistic concurrency model provides the following benefits:

- *Low locking overhead*: Similar to the read-only model, the optimistic concurrency model doesn't hold an (S) lock on the cursor row after the row is fetched. To further improve concurrency, the `NOLOCK` locking hint can also be used, as in the case of the read-only concurrency model. Modification through the cursor to an underlying row requires exclusive rights on the row as required by an action query.
- *High concurrency*: Since locks aren't held on the underlying rows, the cursor doesn't block other users from accessing the underlying table(s). But the modification through the cursor to an underlying row will block other users from accessing the row during the modification.

The following are the cost overhead of the optimistic concurrency model:

- *Row versioning*: Since the optimistic concurrency model allows the cursor to be updatable, an additional cost is incurred to ensure that the current underlying row is first compared (using either version-based or value-based concurrency control) with the original cursor row fetched, before applying a modification through the cursor. This prevents the modification through the cursor from accidentally overwriting the modification made by another user after the cursor row is fetched.
- *Concurrency control without a* `TIMESTAMP` *column*: As explained previously, a `TIMESTAMP` column in the underlying table allows the cursor to perform an efficient version-based concurrency control. In case the underlying table doesn't contain a `TIMESTAMP` column, the cursor resorts to value-based concurrency control, which requires matching the current value of the row to the value when the row was read into the cursor. This increases the cost of the concurrency control.

Scroll Locks

The major benefit of the scroll locks concurrency model is as follows:

- *Simple concurrency control*: By locking the underlying row corresponding to the last fetched row from the cursor, the cursor assures that the underlying row can't be modified by another user. It eliminates the versioning overhead of optimistic locking. Also, since the row cannot be modified by another user, the application is relieved from checking for a row-mismatch error.

The scroll locks concurrency model incurs the following cost overhead:

- *Highest locking overhead*: The scroll locks concurrency model introduces a pessimistic locking characteristic. A (U) lock is held on the last cursor row fetched, until another cursor row is fetched or the cursor is closed.
- *Lowest concurrency*: Since a (U) lock is held on the underlying row, all other users requesting a (U) or an (X) lock on the underlying row will be blocked. This can significantly hurt concurrency. Therefore, please avoid using this cursor concurrency model unless absolutely necessary.

Cost Comparison on Cursor Type

Each of the basic four cursor types mentioned in the "Cursor Fundamentals" section earlier in the chapter incurs a different cost overhead on the server. Choosing an incorrect cursor type can hurt database performance. Besides the four basic cursor types, a fast-forward-only cursor, a variation of the forward-only cursor, is provided to enhance performance. The cost overhead of these cursor types is explained in the sections that follow.

Forward-Only Cursors

These are the cost benefits of forward-only cursors:

- *Lower cursor open cost than static and keyset-driven cursors*: Since the cursor rows are not retrieved from the underlying table(s) and are not copied into the `tempdb` database during cursor open, the forward-only T-SQL cursor opens very quickly. Similarly, the forward-only, server-side API cursors with optimistic/scroll locks concurrency also open quickly since they do not retrieve the rows during cursor open.
- *Lower scroll overhead*: Since only `FETCH NEXT` can be performed on this cursor type, it requires a lower overhead to support different scroll operations.
- *Lower impact on the* `tempdb` *database than static and keyset-driven cursors*: Since the forward-only T-SQL cursor doesn't copy the rows from the underlying table(s) into the `tempdb` database, no additional pressure is created on the database.

The forward-only cursor type has the following drawbacks:

- *Lower concurrency*: Every time a cursor row is fetched, the corresponding underlying row is accessed with a lock request depending on the cursor concurrency model (as noted earlier when talking about concurrency). It can block other users from accessing the resource.
- *No backward scrolling*: Applications requiring two-way scrolling can't use this cursor type. But if the applications are designed properly, then it isn't difficult to live without backward scrolling.

Fast-Forward-Only Cursor

The fast-forward-only cursor is the fastest and least expensive cursor type. This forward-only and read-only cursor is specially optimized for performance. Because of this, you should always prefer it to the other SQL Server cursor types.

Furthermore, the data access layer provides a fast-forward-only cursor on the client side, making the cursor overhead almost disappear by using a default result set.

■ Note The default result set is explained later in the chapter in the section "Default Result Set."

Static Cursors

These are the cost benefits of static cursors:

- *Lower fetch cost than other cursor types*: Since a snapshot is created in the tempdb database from the underlying rows on opening the cursor, the cursor row fetch is targeted to the snapshot instead of the underlying rows. This avoids the lock overhead that would otherwise be required to fetch the cursor rows.
- *No blocking on underlying rows*: Since the snapshot is created in the tempdb database, other users trying to access the underlying rows are not blocked.

On the downside, the static cursor has the following cost overhead:

- *Higher open cost than other cursor types*: The cursor open operation of the static cursor is slower than that of other cursor types, since all the rows of the result set have to be retrieved from the underlying table(s) and the snapshot has to be created in the tempdb database during the cursor open.
- *Higher impact on* tempdb *than other cursor types*: There can be significant impact on server resources for creating, populating, and cleaning up the snapshot in the tempdb database.

Keyset-Driven Cursors

These are the cost benefits of keyset-driven cursors:

- *Lower open cost than the static cursor*: Since only the keyset, not the complete snapshot, is created in the tempdb database, the keyset-driven cursor opens faster than the static cursor. SQL Server populates the keyset of a large keyset-driven cursor asynchronously, which shortens the time between when the cursor is opened and when the first cursor row is fetched.
- *Lower impact on* tempdb *than that with the static cursor*: Because the keyset-driven cursor is smaller, it uses less space in tempdb.

The cost overhead of keyset-driven cursors is as follows:

- *Higher open cost than forward-only and dynamic cursors*: Populating the keyset in the tempdb database makes the cursor open operation of the keyset-driven cursor costlier than that of forward-only (with the exceptions mentioned earlier) and dynamic cursors.
- *Higher fetch cost than other cursor types*: For every cursor row fetch, the key in the keyset has to be accessed first, and then the corresponding underlying row in the user database can be accessed. Accessing both the tempdb and the user database for every cursor row fetch makes the fetch operation costlier than that of other cursor types.
- *Higher impact on* tempdb *than forward-only and dynamic cursors*: Creating, populating, and cleaning up the keyset in tempdb impacts server resources.
- *Higher lock overhead and blocking than the static cursor*: Since row fetch from the cursor retrieves rows from the underlying table, it acquires an (S) lock on the underlying row (unless the NOLOCK locking hint is used) during the row fetch operation.

Dynamic Cursor

The dynamic cursor has the following cost benefits:

- *Lower open cost than static and keyset-driven cursors*: Since the cursor is opened directly on the underlying rows without copying anything to the tempdb database, the dynamic cursor opens faster than the static and keyset-driven cursors.
- *Lower impact on* tempdb *than static and keyset-driven cursors.* Since nothing is copied into tempdb, the dynamic cursor places far less strain on tempdb than the other cursor types.

The dynamic cursor has the following cost overhead:

- *Higher lock overhead and blocking than the static cursor*: Every cursor row fetch in a dynamic cursor requeries the underlying table(s) involved in the SELECT statement of the cursor. The dynamic fetches are generally expensive, since the original select condition might have to be reexecuted.

Default Result Set

The default cursor type for the data access layers (ADO, OLEDB, and ODBC) is forward-only and read-only. The default cursor type created by the data access layers isn't a true cursor but a stream of data from the server to the client, generally referred to as the *default result set* or fast-forward-only cursor (created by the data access layer). In ADO.NET, the DataReader control has the forward-only and read-only properties and can be considered as the default result set in the ADO.NET environment. SQL Server uses this type of result set processing under the following conditions:

- The application, using the data access layers (ADO, OLEDB, ODBC), leaves all the cursor characteristics at the default settings, which requests a forward-only and read-only cursor.
- The application executes a SELECT statement instead of executing a DECLARE CURSOR statement.

■ Note Because SQL Server is designed to work with sets of data, not to walk through records one by one, the default result set is always faster than any other type of cursor.

The only request sent from the client to SQL Server is the SQL statement associated with the default cursor. SQL Server executes the query, organizes the rows of the result set in network packets (filling the packets as best as possible), and then sends the packets to the client. These network packets are cached in the network buffers of the client. SQL Server sends as many rows of the result set to the client as the client-network buffers can cache. As the client application requests one row at a time, the data access layer on the client machine pulls the row from the client-network buffers and transfers it to the client application.

The following sections outline the benefits and drawbacks of the default result set.

Benefits

The default result set is generally the best and most efficient way of returning rows from SQL Server for the following reasons:

- *Minimum network round-trips between the client and SQL Server*: Since the result set returned by SQL Server is cached in the client-network buffers, the client doesn't have to make a request across the network to get the individual rows. SQL Server puts most of the rows that it can in the network buffer and sends to the client as much as the client-network buffer can cache.
- *Minimum server overhead*: Since SQL Server doesn't have to store data on the server, this reduces server resource utilization.

Multiple Active Result Sets

SQL Server 2005 introduced the concept of multiple active result sets (MARS) wherein a single connection can have more than one batch running at any given moment. In prior versions, a single result set had to be processed or closed out prior to submitting the next request. MARS allows multiple requests to be submitted at the same time through the same connection. MARS is enabled on SQL Server all the time. It is not enabled by a connection unless that connection explicitly calls for it. Transactions must be handled at the client level and have to be explicitly declared and committed or rolled back. With MARS in action, if a transaction is not committed on a given statement and the connection is closed, all other transactions that were part of that single connection will be rolled back.

When connecting through ODBC, to enable MARS, include `SQL_COPT_SS_MARS_ENABLED = SQL_MARS_ENABLED_YES` as part of the connection properties. When using an OLEDB connection, you have to set the following property and value: `SSPROP_INIT_MARSCONNECTION =VARIANT_TRUE`.

Drawbacks

While there are advantages to the default result set, there are drawbacks as well. Using the default result set requires some special conditions for maximum performance:

- *Doesn't support all properties and methods*: Properties such as `AbsolutePosition`, `Bookmark`, and `RecordCount`, as well as methods such as `Clone`, `MoveLast`, `MovePrevious`, and `Resync`, are not supported.
- *Locks may be held on the underlying resource*: SQL Server sends as many rows of the result set to the client as the client-network buffers can cache. If the size of the result set is large, then the client-network buffers may not be able to receive all the rows. SQL Server then holds a lock on the next page of the underlying table(s), which has not been sent to the client.

To demonstrate these concepts, consider the following test table (`create_t1.sql` in the download):

```
USE AdventureWorks2008 ;
GO
IF (SELECT  OBJECT_ID('dbo.t1')
   ) IS NOT NULL
    DROP TABLE dbo.t1;
GO
CREATE TABLE dbo.t1 (c1 INT, c2 CHAR(996));
CREATE CLUSTERED INDEX i1 ON dbo.t1 (c1);
INSERT  INTO dbo.t1
VALUES  (1, '1');
INSERT  INTO dbo.t1
VALUES  (2, '2');
GO
```

Consider a web page accessing the rows of the test table using ADO with OLEDB, with the default cursor type for the database API cursor (`ADODB.Recordset` object) as follows (`default_cursor.asp` in the download):

```
<%
Dim strConn, Conn, Rs
    Conn = CreateObject("ADODB.Connection")
    strConn = "Provider=SQLOLEDB;" _
              & "Data Source=FRITCHEYGXP\GF2008;" _
              & "Initial Catalog=AdventureWorks2008;" _
              & "Integrated Security=SSPI; Persist Security Info=False;"
    Conn.Open(strConn)
    Rs = CreateObject("ADODB.Recordset")
'Declare & open a database API cursor with default settings
' (forward-only, read-only are the default settings)
    Rs.Open("SELECT * FROM t1", Conn)
'Consume the rows in the cursor one row at a time
While Not Rs.EOF
  'Fetch a row from the cursor
       Response.Write("c1 = " & Rs.Fields("c1").Value & "<BR>")
  Rs.MoveNext
    End While

'Close the cursor and release all resources assigned to the
'cursor
Rs.Close
    Rs = Nothing
Conn.Close
    Conn = Nothing
%>
```

Note that the table has two rows with the size of each row equal to 1,000 bytes (= 4 bytes for `INT + 996` bytes for `CHAR(996)`) without considering the internal overhead. Therefore, the size of the complete result set returned by the `SELECT` statement is approximately 2,000 bytes (= 2 × 1,000 bytes).

You can execute the code of the preceding web page step-by-step using Microsoft Visual Studio .NET. On execution of the cursor open statement (`Rs.Open`), a default result set is created on the client machine running the code. The default result set holds as many rows as the client-network buffer can cache.

Since the size of the result set is small enough to be cached by the client-network buffer, all the cursor rows are cached on the client machine during the cursor open statement itself, without retaining any lock on table `t1`. You can verify the lock status for the connection using the `sys.dm_tran_locks` dynamic management view. During the complete cursor operation, the only request from the client to SQL Server is the `SELECT` statement associated to the cursor, as shown in the Profiler output in Figure 14-1.

EventClass	TextData	ApplicationName	NTUserName	LoginName	CPU	Reads	Writes	Duration
Audit Login	-- network protocol: TCP/IP set qu...	Microsoft (R...	fritcheyg	CORP\f...				
SQL:BatchStarting	SELECT * FROM t1	Microsoft (R...	fritcheyg	CORP\f...				
SQL:BatchCompleted	SELECT * FROM t1	Microsoft (R...	fritcheyg	CORP\f...	0	34	0	0

Figure 14-1. *Profiler trace output showing database requests made by the default result set*

To find out the effect of a large result set on the default result set processing, let's add some more rows to the test table (`addrows.sql` in the download):

```
--Add 100000 rows to the test table
SELECT TOP 100000
        IDENTITY( INT,1,1 ) AS n
INTO    #Tally
FROM    Master.dbo.SysColumns sc1
       ,Master.dbo.SysColumns sc2 ;

INSERT  INTO t1
        SELECT  n
               ,n
        FROM    #Tally AS t ;
GO
```

This increases the size of the result considerably. Depending on the size of the client-network buffer, only part of the result set can be cached. On execution of the `Rs.Open` statement, the default result set on the client machine will get part of the result set, with SQL Server waiting on the other end of the network to send the remaining rows.

On my machine, during this period, the locks shown in Figure 14-2 are held on the underlying table `t1` as obtained from the output of `sys.dm_tran_locks`.

7	56	14	1303675692	OBJECT		IS	GRANT
8	56	14	72057594064863232	PAGE	1:27651	S	GRANT
9	56	14	72057594064863232	PAGE	1:27661	S	GRANT

Figure 14-2. `sys.dm_tran_locks` *output showing the locks held by the default result set while processing the large result set*

The (IS) lock on the table will block other users trying to acquire an (X) lock. To minimize the blocking issue, follow these recommendations:

- Process all rows of the default result set immediately.
- Keep the result set small. As demonstrated in the example, if the size of the result set is small, then the default result set will be able to read all the rows during the cursor open operation itself.

Analyzing SQL Server Overhead with Cursors

While implementing a cursor-centric functionality in an application, you have two choices. You can use either a T-SQL cursor or a database API cursor. Because of the differences between the internal implementation of a T-SQL cursor and a database API cursor, the load created by these cursors on SQL Server is different. The impact of these cursors on the database also depends on the different characteristics of the cursors, such as location, concurrency, and type. You can use the SQL Profiler tool to analyze the load generated by the T-SQL and database API cursors using the events and data columns listed in Table 14-1.

Table 14-1. *Events and Data Columns to Analyze SQL Server Overhead with Cursors*

Events		Data Column
Event Class	**Event**	
Cursors	All events	EventClass
Security audit	Audit Login	TextData
	Audit Logout	CPU
Stored procedures	RPC:Completed	Reads
	SP:StmtCompleted	Writes
T-SQL	SQL:BatchCompleted	Duration
		SPID
		StartTime

Even the optimization options for these cursors are different. Let's analyze the overhead of these cursors one by one.

Analyzing SQL Server Overhead with T-SQL Cursors

The T-SQL cursors implemented using T-SQL statements are always executed on SQL Server, since they need the SQL Server engine to process their T-SQL statements. You can use a combination of the cursor characteristics explained previously to reduce the overhead of these cursors. As mentioned earlier, the most lightweight T-SQL cursor is the one created not with the default settings but by manipulating the settings to arrive at the forward-only read-only cursor. That still leaves the T-SQL statements used to implement the cursor operations to be processed by SQL Server. The complete load of the cursor is supported by SQL Server without any help from the client machine. To analyze the overhead of T-SQL cursors on SQL Server, suppose an application requirement consists of the following functionalities:

- Identify all products (from the `Production.WorkOrder` table) that have been scrapped.
- For each scrapped product, determine the money lost, where

  Money lost per product = Units in stock × Unit price of the product
- Calculate the total loss.
- Based on the total loss, determine the business status.

The "For each" phrase in the second point suggests that these application requirements could be served by a cursor. You can implement this application requirement using a T-SQL cursor as follows (`app_requirements.sql` in the download):

```
IF (SELECT  OBJECT_ID('dbo.spTotalLoss_CursorBased')
   ) IS NOT NULL
    DROP PROC dbo.spTotalLoss_CursorBased ;
GO
CREATE PROC dbo.spTotalLoss_CursorBased
AS --Declare a T-SQL cursor with default settings, i.e., fast
--forward-only to retrieve products that have been discarded
    DECLARE ScrappedProducts CURSOR
        FOR SELECT  p.ProductID
                   ,wo.ScrappedQty
                   ,p.ListPrice
            FROM    Production.WorkOrder AS wo
                    JOIN Production.ScrapReason AS sr
                    ON wo.ScrapReasonID = sr.ScrapReasonID
                    JOIN Production.Product AS p
                    ON wo.ProductID = p.ProductID ;
--Open the cursor to process one product at a time
    OPEN ScrappedProducts ;

    DECLARE @MoneyLostPerProduct MONEY = 0
       ,@TotalLoss MONEY = 0 ;

--Calculate money lost per product by processing one product
--at a time
    DECLARE @ProductId INT
       ,@UnitsScrapped SMALLINT
       ,@ListPrice MONEY ;
    FETCH NEXT FROM ScrappedProducts INTO @ProductId, @UnitsScrapped,
        @ListPrice ;
    WHILE @@FETCH_STATUS = 0
        BEGIN
            SET @MoneyLostPerProduct = @UnitsScrapped * @ListPrice ;
  --Calculate total loss
            SET @TotalLoss = @TotalLoss + @MoneyLostPerProduct ;
            FETCH NEXT FROM ScrappedProducts INTO @ProductId, @UnitsScrapped,
                @ListPrice ;
        END
```

```
--Determine status
    IF (@TotalLoss > 5000)
        SELECT  'We are bankrupt!' AS Status ;
    ELSE
        SELECT  'We are safe!' AS Status ;

--Close the cursor and release all resources assigned to the cursor
    CLOSE ScrappedProducts ;
    DEALLOCATE ScrappedProducts ;
GO
```

The stored procedure can be executed as follows, but execute it twice to take advantage of plan caching:

```
EXEC dbo.spTotalLoss_CursorBased
```

Figure 14-3 shows the Profiler trace output for this stored procedure.

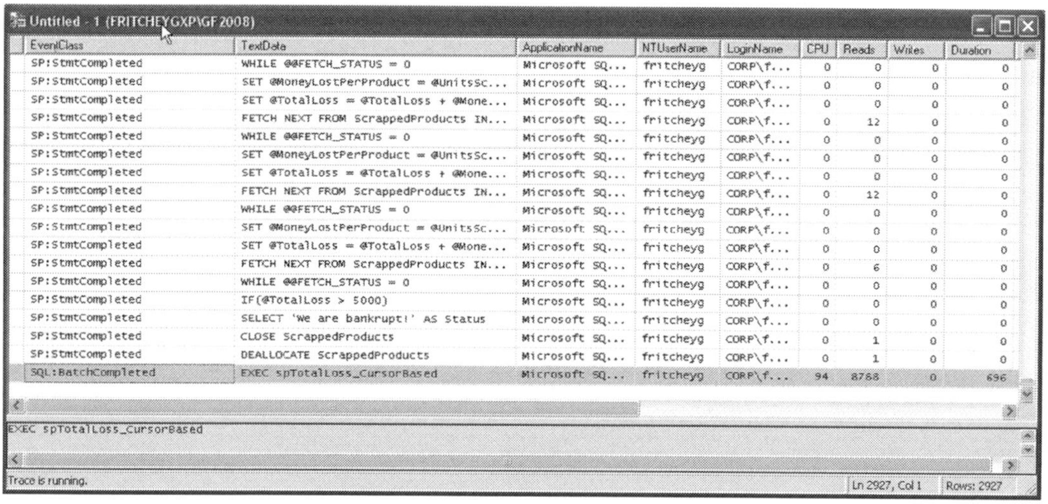

Figure 14-3. *Profiler trace output showing the total cost of the data processing using a T-SQL–based cursor*

As you can see in Figure 14-3, lots of statements are executed on SQL Server. Essentially, all the SQL statements within the stored procedure are executed on SQL Server, with the statements within the WHILE loop executed several times (one for each row returned by the cursor's SELECT statement).

The total number of logical reads performed by the stored procedure is 8,788 (indicated by the last SQL:BatchCompleted event). Well, is it high or low? Considering the fact that the Production.Products table has only 13 pages and the Production.WorkOrder table has only 524, it's surely not low. You can determine the number of pages allocated to these tables by querying the dynamic management view sys.dm_db_index_physical_stats:

```
SELECT  SUM(page_count)
FROM    sys.dm_db_index_physical_stats(DB_ID('AdventureWorks2008'),
                                       OBJECT_ID('Production.WorkOrder'),
                                       DEFAULT, DEFAULT, DEFAULT)
```

Note The `sys.dm_db_index_physical_stats` DMV is explained in detail in Chapter 8.

In most cases, you can avoid cursor operations by rewriting the functionality using SQL queries, concentrating on set-based methods of accessing the data. For example, you can rewrite the preceding stored procedure using SQL queries (instead of the cursor operations) as follows (`no_cursor.sql` in the download):

```
IF (SELECT  OBJECT_ID('dbo.spTotalLoss')
   ) IS NOT NULL
    DROP PROC dbo.spTotalLoss;
GO
CREATE PROC dbo.spTotalLoss
AS
    SELECT  CASE --Determine status based on following computation
                 WHEN SUM(MoneyLostPerProduct) > 5000 THEN 'We are bankrupt!'
                 ELSE 'We are safe!'
            END AS Status
    FROM    (--Calculate total money lost for all discarded products
             SELECT SUM(wo.ScrappedQty * p.ListPrice) AS MoneyLostPerProduct
             FROM   Production.WorkOrder AS wo
                    JOIN Production.ScrapReason AS sr
                    ON wo.ScrapReasonID = sr.ScrapReasonID
                    JOIN Production.Product AS p
                    ON wo.ProductID = p.ProductID
             GROUP BY p.ProductID
            ) DiscardedProducts;
GO
```

In this stored procedure, the aggregation functions of SQL Server are used to compute the money lost per product and the total loss. The `CASE` statement is used to determine the business status based on the total loss incurred. The stored procedure can be executed as follows, but again, do it twice so that you can see the results of plan caching:

```
EXEC dbo.spTotalLoss
```

Figure 14-4 shows the corresponding Profiler trace output.

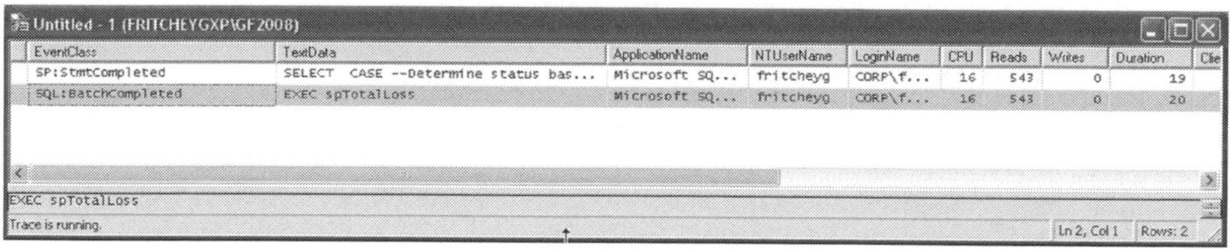

Untitled - 1 (FRITCHEYGXP\GF2008)

EventClass	TextData	ApplicationName	NTUserName	LoginName	CPU	Reads	Writes	Duration	Clie
SP:StmtCompleted	SELECT CASE --Determine status bas...	Microsoft SQ...	fritcheyg	CORP\f...	16	543	0	19	
SQL:BatchCompleted	EXEC spTotalLoss	Microsoft SQ...	fritcheyg	CORP\f...	16	543	0	20	

EXEC spTotalLoss

Trace is running. Ln 2, Col 1 Rows: 2

Figure 14-4. *Profiler trace output showing the total cost of the data processing using an equivalent* SELECT *statement*

From Figure 14-4, you can see that the second execution of the stored procedure, which reuses the existing plan, uses a total of 543 logical reads; however, even more importantly than the reads, the CPU drops from 94 in Figure 14-3 to 16 in Figure 14-4 and the duration goes from 696 ms to 20 ms. Using SQL queries instead of the cursor operations made the duration 34.8 times faster.

Therefore, for better performance, it is almost always recommended that you use set-based operations in SQL queries instead of T-SQL cursors.

Cursor Recommendations

An ineffective use of cursors can degrade the application performance by introducing extra network round-trips and load on server resources. To keep the cursor cost low, try to follow these recommendations:

- Use set-based SQL statements over T-SQL cursors, since SQL Server is designed to work with sets of data.
- Use the least expensive cursor:
  - While using SQL Server cursors, use the `FAST_FORWARD` cursor type, which is generally referred to as the *fast-forward-only cursor*.
  - While using the API cursors implemented by ADO, OLEDB, or ODBC, use the default cursor type, which is generally referred to as the *default result set*.
  - While using ADO.NET, use the `DataReader` object.
- Minimize impact on server resources:
  - Use a client-side cursor for API cursors.
  - Do not perform actions on the underlying table(s) through the cursor.
  - Always deallocate the cursor as soon as possible.
  - Redesign the cursor's `SELECT` statement (or the application) to return the minimum set of rows and columns.
  - Avoid T-SQL cursors entirely by rewriting the logic of the cursor as set-based statements, which are generally more efficient than cursors.
  - Use a `TIMESTAMP` column for dynamic cursors to benefit from the efficient version-based concurrency control compared to the value-based technique.

- Minimize impact on tempdb:
  - Minimize resource contention in tempdb by avoiding the static and keyset-driven cursor types.
  - Minimize latch contention in tempdb. When a static or keyset-driven cursor is opened in SQL Server, the tempdb database is used to hold either the keyset or the snapshot for the cursor management. It creates "worktables" in the tempdb database.

    Creating a lot of worktables can cause latch contention in the tempdb database on the Page Free Space (PFS) or Shared Global Allocation Map (SGAM) page. In that case, the output of the sys.dm_exec_requests DMV will show a last_wait_type of PAGELATCH_EX or LATCH_EX, and the wait_resource will show 2:1:1 (for PFS) or 2:1:2 (for SGAM). Spreading the tempdb database among multiple files generally minimizes the contention on these pages. Just make sure each of the tempdb files is the same size.
  - Reduce or eliminate the autogrow overhead. Set the size of the tempdb database to the maximum size to which it can grow. Generally, I recommend that system databases such as tempdb not be allowed to autogrow, but if they must, then be sure to use set growth numbers, not allowing the file to grow by percentages. That can, in some circumstances, cause excessive blocking while processes are forced to wait for new space to be allocated. You should also be sure to keep the file size the same when using multiple files with tempdb.
- Minimize blocking:
  - Use the default result set, fast-forward-only cursor, or static cursor.
  - Process all cursor rows as quickly as possible.
  - Avoid scroll locks or pessimistic locking.
- Minimize network round-trips while using API cursors:
  - Use the CacheSize property of ADO to fetch multiple rows in one round-trip.
  - Use client-side cursors.
  - Use disconnected record sets.

Summary

As you learned in this chapter, a cursor is the natural extension to the result set returned by SQL Server, enabling the calling application to process one row of data at a time. Cursors add a cost overhead to application performance and impact the server resources.

You should always be looking for ways to avoid cursors. Set-based solutions work better in almost all cases. However, if the cursor operation is mandated, then choose the best combination of cursor location, concurrency, type, and cache size characteristics to minimize the cost overhead of the cursor.

In the next chapter, I show how to put everything together to analyze the workload of a database in action.

CHAPTER 15

Database Workload Optimization

Up to now, you have learned about a number of aspects that can affect query performance, such as the tools that you can use to analyze query performance and the optimization techniques you can use to improve query performance. Now you need to learn how to apply this information to analyze, troubleshoot, and optimize the performance of database workload.

In this chapter, I cover the following topics:

- The characteristics of a database workload
- The steps involved in database workload optimization
- How to identify costly queries in the workload
- How to measure the baseline resource use and performance of costly queries
- How to analyze factors that affect the performance of costly queries
- How to apply techniques to optimize costly queries
- How to analyze the effects of the query optimization on the overall workload

Workload Optimization Fundamentals

Optimizing a database workload often fits the 80/20 rule: 80 percent of the workload consumes about 20 percent of server resources. Trying to optimize the performance of the majority of the workload is usually not very productive. So, the first step in workload optimization is to find the 20 percent of the workload that consumes 80 percent of the server resources.

Optimizing the workload requires a set of tools to measure the resource consumption and response time of the different parts of the workload. As you saw in Chapter 3, SQL Server provides a set of tools and utilities to analyze the performance of a database workload and individual queries.

In addition to using these tools, it is important to know how you can use different techniques to optimize a workload. The most important aspect of workload optimization to remember is that not every optimization technique is guaranteed to work on every performance problem. Many optimization techniques are specific to certain database application designs and database environments. Therefore, for each optimization technique, measure the performance of each part of the workload (that is, each individual query) before and after you apply the optimization technique. After this, measure the impact of the optimization on the complete workload.

It is not unusual to find that an optimization technique has little effect—or even a negative effect—on the other parts of the workload, which hurts the overall performance of the workload. For instance, a nonclustered index added to optimize a `SELECT` statement can hurt the performance of `UPDATE` statements that modify the value of the indexed column. The `UPDATE` statements have to update index rows in addition to the data rows. However, as demonstrated in Chapter 4, sometimes indexes can improve the performance of action queries, too. Therefore, improving the performance of a particular query could benefit or hurt the performance of the overall workload. As usual, your best course of action is to validate any assumptions through testing.

Workload Optimization Steps

The process of optimizing a database workload follows a specific series of steps. As part of this process, you will use the set of optimization techniques presented in previous chapters. Since every performance problem is a new challenge, you can use a different set of optimization techniques for troubleshooting different performance problems.

To understand the optimization process, you will simulate a sample workload using a set of queries. These are the optimization steps you will follow while optimizing the sample workload:

1. Capture the workload.
2. Analyze the workload.
3. Identify the costliest query.
4. Quantify the baseline resource use of the costliest query:
    - Overall resource use
    - Detailed resource use
5. Analyze and optimize external factors:
    - Analyze the use of indexes.
    - Analyze the batch-level options used by the application
    - Analyze the effectiveness of statistics.
    - Analyze the need for defragmentation.
6. Analyze the internal behavior of the costliest query:
    - Analyze the query execution plan.
    - Identify the costly steps in the execution plan.
    - Analyze the effectiveness of the processing strategy.

7. Optimize the costliest query.
8. Analyze the effects of the changes on database workload.
9. Iterate through multiple optimization phases.

As explained in Chapter 1, performance tuning is an iterative process. Therefore, you should iterate through the performance optimization steps multiple times until you achieve the application performance targets, repeating the process after a certain time period when the workload on the database changes.

Sample Workload

To troubleshoot SQL Server performance, you need to know the SQL workload that is executed on the server. You can then analyze the workload to identify the cause of the poor performance and the applicable optimization steps. Ideally, you should capture the workload on the SQL Server facing the performance problems. You will use a set of queries to simulate a sample workload so that you can follow the optimization steps listed in the previous section. The sample workload used in this chapter consists of a combination of good and bad queries.

■ Note I recommend you restore a clean copy of the AdventureWorks2008 database so that any artifacts left over from previous chapters are completely removed.

The very simple test workload is simulated by the following set of sample stored procedures (`workload.sql` in the download) executed using the second script (`exec.sql` in the download) on the AdventureWorks2008 database:

```
USE AdventureWorks2008;
GO
CREATE PROCEDURE dbo.spr_ShoppingCart
@ShoppingCartId VARCHAR(50)
AS
--provides the output from the shopping cart including the line total
SELECT  sci.Quantity
        ,p.ListPrice
        ,p.ListPrice * sci.Quantity AS LineTotal
        ,p.[Name]
FROM     Sales.ShoppingCartItem AS sci
         JOIN Production.Product AS p
         ON sci.ProductID = p.ProductID
WHERE    sci.ShoppingCartID = @ShoppingCartId ;
GO
```

```
CREATE PROCEDURE dbo.spr_ProductBySalesOrder
@SalesOrderID INT
AS
/*provides a list of products from a particular sales order,
and provides line ordering by modified date but ordered by product name*/
SELECT  ROW_NUMBER() OVER (ORDER BY sod.ModifiedDate) AS LineNumber
       ,p.[Name]
       ,sod.LineTotal
FROM    Sales.SalesOrderHeader AS soh
        JOIN Sales.SalesOrderDetail AS sod
        ON soh.SalesOrderID = sod.SalesOrderID
        JOIN Production.Product AS p
        ON sod.ProductID = p.ProductID
WHERE   soh.SalesOrderID = @SalesOrderID
ORDER BY p.[Name] ASC ;
GO

CREATE PROCEDURE dbo.spr_PersonByFirstName
@FirstName NVARCHAR(50)
AS
--gets anyone by first name from the Person table
SELECT  p.BusinessEntityID
       ,p.Title
       ,p.LastName
       ,p.FirstName
       ,p.PersonType
FROM    Person.Person AS p
WHERE   p.FirstName = @FirstName ;
GO

CREATE PROCEDURE dbo.spr_ProductTransactionsSinceDate
@LatestDate DATETIME
,@ProductName NVARCHAR(50)
AS
--Gets the latest transaction against all products that have a transaction
SELECT  p.NAME
       ,th.ReferenceOrderID
       ,th.ReferenceOrderLineID
       ,th.TransactionType
       ,th.Quantity
```

```
FROM    Production.Product AS p
        JOIN Production.TransactionHistory AS th
        ON p.ProductID = th.ProductID
           AND th.TransactionID = (SELECT TOP (1)
                                            th2.transactionId
                                   FROM     Production.TransactionHistory th2
                                   WHERE    th2.productid = p.productid
                                   ORDER BY th2.transactionid DESC
                                  )
WHERE th.TransactionDate > @LatestDate
AND p.NAME LIKE @ProductName;
GO

CREATE PROCEDURE dbo.spr_PurchaseOrderBySalesPersonName
@LastName NVARCHAR(50)
AS
    SELECT  poh.PurchaseOrderID
           ,poh.OrderDate
           ,pod.LineTotal
           ,p.[Name] AS ProductName
           ,e.JobTitle
           ,per.LastName + ', ' + per.FirstName AS SalesPerson
    FROM    Purchasing.PurchaseOrderHeader AS poh
            JOIN Purchasing.PurchaseOrderDetail AS pod
            ON poh.PurchaseOrderID = pod.PurchaseOrderID
            JOIN Production.Product AS p
            ON pod.ProductID = p.ProductID
            JOIN HumanResources.Employee AS e
            ON poh.EmployeeID = e.BusinessEntityID
            JOIN Person.Person AS per
            ON e.BusinessEntityID = per.BusinessEntityID
    WHERE   per.LastName LIKE @LastName
    ORDER BY per.LastName
           ,per.FirstName;
GO
```

Once these procedures are created, execute them using the following scripts:

```
EXEC dbo.spr_ShoppingCart '20621';
GO
EXEC dbo.spr_ProductBySalesOrder 43867;
GO
EXEC dbo.spr_PersonByFirstName 'Gretchen';
GO
EXEC dbo.spr_ProductTransactionsSinceDate @LatestDate = '9/1/2004',
@ProductName = 'Hex Nut%';
GO
EXEC dbo.spr_PurchaseOrderBySalesPersonName @LastName = 'Hill%';
GO
```

The sample workload consists of the different types of queries you usually execute on SQL Server:

- Queries using aggregate functions.
- Point queries that retrieve only one row or a small number of rows. Usually they are the best for performance.
- Queries joining multiple tables.
- Queries retrieving a narrow range of rows.
- Queries performing additional result set processing, such as providing a sorted output.

The first optimization step is to identify the worst-performing queries, as explained in the next section.

Capturing the Workload

As a part of the diagnostic-data collection step, you must trace the workload on the database server. You can trace the workload using the Profiler tool with the events and data columns as recommended in Chapter 3. To be able to follow the logical flow of execution for every SPID, do not use any filters on the events collecting data. Tables 15-1 and 15-2 list some of the important events and data columns that you are specifically interested in to measure the resource intensiveness of the queries.

Table 15-1. *Events to Analyze Costly Queries*

Event Class	Event
`Stored Procedures`	`RPC:Completed`
`T-SQL`	`SQL:BatchCompleted`

Table 15-2. *Data Columns to Analyze Costly Queries*

Data Columns	
Groups	
Columns	`EventClass`
	`TextData`
	`CPU`
	`Reads`
	`Writes`
	`Duration`
	`SPID`
	`StartTime`

■ **Tip** To minimize the effect of the Profiler tool on the server performance, please follow the SQL Profiler recommendations described in Chapter 3.

As explained in Chapter 3, for production databases it is recommended that you use a server-side trace, one that is launched from T-SQL and outputs to a file. To create the SQL script, you can script the trace definition from Profiler as explained in Chapter 3. Using a server-side trace for capturing the SQL workload has the following advantages over using Profiler:

- Since you intend to analyze the SQL queries once the workload is captured, you do not need to display the SQL queries while capturing them, as done by Profiler.
- If the database is already having performance issues, then using the stored procedure technique is more economical than using Profiler, since the stored procedure technique avoids the overhead of the Profiler tool, such as updating Profiler's display as the trace is captured.
- Profiler doesn't provide a very flexible timing control over the tracing process.
- Profiler adds overhead to the server, in the form of latching, that will cause the server to slow down, not something you want to have happen in a production environment.

With regard to timing control, say you want to start tracing at 11 p.m. and capture the SQL workload for 24 hours. Profiler doesn't provide a provision to define the start time, but it does provide one to define the stop time. Since the server-side trace is based on SQL scripts, you can define the trace schedule by modifying the following lines of code in the SQL script file generated by Profiler:

```
exec @rc = sp_trace_create @TraceID output, 0, N'InsertFileNameHere',
@maxfilesize, NULL
```

Replace the preceding line of code with the following lines:

```
-- Schedule the time window for tracing
DECLARE @StopTime DATETIME = DATEADD(dd,1,GETDATE())
exec @rc = sp_trace_create @TraceID output, 0, N'InsertFileNameHere', @maxfilesize,
@StopTime = @StopTime
```

If you want to stop the trace intermediately, you must follow these steps:

1. Determine the `traceid` for the running trace by using the built-in function `fn_trace_getinfo`:

   ```
   SELECT * FROM ::fn_trace_getinfo(default)
   ```

   From the output of `fn_trace_getinfo`, determine the `traceid` referring to your trace file.

2. Subsequently, execute the following SQL queries to stop the trace; 0 stops the trace, and 2 closes it and removes it from the instance:

   ```
   EXEC sp_trace_setstatus <traceid>, 0
   EXEC sp_trace_setstatus <traceid>, 2
   ```

To be able to use the server-side trace for the example, I have modified the SQL script file, setting the DATEADD function to add only two minutes instead of one day (PerformanceTraceForWorkload.sql in the download). Consequently, the trace operation will start immediately on execution of the SQL script file and will run for two minutes.

Analyzing the Workload

Once the workload is captured in a trace file, you can analyze the workload either by using Profiler or by importing the content of the trace file into a database table.

The Profiler tool provides the following two methods of analyzing the content of the trace file, both of which are relatively straightforward:

- *Sort the trace output on a data column by altering the data column property of the trace (in other words, move the data column under the Groups category)*: Profiler rearranges the content in an ascending order on the data column. For nested sorting, you can group the trace output on multiple columns. Sorting the trace output helps you easily locate the slowest-running queries and the costliest queries.
- *Filter the trace output to a selective list of data columns and events*: You can slice the trace output further by applying post filters, as explained in Chapter 3. Slicing the content helps you focus on a selective part of the trace output.

Profiler provides limited ways of analyzing the traced output. For instance, if a query is executed frequently, then instead of looking at the cost of only the individual execution of the query, you should also try to determine the cumulative cost of the repeated execution of the query within a fixed period of time. Although the individual execution of the query may not be that costly, the query may be executed so many times that even a little optimization may make a big difference. The Profiler tool is not powerful enough to help analyze the workload in such advanced ways. For in-depth analysis of the workload, you must import the content of the trace file into a database table as follows:

```
IF(SELECT OBJECT_ID('TRACE_TABLE')) IS NOT NULL
  DROP TABLE TRACE_TABLE
GO
SELECT *, IDENTITY(INT, 1, 1) AS RowNumber INTO TRACE_TABLE
  FROM ::FN_TRACE_GETTABLE('<TraceFileName>', DEFAULT)
```

Substitute your own path and file name for <TraceFileName>. Once you have the traced content in a table, you can use SQL queries to analyze the workload, as you can do with Profiler. For example, to find the slowest queries, you can execute this SQL query:

```
SELECT *
  FROM TRACE_TABLE
  ORDER BY Duration DESC
```

This will show the single costliest query. For the tests you're running in this chapter, it will be adequate. On a production system, although you may want to run a query like this, more likely you'll want to work off of aggregations of data, more like this:

```
SELECT TextData
    ,SUM(Duration) AS SumDuration
    ,AVG(Duration) AS AvgDuration
    ,COUNT(Duration) AS CountDuration
FROM TRACE_TABLE
GROUP BY TextData;
```

With this, you can then order by the fields you're most interested in—say, `CountDuration` to get the most frequently called procedure or `SumDuration` to get the procedure that runs for the longest cumulative amount of time. Microsoft supplies RML tools that can help you with these types of analyses (download the RML tools here: `http://www.microsoft.com/downloads/details.aspx?familyid=7edfa95a-a32f-440f-a3a8-5160c8dbe926&displaylang=en`). You need a method (supplied by the RML tools, but you can roll your own) to remove or replace parameters and parameter values. This is necessary in order to aggregate based on just the procedure name or just the text of the query without the parameters or parameter values, since these will be constantly changing. The objective of analyzing the workload is to identify the costliest query (or the costly queries), as explained in the following section.

Identifying the Costliest Query

As just explained, you can use Profiler or the stored procedure technique to identify the costly queries for different criteria. The queries in the workload can be sorted on the `CPU`, `Reads`, or `Writes` columns to identify the costliest query, as discussed in Chapter 3. You can also use aggregate functions to arrive at the cumulative cost as well as individual costs. In a production system, knowing the procedure that is accumulating the longest run times, the most CPU, or the largest number of reads and writes is frequently more useful than simply identifying the query that had those highest numbers one time.

Since the total number of reads usually outnumbers the total number of writes by at least seven to eight times for even the heaviest OLTP database, sorting the queries on the `Reads` column usually identifies more bad queries than sorting on the `Writes` column. It's also worth looking at the queries that simply take the longest to execute. As outlined in Chapter 3, you can capture wait states with Performance Monitor and view those along with a given query to help identify why a query is taking a long time to run. Each system is different. In general, I approach the most frequently called procedures first, then the longest-running, and finally those with the most reads. Of course, performance tuning is an iterative process, so you will need to reexamine each category on a regular basis.

To analyze the sample workload for the worst-performing queries, you need to know how costly the queries are, again, in terms of duration or reads. Since these values are known only after the query completes its execution, you are mainly interested in the completed events. (The rationale behind using completed events for performance analysis is explained in detail in Chapter 3.)

For presentation purposes, open the trace file in Profiler. Figure 15-1 shows the captured trace output.

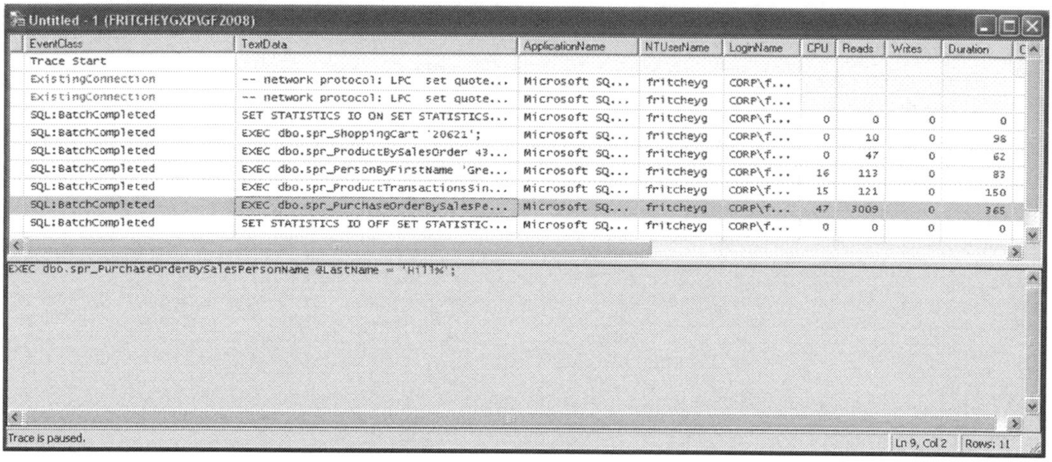

Untitled - 1 (FRITCHEYGXP\GF2008)

EventClass	TextData	ApplicationName	NTUserName	LoginName	CPU	Reads	Writes	Duration
Trace Start								
ExistingConnection	-- network protocol: LPC set quote...	Microsoft SQ...	fritcheyg	CORP\f...				
ExistingConnection	-- network protocol: LPC set quote...	Microsoft SQ...	fritcheyg	CORP\f...				
SQL:BatchCompleted	SET STATISTICS IO ON SET STATISTICS...	Microsoft SQ...	fritcheyg	CORP\f...	0	0	0	0
SQL:BatchCompleted	EXEC dbo.spr_ShoppingCart '20621';	Microsoft SQ...	fritcheyg	CORP\f...	0	10	0	96
SQL:BatchCompleted	EXEC dbo.spr_ProductBySalesOrder 43...	Microsoft SQ...	fritcheyg	CORP\f...	0	47	0	62
SQL:BatchCompleted	EXEC dbo.spr_PersonByFirstName 'Gre...	Microsoft SQ...	fritcheyg	CORP\f...	16	113	0	83
SQL:BatchCompleted	EXEC dbo.spr_ProductTransactionsSin...	Microsoft SQ...	fritcheyg	CORP\f...	15	121	0	150
SQL:BatchCompleted	EXEC dbo.spr_PurchaseOrderBySalesPe...	Microsoft SQ...	fritcheyg	CORP\f...	47	3009	0	365
SQL:BatchCompleted	SET STATISTICS IO OFF SET STATISTIC...	Microsoft SQ...	fritcheyg	CORP\f...	0	0	0	0

EXEC dbo.spr_PurchaseOrderBySalesPersonName @LastName = 'Hill%';

Trace is paused. Ln 9, Col 2 Rows: 11

Figure 15-1. *Profiler trace output showing the SQL workload*

The worst-performing query in terms of duration and CPU as well as reads is highlighted in Figure 15-1 (you may have a different values, but this will likely still be the worst-performing query), and the query inside the procedure is presented here for easy reference:

```
SELECT   poh.PurchaseOrderID
        ,poh.OrderDate
        ,pod.LineTotal
        ,p.[Name] AS ProductName
        ,e.JobTitle
        ,per.LastName + ', ' + per.FirstName AS SalesPerson
FROM     Purchasing.PurchaseOrderHeader AS poh
         JOIN Purchasing.PurchaseOrderDetail AS pod
         ON poh.PurchaseOrderID = pod.PurchaseOrderID
         JOIN Production.Product AS p
         ON pod.ProductID = p.ProductID
         JOIN HumanResources.Employee AS e
         ON poh.EmployeeID = e.BusinessEntityID
         JOIN Person.Person AS per
         ON e.BusinessEntityID = per.BusinessEntityID
WHERE    per.LastName LIKE @LastName
ORDER BY per.LastName
        ,per.FirstName;
```

Once you've identified the worst-performing query, the next optimization step is to determine the resources consumed by the query.

Determining the Baseline Resource Use of the Costliest Query

The current resource use of the worst-performing query can be considered as a baseline figure before you apply any optimization techniques. You may apply different optimization techniques to the query, and you can compare the resultant resource use of the query with the baseline figure to determine the effectiveness of the individual optimization technique.

The resource use of a query can be presented in the following two categories:

- Overall resource use
- Detailed resource use

Overall Resource Use

The overall resource use of the query provides a gross figure for the amount of hardware resources consumed by the worst-performing query. You can compare the resource use of an optimized query to the overall resource use of the nonoptimized query to ensure the overall effectiveness of the performance techniques applied.

You can determine the overall resource use of the query from the workload trace. Table 15-3 shows the overall use of the query from the trace in Figure 15-1.

Table 15-3. *Data Columns Representing the Amount of Resources Used by a Query*

Data Column	Value	Description
`Reads`	3009	Number of logical reads performed by the query. If a page is not found in memory, then a logical read for the page will require a physical read from the disk to fetch the page to the memory first.
`Writes`	0	Number of pages modified by the query.
`CPU`	47 ms	Amount of CPU used by the query.
`Duration`	369 ms	The time it took SQL Server to process this query from compilation to returning the result set.

■ **Note** In your environment, you may have different figures for the preceding data columns. Irrespective of the data columns' absolute values, it's important to keep track of these values so that you can compare them with the corresponding values later.

Detailed Resource Use

You can break down the overall resource use of the query to locate the bottlenecks on the different database tables accessed by the query. This detailed resource use helps determine which table accesses are the most problematic. Understanding the wait states in your system will help you identify where you need to focus your tuning, such as on CPU, reads, or writes. A rough rule of thumb can be to simply look at duration, but duration can be affected by so many factors that it's an imperfect measure at best. In this case, I'll spend time on all three: CPU, reads, and duration. Reads, while a popular measure of performance, can be as problematic as duration. This is why I spend time on all the values.

As you saw in Chapter 3, you can obtain the number of reads performed on the individual tables accessed by the query from the STATISTICS IO output for the query. You can also set the STATISTICS TIME to get the basic execution time and CPU time for the query including compile time. You can obtain this output by reexecuting the query with the SET statements as follows (or by selecting the Set Statistics IO check box in Query Analyzer). In addition, to simulate the same first-time run shown in Figure 15-1, clean out the data stored in memory using DBCC DROPCLEANBUFFERS (not to be run on a production system), and remove the procedure from cache by running DBCC FREEPROCCACHE (also not to be run on a production system):

```
DBCC FREEPROCCACHE();
DBCC DROPCLEANBUFFERS;
GO
SET STATISTICS TIME ON;
GO
SET STATISTICS IO ON;
GO
EXEC dbo.spr_PurchaseOrderBySalesPersonName @LastName = 'Hill%';
GO
SET STATISTICS TIME OFF;
GO
SET STATISTICS IO OFF;
GO
```

The STATISTICS output for the worst-performing query is as follows:

```
SQL Server parse and compile time:
   CPU time = 0 ms, elapsed time = 0 ms.
DBCC execution completed. If DBCC printed error messages, contact your system
administrator.

 SQL Server Execution Times:
   CPU time = 0 ms,  elapsed time = 1 ms.
DBCC execution completed. If DBCC printed error messages, contact your system
administrator.

 SQL Server Execution Times:
   CPU time = 0 ms,  elapsed time = 1 ms.
SQL Server parse and compile time:
   CPU time = 0 ms, elapsed time = 0 ms.

 SQL Server Execution Times:
   CPU time = 0 ms,  elapsed time = 0 ms.
SQL Server parse and compile time:
   CPU time = 0 ms, elapsed time = 0 ms.
```

```
 SQL Server Execution Times:
   CPU time = 0 ms,  elapsed time = 0 ms.
SQL Server parse and compile time:
   CPU time = 0 ms, elapsed time = 0 ms.
SQL Server parse and compile time:
   CPU time = 0 ms, elapsed time = 217 ms.

(1496 row(s) affected)
Table 'Worktable'. Scan count 0, logical reads 0, physical reads 0,
read-ahead reads 0, lob logical reads 0, lob physical reads 0,
lob read-ahead reads 0.
Table 'PurchaseOrderDetail'. Scan count 1, logical reads 66, physical reads 2,
read-ahead reads 64, lob logical reads 0, lob physical reads 0,
lob read-ahead reads 0.
Table 'PurchaseOrderHeader'. Scan count 4, logical reads 2285, physical reads 3,
read-ahead reads 48, lob logical reads 0, lob physical reads 0,
lob read-ahead reads 0.
Table 'Employee'. Scan count 0, logical reads 174, physical reads 2,
read-ahead reads 0, lob logical reads 0, lob physical reads 0,
lob read-ahead reads 0.
Table 'Person'. Scan count 1, logical reads 4, physical reads 2, read-ahead reads 2,
lob logical reads 0, lob physical reads 0, lob read-ahead reads 0.
Table 'Product'. Scan count 1, logical reads 5, physical reads 2,
read-ahead reads 14, lob logical reads 0, lob physical reads 0,
lob read-ahead reads 0.

 SQL Server Execution Times:
   CPU time = 15 ms,  elapsed time = 228 ms.

 SQL Server Execution Times:
   CPU time = 15 ms,  elapsed time = 447 ms.
SQL Server parse and compile time:
   CPU time = 0 ms, elapsed time = 0 ms.
```

Table 15-4 summarizes the output of STATISTICS IO.

Table 15-4. *STATISTICS IO Output*

Table	Reads
Purchasing.PurchaseOrderDetail	66
Purchasing.PurchaseOrderHeader	2,285
Person.Employee	174
Person.Person	4
Production.Product	5

Usually, the sum of the reads from the individual tables referred to in a query will be less than the total number of reads performed by the query, because additional pages have to be read to access internal database objects such as `sysobjects`, `syscolumns`, and `sysindexes`.

Table 15-5 summarizes the output of `STATISTICS TIME`.

Table 15-5. *STATISTICS TIME Output*

Event	Duration	CPU
Compile	217 ms	0 ms
Execution	228 ms	15 ms
Completion	447 ms	15 ms

Once the worst-performing query is identified and its resource use is measured, the next optimization step is to determine the factors that are affecting the performance of the query. However, before you do this, you should check to see whether any factors external to the query might be causing poor performance.

Analyzing and Optimizing External Factors

Besides factors such as query design and indexing, external factors can affect query performance. Thus, before diving into the execution plan of the query, you should analyze and optimize the major external factors that can affect query performance. Here are some of those external factors:

- The batch-level options used by the application
- The statistics of the database objects accessed by the query
- The fragmentation of the database objects accessed by the query

Analyzing the Batch-Level Options Used by the Application

When making a connection to SQL Server, various batch-level options, such as `ANSI_NULL` or `CONCAT_NULL_YIELDS_NULL`, can be set differently than the defaults for the server or the database. Changing these settings per connection can lead to recompiles of stored procedures, causing slower behavior. Further, some options, such as `ARITHABORT`, must be set to on when dealing with indexed views and certain other specialized indexes. If they are not, you can get poor performance or even errors in the code. For example, setting `ANSI_WARNINGS` to off will cause the optimizer to ignore indexed views and indexed computed columns when generating the execution plan. You can use the output from the trace to see this information. The `TextData` column contains the settings used by the connection in the `Audit Login` event and in the `ExistingConnection` event, as shown in Figure 15-2.

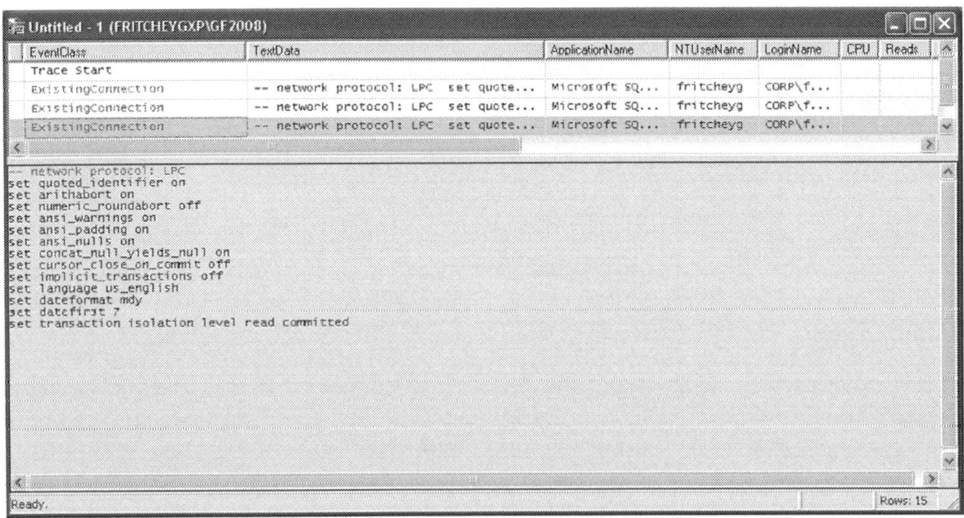

Figure 15-2. *Existing connection showing the batch-level options*

As you can see, not only are the batch-level options displayed, but you can also check on the transaction isolation level to be sure it is as expected. I recommend using the ANSI standard settings. These consist of setting the following to on: ANSI_NULLS, ANSI_NULL_DFLT_ON, ANSI_PADDING, ANSI_WARNINGS, CURSOR_CLOSE_ON_COMMIT, IMPLICIT_TRANSACTIONS, and QUOTED_IDENTIFIER. You can use the single command SET ANSI_DEFAULTS ON to set them all at the same time.

Analyzing the Effectiveness of Statistics

The statistics of the database objects referred to in the query are one of the key pieces of information that the query optimizer uses to decide upon certain execution plans. As explained in Chapter 7, the optimizer generates the execution plan for a query based on the statistics of the objects referred to in the query. The optimizer looks at the statistics of the database objects referred to in the query to estimate the number of rows affected and thereby determines the processing strategy for the query. If a database object's statistics are not accurate, then the optimizer may generate an inefficient execution plan for the query.

As explained in Chapter 7, you can check the statistics of a table and its indexes using DBCC SHOW_STATISTICS. There are five tables referenced within this query: Purchasing.PurchaseOrderHeader, Purchasing.PurchaseOrderDetail, Person.Employee, Person.Person, and Production.Product. You would have to know which indexes are in use by the query in order to get the statistics information about them. That is determined when you look at the execution plan. For now, I'll check the statistics on the primary key of the Purchasing.PurchaseOrderHeader table since it had the most reads, as shown in Table 15-4. When the following query is run:

```
DBCC SHOW_STATISTICS('Purchasing.PurchaseOrderHeader',
'PK_PurchaseOrderHeader_PurchaseOrderID');
```

you'll see the output shown in Figure 15-3.

	Name	Updated	Rows	Rows Sampled	Steps	Density	Average key length	String Index	Filter Expression	Unfiltered Rows
1	PK_PurchaseOrderHeader_PurchaseOrderID	Aug 6 2008 9:18AM	4012	4012	44	1	4	NO	NULL	4012

	All density	Average Length	Columns
1	0.0002492522	4	PurchaseOrderID

	RANGE_HI_KEY	RANGE_ROWS	EQ_ROWS	DISTINCT_RANGE_ROWS	AVG_RANGE_ROWS
1	1	0	1	0	1
2	87	85	1	85	1
3	146	58	1	58	1
4	248	101	1	101	1
5	336	87	1	87	1

Figure 15-3. *`SHOW_STATISTICS` output for `Purchasing.PurchaseOrderHeader`*

You can see the selectivity on the index is very high since the density is quite low, as shown in the `All density` column. In this instance, for this poorly performing query, it's doubtful that statistics are likely to be the cause of poor performance. You can also check the `Updated` column to determine the last time this set of statistics were updated. If it's more than a few days old, you need to check your statistics maintenance plan, and you should update these statistics manually.

Analyzing the Need for Defragmentation

As explained in Chapter 8, a fragmented table increases the number of pages to be accessed by a query. This adversely affects performance. For this reason, you should ensure that the database objects referred to in the query are not too fragmented.

You can determine the fragmentation of the five tables accessed by the worst-performing query using a query against `sys.dm_db_index_physical_stats` (`showcontig.sql` in the download), the first of which is as follows:

```
SELECT  s.avg_fragmentation_in_percent
       ,s.fragment_count
       ,s.page_count
       ,s.avg_page_space_used_in_percent
       ,s.record_count
       ,s.avg_record_size_in_bytes
       ,s.index_id
FROM    sys.dm_db_index_physical_stats(DB_ID('AdventureWorks2008'),
                        OBJECT_ID(N'Purchasing.PurchaseOrderHeader'), NULL, NULL,
                        'Sampled') AS s
WHERE s.record_count > 0
ORDER BY s.index_id;
```

Figure 15-4 shows the output of this query.

	avg_fragmentation_in_percent	fragment_count	page_count	avg_page_space_used_in_percent	record_count	avg_record_size_in_bytes	index_id
1	0	1	42	99.110452186805	4012	82	1
2	33.3333333333333	3	6	90.849196936002	4012	9	2
3	33.3333333333333	3	6	90.849196936002	4012	9	3

Figure 15-4. *`Purchasing.PurchaseOrderHeader` index fragmentation*

If you run the same query for the other four tables (in order Purchasing.PurchaseOrderDetail, Production.Product, Person.Employee, Person.Person), the output will look like Figure 15-5.

	avg_fragmentation_in_percent	fragment_count	page_count	avg_page_space_used_in_percent	record_count	avg_record_size_in_bytes	index_id
1	0	2	64	99.0089201877934	8845	56	1
2	17.6470588235294	4	17	96.3974796145293	8845	13	2

	avg_fragmentation_in_percent	fragment_count	page_count	avg_page_space_used_in_percent	record_count	avg_record_size_in_bytes	index_id
1	30.7692307692308	5	13	92.7999876451693	504	191.793	1
2	50	2	2	85.2606869285891	504	25.392	2
3	66.6666666666667	3	3	99.2257721769212	504	45.817	3
4	50	2	2	71.5838893007166	504	21	4

	avg_fragmentation_in_percent	fragment_count	page_count	avg_page_space_used_in_percent	record_count	avg_record_size_in_bytes	index_id
1	0	1	2	80.9241413392637	504	24	0
2	0	39	765	65.7704101803805	1597	2549.016	0
3	0	NULL	35	80.3007536446751	40	5686.85	0
4	0	1	1	10.6498640968619	32	25	1
5	66.6666666666667	3	3	73.1776624660242	395	43	1
6	0	1	18	93.1403261675315	762	176.128	1
7	0	1	1	1.86557944156165	3	49	1
8	0	1	1	1.19841858166543	3	31	1

	avg_fragmentation_in_percent	fragment_count	page_count	avg_page_space_used_in_percent	record_count	avg_record_size_in_bytes	index_id
1	0.026267402153927	26	3807	85.7145663454411	19972	1320.83	1
2	0.961538461538462	4	104	98.1731529528045	19972	39.388	2
3	0	2	57	99.5413639733136	19972	21	3
4	0	1	3	68.2151470224858	195	82.974	256000
5	0	20	2152	99.6104027674821	301696	55.523	256001
6	0.216294160057678	60	1387	99.5522979985174	301696	35.053	256002
7	0.144300144300144	41	1386	99.6241413392637	301696	35.053	256003
8	0.216294160057678	39	1387	99.5522979985174	301696	35.053	256004

Figure 15-5. *The index fragmentation for the four tables in the problem query*

The fragmentation of the Purchasing.PurchaseOrderHeader table is extremely light, with a fragmentation at 33 percent, and the avg_page_space_used_in_percent is greater than 90 percent for all the indexes. When you take into account the number of pages for the indexes on the table, three or less, you're very unlikely to get an improvement in performance out of defragging the index, assuming you can, as detailed in Chapter 8.

The same can be said of Purchasing.PurchaseOrderDetail, which has very low fragmentation and page count. Production.Product has slightly higher degrees of fragmentation, but again the page count is very low, so defragging the index is not likely to help much. Person.Employee has one index with 66 percent fragmentation, but once again, it's only on three pages. Finally, Person.Person has almost no fragmentation to speak of.

Just as an experiment, as part of the performance-tuning iterative process, try running the index defragmentation script supplied in Chapter 8 and repeated here:

```
DECLARE @DBName NVARCHAR(255)
    ,@TableName NVARCHAR(255)
    ,@SchemaName NVARCHAR(255)
    ,@IndexName NVARCHAR(255)
    ,@PctFrag DECIMAL

DECLARE @Defrag NVARCHAR(MAX)
```

```
IF EXISTS (SELECT * FROM sys.objects WHERE OBJECT_ID = OBJECT_ID(N'#Frag'))
    DROP TABLE #Frag

CREATE TABLE #Frag
(DBName NVARCHAR(255)
,TableName NVARCHAR(255)
,SchemaName NVARCHAR(255)
,IndexName NVARCHAR(255)
,AvgFragment DECIMAL)

EXEC sp_msforeachdb 'INSERT INTO #Frag (
    DBName,
    TableName,
    SchemaName,
    IndexName,
    AvgFragment
) SELECT  ''?'' AS DBName
       ,t.Name AS TableName
       ,sc.Name AS SchemaName
       ,i.name AS IndexName
       ,s.avg_fragmentation_in_percent
FROM    ?.sys.dm_db_index_physical_stats(DB_ID(''?''), NULL, NULL,
                                  NULL, ''Sampled'') AS s
        JOIN ?.sys.indexes i
        ON s.Object_Id = i.Object_id
           AND s.Index_id = i.Index_id
        JOIN ?.sys.tables t
        ON i.Object_id = t.Object_Id
        JOIN ?.sys.schemas sc
        ON t.schema_id = sc.SCHEMA_ID
WHERE s.avg_fragmentation_in_percent > 20
AND t.TYPE = ''U''
AND s.page_count > 8
ORDER BY TableName,IndexName'

DECLARE cList CURSOR
FOR SELECT * FROM #Frag

OPEN cList
FETCH NEXT FROM cList
INTO @DBName, @TableName,@SchemaName,@IndexName,@PctFrag
WHILE @@FETCH_STATUS = 0
BEGIN
    IF @PctFrag BETWEEN 20.0 AND 40.0
    BEGIN
        SET @Defrag = N'ALTER INDEX ' + @IndexName + ' ON ' + @DBName + '.'
+ @SchemaName + '.' + @TableName + ' REORGANIZE'
        EXEC sp_executesql @Defrag
        PRINT 'Reorganize index: ' + @DBName + '.' + @SchemaName + '.'
```

```
+ @TableName +'.' + @IndexName
    END
    ELSE IF @PctFrag > 40.0
    BEGIN
        SET @Defrag = N'ALTER INDEX ' + @IndexName + ' ON ' + @DBName + '.'
+ @SchemaName + '.' + @TableName + ' REBUILD'
        EXEC sp_executesql @Defrag
        PRINT 'Rebuild index: '+ @DBName + '.' + @SchemaName + '.' + @TableName +'.'
+ @IndexName
    END

    FETCH NEXT FROM cList
    INTO @DBName, @TableName,@SchemaName,@IndexName,@PctFrag

END
CLOSE cList
DEALLOCATE cList

DROP TABLE #Frag
```

After defragging the indexes on the database, rerun the query against `sys.dm_db_index_physical_stats` for all five tables to see what the results of the index defragmentation are, if any (Figure 15-6).

	avg_fragmentation_in_percent	fragment_count	page_count	avg_page_space_used_in_percent	record_count	avg_record_size_in_bytes	index_id
1	0	1	42	99.110452186805	4012	82	1
2	33.3333333333333	3	6	90.849196936002	4012	9	2
3	33.3333333333333	3	6	90.849196936002	4012	9	3

	avg_fragmentation_in_percent	fragment_count	page_count	avg_page_space_used_in_percent	record_count	avg_record_size_in_bytes	index_id
1	0	2	64	99.0009201877934	8845	56	1
2	17.6470588235294	4	17	96.3974796145293	8845	13	2

	avg_fragmentation_in_percent	fragment_count	page_count	avg_page_space_used_in_percent	record_count	avg_record_size_in_bytes	index_id
1	30.7692307692308	5	13	92.7999876451693	504	191.793	1
2	50	2	2	85.2606069285891	504	25.392	2
3	66.6666666666667	3	3	99.2257721769212	504	45.817	3
4	50	2	2	71.5838893007166	504	21	4

	avg_fragmentation_in_percent	fragment_count	page_count	avg_page_space_used_in_percent	record_count	avg_record_size_in_bytes	index_id
1	0	1	2	80.9241413392637	504	24	0
2	0	39	765	65.7704101803805	1597	2549.016	0
3	0	NULL	35	80.3007536446751	40	5686.85	0
4	0	1	1	10.6498640968619	32	25	1
5	66.6666666666667	3	3	73.1776624660242	395	43	1
6	0	1	18	93.1403261675315	762	176.128	1
7	0	1	1	1.86557944156165	3	49	1
8	0	1	1	1.19841858166543	3	31	1

	avg_fragmentation_in_percent	fragment_count	page_count	avg_page_space_used_in_percent	record_count	avg_record_size_in_bytes	index_id
1	0.026267402153927	26	3807	85.7145663454411	19972	1320.83	1
2	0.961538461538462	4	104	98.1731529528045	19972	39.388	2
3	0	2	57	99.5413639733136	19972	21	3
4	0	1	3	68.2151470224858	195	82.974	256000
5	0	20	2152	99.6104027674821	301696	55.523	256001
6	0.216294160057678	60	1387	99.5522979985174	301696	35.053	256002
7	0.144300144300144	41	1386	99.6241413392637	301696	35.053	256003
8	0.216294160057678	39	1387	99.5522979985174	301696	35.053	256004

Figure 15-6. *`Production.Product` index fragmentation after rebuilding indexes*

As you can see in Figure 15-6, the fragmentation was not reduced at all in any of the indexes in the tables used by the poorest-performing query.

Once you've analyzed the external factors that can affect the performance of a query and resolved the nonoptimal ones, you should analyze internal factors such as improper indexing and query design.

Analyzing the Internal Behavior of the Costliest Query

Now that the statistics are up-to-date, you can analyze the processing strategy for the query chosen by the optimizer to determine the internal factors affecting the query's performance. Analyzing the internal factors that can affect query performance involves these steps:

- Analyzing the query execution plan
- Identifying the costly steps in the execution plan
- Analyzing the effectiveness of the processing strategy

Analyzing the Query Execution Plan

To see the execution plan, click the Show Actual Execution Plan button to enable it. Figure 15-7 shows the graphical execution plan of the worst-performing query.

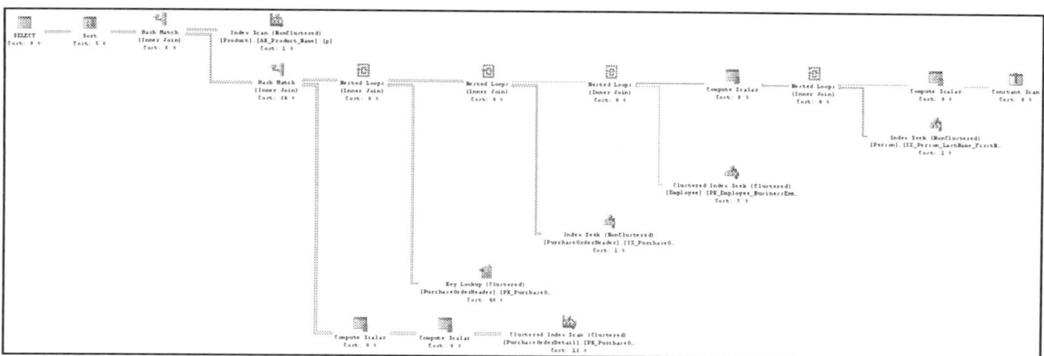

Figure 15-7. *Graphical execution plan of the query*

You can observe the following from this execution plan, as explained in Chapter 3:

- Data access:
    - Index scan on nonclustered index `Product.AK_Product_Name`
    - Index seek on nonclustered index `Person.IX_Person_LastName_FirstName_MiddleName`
    - Index seek on clustered index `Employee.PK_Employee_BusinessEntityID`

    - Index seek on nonclustered index PurchaseOrderHeader.IX_PurchaseOrderHeader_EmployeeID
    - Key lookup on PurchaseOrderHeader.PK_PurchaseOrderHeader_PurchaseOrderID
    - Index scan on clustered index PurchaseOrderDetail.PK_PurchaseOrderDetail_PurchaseOrderDetailID
- Join strategy:
    - Nested loop join between the constant scan and Person.Person table with the Person.Person table as the outer table
    - Nested loop join between the Person.Person table and Person.Employee with the Person.Employee table as the outer table
    - Nested loop join between the Person.Person table and the Purchasing.PurchaseOrderHeader table that was also the outer table
    - Nested loop join between the Purchasing.PurchaseOrderHeader index and the Purchasing.PurchaseOrderHeader primary key with the primary key as the outer table
    - Hash match join between the Purchasing.PurchaseOrderHeader table and the Purchasing.PurchaseOrderDetail table with Purchasing.PurchaseOrderDetail as the outer table
    - Hash match join between the Production.Product and Purchasing.PurchaseOrderDetail tables with the Purchasing.PurchaseOrderDetail table as the outer table
- Additional processing:
    - Constant scan to provide a placeholder for the @LastName variable's LIKE operation
    - Compute scalar that defined the constructs of the @LastName variable's LIKE operation, showing the top and bottom of the range and the value to be checked
    - Compute scalar that combines the FirstName and LastName columns into a new column
    - Compute scalar that calculates the LineTotal column from the Purchasing.PurchaseOrderDetail table
    - Compute scalar that takes the calculated LineTotal and stores it as a permanent value in the result set for further processing
    - Sort on the FirstName and LastName from the Person.Person table

Identifying the Costly Steps in the Execution Plan

Once you understand the execution plan of the query, the next step is to identify the steps estimated as the most costly in the execution plan. Although these costs are estimated and can be inaccurate at times, the optimization of the costly steps usually benefits the query performance the most. You can see that the following are the two costliest steps:

- *Costly step 1*: Key lookup on the Purchasing.PurchaseOrderHeader table: 40 percent
- *Costly step 2*: Hash match between Purchasing.PurchaseOrderHeader and Purchasing.PurchaseOrderDetail: 20 percent

The next optimization step is to analyze the costly steps, determining whether these steps can be optimized through techniques such as redesigning the query or indexes.

Analyzing the Effectiveness of the Processing Strategy

The most costly step is a very straightforward key lookup (bookmark lookup). This problem has a number of possible solutions, many of which were outlined in Chapter 5.

Costly step 2 is the hash match between Purchasing.PurchaseOrderHeader and Purchasing.PurchaseOrderDetail. Figure 15-8 shows the number of rows coming from each of the two tables in the order listed, representing the inner and outer portions of the hash join. As you can see, there are 763 rows coming from Purchasing.PurchaseOrderDetail and 8,845 from Purchasing.PurchaseOrderDetail. Based on these values, it's likely that the hash join is the optimal method for putting the data together. It might be possible to change this through index tuning or query hints.

Actual Number of Rows	763
Estimated Number of Rows	429.748
Estimated Row Size	203 B
Estimated Data Size	85 KB

Estimated Number of Rows	8845
Estimated Row Size	23 B
Estimated Data Size	199 KB

Figure 15-8. *Row counts leading into hash match join*

■ **Tip** At times you may find no improvements can be made to the most costly step in a processing strategy. In that case, concentrate on the next most costly step to identify the problem. If none of the steps can be optimized further, then move on to the next costliest query in the workload. You may need to consider changing the database design or the construction of the query.

Optimizing the Costliest Query

Once you've diagnosed the problems with the costly steps, the next stage is to implement the necessary corrections to reduce the cost of the query.

The corrective actions for a problematic step can have one or more alternative solutions. For example, should you create a new index on a limited number of columns or on a large number of columns? In such cases, prioritize the solutions based on their expected effectiveness. For example, if a narrow index can more or less do the job of a wider index, then it is usually better to prioritize the narrow index solution over the wider index solution.

Apply the solutions individually in the order of their expected benefit, and measure their individual effect on the query performance. You can finally apply the solution that provides the greatest performance improvement to correct the problematic step. Sometimes it may be evident that the best solution will hurt other queries in the workload. For example, a new index on a large number of columns can hurt the performance of action queries. However, since that's not always true, it's better to determine the effect of such optimization techniques on the complete workload through testing. If a particular solution hurts the overall performance of the workload, choose the next best solution while keeping an eye on the overall performance of the workload.

Modifying an Existing Index

It seems obvious from looking at the processing strategy that changing the nonclustered index on Purchasing.PurchaseOrderHeader will eliminate the key lookup. Since the output list of the key lookup includes only one relatively small column, this can be added to the index IX_PurchaseOrderHeader_EmployeeID as an included column (AlterIndex.sql in the download):

```
CREATE NONCLUSTERED INDEX [IX_PurchaseOrderHeader EmployeeID] ON
[Purchasing].[PurchaseOrderHeader] ([EmployeeID] ASC)
    INCLUDE (OrderDate)
    WITH (
         DROP_EXISTING = ON)
ON  [PRIMARY]
GO
```

Now run the costly query again using the Test.SQL script that includes the cleanup steps as well as the statistics information. The output is as follows:

```
SQL Server parse and compile time:
   CPU time = 0 ms, elapsed time = 0 ms.
DBCC execution completed. If DBCC printed error messages, contact your
system administrator.

 SQL Server Execution Times:
   CPU time = 0 ms,  elapsed time = 0 ms.
DBCC execution completed. If DBCC printed error messages, contact your
system administrator.

 SQL Server Execution Times:
   CPU time = 0 ms,  elapsed time = 1 ms.
SQL Server parse and compile time:
   CPU time = 0 ms, elapsed time = 0 ms.

 SQL Server Execution Times:
   CPU time = 0 ms,  elapsed time = 0 ms.
SQL Server parse and compile time:
   CPU time = 0 ms, elapsed time = 0 ms.
```

```
 SQL Server Execution Times:
   CPU time = 0 ms,  elapsed time = 0 ms.
SQL Server parse and compile time:
   CPU time = 0 ms, elapsed time = 0 ms.
SQL Server parse and compile time:
   CPU time = 16 ms, elapsed time = 188 ms.

(1496 row(s) affected)
Table 'Worktable'. Scan count 0, logical reads 0, physical reads 0,
read-ahead reads 0, lob logical reads 0, lob physical reads 0,
lob read-ahead reads 0.
Table 'PurchaseOrderDetail'. Scan count 1, logical reads 66, physical reads 2,
read-ahead reads 64, lob logical reads 0, lob physical reads 0,
lob read-ahead reads 0.
Table 'PurchaseOrderHeader'. Scan count 4, logical reads 11, physical reads 2,
read-ahead reads 0, lob logical reads 0, lob physical reads 0,
lob read-ahead reads 0.
Table 'Employee'. Scan count 0, logical reads 174, physical reads 2,
read-ahead reads 0, lob logical reads 0, lob physical reads 0,
lob read-ahead reads 0.
Table 'Person'. Scan count 1, logical reads 4, physical reads 2, read-ahead reads 2,
lob logical reads 0, lob physical reads 0, lob read-ahead reads 0.
Table 'Product'. Scan count 1, logical reads 5, physical reads 2,
read-ahead reads 8, lob logical reads 0, lob physical reads 0,
lob read-ahead reads 0.

 SQL Server Execution Times:
   CPU time = 15 ms,  elapsed time = 266 ms.

 SQL Server Execution Times:
   CPU time = 31 ms,  elapsed time = 455 ms.
SQL Server parse and compile time:
   CPU time = 0 ms, elapsed time = 0 ms.
```

The number of reads on the Purchasing.PurchaseOrderTable table has dropped from 2,285 to 11. Although this is good, the execution time is almost the same as it was before. This is an example of how simply using logical_reads as a lone measure of performance can lead to false results. This means more tuning of the query is necessary. Figure 15-9 shows the new execution plan.

The key lookup is completely gone, and the query is just a bit simpler and easier to read. The estimated costs on the various operations have now shifted so that the hash match join is now the costliest operation and the clustered index scan against Purchasing.PurchaseOrderDetail is the second most costly.

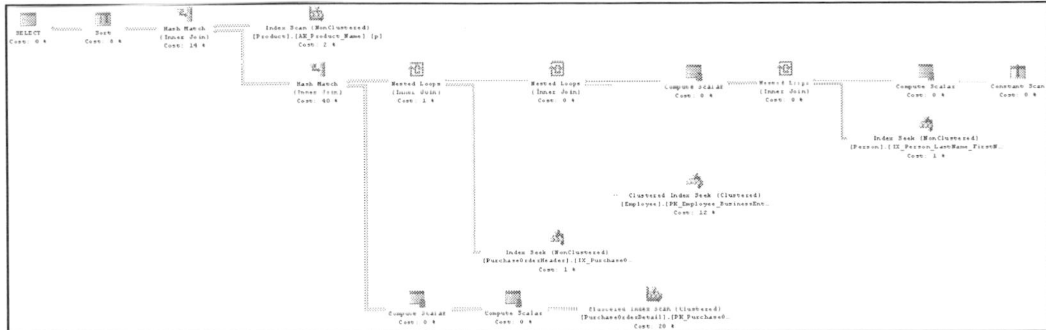

Figure 15-9. *Graphical execution plan of the query after changing the nonclustered index*

Analyzing the Application of a Join Hint

Since the most costly operation is now the hash join, it might make sense to try to change that to a different join. Based on the data being moved, as shown in Figure 15-8, it's likely that the hash match was the appropriate choice. However, to see whether forcing the JOIN to use a LOOP or MERGE might make a performance improvement, you simply need to modify the procedure:

```
ALTER PROCEDURE [dbo].[spr_PurchaseOrderBySalesPersonName]
@LastName NVARCHAR(50)
AS
    SELECT  poh.PurchaseOrderID
           ,poh.OrderDate
           ,pod.LineTotal
           ,p.[Name] AS ProductName
           ,e.JobTitle
           ,per.LastName + ', ' + per.FirstName AS SalesPerson
    FROM    Purchasing.PurchaseOrderHeader AS poh
            INNER LOOP JOIN Purchasing.PurchaseOrderDetail AS pod
            ON poh.PurchaseOrderID = pod.PurchaseOrderID
            JOIN Production.Product AS p
            ON pod.ProductID = p.ProductID
            JOIN HumanResources.Employee AS e
            ON poh.EmployeeID = e.BusinessEntityID
            JOIN Person.Person AS per
            ON e.BusinessEntityID = per.BusinessEntityID
    WHERE   per.LastName LIKE @LastName
    ORDER BY per.LastName
           ,per.FirstName
```

Figure 15-10 shows the resultant execution plan for the worst-performing query.

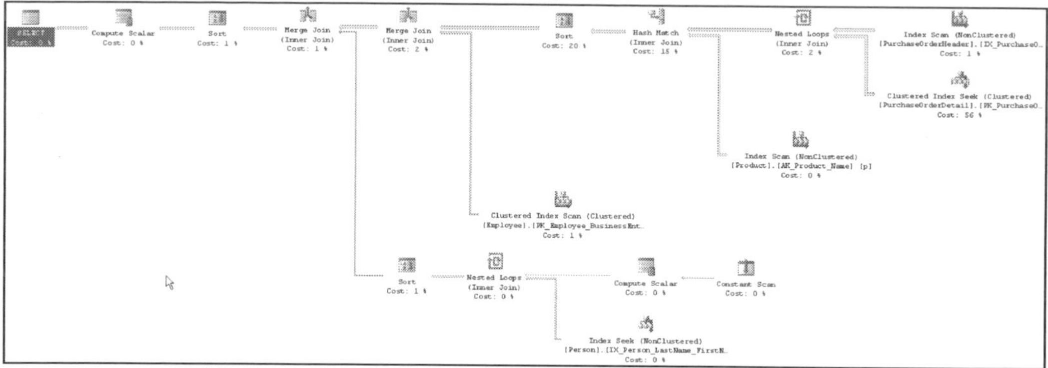

Figure 15-10. *Graphical execution plan of the query with a join hint*

The execution plan gets fairly radically changed. The nested loop allows for a `Clustered Index Seek` against the `Purchasing.PurchaseOrderDetail` table, which, with the elimination of the hash match, you might think that the performance has improved. Unfortunately, looking at the statistics, the number of scans and the number of reads on `Purchasing.PurchaseOrderDetail` have radically increased. The scans increased to support the loop part of the `Nested Loop` operation, and the reads shot through the roof to 9,123 from 66. Performance time almost doubled to 600 ms.

This is clearly not working well. What if the procedure was changed to a `Merge Join`? This time, since there are two hash match joins, I'll try to eliminate both:

```
ALTER PROCEDURE [dbo].[spr_PurchaseOrderBySalesPersonName]
@LastName NVARCHAR(50)
AS
    SELECT  poh.PurchaseOrderID
           ,poh.OrderDate
           ,pod.LineTotal
           ,p.[Name] AS ProductName
           ,e.JobTitle
           ,per.LastName + ', ' + per.FirstName AS SalesPerson
    FROM    Purchasing.PurchaseOrderHeader AS poh
            INNER MERGE JOIN Purchasing.PurchaseOrderDetail AS pod
            ON poh.PurchaseOrderID = pod.PurchaseOrderID
            INNER MERGE JOIN Production.Product AS p
            ON pod.ProductID = p.ProductID
            JOIN HumanResources.Employee AS e
            ON poh.EmployeeID = e.BusinessEntityID
            JOIN Person.Person AS per
            ON e.BusinessEntityID = per.BusinessEntityID
    WHERE   per.LastName LIKE @LastName
    ORDER BY per.LastName
           ,per.FirstName
```

Figure 15-11 shows the execution plan that comes from this new query.

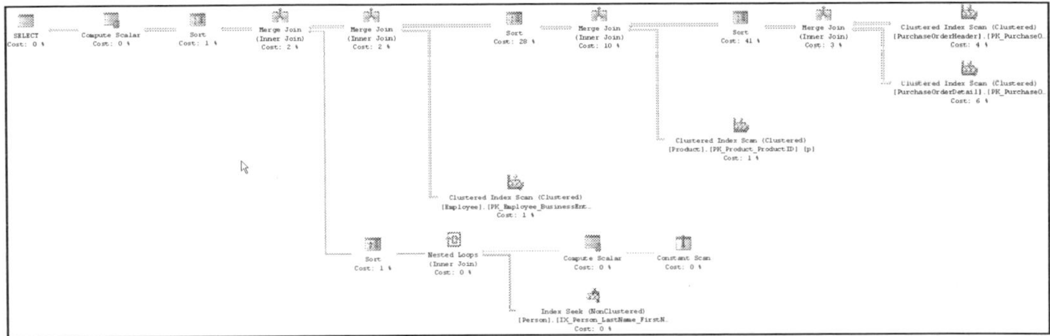

Figure 15-11. *Execution plan forcing merge joins in place of the hash joins*

The performance is much worse in this iteration, and you can see why. In addition to the data access and the new joins, the data had to be ordered because that's how merge joins work. That ordering of the data, shown as a sort prior to each of the joins, ruins the performance.

In short, SQL Server is making appropriate join choices based on the data supplied to it. You can then try attacking the second costliest operation, the scan of `Purchasing.PurchaseOrderDetail`.

Before proceeding, reset the stored procedure:

```
ALTER PROCEDURE [dbo].[spr_PurchaseOrderBySalesPersonName]
@LastName NVARCHAR(50)
AS
    SELECT  poh.PurchaseOrderID
            ,poh.OrderDate
            ,pod.LineTotal
            ,p.[Name] AS ProductName
            ,e.JobTitle
            ,per.LastName + ', ' + per.FirstName AS SalesPerson
    FROM     Purchasing.PurchaseOrderHeader AS poh
             JOIN Purchasing.PurchaseOrderDetail AS pod
             ON poh.PurchaseOrderID = pod.PurchaseOrderID
             JOIN Production.Product AS p
             ON pod.ProductID = p.ProductID
             JOIN HumanResources.Employee AS e
             ON poh.EmployeeID = e.BusinessEntityID
             JOIN Person.Person AS per
             ON e.BusinessEntityID = per.BusinessEntityID
    WHERE    per.LastName LIKE @LastName
    ORDER BY per.LastName
            ,per.FirstName
```

Avoiding the Clustered Index Scan Operation

After eliminating the key lookup earlier, the clustered index scan against the `Purchasing.PurchaseOrderDetail` table was left as the second most costly operation. The scan is necessary because no other indexes contain the data needed to satisfy the query. Only three columns are referenced by the query, so it should be possible to create a small performance index that will help. Use something like this:

```
CREATE INDEX IX_Test ON Purchasing.PurchaseOrderDetail
(PurchaseOrderID, ProductId, LineTotal)
```

Executing the original procedure using the `Test.sql` script results in the execution plan shown in Figure 15-12.

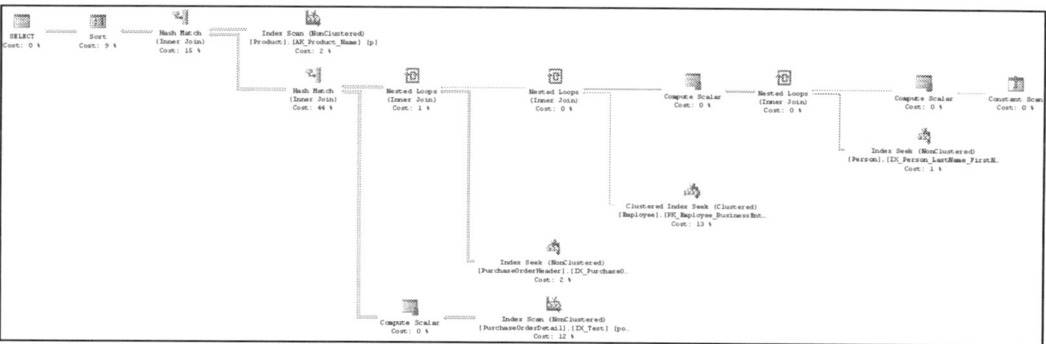

Figure 15-12. *Execution plan after creating a new index on* `Purchasing.PurchaseOrderDetail`

Creating the index results in a couple of small changes to the execution plan. Instead of scanning the clustered index on `Purchasing.PurchaseOrderDetail`, the new index is scanned. One of the `Compute Scalar` operations was also eliminated. This is a pretty mild improvement to the plan.

The real question is, what happened to the performance? The execution time did not radically improve. The reads on the `Purchasing.PurchaseOrderDetail` table dropped from 66 to 28. It's a very modest improvement and may not be worth the extra processing time for the inserts.

Modifying the Procedure

Sometimes, working with the business and the developers to reevaluate the needs of a particular query is one of the best ways to improve performance. In this instance, the existing query uses a `LIKE` clause against the `LastName` column in the `Person.Person` table. After checking with the developers, it's determined that this query will be getting its values from a drop-down list that is an accurate list of `LastName` values from the database. Since the `LastName` value is coming from the database, that means the developers can actually get the `BusinessEntityID` column from the `Person.Person` table. That makes it possible to change the procedure so that it now looks like this:

```
ALTER PROCEDURE [dbo].[spr_PurchaseOrderBySalesPersonName]
@BusinessEntityId int
AS
    SELECT  poh.PurchaseOrderID
           ,poh.OrderDate
           ,pod.LineTotal
           ,p.[Name] AS ProductName
           ,e.JobTitle
           ,per.LastName + ', ' + per.FirstName AS SalesPerson
    FROM    Purchasing.PurchaseOrderHeader AS poh
            JOIN Purchasing.PurchaseOrderDetail AS pod
            ON poh.PurchaseOrderID = pod.PurchaseOrderID
            JOIN Production.Product AS p
            ON pod.ProductID = p.ProductID
            JOIN HumanResources.Employee AS e
            ON poh.EmployeeID = e.BusinessEntityID
            JOIN Person.Person AS per
            ON e.BusinessEntityID = per.BusinessEntityID
    WHERE   e.BusinessEntityID = @BusinessEntityID
    ORDER BY per.LastName
           ,per.FirstName
```

To execute the procedure now, use this:

```
EXEC dbo.spr_PurchaseOrderBySalesPersonName @BusinessEntityID = 260;
```

Running this query results in the execution plan visible in Figure 15-13.

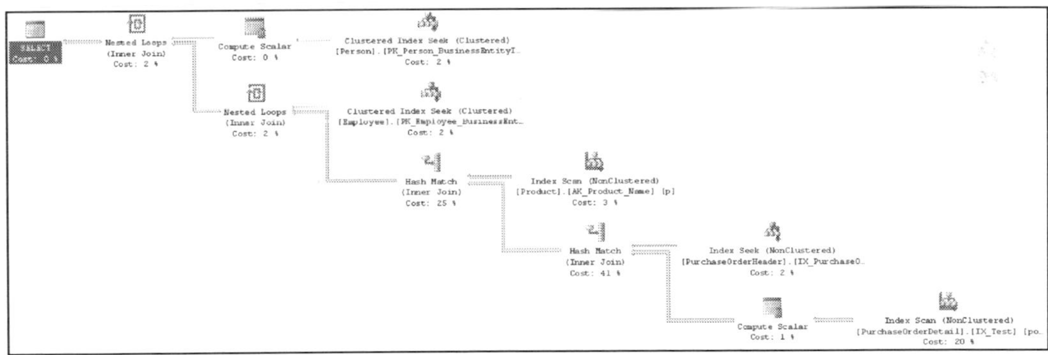

Figure 15-13. *Execution plan after rearchitecting the procedure*

Many of the operations will be familiar, but the costs have changed, the order of events has changed, and the plan is actually much simpler now with close to a bare minimum of operations. Best of all, here are the results from the statistics:

```
SQL Server parse and compile time:
   CPU time = 0 ms, elapsed time = 0 ms.
DBCC execution completed. If DBCC printed error messages, contact your
system administrator.

 SQL Server Execution Times:
   CPU time = 0 ms,  elapsed time = 0 ms.
DBCC execution completed. If DBCC printed error messages, contact your system
administrator.

 SQL Server Execution Times:
   CPU time = 0 ms,  elapsed time = 1 ms.
SQL Server parse and compile time:
   CPU time = 0 ms, elapsed time = 0 ms.

 SQL Server Execution Times:
   CPU time = 0 ms,  elapsed time = 0 ms.
SQL Server parse and compile time:
   CPU time = 0 ms, elapsed time = 0 ms.

 SQL Server Execution Times:
   CPU time = 0 ms,  elapsed time = 0 ms.
SQL Server parse and compile time:
   CPU time = 0 ms, elapsed time = 0 ms.
SQL Server parse and compile time:
   CPU time = 31 ms, elapsed time = 104 ms.

(631 row(s) affected)
Table 'Worktable'. Scan count 0, logical reads 0, physical reads 0,
read-ahead reads 0, lob logical reads 0, lob physical reads 0,
lob read-ahead reads 0.
Table 'PurchaseOrderDetail'. Scan count 1, logical reads 28, physical reads 2,
read-ahead reads 41, lob logical reads 0, lob physical reads 0,
lob read-ahead reads 0.
Table 'PurchaseOrderHeader'. Scan count 1, logical reads 3, physical reads 2,
read-ahead reads 0, lob logical reads 0, lob physical reads 0,
lob read-ahead reads 0.
Table 'Product'. Scan count 1, logical reads 5, physical reads 2,
read-ahead reads 8, lob logical reads 0, lob physical reads 0,
lob read-ahead reads 0.
Table 'Employee'. Scan count 0, logical reads 2, physical reads 2,
read-ahead reads 0, lob logical reads 0, lob physical reads 0,
lob read-ahead reads 0.
Table 'Person'. Scan count 0, logical reads 3, physical reads 3, read-ahead reads 0,
lob logical reads 0, lob physical reads 0, lob read-ahead reads 0.
```

```
 SQL Server Execution Times:
   CPU time = 31 ms,  elapsed time = 222 ms.

 SQL Server Execution Times:
   CPU time = 62 ms,  elapsed time = 327 ms.
SQL Server parse and compile time:
   CPU time = 0 ms, elapsed time = 0 ms.
```

The number of reads across the board has been reduced, and the execution time is down to 327 ms from the original 447. That's about a 25 percent reduction on a query that was already subsecond in its response. The CPU time went up quite a bit to 45 ms, but that still results in an overall reduction in execution time. If you change the test and allow the query to use a compiled stored procedure, as is more likely in most production environments, execution time drops down to 227 ms, and the CPU time drops back down to 15 ms. If you change the test again, to allow for data caching, which may be the case in some environments, execution time drops to 170 ms.

Overall, although not a dramatic improvement because it's being called only once, this can be considered a successfully tuned procedure. If it were called thousands of times a second, getting a 25 percent reduction in time is worth quite a lot. However, more testing is necessary to finally reach that conclusion. You need to go back and assess the impact on the overall database workload.

Analyzing the Effect on Database Workload

Once you've optimized the worst-performing query, you must ensure that it doesn't hurt the performance of the other queries; otherwise, your work will have been in vain.

To analyze the resultant performance of the overall workload, reexecute the complete workload in `workload.sql`, and trace the overall performance using the stored procedure technique (`PerformanceTraceForWorkload.sql` in the download).

■Tip For proper comparison with the original Profiler trace output, please ensure that the graphical execution plan is off.

Figure 15-14 shows the corresponding trace output captured in a trace file in Profiler.

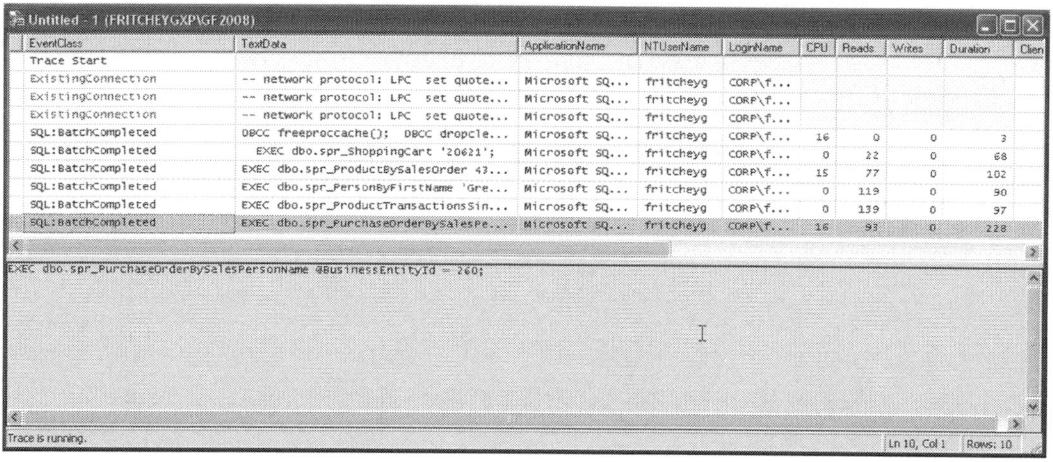

Figure 15-14. *Profiler trace output showing the effect of optimizing the costliest query on the complete workload*

From this trace, Table 15-6 summarizes the resource use and the response time (or `Duration`) of the query under consideration.

Table 15-6. *Resource Usage and Response Time of the Optimized Query Before and After Optimization*

Column	Before Optimization	After Optimization
`Reads`	3009	93
`Writes`	0	0
`CPU`	47 ms	16 ms
`Duration`	365 ms	228 ms

Note The absolute values are less important than the relative difference between the "Before Optimization" and the corresponding "After Optimization" values. The relative differences between the values indicate the relative improvement in performance.

It's possible that the optimization of the worst-performing query may hurt the performance of some other query in the workload. However, as long as the overall performance of the workload is improved, you can retain the optimizations performed on the query.

Iterating Through Optimization Phases

An important point to remember is that you need to iterate through the optimization steps multiple times. In each iteration, you can identify one or more poorly performing queries and optimize the query or queries to improve the performance of the overall workload. You must continue iterating through the optimization steps until you achieve the adequate performance or meet your service-level agreement (SLA).

Besides analyzing the workload for resource-intensive queries, you must also analyze the workload for error conditions. For example, if you try to insert duplicate rows into a table with its column protected by the unique constraint, SQL Server will reject the new rows and report an error condition to the application. Although the data was not entered into the table or no useful work was performed, still-valuable resources were used to determine that the data was invalid and must be rejected.

To identify the error conditions caused by the database requests, you will need to include in your trace or create a new trace that looks for the following events in the `Errors and Warnings` section:

- `Exception`
- `Execution Warnings`
- `Hash Warning`
- `Missing Column Statistics`
- `Missing Join Predicate`
- `Sort Warnings`

For example, consider the following SQL queries (`errors.sql` in the download):

```
INSERT  INTO Purchasing.PurchaseOrderDetail
        (PurchaseOrderID
        ,DueDate
        ,OrderQty
        ,ProductID
        ,UnitPrice
        ,ReceivedQty
        ,RejectedQty
        ,ModifiedDate)
VALUES  (
         1066
        ,'1/1/2009'
        ,1
        ,42
        ,98.6
        ,5
        ,4
        ,'1/1/2009'
        );
```

```
GO
SELECT  p.[Name]
       ,c.[Name]
FROM    Production.Product AS p
       ,Production.ProductSubCategory AS c;
GO
```

Figure 15-15 shows the corresponding Profiler trace output.

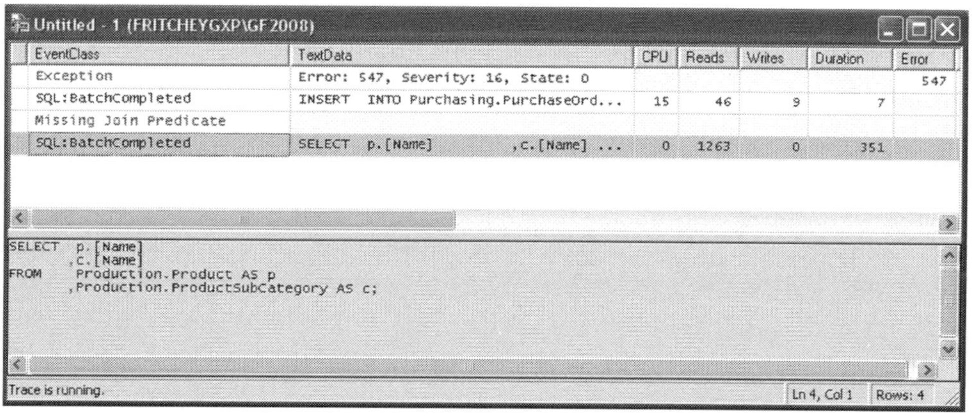

Figure 15-15. *Profiler trace output showing errors raised by a SQL workload*

From the Profiler trace output in Figure 15-15, you can see that the following two errors occurred:

- `Exception`
- `Missing Join Predicate`

The `Exception` error was caused by the `INSERT` statement, which tried to insert data that did not pass the referential integrity check, namely, attempting to insert a `ProductId` = 42 when there is no such value in the `Production.Product` table. From the `Error` data column, you can see that the error number is 547. You can determine the error description for this error number from the `sys.messages` catalog view:

```
SELECT  *
FROM    sys.messages
WHERE   message_id = 547
        AND language_id = 1033
```

Figure 15-16 shows the error description from the `sys.messages` view.

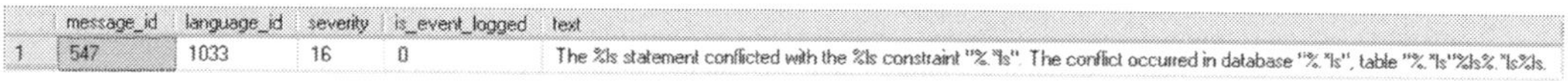

	message_id	language_id	severity	is_event_logged	text
1	547	1033	16	0	The %ls statement conflicted with the %ls constraint "%.*ls". The conflict occurred in database "%.*ls", table "%.*ls"%ls%.*ls%.*ls.

Figure 15-16. *`sys.messages` output showing the description of the error*

The second error, Missing Join Predicate, is caused by the SELECT statement:

```
SELECT  p.[Name]
       ,c.[Name]
FROM    Production.Product AS p
       ,Production.ProductSubCategory AS c;
GO
```

If you take a closer look at the SELECT statement, you will see that the query does not specify a JOIN clause between the two tables. A missing join predicate between the tables usually leads to an inaccurate result set and a costly query plan. This is what is known as a *Cartesian join*, which leads to a *Cartesian product*, or, every row from one table combined with every row from the other table. You must identify the queries causing such events in the Errors and Warnings section and implement the necessary resolutions. For instance, in the preceding SELECT statement, you should not join every row from the Production.ProductCategory table to every row in the Production.Product table—you must join only the rows with matching ProductCategoryID, as follows:

```
SELECT  p.[Name]
       ,c.[Name]
FROM    Production.Product AS p
        JOIN Production.ProductSubCategory AS c
        ON p.ProductSubcategoryID = c.ProductSubcategoryID ;
```

Even after you thoroughly analyze and optimize a workload, you must remember that workload optimization is not a one-off process. The workload or data distribution on a database can change over time, so you should check periodically whether your queries are optimized for the current situation. It's also possible that you may identify shortcomings in the design of the database itself. Too many joins from overnormalization or too many columns from improper denormalization can both lead to queries that perform badly with no real optimization opportunities. In this case, you will need to consider redesigning the database to get a more optimized structure.

Summary

As you learned in this chapter, optimizing a database workload requires a range of tools, utilities, and commands to analyze different aspects of the queries involved in the workload. You can use the Profiler tool to analyze the big picture of the workload and identify the costly queries. Once you've identified the costly queries, you can use Query Analyzer and various SQL commands to troubleshoot the problems associated with the costly queries. Based on the problems detected with the costly queries, you can apply one or more sets of optimization techniques to improve the query performance. The optimization of the costly queries should improve the overall performance of the workload; if this does not happen, you should roll back the change.

In the next chapter, I summarize the performance-related best practices in a nutshell for your ready reference.

CHAPTER 16

SQL Server Optimization Checklist

If you have read through the previous 15 chapters of this book, then by now you understand the major aspects involved in performance optimization and that it is a challenging and ongoing activity.

What I hope to do in this chapter is to provide a performance-monitoring checklist that can serve as a quick reference for database developers and DBAs when in the field. The idea is similar to the notion of tear-off cards of "best practices." This chapter does not cover everything, but it does summarize, in one place, some of the major tuning activities that can have quick and demonstrable impact on the performance of your SQL Server systems.

I have categorized these checklist items into the following sections:

- Database design
- Query design
- Configuration settings
- Database administration
- Database backup

Each section contains a number of optimization recommendations and techniques and, where appropriate, cross-references to specific chapters in this book that provide full details.

Database Design

Although database design is a broad topic and can't be given due justice in a small section in this query tuning book, I advise you to keep an eye on the following design aspects to ensure that you pay attention to database performance from an early stage:

- Balancing under- and overnormalization
- Benefiting from using entity-integrity constraints
- Benefiting from using domain and referential integrity constraints

- Adopting index-design best practices
- Avoiding the use of the `sp_` prefix for stored procedure names
- Minimizing the use of triggers

Balancing Under- and Overnormalization

While designing a database, you have the following two extreme options:

- Save the complete data in a single, flat table with little to no normalization.
- Save the data in fine-grained tables by exploding every attribute into its own table and thus allowing every attribute to save an unlimited number of multiple values.

Reasonable normalization enhances database performance. The presence of wide tables with a large number of columns is usually a characteristic of an undernormalized database. *Undernormalization* causes excessive repetition of data, which can lead to improper results and often hurts query performance. For example, in an ordering system, you can keep a customer's profile and all the orders placed by the customer in a single table, as shown in Table 16-1.

Table 16-1. *Original Customers Table*

CustID	Name	Address	Phone	OrderDt	ShippingAddress
100	Liu Hong	Boise, ID, USA	123-456-7890	08-Jul-04	Boise, ID, USA
100	Liu Hong	Boise, ID, USA	123-456-7890	10-Jul-04	Austin, TX, USA

Keeping the customer profile and the order information together in a single table will repeat the customer profile in every order placed by the customer, making the rows in the table very wide. Consequently, fewer customer profiles can be saved in one data page. For a query interested in a range of customer profiles (not their order information), more pages have to be read compared to that in the design in which customer profiles are kept in a separate table. To avoid the performance impact of undernormalization, you must normalize the two logical entities (customer profile and orders), which have a one-to-many type of relationship, into separate tables, as shown in Tables 16-2 and 16-3.

Table 16-2. *New Customers Table*

CustID	Name	Address	Phone
100	Liu Hong	Boise, ID, USA	123-456-7890

Table 16-3. *Orders Table*

CustID	OrderDt	ShippingAddress
100	08-Jul-04	Boise, ID, USA
100	10-Jul-04	Austin, TX, USA

Similarly, overnormalization is also not good for query performance. *Overnormalization* causes excessive joins across too many narrow tables. Although a 20-table join can perform perfectly fine and a 2-table join can be a problem, a good rule of thumb is to more closely examine a query when it exceeds 6 to 8 tables in the join criteria. To fetch any useful content from the database, a database developer has to join a large number of tables in the SQL queries. For example, if you create separate tables for a customer name, address, and phone number, then to retrieve the customer information, you have to join three tables. If the data (for example, the customer name and address) has a one-to-one type of relationship and is usually accessed together by the queries, then normalizing the data into separate tables can hurt query performance.

Benefiting from Entity-Integrity Constraints

Data integrity is essential to ensuring the quality of data in the database. An essential component of data integrity is *entity integrity*, which defines a row as a unique entity for a particular table. As per entity integrity, every row in a table must be uniquely identifiable. The column or columns serving as the unique row identifier for a table must be represented as the primary key of the table.

Sometimes, a table may contain an additional column, or columns, that also can be used to uniquely identify a row in the table. For example, an `Employee` table may have the columns `EmployeeID` and `SocialSecurityNumber`. The column `EmployeeID`, which serves as the unique row identifier, can be defined as the primary key, and the column `SocialSecurityNumber` can be defined as the alternate key. In SQL Server, alternate keys can be defined using unique constraints, which are essentially the younger siblings to primary keys. In fact, both the unique constraint and the primary key constraint use unique indexes behind the scenes.

It's worth noting that there is honest disagreement regarding the use of a natural key, such as the `SocialSecurityNumber` column in the previous example, and an artificial key, the `EmployeeID`. I've seen both designs succeed well, but they both have strengths and weaknesses. Rather than suggest one over the other, I'll provide you with a couple of reasons to use both and some of the costs associated with each. An identity column is usually an `INT` or a `BIGINT`, which makes it narrow and easy to index. Also, separating the value of the primary key from any business knowledge is considered good design in some circles. One of the drawbacks is that the numbers sometimes get business meaning, which should never happen. Also, you have to create a unique constraint for the alternate keys in order to prevent multiple rows where none should exist. Natural keys provide a clear, human-readable, primary key that has true business meaning. They tend to be wider fields, sometimes very wide, making them less efficient inside indexes. Also, sometimes the data may change, which has a profound trickle-down effect within your database and your enterprise.

Let me just reiterate that either approach can work well and that each provides plenty of opportunities for tuning. Either approach, properly applied and maintained, will protect the integrity of your data.

Besides maintaining data integrity, unique indexes—the primary vehicle for entity-integrity constraints—help the optimizer generate efficient execution plans. SQL Server can often search through a unique index faster than it can search through a nonunique index, because in a unique index each row is unique and, once a row is found, SQL Server does not have to look any further for other matching rows. If a column is used in sort (or `GROUP BY` or `DISTINCT`) operations, consider defining a unique constraint on the column (using a unique index), because columns with a unique constraint generally sort faster than ones with no unique constraint.

To understand the performance benefit of entity-integrity or unique constraints, consider this example. Modify the existing unique index on the Production.Product table:

```
CREATE  NONCLUSTERED INDEX [AK_Product_Name] ON [Production].[Product] ([Name] ASC)
    WITH (
         DROP_EXISTING = ON)
ON  [PRIMARY];
GO
```

The nonclustered index does not include the UNIQUE constraint. Therefore, although the [Name] column contains unique values, the absence of the UNIQUE constraint from the nonclustered index does not provide this information to the optimizer in advance. Now, let's consider the performance impact of the UNIQUE constraint (or a missing UNIQUE constraint) on the following SELECT statement:

```
SELECT DISTINCT
        (p.[Name])
FROM    Production.Product AS p
```

Figure 16-1 shows the execution plan of this SELECT statement.

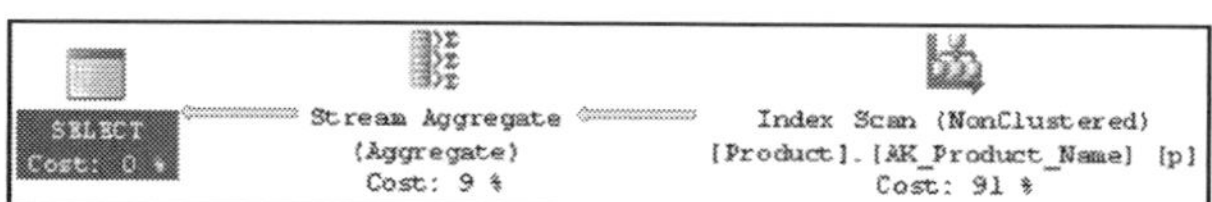

Figure 16-1. *Execution plan with no UNIQUE constraint on the [Name] column*

From the execution plan, you can see that the nonclustered index AK_Product_Name is used to retrieve the data, and then a Stream Aggregate operation is performed on the data to group the data on the [Name] column so that the duplicate [Name] values can be removed from the final result set. The Stream Aggregate operation would not have been required if the optimizer had been told in advance about the uniqueness of the [Name] column by defining the nonclustered index with a UNIQUE constraint, as follows:

```
CREATE UNIQUE NONCLUSTERED INDEX [AK_Product_Name] ON [Production].[Product]
([Name] ASC)
    WITH (
         DROP_EXISTING = ON)
ON  [PRIMARY];
GO
```

Figure 16-2 shows the new execution plan of the SELECT statement.

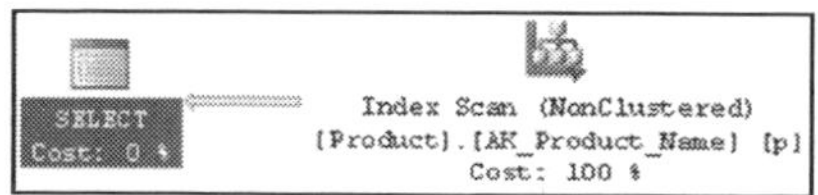

Figure 16-2. *Execution plan with a UNIQUE constraint on the [Name] column*

In general, the entity-integrity constraints (that is, primary keys and unique constraints) provide useful information to the optimizer about the expected results, assisting the optimizer in generating efficient execution plans.

Benefiting from Domain and Referential Integrity Constraints

The other two important components of data integrity are *domain integrity* and *referential integrity*. Domain integrity for a column can be enforced by restricting the data type of the column, defining the format of the input data, and limiting the range of acceptable values for the column. SQL Server provides the following features to implement the domain integrity: data types, FOREIGN KEY constraints, CHECK constraints, DEFAULT definitions, and NOT NULL definitions. If an application requires that the values for a data column be restricted within a range of values, then this business rule can be implemented either in the application code or in the database schema. Implementing such a business rule in the database using domain constraints (such as the CHECK constraint) usually helps the optimizer generate efficient execution plans.

To understand the performance benefit of domain integrity, consider this example:

```
--Create two test tables
IF (SELECT  OBJECT_ID('dbo.T1')
   ) IS NOT NULL
    DROP TABLE dbo.T1 ;
GO
CREATE TABLE dbo.T1
    (C1 INT
    ,C2 INT CHECK (C2 BETWEEN 10 AND 20)) ;
INSERT  INTO dbo.T1
VALUES  (11, 12) ;
GO
IF (SELECT  OBJECT_ID('dbo.T2')
   ) IS NOT NULL
    DROP TABLE dbo.T2 ;
GO
CREATE TABLE dbo.T2 (C1 INT, C2 INT) ;
INSERT  INTO dbo.T2
VALUES  (101, 102) ;
```

Now, execute the following two SELECT statements:

```
SELECT  T1.C1
       ,T1.C2
       ,T2.C2
FROM    dbo.T1
        JOIN dbo.T2
        ON T1.C1 = T2.C2
           AND T1.C2 = 20 ;
```

```
GO
SELECT  T1.C1
        ,T1.C2
        ,T2.C2
FROM     dbo.T1
         JOIN dbo.T2
         ON T1.C1 = T2.C2
            AND T1.C2 = 30 ;
```

The two SELECT statements appear to be the same except for the predicate values (20 in the first statement and 30 in the second). Although the two SELECT statements have exactly the same form, the optimizer treats them differently because of the CHECK constraint on the T1.C2 column, as shown in the execution plan in Figure 16-3.

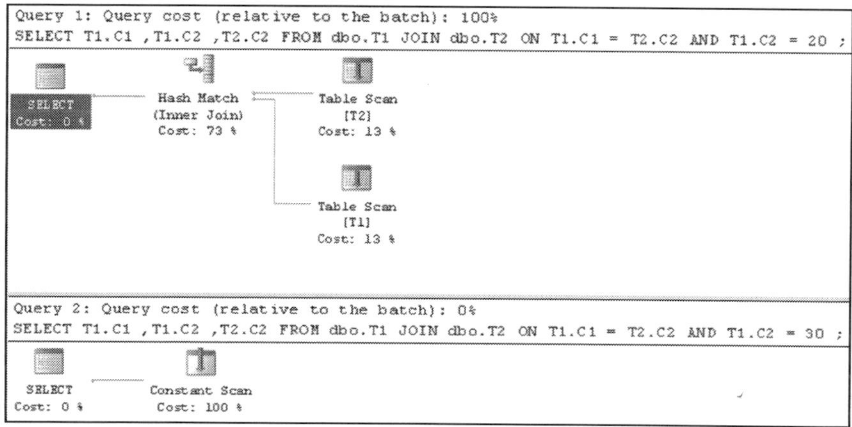

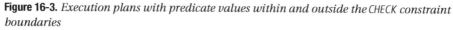

Figure 16-3. *Execution plans with predicate values within and outside the CHECK constraint boundaries*

From the execution plan, you can see that for the first query (with T1.C2 = 20) the optimizer accesses the data from both tables. For the second query (with T1.C2 = 30), since the optimizer understands from the corresponding CHECK constraint on the column T1.C2 that the column can't contain any value outside the range 10 to 20, the optimizer doesn't even access the data from the tables. Consequently, the relative cost of the second query is 0 percent.

I explained the performance advantage of referential integrity in detail in the section "Declarative Referential Integrity" of Chapter 11.

Therefore, use domain and referential constraints not only to implement data integrity but also to facilitate the optimizer in generating efficient query plans. To understand other performance benefits of domain and referential integrity, please refer to the section "Using Domain and Referential Integrity" of Chapter 11.

Adopting Index-Design Best Practices

The most common optimization recommendation, and usually the biggest contributor to good performance, is to implement the correct indexes for the database workload. Unlike tables, which are used to store data and can be designed even without knowing the queries thoroughly (as long as the tables properly represent the business entities), indexes must be designed by reviewing the database queries thoroughly. Except in common and obvious cases, such as primary keys and unique indexes, please don't fall into the trap of designing indexes without knowing the queries. Even for primary keys and unique indexes, I advise you to validate the applicability of those indexes as you start designing the database queries. Considering the importance of indexes for database performance, you must be very careful while designing indexes.

Although the performance aspect of indexes is explained in detail in Chapters 4, 6, and 7, I'll reiterate a short list of recommendations for easy reference:

- Choose narrow columns for indexes.
- Ensure that the selectivity of the data in the candidate column is very high or that the column has a large number of unique values.
- Prefer columns with the integer data type (or variants of the integer data type). Avoid indexes on columns with string data types such as `VARCHAR`.
- For a multicolumn index, consider the column with higher selectivity toward the leading edge of the index.
- Use the `INCLUDE` list in an index as a way to make an index covering without changing the index key structure by adding columns to the key.
- While deciding the columns to be indexed, pay extra attention to the queries' `WHERE` clauses and join criteria columns, which can serve as the entry points into the tables. Especially if a `WHERE` clause criterion on a column filters the data on a highly selective value or constant, the column can be a prime candidate for an index.
- While choosing the type of an index (clustered or nonclustered), keep in mind the advantages and disadvantages of clustered and nonclustered index types. For queries retrieving a range of rows, usually clustered indexes perform better. For point queries, nonclustered indexes are usually better.

Be extra careful while designing a clustered index, since every nonclustered index on the table depends on the clustered index. Therefore, follow these recommendations while designing and implementing clustered indexes:

- Keep the clustered indexes as narrow as possible. You don't want to widen all your nonclustered indexes by having a wide clustered index.
- Create the clustered index first, and then create the nonclustered indexes on the table.
- If required, rebuild a clustered index in a single step using the `DROP_EXISTING` keyword in the `CREATE INDEX` command. You don't want to rebuild all the nonclustered indexes on the table twice: once when the clustered index is dropped and again when the clustered index is re-created.
- Do not create a clustered index on a frequently updatable column. If you do so, the nonclustered indexes on the table will have difficulty remaining in sync with the clustered index key values.

To keep track of the indexes you've created and determine ones that you need to create, you should take advantage of the dynamic management views that SQL Server 2008 makes available to you. By checking the data in `sys.dm_db_index_usage_stats` on a regular basis, once a week or so, you can determine which of your indexes are actually being used and which ones are redundant. Indexes that are not contributing to your queries to help you improve performance are just a drain on the system, requiring more disk space and additional I/O to maintain the data inside the index as the data in the table changes. On the other hand, querying `sys.dm_db_missing_indexes_details` will show indexes deemed missing by the system and even suggest `INCLUDE` columns. You can access the DMV `sys.dm_db_missing_indexes_groups_stats` to see aggregate information about the number of times queries are called that could have benefited from a particular group of indexes. All this can be combined to give you an optimal method for maintaining the indexes in your system over the long term.

Avoiding the Use of the sp_ Prefix for Stored Procedure Names

As a rule, don't use the `sp_` prefix for user stored procedures, since SQL Server assumes that stored procedures with the `sp_` prefix are system stored procedures, which are supposed to be in the master database. Using `sp` or `usp` as the prefix for user stored procedures is quite common. The performance hit of the `sp_` prefix is explained in detail in the section "Be Careful Naming Stored Procedures" of Chapter 11.

Minimizing the Use of Triggers

Triggers provide a very attractive method for automating behavior within the database. Since they fire as data is manipulated by other processes, regardless of the process, they can be used to ensure certain functions are run as the data changes. That same functionality makes them dangerous since they are not immediately visible to the developer or DBA working on a system. They must be taken into account when designing queries and when troubleshooting performance problems. Because they are a somewhat hidden cost, their use should be considered very carefully. Be sure that the only way to solve the problem presented is with a trigger. If you do use a trigger, document that fact in as many places as you can to ensure that the existence of the trigger is taken into account by other developers and DBAs.

Query Design

Here's a list of the performance-related best practices you should follow when designing the database queries:

- Use the command `SET NOCOUNT ON`.
- Explicitly define the owner of an object.
- Avoid nonsarable search conditions.
- Avoid arithmetic operators and functions on `WHERE` clause columns.
- Avoid optimizer hints.
- Stay away from nesting views.
- Ensure no implicit data type conversions.

- Minimize logging overhead.
- Adopt best practices for reusing execution plans.
- Adopt best practices for database transactions.
- Eliminate or reduce the overhead of database cursors.

I further detail each best practice in the following sections.

Use the Command SET NOCOUNT ON

As a rule, always use the command `SET NOCOUNT ON` as the first statement in stored procedures, triggers, and other batch queries to avoid the network overhead associated with the return of the number of rows affected, after every execution of a SQL statement. The command `SET NOCOUNT` is explained in detail in the section "Use SET NOCOUNT" of Chapter 11.

Explicitly Define the Owner of an Object

As a performance best practice, always qualify a database object with its owner to avoid the runtime cost required to verify the owner of the object. The performance benefit of explicitly qualifying the owner of a database object is explained in detail in the section "Do Not Allow Implicit Resolution of Objects in Queries" of Chapter 9.

Avoid Nonsargable Search Conditions

Be vigilant when defining the search conditions in your query. If the search condition on a column used in the `WHERE` clause prevents the optimizer from effectively using the index on that column, then the execution cost for the query will be high in spite of the presence of the correct index. The performance impact of nonsargable search conditions is explained in detail in the corresponding section of Chapter 11.

Additionally, please be careful while defining your application features. If you define an application feature such as "retrieve all products with product name ending in caps," then you will have queries scanning the complete table (or the clustered index). As you know, scanning a multimillion-row table will hurt your database performance. Unless you use an index hint, you won't be able to benefit from the index on that column. However, since the use of an index hint overrides the decisions of the query optimizer, it's generally not recommended that you use index hints either, as explained in Chapter 11. To understand the performance impact of such a business rule, consider the following `SELECT` statement:

```
SELECT  p.*
FROM    Production.Product AS p
WHERE   p.[Name] LIKE '%Caps'
```

In Figure 16-4, you can see that the execution plan used the index on the `[Name]` column but had to perform a scan instead of a seek. Since an index on a column with character data types (such as `CHAR` and `VARCHAR`) sorts the data values for the column on the leading-end characters, the use of a leading `%` in the `LIKE` condition didn't allow a seek operation into the index. The matching rows may be distributed throughout the index rows, making the index noneffective for the search condition and thereby hurting the performance of the query.

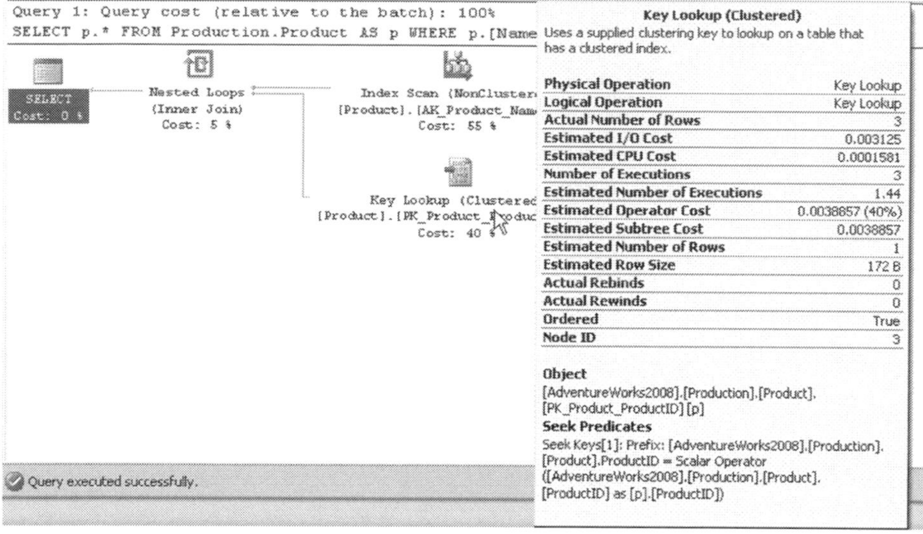

Figure 16-4. *Execution plan showing clustered index scan caused by a nonsargable* `LIKE` *clause*

Avoid Arithmetic Operators on the WHERE Clause Column

Always try not to use arithmetic operators and functions on columns in the `WHERE` and `JOIN` clauses. Using operators and functions on them prevents the use of indexes on those columns. The performance impact of using arithmetic operators on `WHERE` clause columns is explained in detail in the section "Avoid Arithmetic Operators on the WHERE Clause Column" of Chapter 11, and the impact of using functions is explained in detail in the section "Avoid Functions on the WHERE Clause Column" of the same chapter.

To see this in action, consider the following queries (`badfunction.sql` in the download):

```
SELECT  soh.SalesOrderNumber
FROM    Sales.SalesOrderHeader AS soh
WHERE   'SO5' = LEFT(SalesOrderNumber, 3);

SELECT  soh.SalesOrderNumber
FROM    Sales.SalesOrderHeader AS soh
WHERE   SalesOrderNumber LIKE 'SO5%';
```

These are basically the same logic: checking `SalesOrderNumber` to see whether it is equal to `SO5`. However, the first performs a function on the `SalesOrderNumber` column, while the second uses a `LIKE` clause to check for the same data. Figure 16-5 shows the resulting execution plans.

As you can see in Figure 16-5, the first query forces an `Index Scan` operation, while the second is able to perform a nice clean `Index Seek`. This demonstrates clearly why you should avoid functions and operators.

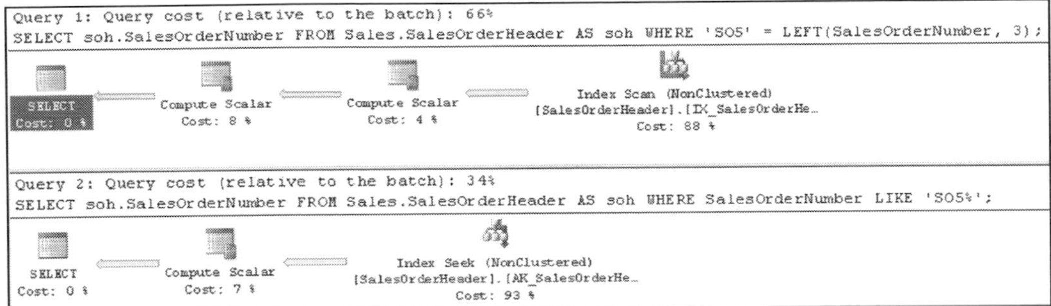

Figure 16-5. *Execution plans showing a function preventing index use*

Avoid Optimizer Hints

As a rule, avoid the use of optimizer hints, such as index hints and join hints, because they overrule the decision-making process of the optimizer. In general, the optimizer is smart enough to generate efficient execution plans and works the best without any optimizer hint imposed on it. The same applies to plan guides. Although forcing a plan in rare circumstances will help, for the most part rely on the optimizer to make good choices. For a detailed understanding of the performance impact of optimizer hints, please refer to the corresponding section "Avoiding Optimizer Hints" of Chapter 11.

Stay Away from Nesting Views

A nested view is when one view calls another view, which calls more views, and so on. This can lead to very confusing code since the views are masking the operations being performed and because although the query may be very simple, the execution plan and subsequent operations by the SQL engine can be very complex and expensive. The same rule applies to nesting user-defined functions.

Ensure No Implicit Data Type Conversions

When you create variables in a query, be sure those variables are of the same data type as the columns that they will be used to compare against. Even though SQL Server can and will convert, for example, a `VARCHAR` to a `DATE`, that implicit conversion will prevent indexes from being used. You have to be just as careful in situations like table joins so that the primary key data type of one table matches the foreign key of the table being joined.

Minimize Logging Overhead

SQL Server maintains the old and new states of every atomic action (or transaction) in the transaction log to ensure database consistency and durability, creating the potential for a huge pressure on the log disk and often making the log disk a point of contention. Therefore, to improve database performance, you must try to optimize the transaction log overhead. Besides the hardware solutions discussed later in the chapter, you should adopt the following query-design best practices:

- Prefer table variables over temporary tables for small result sets. The performance benefit of table variables is explained in detail in the section "Using Table Variables" of Chapter 10.
- Batch a number of action queries in a single transaction. You must be careful when using this option, because if too many rows are affected within a single transaction, the corresponding database objects will be locked for a long time, blocking all other users trying to access the objects.
- Reduce the amount of logging of certain operations by using the Bulk Logged recovery model. Primarily this is for use when dealing with large-scale data manipulation. You also will use minimal logging when Bulk Logged is enabled and you use the `WRITE` clause of the `UPDATE` statement or drop or create indexes.

Adopt Best Practices for Reusing Execution Plans

The best practices for optimizing the cost of plan generation can be broadly classified into two categories:

- Caching execution plans effectively
- Minimizing recompilation of execution plans

Caching Execution Plans Effectively

You must ensure that the execution plans for your queries are not only cached but also reused often by adopting the following best practices:

- Avoid executing queries as nonparameterized, ad hoc queries. Instead, parameterize the variable parts of a query and submit the parameterized query using a stored procedure or the `sp_executesql` system stored procedure.
- Use the same environment settings (such as `ANSI_NULLS`) in every connection that executes the same parameterized queries, because the execution plan for a query is dependent on the environment settings of the connection.
- As explained earlier in the section "Explicitly Define the Owner of an Object," explicitly qualify the owner of the objects while accessing them in your queries.

The preceding aspects of plan caching are explained in detail in Chapter 9.

Minimizing Recompilation of Execution Plans

To minimize the cost of generating execution plans for stored procedures, you must ensure that the plans in the cache are not invalidated or recompiled for reasons that are under your control. The following recommended best practices minimize the recompilation of stored procedure plans:

- Do not interleave DDL and DML statements in your stored procedures. You must put all the DDL statements at the top of the stored procedures.
- In a stored procedure, avoid using temporary tables that are created outside the stored procedure.
- Avoid recompilation caused by statistics changes on temporary tables by using the `KEEPFIXED PLAN` option.
- Prefer table variables over temporary tables for very small data sets.
- Do not change the `ANSI SET` options within a stored procedure.
- If you really can't avoid a recompilation, then identify the stored procedure statement that is causing the recompilation, and execute it through the `sp_executesql` system stored procedure.

The causes of stored procedure recompilation and the recommended solutions are explained in detail in Chapter 10.

Adopt Best Practices for Database Transactions

The more effectively you design your queries for concurrency, the faster the queries will be able to complete without blocking one another. Consider the following recommendations while designing the transactions in your queries:

- Keep the scope of the transactions as short as possible. In a transaction, include only the statements that must be committed together for data consistency.
- Prevent the possibility of transactions being left open because of poor error-handling routines or application logic by using the following techniques:
  - Use `SET XACT_ABORT ON` to ensure that a transaction is aborted or rolled back on an error condition within the transaction.
  - After executing a stored procedure or a batch of queries containing a transaction from a client code, always check for an open transaction, and roll back any open transactions using the following SQL statement:

    ```
    IF @@TRANCOUNT > 0 ROLLBACK
    ```
- Use the lowest level of transaction isolation required to maintain data consistency. The amount of isolation provided by the Read Committed isolation level, the default isolation level, is sufficient most of the time. If an application feature (such as reporting) can tolerate dirty data, consider using the Read Uncommitted isolation level or the `NOLOCK` hint.

The impact of transactions on database performance is explained in detail in Chapter 12.

Eliminate or Reduce the Overhead of Database Cursors

Since SQL Server is designed to work with sets of data, processing multiple rows using DML statements is generally much faster than processing the rows one by one using database cursors. If you find yourself using lots of cursors, reexamine the logic to see whether there are ways you can eliminate the cursors. If you must use a database cursor, then use the database cursor with the least overhead, which is the `FAST_FORWARD` cursor type (generally referred to as the *fast-forward-only cursor*), or use the equivalent `DataReader` object in ADO.NET.

The performance overhead of database cursors is explained in detail in Chapter 14.

Configuration Settings

Here's a checklist of the server and database configurations settings that have a big impact on database performance:

- Affinity mask
- Memory configuration options
- Cost threshold for parallelism
- Max degree of parallelism
- Optimize for ad hoc workloads
- Query governor cost limit
- Fill factor (%)
- Blocked process threshold
- Database file layout
- Database compression

I cover these settings in more detail in the sections that follow.

Affinity Mask

As explained in the section "Parallel Plan Optimization" of Chapter 9, this setting is a special configuration setting at the server level that you can use to restrict the specific CPUs available to SQL Server. It is recommended that you keep this setting at its default value of 0, which allows SQL Server to use all the CPUs of the machine.

Memory Configuration Options

As explained in the section "SQL Server Memory Management" of Chapter 2, it is strongly recommended that you keep the memory configuration of SQL Server at the default dynamic setting. For a dedicated SQL Server box, the `max server memory` setting may be configured to a nondefault value, determined by the system configuration, under the following two situations:

- *SQL Server cluster with active/active configuration*: In active/active configuration, both SQL Server nodes accept incoming traffic and remain available to run a second instance of SQL Server if the other node fails, accepting the incoming traffic for the other SQL Server. Since both nodes must be capable of running two instances of SQL Server, the `max server memory` setting for each SQL Server instance must be set to less than half of the physical memory so that both SQL Server instances can run simultaneously on a single node, when needed. Because of this and other resource shortcomings, active/active configurations are not encouraged (the nickname for active/active is fail/fail).
- *More than 4GB of physical memory*: If a SQL Server machine has more than 4GB of physical memory and the `PAE` switch (in `boot.ini`) is set, then set the `awe enabled` parameter of SQL Server to allow SQL Server to access the memory beyond 4GB, and set the `max server memory` setting to a value approximately 200MB less than the physical memory. The `PAE` and `AWE` settings are explained in detail in the section "Using Memory Beyond 4GB Within SQL Server" of Chapter 2. A 64-bit machine won't have to deal with these same issues because the configuration requirements are not the same to access beyond 4GB of memory.

Another memory configuration to consider for a SQL Server machine is the `/3GB` setting at the operating system level. If the machine has 4GB of physical memory, then you can add this setting to the `boot.ini` file, allowing SQL Server to use the physical memory up to 3GB. Again, this assumes that more memory is not needed for the operating system or other services running on the machine. These memory configurations of SQL Server are explained in detail in the sections "Memory Bottleneck Analysis" and "Memory Bottleneck Resolutions" of Chapter 2.

Cost Threshold for Parallelism

On systems with multiple processors, the parallel execution of queries is possible. The default value for parallelism is 5. This represents a cost estimate by the optimizer of a five-second execution on the query. In most circumstances, I've found this value to be too low, meaning a higher threshold for parallelism results in better performance. Testing on your system will help determine the appropriate value.

Max Degree of Parallelism

When a system has multiple processors available, by default SQL Server will use all of them during parallel executions. To better control the load on the machine, you may find it useful to limit the number of processors used by parallel executions. Further, you may need to set the affinity so that certain processors are reserved for the operating system and other services running alongside SQL Server. OLTP systems frequently receive a benefit from disabling parallelism entirely.

Optimize for Ad Hoc Workloads

If the primary calls being made to your system come in as ad hoc or dynamic SQL instead of through well-defined stored procedures or parameterized queries, such as you might find in some of the implementation of object relational mapping (ORM) software, turning `optimize for ad hoc workloads` on will reduce the consumption of procedure cache as plan stubs are created for initial query calls instead of full execution plans. This is covered in detail in Chapter 10.

Query Governor Cost Limit

To reduce contention and prevent a few processes from taking over the machine, you can set `query governor cost limit` so that any given query execution has an upper time limit in seconds. This value is based on the estimated cost as determined by the optimizer, so it prevents queries from running if they exceed the cost limit set here. Setting the query governor is another reason to maintain the index statistics in order to get good execution plan estimates.

Fill Factor (%)

When creating a new index or rebuilding an existing one, a default fill factor (the amount of free space to be left on a page) is determined with this setting. Choosing an appropriate value for your system requires testing and knowledge of the use of the system. Fill factor was discussed in detail in Chapter 4.

Blocked Process Threshold

The `blocked process threshold` setting defines in seconds when a blocked process report is fired. When a query runs and exceeds the threshold, the report is fired, and an alert, which can be used to send an email or a text message, is fired. Testing an individual system determines what value to set this to. You can monitor for this using events within traces defined by SQL Profiler.

Database File Layout

For easy reference, I'll list the best practices you should consider when laying out database files:

- Place the data and transaction log files of a user database on different disks, allowing the transaction log disk head to progress sequentially without being moved randomly by the nonsequential I/Os commonly used for the data files.

  Placing the transaction log on a dedicated disk also enhances data protection. If a database disk fails, you will be able to save the completed transactions until the point of failure by performing a backup of the transaction log. By using this last transaction log backup during the recovery process, you will be able to recover the database up to the point of failure, also known as *point-in-time recovery*.

- Avoid RAID 5 for transaction logs because, for every write request, RAID 5 disk arrays incur twice the number of disk I/Os compared to RAID 1 or 10.

- You may choose RAID 5 for data files, since even in a heavy OLTP system the number of read requests is usually seven to eight times that of writes, and for read requests the performance of RAID 5 is similar to that of RAID 1 and RAID 10 with an equal number of total disks.

- If the system has multiple CPUs and multiple disks, spread the data across multiple data files distributed across the disks.

For a detailed understanding of database file layout and RAID subsystems, please refer to the section "Disk Bottleneck Resolutions" of Chapter 2.

Database Compression

SQL Server 2008 supplies data compression with the Enterprise and Developer Editions of the product. This can provide a great benefit in space used and sometimes in performance as more data gets stored on an index page. These benefits come at added overhead in the CPU and memory of the system. Take this into account as you implement compression.

Database Administration

For your reference, here is a short list of the performance-related database administrative activities that you should perform while managing your database server on a regular basis:

- Keep the statistics up-to-date.
- Maintain a minimum amount of index defragmentation.
- Cycle the SQL error log file.
- Avoid automatic database functions such as `AUTO_CLOSE` or `AUTO_SHRINK`.
- Minimize the overhead of SQL tracing.

In the following sections, I detail these activities.

Note For a detailed explanation of SQL Server 2008 administration needs and methods, please refer to the Microsoft SQL Server Books Online article "Administration: How To Topics" (`http://msdn.microsoft.com/en-us/library/bb522544.aspx`).

Keep the Statistics Up-to-Date

Although the performance impact of database statistics is explained in detail in Chapter 7, here's a short list for easy reference:

- Allow SQL Server to automatically maintain the statistics of the data distribution in the tables by using the default settings for the configuration parameters `AUTO_CREATE_STATISTICS` and `AUTO_UPDATE_STATISTICS`.
- As a proactive measure, in addition to the continual update of the statistics by SQL Server, you can programmatically update the statistics of every database object on a regular basis as you determine it is needed and supported within your system. This practice partly protects your database from having outdated statistics in case the auto update statistics feature fails to provide a satisfactory result. In Chapter 7, I illustrate how to set up a SQL Server job to programmatically update the statistics on a regular basis.

■ **Note** Please ensure that the statistics update job is scheduled after the completion of the index defragmentation job, as explained later in the chapter.

Maintain a Minimum Amount of Index Defragmentation

The following best practices will help you maintain a minimum amount of index defragmentation:

- Defragment a database on a regular basis during nonpeak hours.
- On a regular basis, determine the level of fragmentation on your indexes and then, based on that fragmentation, either rebuild the index or defrag the index by executing the defragmentation queries outlined in Chapter 4.

Cycle the SQL Error Log File

By default, the SQL Server error log file keeps growing until SQL Server is restarted. Every time SQL Server is restarted, the current error log file is closed and renamed `errorlog.1`, then `errorlog.1` is renamed `errorlog.2`, and so on. Subsequently, a new error log file is created. Therefore, if SQL Server is not restarted for a long time, as expected for a production server, the error log file may grow to a very large size, making it not only difficult to view the file in an editor but also very memory unfriendly when the file is opened.

SQL Server provides a system stored procedure, `sp_cycle_errorlog`, that you can use to cycle the error log file without restarting SQL Server. To keep control over the size of the error log file, you must cycle the error log file periodically by executing `sp_cycle_errorlog` as follows:

```
EXEC master.dbo.sp_cycle_errorlog
```

Use a SQL Server job to cycle the SQL Server log on a regular basis.

Avoid Automatic Database Functions Such As AUTO_CLOSE or AUTO_SHRINK

`AUTO_CLOSE` cleanly shuts down a database and frees all its resources when the last user connection is closed. This means all data and queries in the cache are automatically flushed. When the next connection comes in, not only does the database have to restart, but all the data has to be reloaded into the cache and stored procedures, and the other queries have to be recompiled. That's an extremely expensive operation for most database systems. Leave `AUTO_CLOSE` set to the default of `OFF`.

`AUTO_SHRINK` periodically shrinks the size of the database. It can shrink the data files and, when in Simple Recovery mode, the log files. While doing this, it can block other processes, seriously slowing down your system. Since, more often than not, file growth is also set to occur automatically on systems with `AUTO_SHRINK` enabled, your system will be slowed down yet again when the data or log files have to grow. Set your database sizes to an appropriate size, and monitor them for growth needs. If you must grow them automatically, do so by physical increments, not by percentages.

Minimize the Overhead of SQL Tracing

One of the most common ways of analyzing the behavior of SQL Server is to trace the SQL queries executed on SQL Server. For easy reference, here's a list of the performance-related best practices for SQL tracing:

- Capture trace output using a server-side trace (not Profiler).
- Limit the number of events and data columns to be traced.
- Discard starting events while analyzing costly and slow queries.
- Limit trace output size.
- If you decide to run Profiler for very short tracing, run the tool remotely.
- Avoid online data column sorting while using Profiler.

These best practices are explained in detail in the section "SQL Profiler Recommendations" of Chapter 3.

Database Backup

Although database backup is a broad topic and can't be given due justice in this query optimization book, I suggest that for database performance you be attentive to the following aspects of your database backup process:

- Incremental and transaction log backup frequency
- Backup distribution
- Backup compression

The next sections go into more detail on these suggestions.

Incremental and Transaction Log Backup Frequency

For an OLTP database, it is mandatory that the database be backed up regularly so that, in case of a failure, the database can be restored on a different server. For large databases, the full database backup usually takes a very long time, so full backups cannot be performed often. Consequently, full backups are performed at widespread time intervals, with incremental backups and transaction log backups scheduled more frequently between two consecutive full backups. With the frequent incremental and transaction log backups set in place, if a database fails completely, the database can be restored up to a point in time.

Incremental backups can be used to reduce the overhead of a full backup by backing up only the data changed since the last full backup. Because this is much faster, it will cause less of a slowdown on the production system. Each situation is unique, so you need to find the method that works best for you. As a general rule, I recommend taking a weekly full backup and then daily incremental backups. From there you can determine the needs of your transaction log backups.

The frequent backup of the transaction log adds overhead to the server, even during peak hours. To minimize the performance impact of transaction log backup on incoming traffic, consider the following three aspects of transaction log backups:

- *Performance*: You can back up the transaction log only if the size of the log file is greater than 20 percent of the total size of all the data files. This option is best for the database performance, since the transaction log is backed up only when it is significantly full. However, this option is not good for minimizing data loss, and the amount of data loss (in terms of time) cannot be quantified, because if the log disk fails and the database needs to be recovered from backup, then the last log backup up to which the database can be recovered may be far in the past. Additionally, the delayed backup of the transaction log causes the log file to grow up to 20 percent of the total size of the data files, requiring a large log-disk subsystem.
- *Disk space*: You can back up the transaction log whenever the size of the log file becomes greater than 500MB. This option is good for disk space and may be partly good for performance, too, if the 500MB log space doesn't fill up quickly. However, as with the previous option, the amount of data loss (in terms of time) cannot be quantified, because it may take a random amount of time to fill the 500MB log. If the log disk fails, then the database can be recovered up to the last log backup, which may be far in the past.
- *Data loss*: To minimize and quantify the maximum amount of data loss in terms of time, back up the log frequently. If a business can withstand the maximum data loss of 60 minutes, then the interval of the transaction log backup schedule must be set to less than 60 minutes.

Because, for most businesses, the acceptable amount of data loss (in terms of time) usually takes precedence over conserving the log-disk space or providing an ideal database performance, you must take into account the acceptable amount of data loss while scheduling the transaction log backup instead of randomly setting the schedule to a low time interval.

Backup Distribution

When multiple databases need to be backed up, you must ensure that all full backups are not scheduled at the same time so that the hardware resources are not pressurized at the same time. If the backup process involves backing up the databases to a central SAN disk array, then the full backups from all the database servers must be distributed across the backup time window so that the central backup infrastructure doesn't get slammed by too many backup requests at the same time. Flooding the central infrastructure with a great deal of backup requests at the same time forces the components of the infrastructure to spend a significant part of their resources just managing the excessive number of requests. This mismanaged use of the resources increases the backup durations significantly, causing the full backups to continue during peak hours and thus affecting the performance of the user requests.

To minimize the impact of the full backup process on database performance, you must first determine the nonpeak hours when full backups can be scheduled, and then you distribute the full backups across the nonpeak time window as follows:

1. Identify the number of databases that must be backed up.
2. Prioritize the databases in order of their importance to the business.
3. Determine the nonpeak hours when the full database backups can be scheduled.

4. Calculate the time interval between two consecutive full backups as follows:

   Time interval = (Total backup time window) / (Number of full backups)

5. Schedule the full backups in order of the database priorities, with the first backup starting at the start time of the backup window and the subsequent backups spread uniformly at time intervals as calculated in the preceding equation.

This uniform distribution of the full backups will ensure that the backup infrastructure is not flooded with too many backup requests at the same time and will thus reduce the impact of the full backups on the database performance.

Backup Compression

For relatively large databases, the backup durations and backup file sizes usually become an issue. Long backup durations make it difficult to complete the backups within the administrative time windows and thus start affecting the end user's experience. The large size of the backup files makes space management for the backup files quite challenging, and it increases the pressure on the network when the backups are performed across the network to a central backup infrastructure.

The recommended way to optimize the backup duration, the backup file size, and the resultant network pressure is to use *backup compression*. SQL Server 2008 introduces the concept of backup compression for the Enterprise Edition of the product. Many third-party backup tools are available that support backup compression.

Summary

Performance optimization is an ongoing process. It requires continual attention to database and query characteristics that affect performance. The goal of this chapter was to provide you with a checklist of these characteristics to serve as a quick and easy reference during the development and maintenance phase of your database applications.

Index

Symbols and numerics

A

B

C

E

F

G

H

I

L

N

O

P

Q

T

U

V

W

X

Made in the USA
Lexington, KY
01 October 2012